Regulation and Its Reform

Regulation and Its Reform
Stephen Breyer

Harvard University Press
Cambridge, Massachusetts, and London, England

SIXTH PRINTING, 1994

Library of Congress Cataloging in Publication Data

Breyer, Stephen G., 1938–
    Regulation and its reform.

    Bibliography: p.
    Includes index.
    1. Trade regulation—United States.   2. Industry and
state—United States.   I. Title.
HD3616.U47B68   353.0082   81-6753
ISBN 0-674-75375-5 (cloth)   AACR2
ISBN 0-674-75376-3 (paper)

To Leo Roberts

Preface

On its surface this book is aimed at the topical issue of regulatory reform. But underneath it strives to go beyond the topical, seeking to analyze regulation as a distinct discipline and to help teach it as a separate subject. It does so by developing a basic framework that breaks regulation into a manageable number of categories and then analyzes each category primarily by discussing its typical problems.

This approach to an institution—describing it in terms of purposes and typical problems—is that of a lawyer. But the book does not describe regulation in legal terms: its thesis is that in order to generalize usefully about regulation, one must understand the substance of the regulatory program. Thus, useful generalizations will often call for a knowledge of, for example, economics, as well as governmental administration and law. The discussion of regulation is, however, unlikely to be phrased exclusively in the terms used by any of those individual disciplines.

The result is a framework that in Part I is developed in the context of particular regulatory programs. In Part II the discussion relates that framework to other programs, thereby showing that the basic analysis has general applicability. The discussion in Part III turns back to the topical by illustrating how the analysis can be used to help bring about specific regulatory reform.

The face of regulation is changing rapidly, with major reform initiatives either adopted or under serious consideration in transportation, communication, and other areas. In fact, Congress may pass a "generic" regulatory reform bill at the 1981–82 session. These changes, however, are unlikely to limit the usefulness of generalizations drawn from the history of past regulatory programs. On the contrary, lessons from that experience may be particularly useful as legislators seek to change existing systems and as administrators of new programs seek to avoid past mistakes.

The framework presented here grew out of my work on airline deregulation for Senator Edward Kennedy and the Senate Judiciary Committee in 1975. Partial or skeletal versions have appeared in a paper prepared for the First

Boston Corporation (1977), in Chapters 3 and 4 of the report of the American Bar Association's Commission on Law and the Economy, *Federal Regulation: Roads to Reform* (1978), and in a *Harvard Law Review* article, "Analyzing Regulatory Failure: Mismatches, Less Restrictive Alternatives, and Reform" (1979). This book allows me to present a more detailed version of the framework with concrete illustrations and allows the reader to judge its usefulness more adequately.

I acknowledge here my considerable intellectual debt to Alfred Kahn, many of whose ideas appear in summary form in Chapters 1 and 2, and to Paul MacAvoy. I am grateful as well for the support—intellectual, material, moral—provided by colleagues at the Kennedy School of Government and Harvard Law School, including, among others, Richard Stewart, Clark Byse, Richard Zeckhauser, Chris DeMuth, Graham Allison, and Albert Sacks. The American Bar Association's Commission on Law and the Economy (including its vice-chairman, Richard Smith), the Health Resources Administration of the Department of Health and Human Services, the Ford Foundation, and the Kennedy School itself also provided invaluable aid.

I am particularly grateful for the efforts of Leonard Stein, whose indefatigable research is most apparent in the footnotes of the early chapters and whose editorial skills are reflected throughout. I would also like to thank Patty Saris for her help on Chapter 17, and Michael Aronson and Maria Kawecki for their editorial assistance.

Contents

Regulation and Its Reform

Introduction

Regulation of the American economy has grown enormously since 1887, when Congress established the first modern regulatory agency—the Interstate Commerce Commission—to regulate railroads.[1] Most of this growth has taken place since the mid-1960s. Until then, regulation had consisted mainly of efforts by both federal and state governments to control prices and entry of utilities, communications firms, and transportation companies. The federal government regulated interstate aspects of railroads, trucks, airlines, telephone service, electricity, radio, television, and natural gas, while state commissions regulated the intrastate portions of these same businesses. The federal government also established safety regulation in the transportation, food, and drug industries, and regulated banks and issuers of securities in order to protect depositors and investors.

Beginning in the mid-1960s the number of federal regulatory agencies and the scope of regulatory activity vastly expanded. The federal government began to regulate oil prices and other aspects of energy production; to impose significant controls upon environmental pollution; and to regulate the safety of the workplace, of the highway, and of consumer products. It increased regulatory protection of investors, including pension holders and commodities traders.

By any measure, regulation expanded quickly and significantly. New governmental bureaus proliferated. The number of pages of federal regulations in the federal register grew from 2,599 in 1936 to 65,603 in 1977, with the number tripling during the 1970s. Federal regulatory budgets grew sixfold during the same decade. Permanent full-time positions in regulatory agencies grew from 28,000 in 1970 to 81,000 in 1979.[2] Paul MacAvoy, in a careful effort to measure the effects of regulation, included as "regulated" those industries upon which such "economy-wide" regulation as safety regulation has an unusually important impact (industries in which it accounts for 10 percent or more of investment). He estimates that in 1965, 8.5 percent of the gross national product was produced in "regulated" industries. By 1975 that figure had increased to 23.7 percent.[3] (See Appendix 1 for tables and figures illustrating this growth.)

As regulation has grown, so has concern about regulatory failure. This concern is not new. The Brownlow Committee, established by President Franklin Roosevelt, found in 1937 that the "independent regulatory commissions constitute a serious and increasing problem."[4] Similarly, the Hoover Commission in 1948 and 1955,[5] the Landis Report in 1960,[6] the Ash Council in 1973,[7] and a host of other reports, commissions, and studies have criticized regulatory agencies, programs, and processes.[8] With the growth in regulation, their criticisms have become severe.

The criticisms of regulation are typically of several sorts. First, some critics emphasize the enormous costs of regulation. Estimates of direct governmental expenditure range from $3 billion to $6 billion annually,[9] but estimates of indirect costs, including the costs of compliance, vary from $60–70 billion annually to double or triple that amount.[10] The most careful study of compliance costs, conducted by the Business Roundtable, showed that forty-eight companies, together accounting for about 8 percent of nonagricultural sales, spent $2.6 billion to comply with federal regulations (mostly environmental regulations) in 1977.[11] The largest estimate, made by the chairman of the Federal Paperwork Commission, is over $200 billion a year.[12]

Second, and more important, critics charge that too little is obtained in return for these large expenditures. Thus, MacAvoy argues that the costs of regulation are clear. Before the advent of health, safety, and environmental regulation in the 1970s, for example, the industries that were subsequently particularly subjected to regulation grew faster than others. Now they grow much more slowly (0.4 percent annual rate of growth from 1973 to 1977, compared with 2.1 percent for unregulated industries during the same period). Their prices are significantly higher and output lower.[13] Yet "whether commensurate increases in the quality of work conditions or of the environment have resulted has not been shown."[14] For example, there are numerous statistical studies that seek, but fail to find, any significant effect of workplace safety regulation on accident rates.[15] Although studies of auto safety regulation credit federal regulation with a significant reduction in the number of auto deaths, and the environment is clearly cleaner in some parts of the country, the extent to which regulation can be credited with the improvement and whether its effect is worth its cost are open to debate.[16] Given that many programs have operated effectively for only a few years and given the difficulty of constructing accurate studies to measure and value their impact, the debate over the effectiveness of regulation is likely to continue. At the same time critics of many older regulatory programs, such as those regulating airlines, trucking, and natural gas, have been able to build a strong case that these programs have hurt the general public by bringing about prices that are too high, creating shortages, or both.[17]

Third, critics have complained of unfair and unwieldy regulatory procedures. Some complain that the regulatory process is fraught with delay—perhaps the most famous example being the ten years that the Food and Drug Administration spent trying to set standards governing the percentage of peanuts in peanut butter.[18] Other examples, such as the seven years required to set automobile brake standards, are common. Many complain of a practical inability to participate in the formulation of important policies.[19] Although rules of administrative procedure typically require elaborate hearings when a policy is applied, they grant far less opportunity for confrontation or participation when policy is initially formulated. The "informal" formulation of important governmental policy is sufficiently common and sufficiently distrusted that it has led to increased demand for more open proceedings and greater participation by "public interest" lawyers who seek to represent consumers or consumer organizations. This effort is but the latest in a long series of procedural changes and requirements, now embodied in the Administrative Procedure Act, designed to make the regulatory process a fair one.

Fourth, the regulatory process has been criticized as fundamentally undemocratic and lacking legitimacy.[20] Regulators are appointed—not elected—officials, yet they wield enormous power. How is their exercise of that power to be controlled? At one time, students of the administrative process believed that the congressional statutes themselves would control administrative discretion. If administrators strayed outside their statutory authority, the courts would reverse their action. This hope proved ill-founded, however, for Congress began to delegate authority in very broad terms. At the same time, the courts exercised restraint, hesitating to set aside administrators' action on review. It proved equally illusory to look to regulators as "scientists," professionals, or technical experts, whose discretion would be held in check by the tenets of their discipline. It has become apparent that there is no scientific discipline of regulation, nor are those persons appointed to regulatory offices necessarily experts. Indeed, some of the most successful—as well as some of the least successful—regulators have had political backgrounds and have lacked experience in regulatory fields.

It is currently popular to believe that discretion will be exercised more wisely if representatives of all affected groups participate in the regulatory process, if files and documents are open to the public, and if meetings of regulatory bodies take place in public. Thus, the Freedom of Information Act[21] and the Government in the Sunshine Act[22] have limited significantly the extent to which decisions can be made without public scrutiny. Whether this approach will yield better decisions or limit administrative discretion remains to be seen. Regulators may simply make their decisions without written documentation before the issues are sufficiently formalized for requirements of formal notice and consultation to apply. If so, the regulator will remain vested with nearly uncontrollable discretion, unelected, freed by wide statutory mandates from close judicial scrutiny and unchecked by professional discipline.

Finally, there are those who claim that the regulatory process is unpredictable, even random, in its effects. For example, the process can be used by one competitor to injure another. Western coal producers, for example, may urge the adoption of rules that make it difficult for utilities to burn high-sulfur eastern coal, while eastern producers may urge the adoption of rules making it difficult to stripmine western coal. Given the technical nature of such subjects and the ability of firms to hire excellent counsel to argue for them, it becomes difficult for the agency to separate "the public interest" from the private interest of the parties.[23] However, complexity of regulatory subject matter makes it impossible for regulators to consider all the relevant factors or to predict their likely effects. An environmental regulator who seeks to calculate the cost of imposing a standard likely to require a particular type of antipollution equipment may calculate the expected cost to industry by multiplying the capital cost and operating costs of the equipment by the number of firms in the industry. Yet he cannot readily ascertain the relation of one industry to another, or predict, say, a sudden increase in demand for the equipment, which results in a shortage of pumps, which in turn triggers a demand for a wage increase for pump workers, with rippling effects upon similar workers in other industries. Nor can the regulator readily take account of the added uncertainty produced, which might increase the capital costs of smaller firms, leading them to close down, with the possible effect of changing a competitively structured industry into a highly concentrated one. The more widespread, the more technical, the more costly the regulatory requirement, the more difficult it becomes to predict both the microeconomic and the macroeconomic effects of the change.

These criticisms—high cost; ineffectiveness and waste; procedural unfairness, complexity, and delay; unresponsiveness to democratic control; and the inherent unpredictability of the end result—do not apply to every regulatory program nor to every instance of regulation. They vary in their applicability from one time, place, and program to another. Moreover, defenders of particular programs and of regulation in general can respond by pointing to achievements of individual programs or by claiming that in the absence of regulation, matters would be far worse. Yet it seems fair to say that criticism of regulation has grown apace with regulation itself. There is a perceived public demand for reform, and the reform issue now occupies a place of importance on the nation's political agenda.

The Object and Approach of This Book

Given the large number of regulatory programs and the many criticisms of regulation with their varying applicability, it is difficult to think about regulation in general, to assess the criticisms' validity, and to formulate proposals for reform. Discussions of regulation that focus upon individual programs often appear too individualistic, too parochial, or too "special" to shed much light on regulation in general. On the other hand, efforts to generalize about all "regulation" often appear too abstract or too prone to exceptions to be of use in formulating policy. If regulators, legislators, or others interested in regulation are to learn from past experience with regulatory programs, and if those lessons are to be directly useful and applicable to present programs and present problems, a system of categorizing regulation is needed. That system must contain generalizations about regulation that are broad enough to apply to different circumstances, but specific enough to be useful. A major object of this book is to fill that need. The book presents a framework for analyzing regulatory programs and generalizes about typical problems facing each type of regulation. The framework categorizes regulation and organizes insights about regulation so that a student of the subject can understand more readily the problems facing a conscientious regulator. Understanding these problems, in turn, aids in evaluating the strengths and weaknesses of the regulatory process.

At the same time, the book has a broader objective: the development of the framework and the analysis argue, by example and suggestion, for a particular substantive case-by-case approach to regulatory reform, guided by the analysis set forth. In order to evaluate regulation—to understand its strengths and weaknesses—one must automatically isolate existing areas of regulation that appear likely to need reform. These are areas in which the regulatory weapon is not well suited to deal with the problem at hand. In calling attention to those areas, the book may help legislators and policy makers determine where they might most profitably spend their "reforming" energies. It also may help them decide where or whether to design new regulatory programs and to rely instead upon alternatives to traditional systems of regulation—alternatives that tend to be less restrictive, and less intrusive, than full-blown governmental regulation.

Although several chapters of this book focus on specific regulatory programs, the changes suggested are not meant to be definitive. The framework and analysis of regulation are meant only to identify "candidates" for change. Once a particular program has been selected as a candidate, considerable detailed work is required to determine whether change is in fact warranted and to bring it about. The final part of the book describes this process, using the reform of airline regulation as an example.

The framework is built upon a simple axiom for creating and implementing any program: determine the objectives, examine the alternative methods of obtaining these objectives, and choose the best method for doing so. In regulatory matters, this axiom is often honored in the breach. In part, this may be because there is no widely accepted systematic account of the difficulties that accompany the effort to tackle problems through the use of regulation. While the defects of the free market are well recognized and form an important part of a widely accepted theory,[74] the criticisms of regulation tend to be anecdotal or form part of far more controversial theories. Moreover, the potential alternatives to classical regulation, such as taxation, are often not explored in any detail. Too often arguments made in favor of governmental regulation assume that regulation, at least in principle, is a perfect solution to any perceived problem with the unregulated marketplace. Of course, regulation embodies its own typical defects. One of the book's objectives is to present some of these defects systematically, so that legislators, administrators, and others will find it easier to match regulatory goals with regulatory systems. The reason that it is possible to develop a framework—to find similarities among so many different programs and to fit many different instances of regulation into a few basic categories—is that almost all instances are subject to the same four constraints.

First, the relation between the regulator and the firms affected by regulation is adversarial. In part, this is because the regulator must lead the industry to perform in a way different from that dictated by the incentives of the unregulated market. It may also reflect an American social or political tendency to think, and to act, as if "business" and "consumers" were in a basically adversary relationship. The procedural context and use of lawyers further encourage the framing of issues in an adversary manner, often leading to the characterization of an "industry" position and a "consumer" position, or a set of "positions" stated by the parties involved.

Second, the regulatory agency is itself an institutional bureaucracy. Those working within it are administrators or civil servants. They will act in accordance with their own internal rules and with procedures that can be understood and administered with relative ease. Sociologists, political scientists, and others have described the workings of bureaucracy as involving: a division of activities among workers, each of whom has a duty to carry out his job; the assignment of roles on the basis of technical qualifications that are determined by formal procedures such as tests; the carrying out of activities according to rules; the continuous use of categorization and classification; and the use of technical personnel to attain ends set by others.[25] Scholars have made hosts of interesting generalizations about bureaucracies. Some have tried to develop theories based upon single motivating factors, claiming, for example, that bureaucracies will seek to maximize their budget, their jurisdiction, their output, and their measurable output.[26] Although these theories are controversial, bureaucracies nonetheless resemble one another, and all regulation is characterized by administration through bureaucracy.

Third, despite sudden growth, regulation has in fact emerged gradually over many years. Those fashioning new regulatory schemes tend to copy old ones. Thus, the framers of the Civil Aeronautics Act (1938),[27] the precursor of today's Federal Aviation Act,[28] copied the language of the Interstate Commerce Act (1887), which was in turn modeled on the British Railway Act (1845).[29] Moreover, when administrators seek to implement a statute, they copy the methods of prior administrators. As Chapter 3 will show, for example, the administrators of economy-wide price controls in 1973 copied the methods used by their predecessors during the Korean War, who, in turn, based their methods upon those developed during World War II.

Fourth, decisions are made subject to the requirements of administrative law. The law governing federal agencies is chiefly codified in the Administrative Procedure Act (APA).[30] At a minimum, agencies may make major decisions only after giving advance notice and allowing affected parties to present arguments and evidence for and against the proposed positions. The agency must provide reasons for its action and publicly present evidence in support of its final decision, which the courts may review to determine both whether the decision can be "objectively" supported as rational and whether it has been reached through "fair" procedures. To an ever greater extent, important agency decision making follows the format provided by the APA for either notice-and-comment rulemaking or formal adjudication. These and other administrative law requirements are sufficiently important to warrant further discussion, which as an aid to the interested reader has been placed in Appendix 2.

These basic similarities allow the development of a framework for analyzing and describing "regulation." Nonetheless that framework does not cover every conceivable regulatory program, nor can every part of every program be squeezed comfortably within one or the other of its "boxes." Thus, the justification for the framework does not lie in any theoretical comprehensiveness; rather it lies partly in its ability to suggest useful generalizations—generalizations that are broad enough to cover more than one regulatory program but specific enough to impart useful knowledge. In this way, those interested in one program can learn from the experience of others. The framework's justification also lies in its ability to identify typical regulatory problems, to predict regulatory failures, and to suggest alternatives.

Limitations

There are a number of limitations on the scope of this book—limitations that make it partial and suggestive in nature, rather than a comprehensive effort to deal with all regulation or to propose definitive solutions, even in individual cases.

First, no serious effort is made to define "regulation." The instances discussed constitute "economic regulation" as broadly conceived to deal not only with prices and entry, but also with health, safety, and the environment. The discussion, however, may have only limited applicability to areas that are less obviously "regulatory" (such as the awarding of welfare grants) or that plainly advance noneconomic social goals (such as enforcement of antidiscrimination laws). Efforts to distinguish intellectually between such areas and "regulation"—indeed, to distinguish clearly between governmental "regulatory" action and the entire realm of governmental activity—are difficult and the subject of controversy.[31] This book does not enter or resolve that controversy. But if some of its lessons apply to, or if some of the discussion illuminates, other areas of governmental activity less obviously economic or regulatory, so much the better.

Second, the justifications for regulation listed in Chapter 1 are traditional instances of market failure. Some might argue that there are numerous other justifications for regulatory programs. Through lengthy argument, it should be possible to persuade those who advance other justifications that "market defects" of the sort listed in Chapter 1 lie at the bottom of their claims. No such lengthy argument, however, is attempted here. Rather, those who believe strongly in the existence of other legitimate justifications are asked to begin by evaluating the merits of a program using the analysis to be presented here. Then, having reached a conclusion based on that analysis, they can introduce other justifications to test the conclusion reached—to see if it still holds. Frequently the introduction of other alleged justifications for a regulatory program will not change the result. For example, those advocating airline regulation argued that it might be needed to help support the U.S. Postal Service, or for reasons of national defense. The analysis of the Senate subcommittee that evaluated airline regulation proceeded on the assumption that those justifications were invalid, but it left it open to their advocates to show how and why regulation was needed to secure those objectives. It was not possible to do so.

This approach to the problem of justification avoids the stalemate often produced by looking for the justifications of a regulatory program in its authorizing statute, in the arguments of its supporters, or in the underlying motives of those who fought for enactment of the program. Statutes are typically vague, open-ended, or conflicting in their statements of purpose. The Communications Act urges the Federal Communications Commission (FCC) to seek the "public interest." The Federal Aviation Act ordered the Civil Aeronautics Board (CAB) to keep prices at low competitive levels, but also to promote the expansion of the industry. The arguments of supporters may or may not reflect their underlying objectives, and their true motives are difficult to fathom. One is too often left without standards to judge the merits, either of regulatory actions or of the creation of regulatory programs, unless one looks not to legislative history, statutory language, or the "interests" of various groups but rather to what a consensus of fairly knowledgeable outside observers would consider a reasonable human goal, given our society and our economic and governmental systems. The "market defect" approach, for the most part, reflects such a consensus, at least if the possibility is left open for advocates to interject, to argue for other goals, and to convince those evaluating an action or a program that some other goal is of practical importance.

A third limitation arises out of the fact that the success or failure of individual regulatory programs seems to depend upon so many factors—historical, political, administrative, economic—that an analysis that leaves out some seems incomplete, while one that considers all makes each program seem unique, defying analysis or evaluation in the light of experience gained through regulation elsewhere. This book approaches this problem by initially treating certain relevant factors only superficially. In particular, the politics governing the creation and administration of a specific program, the actual historical reasons for the creation of the program, and such administrative factors as whether the program is run by federal or state administrators, by independent commissioners or Executive Branch department heads, are not treated in detail. Rather, the book's premise is that the comparative merits of alternative methods should be analyzed in terms of the other factors given here, and *then* historical, political, procedural, or (administrative) structural considerations should be introduced to see if, and how, they change one's judgment about the "best" method. Very often they will not. Similarly, this book, in focusing upon individual regulatory programs, says little about the fact that individual firms may be the objects of several *overlapping* regulatory programs—a fact that makes the lives of regulated entities more difficult and influences the probable outcome of any individual program. Yet to analyze regulation initially from the viewpoint of the regulated entity threatens too much complexity in analysis, tending to differentiate each program from all others, making it difficult to learn from experience elsewhere and thus discouraging efforts to match means to ends. This factor of overlapping programs is one that also can be introduced *after* tentative conclusions are reached in light of the analysis here described. Often, doing so will not change the result.

Fourth, the approach of this book is normative. It considers *justifications* for regulation, not causes. It discusses the problems of regulation from the point of view of a conscientious regulator who is trying to do his job well. This approach differs from efforts to produce general causal theories explaining the origin of regulation or its effects.

There are several important types of more general theory. Some writers argue that regulatory programs, initially advanced to serve the "public interest," become distorted because, as an agency or program matures, it becomes "captured" by the very persons or firms it was designed to regulate.[32] Theories of this sort may help explain airline regulation, trucking regulation, and the regulation of electricity in the 1960s. They have greater difficulty explaining the regulation of natural gas, railroads, drugs, environmental pollution, and safety, where industry tends to oppose much regulatory action.[33]

Other writers seek to develop "interest group" theories, which look at regulation as a good "sold" by government officials in return for the votes of those who are benefited.[34] Producers might "buy" protection from competition; small towns might "buy" subsidized airline service;[35] labor unions might "buy" workplace safety rules;[36] and consumers might "buy" lower electricity prices.[37] Such theories wisely direct attention to the political dimensions of the regulatory process. But, of course, regulation is not solely political. Nor can one easily explain the origin or working of a regulatory program solely in terms of the relative political power of the parties—at least not without trivializing the theory.[38]

Recently, several sociologists and political scientists have developed interesting and useful "bureaucractic" theories of regulatory behavior. They seek to use formal models of bureaucratic behavior to explain the creation of some regulatory programs and to predict regulatory outcomes. It is too soon to say whether this approach will offer a persuasive causal or other explanation of regulatory behavior. There is considerable disagreement about what precisely bureaucrats seek to "maximize." Is it their budget? Their jurisdiction? Their bureau's "output"? Some combination? Nor is it clear whether bureaucratic theories can explain different outcomes of different regulatory programs operated by similar bureaucracies.

The most persuasive general theory of regulation, popular among economists and political scientists until the late 1950s, held that regulation grew out of a need for a regulatory program to secure the "public interest" and that regulators sought, to the best of their ability, to secure the public interest as defined in their enabling statutes. This view has been discredited by historians and by economists, who have argued that many forms of regulation, such as trucking or airline regulation, injure the general public.[39] Historians have shown that railroad regulation was brought about not by the general public seeking governmental protection from industry, but rather by the very industry to be regulated. The reaction against this view led some academics to embrace one or another version of the "capture" theory, for they saw transportation regulation (as well as much occupational licensing) as designed primarily to protect those in the industry from competition.

Regardless of the merits of this or any other general theory of resolution, such theories are neither followed nor specifically treated in this book. The book does not provide a general causal theory or explanation of regulation. Instead, it asks what reasonable human goals a program might sensibly have, regardless of its historical origins. It assumes that regulators seek in good faith to attain such goals, regardless of the existence of other possible motives in fact.

Such a normative approach is worth pursuing, despite the fact that political and bureaucratic factors obviously play an important role in the outcome of regulatory programs. Even if the creation (or administration) of existing programs is best explained by the political power of special groups seeking selfish ends—which at least in some cases is doubtful—those who seek to justify those programs must appeal to the public interest. Legislatures, administrators, judges, critics, and the public at large wish to know whether regulatory programs are justified. All of them seek standards against which to judge the success of a program and the merits of specific regulatory actions taken within a program's broad authority. Moreover, the view that regulators or politicians are motivated only by politics or self-interest is far too narrow. Many surely seek the public good and are swayed by arguments on the merits. Bureaucratic behavior is to some extent the behavior of professionals, who will seek through their own actions to carry out a program's legislated objectives. Finally, a description of the problems and obstacles facing regulators as they try to carry out a program in good faith is a useful first step in explaining likely outcomes of regulatory programs. Even the best-intentioned regulator is likely to find it difficult or impossible to carry out many a regulatory statute's mandate; those acting out of purely political motives or seeking to aggrandize are not likely to have an easier time. Understanding the obstacles in the path of the well-intentioned regulator may, then, help to illuminate, even if it does not fully explain, regulatory action. The approach taken here is useful as a guide to implementation and reform, regardless of the validity of other explanations of the derivation of regulatory programs or regulators' actions.

I

A Theory of Regulation

1
Typical Justifications for Regulation

The major objectives of most economic regulatory efforts fall within one of the categories discussed in this chapter.[1] The *justification* for intervention arises out of an alleged inability of the marketplace to deal with particular structural problems. Of course, other rationales are mentioned in political debate, and the details of any program often reflect political force, not reasoned argument. Yet thoughtful justification is still needed when programs are evaluated, whether in a political forum or elsewhere. Usually this justification is one (or more) of the following.[2]

The Control of Monopoly Power

The most traditional and persistent rationale for governmental regulation of a firm's prices and profits is the existence of a "natural monopoly." Some industries, it is claimed, cannot efficiently support more than one firm. Electricity producers or local telephone companies find it progressively cheaper (up to a point) to supply extra units of electricity or telephone service. These "economies of scale" are sufficiently great so that unit costs of service would rise significantly if more than one firm supplied service in a particular area. Rather than have three connecting phone companies laying separate cables where one would do, it may be more efficient to grant one firm a monopoly subject to governmental regulation of its prices and profits. To understand why this may be so, we must examine the underlying arguments.

The Traditional Economic Rationale for Regulation

In a perfectly competitive market, firms expand output to the point where price equals incremental cost—the cost of producing an additional unit of their product.[3] A monopolist, if unregulated, curtails production in order to raise prices. Higher prices mean less demand, but the monopolist willingly forgoes sales—to the extent that he can more than compensate for the lost revenue (from fewer sales) by gaining revenue through increased price on the units that are still sold.[4] The result is waste: Consumers compare the high monopoly price of the monopolized product with the relatively cheaper prices of competitively produced products and buy more of the latter even though (1) they may prefer more of the former and (2) it costs society less in terms of real resources to produce more of the former and less of the latter.[5] Thus, where economies of scale render competition wasteful, the classical economist or regulator will try to set price near incremental cost in order to induce the natural monopolist to expand its output to a socially preferred level—where buyers do not inefficiently substitute consumption of socially more costly goods for consumption of the monopolized good.[6]

Monopolists may also lack sufficient incentive to hold production costs at low levels. They do have some incentive to lower costs, since lower costs will increase their profits. But although there is a "carrot," there is no "stick": they do not feel the pressure of competitors who would threaten to lower their own costs, subsequently lower their prices, and thereby capture sales. For this reason, the monopolist may be lazy about production costs. The extent to which regulation can counteract this tendency is doubtful.[7]

Objections to the Traditional Economic Rationale

There are serious objections to the basic rationale for regulation just described. While none of them suggests outright rejection of the economic model, they do seriously temper the enthusiasm with which we embrace its results.

The "second best" problem. The theory of the "second best"[8] casts doubt on the value of forcing prices down toward incremental costs. Under perfect competition, the price of each and every good reflects its incremental cost; buyers cannot be misled into choosing goods that they desire less but that cost society more to produce; resources are allocated so as to maximize social welfare. However, in the real world, differences between price and true economic cost not only exist, but vary greatly across goods and industries. The theory of the second best posits that one cannot readily determine what sort of price changes are needed to correct the resulting inefficiency. The prices of goods *relative* to one another, not their absolute level, direct purchasing decisions. Thus, monopoly may raise prices, but an equal degree of monopoly throughout the economy should lead to relative prices roughly similar to those of perfect competition. And it should give consumers much the same information about relative production costs as would perfect competition. In an economy in which there are varying competitive conditions and in which there is no accurate, practical method for measuring cost/price differences, one cannot be certain whether lowering the price of a single product will provide consumers with *more* or with *less* accurate information about the relative costs of products. Thus, one cannot be certain whether lower prices and increased production generated by regulation are more or less wasteful of society's resources.

The "second best" argument weakens but does not destroy the classical rationale for regulation. One might confess to uncertainty but still believe that lower regulated prices are more likely to move the economy toward rather than away from allocative efficiency. Large sectors of the American economy are competitive—with prices that are presumably near incremental costs—and unregulated monopoly can raise prices far above costs. In addition, monopoly can significantly distort buying decisions within particular sectors in a way that is entirely independent of its affect on the economy as a whole. Assume, for example, that within the energy sector coal and natural gas are produced competitively but oil is monopolized. Relative prices induce consumers to use some coal that (in relative terms) is more socially costly to produce than equivalent oil. Increased competition in the oil industry improves allocational efficiency within the energy sector regardless of the effect it has on buying decisions elsewhere.[9] In the absence of a strong empirical showing that such proregulation premises are untenable, one may find "second best" considerations ignored in regulatory debates for an important practical reason: agencies and courts need principles and standards to determine the substantive validity of regulatory decisions governing price and other (particularly anticompetitive) practices. The competitive model—based upon the desirability of incremental cost pricing—provides such standards. Given the difficulty of elaborating acceptable substitute standards, it is unlikely that it will be abandoned.

Price discrimination. Without regulation, natural monopolists will not necessarily restrict output, if they can discriminate in price.[10] "Price discrimination" means charging, say, different customers two or more different prices for the identical product. For most producers price discrimination is impractical, because the customer who is charged a low price for a unit of the product can turn around and resell it to the customer whom the producer wishes to charge a high price. The very nature of telephone service, electricity, and natural gas, however, makes it difficult for a user to resell the service he receives. Thus, if the telephone company, electric producer, or natural gas distributing company can discern the relative value of the service to each customer (that is, the maximum price each would pay for the service), it can dramatically increase revenues by raising the price to those who will continue to use its service, while keeping prices low to prevent abandonment by others. There would then be none of the service curtailment that the classical economist/regulator fears the monopolist would bring about without regulation.[11]

The force of this argument depends upon the ease with which the monopoly firm can in fact discriminate. To discriminate in price, customer by customer, is administratively impractical for these firms, as is price discrimination over individual units sold to a single customer. A practical discriminatory pricing system would divide customers into classes, and services into categories. Railroads, for example, charge higher rates to transport more valuable commodities; airlines, seeking to charge business travelers more, give discounts to those who can stay away for a week or longer; electric utilities have "business" and "residential" rates. The unregulated profit-maximizing monopolist presumably would raise the prices of some services across the board within some classes and categories. Thus, to some extent, without regulation service will be curtailed. The seriousness of the classical "output curtailment" problem depends upon the practicality of determining appropriate price classifications, which in turn depends upon the firm's knowledge of how demand responds to price changes. The less accurately the monopolist firm can estimate its customers' response to price changes, the more likely that it would, if unregulated, impose price increases that lead to curtailed service.[12]

Not much market power. A related argument assumes that demand for natural monopoly services is fairly elastic—that is to say, a fairly small increase in price leads to a significant cut in demand for the product. If so, the monopolist will not make substantial price increases for fear that buyers will switch to other products. Alternatively, it may be fairly easy for new firms to enter the market to produce this or a related product, and higher prices may induce new (but less efficient) competitors to enter and attract customers. Thus, the natural monopolist—even without regulation—may be unlikely to raise prices very high, and, in the absence of regulation, production will not be curtailed significantly.[13]

But this argument and the "price discrimination" arguments raise several empirical questions: To what extent is price discrimination possible? How does one go about determining elasticity of demand for different sets of customers over different ranges of price? What is the height of entry barriers? Given the difficulty of answering these questions, it is not surprising that intuitive judgments about them differ when applied to particular industries—just as do estimates of the importance of "inadequate output" as a rationale for regulating monopoly.

The need to pay for investment. The classical "inadequate output" argument may be thought of as an argument for nationalization and not regulation. Consider Hotelling's[14] example of a bridge that costs $25 million to build and will last virtually forever. Assume that the resource cost per crossing—the wear and tear on the bridge—is 50 cents. To charge more than 50 cents will reduce bridge use and prompt inefficient expenditures (such as driving an extra ten miles to avoid the toll). Yet if the bridge owner charges only 50 cents, how is he to pay back the investors who put up the $25 million to build the bridge? The answer, the argument goes, is nationalization. If the government invests $25 million, needed bridges are built, and if it charges a toll of only 50 cents once the bridge is built, no one is unnecessarily discouraged from using it.

Nationalization, however, has its own problems. Consider two common ones related to allocation and efficiency: (1) *How is the government to know when and where to build bridges?* Unless bridge users are prepared to pay not only 50 cents for wear and tear, but also enough additional money to pay the investment cost (whether through tolls or taxes), it is wasteful to build the bridge.[15] A private investor will build bridges only where users can, and will, pay enough to cover investment costs. The government can try to reproduce (or improve upon) the private investor's decision by developing a cost/benefit calculus for each project and investing only in those that demonstrate adequate social returns. However, there is serious doubt as to whether such studies produce results as accurate as those flowing from the discipline imposed upon investors by the knowledge that users must in fact pay sufficient tolls if the investment is to be recovered.[16] (2) *Are nationalized industries less efficiently operated than those run by private firms?* Do they run the risk of undue political interference? Ambrose Bierce, for example, defined a lighthouse as "a tall building on the seashore in which the government maintains a lamp and the friend of a politician."[17]

If nationalization is rejected, then capital must be raised from private sources, and regulators must set prices that allow fixed investment—investment in rights of way or railway beds, representing unrepeatable expenditure—to be paid for and recovered. This need, in the case of a natural monopoly, may well lead to prices that exceed incremental costs. Thus, even when regulation works perfectly, it cannot, by setting prices equal to incremental costs, totally cure the "misallocation" that natural monopoly theoretically might cause, but rather it will aim at setting higher prices that allow recovery of investment costs when incremental cost pricing would not do so.

In sum, the traditional "inadequate output" justification for natural monopoly regulation rests upon the assumption that a natural monopoly, operating without fear of present or future legislation, would set prices not simply higher than incremental cost, but significantly higher. It assumes that the regulated prices (including the recovery of investment) generate product prices (in a sector or in the economy generally) that reflect relative resource costs better than would unregulated prices. Such a proposition is logical, but rests upon a host of empirical assumptions that are unproved or, as a practical matter, unprovable.

Additional Bases for Regulation

In addition to the economically based "increased output" rationale, three other justifications for regulating the natural monopoly are often advanced.

Income transfer. Even if the monopolist maintains output at roughly the competitive level—by practicing price discrimination, for example—he will raise the price of some of his services far above a regulated or competitive level. The effect is to transfer income from the users of the service to investors—an income transfer that is generally believed to be regressive, and hence undesirable.[18] From the investor's perspective, this transfer of wealth takes place only once. If, for example, an electricity company were suddenly deregulated and found it could earn profits equivalent to, say, 50 percent on its equity investment instead of its previous earnings of 10 percent on the stock's market value, the price of the company's shares would rise, so that earnings on the new higher share value would be roughly equivalent to returns earned by other competing investments.[19] Initial investors receive a windfall; future investors, who pay more for the shares, do not. Consumers indefinitely pay the extra charges each year that constitute the increased profits that the firm now enjoys. The more essential the service, the greater the amount that this income transfer is likely to be. Unlike monopoly rents, or patents, or rents accruing to firms that improve their products, there is no natural limitation to the time period over which increased profits are earned, nor is there any obvious social advantage in allowing the firm to earn them. Although the amount of probable income transfer in any specific case is almost always unknown, proponents of regulation may assume it to constitute a strong reason for regulating the prices and profits of the natural monopolist.

Fairness. The competitive market does not provide the firms within it much opportunity for the arbitrary or unjustifiably discriminatory exercise of personal power. If grocery store A hires rude salesmen or provides inadequate service, the customer can switch to store B. If an unregulated telephone company were to treat a customer unfairly, he or she would have no ready recourse. Given the high costs of litigation, courts are not readily accessible. Appeals to higher levels within the firm's bureaucracy may not be very effective when the firm is aware that the customer must continue buying the firm's service regardless of the outcome. The regulatory system, by providing recourse for grievances against the monopolist, offers a remedy that to some extent makes up for the lack of competition's guarantees against unjustified discrimination.[20]

Power. Regulation is also advocated by those who fear concentration of substantial social or political power in the hands of a single firm that controls an essential product. Whether regulation is in fact effective in achieving this end is, of course, debatable. Yet the need to file reports, the fear that improper conduct might prompt hostile governmental action, the feeling of public responsibility that regulation may engender in the minds of the firm's executives—all suggest that regulation may have some effect (for better or worse) on the social or political activities of a large firm. Though the meaning and desirability of "corporate social responsibility" is controversial, it can be argued that regulated firms such as the telephone company will take actions popularly regarded as socially responsible, though there is no empirical data about whether regulation makes such actions more likely.

This survey of the classic case for economic regulation—regulating the prices and profits of the natural monopoly—although brief, suggests that the case for regulation rests partly on economic grounds, partly on political and social grounds, and upon a host of unproved (and possibly unprovable) assumptions. However, enough of these assumptions are plausible to make regulation an apparently reasonable governmental response to the natural monopoly.

Rent Control or "Excess Profits"

What Is a Rent?

Since "economic rent" is often confused with "monopoly profit," the problem of rent control is often confused with that of controlling monopoly power. Yet rents and monopoly profits are very different.

A firm will earn an economic rent if it controls a source of supply that is cheaper than the current market price.[21] It is a rent and not a monopoly profit if the cheap source could not supply the entire market. If, for example, coal sells in a competitive market for $20 a ton, and if Smith finds a small but unusually rich seam that can be mined for $1 a ton, Smith will earn a rent of $19 a ton. Smith's profit is best thought of as a rent because his output is limited. He cannot expand production to the point where he could supply the entire coal market—his seam is too small. Thus, if all non-Smith coal costs $20 to produce, and buyers are willing to pay $20, those buyers will bid the price of Smith's coal up to $20.

Unlike a monopoly profit, the existence of a rent does not mean that there is "inefficiency" or "allocative waste." Assume that the coal industry is highly competitive and sells 15 billion tons per year—including 50 million from Smith's mine—at a price of $20 per ton. By definition, Smith can produce no more; by definition, additional coal will cost $20 or more per ton to produce. To sell coal at $20 equates demand with supply and allows each buyer to see the additional resource cost of supplying his (extra) demand. To force the price of coal down below $20 will yield no more coal, for it costs $20 or more per ton to produce more than the existing 15 billion tons In fact, a price below $20 will bring about a shortage because customers will demand more coal and their demand cannot be satisfied at less than $20. To lower price (below the resource cost of satisfying their demand) causes distortions in the prices of coal and related commodities.

It should be noted that rents are common throughout the economy, in competitive and noncompetitive industries alike. Any firm that finds a more efficient production process, that finds an unusually cheap supply source, that luckily buys a machine at a time when they are cheap, that has unusually effective managers—but that cannot expand to the point of satisfying a significant share of industry demand at prices that reflect its lower costs—earns a rent. To discourage the earning of rents is highly undesirable, for it would impede the search for efficiency. In many instances it seems perfectly fair that rents should accrue to producers who, through talents or skill, produced them.

The Rationale for Regulation

Many of those who demand regulation of rents may not be aware of the precise nature of the problem. They may see large producer profits and believe that they are monopoly profits or they may simply see prices rising, and, without inquiry into the cause, exert political pressure to bring about lower prices through regulation.[22] Mistake, confusion, or political power may cause regulation but cannot justify it. Yet a plausible justification for regulation to control some rents exists. The justification rests upon the desirability of transferring income—from producers to consumers—in a very few instances in which producer rents are large and occur suddenly.

Thus, one finds plausible arguments for rent control made where producers of certain products particularly important to consumers suddenly find that they, through no particular initiative of their own (through luck or change in general economic conditions), have earned very large rents.[23] During World Wars I and II owners of urban housing and property found that increased immigration into cities combined with the curtailment of new building (as construction workers were called to defense work) forced up the price of old housing.[24] Similarly, it has been argued that producers of natural gas that had been found at low cost could earn huge profits—by selling this old cheap gas in a free market, where increased demand and vastly increased exploration costs made natural gas far more expensive.[25] And, of course, between 1973 and 1980 the Arab cartel multiplied the value of existing oil stocks by a factor of ten.

These cases argue for regulation for reasons related not to more efficient use of the world's resources, but to a fairer income distribution. First, it is felt that the extra profit accruing to these producers is somehow undeserved. It does not reflect wise investment decisions—money was not attracted into oil exploration by anticipation of a future Arab boycott. Rather, it reflects plain luck. Second, the income transfer from consumers to producers or to their shareholders that these profits represent is thought to be *regressive*. Of course, the transfer will in part be taxed away—through tax rates on unearned income, for example, that approach 70 percent (compared with a 50 percent rate on earned income). But tax rates may fall, and producers may find ways within the tax laws to shelter the increased income from these high rates of tax. Third, the amounts involved are *large*—so large that the government should intervene to ensure that "windfall" rents are captured for the benefit of the consumer rather than the producer.

The claim for regulation is strengthened if the price of a product increases not just drastically but also *suddenly,* as did, for example, the price of oil during the Arab oil embargo. The uncontrolled market price of $10–12 per barrel was five to six times the preembargo price; and the increase took place within a period of weeks. Such jumps obviously generated high rents for those controlling oil stocks. The rents were arguably "undeserved"; the transfer was regressive, and the amounts involved were large. Moreover, the *suddenness* of this rise might have required consumers to cut back other expenditures drastically in order to pay increased oil bills without significantly eroding their savings. The net result might have been to hasten economic recession.

In essence, rent control is aimed at transferring income and is undertaken for reasons of "economic fairness." It may also seek to avoid certain adverse social effects—dislocation and hardship—of a significant increase in the price of an essential household item. These hardships may result from the suddenness of the price increase rather than the existence of the rent.

Compensating for Spillovers (Externalities)

What Are Spillovers?

A considerable amount of regulation is justified on the ground that the unregulated price of a good does not reflect the true cost to society of producing that good. The differences between true social costs and unregulated price are "spillover" costs (or benefits)—usually referred to by economists as "externalities."[26] If a train emits sparks that occasionally burn the crops of nearby farmers, the cost of destroyed crops is a spillover cost imposed upon the farmers by those who ship by train—so long as the shipper need not pay the farmer for the crop lost.[27] Similarly, if honeybees fertilize nearby apple orchards, the beekeepers provide a spillover benefit to the orchard owners—so long as the latter do not pay the former for their service.[28] Spillover benefits have sometimes been thought to justify government subsidy, as when free public education is argued to have societal benefits far exceeding the amount which students would willingly pay for its provision. Yet when one considers regulatory systems, spillover costs—not benefits—are ordinarily encountered.

The Classical Rationale for Regulation

Like the regulation of natural monopoly, the regulation of spillover costs is justified by the desirability of avoiding economic waste. Suppose a factory can produce sugar either through production method A or production method B. Method A costs 9 cents per unit of production but sends black smoke billowing throughout the neighborhood to the annoyance of neighbors for miles around. Method B costs 10 cents per unit of production and produces no smoke at all. The profit maximizing factory owner adopts A although, if those injured by the smoke would willingly pay more than 1 cent (per pound of sugar) to be rid of it, method A is socially more expensive. Then B, not A, should be chosen, because its total social costs—including costs of harm inflicted—are lower. As long as the affected public prefers reduced pollution to its noisome effects, it should bribe the producer to choose method B. Where the public prefers reduced pollution yet finds no practical way to bribe the producer, too many of society's resources are attracted (by lower prices not reflecting the cost of pollution) into polluting processes and products, and too few are attracted into pollution-free products and processes. Government intervention arguably is required to help eliminate this waste.

Objections to the Classical Rationale

It can be argued that spillover costs do not call for government intervention but, rather, for a rearrangement of private property rights.[29]

First, as Ronald Coase[30] has pointed out, if bargaining were costless, spillovers would not exist. Those suffering the pollution in the example above would simply band together and offer to pay the factory to use process B rather than A. The factory owner would switch only where the coalition was willing to pay more than 1 cent per pound. Precisely the same result would occur if the factory were required to compensate residents for pollution damage (both physical and psychological) it created, or if the government intervened and stopped pollution precisely and only in each instance where the public would rather pay abatement costs than suffer the effects of pollution. Thus, one might argue, why not let people bargain privately to abate pollution rather than introduce government regulation?

The answer to this question is that bargaining is not costless. Thus, the residents may suffer the pollution despite a willingness to pay more than 1 cent per pound to avoid it, simply because it is too difficult for them to band together. As the number of affected people increases, communication becomes more expensive, bargaining becomes more complicated, and a clear consensus is harder to obtain.[31] Furthermore, there is the added problem that some participants may systematically underestimate the true value of abatement to them in the hope of minimizing their contribution to the cost of abatement.[32] Thus, transaction costs may permit the continuance of spillover costs even though society would be better off without them.

Second, one may object to the classical rationale for regulation on the grounds that inefficient spillovers could still be eliminated by allocating relevant property rights to those who are most likely to achieve the efficient result through bargaining (were bargaining practical). For example, making the factory liable for the damage it causes will prompt it to switch to process B where doing so is cheaper than compensating sufferers. Freeing the factory of liability places the burden of organizing on the sufferers, so that they can bribe the producer to switch to B—an impractical alternative.

Third, one might argue that rather than introducing governmental regulation, it might be better to create liability rules to allocate the burden of paying for the harm of pollution in a way that leads to "efficient" solutions. However, court-administered liability rules, although they may indeed have theoretical and practical merit for dealing with some spillovers, cannot adequately deal with others. For one thing, government officials must determine the precise shape and location of liability rules. This in itself may prove a herculean task. For example, should liability be placed upon the party best able to calculate the relevant costs?[33] Upon the party best able to organize? Upon the party most likely to reach the socially optimal result? It may be as difficult for a "liability rule maker" to determine the correct response in a particular instance as for a central administrator to choose between process A and process B. Moreover, the court enforcement of liability rules may be nonuniform, expensive, and have as many harmful side effects as central administrative direction. Thus, despite the theoretical existence of a system of private rights to deal with spillovers, direct governmental intervention is often believed desirable.

Another, less serious objection to governmental regulation rests upon the belief that spillovers do not exist. Undesired air pollution, for example, is caused not only by a process that sends smoke up the stack but also by the presence of nearby residents who breathe the smoke. The discomfort is as much a result of living near the factory as of using process A: while the cost is external to the good produced by A, it is internal to those who live near the factory and affects the behavior of those thinking of moving. And moving away eliminates the problem just as would the factory's switch to process B.[34]

This objection, however, misses the point. As a technical matter, externalities (or spillovers) are defined in relation to particular products. That is to say, air pollution is spillover in relation to the production of sugar; it is not claimed to be a spillover in relation to living near a sugar factory. Moreover, the justification for governmental intervention to deal with this spillover rests upon the judgment that society is better off where firms are encouraged to control polluting processes than where persons are encouraged not to live near polluting factories. Insofar as this justification relates to the spillover, it reflects the belief that those affected by air or water pollution would rather pay the cost of reducing the pollution than suffer from the pollution itself. Furthermore, the difficulties of organizing coalitions to bribe producers are just too great under the present allocation of private rights and liabilities. Thus, governmental intervention is likely to approximate better the amount of pollution that affected consumers are willing to pay for.

Of course, intervention itself is not costless. Moreover, intervention—or rearrangement of rights and liabilities—changes the distribution of wealth and income. Those who buy sugar (and the owners of sugar factories) are made poorer and those who suffer pollution are made richer by intervention or liability adjustments leading to reduced pollution. Insofar as intervention is designed to produce the result that would be paid for were bargaining feasible, those suffering pollution will gain more than the others lost. Whether this is a sufficient basis for intervening or altering liabilities may be debated. Traditionally it has been argued that changes should be made when the beneficiaries can compensate the losers out of their gains and have some gain left over; others have claimed that since the compensating is only hypothetical and not actually carried out, there is no clear justification for making the change. Regardless of the merits of these arguments, it is sufficient to note here that this rationale is one of "economic efficiency." To satisfy it is to move closer to a world in which all resources are used in a manner that maximizes the welfare of the world's individuals as measured by their preferences revealed in the marketplace. And it is the same rationale of allocative efficiency that underlies many governmental economic decisions and actions, including regulation of natural monopolies.

In sum, a spillover rationale must be phrased in terms of a particular product; it must assume that obstacles to bargaining lead to significantly greater use of a product (or production process) than would be the case if costless bargaining were possible; and it must assume that the result of intervention (taking into account the costs of intervention) will better approximate the bargained-for solution. If these assumptions are correct, then intervention will reduce allocative inefficiency.

A Caveat

One can too readily classify as a spillover cost or benefit almost any policy reason for taking actions that lead to results other than those dictated by existing market arrangements. Thus, law enforcement can be seen as securing the "external benefits" of security, or the laws prohibiting blood feuds can be justified as elimination of the "external costs" of chaos and disruption. Where it is used to describe those commodities, the value of which is incapable of even rough monetary estimation—commodities such as justice, security, and so on—the "spillover" notion is virtually useless. The more readily monetary values of the commodities or objectives can be estimated, the more directly useful "spillover" characterization is likely to prove. In other cases, one is better off speaking directly of noneconomic reasons for and against taking a particular action rather than explicitly invoking the notion of "spillover."

Moreover, since there is always some possible beneficial effect in reversing a market-made decision, one can always find some (broadly defined) spillover cost rationale for regulating anything. Thus, the rationale, if it is to be intellectually useful, should be confined to instances where the spillover is large, fairly concrete, and roughly monetizable.

Inadequate Information

For a competitive market to function well, buyers must have sufficient information to evaluate competing products.[35] They must identify the range of buying alternatives and understand the characteristics of the buying choices they confront. At the same time, information is a commodity that society must spend resources to produce. The buyer, looking for alternative suppliers, spends time, effort, and money in his search.[36] The seller spends money on research, labeling, and advertising to make his identity and his product's qualities known. In well-functioning markets, one would expect to find as much information available as consumers are willing to pay for in order to lower the cost or to improve the quality of their choices.

The Classical Rationale for Regulation

Markets for information may on occasion not function well for several reasons. First, the incentives to produce and to disseminate information may be skewed. Like the bridge in Hotelling's example, some information (particularly that requiring detailed research) is expensive to produce initially but very cheap to make available once produced. Since it can be repeated by word of mouth, televised, or printed and reprinted at low cost, it may easily benefit many recipients who never pay its original producer. Thus, those in the best position to produce the information may not do so, or they may hesitate to disseminate it, for fear that the benefits will go not to themselves but only to others.

The importance of this problem varies considerably depending upon the type of information and its use. A firm that manufactures breakfast foods, for example, would have every incentive to produce information showing that its cereal was more nutritious than that of its competitors and to disseminate that information widely. Moreover, the production, use, and dissemination of much information is protected by copyright and patent laws.[37] Further, the inadequate incentive to produce information typically leads to a demand not for regulation but for governmental support of production and dissemination.

Nonetheless, occasionally the problem may lead to a demand for regulation. Drug manufacturers, for example, are required to print the generic (general scientific) name of their product, as well as the brand name, on the label. Thus, the buyer sees that a host of competitors in fact offer to sell the same product. This labeling requirement can be seen as lowering the cost to buyers of searching for competing sellers,[38] by quickly making them aware of the competitors' existence. And it does so by requiring those with the information most readily at hand to make it available.

Second, one of the parties to a transaction may seek deliberately to mislead the other, by conveying false information or by omitting key facts. A seller of securities may lie about the assets of the company; a seller of a used car may turn back the mileage indicator. Of course, false statements or active misrepresentations may be grounds for rescinding a contract or suing for damages. Yet the cost of court action is often high enough to weaken it or give it minimal effect as a deterrent. Nor can one necessarily rely upon fear of declining reputation to act as a deterrent. The importance of reputation in securing sales depends upon the particular product, the particular seller, and a host of other circumstances. The rationale for governmental action to prevent false or misleading information rests upon the assumption that court remedies and competitive pressures are not adequate to provide the consumer with the true information he would willingly pay for. Thus, the Securities and Exchange Commission (SEC) regulates the issuances of securities, while the buyer of used cars is typically left to his basic judicial remedies.

Third, even after locating potentially competing sellers, the buyer may not be able to evaluate the characteristics of the products or services they offer.

The layman cannot readily evaluate the competence of a doctor or lawyer. Nor can he, unaided, evaluate the potential effectiveness or dangers of a drug. And he is unlikely at the time of purchase to know if a car is a lemon. Formal or informal understandings among those on the supply side—whether doctors, lawyers, or drug producers—may make difficult or impossible the creation of objectively applied labels that aid evaluation.[39] Governmental intervention may be desired to prescribe the type of information that must be provided, as well as to help buyers evaluate the information that is being supplied.[40]

Fourth, the market may, on the supply side, be insufficiently competitive to provide all the information consumers would willingly pay for. Until the government required disclosure, accurate information was unavailable to most buyers concerning the durability of light bulbs, nicotine content of cigarettes, fuel economy for cars, or care requirements for textiles.[41] In the 1930s automobile manufacturers advertised the comparative safety of their product. Subsequently this advertising disappeared, since auto makers felt that calling attention to safety problems hurt the industry more than it benefited individual firms. For similar reasons one does not find individual airlines advertising safety records. Since the airline industry is highly competitive in many respects, this fact suggests that tacit understandings not to supply certain varieties of information may be easier to reach (the industry need not be highly concentrated) than are tacit agreements not to compete in price or in service quality.

Criticisms of the Rationale

Criticisms of the rationale for regulating the provision of information usually focus on whether the rationale applies to the particular case at issue. Critics may claim, for example, that in a particular case the market is functioning competitively, consumers are sufficiently capable of evaluating a product's qualities, or there is little deliberate deception. They may argue that a particular agency's efforts to provide information are too expensive, that the information is unnecessary, that disclosure itself may mislead consumers, or that it may interfere with the competitive workings of the marketplace. For example, the efforts of the Federal Trade Commission (FTC) to require that imported products have a "country of origin" label have been criticized as at best a waste of time and at worst as an effort to protect American manufacturers from foreign competition by imposing costly labeling requirements on foreigners.

In sum, there is little quarrel with governmental efforts to help consumers obtain necessary information when the information is in fact needed and the intervention lowers the cost of providing it. Critics of intervention tend in particular cases to quarrel with the claim that regulation will lower the costs of its provision.

Excessive Competition: The Empty Box

A commonly advanced rationale for regulation of airlines, trucks, and ships is that competition in those industries would otherwise prove "excessive." This rationale has been much criticized as incoherent or at least inapplicable to the transportation regulation it is meant to justify. In fact, the difficulty with the term is that it has been used to describe several different types of rationale—some of which are no longer acceptable justifications for regulation. The notion common to all those rationales is that prices, set at unprofitably low levels, will force firms out of business and result in products that are too costly.

Historical Use

The history of airline and trucking regulation offers some insight into two possible uses of the term "excessive competition."

Airlines. The federal government began to regulate prices and profits of the airline industry in the 1930s, when it was still subsidizing the industry to encourage its development. The subsidy consisted of contracts to carry airmail at prices that exceeded the cost of carriage. A major scandal arising out of subsidy awards by the United States Postal Service led Congress, first, to transfer subsidy authority to the Interstate Commerce Commission (ICC), and, second, to consider comprehensive change of the subsidy system. The ICC administered the subsidy by asking the airlines to bid for the right to carry U.S. airmail. It awarded the contract to whichever line was willing to fly for the lowest subsidy. But the airlines believed that once the government awarded a contract to a particular carrier, it would increase the subsidy should the initial payment prove insufficient to cover the airline's costs. As Colonel Gorell, an industry representative, testified before Congress in 1937, "The law put a premium upon an unreasonably low bid since there is always the possibility that later on, a rate first put unjustifiably low will be raised by the action of the Interstate Commerce Commission . . . [which] is ultimately under the duty of fixing a reasonable rate."[42]

As a factual matter, it is not clear that competition in the 1930s was "excessive" in any sense. Colonel Gorell also testified before Congress in 1937 that excessive competition had not actually occurred, but that it had been "much closer than I would like to talk about."[43] Moreover, the classical price and profit regulatory provisions of the act may reflect the fact that its framers borrowed many of its provisions from the act governing the ICC.[44] But, at least in theory, a subsidy offer provides one perfectly sensible rationale for "excessive competition": the airlines' belief that the ICC would increase the subsidy award to a firm under contract provided an incentive to bid for the initial contract at a price well below cost. By doing so, an airline could expand the size of its route system, with the government making up the difference. Indeed, each airline would charge low prices to all customers, for the objective of each would be to expand system size and not to earn profits or to minimize losses. Thus, a government seeking to minimize the amount of subsidy required would have to prevent prices that were "unreasonably low," and regulation would be justified in order to minimize government outlay.[45]

This rationale for regulation, while coherent, is not applicable today, when almost all airlines are unsubsidized.

Trucks. Demand for regulation of trucking prices, profits, and entry arose in the 1930s for three reasons. First, the railroads, regulated by the ICC, complained that truckers were undercutting their prices. They did not argue that trucking prices were below costs, but rather that the ICC required the railroads to charge more than incremental costs on routes where they could compete with trucks; thus, the trucks took away business that, on a "least cost" basis, should have belonged to the railroads. This argument does not offer a strong rationale for regulation of trucking, but rather suggests the need for changing the way railroads are regulated.

Second, the truckers argued that an unregulated market would lead some firms to cut prices and drive others out of business. Regulation would keep more firms in business and provide more employment. In principle, however, competition drives firms out of business because the survivors can do the same job better, more efficiently, or with fewer employees. To keep *unnecessary* firms in business is likely to sound more reasonable at a time of very serious depression (like the 1930s) than today.

Third, in the 1930s the competitive process itself was often blamed for the Depression. The framers of the National Industrial Recovery Act, for example, believed that agreements among firms not to cut prices would increase profits, encourage investment, and maintain employer purchasing power. Thus, ordinary competition in many industries was viewed as "excessive." The NIRA cure for recessions, however, has been discredited. In a world in which competition is the desired norm and regulation the exception, the NIRA theory does not provide a coherent rationale for selective regulation.[46]

Current Use

Currently, "excessive competition" might be used to refer to any of three alleged justifications for regulation.

The "natural monopoly." The "excessive competition" argument would make sense as applied to an industry that is a natural monopoly. One might claim that, without regulation, too many firms would seek to enter, and the resulting fight for market share would lead to the demise of all but one—the one that obtained the lion's share of the market by achieving the lowest unit costs.[47] According to the argument, this competitive process is wasteful of resources; a regulator should make certain that only one firm enters the industry and others do not seek to displace it.

Those opposed to regulation argue the opposite. They claim that any potential waste is justified by (1) the ability of the competitive process to pick the "best" firm out of the contenders; and (2) the tendency of the competitive battle to demonstrate empirically whether or not the industry is in fact a natural monopoly.

Regardless of the outcome of this argument, it does not apply to airlines, trucks, or ships, because those industries are generally conceded to be structurally competitive—not natural monopolies. Yet it is in the case of airline, trucking, and ocean shipping regulation that one finds the excessive competition argument used.

The cyclical nature of demand. "Excessive competition" might refer to a claim that, unless a particular industry is regulated, the cyclical nature of demand for its product will produce waste. When demand falls during, say, an economic downswing, competition among firms results in prices that cover only short-run incremental costs and prompts capacity curtailment. When the next upswing occurs, a firm will have to reopen its plant or rebuild its capacity. It might be argued that, rather than have firms go through the expensive process of closing and reopening plants, the government should set minimum prices— or allow firms to agree on minimums. Prices would remain high enough to cover fixed costs and plants would continue to operate during the recession. The extra costs of the agreements to consumers, one might claim, would be less than the cost of closing and reopening during the business cycle.

This argument assumes, however, that firms cannot raise sufficient funds in the capital markets to support excess capacity during periods of soft demand. If capital markets are functioning well, the firm ought to be able to attract funds to keep its plant open during the downswing on the basis of the expected future profits in the upswing. If it cannot do so, perhaps the capacity ought to close permanently, for consumers will not pay enough for the product (in the upswing) to justify maintaining it (in the downswing). Only if markets fail accurately to reflect the firm's future earning ability is it desirable to keep the plants operational.[48]

Moreover, to prevent excessive competition by maintaining higher-than-competitive downswing prices may easily encourage overinvestment. Firms would be prevented from the otherwise unprofitable consequence of overpredicting demand for the industry and product. Any resulting overinvestment is a wasteful byproduct of an effort to prevent "waste."

In any event, this excessive competition argument applies to industries with large fixed investments and comparatively small variable costs—industries such as steel or copper.[49] One can understand that a recession might drive copper prices so low that mines must close, that the expense of reopening them may be great, and that capital markets may be unwilling to finance them so that they could remain open. But the argument does not apply to trucking, where fixed costs are low, or to airlines, where fixed costs can be reduced by leasing or storing planes during the downswing in the cycle.

Predatory pricing. Another variation of the excessive competition argument is that a particular industry is subject to "predatory pricing." Competition leads some firms to price below costs, driving their competitors out of business. The remaining firm then raises its prices to excessive levels, leaving the public worse off than before.

For a firm to have an incentive to price predatorily, however, two preconditions must be met: (1) the predator must be powerful enough to outlast its competitors once prices are cut below variable costs; and (2) reentry into the market must be so difficult that the predator can maintain prices well above costs long enough to recoup its prior losses. Unless a firm is reasonably certain that both these conditions will obtain, it is irrational for it to attempt predatory pricing.[50]

For this reason, it seems unlikely that predatory pricing will ever justify regulation. In fact, regulation can make predatory pricing easier, since it often provides the barriers to entry necessary for a potential predatory pricer to succeed. Furthermore, the antitrust laws make predatory pricing unlawful.[51] Those firms suffering its consequences can bring antitrust suits and appeal to enforcement agencies. Of course, the enforcement agencies may not be effective, but that is no argument for regulation since the regulatory agency is as likely to be ineffective.

Moreover, unfortunately, ordinary price competition is easily confused with predatory pricing. The former generally involves low-cost firms charging lower prices that take business from higher-cost firms;[52] the latter involves short-term prices well below costs, set with the object of destroying competition and later recouping losses through prices well above cost. Those advocating regulation on these grounds in the transportation field may well have confused the two.

Other Justifications

The reader should be aware of several other possible justifications for regulatory systems. While important, they have been used less often in the United States than elsewhere to justify governmental regulation of individual firms.

Unequal bargaining power. The assumption that the "best" or most efficient allocation of resources is achieved by free-market forces rests in part upon an assumption that there is a "proper" allocation of bargaining power among the parties affected. Where the existing division of such bargaining power is "unequal," it may be thought that regulation is justified in order to achieve a better balance. It is sometimes argued, for instance, that the "unequal bargaining power" of small sellers requires special legislative protection. While in principle one might regulate the "monopoly buyer" in order to protect these sellers, the more usual congressional response is to grant an exemption from the antitrust laws, thus allowing the sellers to organize in order to deal more effectively with the buyer. This rationale underlies the exemption granted not only to labor, but also to agricultural and fishing cooperatives.[53]

Rationalization. Occasionally governmental intervention is justified on the ground that, without it, firms in an industry would remain too small or would lack sufficient organization to produce their product efficiently.[54] One would ordinarily expect such firms to grow or to cooperate through agreement, and to lower unit costs.[55] But social or political factors may counteract this tendency.[56] In such circumstances, agencies have sought to engage in industry-wide "planning." In the 1960s, for example, the Federal Power Commission argued that increased coordination in the planning and operation of electric power generation and transmission facilities would significantly lower unit costs. The commission felt that environmental, political, regulatory, and managerial problems make it difficult for firms to plan jointly. The result was a relatively unsuccessful federal agency effort to encourage industrywide rationalization.[57]

Moral hazard. The term "moral hazard" is used to describe a situation in which someone other than a buyer pays for the buyer's purchase.[58] The buyer feels no pocketbook constraint, and will purchase a good oblivious to the resource costs he imposes upon the economy.[59] When ethical or other institutional constraints or direct supervision by the payer fail to control purchases, government regulation may be demanded.

The most obvious current example is escalating medical costs.[60] As medical care is purchased to an ever greater extent by the government or by large private insurers (with virtually no constraint on the amount demanded by the individual users), medical costs have accounted for an ever greater proportion of the national product.[61] The fact that purchases are paid for by others frees the individual from the need to consider that using more medical care means less production of other goods; thus, he may "unnecessarily" or "excessively" use medical resources. If one believed that too much of the gross national product is accounted for by medical treatment, and also believed that the problem of moral hazard prevents higher prices from acting as a check on individual demand for those resources (which in turn reduces incentive to hold down prices), one might advocate regulation to keep prices down, improve efficiency, or limit the supply of medical treatment.[62]

Paternalism. Although in some cases full and adequate information is available to decision makers in the marketplace, some argue that they nevertheless make irrational decisions and that therefore governmental regulation is needed. This justification is pure paternalism: the government supposedly knows better than individuals what they want or what is good for them. Such distrust of the ability of the purchaser to choose may be based on the alleged inability of the lay person to evaluate the information, as in the case of purchasing professional services, or the belief that, although the information could be accurately evaluated by the lay person, irrational human tendencies prevent this. The latter may be the case where small probabilities are involved, such as small risks of injury, or where matters of life and death are implicated, such as when those suffering from cancer will purchase a drug even though all reasonably reliable information indicates that it is worthless or even harmful. Whether the brand of paternalism based on mistrust of consumer rationality is consistent with the notions of freedom of choice that underlie the free market is questionable. However, it plays an important role in many governmental decisions.

Scarcity. Regulation is sometimes justified in terms of scarcity.[63] Regulation on the basis of this justification reflects a deliberate decision to abandon the market, because shortages or scarcity normally can be alleviated without regulation by allowing prices to rise. Nonetheless, one might decide to abandon price as an allocator in favor of using regulatory allocation to achieve a set of (often unspecified) "public interest" objectives, such as in the case of licensing television stations. Sometimes regulatory allocation is undertaken because of sudden supply failures: to rely on price might work too serious a hardship on many users who could not afford to pay the resulting dramatic price increases, as in the case of the Arab oil boycott. "Scarcity" or "shortage" calling for regulation may also be the result of the workings of an ongoing regulatory program, as when natural gas must be allocated because of rent control or when an agency awards licenses to enter an industry.

The Mixture of Rationales

Many existing regulatory programs rest upon not one but several different rationales. Thus, for example, one might favor regulation of workplace safety for several reasons. One might believe that employers and employees can bargain fairly and equally for improved workplace safety (greater safety expenditures), but argue that accidents impose costs on others who are not represented at the bargaining table; thus, bargaining alone will produce inadequate expenditures for safety devices. This is a *spillover* rationale. Or one might believe that the worker does not know enough about the risks or consequences of accidents, so that he will fail to insist upon adequate safety expenditures. This is to argue that there is an *informational defect* in the market. Or one might feel that the worker is too poor or too weak to bargain for the safety he needs— that he has *unequal bargaining power*. Finally, one might claim that workers (indeed, all people) are simply incapable of understanding their likely future feelings about accidents that hurt them. They inevitably underestimate the risk. If regulation is an effort to give them what they "really" want (contrary to their expressed views), a *paternalistic* rationale is at work.

The importance of distinguishing rationales lies in the extent to which different rationales may suggest different remedies. Thus, one who believes that the primary problem is informational will tend to favor not classical regulation, but governmental efforts to provide more information. Although one who accepts a paternalistic rationale may disagree with one who believes the problem is informational, the clear statement of their points of difference can form the basis of empirical work that will lead them toward agreement upon the basic rationale and thus help choose the regulatory weapon best suited to the problem at hand.

Similarly, the debate over the need for regulation of medical costs might be clarified if its proponents specified the rationale, or mixture of rationales, for regulation and the relative importance of each. To point to the increased price of medical care does not, by itself, suggest a need for regulation. The increased price might reflect cost increases due, for example, to medical advances. If scientific progress means that few older people die of pneumonia, more will (eventually) die of cancer or strokes, which require more expensive care and treatment. Moreover, labor costs may be increasing, as well as the costs of technology. Demand may increase because people have more money to spend on medical care. If rising prices reflect no more than increased demand for medical care (greater relative desire for medical care compared with other goods, greater ability to pay for it) and increased costs of supply (more technology, higher labor costs), regulation of these prices would not rest upon a "market failure" rationale. Indeed, rising prices might be a consequence of highly desirable actions taken by governments on grounds of equity—namely, supporting medical care for those who cannot readily afford it.

The proponent of regulation might cite other factors, however. He might argue that there is excess demand because so many patients do not pay their own bills—a problem of *moral hazard*. He might point to the difficulty potential patients have in determining whether they need care or what sort they may need. He might add that doctors themselves may not fully comprehend the economic costs of the treatment choices they make and thus choose treatment that is too expensive. All these are *informational problems* Finally, he might fear that sudden increases in demand for medical care will lead to higher profits for hospitals, which, being "nonprofit" institutions, invest the "excess" in new, more expensive technology and plants. This is a problem akin to *rent control*.

Again, a breakdown by rationale does not determine whether hospital prices ought to be regulated. To know that, one would have to obtain empirical confirmation that the rationale is empirically important. Nonetheless, analysis may help clarify and focus the debate and thereby help policy makers reach more sensible conclusions.

This chapter has surveyed the major economic rationales for regulatory programs. Individually or in combination they underlie most major regulatory programs, which are themselves of several different types. The next six chapters each describe one major type of regulation. Together with this chapter, they provide a survey of most major types of regulatory programs and the economic justifications that underlie them.

2
Cost-of-Service Ratemaking

The first of the six regulatory modes to be described is cost-of-service ratemaking. When the government has sought to regulate the prices and profits of firms in a particular industry, it has almost always done so through this system. The system has been applied to natural monopolies, such as local telephone service and electricity generation, as well as to competitive industries, such as natural gas and airlines. The system ordinarily is applied under a statute that requires a regulator to set "just and reasonable" prices.[1]

The System

Except for the objectives of cost-of-service ratemaking, the system is an administrative effort to apply a fairly simple pricing formula through a series of mechanical steps. The regulator, in determining prices, proceeds as follows:

1. He selects a test year for the firm (t).
2. He adds together that year's operating costs (OC), depreciation (D), and taxes (T).[2]
3. He adds to that sum a reasonable profit, determined by multiplying a reasonable rate of return (r) times a rate base (RB), which is determined by taking total historical investment $(\Sigma_0^t\ I)$ and subtracting total prior depreciation $(\Sigma_0^{t-1} D)$.
4. The total so far equals the firm's revenue requirement (RR). The regulator now sets prices so that the firm's gross revenues will equal its revenue requirement.
5. If the firm provides several different classes of service or serves different classes of customers, the regulator may also determine the percentage each will contribute to the total revenue, in effect determining the firm's "rate structure."

Thus, the regulator must determine profits, add on other costs to fix a "revenue requirement," and set prices to yield that requirement.[3]

While the mechanics of applying these formulas vary from one agency to another, a typical statutory system works as follows. The regulated firm must file tariffs containing proposed rates and may not lawfully charge any rate not contained in a filed tariff. The agency has the right to suspend any new filing for, say, ninety days, during which time it may hold a hearing and investigate the reasonableness of the charge. After ninety days the agency can accept the tariff, reject it as unreasonable, or continue to investigate. If it continues, the tariff takes effect subject to a possible obligation to refund any amount the agency later finds was "excessive."[4]

The agency also has the right to order hearings to investigate the *continued* reasonableness of charges already accepted. In that case, the tariff stays in effect during the investigation and there is no refund obligation.

Full investigations of existing rates are rare because they are time-consuming. The agency is more likely to investigate an application for a change in rates. Note one effect of such a system: if costs are rising, the agency will face, and must pass upon, a series of company requests for rate increases. If costs fall, however, the company will take no action, and it is unlikely that the agency will pursue it. Rates stay the same and the firm's profits increase.[5] With steady prices, consumers and others are less likely to notice an "excess rate" problem. Also, the statute works against the commission procedurally. The firm is free to keep any excess profit earned during the lengthy commission-initiated hearing; by the time the hearing is complete, facts may have changed, provoking a new company request for a rate increase.[6]

The Problems

While the precise objectives of cost-of-service ratemaking vary depending upon the particular regulatory system, regulators would agree that such systems ordinarily should seek goals such as the following: (1) preventing excess profits; (2) holding prices down to costs (including reasonable profit); (3) avoiding economic allocative waste—that is, minimizing shortages and surpluses as well as directing resources to where they satisfy the greatest demand; (4) eliminating inefficient production methods; and (5) assuring administrative ease. Taken individually, none of these goals offers concrete standards for criticism or guidance. "To hold price at cost," for example, does not indicate how to measure costs, nor does "preventing excess profits" indicate when profits are excessive or at what level of output the firm should produce. Taken together, however, the first four goals offer effective criteria for judgment. They do so because a well-functioning, competitive marketplace tends to achieve all four. Thus, one often hears that the objective of cost-of-service ratemaking is to replicate a competitive marketplace—that is to say, to reproduce the price, profit, output, and efficiency levels that would exist were the regulated market in fact competitive and well-functioning. (Any other objective would have to be specifically stated and justified as a modification of these goals.) The fifth goal, administrative ease, ofttimes directly conflicts with economic efficiency and makes the first four difficult to achieve with precision, if at all.[7] Typically, five sets of problems force the regulator away from economic objectives and make cost-of-service ratemaking a highly imprecise undertaking—which often functions as badly as an imperfectly competitive market. These five sets of problems and how regulators have dealt with them are briefly described below.

Determining the Rate Base

A key step in determining the amount of profit a regulated firm is allowed is determining its rate base—its investment upon which profit will be earned. Regulated prices will differ from the competitive market prices, since regulators almost uniformly assume that a firm's rate base (which determines the allowable profit) equals the book value of its *historical* investment.[8] A competitive marketplace values assets, not at their historical price, but at their *replacement* value—the present cost of obtaining the identical service that the old asset provides. Thus, for example, firm A's old pipeline right-of-way, bought cheaply in 1950, would be worth precisely what it would cost the owner of pipeline B to buy a similar right-of-way today. If the price has risen, B will have to charge more to its customers. In competitive markets, unregulated producers such as A could match B's price, earning a windfall for their shareholders. Alternatively, if B buys new, cheaper equipment that, thanks to new technology, does the same job as A's old equipment, in a competitive market A can charge no more than B, and its old expensive plant or equipment would be worth no more.

Moreover, note what may happen if firm A departs from competitive principles and sets its price to reflect historical cost. In the first instance mentioned (when B's new cost is higher than A's old cost), consumers seek A's gas, not B's, to the point where A's pipeline is used to capacity (without satisfying all demand). The regulator would have to allocate A's gas and would probably do so on historical, not market-based, principles. In the meantime, firms would have been encouraged unnecessarily to move from near B to near A. In the second instance mentioned (when B's new cost is lower than A's old cost), the historical system would allow A to overstate its plant's present or true value and keep its prices high, thus collecting the monopoly profits that regulation seeks to proscribe.

Why then do regulators not value rate base at replacement, rather than historical, cost? Indeed, for many years they sought to do so,[9] but the change to historical cost reflects one important administrative fact: to determine the replacement cost of a plant or equipment is too complex a task for an administrative process.[10]

Consider, for example, a public utilities commission trying to value a coal-fired 200-megawatt power station built in 1920 and located one hundred miles north of Boston. Its replacement value equals the cost of producing the 200 megawatts from a modern plant with efficient, modern equipment. But to establish that cost one would have to determine, for example, (1) whether the new plant would use coal, oil, natural gas, or nuclear fuel, (2) whether the plant would be 200 megawatts in size or larger, (3) where the plant would fit within the multistate integrated network of power plant facilities, (4) the cost of the land used for the plant, (5) expected construction delays, (6) the effect of the new plant upon the optimal cost configuration of other future plants, (7) what environmental safeguards would be necessary, and (8) the cost of likely delays in obtaining regulatory permissions. Each of these decisions—including those governing site-acquisition costs and the restructuring of the total network of plants and transmission lines, which becomes desirable once one assumes a new plant rather than an old one—would be made hypothetically. But each is necessary to determine the hypothetical cost of a new plant and therefore the valuation at current market price of the old plant.

The problem is not limited to electricity. How should a regulator determine the replacement value of an airplane that costs $10 million when new? Its value (if the regulator's objective is to replicate competitive prices) is the cost of new equipment that would do a similar job—say, carry 150 passengers from Boston to Atlanta. But this cost is not necessarily the $10 million price for a new plane, for, if replacement were at issue, the company might change its route or fleet configuration or simply shrink its fleet size. Indeed, if fewer planes could do the same job as effectively (by increasing the load of each plane), the replacement value of any individual plane is arguably zero.

In any event, one can see how highly qualified experts could argue both sides of these questions in great detail, with "company experts" placing a high value on the plant and "consumer experts" a low one. The arguments would be lengthy, the technical evidence extensive, and the result largely a matter of judgment. The possibility of court review finding the judgment "unreasonable" would make ratesetting uncertain.

To avoid this uncertainty, commissions using a "reproduction cost" rate base in the early part of this century defined "reproduction cost" as the actual cost of reproducing brick by brick the very plant under consideration.[11] Although this approach allowed accountants to give a specified determinable answer to the question "What is the value of the plant?" it destroyed the value of a replacement cost approach. It would, for example, allow inclusion of an expensive plant in the rate base despite technological change that destroyed the value of the existing plant. The more obsolete the plant, the higher might be the rates.

To avoid both uncertainty and this result, the United States Supreme Court authorized commissions to use historical costs to determine the rate base.[12] Historical cost has the virtue of ease in calculation, and its simplicity led most commissions to follow it. Its use does create the economic problems sketched at the beginning of this section, but modern commissions have chosen to incur them as the lesser evil.

Where the economic problems created by the use of historical cost valuation become serious, special modifications must be made in the process. Consider, for example, the effect of inflation upon the rates charged by a firm with a historically determined rate base. The rates will be set uneconomically low— lower than the cost of building additional new capacity—and they will encourage excessive electricity consumption. The firm will realize that not only must it build additional capacity but that it will be more expensive to replace existing capacity as well. Instead of using revenues to replace existing equipment (effectively "borrowing" its depreciation account back from its shareholders), it will be forced to finance replacement by selling more shares or issuing bonds.

In principle, the cost of borrowing should be borne by those who will use the additional new capacity. Future users should bear the costs even of land that the firm buys now and holds in reserve. If the firm must borrow to finance the land or to pay interest on the debt, that too should be financed by the future consumers—the eventual beneficiaries. Thus, borrowing requirements become extraordinarily high. The large borrowing requirements, aggravated by the historical rate-base method of accounting, have been alleviated by special statutory provisions that allow firms to include "interest during construction"[13] or the costs of land held for future use in the present rate base, effectively charging present customers part of the cost of future service. Such devices only imperfectly compensate for the economic undervaluation of the present rate base.[14]

Determining the Rate of Return

The rate of return and the rate base are related in that multiplying them together produces a pool of money profits that in principle belongs to the investors. The basic regulatory question is how large that pool ought to be. To decide, for administrative reasons, that the rate base will equal historical net investment does not by itself determine the amount of profit, for the commission must also specify the rate of return—an endeavor that occupies much of the agenda of modern commissions. In doing so, commissions are moved by three considerations: (1) fairness to shareholders and investors, (2) the need to attract roughly that amount of investment that competitive market considerations would dictate,[15] and (3) administrative simplicity.

Some of the commissions' problems can be readily solved. Bondholders are paid a fixed coupon rate of interest. Thus, people buying 8 percent bonds will be paid back 8 percent per year on the dollars they invested,[16] and the utility will be allowed to earn enough profit to pay them. Unregulated firms in competitive markets would treat their bondholders no differently. Such a payment is fair, readily calculable, and consistent with valuing the rate base—the plant and equipment that the borrowed money was used to purchase—at historical cost.

The more difficult problem is calculating a fair return on equity. That is to say, how large should the profit pool be, over and above the amount needed to pay bondholders? Put somewhat differently, what price should the company charge so that its return on total investment (valued at historical cost), after subtracting payments to bondholders (and the book value of the bondholders' investment), leaves enough to pay a "fair" or "proper" return to equity holders (which equals the remainder of the firm's book value)?

Since the accounting concepts suggested make this question appear confusing, consider a simple balance sheet. The firm has borrowed $10 million—$6 million in debt and $4 million in equity. It has invested that money in plant and equipment worth $10 million. The debt carries different coupon rates of interest—half at 6 percent and half at 8 percent—because the money was raised at different times. The rate of return that is allowed the firm on its $10 million book value must be sufficient to allow it to pay its bondholders: $420,000 [($3 million × .06) + ($3 million × .08)]. Any profit in excess of this amount constitutes a return to equity holders. The issue is how much higher the rate ought to be—in other words, what constitutes a proper return on shareholders' equity.[17] The overall rate of return that the regulator allows the firm on its $10 million will simply equal the weighted average of the individual rates of return on debt and on equity. (Thus, if the commission determines that the rate of return on equity should be 10 percent, $400,000 will have to be earned for the firm's shareholders, and $820,000 will have to be earned overall. The allowed rate of return in this case will be 8.2 percent. See Table 1.)

One can easily do the arithmetic once one determines the proper rate of return to equity. But what *is* the proper rate? How is it determined? In trying to measure the proper rate of return to equity holders, one might, at first, favor

Table 1. Determining the rate of return on $10 million.

Assets (rate base or *RB*)	Net worth	
	Instrument	Cost
$10 million	6% bonds	$3 million
	8% bonds	$3 million
	Common stock	$4 million (at book value)

Rate of return = 6% × 30% *RB* = 1.8 bonds
8% × 30% *RB* = 2.4 bonds
10% × 40% *RB* = 4.0 stocks

Allowed return on total *RB* = 8.2%

a deceptively simple standard: pay equity holders precisely that amount that will induce them to put up necessary investment and no more. To pay more would grant unnecessary profits to investors; to pay less would not raise adequate capital.

This rule sounds reasonable at first blush. But it must be modified because it does not, in fact, set out an unequivocal standard. A firm might pay its shareholders more without increasing profits to new investors; it might also pay them less but still raise the money it needs. This is so because the securities market is itself competitive and securities prices fluctuate. Thus, suppose a regulated firm seeks $2 million in new investment, and suppose that the competitive rate of return (considering comparative risk and attractiveness of other securities on the stock exchange) for its shares is 10 percent. The firm can still attract $2 million by offering not 10 percent but 8 percent. The shares simply decrease in price, so that the investor's return on his purchase price is still 10 percent. The firm seeking $2 million in new money and offering 8 percent offers $160,000 as an annual payment to investors. That $160,000 will buy it not 2 million new dollars, but only $1.6 million. To obtain the additional $400,000 it seeks, it will have to offer more shares to the public. When it does so, the extra money it pays as a return comes from the pockets of existing shareholders.

Assume that the firm seeking 2 million new dollars owns an existing plant worth $2 million and has 20,000 existing shares of stock. Suppose it obtained the money needed to pay for this at 8 percent. It sold 20,000 shares (at 8 percent) for annual payment of $160,000. If the competitive rate of return has risen to 10 percent, it will find that to raise an additional 2 million new dollars it has to sell many more than 20,000 new shares. If the regulator permits only an 8 percent return, it will allow a total profit pool (on $4 million) of $320,000. This must be sufficient to pay 10 percent on the market value of all shares, both old and new. Thus the shares' total market value must be $3.2 million. To raise the new $2 million will require issuing enough new shares so that the new shareholders own the firm's assets in the ratio of 2 to 3.3. Thus the firm, to raise the $2 million, will have to issue 33.3 thousand shares, which will each sell at $60; the value of the old shares will also sink to $60; and the old shareholders will own less than two fifths of the company, though they advanced as much money as the new shareholders. The above example is meant to show that money sometimes can be raised at a lower than market rate by diluting the equity of existing investors.[18]

Conversely, if higher than competitive rates of return are offered to new investors, the price of the shares is bid up; the total market value of the shares exceeds their book value (in the above example the total market value of all shares was *less* than book value); and existing shareholders earn a windfall profit (instead of incurring a windfall loss).

Thus, our initial standard—pay equity investors the minimum they insist upon to put up the money—is insufficient unless one adds: provided that there is no dilution of existing equity (nor any increase in the value of existing equity). Under this standard, the return to equity equals the market price of new investment in the regulated firm. That price keeps the market value of the firm's shares equal to the book value of the investment they represent.

One should note that this standard, while specific and fair, does not necessarily reflect what would occur in competitive markets. In competitive markets, existing share prices of any individual firm might rise above book value or sink below it. Economic considerations such as the increased (or decreased) value of an existing plant may bring about windfall gains or losses to shareholders. Unusually efficient (or inefficient) corporate management could also cause profits and stock prices to fluctuate. Here, let us assume that it is reasonable to aim toward earning a return on equity that reflects the market price of new investment in the firm.[19] Let us assume that the standard as modified sets forth roughly what we are trying to achieve. And let us ask how a commission is to determine the price of capital that meets the standard.

The "comparable earnings" method. According to the traditional method of determining a proper return on equity, the commission examines rates of return in "comparable" industries.[20] Of course, this procedure requires the regulator to determine what industries are comparable.

Consider two examples. First, a Federal Power Commission (FPC) staff expert in 1972 determined the appropriate return for a pipeline transmission company by placing it on a scale of "risk comparability." The other firms and industries in that list, with which the pipeline company was compared, included (1) general industrials as a background; (2) defense industries which, like utilities, are least affected by economic cycles; (3) utilities as a whole; and (4) other pipelines.[21] The expert concluded that the pipeline company was entitled to a return of 9.66 percent. Second, an industry expert testifying at airline rate hearings in the early 1970s argued that between 1958 and 1969 electric utilities earned between 10 percent and 14 percent on book value attributable to common stock, and that between 1965 and 1969 gas pipelines earned 15 percent, truckers earned 15 percent, and food processors earned more. Therefore, airlines—being subject to more risk—should earn 18 percent.[22]

These examples suggest that comparisons may help to set outer limits, yet they cannot possibly point to so precise a rate of return as the 9.66 percent suggested by the FPC staff member.[23] For one thing, the industries with which the regulated firm is compared may themselves earn higher than competitive returns. The fact that gas pipeline shares between 1965 and 1969 sold at nearly twice their book value suggests that the return earned was quite sufficient to induce investment. For another thing, to compare one regulated industry with another is circular if the practice is generally adopted by regulators.

Finally, the return needed to induce investment depends upon risk, but risks vary widely among industries and over time. Truckers earning 15 percent were the successful truckers who remained in business. To what extent should that risk be discounted by the possibility of business failure? And how should the resulting figure be compared with the airline industry, where *no* major firm was allowed to fail since 1938 when regulation began (though of sixteen original firms, six were allowed to merge into the remaining ten)? Risks for shareholders are not the same as those for firms, because shareholders can diversify their portfolios. To what extent should the regulator take this fact into account? While one industry may be perceived as more or less risky than another, there is no precise way to translate this observation into a specific amount of more (or less) profit needed to attract capital to the regulated firm.[24]

The discounted cash flow method. The discounted cash flow (DCF) method forces the regulator to ask the relevant question: What is the minimum return that must be paid (without dilution of existing equity investment) to obtain the needed capital? This method determines the return a firm must pay equity holders now or in the future by examining the yields investors have required in the past.[25]

One can determine what rate of return a shareowner expects to earn by comparing the price of his share with the stream of profits that it is expected to yield. The rate that "discounts" this stream—that makes it equal—to the present share price is the investment's current rate of return. The regulator would set the regulated firm's allowable rate of return equal to a number such that investors would expect a stream of profits from the regulated firm precisely equal to that which they might earn on other investments of equivalent risk.

Of course, how is one to determine the stream of profits that an investment is expected to yield its owners? That stream is *not* the stream of dividends, for most investors expect dividends per share to grow over time, both from reinvested earnings and from other factors.[26] Nor can it be viewed simply as the stream of earnings, for investors expect earnings to vary and to grow over time. One can view the expected stream of profits as equal to current dividends, adjusted for expected growth (or decline) in dividends. But can one go further? Can one measure investors' subjective assessment of expected growth in dividends or earnings? If so, one could determine their total expected return. Some economists and ratemaking experts have sought to measure this highly subjective expectation.[27]

Most commonly the expert prepares elaborate models correlating, for example, the dividend/price ratio of many different stocks in the stock market with a series of objective components related to expected growth, such as *past* average growth in earnings, dividends, book equity, revenue, or net plant. He then finds that some combination of these components correlates well with increasing dividend/price ratios. That is to say, he finds that the greater the past average growth in, say, net plant, the lower the dividend that a buyer will accept when buying a, say, $20 share. After working out the precise correlation of this bundle of components with the dividend/price ratio, he announces that the bundle (or, more accurately, some numerical operation on the bundle, such as .127 times past plant growth, plus .837 times past income growth, plus . . .) equals factor *g* (expected growth), which investors pay for along with dividends when they buy their shares. Then, by examining past values of the bundle for the regulated firm, the expert determines investors' prior expected growth in earnings, and, by comparing the bundle + dividends with the share price of the regulated firm's stock, estimates the actual total rate of return that investors insisted upon. By projecting bundle components into the future, the expert estimates the rate of return the firm must earn to give equity holders that same subjective rate of return on future investment.

There are several serious problems with this approach. First, and most obviously, attempts to correlate measurable variables with investors' expectations of growth in earnings or dividends must be imprecise. So many factors affect those expectations, and their importance may change so radically over time, that despite past successes with the model it is uncertain whether the factors used comprise all, or even the more important, factors that determined expectations of future growth in earnings or dividends.

Second, one cannot safely assume that the objective criteria that investors used to predict growth rates in the past will continue to be used in the future. Changes in general economic conditions, in expectations about the stock market, in expectations about governmental regulatory or tax policy may dramatically change the way in which the investor translates a history of, say, past growth in net plant into expected future earnings growth.

Third, the investors' required rate of return may also change radically with changes in economic conditions, governmental policy, or stock market expectations. This fact casts doubt on the usefulness of one proposal (the earnings-price approach) for setting rates of return. The authors of that plan[28] point out that a regulator can tell if he has allowed shareholders an incorrect return in the past. If the market price of the firm's shares rose above book value, a greater return was offered than needed to attract required investment, and the contrary if market value dipped below book value. The authors' suggest that the regulator should then adjust the rate of return accordingly, lowering it if market value of the stock exceeded book value, and raising it if market value sank below book value. This suggestion is of limited use, however, because market conditions and investor demands change. Thus, a 9 percent return for 1974–79 may have been too high, with share prices exceeding book value, yet for 1980–85 it could be too low. A regulator, lowering the rate in 1979, might then compound the error, not correct it.

Fourth, commissions using the DCF model must realize that the choice of regulatory policy will itself affect investors' expected return. And a commission cannot predict how the market will translate an allowed rate of return for the firm into an expected return to the shareholder. Thus, airline shareholders may have insisted upon an expected 16 percent return in the 1960s. Yet if the Civil Aeronautics Board (CAB) had changed its regulatory policy to allow the firms to earn 16 percent on equity, that policy itself would have affected earnings expectations. The industry may become less risky, and, as a result, investors may then expect less than 16 percent.

The capital asset pricing model. Regulatory commissions have begun to use a third method for determining return on equity, a method derived from an academic model that relates returns on investments in common stock portfolios to their risks.[29] The theory essentially states that an investor, by buying a portfolio of stocks instead of just one, can, by diversifying, avoid many risks attached to concentrating investment in an individual firm (for example, bankruptcy or raw material shortage). He cannot avoid the risk that the stock market as a whole will decline (or rise). For this reason, investments in common stocks tend to pay higher returns than risk-free assets (such as Treasury bills and savings accounts). Portfolios of volatile stocks (which sink lower than the average in bad times, but rise higher than the average in good times) tend to vary in their performance more than the stock market as a whole and tend to pay a higher return. In general, the potential investor will require an expected return equal to the risk-free rate of return plus a premium for investing in a risky stock.[30] This premium must equal the average premium for all stocks if the returns paid by the stock vary in just the same way as the stock market in general;[31] the premium can be less if the stock varies less, but it must be more if the stock is likely to vary more (if its performance is supercyclical). If the theory is right, the regulator can determine the expected return necessary to prompt investment in utility shares (R_u) by determining the risk-free rate (R_f), the stock market risk premium (R_m), and the comparative variability of the utility stocks and the market in general (typically referred to as the coefficient beta, β). $R_u = R_f + \beta_u(R_m - R_f)$.[32] Regulators sometimes set the firm's return to equity at this level.

This system raises two sets of serious problems. First, there are obvious measurement problems resembling those that plague the DCF model. The rates of return used are expected rates of returns. How can the regulator know what rate of return investors actually expect in the stock market, or, for that matter, when they buy risk-free securities? Hindsight is not a very good guide to expected future performance. The average performance (Standard and Poor's common stock index) varies considerably depending on the time at which the investment was made. An investment in this market portfolio consisting of the stocks that make up that index, held for ten years, for example, would have averaged an annual return of about 16 percent if made in 1951, 1 percent if made in 1965, and 7 percent if made in 1967.[33] Which return most accurately reflects investors' present expectation of future returns from a ten-year stock market investment? Estimates by investment houses of expected future returns differ. Nor is the risk-free nature of an investment in, say, short-term Treasury bills certain in time of inflation.[34] Further, estimates change rapidly over time. Wells Fargo's estimates of future annual average returns on common stock, for example, varied from 11 percent to 16 percent during the year 1974.[35] Treasury bill rates also change rapidly. The cost of capital might also be affected by the specific time period selected to measure the risk-free return and risk premium.

Second, suppose that investors' required return on investment and the expected beta of utility stocks were known with certainty. Assume, for example, that one knew that investors expected an average return of 10 percent from the stock market, but because utilities stocks are countercyclical (say, a beta of .8),[36] they would insist on only 8 percent to buy utility stocks. What rate of return should the regulator allow the firm on its assets? Suppose he allows the firm to earn 8 percent on its equity investment. Investors may or may not then expect to earn 8 percent on average on their investment in shares, since what they expect to earn on their investment depends on factors other than dividends or earnings. These include investors' expectation of both future stock market performance and utility stock performance in relation to other segments of the market.

This simply indicates that betas themselves are notoriously difficult to measure. While one can measure past performance of utilities' stocks, the issue here is how they are likely to perform in the future. Since future expected comparative performance depends upon a host of factors—expected regulatory policy, expected economic conditions, expected attitudes toward risk, inflation, equity investments—past betas may be only very weak evidence of future ones. Reliance on past performance is particularly risky in an era of energy crunches, nuclear plant accidents, and major changes in governmental policy which may suddenly force various windfall losses on energy investors.

In sum, the capital asset pricing model, despite its academic elegance, is difficult to apply to the actual world. In application it seems as filled with guesswork as any of the other methods of fixing a fair rate of return on equity.

Conclusion. This discussion is meant to suggest that setting a rate of return cannot—even in principle—be reduced to an exact science. To spend hours of hearing time considering elaborate rate-of-return models is of doubtful value, and suggestions of a proper rate, carried out to several decimal places, give an air of precision that must be false. All this assumes that one accepts the standard of giving the investor just that return he insists upon to put up his investment and no more. In fact, even if it were feasible, there is one very good reason for not following the standard: it seeks to equate book and market investment values. Should one succeed in practice in doing this, the firm would have no incentive to increase efficiency.

Efficiency

In a competitive industry, firms are motivated to produce efficiently—to find ways to cut production costs—by the hope of increased profits and by the fear that failure to keep costs low will cause more efficient firms to capture their customers by lowering price. In a regulated industry, the stick is usually unavailable. The carrot has diminished influence, for, if ratemaking is based upon actual costs and is performed accurately and promptly, firms do not benefit by adopting cost-saving devices; the total saving produced by increased efficiency flows to the consumer.

Regulators have tried to deal with the problem in several ways. First, they have relied upon the "rate-setting lag" to provide an incentive for efficient production.[37] If prices set in year one remain in effect for at least three or four years, the firm is able to keep any extra profits earned in the interim. Thus, it will try to lower its costs to generate extra profit.[38] If costs are rising (due to inflation), the lag between the time it applies for a rate increase and the time it is granted may put extra pressure on the firm to hold down costs to avoid losses. If it cannot do so, it will earn less than its allowed rate of return.[39]

How well this crude incentive system works is debatable. Commissions do not set rates at regular intervals. Rather, commission-initiated rate investigations are rare;[40] commissions ordinarily consider rates when firms seek approval of newly filed tariffs—that will raise rates. Thus, when costs are rising, a firm may seek to contain them where it seems possible to avoid a rate review, but once it becomes clear that it will have to seek some rate increase, it no longer has an incentive to keep costs down (say, during a potential test year), because it must provide evidence of high costs to obtain the rate increase.[41] When costs are falling, the firm's desire to increase productivity and cut costs even more will be tempered by its fear of earning sufficient profit to provoke a rate investigation by the commission. In addition, a lag at best produces incentives to find short-run productivity savings. Investment in research, for example, that will produce only long-run savings is discouraged, because the regulator is far more likely to take the latter into account in determining costs; thus, its benefits flow directly to the consumer, not to the firm.[42] In general, the incentives produced by varying regulatory lags are complex and quite different from those of a competitive market.

Second, regulators have sometimes tried to take increased efficiency into account when setting a rate of return. Firms judged to be more efficient are sometimes given a bonus, by being allowed extra profit above the cost of capital.[43] Or sometimes the cost of capital is determined on an industry, rather than a firm, basis, allowing firms of above-average efficiency to earn more and others less. The District of Columbia has used a sliding scale, permitting a firm that earned more than the allowed rate of return in period X to obtain a small increase in the allowed rate of return for the next period. Yet how could the commission determine whether the profit increase was due to increased efficiency or to other factors? Moreover, what was the commission to do about inflation, which would obscure any efficiency saving? More generally, how should a commission determine the amount of the bonus? If it uses industry averages, how does it know whether below-average performance flows from below-average efficiency or from an uncontrollable feature of firm life (for example, a worse route structure for an airline)? Do firm managers believe that receipt of the bonus is predictable? Such questions suggest the imprecision inherent in the bonus method. Still, some informal rate of return reward for special efficiency has been fairly popular among state commissions, which feel that it represents a practical, albeit crude, way to lower production costs. Of course, if such a system proves unworkable, regulators can still provide more direct monetary incentives for increased productive efficiency by paying bonuses directly to workers—a system that has roughly the same virtues and drawbacks with both regulated and unregulated firms.

Third, regulators sometimes directly disallow expenses they consider unreasonable, striking them from operating costs. Thus, when an executive has been overpaid or when utilities have unnecessarily paid for convention expenses, commissions have disallowed those expenses and been upheld in the courts.[44] Such disallowances, however, tend to involve extreme instances of expenses far removed from the production process.[45] Normally, commissions are reluctant to substitute their judgment for that of management, and the courts have tended to define management prerogatives with sufficient breadth to make it difficult for regulators to intervene in the daily workings of the firm.[46]

Fourth, regulators sometimes compare the utility under consideration with other utilities in order to determine comparative efficiency. They may use such measurements as output per employee, number of employees per customer, or the dollar revenue.[47] Such comparisons produce arguments about the usefulness of the standard, the appropriateness of the comparison (is a government-owned power company a proper yardstick?), or the special circumstances of the utility under examination.

It is also argued that the regulatory process itself encourages firms to produce inefficiently. Regulatory lag may lead the utility to skimp on product quality. If it can cut costs by doing so, it will be able to keep the extra profit. Thus, for example, a utility might provide fewer back-up facilities or use less reliable equipment than is warranted.[48]

Economists have debated vigorously whether the regulatory process leads utilities to overinvest, to use too much capital in production, and to provide more product quality than is called for. The tendency to overinvest has come to be known as the Averch-Johnson (AJ) effect.[49] Its proponents argue that the utility tends to invest extra funds and expand its rate base because the regulator will allow it a fair rate of return on the additional investment. If the actual cost of the investment is even slightly less than the allowed rate of return, the utility makes the investment, because the difference is pure profit. The utility need not worry about whether the investment is necessary, for its customers will pay for it regardless. That is to say, they are willing to pay more for the electricity they already receive; hence, if the regulator allows a price increase, the firm will be able to accomplish it.[50] To use an extreme example, Michigan Electric Company would be delighted to borrow $10 million at 7 percent to build Egyptian pyramids if the fair rate of return is 8 percent. If the regulator approves, it will collect an additional $800,000 from its Michigan customers, pay $700,000 to its bondholders, and keep the difference.[51]

As the example suggests, whether the AJ effect exists in fact is controversial. Regulators must approve the firm's investments, and they would obviously disapprove an investment in pyramids. Whether they would disallow an investment in newer, sturdier telephone poles or longer-lasting telephone cable, however, is more problematic. In addition, the added unnecessary investment benefits the firm only if the allowed rate of return exceeds the cost of capital. Whether in times of inflation that is likely is highly debatable. Hence, it is not surprising that economists' empirical studies of the question have reached conflicting conclusions.[52]

Fifth, commissions sometimes have defined performance standards that prevent firms, for example, from recovering costs in excess of the standard. There are several obvious difficulties with this approach: Which company practices should be subject to such standards? Who should draw them up? How will they be applied and enforced? Obviously, the more detailed the standard, the more complex its creation and administration. But the more general it is, the more difficulty the commission will have in improving the firm's behavior. At some point, detailed standards become so complex as to require the commission to possess almost enough expertise to run the company itself. If so, one might ask, why duplicate experts? Why not simply have the commission run the firm? (Of course, nationalization has its own problems.) This tension—between the fact that information and skill rest primarily within the firm and the fact that greater motivation (here for cost-cutting) is generated within the commission— is common to the setting of standards through an adversary process. It will be discussed in more detail below, but it should be noted that there is no solution to the problem within a regulatory system.

The "Test Year"

Commissions determine future operating costs by looking to past costs, and the rates so determined remain in effect for some time although operating costs may well have changed. Thus, if costs increase after rates are set (as in the electricity industry in the early 1970s), the company will earn a lower return than the commission has allowed. If costs fall (as in gas pipelines in the mid-1960s) the company may charge a higher than competitive price and earn excess profits.[53] Commissions base costs upon a test year due to the need for certainty—the need to avoid unresolvable factual disputes that threaten lengthy proceedings, arbitrary decisions, and court reversals. Although last year's prices will differ from likely future prices, at least they are known. One thereby avoids what would be an endless and unresolvable argument about what future costs will probably be.

Commissions make some effort to adjust to known inflation. Thus, the Civil Aeronautics Board allowed the industry to annualize the costs incurred at the end of the test year, instead of averaging costs throughout the entire year.[54] And some public utilities commissions allow firms to assume higher future labor costs—at least if those costs are already the subject of a negotiated contract.[55] Fuel adjustment clauses allow utilities to pass on fuel cost increases as they are incurred.[56] Still, using test-year costs often leads to prices different from those that would be set in an unregulated, competitive marketplace.

The difference between regulated and competitive prices is aggravated by the tendency of commissions to use test-year quantities in determining how changes in price levels will affect firm revenues. If a firm's revenue requirement increases by $1 million, the regulator is likely to divide the $1 million by the quantity sold during the test year and raise unit prices by the result. Such a calculation assumes that the price change will not itself affect the number of units sold—a most unreasonable assumption.

Why then have regulators only rarely tried to take account of the way in which demand responds to changes in price? Partly because estimating demand elasticities is so difficult.[57] After extensive hearings, for example, the CAB determined that demand elasticity for airline travel equaled .7. This number assumes that as price falls (rises), demand will rise (fall) less than proportionately. Academic economists strongly criticized the result, claiming that a figure of 1.2 or 1.0 would reflect the response of demand more accurately.[58] They noted, for example, that when Pacific Southwest Airways (PSA) entered the Sacramento–Los Angeles market in 1967 offering a 25 percent reduction in fares, traffic over the route doubled.[59] Yet arguments were made that each example of high elasticity is a special case. Thus, for example, the PSA experience may reflect the increased demand for air travel in general or the increase in the importance of Sacramento, rather than the price cut. In the words of one experienced airline financial analyst, "There has never been a study which satisfactorily removed the non-price determinants of demand while successfully freezing the price determinants for a sufficiently long period of time to produce results which could be deemed extrapolatable."[60]

In other industries, such as electricity, it may be reasonable to assume that demand is highly inelastic. Thus, use of the test year's quantity figures may provide as accurate a result as more elaborate, inevitably controversial demand studies. Thus, using a demand estimate based on a test year, like basing costs on a test year (with rough adjustments), frequently represents what is, administratively speaking, the least bad alternative.

Rate Structure

Once a firm's revenue requirement is determined, prices must be set to yield that revenue. Several difficulties of estimating precisely what revenues a particular set of prices will yield have already been mentioned. How do price changes alter demand? Will costs change while the rates are in effect? In addition, a regulator must resolve policy issues related to the structure of rates. Should one group be charged more for certain types of service?[61] Should prices be higher or lower at certain times of the day? In a competitive world, prices will move toward long-run incremental costs; in doing so, they will help direct resources to where they can be most efficiently used.

Welfare economics describes the effects of prices that equal marginal cost. The major virtues have already been described: When prices throughout the economy equal incremental costs (as is the case in most competitive industries), consumers face a set of relative prices that tells them the true cost to the economy of consuming a bit more of A or a bit less of B—a fact that tends to make buying and selling choices economically efficient.[62] Where the prices of some commodities equal incremental costs and the prices of others do not, consumers are given a misleading set of price signals that can lead to economically inefficient production and consumption decisions. Suppose that the price ($1) of one product (A) is far in excess of its incremental cost ($.50), while the price of other products is equal to their incremental cost ($.75), which is somewhat higher than that of A. Consumers compare the price of A with that of B and C and choose relatively more of B and C, even though they would prefer relatively more of A if its price were equal to incremental cost, and it would cost society less in terms of resources expended to produce more of A and less of B and C.

Whether one ought always to price at incremental cost—particularly in a world where differences between cost and price may vary among industries, is much debated. But the ability of such prices to inform consumers about the true economic cost of buying more or less of the regulated product—and thus direct buying decisions toward the cheapest way to satisfy preferences—is a strong point in their favor.

Despite the virtues of incremental cost pricing, the regulator often finds that he cannot set prices equal to incremental cost. He cannot use incremental cost as a standard for judging proposed utility prices, nor can he seek prices that will "replicate" competitive markets. The following three problems illustrate this point and are typical of rate design problems that arise.

Distributing fixed costs. Because many regulated firms, particularly natural monopolies, often have large fixed costs and declining incremental costs, prices that are set to equal incremental costs will fail to produce sufficient revenue to earn a return on investments. Thus, an extra charge must be assessed to cover fixed costs and the regulator must decide who will pay the charge.

Recall the hypothetical bridge problem discussed in Chapter 1. The bridge costs $25 million to build but will last forever. The resource cost of one person's crossing—the wear and tear on the bridge—is 50 cents. To charge more than 50 cents will prevent some potential users from crossing, leading them to spend their money on less preferred alternatives that cost society more to produce. Yet if the bridge owner charges only 50 cents, how is he to pay back the investors who put up $25 million to build the bridge?

Assume the bridge was built by private enterprise. Assume further that, in order to provide investors a return on the capital invested to build the bridge, an extra $1 million must be raised, over and above the revenues generated by a 50 cent toll to cover incremental operating expenses. How should tolls be set to raise the needed extra revenue?

At first, one might think that everyone should be charged the same, because each obtains the same service from the bridge—namely, one crossing. Yet to charge each crosser equally can have several pernicious effects. For one thing, some potential crossers, willing to pay, say, 80 cents but not one dollar for bridge crossing, will stay at home—a pity, in that the economy could give them what they value at 80 cents for an economic expenditure of only 50 cents worth of additional resources. Furthermore, with a one dollar toll they might buy something other than a bridge crossing for 80 cents—say, a ferryboat ride—and thereby require the economy to use 80 cents worth of resources to give them less satisfaction than it might have obtained (through bridge cross- ing) with an economic expenditure of only 50 cents worth of extra resources. And one can imagine the waste involved if a host of "80 cent cost" ferryboats were to appear, attracting passengers from the "50 cent cost" bridge because of its one dollar price. To minimize this waste, some economists advocate charging prices that allocate fixed costs in inverse relation to elasticity of de- mand—called "Ramsey pricing."[63]

Those to whom bridge use is worth more are charged a higher proportion of fixed costs; those to whom it is worth less are charged less, and, as a result, they are less likely to stop using the bridge or to switch to a ferryboat. The resulting pattern of resource use is more likely to resemble what it would have been if prices had been set equal to incremental cost. The Interstate Commerce Commission, for example, has traditionally allowed railroads to charge more for shipping valuable items than for shipping inexpensive items, presumably because a small extra charge is less likely to affect the shipping behavior of those who send expensive items.

Aside from a theoretical point—that this type of pricing does not always minimize economic waste[64]—this effort to minimize waste when allocating fixed costs often founders on administrative obstacles. As previously men- tioned, to measure demand elasticities is extremely difficult. This problem is compounded by efforts to classify customers or services into administrable cat- egories that correspond, even roughly, to demand elasticities. Thus, for exam- ple, the ICC's system of varying rates according to value of the product shipped may bear only a distant relation to the inverse demand elasticity it is supposed to represent. Do shippers of diamonds, in fact, care less about trans- portation cost per pound than do shippers of salt? Perhaps so, for transportation is a smaller proportion of their final selling price. Yet their willingness to ship at a higher price depends directly not upon the proportion of transportation costs in final value, but on the state of competition in the diamond market and the availability of alternative transport. If diamond selling is fiercely competi- tive—to the point where sellers look for any and every cost-saving device, and if equally good truck transport is readily available, even a small increase in rail prices will lead them to use trucks. On the other hand, a noncompetitive salt industry, without ready alternatives, may be willing to pay quite high rail prices before salt shippers would use other modes of transport. The use of "value of commodity'' as an administrable substitute for elasticity of demand is understandable, but highly inaccurate.[65]

A typical ICC rate problem, based on Kahn's example,[66] illustrates some of these rate-structure difficulties. Assume that a railroad builds a track connecting A, B, and C. Assume that the track costs $5 million. Assume further that, once the track is built, it costs an additional $2 million to buy special cars for carrying oil from A, through B, to C. Suppose that points A and C are connected by a river, plied by barge lines. The *incremental cost* of carrying the oil by rail from A to C is $2 million—the amount needed for cars to carry oil from A to C. The *fully allocated* cost of carrying the oil by rail from A to C, however, includes a "fair" portion of the overhead necessary to supply any rail transport between A and C whatsoever. In particular, it includes a proportionate share of the rail bed cost—a sunk cost that need never be incurred again. Let us assume that the fair share of the overhead is $1 million. In that case, the railroad's fully allocated cost of carrying oil between A and C is $3 million, and the incremental cost is $2 million.

Suppose that a barge can carry oil from A to C at a cost of $2.5 million. Should the railroad be allowed to cut its price for carrying oil from A to C, let us say, to $2.2 million—a price near incremental cost? Or should the ICC insist that it keep its price at $3 million? The major economic arguments for allowing the railroad to cut its price are based on the virtues of incremental cost pricing. First, unless the railroad cuts its price, all oil will be carried by barge. That means that the portion of fixed costs previously borne by the A to C oil shippers will no longer be borne by them; the fares that the railroad charges other shippers must rise to recover the additional fixed cost. In our example, if the railroad cut its price to $2.2 million, the oil shippers still contribute two hundred thousand dollars to overhead. If these shippers are lost to the barge lines because the railroad is not allowed to cut its price, this $200,000 must be made up by other railroad customers.

Second, since the railroad's fixed costs are in place (the roadbed will never have to be built again), the extra resources that the economy must put forth to carry the oil from A to C by rail amount to $2 million worth of resources. To carry that same amount from A to C by barge, however, requires $2.5 million worth of extra resources. Thus, we can do the same job and save the $500,000 worth of resources that will be left over if the shipper sends his oil by rail.

These economic arguments are well known and widely accepted.[67] Other economic arguments, however, suggest that in some circumstances the commission should not allow the railroad to price at incremental cost. First, suppose that the barge line's costs of $2.5 million include a fee of $1 million that the barge line must pay to the government to cover the cost of initially improving the river or digging a canal. If those costs are nonrepeatable, that fee of $1 million also represents payment for a fixed cost, and the true incremental cost for barge line carriage is $1.5 million—in other words, the barge line's incremental costs are lower than the railroad's, but it may not be legally possible for the barge line to lower its prices to its own incremental costs. In such a situation, it may be economically sensible for the ICC to prevent the railroads from charging a fee equal to the railroad's incremental cost—when that cost is greater than the barge line's incremental cost but less than the barge line's fully allocated cost. Second, barge transport may serve some other social purpose; for example, it may augment national defense, add to the scenic beauty of the countryside, or help people in other ways not reflected in the price charged for the service. In order to serve this other social goal, the ICC may insist that the goods be moved by barge rather than by rail.

Finally, consider an oil-using widget producer located at B in competition with a similar oil-using widget producer located at C. If the railroad is allowed to cut its price for oil transport to C due to riverboat competition, the B producer will end up paying a higher price for oil than C producers (though incremental costs of shipment are lower) and widget producers will tend to locate at C, not B. This discrimination results because fixed costs must be collected from someone, and we have chosen B in order to prevent a rail/barge shipping misallocation; in doing so, we create a B/C producer-location misallocation. It may be of some comfort to realize that even if the regulator keeps the C rail prices high, B is not helped. Oil will then go by barge to C and so will the oil-using widget makers.

Does the situation change any if, instead of a barge, another rail line runs between A and C? Now to let rail line number 1 lower its A-C price to incremental costs not only hurts B, but also seems unnecessary. It is unlikely that the incremental costs of lines 1 and 2 for the A-C oil run differ significantly. Moreover, the regulator can control the prices of each. Thus, a refusal to let line 1 lower its A-C price is unlikely to end up with oil shippers using a higher incremental cost mode of transport, because the regulator can also control the price of line 2. Thus, the discriminatory harm to B is not counterbalanced by so clear an allocative good.

The upshot is that the ICC, in fixing relative prices for regulated service, must consider the allocative effects of these prices.[68] Economics can prove a helpful guide in doing so, yet because of administrative considerations economic rules are not determinative. And it is unlikely that such prices will replicate those of a competitive marketplace.

Distributing joint costs. When two products share a certain ingredient—as, for example, chicken necks and chicken breasts share the cost of the grain that fed the chicken—regulators have an unusually difficult time allocating the cost of the common ingredient between them. In competitive markets the relative prices of two such products would depend on the relative demand for them. The relative price of chicken necks and breasts does not depend upon the weight of the grain absorbed by a neck compared with that absorbed by the breast. Rather, the price received for neck and for breast each would have to cover any *incremental* cost of producing each for market. (This cost would be very low, as growing a neck automatically involves growing a breast, and vice versa). The total price received for each chicken would have to cover its total production costs. Indeed, chicken prices would equal the cost of producing the "incremental" chicken—the last chicken produced—because farmers would add to chicken production so long as prices are higher; but within these constraints, comparative neck/breast prices would be determined by comparative demand. Neck prices would fall and breast prices would rise, until the same number of each is sold.

Once again, regulators might try to replicate competitive market prices and conditions, but to do so they would have to estimate demand for each product under varying price assumptions. The difficulties of estimating demand—severe enough when only a single regulated product is at issue—are multiplied when several products or some regulated and some unregulated products are involved. Thus the Federal Power Commission, forced to allocate drilling and exploration expenses between the (regulated) gas and the (unregulated) oil that a well produced, allocated costs in proportion to BTU's (heat units) produced by each fuel—an economically irrelevant figure. In fact, oil prices were high and most oil well producers recovered almost all exploration costs from oil sales. Thus, the FPC's allocation of exploration costs according to the comparative heat content of a barrel of oil and a cubic foot of natural gas led it to allocate a large share of exploration costs to gas. This fact, in turn, led the FPC to allow a high gas price—higher than the gas producers were currently charging. The advocates of natural gas regulation were shocked when the FPC found in its first major gas price investigation that Phillips Petroleum's gas prices were *below,* not above, a "reasonable" level.[69]

These advocates thought the FPC was dishonest. The results showed not dishonesty, however, but only the effects of a totally artificial allocation formula. Commissions, when dealing with joint costs, may ask the right questions about relative demands, but then they must guess at the answers. Or they may ask the wrong questions—about, for example, relative heat content—which they can answer precisely.

Off-peak pricing. Regulators must often decide the proper relation of peak and off-peak prices for, say, electricity[70] or transport. Economists argue that, in principle, off-peak prices should fall until either the peak is ironed out or the price reaches variable cost (not including the cost of plant). As a result, the charge to off-peak customers may be very small compared with the charge to peak users.[71]

The charging of low off-peak prices is efficient and fair. If there is extra space in a pipeline or extra capacity in a generator, there is no need to build new plant so long as potential peak users can be attracted (by a lower price) to off-peak use. Thus, off-peak discounts save resources. Moreover, investment in new additional plant is made primarily to serve peak customers, for if peak customers were willing to use off-peak facilities, the new plant need not be built or it could be smaller. Thus, it is fair to charge a price that reflects the need for extra capacity to all peak customers (even if doing so means that they will pay the entire cost of the plant).[72]

Peak-load pricing, however, is far more complicated in practice than the simple theory suggests. For one thing, in the electricity industry, it is not quite true that additional plant is built only to serve peak users. Because a system must be more reliable the more it is used, additional off-peak users may also require the building of some extra plant, though precisely how much (compared with additional peak users) is open to debate.[73] Furthermore, plant and other costs are difficult to determine and allocate. How much revenue will higher peak prices obtain? To know this, one must know demand elasticity; without such elusive knowledge, the firm cannot know in advance how much of its plant costs it will in fact recover from its peak revenues. Similarly, off-peak variable costs partially depend on off-peak demand; more demand may mean using oil burners, which are more expensive to run per kilowatt than coal or nuclear generating capacity.[74]

Further, in implementing peak-load pricing systems, the utility must beware of the "shifting peak" and the "needle peak." The shifting peak will occur if low nighttime electricity prices, for example, encourage so great a shift to storage batteries that lower off-peak rates do not shave the peak. Instead, they just shift the hour of peak demand. The same peak occurs but at 4 A.M. instead of 4 P.M., and no plant costs are saved. As much capacity as ever is needed, but peak demand simply occurs at a different time of day. The needle peak occurs if high electricity prices on, say, summer afternoons discourage the use of air conditioners until the temperature reaches, say, 102°, at which point everyone turns on the air conditioner. The result would be a sudden blackout unless more plant is built.[75] Moreover, the practicality of peak pricing systems will depend on the cost of metering. If a necessary residential meter costs $30 per year, but residential users are not likely to shift to the point of saving $30 of plant costs per user, the meter and the system are not worth the cost (for them).[76] Finally, a peak-load system with rates that approximate incremental costs may (if capacity costs are rising) generate more than the firm's revenue requirements. This fact could create serious political problems, as many different groups of users, investors, and administrators seek to obtain the excess revenue for their programs or for themselves.

Despite these practical difficulties, peak-load pricing is used extensively in Europe. France, for example, has different prices not only for different times of day but also for different seasons of the year.[77] Several American experiments designed to measure demand under such pricing arrangements suggest that its introduction is warranted. (Data from those experiments support the use of peak-load pricing in Massachusetts for commercial and industrial customers, for example, but not for residences).[78] And peak-load pricing is now required in almost half the states.[79] Yet regulators have been led to introduce this system by inflation, the energy crisis, the environmental movement, and the consequent search for cost-cutting and capacity-saving devices, rather than as a response to the system's economic merits.[80]

It is reasonable to believe that variable pricing systems are introduced more rapidly in competitive than regulated industries. Of course, firms in competitive industries have many of the practical problems listed above—most of which are related to the difficulty of predicting demand elasticity. But in competitive industries, pricing experimentation is easier and better rewarded. Rate changes are not the subject of public hearings at which adversely affected parties oppose them, nor need they be "cost-justified" on the basis of a written record. Nor will a regulator seek to take from the "competitive" firm any extra profit earned by a correct guess about demand.[81] Nor will the unregulated firm have a built-in incentive to expand the *amount* of investment, regardless of its profitability. These facts may in part explain the difficulty that off-peak pricing systems have had winning acceptance among regulators.

The rate structure problems mentioned are not the only problems to arise in determining rate structure, yet they illustrate the fact that the economist's ideal of price reflecting long-run incremental costs is not easy to attain in a regulated environment. The types of problems mentioned are endemic to that environment, and, like the problems of imperfect competition in the unregulated world, inevitably produce a certain amount of economic waste.

Conclusion

The five sets of problems discussed above—rate base, rate of return, efficiency, test year, and rate structure—are typical of those that arise where cost-of-service ratemaking is practiced. They do not show that such regulation is undesirable. They do show that the need for administrative practicability and the difficulty of economic prediction, particularly about demand responses, make it virtually impossible for the regulator to replicate the price and cost results of a hypothetically competitive industry.

Certain important differences are inevitable. In the competitive world, prices adjust rapidly; investors earn rents when the price of reproducing old equipment increases; they may suffer windfall losses when technology lowers reproduction costs; prices tend to be based upon present costs, not those of a test year; changes in demand resulting from change in price are taken into account as they occur; and firms can experiment with different price structures. In the regulated world, on the other hand, prices remain stable for fixed periods of time; the prices set may not yield the amount of revenue that the regulator expects; and as costs increase or decrease due to added efficiency, prices do not change; nor do prices change to reflect possible increases or decreases in the cost of supplying similar service, and firms find price experimentation difficult.

Two conclusions should be drawn. First, efforts to obtain economic precision in the regulatory process—estimates, for example, of a "proper" rate of return carried out to one or two decimal places—are unlikely to be worth the effort expended. The standard to which such efforts implicitly appeal is that of overcoming "distortions" produced by competitive market failure—the standard of trying to replicate what would occur without such a failure. Yet in trying to overcome such failures the regulatory process introduces so many distortions of its own, that one should be satisfied with gross estimates and not insist upon refined economic calculations. Second, insofar as cost-of-service ratemaking is advocated as a "cure" for market failure, one must believe that the unregulated market is functioning quite badly to warrant the introduction of classical regulation. That is to say, the regulatory process—even when it functions perfectly—cannot reproduce the price signals that a workably competitive marketplace would provide. Thus, only serious market failure will, even arguably, warrant the adoption of cost-of-service ratemaking as a cure.

3

Historically Based Price Regulation

The only practical alternative to cost-of-service ratemaking—indeed the only practical method for setting the prices of large numbers of firms with disparate costs—is a system based not upon cost but upon historical prices. Such a system has been used to implement economy-wide price controls [1]—to regulate oil prices; [2] and it has been suggested as a method for containing hospital costs. [3] Over time, however, the system's drawbacks become more aggravated and the system itself begins to resemble cost-of-service ratemaking. The longer such a system stays in effect, the less advantageous it becomes, and the more serious become its defects. Thus, historically based pricing systems are used infrequently and provisionally.

The System

The basic principle of the system is simple. Each firm is allowed to charge for its product whatever price it charged on a certain past date. Typically this price is the highest price charged during a "base period"—say, the month before the freeze took effect. Thus, in World War II the General Maximum Price Regulation (GMPR), issued April 22, 1942, provided that the seller's maximum price for a good or service would be the highest price he charged for that commodity or service to a purchaser of the same class in March 1942. [4] In the Korean War the General Ceiling Price Regulation (GCPR), issued January 26, 1951, froze prices at their highest level in the preceding month. [5] And on August 17, 1971, the president froze prices for ninety days "at levels not greater than the highest" charged "during the 30 day period ending August 14, 1971." [6]

In each instance the regulators immediately had to make exceptions to fit the circumstances of special products or sales. How would a seller price seasonal products not sold, or sold at special prices, during the preceding month? What about a seller who had sold at "introductory" prices or whose goods had been "on sale"? What about sellers such as certain steel fabricators, who tailor their products to meet the special needs of individual purchasers and who charge accordingly? What about sellers who had signed contracts for future delivery that contained provisions for increasing prices? What constituted the "same" product or service? What is a sale to the "same" class of purchasers? These questions were answered through the choice of a base period long enough to minimize their scope, special rules and regulations, and a special case-by-case exception procedure.

For these and other reasons, a pure historical price freeze has never been imposed for long. The historical price rule has tended to be formulated as "permitted price" equals "historical price plus (certain allowable) costs." In the case of economy-wide price controls this change took place primarily because of concern for sellers who were squeezed between rising costs and frozen prices. But, why was there a squeeze? Why, if prices were frozen, were costs rising? For one thing, certain prices were exempt from direct regulation. Congress exempted common carriers, real property, newspapers, insurance, and professional fees from Korean War controls. The Price Commission went on to exempt other products for administrative reasons. Agricultural commodities, for example, were exempted because their marketing characteristics (perishability and dependence on weather) made their prices subject to sharp and unforeseeable fluctuations. Controls would produce capricious and unfair results. Certain defense items were exempted to provide a strong incentive for their production. Eventually rising prices for exempt commodities meant higher costs for many producers of controlled products. For another thing, costs gradually rose as producers found ways to fit their claims within exemptions, as they substituted slightly lower-quality items or services, and as wage rates (subject to a different set of controls) rose slowly or work quality declined.

The squeeze placed the regulators in a dilemma, for to allow cost passthroughs threatened to erode the general price ceiling. But to refuse to do so not only seemed unfair, but also meant that producers might discontinue particular product lines or fail to reinvest. For example, in World War II the cost squeeze led producers to sell sports shirts, but not white shirts; three-inch boards, but not one-inch boards; apple jelly with sugar, but not sugar alone.[7] Shortages during World War II were aggravated when differences in squeezed profit margins led producers to switch products. And even during the brief 1972–73 control period, shortages developed in several industries.[8]

The result is that in each instance of economy-wide price controls, the regulators gradually began to allow the pass-through of "justified" cost increases—a category that expanded over time. During World War II the Office of Price Administration (OPA) allowed certain firms, such as grocery stores, to set prices based upon their costs plus a formula mark-up. Without such a formula there would have been no way for a store to adjust to unregulated raw agricultural prices.[9] The formula method spread to many industries;[10] it was supplemented by occasional special authorizations to raise prices.[11] And finally in 1946, just before the expiration of controls, Congress enacted the Barkley-Taft Amendment, which specifically stated that maximum prices would have to include "the average increase in cost" in the individual industry since 1942.[12] Similarly, during the Korean War the price regulators first began to allow the pass-through of agricultural and certain transportation costs.[13] The pass-through was extended to import costs[14] and to distributors whose supply costs had increased.[15] Manufacturers were allowed, by the Capehart Amendment, to pass-through cost increases incurred up to six months after controls took effect.[16] And, the pass-through principle was adopted in part by the regulators when they developed numerous standards tailored to industries or to individual firms; they allowed such adjustments when the industry's or firm's profits were unreasonably low.[17] In 1972, after the initial ninety-day freeze, the regulators allowed manufacturers and retailers to pass-through "allowable" cost increases, provided they were not earning profits that were too high.[18]

Thus, as economy-wide price controls were administered in practice, the historical price principle gradually came to approximate "historical price plus (certain) additional costs." When the historical system has been applied not on an economy-wide basis but to a single industry such as oil or hospitals, the historical price principle usually has been stated outright as a principle of "price plus cost increase." Since price controls apply to only one sector, the regulator knows that input costs will rise, and that he must allow for their pass-through. Thus, in the case of oil, the system provides for vintaging: a low price ceiling is imposed upon older oil, based upon its historical price; a higher price ceiling is imposed upon newer oil, based upon its higher expected costs.[19] In the case of proposed hospital cost containment provisions, historical prices would be allowed to rise by a fixed percent each year.[20]

Despite the difficulties involved, compared with cost-of-service ratemaking the historical price principle—even when it takes the form of "price plus allowable costs"—has the initial advantage of administrative simplicity, particularly when applied to vast numbers of firms with different costs. The comparative simplicity obtains because (1) historical prices are usually ascertainable, (2) producers can determine cost increases fairly readily, (3) the same rule can apply to all industry, and (4) the rules are understandable and to some extent self-enforceable. Initially, of course, the system is likely to exist in its administratively simplest form—the historical price freeze. Over time, however, as cost squeezes become intolerable, the system will be modified. But modified systems based on "historical price plus cost increases" face several typical and serious difficulties—difficulties that over time deprive the system of its initial administrative advantage, bring about an evolution toward cost-of-service ratemaking, and may lead to breakdown.

The Problems

Despite its apparent simplicity, a historically based pricing system generates economic and administrative problems that are more serious than those of cost-of-service ratemaking. The problems are typical of such systems, they are un-avoidable, and they worsen over time. They may be grouped into five cate-gories.

Categorization

The basic virtue of a historical pricing system consists of its ability to use general rules, instead of individual investigations of each manufacturer or sup-plier, to determine costs and prices. This approach brings with it the difficulty of defining appropriate categories and inevitably creates serious controversy as individual parties dispute the applicability of the lines that have been drawn.

The wartime price controllers found that their most serious problem was determining, through the use of general standards, when a firm could pass-through increased costs. The standard for distributors, for example, in allowing the pass-through of cost increases, also allowed the distributor to add a usual mark-up to the cost of a new or increased-cost product. This is reasonable, for otherwise the sale would not contribute to the dealer's overhead and profit. However, the only readily administrable way to determine a proper mark-up is as some customary percentage of the item's cost or selling price. Yet to allow a distributor, with a fixed investment, to mark up his costs by a percentage of those costs leaves him no incentive to keep these costs down. On the contrary, the higher his dollar sales volume (the higher his costs or ceiling prices), the more money a given percentage mark-up will yield. With a fixed investment, the more dollars the distributor earns, the higher his profit as a percentage of investment—the profit figure that primarily interests investors.

In the manufacturing sector regulators sought to overcome this problem by not allowing price increases, even when costs went up, unless a price increase was needed to maintain "reasonable" industry profits. But then they had to determine what profits were reasonable. To do so without examining each firm, they categorized firms by industries, sought to determine "normal" profits for the industry, and allowed price increases when profits fell below this normal level. Aside from difficulties in categorizing firms, the regulators had to decide how to measure profits—on total investment? net worth? sales?—to determine what was normal, to decide why (as well as whether) profits were below nor-mal, and to determine how to treat allegedly unprofitable lines of product in a profitable industry.[21]

Categorization produced an occasional absurdity, as when chicken feathers were sold at different prices depending on whether they came from live chick-ens (and were agricultural) or dead chickens (and were industrial).[22] But, more important, it produced endless controversy. Often the line had to be drawn arbitrarily, as when various "raw" agricultural commodities (exempted) had to be distinguished from "processed" commodities (covered). The category was difficult to apply to certain cases. (Is a hula hoop a new product? Is it a product for which a manufacturer already has a system for determining a price?) And the policy decisions involved in categorizing were often complex. If, for example, the price of "old" oil is held to its historical price, the regulator must define "old." Does it include oil from existing wells? Suppose the well owner shuts down an existing well and drills a new well nearby. Should a geographic boundary be drawn around existing wells? How far from the well is its perimeter? How should the regulator treat "extra" oil flushed out of an old well through a new process?[23]

These questions can be resolved through further categorization, yet several features of this process should be noted. First, each categorization produces a set of special prices and production incentives likely different from those of a free market. If, for example, "new" oil is separated from "old" oil on the basis of a circle drawn around each existing well with a two-and-a-half-mile radius, firms will neither deepen an existing well nor drill for new oil within the circle. Second, the policy decisions needed to apply a system of categories are likely to be made only after hearings, or at least after some informal presentation of evidence and argument by lawyers for interested parties. Third, the pressure to increase the number of categories and subcategories increases as more special facts and special cases are found. Fourth, the greater the proliferation of categories, the less the advantage of a historical pricing system compared with traditional cost-of-service ratemaking. Proliferation of rules and categories destroys the advantage of a fairly clear general principle intended to avoid the need for case-by-case determinations. Yet sticking to the principle threatens increasing economic harm as well as unfairness.

Cost-of-Service Ratemaking

After a period of time, it is virtually impossible for the regulator to avoid the very same problems that plague cost-of-service ratemaking. In one area after another, price regulators discover that they must set prices on the basis of an individual firm or industry. How, for example, should a firm set its prices for a product that it had not previously sold? During the Korean War, new commodity prices were set by allowing the seller (1) to set prices in line with those of comparable products that he sold previously, or (2) to set prices in line with those of a direct competitor selling the item, or (3) to apply for a special price set individually by the regulator.[24] Regulators used similar techniques during the 1972–73 period.[25] The result eventually was a tendency to set prices on an individual, case-by-case basis.

In part, this was because the categorization problems were severe, particularly when a manufacturer offered a brand-new product. Was a skateboard a new product? If so, was it unique or was it comparable to the roller skates or sleds produced by the same, or competing, manufacturers? How should the World War II regulators treat "butter spreader" (a butter substitute) or such goods as paper garbage cans, glass utensils, or products with wooden rather than metal parts? Even if they surmounted these categorization problems, however, the regulators still had to decide when a price was in line with that of comparable products sold previously or elsewhere. They recognized that if they required an *identical* price, the seller might not offer the new product, for his start-up costs were likely to be high. Thus, regulators during the Korean War allowed a manufacturer to take each item's direct costs—defined as the direct labor and direct material cost of replacing the item—and add a percentage mark-up equal to that earned on his own previous sales (or his competitor's sales) of comparable items. Similarly, retailers and wholesalers were allowed to add the percentage mark-up received on comparable items to the item's invoice costs.

This approach, although administratively workable, produced unfair results. As firms used capacity more fully,[26] a mark-up based on a fixed percentage of direct cost meant even higher profits. To use a simplified example, a firm with a total investment of $1 million and direct costs of $2 million which sells its output for $2.2 million earns a 10 percent return[27] on costs and a 20 percent return on its investment. If it can increase its output by 50 percent without additional investment, it will sell that output for $3.3 million, still earning a 10 percent return on costs but increasing its return on investment from 20 percent to 30 percent. Moreover, as previously mentioned, this approach gives the firm a perverse incentive, for it permits the firm to increase its return on investment by increasing (through, say, high wage settlements) its direct costs (for the same output) from $2 million to $3 million.

It is, then, not surprising that regulators hesitated to use the mark-up approach,[28] and often relied instead upon individual case proceedings.[29] During the Korean War individual prices for many new products were set by letter order. During World War II there was considerable individualized price setting, though not necessarily based upon cost. In fact, certain OPA staff members "argued that they could feel, bend and smell a product for a few minutes and come within a few cents of the in-line retail price without ever knowing the manufacturer's cost."[30] In 1972 the price regulators effectively gave up; they modified their regulations to provide that when no "comparable" item had been previously sold, the seller could "use any customary pricing practice" he had previously used or "any other pricing practice commonly used" by others.[31] Essentially regulators, seeking to avoid arbitrary decision making, felt that they had to examine costs case by case, and the only reasonably fair and workable set of principles for such an examination are those of cost-of-service ratemaking.

A similar problem arose for firms losing money or earning low profits when controls took effect. If demand for their product grows, those firms could not be required to lose money indefinitely. The OPA's policy was to "afford relief in any special situation where ceiling prices resulted in undue hardship."[32] Regulators during the Korean War also allowed exceptions when the ceilings would produce an overall loss.[33] In making adjustments, prices were to reflect costs, including a reasonable profit. And the regulators gradually began to judge the reasonableness of profits by looking at return as a percentage of investment, not of sales. In other words, they began to move toward a cost-based price-setting approach.

Finally, the regulators had to consider new investment by firms opening a new plant or entering a new field of production. To freeze their prices at existing levels would prevent expansion, though an existing shortage, suggesting a demand at higher prices, may have motivated it. During World War II this did not pose a serious problem, for the government wished to control most new investment and channel it into war production. During the Korean War a set of special exemptions freed essential defense production from price controls. Regulators initially were not concerned with nondefense investment. Eventually, however, they began to regulate the prices of items produced through new investment. To do so, they had to determine costs—operating costs plus capital costs. And the cost of capital was represented by a fair return on investment.[34] The alternative to arbitrary decision making or ineffective regulation was a process that resembled cost-of-service ratemaking problems.

In short, some firms will seek over time to make major new investments and to introduce new products; others, previously losing money, will find it within their power to earn a profit by raising prices. Historical prices or comparative prices do not help the regulator determine what prices such firms should be allowed to charge. The problem can be avoided for a time through the use of essentially arbitrary price comparisons. But eventually the regulator will seek to set prices that can be justified as reasonable. He will then seek a cost-based price, individualized price setting will proliferate, and the problems of cost-of-service ratemaking will be imported into the historically based system. Thus, a regulator during World War II wrote of the historical price system: "Its maximum utility was achieved at the moment it was imposed and its utility diminished steadily as the time span since the base period increased. Inevitably, there were new products, new sellers, new types of buyers, new selling areas, new conditions of sales, new volume conditions, new container types and sizes. Experience showed that to meet such problems the freeze approach, even when strengthened by the use of price bridges, had to be supplemented by other and more flexible techniques." Those techniques were cost based.[35]

Allocation

After a time, a historical price control system threatens shortages, and the regulator is forced to consider how to allocate the product in short supply. These shortages may arise for several reasons. First, as previously discussed, an economy-wide price freeze can bring about shortages by refusing to allow sellers to pass-through increases in cost. Sellers hesitate to make new investment, discontinue unprofitable product lines, or even go out of business.[36]

Second, even if the price regulator allows cost pass-throughs to avert a serious shortage or to encourage new investment, typically the firm must apply for individualized consideration. Then the process itself, with its attendant delay, inhibits the pass-through with subsequent undesirable effects. In both World War II and the Korean War the exception procedure involved delay. "Although strenuous efforts were made from time to time to bring up-to-date the pending applications for prices by specific authorization, and in fact such drives were made with what seemed to the staff to be distressing frequency, the backlog [of World War II applications] was never cleaned up until the hiatus period of July 1946."[37] The delay can be overcome only by allowing firms to make their own price adjustment—even though doing so severely threatens the system's effectiveness. Thus, during the Korean War, in the case of small business "a trend developed to make adjustment applications self-executing, generally after a waiting period. The agency reserved the right to review the file and modify or deny the adjustment of it found good cause."[38] In 1971–73 the regulators compromised, allowing firms with less than $100 million in revenues to make price adjustments automatically, but requiring larger firms to obtain prior approval.[39]

Third, even if regulators could avoid the first two problems by setting cost-based prices, they would still find shortages occurring. In allowing prices to rise to reflect cost increases, regulators will bring about price "tiers" or "vintages." The bicycles or tables or refrigerators already in stock or made with inventoried materials will be cheaper than the newer items made with higher-cost inventory replacement or from new plant. The price freeze will itself add to the vintaging problem by freezing producers at a different price for the same goods. The problem may be aggravated by categorizations or rules that allow different prices for very similar products. During World War II manufacturers of upholstered furniture were allowed to charge different prices depending upon the economically irrelevant fabric covering. The rules during the Korean War, designed to take account of transportation and taxes, produced price vintages by allowing producers who sold at prices net of freight costs or excise tax to pass on increases in transportation or taxes but denying that right to producers who sold at prices that included freight or taxes. Finally, the problem is aggravated by cost-based new-product rules which will encourage firms to switch production from old lines to new so that they can raise their prices to reflect their actual costs.[40]

The first two sets of problems might be overcome in principle. The shortages caused by a freeze that does not allow the pass-through of cost increases can be alleviated by allowing those adjustments. The argument against doing so is that unless firms can be forced to swallow cost increases, economy-wide controls will not be very effective. Similarly, shortages caused by administrative delay in making adjustments might be alleviated through "better" administration. Yet here too, as a practical matter, the regulator cannot readily administer adjustments affecting large numbers of firms.[41] And simply allowing each firm to make adjustments on its own threatens the system's effectiveness.

The third set of problems is unavoidable, even in principle, for price differences, tiers, or vintages automatically raise an allocation problem. Who will receive the older or cheaper items? Everyone will want them, but there must inevitably be an inadequate supply. The closer the regulator comes to setting prices that equal costs, the more vintages he creates and the more serious his shortage problems. Yet failure to set prices that approximate costs also creates shortages.

The methods open to the regulator to deal with the allocation problem will be discussed in Chapter 5. The most common alternative is some sort of formal or informal rationing system, administered by the firm itself or by the regulator if the shortage is sufficiently serious. Indeed, one student of the subject argues "that serious controls, which attempt to keep prices well below market clearing levels, can only be successful if accompanied by rationing." Of course, rationing can lead to a black market, which exacerbates the shortage of low-priced goods by drawing off goods into illicit channels. Dairy industry representatives testified before Congress in 1946 that between 50 percent and 80 percent of all butter was sold on the black market.

An alternative allocation method is to set a single uniform price, midway between low and high price vintages. The regulation of oil prices illustrates this system: domestic oil is sold at a "rolled-in" price between the low ceiling price for old oil and the higher price for new oil. This system involves the regulator in efforts to use the extra profits on the old oil to finance production of new oil. In practice, regulators may set essentially arbitrary uniform prices, based on neither historical price nor cost. Yet as the regulatory system becomes more bureaucratized, operating through rules and subject to court review, this becomes progressively more difficult to do.

Enforcement

Historical price setting is created to hold prices of large numbers of producers with disparate costs below the prices that an unregulated market would set. Producers can charge higher prices and earn higher profits; they will seek to do so; and their large number and disparate costs will make enforcement of lower price ceilings particularly difficult.

Producers ingeniously find loopholes that effectively allow price increases. During World War II, for example, Kraus Brothers, a poultry firm, sold chicken breasts and chicken skin, each at the ceiling price, requiring buyers who wanted breasts also to buy unwanted skin. Stopping the proliferation of ingenious evasion schemes by forbidding them in advance is difficult, for the agency cannot determine what producers (and their lawyers) will concoct. Should all tie-in sales be forbidden? What about washing machine sellers who have traditionally sold soap at low prices as an inducement to buy the machine? What about those who sell combs and brushes as a set? In any case, Kraus might then stop selling chicken parts and sell only whole chickens.[42]

A more serious problem is the gradual deterioration of product quality. The regulations forbidding price increases cannot easily require the supermarket to continue to provide free parking space, or forbid the drugstore to deliver to homes less frequently. The hardware store may stock fewer items, the quality of appliance parts may decline, the lawyer may work more slowly and charge for additional hours. Occasionally the regulators may seek to prevent noticeable and dramatic changes directly related to price, as when they forbid supermarkets from discontinuing trading stamps. But more often they are unable to deal with the problem of gradual decline. Korean War regulations, for example, exempted professional services (leading to considerable argument over the definition of "professional service").

Finally, the large number of producers that prompted a simplified historical approach is itself an obstacle to effective enforcement. Enforcement staff may be relatively small, particularly in wartime. In 1943, for example, there were only one thousand investigators for enforcement of all food price and rationing regulations at all levels of production and distribution.[43] Violations may be widespread. Indeed, during the 1971 ninety-day freeze, there were 46,387 violations reported to the federal regulators—and obviously many more went unreported.[44] Elaborate record-keeping requirements may help detect violations, yet it is unrealistic to expect all retailers to keep detailed records of all transactions or restaurants to keep all old menus.[45] Inevitably the system depends heavily upon voluntary compliance for its effectiveness, yet there may be considerable disregard for the regulations. During World War II a black market sprang into existence. During the Korean War field officers conducting spot "compliance drives" found between 25 percent and 55 percent of the thousands of establishments visited to be in violation of the pricing rules.[46] As time passes, the rules may become more complex, and patriotic motives to comply may become less forceful. Those willing to comply find it more difficult to know what they are supposed to do; those unwilling to comply find it easier to justify higher prices.

New Investment

Insofar as a historically based system holds the price of items below the cost of the *new* investment needed to produce them, it will obviously discourage new investment and bring about a shortage. Yet even if the system gradually adjusts and becomes a cost-based system, investment in new products still may suffer. Without regulation, shortages would be accompanied by high prices and high profits, which would attract needed investment. Moreover, firms would seek new products or anticipate shortages with the hope that by discovering new demand (or by anticipating a shortage) they will earn unusually high profits. Under a price controlled regime, they will at best be able to earn no more than a "normal" return, which is unlikely to include any special premium for added risk. Thus, the response to changes in consumer taste or need is likely to be sluggish.

In practice, regulators have responded to perceived needs for increased investment by moving from a historical price method to a cost-based method of price determination. Thus, in 1951 the machine tool industry was unable to attract sufficient investment and became a defense bottleneck. A general overriding regulation was enacted to relieve some of the price squeezes. Indeed, a general regulation later allowed firms to earn their costs plus ordinary profit on items essential to the defense industry.[47] Regulations have occasionally gone further and exempted certain sectors entirely from the regulation, presumably in order to direct investment in that direction. Thus "sales of military and strategic commodities" were basically exempted during the Korean War, and discoveries of new oil have been wholly or partially exempted from historically based oil price regulation.[48] Insofar as the regulators adjust prices deliberately to encourage or to discourage new investment, their role becomes closer to that of the economic planner. Determining where to raise or to remove a price ceiling is difficult, and obviously more difficult in peacetime than during a war (where defense has top priority). The need to make such adjustments for major investment purposes, however, may grow gradually over time.[49]

Conclusion

The problems that accompany historically price-based pricing methods are serious and increase in severity the longer regulation stays in effect. Misallocation, shortage, and enforcement problems become increasingly serious. Categories proliferate. The system evolves toward cost-based pricing methods and the regulators find themselves faced with many of the difficulties that accompany cost-of-service ratemaking. The virtues of the system are apparent during wartime, when citizens are more prepared to cooperate voluntarily and when they will tolerate the unfairness of broad rules. The system's problems are more apparent in peacetime. Indeed, "as the threat of a full-scale shooting war on a world-wide scale lessened, OPS [the Korean War regulator] was increasingly beset by hostile critics. Like OPA it found that without widespread public support, engendered by an actual or clearly imminent global shooting war, price control, at least in a democracy, did not function well."[50] Nonetheless, the virtue of the historically price-based system rests in its ability to control the prices of hundreds or thousands of producers and products, while avoiding the firm-by-firm approach of cost-of-service ratemaking. It is difficult to see, in the case of economy-wide controls, any practical alternative.

4

Allocation under a Public Interest Standard

Regulators frequently must allocate a scarce resource, such as a television license, a liquor license, a right to fly an airline route, or natural gas among competing qualified applicants. One typical method of doing so is to award the item to the "best" applicant, as determined after hearings that weigh comparative merit. This method can be called "allocation according to a public interest standard."

Public interest allocation is used when the following three conditions are met: (1) The demand for the item by qualified applicants exceeds supply. It does not matter whether this scarcity is "natural," as in the case of television, or "artificially" caused by government, as in the case of airline routes.[1] (2) The agency cannot solve the allocation problem by promulgating simple rules, either of qualification or for allocation. More airlines, for example, meeting minimal financial requirements, want routes than are available. Allocating in accordance with simple historical principles will prove inadequate. (3) The agency can neither auction the commodity to the highest bidder nor dispense it by lot. Sometimes the enabling statute, such as the 1934 Communications Act,[2] (or past agency practice) is inconsistent with an auction or lottery.[3] In other instances, such as airline routes or natural gas, the agency is pursuing regulatory objectives that auction or lottery would tend to thwart.[4]

Thus, public interest allocation, while sometimes involving "licensing," cannot be equated with this term. Rather, licensing covers a broad range of regulatory activities and its usefulness as an analytic category is limited. Sometimes the primary licensing task involves setting standards, such as those that govern the fitness for practice of airline pilots or chiropodists, or those that limit chemical additions to the food supply. In other instances, licensing agencies screen doctors, lawyers, or drugs to weed out the unfit or unsafe. These activities will be discussed in separate chapters.

Moreover, public interest allocation is not used when regulators can develop a simple standard to solve the allocation problem. Energy regulators, for example, sought to regulate oil on historical principles, sharing the burden of the shortage in proportion to applicants' prior use. This allocative method will also be discussed separately, for it presents a quite different regulatory approach to the allocation problem. The present discussion focuses on allocation among qualified applicants where no single standard does the job.

The System

This method for awarding licenses, routes, and a host of other scarce commodities is characterized by the regulators' need to decide, first, what precisely to give away; second, what threshold criteria will weed out those not minimally qualified; third, which remaining applicant is "best"; and, fourth, how long the winner is to retain the license or right to a commodity.

The first step—deciding what exactly to give away—is often determined by formal hearings. The Federal Communications Commission (FCC), for example, controls not only radio and television licensing but the use of the entire electromagnetic spectrum. It set aside for major commercial broadcast use about .1 percent of the spectrum, dividing it into radio service (AM, FM) and television service (twelve VHF channels and fifty-six UHF channels).[5] The FCC then had to decide the following: Should it divide the country into regions and allot the twelve VHF channels so as to allow six or seven VHF stations broadcasting throughout each region, alternating with empty channels to prevent interference?[6] Or should it place more stations in local communities, despite the fact that most viewers would then receive only three or four VHF channels? (This would be because potential interference from nearby communities requires more empty spectrum space between channels.) The former would allow viewers greater choice; the latter would permit more local station ownership and program origination. Thus, important policy questions were embedded in the FCC's determination of precisely what type of station license it would allocate.

The Civil Aeronautics Board faced a similar definitional problem when allocating aviation routes. The decision as to what to give away led it to determine patterns of service among many possible configurations, or networks of city pairs.[7] Even awarding so specific a commodity as natural gas involves difficult definitional questions. The agency awards a right to acquire the commodity. But how long should that right last? What amount does it involve? And what product quality is specified?

The second question—setting minimum fitness standards—is often the easiest. The agency promulgates basic criteria of qualification, and then its staff administers their application. The FCC, for example, requires applicants to provide information[8] related to:

1. *Legal qualifications:* citizenship, history of any violations of law, compliance with cross-ownership rules (other broadcasting or newspaper ownership), compliance with other ownership rules, and so on.

2. *Financial qualifications:* source of capital, amount of capital, estimated costs, revenues, construction expenses, and so on.

3. *Proposed program service:* efforts made to determine community needs (surveys), proposed programming (time devoted to news, public service, local programming), proposed method of operation, and so on.

4. *Engineering qualifications:* frequency, transmitter height, terrain, antennae, and so on.

Similarly, the Civil Aeronautics Board determined whether a route applicant was "fit, willing, and able" to fly—whether the applicant has sufficient safe airplanes and adequate financial resources.[9] With commodities, the preliminary inquiry may be as simple as determining whether the applicant had previously used the commodity—say, natural gas.

Whether or not the list of preliminary qualifications is lengthy, applying them is likely to be a routine matter. The television license applicant routinely fills out the application and satisfies each condition. Often there is more than one qualified applicant for each frequency (or route, or unit of natural gas) with commercial value.

The third step—the selection of the "best" among several qualified applicants—is the most difficult. It typically involves a lengthy hearing, often "comparative,"[10] at which all parties are represented and each argues that it is superior to the others. The hearing is characterized by its open texture. The specific relevant issues may themselves be in dispute and vary from one hearing to another.[11] Thus, one television license applicant, with excellent programming proposals, will argue that the award should turn upon program proposals, while another, perhaps with many black employees, will argue that affirmative action plans should constitute a major determinant. One airline, applying for a route, may urge the CAB to examine comparative employment effects; another might urge the board to examine comparative fuel savings.[12] Parties will also dispute the weight to be given individual criteria. Even if program proposals and affirmative action are both relevant, their comparative importance will be argued and redetermined in each case. In addition, there are likely to be lengthy lists of potentially relevant criteria. This allows the parties to argue about what criteria are relevant and which are more important, at the same time as they argue about who better satisfies them.[13] The agency, to simplify the proceedings, often develops a prehearing procedure to determine the relevant issues in the particular case.[14]

The hearing consists of lengthy presentations of evidence on each of the many potentially relevant criteria. Much of this evidence will already have been presented during the prehearing procedure.[15] Finally, the agency exercises its subjective judgment, based on the hearing record to determine which applicant is best. Its decision is subject to court review, essentially to determine whether the decision is "reasonable."[16]

The final stage of the process—determining the length of the award—may take place years later, as those who have been awarded a license or commodity seek to keep it. Whether incumbents should receive priority for additional supply will be decided in future hearings focusing upon renewals (say, for broadcast license) or additional applications (say, for scarce natural gas).

Problems

Many of the problems plaguing public interest allocation arise from two conflicting drives that the system generates. First, the regulator's desire to find objective standards to select the winner from the final group often conflicts with his belief that he must exercise his subjective judgment, for *no* set of standards can consistently select winners who are best in terms of the regulatory program's objectives. The FCC, for example, has developed standards emphasizing "diversity of media ownership" and "integration of management and ownership." Yet, if rigorously applied, the first would favor General Motors' application to open a Detroit broadcasting station over that of an Albuquerque newspaper. The second would favor managers rich enough to supply their own capital. Of course, the FCC modifies its application of these standards by considering other factors, but then subjective judgment, not the standards, decides close cases. More important, standards sufficiently objective to select winners are likely to deflect the decision from a major statutory objective—"good programs" in the case of the FCC. A regulator who takes this objective seriously may believe that it is a function of many different qualities of the applicants, such as experience, financial backing, character, program plans, and imagination. Yet to work with such factors to reach a judgment is more a managerial than a legal skill. It requires the exercise of subjective judgment—a managerial activity often at war with the legal drive toward certainty and rational justification.

The second difficulty is the conflict between the need for decisions that comply with certain legal principles of fairness and the effort to implement the statute's major purposes. For example, the need to treat like cases alike—a basic principle of fairness in law—pushes the agency toward developing uniform rules and standards. Yet when deciding individual cases, agencies make exceptions or blur standards to better attain the statute's purpose. This latter drive also exemplifies an aspect of fairness found in courts of equity, by relieving parties of strict general rules that might work injustice in the particular case. In fact, the tension between uniform rulemaking and deciding each case on its merits is reminiscent of the historical conflict between law and equity.

Moreover, the difficulty of developing clear, objective, substantive criteria leads the agency to emphasize principles of fairness, familiar to lawyers and administrators, often using them to decide cases. One such principle is "historical fairness"—the protection of reasonable expectations that parties develop over time. Regulators tend, for example, in the absence of other determinative criteria, to rely upon historical allocation as a starting point for a new allocation decision. A second principle is that of "procedural fairness," which essentially requires that all affected parties have an equal opportunity to convince the decision maker.[17]

The extent to which these conflicts are embedded in the public interest allocation system and the difficulties they pose can be made clear by examining several basic problems of this system. The FCC's allocation of television licenses provides an excellent example, though similar problems arise when the CAB allocates airline routes or when the ICC grants trucking licenses.[18] These problems exist because (1) the marketplace is not used to allocate the right or commodity, (2) there are no clear standards to determine winners, and (3) a legal/administrative system awards the right or commodity. These elements produce problems that plague the agency through each stage of its decision-making process.

What Is to Be Allocated?

Defining the commodity to be allocated is sometimes easy, as in the case of oil or natural gas. But more often division of the commodity, such as broadcast spectrum space or airline routes, raises difficult policy questions. And when the commodity is awarded under a public interest standard, a special difficulty arises. That special problem is the interrelationship between *what* is to be given out and *who* is to receive it.

This relation of the "what" question and the "who" question poses a dilemma for the agency. The more it separates the questions—by defining what is to be given away in advance, through rules or precise specifications—the greater the risk of disqualifying applicants to whom an award would further the goals of the allocation system. Yet the more flexible the definitional standard, the more complex the determination of who should receive the rights, for each party in the "who" proceedings will argue a definition of "what" that favors its own cause.

The CAB took the approach of leaving the definitional question open. In awarding airline routes, the board had to decide both what route to award and who will receive it; the two decisions are interrelated. Suppose, for example, that airline A serves several cities in the Southwest, flying between them and Florida. Airline B serves the Northeast, flying between Boston and New York, as well as to Florida, Texas, and Southern California. Airline A now applies to fly between Los Angeles and Miami, with connecting service through Phoenix and Dallas. Airline B applies to fly between Boston and Los Angeles, with the right to stop in Phoenix and Dallas. Airline A will urge the board to create, and to award, a new Miami–Los Angeles route; airline B will seek the creation and award of a new Boston–Los Angeles route. Each may be the only applicant for its route. Yet the decision to create one or the other route will effectively determine which airline will fly between Phoenix and Dallas, common points on both proposed routes, for it is logical to award that segment to a line already flying between them and Los Angeles. (Indeed, the Phoenix-Dallas segment may have been the main objective of each proposal.)[19]

The configuration of an airline's route system significantly affects the probability of its being awarded a particular route segment. Airlines were fully aware of this and planned their applications strategically with future applications in mind.[20] Until the mid-1970s, interaction of past awards, present planning, and future applications determined what routes the board would award, which, in turn, would help to decide which carrier would fly them.

The CAB dealt with this problem by considering the "who" and "what" questions in the same proceeding. It would consolidate all route applications that might conflict into a single set of hearings, entitled, for example, "Service to the Southwest." Such proceedings might consist of tens, or even hundreds, of conflicting applications. These hearings were not only complex but often highly political, for each applicant encouraged testimony by public officials of towns that would receive service along the proposed routes.

The FCC dealt with a similar problem in a quite different way. After a series of rulemaking proceedings, it reserved a portion of the spectrum for AM, FM, UHF, and VHF licenses and developed a table of assignments for both FM and TV broadcasting.[21] This table, together with station separation requirements, determines approximately where each FM station and each television station will be located. While several applicants may compete for a certain frequency in a certain area, it is unlikely that an application to serve one community will conflict with an application to serve another. (AM radio stations present a more complex problem because AM radio waves, reflected by the atmosphere, can carry over a much longer distance than FM or TV. Thus, to award to one applicant a "clear channel"—permission to broadcast with considerable power—may conflict with another applicant's efforts to serve a local community over the same frequency.)[22]

Despite the table of allocations, AM radio applications and certain FM and television applications to serve different communities may still conflict, particularly when applicants seek to locate stations at the borders of a community. When such conflicts occur, the FCC will first decide which community will obtain service.[23] Then it will choose among competing applicants to serve that particular community. In deciding among communities, the FCC holds a hearing and uses as its standard of judgment Section 307(b) of the Communications Act, which requires a "fair, efficient and equitable distribution of radio service" among "the several states and communities." The hearing examines the communities' relative needs for new service; it does not consider the comparative merits of the applicants.[24]

The FCC's procedure for dealing with the definitional problem has a decided administrative advantage over that of the CAB: it simplifies the proceedings. Separation of these issues into different proceedings has allowed the FCC to develop standards to determine the more "deserving" community.[25] These standards, based upon a preference for local broadcasting, make it more difficult for an applicant to manipulate the "what" issue to obtain a favorable result.

However, certain important defects in the FCC's system should be noted. First, the standards that the FCC uses to pick among communities are sometimes not precise enough to decide the issue. Nor has its policy favoring local origination of programming always been implemented. New Jersey, for example, despite its large population, has no local VHF television station, because all available spectrum space was allocated to New York and Philadelphia.[26] When the allocation standards are not determinative or have not been met, allocation hearings can still prove lengthy and complex, and parties, such as New Jersey, may seek to inject the allocation issue into a licensing proceeding, thus recombining the "who" and the "what" issues.

Second, and more important, the FCC purchases simplicity and procedural logic at a price: it cannot easily allow a superior applicant to overcome the needs of a community with comparatively less service.[27] If community A has three stations and B has four, A will receive the next station even though the applicant wishing to serve B may be far superior to the applicant seeking to serve A. Where the commission attempts to circumvent this dilemma, it runs into the "complex procedure" problem typified by the CAB's proceedings.

Third, critics have claimed that the policy of localism, which makes separation of the "what" and "who" issues practical, is undesirable.[28] Studies of viewer behavior suggest that the policy may bring the viewer few practical benefits.[29] Local programming is unprofitable for local stations because viewers prefer national network programming. By pursuing a policy of maximizing the number of communities with local broadcast outlets, the FCC has made it impossible to have regional stations—though a policy of regionalism would offer more channel choice to viewers (especially those in rural areas). At the same time, the localism policy has compelled station separations that are greater than the technical characteristics of the spectrum require (to ensure viable allocations to sparsely settled areas), thus decreasing the options in densely populated areas.[30]

If these criticisms are accurate, the FCC has developed standards for allocating channels among communities, which may conflict with its broader public interest mission—a mission that includes securing "good" television programming.

The point here, however, is not to criticize localism, but to point out that a dilemma can readily arise as an agency tries to work out the relationship between the "what" and "who" questions. On the one hand, a procedure that specifically recognizes the relation and tries to determine both together threatens to become lengthy and very complex, with competing applicants searching for allies who will help achieve a favorable "what" determination. On the other hand, a procedure that separates the two questions threatens to produce a result that is only formally satisfactory. It may flow from a set of policy criteria, but separateness makes it difficult for the agency to consider "who" factors when deciding a close "what" issue. The net result may be worse in terms of the agency's overall objective.

There is no solution to this problem. There is only the practical cliché that the individual agency should recognize conflicting tendencies and fashion an optimum solution.

The Selection Process

The preparation of criteria that weed out unqualified applicants is usually not as difficult as selecting a winner from those who remain. This latter process typically raises the following difficulties.

Coherent standards. Lawyers and judges have criticized agencies, such as the FCC and the CAB, for their failure to develop and to apply consistently coherent selection standards. The Landis Report, for example, complained of the FCC's failure to plan.[31] Judge Henry Friendly, in a well-known critique of agency procedures, wrote that the FCC uses "an arbitrary set of criteria whose application . . . is shaped to suit the cases of the moment." He argued that both the FCC and the CAB needed a "better definition of standards."[32] Others have argued that FCC proceedings are "unpredictable, excessively discretionary, complex and baffling, deficiently consonant with the rule of law, and producing results that seem inconsistent from case to case."[33] The CAB's route-award procedure was characterized as "disturbing" because the board had "no fixed standards for determining . . . what carrier will be awarded a route."[34] Indeed, the board itself described its results in route-award cases as "random."[35]

The critics do not claim that these commissions work without standards. On the contrary, they argue that the agencies have too many standards, not too few. For example, the FCC announced for many years that it would take the following into account in comparing minimally qualified applicants:

1. the extent to which the station would be locally owned
2. the extent to which management and ownership is integrated (that is, do owners participate in management?)
3. the extent to which owners have diverse backgrounds
4. the extent to which owners have participated in civic affairs

5. proposed program policies
6. the carefulness of operational planning
7. relative likelihood of the station carrying out its program proposals
8. broadcast experience
9. past broadcast record
10. the adequacy of technical facilities
11. the background and qualifications of the staff
12. the character of the applicants
13. the areas and populations to be served
14. avoiding concentration of media control.[36]

Similarly, the CAB asked:

1. Can the carrier render effective service responsive to the public's needs?
2. Can it provide benefits to beyond-segment traffic?
3. Will there be route integration?
4. What points are involved?
5. Has the carrier historically participated in this traffic?
6. Will traffic be diverted from other carriers?
7. Does the carrier need strengthening?[37]

The effect of many standards, however, is virtually the same as having none at all. There is no clear indication of which standards are more important, how they are to be individually applied, or how varying degrees of conformity are to be balanced. The existence of so many standards effectively allows the agency near-total discretion in making a selection.

What leads jurists to demand, but not receive, more definite standards stems not from incompetent or malicious regulators but from problems deeply embedded within the public interest allocation system. For one thing, some of the factors that led Congress to enact so broad a standard as "public interest" or "public convenience and necessity" reappear at the agency level. These include disagreement about what agency goals should predominate. Some congressmen may have felt that air routes should be awarded as incentives to encourage system expansion; others may have favored economic efficiency; still others may have wanted to promote lower fares. Their disagreements will be reflected in commission decisions that compromise differing views and change over time.

Alternatively, the subject matter itself may make articulation of clear, specific criteria unusually difficult. To award a television license in the public interest, for example, requires consideration of "good programming." Programming is, after all, the final product that television provides for the public.

Yet how is the FCC to take this basic objective into account? On the one hand, it seems impossible to specify program content through detailed standards; on the other, good programming as an objective is impossible to ignore.

This dilemma is hardly surprising, for there is no consensus about what constitutes good or bad programming. However, most people acknowledge that program quality, like many other questions of taste, aesthetics, or morals, *can* be discussed rationally and that conclusions (within limits) can be reached. Yet they also acknowledge difficulty in reaching agreement, as well as the great danger in allowing the government to enforce conclusions that have not been generally agreed upon. Thus, it would be almost universally agreed, for example, that a television station that shows the same grade B film—called *Twenty Thousand Buckets of Blood*—eleven times each week is doing a poor job of programming, and not just because of the repetition involved. But it is also generally recognized that a debate about what constitutes good programming for children is unlikely to produce a clear consensus.

The result is FCC ambivalence and obscurity. The commission promulgates criteria, some related to good programming, but it cannot tackle the question directly. Consider the criteria for license awards listed above. Judge Friendly wrote that they reflect two basic policy objectives: the "community should have the programs best adapted to its needs, and this goal should be achieved in a manner that will avoid undue concentration of the media."[38] The phrase "programs best adapted to its needs" is vague, but if interpreted to include local ownership, program diversity, programs reflecting local interests and problems, and programming that is also otherwise "good," the criteria seem aimed at the objectives. Some of the criteria reflect these goals directly—for example, "concentration of media ownership" and "proposed program policies." Others seem to require evidence of quality and diversity of programming—for example, "broadcast experience," "applicant character," "technical facilities," "staff qualifications," "planning," "broadcast record," and "likelihood of follow-through." Still others seem related to local program origination and the reflection of local interests—for example, "diversity of owners' backgrounds," "participation in civil affairs," "local ownership," and "integration of management and ownership."

Throughout this list one perceives a definite, but uncertain, striving toward program quality.[39] But how could this be otherwise? The courts have interpreted the FCC's licensing mandate to have something to do with program quality. The United States Court of Appeals for the District of Columbia has written that "in a comparative consideration . . . comparative service to the listening public is the vital element and programs are the essence of that service."[40] At the same time, the commission's judgment of program quality must remain obscure, hampered by the nature of the issue, the lack of consensus, and First Amendment considerations that warn against entrusting such decisions to the government.[41]

The problem confronting the FCC and CAB is neither unusual nor beyond solution. In many areas of life, human beings deal with similar problems on a daily basis. Broad, abstract objectives are broken down into components through the use of criteria which are then applied to alternatives, and selections are made. Yet such decisions are not comfortably made through formal administrative or legal decision-making processes. Rather, they are typically reached through the exercise of intuitive, highly subjective judgment, and they are more often the subject of business than of legal decision making.

A subjective approach is commonly used, for example, by managers, particularly when filling job vacancies. Minimum criteria are supplemented by general lists of "desirable qualities" applied by a single manager, who uses his or her judgment to determine which candidate, all things considered, is likely to do the best job.[42] If the FCC were to use this "subjective" approach to the "good programming" problem, it would review the evidence about the quality of those owning and managing a station, their program proposals, connections within the community, past records, and so forth. It would subjectively weigh all factors, and then intuitively or instinctively judge which applicant was likely to do the best job.[43] Similarly, the CAB would simply review its candidates, apply its criteria, and choose.

The subjective approach, however, means unchecked discretion. Thus, the administrative and legal surroundings in which the agencies work encourage them to develop and to formalize selection criteria, minimizing subjective judgment and choosing that applicant which the formal criteria tend to select.[44] This "objective" approach, while often considerably fairer, can lead the agency away from achieving its primary goal.

Consider the FCC's efforts to develop more definite standards. Stung by criticism of irrationality, unfairness, inconsistency, and favoritism, in 1965 the FCC announced the selection of new criteria. The two primary criteria were "diversification of control of the media" and "integration of ownership and management." This policy statement has been characterized as "a change in the philosophies of license allocations away from predictions of programming content and toward structural policies."[45] The commission constructed an objective model of the type of station most likely to program in the public interest—a station whose owners do not have interests in other stations or newspapers, but who instead come from the locality to be served, remain in touch with civic leaders, and run the station themselves. The applicant who came closest to this "structural" ideal would be awarded the license.

There were three major difficulties with the 1965 approach. First, the standards remained highly subjective. Scaling was difficult within each category. To measure the "concentration" factor, for example, one must weigh the number of stations owned, degree of ownership, nearness to the station applied for, importance of the stations, and so on.[46] How these subsidiary factors should be measured and weighed and how they should affect the award of a preference remained unclear. Nor did the commission state how integration and concentration were to be balanced.[47] Moreover, since these major factors might have appeared evenly balanced, the minor factors reassumed major importance and the parties sought to raise hosts of subsidiary issues.

Second, the major factors did not determine the outcome of specific cases. Noll, Peck, and McGowan examined the FCC's awarding of applications for sixteen new television broadcast licenses between 1965 and 1973. The forty-five applications for these licenses were ranked in terms of the factors mentioned in the 1965 policy statement. After regressing these factors against the award of the license, Noll et al. found local ownership, local origination of programming, and news and public affairs programming to be negatively correlated with the award of the license, while ownership of other broadcast facilities was slightly positively correlated. In other words, the greater an applicant's local ownership, local origination of programming, or public affairs programming, the *less* likely he would be to receive the award. Cross-ownership made the award *more* likely—just the opposite of what one would expect from the policy statement.[48]

Third, if the criteria had been still more specific and had been rigorously applied, they would have yielded an absurd result. An owner with however little experience, managing his own station, would have been preferred over an absentee owner no matter how experienced the manager he hired.

Moreover, the objective standards bear only a distant relation to the development of quality programs. When the FCC tried to specify "quality" programming, it used numerical standards relating to *type* of program. When it considered license renewal standards, for example, the FCC considered whether stations had devoted 3–5 percent of their prime time hours to public affairs, 5–10 percent to news, and 10–15 percent to local programs.[49] Yet Noll, Peck, and McGowan concluded that there is little local programming because (with the exception of news) "locally produced programs . . . have low audience ratings, and their advertising revenues are correspondingly low"; thus, they are "not as profitable for station owners as national programming."[50] In sum, viewers do not want to watch them.

It is not surprising, then, that some commissioners have argued for *less* objectivity: Commissioner Hyde well summarized the argument for less definite standards in dissenting from the 1965 policy statement. The statement, he (perhaps unnecessarily) feared, "would press applicants into a mold, . . . thus deterring perhaps better qualified applicants from applying; it would preclude significant consideration of material differences among applicants and result in automatic preferences of applicants slavishly conforming to the model and eventually for the Commission to decide cases on trivial differences among applicants." He added:

I know of no two where the underlying facts [or] . . . differences among applicants are identical. Therefore, the significance to be given in each decision to each difference and to each criterion must of necessity vary and must necessarily be considered in context with the other facts of the individual case . . .

The Commission is . . . placing legislative-like restrictions upon . . . the responsibility Congress intended it to [perform] with broad discretion. It would appear we do not trust Commissioners to exercise judgment with as much discretion as Congress intended to repose in the agency.[51]

Thus, the desirability as well as the practicality of more definite standards is debatable.

Unmanageable procedures. Critics of the FCC's and CAB's (preregulation) license award procedures complained of the length of time, delays, and complexity involved. These complaints did not reflect agency mismanagement so much as they indicated procedural difficulties that arose out of the nature of the agency's task. The conflict between "objective standard setting" and "subjective managerial judgment" described above leads inexorably to complicated procedures. Insofar as the two agencies seek subjectively to determine the best applicant, the range of possible issues broadens and the amount of relevant evidence grows exponentially. The result, in the case of contested license proceedings, is a typical duration of well over two years, with many hotly contested applications lasting much longer. A recent Florida broadcaster's renewal application, for example, took six years to reach a final decision,[52] and the famous WHDH initial application and renewal proceedings took twenty-four years from start to finish.[53] Similarly, route proceedings before the CAB that lasted for five to nine years were not uncommon.[54] These proceedings can cost the parties hundreds of thousands or millions of dollars[55] and can result in enormous backlogs in agency dockets. Many times it takes months or years before the case is even heard.

The manner in which the nature of the task creates procedural complexity is well illustrated at the FCC, which has struggled to streamline its procedures, but with only limited success. In a comparative proceeding, the FCC's Broadcast Bureau, under delegation of authority from the commission, examined each application. It determined, first, whether an application met the minimum criteria (those that would allow a license if the application were uncontested), and, second, whether a party's request to add specific issues (such as "character of the applicants") to the comparative hearing should be granted. If the answer to the first question was yes, and if there were no requests to add issues, the case proceeded to a hearing on issues designated in a hearing order. The hearing focused on the "standard comparative" issue: "to determine which of the proposals would, on a comparative basis, best serve the public interest," using the criteria specified in the 1965 policy statement. The Broadcast Bureau, however, may add specific issues, or the commission may itself specify which issues will be heard, including not only the "standard comparative" issue but also issues related to minimum qualifications, as well as any "specific comparative" issue it believed important.[56]

A hearing examiner conducted the initial hearing. The parties, even during the hearing,[57] might, and often did,[58] file petitions to enlarge, modify, or delete issues specified in the hearing order, and they would appeal unfavorable rulings.[59] The hearing examiner eventually made an initial decision to award the license. This decision was inevitably appealed by the losing parties to the Review Board, to the commission, which tended to relitigate major issues,[60] and finally to the courts, which examined the decision for reasonableness and procedural error.

The complexity of the hearing process in part reflects the procedural difficulty of defining the relevant issues *and* deciding who prevails upon each. But even when the issues are narrowed to the most basic ones—media concentration and manager/owner integration—the hearing is complex, lengthy, and open-textured. In considering manager/owner integration, for example, the commission considered the owners' acquaintance with the community and their participation in civic affairs. Thus, each party could present testimonials about its owners' civic virtue. Witnesses, including the town mayor, could testify. One recent case included not only many letters of commendation from local citizens but also large glossy photos of numerous awards the owner had won.[61] Shares of stock might be given to persons of recognized civic virtue so that they would count as "owners." Naturally, opponents attacked their rivals' civic virtue and argued that such ownership was a charade.[62]

In practice, it was not possible to limit the issues to integration and concentration. Two or more applicants might be evenly balanced as to these, and other issues might become relevant. The parties were likely to petition the Review Board to add issues, in any event, perhaps in the middle of the hearing. The petitions themselves contained affidavits with most of the evidence, so that the evidence remained in the record and could be used on appeal to the commission even if the petition to add an issue were denied.[63]

Subsidiary issues offered fertile ground for the legal imagination. Consider, for example, the issue of program proposals, which were judged primarily on the basis of their responsiveness to community needs. The applicant for a new license was to provide the commission with: "(a) full information on the steps the applicant has taken to become informed of the real community needs and interests to be served; (b) suggestions which the applicant has received as to how the station could help meet the area's needs; (c) the applicant's evaluation of these suggestions; (d) the programming which the applicant proposes in order to meet those needs as they have been evaluated."[64] Each requirement allowed room for argument. An applicant's lawyer might claim, for example, that his client interviewed the "true" community leaders while his rival interviewed mere toadies; his client conducted personal interviews, while his rival only sent mail questionnaires;[65] his client had more, or better, community leaders on his board of directors; his client responded more directly (or more intelligently) to the suggestions of community leaders;[66] and so forth.[67] The number of claims that could be pursued was limited only by the applicants' financial resources.

Just as hearing officers and the commission found it difficult to limit the number of issues, so they found it difficult to limit the evidence introduced on each. The candidates, evenly matched in terms of the basic requirements, also satisfied any other objective criteria on subsidiary issues. Thus, they were likely to have taken adequate surveys of community opinion and to have prepared program proposals on the basis of those surveys. The commission's renewal form lists nineteen community "elements" or "institutions" (civil organizations, military groups, elderly groups, women's groups) and five minority groups (blacks, Hispanics, Indians, Orientals, women) that should be surveyed.[68] Rival applicants would contact all of them. Trivial differences between the rivals then began to matter.[69] Moreover, cumulative evidence on program proposals, reliability, experience, and character issues was useful if subjective judgment were to be exercised, for as such evidence cumulates, a "picture" of the applicant (or its owner) begins to emerge. Thus, it is not surprising that in the record and hearing transcripts, more pages were devoted to the background and character of the principals than to any other single issue.[70]

Finally, after the hearing examiner made an initial decision and the Review Board decided the initial appeal, the parties appealed to the commission itself. Despite totally discretionary authority to deny review,[71] commissioners tended to conduct a full de novo hearing based on the record, often changing the result.[72] The fact that commissions were unwilling "to forego a second de novo review of every decision" appealed from the Review Board[73] is not surprising, given the nature and importance of the task.

As the commission states in its application, "programming is the essence of broadcasting." The primary method open to the commission to affect broadcast quality is by choosing people who will themselves choose, and broadcast, good programs. Thus, they may well see the selection of the best broadcasters as lying at the heart of their mission. Given their inability to devise specific objective criteria that will select "best" broadcasters, they may not only see the need for the exercise of subjective judgment as necessary but also as a major part of what they as commissioners were appointed to do. They are, then, no more likely to delegate the ultimate selection of initial licensees than the president of the United States is likely to delegate his responsibility for choosing cabinet members, a board of directors theirs for choosing a new company president, or any top manager his for choosing key officials. And a several-stage process for initial applicants is likely to continue. (Renewals present a special problem.)

In other words, each part of the complex, lengthy hearing process before the FCC can be seen as a plausibly necessary effort to respond to the basic problem the agency faces: the awarding of a license to the best applicant through the use of adversary procedures. The CAB's procedures for route awards were also complex.[74] Indeed, one would expect lengthy, complex, barely manageable procedures whenever an agency seeks to impose standards of objectivity and fairness on this subjective process—whenever it tries to control in this way the discretion to exercise that judgment that public officials otherwise might enjoy.

Inconsistency. The mix of subjective judgment and objective standards that characterizes public interest allocation leads to inconsistent decision making. The inconsistency appears when two decisions made under similar standards and similar facts reach opposite results. For example, according to Judge Friendly, when the FCC has awarded TV licenses, sometimes the fact that an applicant owned a newspaper seriously hurt his chances, while other times this fact was neutral[75] or may even have helped the applicant.[76] Similarly, the random nature of the CAB's route-award process meant that the strength of an applicant's existing route network sometimes may have helped and other times may have hurt his chances.[77]

The manner in which inconsistency can arise is well illustrated by an FCC case awarding a television broadcast license to the Biscayne Television Corporation over several other applicants.[78] The commission found the applicants quite evenly balanced. Biscayne's competitors argued that Biscayne ought to be given a demerit because its key executive previously had been president of a network and because that executive would continue to be paid a large consulting fee by the network while working for Biscayne. In previous cases the commission had given demerits on the grounds that it was undesirable that persons connected with a network also own part of a local station, because the network might then favor the local station over its local competitors, or the local station might favor that network. In one of these cases, a substantial shareholder of the applicant was also a network vice-president; in another, the shareholder was also a network officer and director. The Court of Appeals reversed the commission's award to Biscayne on grounds of inconsistency: the commission had neither distinguished its earlier cases nor explicitly overruled them. Hence it must redetermine its license award. The commission made the redeterminations and gave Biscayne a demerit for the "conflict of interest," but nevertheless awarded it the license.

The evils of inconsistency are several. For one thing, the factors that the commission articulates as its reasons for its decision may not be the real factors. An impermissible factor—one that Congress did not wish the commission to use—may well have crept in. In the case of the FCC, for example, this factor may relate to the content of the station's programs. Even if the commission does not, in fact, consider the applicants' political views, the applicants may come to fear that it does. They may then censor their own broadcasts for fear of the commission's future reactions—contrary to the intent of Congress.

In addition, if the inconsistency simply reflects change in commission policy,[79] the alteration has been made without the commission specifically focusing upon its wisdom. People affected by the change have not had an opportunity to present their views to the commission; the commission has not openly debated the issue; and it has not explicitly thought about whether it is wise.

Moreover, the inability to perceive key factors, produced by inconsistent decision making, leads applicants to depend upon the views of insiders—the expert Washington lawyers or commission staff members—to try to learn what is truly important. They may act on rumor, suspicion, or guess about what individual commissioners feel, sometimes seeking academics for their boards of directors, at other times blacks or Catholics. The greater the importance of this inside knowledge, the more tempting it is for an FCC staff member to see his position as a stepping stone to a lucrative career in the specialized agency bar.

The result is unfairness, between applicants with greater and lesser access to inside knowledge and between equally qualified applicants who are treated differently. The result is unpredictability in decision making and uncertainty as to how one can obtain a license. It is also cynicism, as the public comes to believe that the articulated criteria are not the real ones. Finally, it is abuse of power, as the courts find it difficult to keep the agency within the bounds of its legislated discretion.

There is no easy way to overcome the inconsistency problem. As the Biscayne controversy makes clear, when the courts find clear examples, they can remand to the commission. Yet the commission can then distinguish past cases, change its policy, or, without doing either, simply reach the same result by balancing the host of other relevant factors. Though the remand forces the commission to focus upon the relevant policy issue, it does little to cure unpredictability, unfairness, or the suspicion of impermissible factors at work.

The FCC has taken two procedural steps to meet the problem, perhaps in response to Judge Friendly's criticism that changes of position were "slipped into an opinion in such a way that only careful readers would even know what happened, without articulation of reasons, and with the prior authorities not overruled."[80] First, it turned over much of the job of reviewing initial license decisions, and of deciding the relevance of issues, to an intermediate Review Board.[81] This seems to have helped. One student of the subject writes: "Among lawyers who regularly appear before the Commission, there seems to be general agreement that decisions of the Review Board are more predictable than were the decisions of the Commission . . . . They reach results that are significantly more consistent with precedent and existing policy and that adhere more closely to the record facts."[82] Second, the commission has begun to require that individual commissioners write, or at least supervise the writing of, the opinion that articulates the reasons for an applicant's selection.[83] This requirement helps overcome one major defect in its previous practice of having an "opinon-writing" staff write the opinion— namely that those aware of this practice suspected that the decision simply rationalized, ex post, a decision reached on other grounds.

These changes, however, have not eliminated the problem. The FCC still reviews major decisions of its Review Board; the Office of Opinions and Review continues to be primarily responsible for shaping opinions; and the commission continues to be criticized for inconsistency.[84] This fact is not surprising, for reasons pointed out earlier. Inconsistency arises out of the exercise of subjective judgment. Indeed, the judgment of different individuals or even the same person about who is best may differ from time to time among cases that ostensibly meet the same objective criteria. This suggests that inconsistency could be eliminated only by rigorous adherence to objective standards. This course of action has been advocated by those who see inconsistency as the commission's greatest problem,[85] yet to do so compromises the larger goal of bringing about better programming. No set of objective criteria can be consistently applied to reach that goal. The opposite approach—to rely *explicitly* upon subjective judgment—would eliminate hypocrisy and ease judicial review of consistency in the application of standards. Yet it would neither prevent inconsistent decisions in practice, nor cure the other vices of inconsistent decision making. In sum, the public interest allocation process cannot readily avoid this significant defect.

Corruption. A fourth problem, directly related to the preceding three, lies in the vulnerability of a subjective process to corruption. The standards promulgated by the FCC are not too few but too many. They do not confine the commission's discretion, but leave it free to pick and choose among applicants for unarticulated reasons. Consequently, its good-faith exercise of subjective judgment can easily become (or can be viewed as) the bad-faith consideration of impermissible factors.

Thus, commentators have concluded that the FCC's awards of television licenses simply reflected the applicants' political views. All awards to newspaper applicants from 1952 to 1959, for example, allegedly went to newspapers that had supported the president politically.[86] And the Nixon tapes reveal that at least one president was willing to try to use the FCC to punish political opponents. Similarly, the recent congressional investigation of the airlines was replete with allegations of corruption, special favors, and special treatment provided commissioners.[87]

There are three ways in which commissions might deal with the corruption problem. First, commissioners can be appointed who are above suspicion. Identifying these persons and securing their appointment may prove difficult. Yet the large number of persons appointed to administrative commissions with little prior experience except a background in politics leads some to suggest that this approach may not have been given a fair opportunity.

Second, Congress and the commissions have sought to prevent commissioners from personally benefiting from their decisions. Conflict-of-interest rules are designed to prevent financially interested persons from deciding cases. Other rules prevent commissioners (for a time) from later accepting employment that brings them back to practice before the commission.

Rules of this sort, which will be discussed in Chapter 17, are difficult to draft and to enforce. To prevent a commissioner or staff member from ever working for or with the industry in which he has (or will) become a leading expert seems unduly harsh and impractical, given the existing structure of the civil service. Moreover, commissioners can benefit personally from their decisions in nonfinancial ways. For example, the media are of paramount importance in the election of congressmen and presidents. Commissioners tend to include those who have political experience and personal political ambitions, and who are grateful to the politicians who appointed them. It would thus seem impossible to isolate the commissioner from at least the appearance of potential personal benefit.

Third, commissioners, Congress, and the courts have created rules designed to make the decision-making process as open as possible. Ex parte communications are forbidden; sunshine laws require open meetings. The courts, sensitive to charges of improper influence, have reversed cases because, for example, a commissioner accepted a Christmas turkey[88] or because an applicant's major shareholder privately stated to a commissioner his views about legislation pending in Congress.[89]

The effectiveness of these methods for removing the suspicion of corruption appears limited, however, because the system itself gives rise to it. The licenses that commissions award are extremely valuable. The commission awards them under a system that cannot be readily reduced to clearly articulated, determinative standards. Hence, the award seems to depend upon the exercise of subjective, uncontrollable discretion. Under these circumstances, suspicion of corruption and its occasional appearance are inherent in the process.

The Renewal Process

Television stations must renew their licenses every three years. Pipelines from time to time must receive new allocations of natural gas. Airlines with permission to fly a route need not renew their certificate, yet as a practical matter the certificate may become worthless if too many other airlines are awarded rights to fly the same route. In each case, the agency must decide issues involving a winner's "security of tenure" in what it has previously awarded. In each case, the agency will have to face two general policy issues.

First, the agency must determine what weight to place upon the reliance of the firm in maintaining its existing right or that right's exclusivity. To what extent is renewal needed to protect existing investment or to encourage future investment? To what extent is that investment desirable? To what extent is termination unfair? Second, the agency must consider whether a refusal to renew will encourage competition and whether such competition is desirable.

Thus the FCC, for example, must ask: Would (should) renewal help protect license investment? Would nonrenewal lead to competitive pressure for better programming? The CAB might ask whether it should pursue a more open entry policy. Would fear of more entry by new airlines help promote desirable price competition? The energy agencies must determine the extent to which security of gas or oil supplies is needed in order for firms to plan production, as compared with the extent to which giving some firms that security would prevent increased competition from other firms entering the industry.

Critics have complained that agencies involved in public interest allocation tend to favor the status quo. They protect existing firms at the expense of new ones. Thus, the FCC almost always renews an applicant's license. Similarly, the CAB allowed no new firms into the airline industry for many years, at the same time limiting the new routes it would award to existing firms.[90] Thus, it is reasonable to ask whether the public interest allocation process itself contributed to this automatic renewal tendency—to protect those who have already received the allocation.

Again, the FCC provides an excellent example of this process. The Communications Act specifies that a television license is granted for three years.[91] It also states specifically that the license does not "create any right beyond the terms . . . and periods of the license."[92] In the *Hearst Radio* case,[93] however, the commission wrote that it would give an advantage in a comparative renewal hearing to an incumbent with a good record. Given the poor performance record that it used to justify its renewal of Hearst's license, the industry took the case as a signal that in a renewal proceeding the incumbent always wins.[94]

Until 1969 only one application for renewal of a television license was denied over the applicant's objection.[95] In fact, no regular television renewal applicant faced a comparative hearing in the 1950s or 1960s. (The commission denied WHDH's application in a departure from that policy.)[96] Since 1969, however, there has been only one major instance of a failure to renew a television license (the denial of Lamar Broadcasting's application for a Jackson, Mississippi, license because it had pursued racist policies),[97] though four other license renewal applications have been denied for technical reasons.[98] Since then, most observers feel that the commission has returned to its "incumbent wins" policy.

The commission has made efforts to change that policy. In 1970 it directly faced the question of how much preference it would grant an incumbent. It concluded that an incumbent whose program service had been "substantially attuned to meeting the needs of the public" and was without "serious deficiencies" would "be preferred over the newcomer."[99] This standard appeared strongly to favor incumbents, but it seemed to open a practical possibility that, in some instances, incumbents could be successfully challenged. The Court of Appeals held this standard unlawful, for it deprived challengers of their right to a hearing.[100] The court suggested that the commission might grant a considerable advantage in a renewal proceeding to an incumbent with a "superior" performance. The court added that, in determining superior performance, the commission might consider (1) eliminating excessive and loud advertising, (2) delivery of quality programs, (3) the extent to which the incumbent reinvested its profit in public service, (4) diversification of mass media ownership, and (5) independence from government influence in promoting First Amendment objectives.

The FCC then sought to develop standards to define "superior" performance, tentatively suggesting quantitative standards based on the proportion of viewing time devoted to local programming, news, and public affairs.[101] After six years of hearings, the commission gave up. It recommended to Congress the abolition of comparative renewal hearings, effectively giving existing stations security of tenure.[102] It announced a return to its prior policy of taking all factors into account in renewal hearings.[103] Its practice suggests a continuance of the policy that the incumbents will receive a special consideration, or a plus of major significance for a solid, substantive past performance, even where that performance is not significantly better than average.[104] Ultimately, the incumbent will almost always win.

For example, the commission was criticized for manipulating factors so as to favor incumbents in discussing the renewal of KIIJ (an RKO subsidiary). One commentator argued that RKO's substantial antitrust violations were equated with (the challenger) Fidelity's failure to reveal a small interest in suburban newspapers that one of its shareholders acquired; that RKO's financial interest in newspapers and eighteen other broadcasting stations was not heavily penalized; and that RKO's lack of owner/management integration was overlooked because RKO gave its local managers programming authority.[105] When the commission went on to renew the incumbent's license in the next renewal case, a dissenting commissioner argued that the commission had characterized an average record as "superior," and commented that the case "should set to rest any lingering fears that the Commission intends to use the comparative process to dislodge incumbent licensees."[106]

Before concluding that the FCC shows an unusual bias in favor of incumbents, one should recall a similar tendency in other agencies. Out of seventy-nine applications made by new airlines between 1950 and 1974 to enter the trunk domestic industry and to challenge existing firms, the CAB granted none.[107] When existing firms sought to fly new routes, the board granted licenses under standards that guaranteed the existing firms would not suffer financially from this new competition.[108]

Two propositions help explain the FCC's continued granting of renewal applications. First, a policy favorable to incumbents has something to be said for it on the merits.[109] It desirably encourages broadcasters to invest money in developing markets. Public interest programs today may improve the reputation of a station, but only indirectly provide benefits several years in the future. Stability and likely license renewal would increase the profitability of the long-term investment. Nonetheless, it is difficult to see how even this view of the merits could justify as much license stability as the FCC has provided. Are there not some stations that seek to "milk the market"? Is the "competitive spur" theory—that license insecurity encourages better programming—totally without merit?

In addition, political factors are at work. The broadcasters' political power is great; there are few in Congress who do not depend upon them for election. Thus, after the 1969 WHDH license decision, there was activity in Congress suggesting the likelihood of a law that would have limited the commission's power to deny license renewal.[110] Moreover, even without threatening legislation, the chairmen of congressional communications subcommittees have the power to reward or to punish broadcasters through the committees' reviews of the FCC's appropriation requests, their ability to conduct oversight hearings, and their power to make politically visible those commission actions that might prove either politically rewarding or politically embarrassing.

Alongside these factors, there is another set of considerations that helps explain the FCC's renewal policy. These factors are embedded in the public interest allocation system itself.

First, the agency's protectionist policy reflects a tendency present in all administrative and legal institutions—a tendency to protect an individual's reasonable expectations.[111] The importance of this fact is revealed by contrasting an administrative system with a market-based system. The market does not protect reasonable expectations; it impersonally destroys some firms, workers, and investments so that others may prosper. Regulation substitutes for this impersonal force human beings who are able to protect reasonable expectations, who will wish to do so, and who can (and will) be blamed if they do not do so.

In the case of broadcasting, there is little doubt that the amount of reliance is great. The station owners invest millions of dollars in obtaining a license, developing local programs, establishing local contacts, and so forth. Similarly, their employees invest their time and energies in developing their careers with the station. Suppliers and customers also commit time, energy, and perhaps money. Thus, all have a vested interest in the renewal of a license.

Whether the amount of reliance on the expectation of renewal is *reasonable* raises a more difficult question. The statute specifically denies the existence of any right to renewal. Yet years of automatic renewal create contrary (reasonable) expectations. Moreover, it may be nearly impossible to prevent such expectations. Consider, for example, an inexperienced climber who seeks to scale a mountain cliff in the face of repeated warnings not to do so and threats by rangers and others that they will not risk the lives of rescuers should the climber get into trouble. The climber knows full well that no matter what the ranger says, if he gets stuck, a rescue party will be sent out; and he is right. He may behave very badly in relying upon this expectation, but is he not reasonable in doing so? The example suggests that certain expectations cannot readily be destroyed by prior announcements. No matter what Congress or the FCC says, firms and individuals will invest time, effort, and money to obtain and develop broadcasting rights. Once they have done so, administrators whose policies will affect that investment are likely to feel some obligation to protect it.[112]

Second, once the agency decides to grant investment, reliance, or incumbency some advantage, how is the agency to decide how much advantage to give it? The agency's inherent inability to specify how various relevant factors are to be weighted makes it difficult to specify how all other factors are to be compared with incumbency.[113] Moreover, incumbency implies not only the reliance (and political and pragmatic) features just mentioned, but also the fact that the average incumbent has actually produced programs acceptable to the community it serves. The challenger is inevitably associated with uncertainty and risk. The FCC knows that applicants frequently fail to live up to their promises.[114] Further, it realizes that all of its knowledge about the challenger is based upon an advocates' hearing, which must involve some distortion. It would seem natural then, insofar as the commission judges who is likely to do the best job, to favor the applicant who has already performed adequately rather than those whose selection inevitably involves risk and whose true abilities are ex ante unknowable.

Third, the problem is exacerbated insofar as the promulgated standards are unable to fully embody the commission's congressional mandate. In the FCC's case, the problem is serious because of the discrepancy between its basic selection criteria and good programming. Once incumbency and at least average programming are shown, the incumbent is judged comparatively on the basis of the amorphous, problematic criteria previously discussed. These include such "structural" criteria as ownership diversity, local ownership, and management/operator integration. Even if the use of such criteria is no more unfair than the use of a random lottery, its fairness is questionable when an existing license holder (with some equity attaching to possession) is involved, for random selection then no longer seems justified. Indeed, the renewal hearing and criteria may serve simply to place a weapon in the hands of potential challengers seeking to obtain concessions from the license holder—concessions that may or may not mean better programming.[115] Yet unless the criteria can be shown likely to produce a better broadcaster, their use to supplant a present broadcaster seems unjustified.

The United States Circuit Court of Appeals for the District of Columbia in *Citizens Communications*[116] unwittingly illustrated this last problem when it suggested such standards as the elimination of excessive advertising, the delivery of quality programs, and promoting First Amendment objectives. The court did not explain how its standards were to be elaborated or applied. How are quality programs to be determined? What standards other than those based on, for example, percentage of prime time devoted to public affairs, might be used? How can the FCC directly involve itself in programming consistent with the First Amendment objectives the court seeks to advance? How could the commission promulgate a First Amendment standard that would not itself conflict with its own objective? These problems of definition and administration, as previously pointed out, have led either in the direction of more definite but less directly relevant standards,[117] or in the opposite direction of increased reliance upon subjective judgment.

One can see how a commission, feeling strong pressures to avoid reliance upon subjective judgment, would welcome (average) incumbency as a steady beacon in a storm—an objective fact directly related to fairly unobjectionable programming and a fact that for reasons of equity, policy, and politics would tend to sway subjective judgment. How under such circumstances a commission could give weight to incumbency, but not give it too much weight, then remains one of the more intractable problems facing an agency engaged in public interest allocation.[118]

Conclusion

The problems discussed here result from the fundamental fact that an administrative rather than a market process is used to allocate a commodity in scarce supply. The process inevitably tends to rely upon lawyers and hearings. A tension similar to that between law and equity arises. Standards hinder the agency's ability to apply the statute directly in an individual case and to choose the applicant who is best in terms of the statute's ultimate purposes; yet if the agency forgoes standards it will create unfairness, inconsistency, and injustice among applicants in individual cases.

It is not surprising, then, to find those who are particularly disturbed by these problems advocating abolition of the public interest allocation process altogether. Thus, the Senate subcommittee studying the CAB noted that the board might simply do away with allocation by allowing any "fit, willing, and able" firm to fly or by awarding the route to whoever would charge the lowest price. The subcommittee noted:

Having rejected competition and lower fares as automatically desirable, the agency is tempted to forge standards out of its overriding instinct to protect existing carriers. And, since entry invariably threatens the profits of existing carriers, any such standard will be highly restrictive . . .

In fact, before 1969, the Board awarded routes by giving different weight at different times to its desire to protect existing carrier revenues, its desire to build an efficient route network, its desire to supply the service requested by various cities and towns, and its desire somehow to even out carrier profitability. Given this broad range of rather abstract factors and many claimants, it is hardly surprising that a route case resembles an instance of political, rather than judicial, decisionmaking. Different sorts of arguments relating to different, and sometimes conflicting, standards are made by a host of claimants: existing carriers, cities, towns, new carriers, trade unions, airport representatives, and others. Proceedings last for years. A decision finally emerges and that decision is written into an opinion, not by the Board itself, but by the Board's opinion writing section. The result is usually an opinion that lists a set of factors followed by the result.

Of course, it is difficult and dangerous to award such valuable commodities as routes through such a process. Yet, in fairness to the Board, it is equally difficult to see how coherent, consistent standards, readily applicable, can be created as long as the object is to administer a *restrictive* route policy.[119]

As will be discussed in Chapter 14, the subcommittee recommended abolishing the form of regulation that restricted access to routes and that created the need for public interest allocation.

Similarly, some critics of the FCC's policies have argued that the comparative license award system should be abolished. Some have advocated auctions or lotteries. Others, including the FCC itself (in 1976),[120] have argued that comparative renewal hearings should be abolished and existing license holders should be granted security of tenure. There are, of course, strong arguments made against each of the alternatives. An auction, awarding the license to the highest bidder, might effectively compel the winner to concentrate on maximizing profits to the detriment of better or public interest programming. FCC programming standards would be arguably insufficiently specific or enforceable to counteract this tendency. To grant tenure to existing license holders, it may be claimed, would remove the FCC's last available weapon to encourage improved programming. It would also prevent potential challengers from using the threat of challenge to force the station to pay greater attention to local needs.

These arguments are mentioned to indicate that one cannot readily conclude, in a case such as the FCC, whether or not public interest allocation should be kept or abandoned. Rather, the discussion here is meant only to describe the flaws inherent in the system. Whether such a system is nonetheless preferable to the alternatives is a matter that would require considerably more detailed examination.[121]

5
Standard Setting

Another classical method for regulating industry's behavior is the setting of a standard. Standards are aimed at objectives as diverse as increasing workplace and product safety, producing a cleaner environment, and providing consumers with better information. They may be enforced through criminal sanctions, withdrawal of a license, civil fines, or adverse publicity. They may be written broadly or narrowly, with widespread or limited application. In view of their diversity of objective and type, to generalize about the method of creating standards risks ignoring many counterexamples or generalizing too abstractly. Despite these risks, there are certain features that are characteristic of much standard setting, and certain problems that are endemic to the process.

This chapter examines the general characteristics of the standard-setting process. In doing so, it will base its discussion upon several specific examples drawn from the experience of the National Highway Traffic Safety Administration (NHTSA). During the late 1960s and 1970s NHTSA had to develop both safety and fuel economy standards. The subject matter was technical, involving moderately difficult scientific and engineering questions. The agency regulated a small group of large, politically powerful producers. It sought to protect a large number of consumers, who provided the agency with considerable public and congressional support. Thus, its experience ought to resemble that of similar agencies concerned with environmental and other safety areas.

The NHTSA standard setting activities to be considered here include the following:

Preliminary standards. As required by statute, in January 1967 the agency promulgated twenty preliminary safety standards—four months after the "Safety Act"[1] became law. These standards were copied from various existing standards and were used as a starting point for further work.

Head restraints. The object of a head restraint standard is to prevent whiplash injuries by stopping the head from jerking backward when a car is hit from the rear. NHTSA began working on a standard in 1967 and the standard took effect two years later. A series of studies begun in 1971, however, suggested that the standard had little or no effect. NHTSA proposed a new standard in 1974, but then abandoned modification efforts.

Brakes. In 1967 the agency began to develop brake standards for trucks and buses. Its object was to try to reduce the stopping distances of these heavy vehicles to prevent them from running into the rear ends of lighter passenger cars in an emergency. After three years NHTSA proposed a strict standard that effectively required the redesign of all existing brake systems and the use of a new braking technology. It modified these requirements over the next four years, but a final standard was to take effect in 1974. By then, however, a host of practical problems prevented the new system from working properly. Quality variations within each batch of brakes forced manufacturers to overdesign, so that the worst brakes would meet the standards. Mechanics were uncertain how to maintain the brakes; test equipment could not be readily obtained; engineering experience developed slowly; and fragmentation of the industry among brake manufacturers, chassis makers, and truck assemblers created uncertainty about where responsibility rested. Despite several more years of modification, in 1978 a court of appeals set aside the 1974 standard as arbitrary.

Passive restraint devices. NHTSA made a major effort to develop a standard for a device to prevent passengers from flying forward in a crash, colliding with the dashboard or windshield. In 1967 it required passenger-operated seatbelts. In 1971 it promulgated a standard requiring airbags that inflated on impact: this standard was to take effect in 1973. In the meantime NHTSA required a seatbelt with an "interlock" to the car, preventing it from running unless the belt was fastened. A court of appeals set aside the airbag standard, however, because the testing system was inadequate. Congress, aroused by the unpopularity of the seatbelt interlock, enacted a statute forbidding it. After several years of additional work, NHTSA adopted a new rule in mid-1977 that required passive restraints—either seatbelts or automatically fastening seatbelts—on a phased-in schedule to take effect in 1984.

Tires. NHTSA's tire standards were aimed at helping buyers make more rational purchasing decisions. NHTSA began work in 1967 and in 1971 it proposed a standard that required label information about temperature resistance, impact, endurance, and treadwear performance. Consumer groups opposed the requirement as too complex, arguing that buyers wanted a simple system for comparing blowout resistance, traction, and treadwear. Despite a court suit and an order requiring NHTSA to act speedily, it did not set a final standard until 1975. After further modification, the standard took effect for bias belted tires in 1979 and for radial tires in 1980—more than twelve years after NHTSA began to work on the project.

Bumpers. NHTSA's bumper standards were primarily designed to save auto repair costs. NHTSA began to develop a standard in the late 1960s, and in 1971 it issued a requirement that bumpers withstand front-end collisions of 5 miles per hour (mph) and rear-end collisions of 2.5 mph without damage. After enactment of a new law increasing its authority, NHTSA made a stronger proposal in 1973 that simply would have required no damage in collisions of 5 mph or less. This proposal led to considerable discussion, including criticism that it was too expensive, and, since consumers did not notice microscopic dents, too strict. After debate and several further modifications, a new NHTSA standard took effect in 1979. It applied to 5-mph crashes, but allowed tiny dents in the bumper.

Fuel economy. Congress required manufacturers to make fleets of cars that each year, on average, satisfy a specific miles-per-gallon fleet efficiency standard. NHTSA's limited task was to set provisional yearly standards, starting from 1980, which the law set at 20 miles per gallon (mpg) and stretching to 1985, by which time the law requires 27.5 mpg. NHTSA began work in 1976. It based its proposals on two in-house studies, which the industry criticized because they were industry-wide studies and did not deal with the implementation problems of individual firms. Some firms also argued that the feasibility of a gas mileage standard depended on what emissions standard the Environmental Protection Agency (EPA) would set—a factor not yet known. NHTSA promulgated a final rule in mid-1977 setting standards of 22 mpg for 1981, 24 for 1982, 26 for 1983, and 27 for 1984. It recently rejected an industry request for relaxation.

In sum, NHTSA set standards with various aims. Some sought to increase safety, others to provide consumers with more information, and others to cut costs. NHTSA had to develop technical expertise and had to deal both with industry and consumer groups. NHTSA found its task difficult, for most of the standards took a decade or more to develop and to take effect. Moreover, in some instances the standards proved ineffective or impractical; in others they seemed helpful and workable. Thus, NHTSA experience provides a reasonably typical basis for a general description of the standard-setting process—a process that is used to achieve many of the difficult objectives described in Chapter 1.

The System

It is tempting but misleading to think of the standard-setting process as it might exist in the idealized world of the rational policy planner. In such a world a legislator or an administrator with broad statutory authority would first define the adverse effect, such as pollution or highway deaths, that he seeks to control. The administrator would then use a preliminary, rough cost/benefit analysis to select the specific part of the general problem that he should attack initially in order to obtain the greatest improvement at the lowest cost. Next, the administrator would obtain information and design a standard that would reduce the targeted adverse effects to an economically reasonable level in the least expensive way available. He would enforce that standard, developing means to ensure compliance. Finally, he would monitor enforcement, evaluate the standard's effectiveness, and revise it in light of his findings.

This description is misleading, because it cannot account for elements that even a cursory description of NHTSA experience suggests are typical of the standard-setting process. The process in practice appears to rely heavily upon precedent for the content of its standards; it is characterized by continued negotiation, modification of proposals, and long delays. Yet its standards, once in place, prove surprisingly resistant to change, even when, as in the case of head restraints, experience suggests they are ineffective.

This chapter will present a more practical description of standard setting and will discuss several major problems that are endemic to the process.

The Procedural Background

Most standard setting takes place in accordance with the procedure prescribed by law for "informal" or "notice and comment" rulemaking. While a general knowledge of those procedures is important to an understanding of the standard-setting process, it is not sufficient, because the law's procedural constraints are few and highly general. The Administrative Procedure Act states that an agency, before it promulgates a rule, must provide public notice and offer opportunity for comment. When it promulgates a rule, it must supply a "concise general statement" of the rule's "basis and purpose."[2] The rule can be set aside by a court if it is "arbitrary, capricious, or abuse of discretion."[3] The law thus lays down no more than a few general background constraints, within which the standard-setting process must operate. The procedures that NHTSA followed are typical of those used by other agencies, such as the Environmental Protection Agency and the Consumer Product Safety Commission.

Before presenting proposals for a rule, NHTSA would gather preliminary information. Sometimes it did so informally through meetings among members of its staff, with outside experts or with members of the industry and the general public. It kept written summaries of most of these meetings and made them available for public comment. In other instances NHTSA published an "Advance Notice of Proposed Rulemaking" (ANPRM) requesting comments and information from the industry and the general public about a particular subject—say, brake standards. The preliminary information was then used to develop a proposed standard.

Next, NHTSA formulated a preliminary standard and issued a "Notice of Proposed Rulemaking" (NPRM) describing it. The industry, consumer groups, and others submitted comments, information, and suggestions for modification. NHTSA held informal hearings, or public meetings, at which interested persons read statements and submitted to questioning by agency staff and by members of the audience.

NHTSA then modified its proposal. It had to publish its proposed modifications, however, and allow comment upon them, in order to satisfy the law's "notice and comment" requirement. Further modification and further comment might then be necessary. Eventually, the back-and-forth procedure would come to an end, and NHTSA would publish a final rule. Interested persons could still file petitions for reconsideration or further modification, but NHTSA would grant or deny them without further hearing.

Finally, any party to the proceeding could obtain judicial review of the final rule by appealing to the courts. As previously mentioned, a court would examine the proceedings and the rule to determine whether (1) NHTSA had committed procedural errors, (2) its factual findings were supported by substantial evidence, and (3) the rule was reasonable.

Of course, not all standard setting need take place within the context of informal rulemaking. An agency may set a standard in an adjudicatory proceeding, just as a court, in deciding an individual case, lays down rules in the form of precedents that guide future conduct. Indeed, the basic rule of law is that the choice between proceeding by general rule or by individual, ad hoc litigation is one that lies primarily with the informed discretion of the agency.[4] The National Labor Relations Board, for example, has promulgated nearly all of its policies in the form of rulings in adjudicatory proceedings. Indeed, adjudication has certain advantages, because it is easier for the agency to test, to modify, or to withdraw a rule that has been set forth in the form of an adjudicatory precedent.[5]

At the other extreme, certain statutes require that an agency promulgate rules in formal rulemaking proceedings. When an agency must do so, its decision must be made on the basis of a record, which is created at a hearing. The hearing is presided over by an agency employee, who typically takes evidence, hears witnesses, and allows cross-examination. Only a few statutes, however, contain the words "after a hearing on the record," which trigger the formal hearing requirements.[6] Similarly, agencies do not often use adjudication to set major policies or to promulgate standards.[7] Informal rulemaking has gradually become the preferred mode of proceeding.

The precise legal requirements of the informal rulemaking process are currently matters of debate and are in the process of evaluation. Lawyers and judges are uncertain about the extent to which agencies should be allowed to consult off the record in developing standards and the extent to which they should be required to make the information available to all interested persons for comment. Thus, one court of appeals has held that, in certain instances, once an agency has promulgated a notice of rulemaking, it must make public all relevant communications that it receives from outside.[8] Other courts, in environmental cases, have required the agency to set forth in detail the reasons for its decision and to respond to criticisms and contrary evidence. Thus, the agency has had to deal with the documentary evidence submitted to it in comments; lawyers for the parties have also been able to obtain internal documentary studies from the agency and have introduced them into the record for court review. The result is that in technical environmental cases there has developed a requirement of a "paper hearing," with all parties seeing the relevant documentary evidence and having an opportunity to respond to it.[9]

Lawyers and judges are also uncertain about the degree of deference or involvement that a judge ought to exhibit when reviewing the agency standard. How closely should the judge examine the agency decision to see whether it is arbitrary? The problem plagues highly technical areas in which judges will have difficulty determining whether, for example, a statistical scientific study makes sense. Some courts have sought to avoid the problem by requiring more formal procedures in technical cases, but the Supreme Court has recently held that courts cannot do so, in informal rulemaking, over the agency's objections.[10] Thus, judges' standards of review appear to vary, particularly in technical cases. Sometimes they appear to intrude deeply into the agency's standard-setting process, while at other times their review seems more superficial.

These procedural issues will be discussed more fully in Chapter 17. It suffices here to note that procedural requirements cast agency standard setting in a back-and-forth, adversary mode. Proposal is followed by response by modification by response until a rule is finally promulgated. The procedural requirements themselves, however, are normally few. Thus, to describe the procedures is to describe only the background against which standard setting normally takes place. It is not to describe the process itself.

The Standard-Setting Process

The typical standard-setting process can be divided into five stages: setting an initial agenda and preliminary standards, obtaining detailed information, formulating a basic standard, bargaining over modifications, and implementing a final standard.

Setting an Initial Agenda and Preliminary Standards

Few agencies can afford to begin setting standards under a new regulatory program by first conducting a cost/benefit analysis to establish priorities. It is unlikely that there will be adequate time. In any event, the agency is aware of the debate before Congress that led to the enactment of the program. That debate will be filled with specific instances of problems that Congress will expect the agency to try to solve. Since the head of the agency knows he will be questioned by Congress about those problems, they are likely to help shape the initial agenda.

NHTSA, for example, did not simply consider how it might best save lives. Had it used even a very rough cost/benefit analysis to do so, instead of starting with head restraints, it might have worked on mandating special devices to stop illegal speeding, such as flashing lights on the outside of a car that would indicate a speed above 60 mph.[11] A cost/benefit analysis might also have suggested that instead of mandating an elaborate new truck brake technology, NHTSA should have tried to improve brake maintenance. Yet auto and truck technology, not speed control or repair shops, formed the context of the political debate out of which NHTSA emerged, and it is not surprising that NHTSA turned to that debate for an initial agenda.

Similarly, existing precedent and existing related standards help shape the content of the agency's initial proposals. In part, this fact reflects a need for speed, as Congress often orders an agency to promulgate preliminary standards in a short time—in NHTSA's case, four months. It also reflects a natural tendency to use work that has already been done. Thus, NHTSA promulgated twenty preliminary standards in 1967 culled from a list of forty-eight existing standards, about half of which were used by the General Services Administration and the other half of which were voluntary practices recommended by the Society of Automotive Engineers.[12] Similarly, the EPA based its initial air pollution standards upon those that had already been developed in California and elsewhere. The Occupational Safety and Health Administration (OSHA) based many initial rules upon standards contained in the previously existing Walsh-Healy Act setting minimum requirements for firms doing business with the government and upon consensus standards worked out over the years by industry committees for industry's voluntary use.[13]

Basing mandatory standards upon preexisting voluntary standards, however, can create serious problems. The development of voluntary standards by industry groups involves little risk of harm to the firm through error, for their voluntariness allows individual firms to reject the standards if they are absurd, inappropriate, or simply wrong. When a "should" in such a standard is changed to a "must," however, the risk of harm increases. Standards must then be reviewed and updated to make certain that they continue to make sense, that they are fair, and that they are enforceable. This review may itself be time-consuming to the point where much of the administrative advantage of relying upon the preexisting standard is lost.

This type of reliance upon preexisting work is responsible for many of the problems that plague OSHA. In an effort to comply with a congressional mandate to "promulgate all national consensus standards," the agency adopted thousands of voluntary industry standards wholesale. Within six months of its creation, OSHA regulations occupied an entire volume of the Code of Federal Regulations. The regulations included such absurdities as forbidding workers to put ice in drinking water (from a nineteenth-century rule aimed at preventing contamination back in the days when ice was cut from ponds), and twenty-two pages of fine print mandating certain construction for ladders (adopted from an industry manufacturing specification that was not related to safety).[14]

Obtaining Information

As an agency begins to focus on developing a detailed, permanent rule, its initial and most important task is to obtain accurate, relevant information. It will obtain the information, in part, through research by agency staff, as they consult research literature and talk to employees of other agencies. Before the agency formulates an initial proposal, the staff may consult widely outside the agency as well. Staff members will telephone, write letters to, and arrange meetings with independent experts, industry experts—in fact, anyone they consider knowledgeable. Once the Notice of Proposed Rulemaking is promulgated, however, staff members may feel less free to consult widely. Information is then more likely to flow in the form of comments submitted to the agency by lawyers for parties. The staff will seek primarily to test the validity of that information.

Obtaining accurate, relevant information constitutes the central problem for the agency engaged in standard setting. It has difficulty finding knowledgeable, trustworthy sources. It may find that it has taken a totally wrong turn due to the fact that its initial proposals determine what information is produced, which in turn determines the content of future proposals. It may find relevant information impossible to obtain when most information depends upon the action of other governmental agencies, as when an auto firm's technical ability to satisfy fuel saving requirements depends upon the environmental standards to be promulgated by a different agency. There are a variety of problems involved in this activity.

Formulating the Standard

Once the agency has gathered sufficient information, it can proceed to the formulation of a proposed standard. In doing so, it must answer several questions.

1. *Should the standard aim directly at the evil targeted by the regulatory program or should it aim at a surrogate?* Frequently a standard that aims directly at the evil a program seeks to eliminate would be too complex to administer. To obtain the necessary simplicity, the standards must aim at a surrogate instead. Environmental standards used to control water pollution, for example, are frequently written in terms of the pounds of BOD (biological oxygen demand) that a firm may discharge into a stream. BOD refers to the oxygen that the substance will demand from the water as it undergoes chemical change. Obviously, the more oxygen demanded by the waste, the less is available for fish and plants. The amount of pollution that a given amount of BOD can cause, however, varies with other factors. A fast-running stream replenishes its oxygen more quickly; the number of other pollutants also can change the consequences of adding a given amount of BOD. Yet because standards tailored to exact polluting effect would have to be written stream by stream, and possibly day by day, the agency may choose to write its standard as if the effect of adding a given amount of BOD were the same, regardless of time or place. Thus, pounds of BOD becomes a surrogate for the pollution at which the statute is aimed.

Less obviously, safety standards that seek to save lives, or reduce the number of accidents, may in fact be aiming at a surrogate. The argument that this is so rests upon the premise that no one wants absolute safety; some risk is inevitable in any society and cannot be eliminated at any reasonable cost. Thus, safety statutes must seek to eliminate unreasonable risk, regardless of their language. And to aim at reducing the number of deaths is to aim at a surrogate for the actual object, which is to reduce the unreasonable number, or excess number of deaths. Because of disagreement about what constitutes "unreasonable" or "excess" or "too much" risk, it is simpler to write a standard that just reduces accidents.

As a general matter, the use of surrogates will prove undesirable if it leads the agency to forget its primary aim. If, for example, reduction of BOD to near zero becomes the EPA's objective, it will spend money in some areas where it makes little difference (fast-running streams with some BOD) instead of spending it elsewhere where it might do more good (slow streams with less BOD). Similarly, safety agencies have been criticized for enacting rules that require enormous expense to lower risk only slightly, while ignoring other ways of spending the same money to save more lives.[15] If the agency recognizes that the surrogate is not its basic aim, however, but an administratively compelled substitute, its rules are less likely to be pushed to extremes and its program will be administered more flexibly.

2. *What degree of specificity should the standard embody?* Typically the agency has a choice of writing regulations that are more general or more detailed. It must choose between the greater control and involvement that detailed regulations imply and the administrative simplicity and greater flexibility of the more general rule. Consider, for example, the task that Congress delegated to the Interstate Commerce Commission (ICC) when it instructed the commission to "formulate regulations for the safe transport . . . of explosives . . . in accordance with the best known practicable means for securing safety in transit."[16] How detailed a set of regulations should the commission write? Should it seek to license each shipment of explosives—an enormous administrative task? Should it examine a route map of the nation's highways and determine which were safe routes for explosives? If so, the commission would have had to hold hearings, state by state, city by city, to resolve the issue of which streets explosives-bearing trucks should be allowed to travel—a prospect that would have provoked a certain hostility among the residents of the chosen streets. The commission might have tried to set standards in terms of the general characteristics of the bridges or the tunnels that might be used. Yet practical standards may have been difficult to write because of varying travel conditions and varying need for explosives. The ICC eventually chose one highly general standard, which told drivers to "avoid so far as practicable . . . driving into or through congested thoroughfares, places where crowds are assembled, streetcar tracks, tunnels, viaducts, and dangerous crossings." The use of the words "so far as practicable" makes the standard highly general and effectively adopts the industry standards of safe conduct as the commission's own. Yet the ICC may have believed such a general, though weak, standard was necessary, given the administrative difficulties of developing more detailed standards and the other calls upon its administrative resources.[17]

3. *Should there be a performance standard or a design standard?* When developing a standard for a technical subject matter, the agency must decide whether to phrase the standard in terms of performance or design. A design standard specifies precisely how, say, a machine must be built. OSHA regulations, for example, state precisely what the distance must be between rivets used to attach guards to pulleys.[18] A performance standard, by contrast, states its obligations in terms of ultimate goals that must be achieved. The firm then is free to achieve those goals in any appropriate way. An NHTSA standard that requires head restraints that keep a test dummy's head upright is phrased in terms of performance; the manufacturer can achieve that goal as he sees fit.

In principle, design standards are easier to enforce than performance standards. If a safety standard describes the specific head restraint that must be used or an environmental standard describes in detail the electricity generator it requires, manufacturers know precisely what they must do and an inspector can determine compliance simply by looking to see if they are using the mandated equipment. On the other hand, design standards limit the firm's flexibility. A firm that finds a cheaper or more effective way of achieving the regulation's objective must undertake the heavy burden of forcing a change in the standard before it can use its new method. It thus has diminished incentive to look for better methods. For the same reason, a design standard tends to freeze existing technology and to favor those firms already equipped with that technology over potentially innovative new competitors.

A performance standard permits flexibility and change. It is directly addressed to the problem that must be solved. And since the agency must, in any event, consider the comparative performance of different machines in order to write a design standard, it may be as easy for the agency to write its standard directly in terms of performance goals, such as cleaner air or fewer injuries. On the other hand, performance standards are often difficult to enforce, because they lead to complex arguments about the appropriate testing procedure for differently designed machines.

In practice, the notions of "performance" and "design" tend to converge. Congress, for example, insisted that NHTSA write only performance standards. Yet it was not difficult for the agency to write performance specifications that could be met only by a machine of a certain design. When NHTSA initially set passive restraint standards, it insisted that manufacturers satisfy performance tests that effectively required them to use airbags.[19] Similarly, it set bumper standards that could not be met by metal bumpers, thereby requiring the use of "soft-face" bumpers. Alternatively, an agency, in setting design standards, will pick that design which best meets certain performance criteria, and if the agency changes the standards readily as technology changes, the use of the design standard may not differ significantly from the use of performance standards.

Despite the agency's theoretical ability to transpose performance and design standards, the underlying tension remains. There is a fundamental tension between flexibility, embodied in a statement of goals that allows maximum freedom to the industry to meet them, and enforceability, which points in the direction of specific, usable, recognizable detail. The agency must consciously balance these two objectives.

4. *Should the agency adopt a technology-forcing standard?* Agencies are often tempted to write standards that cannot be met using current technology, thus forcing the industry to develop new technology in order to comply. The temptation arises from the fact that many firms will already meet whatever standards are based on existing technology; "progress" requires a stricter standard and new technology to meet it. Moreover, the agency may distrust the industry when it argues that developing, say, safer workplaces or pollution-free cars, is too costly or impossible. It may feel that if the industry were forced to do so it could comply.

The major difficulty with technology-forcing standards is that the agency is in the dark. It cannot know in advance whether the industry will or will not be able to comply. NHTSA experience provides two contrasting examples: it guessed right about bumper standards and wrong about brake standards. The industry opposed NHTSA's bumper standard of no damage in a 5-mph collision, and amassed considerable data showing that it was impractical. In the industry's view, the standard would require steel bumpers that were too heavy and would drive up fuel costs. NHTSA's technical staff initially agreed. But after political opposition to a weaker standard developed, NHTSA's staff did a new study suggesting that a stronger, technology-forcing standard was practical. This study, described by one of its authors as a "very cursory analysis, . . . a crash effort," used a few Society of Automotive Engineers (SAE) reports as a basis for suggesting the use of soft-face, lightweight bumpers. The industry had never used soft-face bumpers previously and had no available estimate of their cost. NHTSA then estimated costs crudely by taking cost per pound of material and multiplying by the number of pounds in the bumper. NHTSA based its standards on this soft-face bumper information. It guessed. But its guess was right, and that technology has proved practical.[20]

NHTSA's technology-forcing approach worked very badly, however, when it required new interlocking devices on truck brakes. The new standard led the industry to embark upon a crash effort to develop antilocking devices within the time limit specified. It developed devices, but they did not work for a variety of reasons. Rockwell International's antilock system for buses had a tendency to release the brakes when the bus stopped. It eventually had to be disconnected after having been installed on all new buses. Other systems proved difficult to maintain; mechanics were unfamiliar with them, preventive maintenance was required, and the systems changed too rapidly for mechanics to adjust. Both the agency and the industry were wrongly optimistic about how much could be quickly accomplished.[21]

The very lack of information that may lead the agency to choose a technology-forcing standard means that it will not be certain precisely why such a standard fails. If the industry was unable to comply, was compliance impossible or did the industry just call the agency's bluff? Congress, for example, enacted very strict auto pollution standards into law—standards that required the development of new technology. When several years later the industry stated that compliance was impossible, Congress relaxed the standards rather than put the firms out of business. Was the industry correct throughout when it said compliance was impossible, or did it not try hard enough? It is difficult, if not impossible, for the agency to know.

Negotiating a Final Standard

The development of a final standard often includes a process best described as a form of negotiation. Several parties participate. Each group has its own goals. Each has weapons other than rational argument to bring about a more acceptable result. The negotiating may begin prior to development of an initial proposed standard, but it is likely to prove most important in securing modification.

The parties involved in NHTSA standard setting included the auto industry, its suppliers, consumer groups, members of Congress, and NHTSA itself. Each of these parties had different objectives. Of course, none sought accidents or death, nor did any deliberately seek to impose unreasonable costs. All sought the same ultimate objective: the speedy creation of a standard that would save lives without unduly enhancing costs, encourage the development of lifesaving technology, allow smooth adjustment of the production process, and prevent unfair competitive advantage. Each party, however, emphasized different aspects of the general objective. Thus auto manufacturers emphasized the costs and adjustment lags; suppliers, competitive fairness; consumer groups, life saving and speed. The agency wanted to appear effective and emphasized enforceability; members of Congress wished to be seen as taking action that the public believes important (which may at different times consist of saving lives or saving costs).

Moreover, each party used a specific weapon in the bargaining process. The agency had the legal power to promulgate a standard that would help or hurt other parties. The industry members (and suppliers) possessed information which they could make available to the agency with greater or lesser ease. They could make greater or lesser efforts to suggest standards. They could threaten court proceedings. And they could, in some cases, threaten political retaliation, by, for example, unanimously arguing that the agency's action would vastly increase costs, destroy jobs, or injure the consumers it ought to help. Consumer groups could also invoke political weapons, such as appeals to Congress or to the public through the press. They could bring court actions to force the agency to act more quickly or to modify standards.

The tire-standard example illustrates the use of some of these weapons. Initially the industry, insisting that a standard was unnecessary, would not provide NHTSA with technical data. Then, as NHTSA developed its own data base, the industry—maintaining a united front throughout—argued that NHTSA's proposals were impractical; they made counterproposals which NHTSA lacked the technical skill to evaluate. Initially, they argued that NHTSA could not promulgate a standard without an effective means of testing compliance, and, they added, only use of a special "control tire" would adequately measure compliance. When NHTSA agreed and decided to use control tires to test compliance, it found that the industry was unwilling to supply control tires on NHTSA's terms. The standard then had to be delayed and rewritten. Only when a tire firm (Uniroyal) broke ranks and submitted its own proposal for rating treadwear, traction, and blowout resistance was NHTSA able to develop a meaningful standard. It built that standard around the Uniroyal proposal. In fact, even then NHTSA might not have acted, had it not been for a court order issued at the request of a consumers' group.[22]

Bumper standards reflect, more directly, a negotiating process. NHTSA originally proposed a standard of no damage in 5-mph collisions. The industry, countering with a "slight damage" standard, argued high cost. When the agency moved in the industry's direction—supported by its own cost/benefit analysis, Congress, at the behest of consumer groups, intervened. The agency moved back toward a stricter standard. Suppliers, arguing that they would be put out of business, helped persuade the agency to adopt a standard of slight damage in 4-mph collisions, with sufficient lead time to win at least grudging acceptance from all concerned. The standard arguments and power of the parties, not the merits of the case, led to a final standard. The airbag controversy also has involved Congress as well as the agency, courts, and consumer groups in an effort to find a standard that accommodated the most important objectives of each.

The negotiation involved in standard setting does *not* turn that process into a form of collective bargaining. The parties do not all meet and trade specifics in order to find general agreement. Rather, the negotiation consists of efforts by the parties to use their weapons to shape the final standard other than through rational analysis. The result is a standard that departs from the policy planner's ideal insofar as it is designed to secure the parties' reluctant agreement, or at least a reduction in the vehemence of their opposition. To this extent, the ideal of the rational standard is sacrificed to the criteria of the negotiator—sometimes to the point where the net result is an agreed-upon but ineffective standard.

Implementing the Standard

As noted above, before an agency can implement the standard, it must survive judicial review. And the process of review may take several years. The courts do not often strike down agency action; they are far more likely to accept than to reject the agency's standard. And in any event, the agency is usually free to enforce the standard during the review process. In important and controversial cases, however, the courts may stay enforcement of the challenged rule, thus adding significantly to agency delay.

The effectiveness of the standard will obviously depend on the agency's ability to enforce it. Critics of OSHA complain, for example, that it has too few inspectors and that fines are so low—one thousand dollars for a serious violation—that employers do not worry about being caught. Employers, on the other hand, argue that they would comply voluntarily more often if OSHA would advise them about whether their proposed improvements in machinery or plant comply with the laws, but the statute inhibits OSHA from giving advisory opinions. In most agencies these later problems of implementation will affect the way in which the agency writes the standard. If the agency must rely on voluntary compliance, for example, simplicity and comprehensibility will be more important than precise accuracy, and the agency will be tempted to give the industry a larger role in the standard-setting process.

Problems Inherent in the Process

The deviations from the ideal that characterize standard setting in practice arise partly out of certain problems endemic to that process. In particular, there are four sets of problems that will plague even the most competent and honest administrators. The existence of these problems helps explain why the process works as it does—why it is characterized by reliance on precedent, negotiation, delay, and a certain inflexibility.

Information

The central problem of the standard-setting process and the most pressing task facing many agencies is gathering the information needed to write a sensible standard.

The Source Problem

The agency has five possible sources for this information: the industry, government staff, independent consultants, academics, and consumer groups. Each source suffers from serious drawbacks, which NHTSA experience illustrates as typical of the standard-setting process.

The industry. Most of the specific information needed by NHTSA lay in the hands of the industry to be regulated. In such a case, obtaining information is often difficult. First, the industry can try to use the information it controls to influence the agency in its favor. When NHTSA set tire standards, for example, it knew the qualities that consumers wished to know about: blow-out resistance, stopping distance, and tire life. NHTSA's main problem was devising fair, practical tests for these qualities. It assumed that such tests already existed in the industry, but it discovered that it was wrong. Thus, the cost of developing such tests became an issue. The firms were asked to make estimates. And it was easy for a firm—with total honesty—to produce a high cost estimate, simply by telling its engineers to make "high-quality" assumptions. How was NHTSA to gauge the accuracy of those estimates?

Consider further a related issue: Should tires be tested on a single track rated by NHTSA or by means of a control tire sold to the companies and compared with company tires? The single track would require careful construction to guarantee that it typified ordinary road conditions; adjustments would be made for temperature and moisture through the use of a "course monitoring tire." These facts would produce considerable argument about what constituted an appropriate track and course monitoring tire. On the other hand, to use a control tire would produce argument about its characteristics. Moreover, manufacturers might reach different results with the same control tire by running their tests on different courses; in fact, a 5,000-mile test might favor a tire that wears out slowly at first and then quickly, whereas a 10,000-mile test might favor a different tire which wears out quickly at first and then slowly.

To resolve issues of this sort, NHTSA needed access to technical, scientific facts. Yet the experts who could deal with these questions were in industry. Moreover, they might reach different conclusions on these issues depending on how questions were put to them and on their own biases.[23]

Second, the industry may use its control of information as a bargaining weapon with the agency. The tire-standard example illustrates the agency's difficulty. Until Uniroyal broke ranks and suggested a tire grading system, NHTSA had to make proposals on its own. It was relatively easy for industry experts to point to serious flaws in each NHTSA proposal. To produce a workable proposal, NHTSA had to satisfy industry's technical experts. If the industry claims its information is confidential, its bargaining position is still stronger, for the agency either must work out a method to keep the information secret or do without it—and risk the industry's later technical criticisms of the agency's proposals.

Third, it is particularly difficult to gather needed information through adversary proceedings. Consider, for example, NHTSA's efforts to determine the costs and benefits of its proposed bumper standards. No one knew initially how much money a "5 mph/no damage" standard would save or what it would cost. Only elaborate surveys concerning such factors as dents, chipping paint, time lost in repairs, bumper weight, lead time costs, and costs of new manufacturing processes could provide this information. The estimates would relate directly only to the standard proposed—"5 mph/no damage"—not to alternative standards. Thus, if the information suggested abandoning the standard, new information would have to be collected relevant to an alternative. NHTSA sought to speed the information-gathering process by proposing five different standards (for example, "no regulation," "5 mph with no safety damage," "5 mph/no damage," and so on), and to gather cost/benefit data for each. It obtained the industry's cooperation in securing the data, yet the data left it uncertain as to which standard was cost-justified. Ultimately it decided to use a standard based on soft-face bumper technology—a decision that required redoing the cost/benefit analysis.

The adversary process requires the agency to propose a standard; the industry responds to questions related to the proposed standard. To shift the proposed standard requires a new set of questions. The more hostile the industry, the more narrowly responsive will be its answers, the more strictly the questions will be interpreted, and the less likely it is that the information provided in response to the first set of questions will help when the agency shifts to the second set. While the adversary process can determine whether a specific proposed standard is good or bad, it cannot readily show which of the myriad of unproposed standards is preferable. To use it to test each plausible alternative standard would take forever. The adversary process is likely to help develop information only if different segments of the industry are adversary, one to the other, and if each can be relied upon to test the other's information.

In-house. Developing information within the agency avoids the taint of industry self-interest, but the agency may lack the requisite technical ability. NHTSA was unable to develop fuel conservation standards, for example. NHTSA tried to use two highly qualified in-house staff groups—the Transportation Systems Center (TSC) and a special task force.[24] These groups were able to develop models based upon existing industry-wide statistical information, but they lacked firm-specific information. They could not determine how a particular standard (applied to an individual firm) would affect that firm's costs or fuel economy. So the study's value was limited, because an agency must examine particular effects on particular firms before it can responsibly promulgate a standard. To obtain that sort of information, it has to rely on the firms involved.

Independent experts. Relying upon independent outside consultants or academic experts does not necessarily solve the agency's problems. The independent consulting firm is expensive. Moreover, the consulting firm must itself go to the industry for detailed cost and performance information. There may be no academic experts with relevant detailed expertise. If there are, it is likely that they consult frequently for industry. Unless they have industry connections, they may have to base their work on older data or on statistical data, drawn from public sources, using industry averages. They will then produce models that are not firm-specific. Academic and independent experts often are not as good at generating data as at reviewing data, assessing their reliability and objectivity.

Consumer groups. Consumer groups typically have less information available than does the agency. They may help find experts, but they are rarely experts themselves. Their information may also suffer from an anti-industry bias.

In essence, the agency fears that industry information is biased, outside sources must themselves rely on industry information, and in-house sources are inadequate. The fact that the agency fears its information is inadequate or incomplete will push it toward compromise.

The Coordination Problem

The information source problem, together with the adversary mode of gathering much information, makes coordination of related standard-setting activity among agencies particularly difficult. Imagine, for example, one agency proposing a fuel standard, another an emissions standard, and a third a speed limit for trucks. The industry will respond to each proposal through back-and-forth adversary dialogue. It is likely to respond to information requests in one area by stating that much depends on what the other agencies do. Thus, it will have a range of discretion in shaping its answers, and information it provides will become more suspect. At the same time, the adversary mode makes it difficult for all parties to deal with all related proposals simultaneously and informally.

In sum, the information problem is central and endemic to the standard-setting process, and agencies grapple with it in various ways. The Environmental Protection Agency, for example, divided the problem of setting water pollution standards among several of its divisions; it staffed different divisions with people possessing different professional backgrounds (lawyers, business graduates, scientists); and it deliberately encouraged argument among them, in hope of giving top decision makers a more objective view. NHTSA and the EPA also encouraged informal meetings between staff and industry scientists and engineers in the hope that direct contact among professionals would avoid the posturing that occurs when lawyers and top executives testify in formal meetings. Although these techniques have helped, they still cannot provide problem-free information sources. In technical areas, the agency to some extent inevitably works in the dark.

Enforcement

Standards must be enforceable. The agency must develop practical compliance tests capable of easy, widespread application. The need to write standards with an eye toward enforcement raises difficulties that often compel the agency to write standards that do not meet the statute's primary objective.

Developing the test. Since manufacturers who violate a standard may be penalized severely (even subjected to criminal prosecution), tests must be fair and objective. "Objective," in the view of one court of appeals, means that "tests to determine compliance must be capable of producing identical results when test conditions are exactly duplicated, that they be decisively demonstrable by performing a rational test procedure, and that compliance is based upon the readings of instruments as opposed to the subjective opinions of human beings."[25] A test is unfair or arbitrary if, for two manufacturers with equally safe systems, it failed one and passed the other.

These simple criteria, requiring objectivity and fairness, create serious problems for agencies seeking to develop tests in complicated technical areas. Consider, for example, NHTSA's efforts to develop its tire standard. NHTSA knew from the beginning that consumers want to know about a tire's traction and treadwear performance. Its initial proposed standards did not provide for effective disclosure of those characteristics because it feared that it could not adequately test them. NHTSA later changed its mind, under pressure from a consumers' lawsuit[26] and the president's consumer advisor.[27] But events showed that its earlier concerns about finding a fair testing system were well founded. As previously mentioned, NHTSA proposed the use of a control tire to compare different manufacturers' tires in all relevant respects. This approach collapsed, however, when NHTSA found that it could not obtain a proper control tire from industry. It then turned to a "standard track" testing system. But, here it faced claims that results based on a standard track might vary depending upon the month and the weather. NHTSA then developed a course monitoring tire that could be used to correct for variations among standard tracks or between standard tracks and "ordinary road conditions." Finally, several years later, a court of appeals held that NHTSA must consider whether its course monitoring tires were sufficiently uniform or whether it must correct for possible variations among them.[28] There were sufficient plausible objections to the fairness of each proposed testing procedure to force NHTSA either to spend enormous time on the testing problems or abandon its basic effort to inform consumers about relevant tire characteristics.

Similarly, in developing a standard for a passive restraint system, NHTSA had to develop a test to determine whether a manufacturer's system was adequate. The test required the system to restrain a specified test dummy. NHTSA then had to determine the characteristics of the test dummy. But it found scientific uncertainty about what specifications for the dummy's head, neck, and chest, for example, would make it act most like a human being. Given this uncertainty, if NHTSA wrote precise neck specifications, it would run the risk that the test treated equally safe systems differently. If NHTSA wrote no neck specifications, or made them imprecise, it ran the further risk that a system might pass or fail depending on which of two equally "qualified" dummies was used to test it. Yet any NHTSA effort to resolve the scientific uncertainty about the relation between test dummies and humans might take months or years. In fact, NHTSA did not specify definite criteria for constructing the dummy's head, neck, and chest. And the court of appeals found the NHTSA standard arbitrary for this reason.[29]

Another problem that NHTSA faced in developing its tests was deciding how much variation to allow within batches of tires, brakes, or safety systems. There is inevitable quality variation within the batches of any product. Thus, if NHTSA required each individual tire to pass a specific test, the tires actually tested, which are representative of the batch, would have to surpass the test's standard by far; otherwise some tires in the batch would be unable to meet it. (In fact, in the tire case, if *all* in a batch had to meet the standard to warrant a label specifying a certain quality, the label might mislead consumers, because almost all the tires in the batch would in fact be of higher quality.) As a practical matter, the test and the degree of variation permitted can make the actual substantive standard in practice quite different from the standard the agency promulgates in writing.

Applying the test. The fact that a test must be easy to apply and inexpensive will significantly influence the initial standard and its practical effect. NHTSA's experience with brake standards suggests what can happen when these needs are not taken into account.

NHTSA initially did not consider the complexity of the industry and how difficult that complexity would make compliance. Truck brakes are made by specialized brake companies, which sell them to chassis manufacturers. Other manufacturers assemble chassis and other truck components, designing them especially to fit diverse customer needs. NHTSA required that the final manufacturer test and certify truck brakes, but it was beyond the final manufacturer's power to adjust, redesign, or modify brakes when necessary, because the brakes were already in the chassis. The final manufacturer was an assembler, typically with a small engineering staff.[30] It was also difficult to determine who should be responsible for compliance, because trucks that initially complied might soon cease to do so. The NHTSA standard required antilock devices that in turn required strong front-end brakes.[31] Drivers were not used to those brakes; many disliked them and disconnected the brakes, destroying the standard's effectiveness. Yet new, tamper-proof equipment would have introduced new complexity into the process. In fact, introducing the compliance problem (ensuring use of the new brakes) into the initial standard-setting process would have made it still more unwieldy. Yet failing to do so meant significantly diminished agency effectiveness, for the standard would not have been followed.

Voluntary compliance. Many agencies, such as NHTSA, must rely heavily upon voluntary compliance to enhance the standards they promulgate. NHTSA would need an impossibly large enforcement staff to police factories, auto repair shops, and individual trucks and cars to determine compliance. Moreover, the discovery of a violation marks the beginning of elaborate administrative and court proceedings, not the immediate assessment of a penalty. The agency may bear a heavy burden of proof in showing a violation.[32] It may also have to defend the standard itself from an attack on its validity. The court, not the agency, is likely to determine an appropriate sanction and enforce it. The elaborate nature of the proceeding and the risks it creates for the agency as well as the defendants lead to bargaining between agency and defendants and small penalties for an initial violation. Thus, if firms strictly weigh costs and benefits, they may disobey a standard with which they disagree.

This provides another reason for an agency to promulgate simple standards—so that those who wish to comply voluntarily can readily understand what they are to do—and to seek negotiated standards that all parties feel are reasonable, so that firms will not resist compliance.[33]

Anticompetitive Effects

The creation of a standard can adversely affect competition in several ways.

Barriers to entry. The added cost of compliance with a standard automatically raises barriers to entering the industry. While individual standards may not raise barriers significantly, a series of several standards—say, safety, emissions, and fuel standards—may well raise costs to the point where new firms will find it difficult to assemble sufficient capital to enter. This problem, particularly severe in the case of concentrated industries, tends to be given less attention in agency proceedings than it warrants.

Present competition. A new standard is likely to affect competition among firms already in the industry.[34] The agency may favor an existing firm, for example, by writing standards with which only one firm presently complies. A standard may also favor some competitors over others by setting particular lead times that allow only some firms to achieve compliance.

Precisely which firm a standard will favor may not be knowable in advance. NHTSA's brake standard, for example, turned out to require substantial redesign of the front ends of many trucks. This fact, given the large number of firms in the truck manufacturing industry and the industry's complexity, made it impossible for NHTSA to know how much compliance would cost each truck manufacturer or supplier. In the other five examples, in which NHTSA dealt with the large, integrated auto manufacturers, the differential cost effects of standards were usually knowable, though NHTSA had to rely upon the industry for its information. NHTSA typically allowed sufficient lead time to help the weakest manufacturer, but in doing so, it had to delay the standard's effective date.

Future competitors. It is more difficult for an agency to determine whether its standards will injure firms that are potential entrants but not now in the industry. Existing firms, including suppliers, immediately complain to the agency if a proposed standard threatens them. Thus, Houdaille, Inc., a steel bumper manufacturer, quickly pointed out to NHTSA that a "no damage" bumper standard would put it out of business.[35] But the firms that might have produced the soft-face bumper were not as likely to oppose a steel standard, for it would not cost them present business. Instances of deliberate use of standards for anticompetitive purposes have been alleged. An initial bicycle standard proposed by the Consumer Products Safety Commission allegedly would have inhibited the marketing of foreign bicycles. Trade associations similarly have been accused of manipulating standards for anticompetitive purposes.[36] The danger is greatest when the agency has no one before it who will be presently hurt—when the injury is to future competition rather than present competition.

Freezing technology. As previously pointed out, an agency that uses design standards (or performance standards that function as design standards) will freeze technology. Firms will not compete to make differently designed products that better fulfill the statute's objective. They may also be inhibited from competing by the fear that technical improvements will lead the agency to tighten its standard. In fact, the industry also knows that the less technical information that is available, the stronger will be its bargaining position with the agency. For this reason, firms may hesitate to conduct research unless true performance standards encourage them to do so.

These competitive concerns support "weaker" standards that may be less readily enforceable. The agency must weigh them against other considerations. But precisely how it weighs anticompetitive factors is less important than the simple fact that it does so, for too often they are ignored entirely. To learn about anticompetitive effects the agency must rely upon the parties involved, upon staff from other government agencies (the Federal Trade Commission or the Antitrust Division of the Department of Justice), or upon internal staff. The parties are likely to provide a lopsided view, due to their individual competitive interests. Government agencies, such as the Antitrust Division, appear formally before some agencies (such as the ICC, CAB, and FCC) and sit informally on numerous interagency task forces. This method has worked well and is limited only by the size of the division's staff. The EPA has successfully relied upon internal staff to analyze potential anticompetitive effects. It specifically placed economists and business graduates on its staff to do so.

Judicial Review

Although the criteria applied by judges in reviewing agency decisions seem reasonable, leaving the agency with great discretion,[37] the prospect of judicial review, even under such broad criteria as these, creates several problems for the agency.[38]

Adversary proceedings. The procedural requirements of "notice and comment" rulemaking encourage the agency to use a back-and-forth adversary trial-and-error approach to obtain information and develop standards. Consider one example of how the "notice" requirement itself leads to complexity and delay. In January 1970 NHTSA published a notice of its intent to amend FMVSS 108, which governed turn signals and hazard warning flashers.[39] The NPRM did not refer to changing testing criteria for flashers. After receiving comments, NHTSA decided to change those criteria.[40] NHTSA wanted to eliminate testing by sampling, which would have allowed variations within batches. One party objected to the lack of notice. NHTSA then published a new notice and received more comments.[41] In August NHTSA published a final rule eliminating the sampling procedure (and requiring 100 percent compliance); at the same time, it weakened the performance criteria in order to make compliance easier.[42] On review, the court held that NHTSA's notice was defective because the notice had not mentioned the possibility that NHTSA would weaken the substantive standards.[43]

The court's decision seems procedurally fair. The affected firms might not know what comments to make in response to a notice that did not speak explicitly about the "weakening" possibility. Yet the decision makes it difficult for the agency to use information gathered either to promulgate an optimum standard or to make revisions expeditiously. Fairness in terms of an ability to hear and to meet arguments can be combined with effectiveness only if all interested parties can meet informally and make various suggestions until agreement is reached or all considerations are out in the open. But this discussion cannot take place through back-and-forth, notice/comment/revise procedures. This back-and-forth process may prevent the agency from revising the standard optimally in light of the last set of comments for fear of provoking new hearings. The agency may determine the standard's content initially through informal meetings and negotiation with those affected, later "ratifying" the decision with a more formal procedure. The courts may hold this process unlawful, however, as an effort to circumvent the law's procedural requirements.[44]

The need to keep records. The possibility of court review has led agencies to keep records demonstrating the basis of their decision and the fact that all the relevant issues were explored.[45] By doing so, the agency shows that its decision was rational. Yet the agency may find it difficult to keep a thorough set of records. Given the multifaceted nature of most problems, the uncertain quality of the information, and the need to consider a broad range of uncertain factors, many technical decisions (such as the decision to try to force development of a soft-face bumper technology) may reflect only an inspired engineering guess. The engineer may not know precisely where or how the decision emerged—even in his own mind—nor can he necessarily write down a justification for the decision at the time he made it. Thus, records for court review are often made ex post. The agency's lawyers insert into a public record sufficient information to show rational support for each key decision. Cost/benefit analyses are often prepared to support decisions already reached rather than to help determine what future decisions ought to be made. When an agency makes a serious effort to keep contemporaneous records, they are often sketchy and informal.[46]

Rationality and "hard" information. An agency decision must appear rational or nonarbitrary to a court in light of the information in the record. Yet an agency staff member or engineer may not agree with a judge or lawyer about what is rational. Given the uncertainties and complexities described above, it may appear perfectly reasonable to an engineer to rest a decision to require soft-bumper technology on an inspired guess. That same decision might appear irrational to a judge to whom the parties have explained how much time, effort, and money that inspired guess will cost them. Judges may not fully appreciate the agency's need to make decisions under conditions of uncertainty. Modifications made to help secure agreement may strike them as irrational because of the agency's inability to explain them through logic. They may not sympathize with the agency's wish to promulgate a standard before working out all the details. Thus, one court set aside NHTSA's passive restraint standard because of inadequate specification of test dummy characteristics.[47] The issue involved very minor aspects of the basic standard.

NHTSA concluded that hard factual support for its standards was needed to show that its standards were rational. Hence, it asked its staff to document: (1) the safety problem in the area that the standard is designed to affect, expressed as far as possible in quantitative terms of deaths and injuries; (2) the aspects of performance sought to be improved by the standard, and the intended effect in performance terms; (3) the expected benefit flowing from the standard; and (4) the correlation of the standard's requirements with the problem to achieve the benefit.[48] These criteria will influence NHTSA to set standards that can be documented with readily available or easily obtainable, noncontroversial, factual information. Yet there is no reason to believe that areas where such readily supportable standards can be drawn are those in which the most lives can be saved.

Delay. Judicial review is time-consuming, possibly taking years. Courts are crowded, delay is inevitable, and any serious confrontation may lead to an injunction postponing the effective date of the standard until the legal issues are resolved. This fact helps explain why modification of standards once set is difficult. It also reinforces the need for fairly simple standards that will last for many years without becoming obsolete.

Conclusion

The four sets of problems just described—related to information, enforcement, anticompetitive effects, and judicial review—help explain why the standard-setting process inevitably deviates from the policy planner's cost/benefit model. They also explain why the process resembles negotiation, why standards are so closely tied to precedent, why the process is time-consuming, and why standards once set (even when they are as ineffective as NHTSA's head-restraint standards) prove relatively immune to revision.

One sees, for example, obvious major advantages for the agency in achieving mutually satisfactory ("negotiated") solutions, given the agency's comparative inability to secure necessary information—particularly as to costs and competitive impacts, the desirability of securing voluntary compliance and industry cooperation in developing enforcement procedures, and the time and effort saved if judicial challenge can be avoided. One can understand the temptation to build from preexisting standards once one sees the difficulty of developing information that allows radical departures, the security that preexisting rules provide the agency in terms of feasibility and enforceability, and the greater probability of its developing studies to show they are not arbitrary. One sees the time needed to develop standards as stemming in part from the difficulties of obtaining appropriate information and the need to force a multifaceted or "polycentric" problem into an adversary mode. Finally, given the other difficulties, a standard's resistance to change becomes inevitable, because only a very dramatic need would justify redoing the complex standard-setting procedure.

None of these problems warrants abandoning the standard-setting process, nor do these difficulties pose insurmountable obstacles. They are simply tendencies—likely to be present—that administrators must take into account when planning strategies for developing workable sets of standards.

6

Historically Based Allocation

Just as history can provide a standard for temporarily circumventing cost-of-service ratemaking, so it can help to circumvent the complexity of standard setting and public interest allocation.[1] Goods temporarily in short supply—such as oil in 1973, California water in 1976, and natural gas in 1977—can be allocated provisionally according to historical use in a specified preceding year, less X percent. The shortage may result from nature together with a reluctance to let the market allocate through a price rise, as in the case of water or oil, or it may constitute the by-product of a preexisting regulatory program, as in the case of natural gas. Regardless, historically based allocation offers provisional relief—but at a price. The system, like historically based price setting, is unstable. It soon evolves toward either standard setting or public interest allocation. And it soon develops the problems that plague these other two regulatory forms.

The System

The system itself appears to be deceptively simple. As indicated, the regulator looks at the total supply for the product, compares it with total demand, and allocates the shortfall pro rata in accordance with each customer's use during the base period. The rule is simple, and appears fair enough to win support from regulators and regulated alike. Thus, during the 1973–74 oil shortage energy specialists, the oil companies, the Treasury Department, independent gasoline retailers, dealers, and others all endorsed the approach. (Indeed, the major oil companies had already begun to use such a system to allocate among their customers.)[2] Yet the rule is a standard and suffers from certain standard-setting problems that automatically require some modification in the rule.

In the case of oil and natural gas, information about the supplies available and the amounts each customer had previously demanded was in the hands of the major suppliers. Moreover, only the suppliers could enforce a rule that customers are to receive, say, 75 percent of their previous demand. The regulating agency itself could not effectively determine the demands or past usage of thousands or millions of prior customers, nor could it, as a practical matter, force the customer to obtain less without the cooperation of the supplier. Thus, a rule based upon historical use was in practice tied to individual suppliers: each supplier allocated its available supply in accordance with historical use.

Basing a reduction upon the supplier's available product will make the system far less fair when different suppliers have different amounts available. If, for example, supplier A provided customers X, Y, and Z with 50,000, 30,000, and 20,000 gallons of gasoline in 1972, and if in 1973 he had 60,000 gallons available, he would divide the supply, using an "allocation fraction" equal to his current supply divided by his base-year supply. In this case the fraction is six tenths, so he would give 30,000 to X, 18,000 to Y and 12,000 to Z. If by chance these three customers had been supplied by B, who had only 30,000 gallons available in 1973, and used an allocation fraction of three tenths, each would receive only half as much. To treat customers equally would require assuring suppliers of proportionally equal supply—an assurance that could not be made for oil or gas, where supplies depend upon physical connections to production facilities.

In addition, it is apparent that, except for a very temporary shortage, a single simple historical standard provides no way to register the intensity of a customer's need for the product. Some system of priorities is necessary to avoid treating frivolous and critical needs alike; otherwise the use of gasoline for driving tractors and for pleasure trips, the use of water for drinking and for the garden, the use of natural gas for heating hospitals and heating boilers will be treated alike.

Thus, actual systems of historically based allocation have been supplemented with priorities—sometimes worked out on an ad hoc basis and sometimes embodied in standards. The emergency oil allocation system in late 1973, for example, set special priorities for farmers, truckers, and others. Farmers and truckers, for example, were to receive 100 percent of their current needs before the remaining oil available to the supplier was divided according to its allocation fraction.

The working out of priorities through standards presents the same problems discussed in the preceding chapter, with one addition: when standards are used to set priority categories for commodities, it is likely that no set of categories will accurately reflect comparative need. After all, not all farmers need oil, nor do all hospitals need natural gas; some might easily switch to other fuels. Thus, categories will always appear somewhat arbitrary, as when truckers are placed in a top-priority category but rural nutrition programs and public health nurses are not.[3] Moreover, the apparent arbitrariness makes it more likely that the regulator's priorities reflect outside political pressures. For example, the initial proposed Federal Energy Office (FEO) regulations provided that farmers would receive 100 percent of their current needs for gasoline, but only 110 percent of their base-period use (a lesser amount) for middle distillates, such as diesel fuel.[4] Initial FEO regulations gave truckers, too, 110 percent of their base-period use.[5] In both cases, the regulations were changed to allow farmers and truckers a greater amount—100 percent of their current needs.[6] Since other important users—such as those making hospital supplies from plastic—were treated less favorably,[7] it seems likely that political pressures, in the form of congressional hearings[8] and truck stoppages and strikes,[9] account for FEO's change of heart.

Nonetheless, one might claim that a historical principle is a useful adjunct to a system of priorities, because it allows that system to be limited to particularly needy instances. The remainder of the commodity can be allocated in accordance with a simple historical rule. Even as modified by the priorities, however, the historical system is unstable and soon develops serious problems—problems that force the promulgation of even more complex standards, or a movement toward public interest allocation, or both.

The Need for Exceptions

The problems of historically based allocation arise out of two sets of factors. First, "history" as a basis for fairness conflicts with the substantive economic aims of allocation and with "fairness" seen in terms of achieving those ends efficiently. It makes no sense to give oil to an old firm that does not need it, while depriving a new firm of any allocation. Second, economic conditions change continually; what made sense in 1972 may make no sense in 1974. Thus, regulators using a historical system face several serious difficulties—difficulties that call for exceptions. This continuous and growing need for exceptions soon destroys the major advantage of simplicity that characterized the system.

The need for priorities. A system without priorities would sacrifice, contrary to the apparent fairness of a simple rule, the more substantive aim of providing product where it is most needed. The pressure to do just this requires continuous modification of priorities as individuals seek to place themselves in high-priority categories and regulators seek to stretch their definition in order to provide a product, such as oil, to those who seem to need it. Thus, the high priority for agriculture, according to one FEO official, was intended to include all steps "from the field to the table."[10] "Agriculture" might thus include potato chips, candy, or cotton. Manufacturers of both alcoholic and soft drinks laid claim to this priority.[11] In some regions truckers of agricultural commodities were held to be included; in other regions, they were not.[12] Regional officials admitted that they tried to stretch the meaning of the term to allow special allocations that they thought were necessary: "We didn't want anyone to go cold; we didn't want anyone to go without." As a result, "within your limited ability you would stretch [the priority categories] to be covered."[13] Insofar as the categorization problem led to continuous redefinition and refinement through rule,[14] the regulator faced standard-setting problems. Insofar as priority categories were broadened to serve as umbrellas beneath which officials exercised discretion, they faced problems similar to those of public interest allocation.

Special and changing circumstances. As was true of historically based price regulation, the choice of a base period poses difficult problems. Any base period will prove unfair to someone. Fuel allocation regulations, for example, were based upon use in the year 1972. Farmers pointed out that the fall of 1972 had been unusually wet in California, central Texas, and Louisiana. Farmers there had not used their tractors in the field very often. The fall of 1973, however, was dry and they were anxious to obtain more fuel to plant their crops.[15] Gasoline station operators in Pennsylvania, Maryland, and New Jersey noted that Hurricane Agnes had disrupted normal gasoline deliveries and use in fall 1972, resulting in a low base volume.[16] Construction contractors argued that their needs varied, depending upon the contract on which they happened to be working at the moment; their needs in 1972 provided no evidence of their needs in 1974.[17]

In each instance, the agency had to depart from the historical principle to make an adjustment. Farmers were given priority. The construction industry was exempted in its entirety from the historical base-period regulations. Each new project was treated as a new customer and assigned a base volume without regard to past historical use.[18] In each instance, new rules or increased discretion was required.

It was still more difficult for the regulators to deal with changes in demand caused by shifts in population. Florida's population, for example, increased by half a million between July 1972 and July 1974. Gaithersburg, Maryland, grew by 50 percent between 1972 and 1974. Arizona and southern California grew massively.[19] Drivers increased their use of gasoline: in 1973 the increase was 34 percent. But the increase varied in different parts of the country. Any system that relied on historical use could not take into account these shifts in population and regional demand (unless it could determine and adjust the use pattern of each individual consumer—an impossible task when the product is used by millions). Unless regulators could devise a system of adjustment that would take these shifts into account, severe shortages were inevitable. Indeed, the gasoline shortages of 1974 were not distributed equally. Despite severe shortages in some areas of the country, many gasoline dealers in the Southeast obtained gas.[20] A Georgia congressman reported that coastal gasoline stations in his state had gas; inland stations did not.[21] Eventually FEO sought to even the shortages, varying the amounts shipped to each state in order to provide equal treatment on a state-by-state basis.[22]

Administrability and fairness. A historically based system, in principle, would look to the base-period demand of each end user and curtail each by an equal percentage. As previously pointed out, however, enforcement considerations make this approach impractical. To implement it the regulator would, for example, have to distribute coupons to end users based upon prior use. Yet to find out how many coupons to give each user, he would have to examine the records of each supplier—an enormous task. Moreover, since different suppliers may have different amounts of end product available, he would have to shift the product among them to make certain they were treated alike, each bearing a proportionate share of the shortage.

It is far easier to allow each supplier to administer the curtailment system itself, each distributing its available supplies proportionately to its customers. Yet such a system seems unfair, particularly if a historical allocation rule is coupled with a system of priorities. For example, in March 1974 Shell Oil Company had an allocation fraction of 7. It had 70 percent of its 1972 supplies available. Exxon's fraction, however, was 8.3 and Gulf's was 9.0. Thus, customers supplied by Gulf would be far better off than those supplied by Shell.[23] The problem is exacerbated for nonpriority customers, because a supplier serving many farmers (who were entitled under the priority rules to all their current needs) would have far less oil to divide among its remaining customers than a supplier who served only urban users.

FEO dealt with the problem through a series of ad hoc adjustments. It required each supplier to set aside a certain amount of oil as a reserve and ruled that, "to meet imbalances," it would order "the transfer of specified amounts" of any oil product "from one region or area to another."[24] It then sought to bring the states into balance, so that no single state experienced too severe a shortage.

FEO used a variety of formulas. It set as a goal that no state would have an allocation fraction greater than 95 percent of its 1972 level or less than 85 percent. In fact, by April 1974, when the oil shortage eased, one state received 106.6 percent of its 1972 demand, another received 90 percent, and the remaining states received something in between.[25] FEO considered the mix of priority users and apparently allocated more oil to states with more priority users.[26] But, to quote one student of the subject, it looked as if "FEO was simply determining where the shortages were and then creating a formula that would provide gasoline for these hard-hit areas."[27] Thus, continuous complaint by Pennsylvania authorities, both in and out of court, led to a higher allocation fraction adjustment in its favor.[28]

It is important to see that ultimately the need for ad hoc adjustments and the limitations on their success were the result of an enforcement problem: the need to rely upon individual major suppliers to enforce the allocation. That need partly stemmed from the physical difficulty of shipping oil back and forth between major suppliers to make certain each began with a proportionately equal amount. The ad hoc adjustments increased reliance upon "perceived need" rather than "historical use" as a basis for receiving oil.

Two other enforcement problems added to the difficulty of administering the historically based oil allocation system. First, records of purchases made in 1972 were sometimes unavailable, even to suppliers. Poor people heating their houses with number 2 fuel oil sometimes did not have regular oil deliveries, but instead bought oil for cash when they had sufficient funds available. A strictly enforced historical rule based on records would have forced these customers to go without heat. Thus, FEO simply authorized dealers to make deliveries to cash customers as needed.

Second, widespread allocation controls, like widespread price controls, are usually temporary. This produces a perverse incentive to raise prices or increase consumption before controls are imposed, so that the user's base is higher when they take effect. This makes it more difficult for the regulator to find a "normal" base period against which he can measure the present allocation. It also accounts for the price controller's efforts, in the Korean War period, to roll back prices and not just to freeze them. Yet the further back in history one must search to find a base period unaffected by the possibility of shortage, the more out of date the base period becomes and the less likely it is to reflect current needs. Again, these factors push regulators in the direction of abandoning a historical method in favor of standards or ad hoc exemptions based upon need.

Interference with the competitive process. Regulators must make ad hoc exceptions or develop special rules in the historical system of allocation to avoid injury to the competitive process. The historical system can interfere with the ordinary workings of the marketplace in several important ways.

First, some account must be taken of the new entrant—the firm that was not in business during the base period. The oil allocation regulations allowed new entrants to apply to be assigned to a supplier and to be assigned a base-period volume. The standards governing the assignment, however, were unclear. It was fairly easy to deal with firms that had entered the market during 1973, because their sales at that time provided a standard. But firms seeking to enter after the allocation regulations took effect essentially had to rely upon the discretion of an administrator. The administrator, in turn, might be moved more by the pleas for oil of existing firms with investment in and reliance upon the oil business than by the request of a new entrant without preexisting reliance.

Second, a historically based system tends to freeze the existing market shares of industrial customers. American Motors, a far smaller company than General Motors, obviously used fewer petroleum products than GM in 1972. This would have prevented AMC expansion in 1974, for it would have been unable to obtain the petroleum products needed to do so. The same problem would face dynamic smaller firms in every industry that used oil. The FEO regulation took account of the problem where it was unusually serious—in construction, for example, where past construction needs bore little relation to present needs. But FEO did not use its job-by-job method of determining oil needs elsewhere.

Third, a strict application of a historically based system administered by suppliers would distort existing supply relationships. This problem arises because the supply relationship will have changed between the base period and the time of allocation. If a supplier in 1974 is asked to go back to its 1972 books to determine which customers to serve, it may find that it has kept very few of those customers, particularly if it no longer serves the same marketing area. Indeed, during 1973, Sohio had closed two hundred dealerships; Phillips Petroleum, Tenneco, and Gasland had all left the Northeast; and six suppliers had left Maine and Illinois since 1972.[29] Had the oil and gasoline markets been left to work as organized in 1973, the distribution system would have been very different from that which had existed the year before.

To rely on the new supply arrangement would have forced FEO to reflect a base year of 1973—a year that already reflected the effects of the forthcoming shortage. It would have had to move the base period too close to the allocation period to determine a normal pattern of use. Indeed, some of the oil suppliers' 1973 withdrawal represented a retrenchment by major oil companies, which, given a potential shortage, could stop supplying independent outlets and concentrate instead on supplying their own gasoline stations. To implement this arrangement with a 1973 base period would have prevented many independent stations from obtaining supply.[30] Yet how could FEO determine the 1972 pattern of use of a customer whose 1972 supplier had left the area? To avoid a case-by-case reassignment of customers to suppliers and redetermination from customer records of 1972 purchases, FEO simply ordered suppliers to reclaim their 1972 positions.

For a major gasoline or oil supplier to reenter a market, however, was not easy. Three to six months' lead time is usually needed to schedule the shipment of petroleum products through a pipeline. It was still more difficult to find excess pipeline space if the supplier had previously terminated its contract with the pipeline. Tenneco, for example, had supplied the New England market with 100 million gallons of gasoline in 1972. It left the market in 1973. It was ordered to reenter New England on January 30, 1974, but several weeks went by before the oil itself could be transferred.[31] The net result of ordering reentry was to transfer the shortage—from the area that the supplier had left to the area where it currently did business. The net result was to sacrifice both the efficiencies represented by current distribution arrangements and the equity involved in allocating shortages in accordance with current use patterns to the administrative convenience of basing an allocation order upon the 1972 supply network.

Fourth, the rules developed by FEO to take account of changes in customer needs between 1972 and 1974 distorted competitive relationships. FEO's regulations allowed wholesale purchasers adjustments in their allocation for growth of greater than 10 percent between the base period (1972) and the effective date of the regulations (January 15, 1974). Thus, if a wholesaler's sales volume had grown by, say, 40 percent—from 10 million gallons in 1972 to 14 million in 1973—it would be allowed a 30 percent increase or 13 million gallons as a base.[32] This rule, although necessary to reflect changes in demand, probably injured the independent oil suppliers and helped the major companies, for in 1973 the effects of the forthcoming shortage were beginning to be felt, the independents had difficulty finding supplies, and the majors often increased their market share at the independents' expense. The 10 percent rule embedded that expansion by inhibiting the efforts of the independents to regain their 1972 position.

Fifth, historical allocation of a good in scarce supply typically requires price controls. Indeed, price controls may be responsible for the scarcity. Controls bring with them the problems discussed in Chapters 2 and 3. If controls are not instituted, however, allocation simply allows those with historical rights the power to earn rents as they transfer, for example, taxi medallions or liquor licenses to those who will pay the most for them. Only where controls are temporary and resale is impractical (as with California's water rationing) can this problem be avoided.

Finally, historical allocation may impede the flow of resources to the areas where they can be used most efficiently. For example, firms that might have produced more efficiently with a more oil-intensive process (even at world prices) may not be able to obtain the requisite allocations in order to bring this process on line. Supplies wind up in the hands of those who arguably were the most efficient users in the preallocation period. This distribution will become inefficient as the changing marginal productivity of oil across consumers and over time alters the optimal allocation of the resource. The result is that those who *used to* need the oil the most—and not those who *currently* need the oil the most—end up with an inefficiently large supply of the resource

The Exception Process

The need for exceptions leads the regulator toward standard setting, public interest allocation, or some combination of the two. The oil allocation program, for example, relied heavily upon standard setting to set priorities and to develop rules governing exceptions. Major FEO rules governing departures from the historically based system have been described. Those rules were not adequate to deal with the need for exceptions.

The inadequacy of standards is not surprising, given the nature of the problem. The regulator turned to history to allocate because history offered a rule of thumb that seemed reasonably fair and reasonably efficient. As time passes, the historical period becomes less fair and interferes ever more with economic efficiency. Yet to develop a different set of standards that seek to allocate an industrial product, the regulator must second-guess the market; he must explicitly deal with the fairness claims of past reliance, the economic claims of future need through the creation of categories, rather than through a bidding process that ranks individual claims.

Inevitably the regulator begins to rely more heavily upon subjective judgment. Certainly the FEO authorizing statute foresaw the use of that judgment. It simply listed a set of objectives, such as protecting the public health, safety, and welfare, maintaining agriculture, preserving a sound petroleum industry, minimizing economic distortion, maintaining the viability of independent suppliers, and so on. And the congressional conference report stated that this list did not create "an order of precedence"; rather, "it may be impossible to satisfy one objective without sacrificing . . . another," and so the regulators may "permit the regulation to be constructed so as to accomplish the enumerated objectives to the maximum extent practicable."[33] Moreover, the regulators promulgated criteria governing the creation of exceptions, which in essence repeat the conflicting goals of the statute.[34] Thus, in addition to creating numerous standards creating priorities, FEO created a form of public interest allocation.

Essentially, any person dissatisfied with his assignment of supplier or the amount assigned could apply to FEO for a new assignment or an adjustment. In this way, FEO would take into account the need for new entry and changed circumstances. Once FEO abandoned automatic rules, such as granting an adjustment for increases in business above 10 percent in 1973, it found that it was effectively administering a public interest allocation system.

To some extent, the outlines of such a system became apparent when FEO assigned new suppliers. A new entrant needed a new supplier. In addition, oil price control, which effectively froze the price of old oil, meant that different suppliers had different prices depending on their mix of old, new, domestic, and imported oil. Thus, customers of different suppliers might have different supply costs and yet end up competing to resell gasoline. Frequently firms with high-cost suppliers requested a change of supplier.

A review of new supplier applications suggests that FEO had no fixed standards for determining when a new supplier would be assigned or which firm would be ordered to supply. Suppliers often objected to a new assignment, arguing that there would be less oil available for other customers. When it rejected this argument, FEO wrote that "it is certainly not unreasonable to expect that some sacrifice be made by all and that available supplies be shared."[35] When it accepted the argument, it wrote of the importance of being able "to supply the new purchaser without unduly affecting the amount of fuel which the supplier's base-period customers are entitled to receive."[36] Regional offices sometimes drew up lists of suppliers and simply assigned new firms to suppliers in order. But exceptions had to be made when a supplier had "too little" supply, and to some extent the regulator had to take account of the desirability of assigning independent gasoline stations to independent suppliers, rather than the major oil companies. They also had to decide when a claim of high price justified a change of supplier. No clear standards or directions on these issues ever emerged.[37]

The existence of a public interest system was still more apparent, however, when the regulators faced the question of "how much." What additional allocations were required by new entry or any other special or changing circumstances? The "10 percent increase" standard discussed earlier did not deal with these problems. Firms could apply for extra allocation by claiming that they or their customers were entitled to a priority. But this was inadequate. To deal with the exceptions problems, FEO promulgated an additional standard, Section 211.13(e),[38] which allowed extra allocation for unusual growth since the promulgation of the regulations in January 1974 or in other special circumstances.

The standard established numerous, sometimes conflicting criteria, reminiscent of the FCC's standards for allocating television licenses. FEO wrote that in processing applications for adjustments, it would consider "unusual conditions that indicate a need for increased amounts over base-period volumes, such as plant expansions, new population, industrial growth in an area, or unusual growth problems such as could occur at truck stops on highways." In an effort to clarify the rules, Region I (New England) administrators wrote:

Situations deemed by this office to indicate *possible* need for base period adjustments due to unusual conditions or changed circumstances include, *but are not necessarily limited to,* the following:

A. Permanently closed station(s) in the trade area causing significantly increased demand upon the remaining retail sales outlets and/or unusual changes in the local economy and trade area due to housing development, new plant construction or expansion, significant changes in traffic patterns due to road changes or construction, etc.

B. Significant new investments for gasoline distribution.

C. Unusual growth in demand for "100% of current requirements" type end users who have historically purchased from gasoline retailers.[39]

Efforts to convert these standards into formulas failed, because there was no usable method for deciding what dollar level of renovation or amount of increased traffic warranted a specific gallon adjustment. Administrators report that the standards were applied judgmentally and subjectively by FEO officials.[40]

The result was uncertainty about what would support an increase. Applications proliferated and became lengthy. Gas stations would try to get support from as many priority or important customers as possible (one applicant enclosed letters from local factories, car dealers, contractors, and a U.S. senator, all testifying that they relied on the applicant for gas).[41] Decisions were delayed while awaiting documentation.[42] Cases that appeared similar were treated differently: adjustments were allowed one station because of an increase in construction vehicles; another was denied an adjustment despite a similar increase in pulp-hauling vehicles.[43] An adjustment was granted one firm to supply the needs of farmers, school buses, rural mail carriers and doctors, but was denied another firm seeking to supply farmers, public transportation, and a municipality.[44]

At the same time, the number of applications for special treatment grew. Hundreds of people in New England alone were applying for special treatment adjustments to their base-period volumes.[45] This took place during less than four months; the shortage was over in April. During so short a period—particularly given the emergency—FEO employees made decisions subjectively with procedures that were informal and limited.[46] Yet had the shortage continued, more formal procedures—hearings, appeals—would have been necessary. And the process would have come to resemble still more that before the FCC (described in Chapter 4).

Conclusion

The historically based allocation system is unstable—nearly as much as the historically based pricing system that may accompany it. The need for exceptions proliferates, erodes, and soon destroys the advantage of simplicity that the historical rule appears to offer. Regulators must then use standards or turn to public interest allocation to deal with the exceptions. The most important point is that distortions in the flow of resources and the need for exceptions grow rapidly and the problem becomes ever worse over time. Thus, a historically based oil allocation program can develop the characteristics of the two alternative forms of regulation, overwhelming the historical system within a few short months. It seems unlikely to retain separate identity as a system for a longer period of time.

7

Individualized Screening

The success of a standard-setting process depends upon the ease with which fairly precise standards can be formulated and applied. In many cases, it is not possible to develop standards that are precise, that fulfill regulatory goals, and that can be readily applied. As a result, an agency may resort to highly general standards (for example, "qualified doctors") to screen out, *on a case-by-case basis,* those individual products or persons that are unacceptable. This process is very different from public interest allocation described in Chapter 4: public interest allocation consists of selecting a few winners from many qualified applicants, whereas this process consists of screening out unfit applicants from a larger group. Although the two results sound like mirror images, the processes differ significantly.

Agencies have applied individualized scrutiny to airline pilots, doctors, lawyers, food additives, prescription drugs, toxic substances, pesticides, and nuclear power plants. In the case of chemicals (drugs, additives, pesticides) and nuclear power plants, many difficulties arise because a vague, highly general safety standard, requiring considerable expertise to apply, is used. An exploration of one of these areas—food additives—illustrates how individualized screening works and what typical problems arise when it is applied in areas of scientific uncertainty.

Before turning to a discussion of the process, three issues should be noted. First, the problems discussed appear as the regulator begins to insist upon strictness and accuracy in application of the standard. As long as an examiner, for example, is satisfied with screening out only *obviously* unfit candidates for the bar, he can devise an examination and a character test that work fairly well. If, however, he tries to screen out *all* who are unfit or pose risks of unfitness, he will face many of the problems of those who screen out unsafe power plants or drugs.

Second, when safety screening is at issue—say, in the case of chemicals or power plants—regulators seek just such strict and accurate screening, for several reasons. As pointed out in Chapter 1, there is no general agreement about the objectives of safety regulation. Some argue that consumers do not have adequate information to evaluate the safety of the product; regulators should supply them with information that the market does not offer. Others claim that market prices do not reflect the costs of accidents or disease that they may bring; regulators should correct for this adverse spillover. Others believe that individuals, even when fully informed, have inadequate ability to bargain for the result they want. And still others may seek safety regulation on grounds of paternalism—the necessity to give buyers what they "really" want, despite their efforts to choose a more dangerous alternative (say, a properly labeled risky food product). Sometimes, those advancing this last claim argue that the public expects the government to screen out and to ban dangerous products. Thus, the mere appearance of a food product at the grocery store announces its safety, regardless of the label. Disagreement about the specific rationale for safety regulation can lead all involved to submerge their differences and agree that the objective is simply "safety." Yet this very agreement suggests that more safety is always better, despite the fact that safety is always bought at a price and some risks are clearly worth running. (Who, for example, would want to make the Grand Canyon 100 percent risk-free?) Instead of seeking the "right amount" of safety, the safety goal suggests the elimination of all risk.[1] The tendency to make safety an absolute rather than relative goal may lead the regulator to press ever further to eliminate smaller and smaller risks, remaining always dissatisfied with an imperfect screening process.

For another thing, there are severe political pressures on regulators, stemming in part from the fact that certain of their actions may receive publicity. Simple human interest in death, disease, and accident means that a regulatory action allowing a product that subsequently causes death or accidents will receive adverse publicity. An action that keeps a product off the market, on the other hand, is likely to receive considerably less adverse publicity, particularly if the product is new. Thus, regulators have a personal incentive to err, if at all, on the side of eliminating small risks. This political problem is particularly serious when such emotive issues as cancer or nuclear accidents are involved.

Further, there is a generally held view of science that leads the public to believe that scientists can produce specific, certain information about the likely effects of most individual products. This view, however, is probably exaggerated. The problems of specifying objectives, political pressure, and imperfect information lead regulators in the safety area to seek ever more elaborate screening procedures to protect against ever smaller or less likely risks of disease, death, or accident. Hence, regulators face the problems described below, inherent in many instances of individualized screening.

Third, the individualized screening process is another, and final, aspect of licensing. Licensing has not been treated as a separate category of regulatory activity because the categorization used here more clearly illustrates typical regulatory problems. Licensing sometimes involves allocation under a public interest standard, as with television licenses. Sometimes it involves the problem of standard setting, as with much occupational licensing. And sometimes it involves individualized screening. Of course, any specific regulatory program may involve several of the regulatory activities described here.

The Food Additive Screening System

Administration of the law governing food additives provides a good example of the individualized screening process. That law is contained in the Food, Drug, and Cosmetic Act (as amended in 1958).[2] It can best be understood by dividing food additives into four categories: natural constituents of food, unavoidable added contaminants, direct food additives, and indirect food additives.

The Food and Drug Administration (FDA), which administers the act, can proceed against the first of these—natural constituents of food, such as vitamin C in orange juice—whenever the food "bears or contains any poisonous or deleterious substance . . . if the quantity . . . ordinarily render[s] it injurious to health."[3] The FDA will typically proceed by bringing a court action to seize the harmful food or to forbid its sale.[4] No prior approval is needed to market natural constituents of food.

The second category—unavoidable food contaminants—consists of food constituents that occur unavoidably when certain foods are harvested or manufactured, such as aflotoxin in peanuts and mercury in swordfish. The act requires the FDA to set a standard or tolerance level that considers "the extent to which the use" of the substance "is required or cannot be avoided" and the ways in which it may harm the consumer.[5] The FDA's role here is primarily one of setting a safety standard. The procedures required for setting the standard are elaborate; once it is set, the FDA will bring court actions to seize products that violate it.[6]

The most important category of additives is the third—intentionally added ingredients, such as food preservatives or artificial sweeteners. No such food additive can be marketed unless there is "in effect . . . a regulation . . . prescribing the conditions under which . . . [the] additive may be safely used." The regulation shall be issued only if "the data" establish "that the proposed use of the food additive . . . will be safe."[7] Thus, before anyone can market a food additive, he must obtain permission from the FDA by showing that the individual substance meets the general standard of "safe."

The procedures for obtaining approval as safe are complicated. A petition for approval must be filed. Then, after informal rulemaking procedures, the FDA decides whether to grant, deny, or conditionally grant the petition. Any dissatisfied person can demand a second, formal, on-the-record hearing on the same issue, and the FDA's decision will be final only after the second set of hearings and court review (but its provisional decision will take effect in the meantime).

The burden on the manufacturer is heavy. He must show that the additive is effective and safe by producing at least four and possibly more than ten valid studies involving rodent and nonrodent toxicity, cancer, and other tests.[8] Moreover, no additive can be approved as safe "if it is found . . . to induce cancer in man or animal."[9]

Before marketing, such a substance must receive FDA approval. Once marketed, the FDA can withdraw its permission if it subsequently believes that the substance is unsafe. The withdrawal procedure is similarly elaborate. First, the FDA must informally come to the view that the substance is unsafe. Second, it must conduct a "notice and comment" informal rulemaking proceeding to issue a rule withdrawing the approval. Third, it must (on request) go through a second, formal, on-the-record proceeding before its withdrawal of approval becomes final.[10] Given the difficulties of obtaining approval and of withdrawing approval once given, it is not surprising that few new additives are approved and still fewer have their approvals withdrawn.[11]

There are two important exceptions to the "prior approval" requirement for direct additives. The requirement does not apply to substances "generally recognized, among experts . . . [as] safe" (GRAS)[12] nor does it apply to "grandfathered" additives—those that had received informal government approval before the 1958 amendments to the act.[13] There are hundreds of GRAS additives. The FDA keeps a GRAS list, which it recognizes as incomplete and which often includes limitations on the use of particular additives.[14] Should a scientific controversy develop about a particular GRAS item, the FDA will declare that it is no longer GRAS, requiring the manufacturer to begin the lengthy approval procedure.[15] (If the manufacturer disagrees about whether the item is GRAS, the FDA may bring a court action and seize the food, by showing that it contains an unapproved, non-GRAS additive.) Grandfathered ingredients are never considered additives; the FDA can proceed against them only by showing in court that they are "injurious to health," as in the case of natural constituents of foods.[16]

The fourth category—indirect food additives—consists of packaging materials (whose molecules migrate into food), residues of animal drugs, and residues of pesticides. The first is treated like a direct food additive,[17] and the other two are regulated under separate statutes.[18]

Essentially, the FDA screens food additives individually to determine whether each should be allowed on, or removed from, the market. Despite the complexity of the statutory procedural scheme, the key step in the process is the informal decision made within the FDA about whether to proceed against or to allow a particular substance.[19] To help it make this determination, the FDA often convenes special advisory committees—expert, scientific committees organized by the National Academy of Sciences (NAS) or the Federation of American Societies for Experimental Biology (FASEB). These advisory committees, as a practical matter, often make the crucial decision, because the FDA tends to take their advice and it ordinarily can produce sufficient supporting evidence to win whatever legal proceeding is appropriate. Once the agency has decided to bring proceedings to allow or to ban a particular item on the strength of this recommendation, it is likely that it will reach the same ultimate result as the panel. The courts tend to give considerable weight to agency decisions in this highly technical area.[20]

This key step, partial delegation of authority to an expert advisory group, is also followed by the Nuclear Regulatory Commission when it licenses atomic power plants. The commission refers an application to build a nuclear power plant to a nongovernmental group of technical experts—the Advisory Committee on Reactor Safeguards (ACRS).[21] Its report then becomes part of the record when the application is later heard by the Atomic Safety and Licensing Board, and it carries considerable weight.[22] In fact, some form of delegation to experts is commonly found wherever individualized screening in technical areas takes place. The decision to admit lawyers to practice, for example, is made by unpaid boards of bar examiners, composed of lawyers. Doctors' admissions are handled similarly.

Criticisms of the food additive screening process echo those made in other instances of such regulation.[23] (1) The agency acts inconsistently. It acts arbitrarily in selecting items on the market against which to proceed, often taking action against less dangerous substances while leaving more dangerous substances on the market. Moreover, the standards used for deciding whether new additives should be allowed are far stricter than those applied to determine whether presently marketed additives should be removed.[24] (2) The agency's decisions are inexpert and do not adequately reflect the state of scientific knowledge. (3) The agency does not adequately consider potential benefits. It tends to ask only whether an ingredient with even the slightest risk attached is essential. If the ingredient is not essential, the agency will ban it.[25] (4) The agency's rules prevent the introduction of new, desirable, ingredients or products.[26] (5) Conversely, the slowness of the agency's procedures and inadequate testing often allow dangerous products to remain too long on the market.

These criticisms grow out of certain problems endemic to individualized screening.

Problems with This Form of Regulation

We will examine the problems that can arise as screening is conducted under a general standard, in an area of scientific complexity, and by an agency anxious to screen vigorously and accurately. We will look at a difficult case—the testing of food additives to see if they cause cancer. Regulating carcinogens has become a major part of safety regulation. At the same time, carcinogens present a severe case of regulatory difficulty because (1) the way in which a carcinogen works is essentially unknown, (2) the length of time between exposure and disease may be twenty years or more, and (3) the number of persons for whom disease follows exposure may be very small. The difficulties concern the determination of risk, the use of experts, the weighing of benefits, and the effort to treat ingredients consistently.

Developing a Test for Risk

The notion that there are clear, relatively simple scientific methods for determining safety risk and screening out unacceptable risks is incorrect. In fact, the single most difficult problem for the regulator is to obtain even a rough idea of the health or safety dangers that may surround a particular substance.

The number of individual substances subject to most screening programs is enormous. There are 63,000 chemicals in common use in the United States.[27] There are an estimated 13,000 components of the food supply.[28] There are an estimated 3,000–4,000 direct food additives, 10,000 indirect food constituents,[29] and about 1,200 GRAS additives.[30] At the same time, individual testing is time-consuming and expensive. The National Cancer Institute suggests that two strains of animals should be used and that treatment with chemicals should continue for twenty-four months; five hundred animals are ordinarily required. "The total time required is at least 3.5 years or more and the cost is at least $250,000 per substance,"[31] though it may easily reach $500,000.[32] There is an insufficient amount of personnel, time, money, and laboratory animals to test all these substances in detail.

In addition, even as to those substances that are to be tested in detail, there is often no test procedure that will produce unambiguous results. Practical considerations make it impossible to avoid making highly subjective judgments—almost guesses—about a substance's risks, particularly where, for example, one is testing for carcinogenicity.[33]

Epidemiological tests. The most accurate type of test, in principle, is a prospective epidemiological test on a human population. One group receives the substance; a carefully selected control group does not. The test is "double blind," in that neither administrator nor recipient knows who receives which substance. Results are matched to see whether the exposed group is more likely to contract the disease.

While such a test might work for a large, immediate risk, it is impractical in the case of a small, delayed risk, because the number of controls needed is too great and the time of observation too lengthy. To obtain a rough idea of the magnitude of the problem, imagine that the risk of a person in the population at large getting bladder cancer is 1 in 6,000. If one wishes to test a substance that in reality doubles the risk of bladder cancer, a test group of 6,000 and a control group of 6,000 are far too small. One could not be certain whether a result showing that two exposed persons and one control person developed bladder cancer was not just chance—like heads on a coin flip coming up twice in a row. To know that there are fewer than 5 chances out of 100 that this result is due to chance alone (which statisticians call the 95 percent confidence level), one would need close to 50,000 exposed persons and 50,000 controls.[34] To follow so large a group for twenty years or more would be impossible.[35]

The epidemiologist may seek to avoid this practical problem by observing groups in the society at large. He may observe a large naturally exposed selected group—say, those who use saccharin—and match them against others who do not use saccharin. Yet if the groups are not artificially selected, he will not know whether saccharin is the cause of any small increase in bladder cancer observed among the exposed. The higher cancer rate could be caused by obesity or any of hundreds of other factors correlated with saccharin use. The test groups have then been selected by nature not man, so they need not have been selected at random.

For these practical reasons, epidemiologists prefer to use retrospective testing. The epidemiologist will take a group of people with disease and match them against identical controls without disease; he will then note whether those in the first group have used more of the suspect ingredient than those in the second. If he takes a group of two hundred persons with bladder cancer and a matched group of two hundred without, and if in fact saccharin doubles the risk of getting bladder cancer, he will find that far more people in the first group use saccharin than in the second. (The ratio of saccharin users to nonusers in the first group will be twice as great as in the whole four hundred taken together.)[36] One can be 95 percent certain that such a result is not due to chance with far fewer cases than in a prospective study. The number depends on the likelihood that controls use saccharin and the extent to which saccharin in fact increases the risk of cancer. But if saccharin is used by 10 percent of the population, one could detect a doubling of cancer risk with a few hundred cases and controls, not tens of thousands.[37]

Retrospective epidemiological studies raise formidable problems when small risks of diseases with unknown etiologies (such as cancer) are at issue. For one thing, the cancer group may be specially selected. For example, those interviewed are more likely to be found in hospitals; they are sufficiently well educated to recognize and report their disease; and perhaps saccharin is used more by educated people. Alternatively, controls may not be well matched. Have they come from a particular area or social, economic, or cultural group that is less likely to use saccharin?

The fact that the biological causes of cancer are unknown makes it particularly difficult to account for all possibly relevant factors. Suppose a retrospective study among diabetics (heavy saccharin users) shows no increase in the incidence of bladder cancer. Does this fact show that saccharin is safe? Or is there something about diabetics that counteracts saccharin? Are diabetics more likely to get medical checkups, which tend to stop cancer? Are they less likely to smoke or to drink coffee, which lessens their cancer risk? Alternatively, assume that such a study shows an increased risk of cancer associated with saccharin use. Is saccharin then dangerous? Or are those who use it more likely to be overweight? To smoke? To drink coffee? Are there other factors more closely related to the problem? Designing a study with controls that can take into account smoking, occupation, coffee drinking, medical history, social status, type of water supply, and other factors is extremely difficult—particularly when the mystery of cancer means that the epidemiologist does not know what all those factors are.[38]

Further, obtaining the necessary objective information for the study is difficult. The most serious cancer cases may die quickly, making access to case histories difficult. Others may be incorrectly diagnosed. Controls may not accurately report saccharin use, particularly in the form of diet soft drinks, over a period of twenty years or more. Cancer victims, on the other hand, may remember the use of any suspect substance more vividly, for they tend to mull over possible causes of their disease. Mail questionnaires are plagued with poor response rates, selective returns, and differences in interpreting questions. Yet personal interviews risk that interviewers may unconsciously project personal biases.[39]

Finally, one can never be certain whether cases and controls together constitute a special group such that the relationship between them does not apply elsewhere. Thus, a saccharin/cancer relationship, established in Japan where everyone eats fish containing iodine, may not exist in Mexico where the people do not eat much fish.

These problems may not be serious where a study establishes a strong relationship between substance and disease, where the relation is confirmed by other studies, where fairly short time periods are at issue, or where the relation is biologically understood and plausible. But they are very serious when the relation is weak, when long time periods are involved, when the biology is not well understood, and when many confounding factors are at work.[40] The result is that epidemiological tests will not necessarily relieve the regulator of highly subjective judgments when he is, scientifically speaking, in the dark.

Animal tests. Given the difficulties of epidemiological testing, most tests for small risks are carried out on animals and the results extrapolated to human beings. But the precise relevance of animal tests is highly uncertain. The statistical need for large test populations still raises practical difficulties. Since prospective testing is ordinarily used, one must ask how many treated animals and controls are needed to obtain 95 percent confidence that a result is not due to chance. When asked how many animals (n) are needed to have confidence that a given substance is not toxic, a leading group of scientists responded:

If n is 1000 an upper limit of 2.3 affected animals would give a 90% confidence of the absence of toxicity. Such a degree of assurance, however, would hardly be comforting to the average person as far as cancer is concerned. [Since a specific type of cancer may attack fewer than one person in a thousand] he or she would prefer a much higher confidence, together with an associated incidence of, say, less than 1 tumor per

500,000 test animals. To obtain such a projection with 0.999 confidence would require negative results in over 3,000,000 test animals.[41]

Because of this practical problem, scientists typically use fewer animals but feed them higher doses of the test substance. Positive results are then extrapolated backward to determine a safe low dose level for a human being.[42] One commonly used method is to take the highest dose at which no adverse effect is observed in an animal and divide it by 100, after taking into account relevant weight and other differences between man and animal. The result is a somewhat arbitrary but cautious safe limit for human consumption.[43] The methods used to extrapolate work well in many cases, but they are highly controversial with low-risk substances consumed in small amounts and related to a disease about which little is known.

Consider the problem of extrapolating from a positive finding in a Canadian saccharin/cancer rat study to even a rough estimate of the danger saccharin poses for human beings. The Canadian study showed that saccharin doses of 5–7.5 percent of a rat's diet, when fed to two rat generations (mother and child), produced tumors in about 27 percent of the children.[44] The daily rat dose (1.5 grams per 500 grams of body weight) was equal to the amount found in twelve bottles of diet soft drink. Since a typical human weighs about 140 times as much as a typical rat, the rat dose per pound per day was over 1,000 times the amount a human is likely to consume. What is the significance of this difference? What is the proper way to extrapolate from a high animal dose to a lower human dose? First, how are smaller doses likely to affect rats? Second, how are rat effects likely to compare with human effects?

There are several mathematical models that extrapolate effects from high to low doses. One assumes a simple linear relation between dose and response: if a 5 percent saccharin diet causes tumors in 30 percent of all rats, a .5 percent diet presumably would affect 3 percent and a .0005 percent diet would affect .003 percent. Another model uses a different mathematical curve relating dose and response such that lower doses adversely affect slightly more than a proportional percentage of the population. Still another model presumes a dose threshold below which the substance causes no adverse effect.[45]

Each of these models is mathematical, not scientific, biological, or medical. The model used depends upon the user's view of the scientific nature of the disease and the substance at issue. Suppose the user believes that cancer occurs when a susceptible person comes into contact with a carcinogen. Suppose, further, he believes that susceptibility is a matter of sensivitiy to a particular substance and that it is distributed in the population normally and at random. Such a user might believe that the first model accurately depicts the effects of small saccharin doses. Another user might, for a variety of reasons, have a different view about the distribution of susceptibility in society, which would make the second model appropriate. A third might believe in the existence of a threshold exposure below which the additive has no deleterious effect. After all, sugar when fed to rats in high doses (say, 25 grams for each kilogram of body weight) can kill them through dehydration, yet low doses are helpful not harmful to human beings. Indeed, iodine, which kills both man and animals in high doses, is not merely harmless, but *necessary* for life, in low doses.[46] Thus, proper extrapolation from high dose to low requires a knowledge of the etiology of the disease and the chemical and biological effects of the substance. When this knowledge is uncertain—as in the case of cancer and several other diseases—one cannot be certain of the validity of the extrapolation.

To extrapolate from animal to man is equally difficult. Obviously chemicals and diseases follow different courses in animals, but beyond that obvious point, how should one take into account the weight differences between man and animals? A human weighs about 140 times as much as a rat. Does this fact mean that an equivalent human dose is 1/140 of a rat dose? Humans also live about 35 times as long. Does this fact mean that the equivalent human dose is 35 times 1/140, or ¼ the rat dose? Much depends on whether one expects saccharin's effects to depend upon weight, body area, or accumulation. That, in turn, depends upon the biological causes and characteristics of cancer. Further, to what extent should one consider the fact that laboratory animals are genetically homogeneous? Or the fact that humans are exposed to many more carcinogens than laboratory animals?

For these and similar reasons, the National Academy of Sciences concluded that the "question of scaling from animals to humans . . . has never been fully resolved."[47] Yet scaling and dose extrapolation are of overwhelming importance. Depending upon which of several reasonable extrapolation methods one chose to use, one could extrapolate from the Canadian saccharin/rat study that saccharin might lead either to less than one case or to more than three thousand cases of cancer per year.[48] In other words, the uncertainty surrounding the extrapolation of animal test results is not mere scientific hedging. Rather, it is fundamental, leaving the conscientious regulator genuinely uncertain about the result.

In vitro tests. A range of short-term, relatively inexpensive tests may be used to help determine whether a substance is a carcinogen. These vary in cost from a few hundred dollars to about $10,000 and take a few days to a few months to perform.[49] Essentially, they measure whether a specific chemical is likely to alter the DNA in a cell. Thus, in the most famous of these tests—the Ames Salmonella test—the chemical is given to a special group of bacteria lacking an essential amino acid (histidine). They will grow only if histidine is added artificially. If treatment with the chemical causes bacterial growth without added histidine, the tester infers that it enabled them to make their own histidine. Thus, the chemical must have caused a backward mutation; thus, it has the power to alter DNA; thus, it may cause cancer.

The Ames test and other short-term tests, however, can give both false negative and false positive results. While they can help pinpoint substances for further study, most scientists believe they are not sufficiently accurate to constitute the basis for a regulatory decision.[50]

The Use of Experts

The agency, faced with a difficult scientific issue and without any simple testing method to determine risk, frequently delegates decision-making responsibility to a panel of experts. The desire to rely upon experts is understandable. Even if the experts themselves are uncertain, theirs is a more informed uncertainty than that of the lawyer, politician, or bureaucrat who must make the regulatory decision. Sometimes expert panels are formally given decision-making responsibility, as when doctors administer licensing tests or lawyers admit new members to the bar. Often, however, particularly when safety is at issue, the panel of experts is advisory. The regulator solicits an outside group of experts for its opinion. In practice, it acts on the basis of that opinion.

The FDA's use of panels of outside experts to screen drugs is illustrative. The 1962 amendments to the Food, Drug, and Cosmetic Act[51] required the FDA to screen drugs for efficacy as well as for safety. To determine the effectiveness of drugs that had been approved since the original 1938 act was an enormous job. The FDA needed to review 4,349 drug products with 10,000 different "indications."[52] Its staff was numerically inadequate, and many outside critics felt that it lacked the necessary scientific competence. A Smithsonian Institution study observed that the "medical officer group within FDA attracted few physicians with credentials in experimental design and evaluation for lack of creative incentives. Hence, an adverse selection factor operated in attraction and retention of staff."[53] To ease logistical problems, to obtain more accurate decisions, and to make decisions publicly more acceptable, the FDA asked the National Academy of Sciences to conduct the efficacy review. Thirty panels of outside experts, selected by the NAS, categorized each of these thousands of drugs as "effective," "probably effective," "possibly effective," or "ineffective." The FDA removed from the market drugs placed in the fourth category.[54]

The statute, however, delegated the power to remove drugs to the FDA, not the NAS. Moreover, it mandated complex procedures for removal: the FDA had to promulgate a rule (after "notice and comment" procedures) to remove the drug, and the rule became final only after a full on-the-record hearing.[55] The FDA circumvented this requirement by promulgating a more general rule stating that a drug company could show efficacy only through prospective, double-blind testing. Since few existing drugs had been tested this carefully, the FDA could remove drugs without a hearing, because in its view there was nothing to have a hearing about—the fact of no double-blind testing was undeniable. Of course, the FDA did not proceed against *all* inadequately tested drugs, but only against those that the NAS panel rated as ineffective. Hence, despite the statute, the FDA effectively delegated decision-making power to the outside experts.[56] These rather doubtful procedures were upheld in the courts.[57]

In the area of food additives, the FDA similarly effectively delegated screening power to outside experts. In 1972 the FDA contracted with FASEB to review 1,200 GRAS food additives. By 1977 FASEB panels had reviewed 229 substances.[58] When the panel questioned the safety of a substance, it was taken off the GRAS list (by definition). The manufacturer then had to overcome serious procedural obstacles to obtaining FDA marketing approval.

The FDA is not the only agency to rely heavily upon the informal advice of outside experts in making its basic regulatory decisions. The Nuclear Regulatory Commission asks outside panels to review the safety of proposed reactors.[59] The Environmental Protection Agency has relied upon outside expert advice to determine whether to waive environmental requirements in order to allow certain reactors to be built.[60]

This use of outside expertise by agencies may appear to eliminate many defects that characterize individualized screening. After all, such a group will in principle reach a conclusion that reflects the scientific state of the art—an objective, nonpolitical decision, soundly supported by whatever evidence currently exists. In fact, however, the use of experts is itself beset with difficulties, sufficient to shake one's confidence in the objectivity of their decisions and in subsequent regulatory judgments based upon them.[61]

First, selecting members of the expert panel is difficult. The agency tries to avoid obvious conflicts of interest. This results in drug or food additive panels consisting of academic scientists rather than those directly connected with industry. However, detailed firsthand expertise will tend to reside in industry. There may well be no academic scientists with firsthand experience of the health aspects of adipec acid, rennet, or papain.[62] To avoid this difficulty, the FDA recently created panels without formal industry representation, but with industry observers or participants who present information to the panel. Moreover, the tentative views of the panel can be made available for public comment. Yet expert scientists may feel a need for secret deliberations if they are to risk their reputations by expressing frank views in an area of inadequate information.[63] In closed sessions the presence or absence of industry experts can make a difference.

Moreover, the make-up of the panel creates bias. If industry experts are included, their views may reflect the interests of their firms. But if they are not, a reverse bias may be created. Academic scientists may distrust industry experts. Academics may also place more confidence in scientific tests than an industry expert would. Or they may discount practical experience more than would a practicing physician. Take the case of Panalba, for example. Panalba was a combination antibiotic which was no more effective than its constituent ingredients, which were sold separately. Its manufacturer argued that it was effective because many physicians might not make a detailed accurate diagnosis and choose the proper noncombination antibiotic; they would simply reach for the nearest antibiotic at hand. And Panalba, a broad-spectrum antibiotic, would likely do for many different diseases. The FDA's scientific advisory NAS panel rated Panalba ineffective. The scientists believed that doctors *should* make precise diagnoses and use antibiotics more precisely designed to fit the disease. A different panel with more practicing physicians and fewer academics might have been swayed by the claim that what matters is what doctors *will* do, not what they *should* do. Given a propensity to misdiagnose, Panalba might cure some illnesses that might not be cured in its absence.[64]

Finally, panel members must devote a great deal of time and effort to the panel's task. A member of one GRAS panel had to donate four full days a month for several years to this work. The work is unpaid and does not lead directly to professional advancement. Hence, recruiting can be difficult. Nor can the panel's organizers exhort panel members to spend additional time doing research or reading. The basic literature searches and evaluations are thus done by the panel's professional staff. In fact, if the panel is not conscientious, much of the value of turning the problem over to the experts is lost.

Second, the experts may find little information available and what they find may be limited, or difficult to digest. For example, the members of one FASEB panel that was evaluating GRAS substances found that they themselves did not have expert knowledge about most substances they evaluated. A panel of ten or twelve was unlikely to contain a member who had worked directly with carnauba wax, or even vitamin A. Thus, panels had to draw their information from the literature about the substance. They found that the literature varied enormously in quantity, quality, and accessibility. A search of fifty years' worth of literature on carnauba wax, for example, uncovered only twenty-three reports, while a search for references to vitamin A produced over twenty thousand. Moreover, in searching the literature, panels found lags of months or years between research activity and publication; indexing systems that listed even simple substances such as sugar under numerous different names; information that might be deposited in any of half a dozen data banks; and references to reports that were often obscure and conflicting. Moreover, after hiring researchers under contract to complete references and to summarize their conclusions objectively, the panels found that researchers often wrote their own views about safety into the compilation. Panels found that in many cases they simply could not draw firm conclusions, because the underlying data were inadequate, conflicting, or incomplete.[65]

As a result, panel members would consult informally, "inquiring of those currently active or productive in the field" for information about the substance.[66] Such inquiry limits the effectiveness of conflict-of-interest criteria that govern panel composition. More important, the unavailability of good information increases the likelihood that the subjective point of view of individual panel members, rather than objective analysis, will influence the result. That is to say, if academics tend to distrust practitioners, the less information there is available the more that distrust is likely to affect the panel's decision.

Third, expert scientific panels may reach only very limited conclusions, particularly if they know that their conclusions will be made public. Scientists are trained to express judgments in terms that are very different from those used by policy makers. Good scientific work tends to hold constant a broad range of variables and to investigate very carefully the effect of X on Y. The merit of the work often lies in the care and thoroughness with which the narrow, specific investigation is done. A good piece of legal or policy-related work, however, tends to consider *all* relevant factors. The author need not produce convincing or conclusive evidence regarding each. He is expected to do the best he can with whatever evidence he has available, even if that evidence is of poor quality. A lawyer or policy maker does a poor job when he leaves out some relevant factor; a scientist does a poor job when he fails to analyze thoroughly those factors within his study. A lawyer is expected to recommend a result; a scientist need not say more than that the evidence is inconclusive. Thus, panels of scientists are reluctant to draw conclusions in areas where detailed studies are weak or nonexistent. They are reluctant to provide any conclusion or recommendation when any such conclusion would rest not upon scientific studies but upon their own impressions.

The NAS report on saccharin is a good example of scientists' reluctance to commit themselves to judgments in the absence of high-quality scientific evidence. Congress and the FDA hoped that the NAS report would help determine whether saccharin should be banned.[67] To make this decision, one must judge at least whether banning saccharin is likely to kill more people than allowing it. If saccharin is permitted, some users may die of bladder cancer; if it is banned, others may gain weight and die of heart attacks or strokes. Obviously, some rough scientific judgment about the magnitude of each of these risks is critical. Yet the NAS panel felt unqualified to make any such assessment.

The panel reported that although epidemiological studies were inconclusive, animal studies showed some connection between saccharin and bladder cancer. The Canadian saccharin/cancer study mentioned above shows that high doses led to tumors in second-generation rats. After pointing out the difficulty of extrapolating from rats to humans, the panel report implies that the saccharin risk is moderate compared with that of other carcinogenic chemicals.[68] It does not tell the reader, even roughly, how many of the 7,500 male bladder cancer deaths per year any or all of the panel members would judge to be due to saccharin. Moreover, when it describes saccharin's health benefits—benefits achieved through weight control—the study is still less helpful. It surveys studies of weight reduction and determines that they are inadequate. It dismisses as unscientific the opinions of doctors whose patients use saccharin to control weight. It concludes that there is no *scientific* evidence that saccharin helps control weight.[69]

The scientists' report, when read carefully, does not provide a judgment about the risks and benefits of saccharin. Rather, it assesses the scientific quality of the evidence advanced in support of claims that saccharin is dangerous or beneficial. The assessment demonstrates that much evidence does not meet high scientific standards. But the report fails to assess the quality of nonscientific opinions of practitioners. Might not the panel have gone on to discuss other, less scientific evidence? Might it not, in particular, have sought to assess the impressionistic judgments of the usefulness of saccharin provided by medical practitioners?

Such an assessment would have been helpful, for evidence can be strong even though it fails to meet scientific canons. Decisions—such as whether to eat an egg with a spot on it, whether a defendant should be found guilty of running a red light, or whether an inner-city investment program will reduce crime—are frequently made on the basis of common experience, opinion, hearsay, or suggestive (but different) experience elsewhere. Within each of these categories some evidence is better than others. Waiting for scientific studies would prevent action. Nonetheless, it should not be surprising that a group of eminent scientists, when asked to produce an important public report, will not go beyond evaluating the scientific quality of the evidence. Their professional training makes them hesitate to go beyond what has been proved. They tend to view judgments that rest upon impressions, anecdotes or opinion as speculative. The result is a report that is accurate scientifically, but that cannot decide the policy issue.

Fourth, reliance upon an expert panel may produce a policy judgment that does not reflect a comprehensive evaluation of likely risks. The expert panel may accurately report whether or not there is good scientific evidence that a product is safe. To the extent that good scientific evidence is not available about certain risks attaching to the use of saccharin or to its abandonment, a regulator should, in principle, turn to less good evidence, such as medical opinion or impressions from common experience, before making a decision. Yet the regulator may not do so, particularly if he has referred the matter to the panel so that they, not he, will make the decision. He will be tempted to take the panel's conclusion on a different issue (the quality of the evidence on safety) as if it were a conclusion about the ultimate question (whether the substance should be banned).

Panel members, while restrained by their professional discipline from going beyond the scientific evidence, may be aware of what the regulator is likely to do and they may therefore seek to write their ultimate policy views into the report "between the lines." Thus, the tone of the report may reflect the subjective views of panel members, rather than the objective evidence. For example, the NAS found that although the few scientific studies of saccharin and weight control that had been made were inconclusive, many doctors treating obesity feel that saccharin is effective. An initial draft of the NAS panel report, written and supported by those who seemed hostile to saccharin, summarized the findings as follows: "It has not been demonstrated that saccharin is a beneficial aid in caloric control or regulation of food intake, both of which are key factors in the prevention or treatment of obesity and diabetes. The available scientific evidence does not indicate that saccharin is useful in weight control or dietary compliance."[70] Those more favorable to saccharin, who considered themselves subjectively neutral, objected to this language and substituted the following: "Scientific evidence does not permit assessment of the role that saccharin plays in weight control or dietary compliance, both key factors in the prevention or treatment of obesity and diabetes. Five studies on management of obesity with non-nutritional sweeteners and three studies pertaining to diabetes were reviewed by the committee. It considered the design of the studies to be inappropriate for assessing the efficacy of saccharin in weight control or diabetic management."[71] When read closely, these two statements are roughly equivalent, yet heated debate took place because of differences in their tone, with individual members seeking to create a tone that suggested their view of the proper policy outcome.

The GRAS panels also recognized that their description of the efficacy of scientific evidence would in fact determine whether a substance would be banned. The panel was asked to place each substance into one of five categories:

1. There is no evidence suggesting a safety risk at present consumption levels.
2. There is no evidence suggesting a safety risk at present consumption levels but more evidence is needed to determine whether increased consumption would present a risk.
3. There is no evidence suggesting a safety risk at present consumption levels but there are uncertainties which suggest a need for further studies.
4. The evidence is insufficient to determine that the item is not harmful.
5. There are so few studies, the panel cannot evaluate the item.

In categorizing substances, the panels knew that the FDA would ban those in the fourth category and possibly in the third. Members, when faced with a paucity of evidence, tended to divide into those who would categorize in accordance with what looked like the trend of empirical findings and those who tended to categorize in a way likely to result in least harm through disease. Their differences of view reflected differences in the philosophy between those who felt that food additives are generally not desirable (so, when in any doubt, ban) and those who felt that an additive should be allowed in the absence of real evidence that it is harmful.[72]

As previously indicated, there is often wide scope for subjective views to influence a panel's judgment. Objective evidence may be sparse. Toxicity is related to dose, yet extrapolating from large doses, or those administered to animals, to small doses and human effects is fraught with uncertainty. Efforts to make this extrapolation more objective by, for example, equating toxicity with *any* positive response, regardless of "quantity, concentration or dose reported for any length of time,"[73] are doomed to failure given the vast number of common foods that can injure animals given a large enough dose. Nor is there an objective way to determine how much of a dangerous substance the FDA should allow in foods. The FDA cannot readily use the objective standard "none," for sensitive equipment reveals that a few molecules of carcinogenic plastic bottling material may migrate into a soft drink. Should that material be banned, the alternative is glass bottles, which lead to thousands of serious accidents each year.[74] Also, how can the panel be sure that a substance that is ordinarily consumed in small quantities is not consumed by some small group (say, vanilla-bean freaks) in large quantities?

The problem is not the panel's use of subjective judgment, but the indirect, disguised way in which the subjective element is communicated to the regulator. He does not know whether it reflects a judgment of the science, to which he should defer, or a philosophical view, with which he might disagree.

These problems might be overcome through informal communication between the regulator and the panel. Basically, the regulator wants to find out from the panel how he should treat the substance. Should he approve the additive (or atomic power plant) or not? Despite the potential biases of the panel, the regulator may still feel it will make as wise a decision as he would himself. Thus, he may ask the panel directly what he should do. If asked for an *informal* opinion, most scientists or other experts, while stressing that they are speaking in their capacity as individuals, would be willing to tell the administrator what they think he should do.

This approach, however, is ad hoc and informal. Courts have asked whether it is either fair or lawful for a critical element in the decision-making process to take place secretly, particularly when it involves an individual (the expert) who cannot be cross-examined about what he has told the regulator.

Thus, in *Moss* v. *CAB*[75] the District of Columbia Court of Appeals held unlawful a regulator's rate decision that was the result of informal advice given privately before the rate case began. In *Home Box Office* v. *FCC*[76] that same court held that once an agency gave notice of a rulemaking proceeding, it could not consult informally off the record. If that is the direction of future law, informal consultation will prove difficult. Experts, unwilling to subject themselves to cross-examination, will hesitate to express informal opinions. Administrators will have to rely upon formal, guarded reports with limited conclusions or with broader conclusions hidden between the lines.

The Effort to be Comprehensive: Calculating and Weighing Benefits

A third set of problems arises when the agency seeks to weigh benefits against risks. The agency need not do so when it proceeds against obviously dangerous items—defective bridges or airplanes. Nor need it do so when it is satisfied with less-than-perfect results, as when it screens out potential lawyers or doctors as unqualified. In the case of food safety and related areas, items carry very small risks. At the same time the agency realizes that absolute safety—the absence of all risk—is an impossible goal. Hence, it must decide when a very small risk is too risky, and it is tempted to assess benefits and to weigh them against risks in order to make this judgment.

Any agency that decides to examine benefits must first determine which benefits to consider and then decide how to measure them. Where the risk involved is to health, it is often argued that only health benefits should be taken into account.[77] Yet identifying health benefits may be substantially more difficult than identifying health risks. How can the regulator predict public behavior if he restricts access to, say, saccharin or peanut butter or even cigarettes? Will some, many, or all former consumers turn to other riskier products? Might former smokers turn to alcohol or former saccharin users eat more sweets? Predicting the alternative forms of behavior is unlikely to be scientific and will involve rough guesses.

A reasonably thorough study would require a risk analysis of any major substitute for the item banned. If those who no longer drink diet cola turn to coffee, some effort should be made to measure the carcinogenic effect of caffeine and compare it with that of saccharin.[78] Thus, an effort to consider health benefits will involve the very difficulties that plague the determination of health risks, but multiplied across all possible risky alternatives to the banned substance.

Finally, many health benefits are intangible or difficult to measure. Consider, for example, the connection among increased physical vitality of the population, better eating habits, lower-cost food, and animal drugs that lower farming costs (while perhaps leaving small-risk residues in the food). How are these potential health benefits to be estimated?[79]

The problem is illustrated by the NAS effort to measure the potential benefits of saccharin. To determine whether a partial ban on saccharin would increase the risk of death, the panel must consider the potential effects of a ban on weight control. To do this it must determine several things. (1) To what extent is being overweight itself a cause of death because of increased risk of heart attack, strokes, or other diseases? There is some scientific evidence about the relation between weight and disease, which could be used to determine at what point increased weight is as risky as saccharin. (2) If saccharin users substitute sugar for saccharin, how much weight are they likely to gain? Evidence is sketchy or unavailable on this point. No one is sure whether those who eat more sugar will eat less starch, thereby keeping their weight constant. (3) To what extent would a saccharin ban lead users to switch to sugar or switch from diet cola to coffee or tea? There is virtually no evidence available here.

The panel believed that the second and third of these questions could not be answered without considering nonscientific, impressionistic, or anecdotal evidence. They concluded that it did not have sufficient scientific evidence available to answer them, and so it did not try to do so.[80] A regulator, however, would have to make some rough judgment about these answers before imposing a ban. To fail to do so can lead to tragic results. Those who promulgated regulatory rules designed to make children's sleepwear less flammable did not consider that the manufacturing process for doing so involved the use of TRIS, a flame-retardant chemical that turned out to be seriously carcinogenic.[81]

Calculating nonhealth benefits may be slightly easier. Many such benefits are reflected in the amount of money users would pay for the product. The extra value of the product to each purchaser, for example, is reflected in the extra amount he would pay for it rather than make do with its closest substitute. Obviously, it is difficult to estimate these amounts—particularly for a new product not yet marketed, as well as for an existing product that some users may value at much more than its present price. The problems of valuation are roughly comparable to those facing rate regulators who seek to measure demand elasticity. The practice of cost/benefit analysis, however, was developed in the context of evaluating government dams and irrigation projects,[82] and its practitioners developed methods of placing rough values on benefits for which there might be a market, such as "irrigation, navigation, flood control and municipal and industrial water supplies."[83] Thus, market information can help place a rough value on the benefits of items designed to be sold. These techniques do not work well—even for measuring economic benefits—when the benefits are diffused in many different markets and involve fundamental changes in technology. The benefits of nuclear power plants are unusually difficult to measure, given the changes they would require in numerous supplying and customer markets, and the irreversible quality of those changes (preventing retreat from nuclear technology).[84] The fact that there is little available market information to help evaluate many of these benefits—such as the elimination of the harmful environmental impact of alternatives to nuclear power, such as coal—makes the estimate all the more difficult. Yet unless such an estimate is made, a regulator might ban a nuclear plant while ending up with environmentally harmful (and possibly unsafe) coal plants instead.[85]

A second and still more difficult problem for the regulator is making various sorts of risks and benefits commensurable so that some sort of global estimate of each can be reached, allowing them to be weighed against one another. Economists' tendency is to reduce each to dollar equivalents, because "monetization is virtually the only way to arrive at common, comparable terms for summation of various kinds of benefits and summation of various kinds of costs."[86] Yet monetization as an effort to fund commensurability faces intractable difficulties.

One cannot easily make benefits (or risks) commensurable when they are distributed differently among groups of people. Suppose that a food additive that benefits many people places one small group of the population at risk. Many economists tend to favor actions that yield a *net* increase in benefits—the gainers might compensate the losers and have added benefits to spare.[87] Even if the compensation is never actually carried out, proponents would argue that economic transactions produce vast numbers of these changes, with benefits and burdens spread randomly throughout the economy; losers in some instances will be gainers in others. Moreover, the entire economic system provides significant benefit to all in the form of increased productivity, innovation, and efficiency.[88] One might accept all these arguments and still hesitate to allow decisions that impose serious risks to health on one group while helping another or that involve benefits (or risks) that are very large in amount and very badly distributed, when the compensating transaction is never actually made.

This problem is particularly severe when the risks and benefits are distributed unevenly across time. When private persons or governments make economic decisions affecting the future, they discount those effects. This discount is often reasonable, as long as those wishing to use money now (and the resources it represents) will pay others for its use. One could always invest a small amount of money now which would grow to compensate for a larger harm that occurs in the future. Similarly, as long as people have to be paid to defer enjoying a present benefit, a future benefit is less valuable than a present one. A discount rate, however, when applied to future costs and benefits, soon reduces their size so greatly that the effect of a present action on future generations becomes irrelevant in any cost/benefit analysis. (A dollar's worth of harm, for example, one hundred years from now, if discounted at only 3 percent is equal to 6 cents today.) Leaving future generations out of account when considering an action that may harm them is sometimes justified on the ground that they are also left out when we consider actions that may benefit them. We may leave them with a dirtier environment, but we will also leave them with a large stock of capital equipment. Nonetheless, as one considers actions that may have serious, irreversibly harmful effects upon future generations, the justification for doing so (without actual compensation) becomes more questionable.[89]

Aside from the distributional problems that traditionally have plagued cost/benefit analysis,[90] the regulator must consider how to weigh risks to human life against economic or nonhealth benefits. It is sometimes argued that such a weighing is improper—that no amount of money is too great to save a human life.[91] This argument seems less convincing, however, as soon as one considers risks to life, instead of certainty of death, and when large amounts of money become involved. Though ethical principles may require rendering vast sums to save an identified individual facing death—a trapped coal miner or astronaut—those principles do not dictate expenditures of 10 percent of the gross national product to fence in the Grand Canyon or to wrap all machines in soft plastic.[92] Indeed, to spend huge amounts of money to lower statistical risk and thereby save a single human life (say, by putting foam rubber under the Empire State Building) would waste lives, for the same money would buy far more safety when spent elsewhere.

How, then, should dollars be weighed against lives? Some have tried to measure the value of a life as the discounted value of the earnings forgone. Yet such an approach makes the value of the individual depend upon how well he is paid.[93] The life of the housewife would be worth less than that of the salesman; the movie star's life far more than that of the serious novelist; the unemployed man would appear better off dead. Nowhere would this measure take into account the individual's worth to himself, to his family, or to his friends.

On the other hand, to value a life on the basis of what a person would pay to save it or would accept to forgo it is equally unworkable; he may be willing to pay all his assets to save his life and there may well be no monetary price high enough to make him give it up.[94]

A more successful approach focuses upon what agencies actually seek when they screen out substances: the lowering of statistical risk of sickness, injury, or death. It asks not what a person would pay to save his life, but rather what he would pay to lower the risk of sickness or death.[95] Still, how is one to measure this willingness to pay? Some have looked to comparative wage rates for a rough indication. The fact that they are higher in riskier jobs suggests roughly what extra compensation employers must pay to lead workers to accept added risk.[96] Yet differences in wage rates may reflect degrees of unionization or other job differences that make extrapolation to other circumstances difficult.[97] Others have looked at the time that people spend lowering risk by, for example, fastening auto seat belts; they have valued the time and thus estimated the value of lower risk.[98] This approach, too, obviously gives only the roughest idea of the value of lowered risk.[99]

The problem of valuing lowered risk is intensified by the fact that individuals do not know how to react to changes in very small risk.[100] Moreover, an individual's reaction—and society's view of a proper response—to a particular degree of risk varies with the individual, the type of risk, and the substance at issue. Regardless of countervailing benefits, people are less concerned with risks that they voluntarily assume than with those forced upon them, and they may be more concerned with food purity than with safety in the workplace. Some of the factors that affect the value of a particular degree of lowered risk are shown in Table 2.[101]

Table 2. Some countervailing factors affecting individual assumption of risk.

Factor	Countervailing factor
Risk assumed voluntarily	Risk borne involuntarily
Effect immediate	Effect delayed
No alternative available	Many alternatives available
Risk known with certainty	Risk not known
Exposure is an essential	Exposure is a luxury
Encountered occupationally	Encountered nonoccupationally
Common hazard	Dread hazard
Affects average people	Affects especially sensitive people
Will be used as intended	Likely to be misused
Consequences reversible	Consequences irreversible

Source: W. Lorence, *Of Acceptable Risk* (1976).

One way to avoid the difficulties of reducing risk and benefits to a dollar value is for the regulator to resort to a subjective weighing of the relevant factors. First, the regulator compiles several lists containing different varieties of risks and benefits. He then arranges the risk and benefits under alternative courses of action available to him. Finally, he chooses the best action on the basis of his subjective valuation and weighing of each alternative.

The virtue of this approach is that it makes explicit the subjectivity and uncertainty involved in efforts to monetize and to compare incommensurable elements. Its major vice is that it explicitly grants nearly uncheckable discretion to the regulator. The problems are similar to those discussed in the allocation of broadcast licenses or airline routes in Chapter 4. As one participant in this type of process complained: "How [the agency] . . . reached its decision I have no idea. On what basis it compared micro- and macro-economic benefits with health risks I do not know. And . . . added to the disappointment that naturally follows from losing a case was the dissatisfaction that comes from losing for reasons that are not (and, indeed, could not be) fully explained."[102]

Yet the alternatives are often still less desirable. Using essentially arbitrary formulas to place dollar values on the relevant elements may prevent the regulator from using common sense. Refusing to consider benefits at all may lead to equally bad results, such as health or safety rules that end up killing more people than they save. In fact, the regulator's plea that he does not know how to weigh incommensurable risks and benefits is not a claim that they should not count; he must make a decision that inevitably implies some trade-off among them. Rather, his is a plea not to be made accountable; he wishes to avoid responsibility for the trade-off. To heed his plea is to leave the weighing to the arbitrary workings of an anonymous process—an undesirable result.

A third problem is the difficulty of devising a practical hearing procedure. The general counsel of the Food and Drug Administration has described the hearing procedure followed by the EPA in deciding whether to ban two pesticides (heptachlor and chlordane) as follows. The agency considered a wide range of risks and benefits, including *risks* "to workers who handled the pesticides," to those living nearby and subjected to the runoffs in streams, to the general population "from ingestion, inhalation, and absorption," and to animals. It considered the economic *benefits* to farmers, processors, distributors, localities, regions, and the nation as a whole.[103] The procedure—a suspension hearing—was expedited and preliminary.

Everyone understood that the hearing did not address any of the issues fully. Nevertheless, the hearing took 40 trial days of live testimony— even though all the direct testimony was submitted in writing. The record ran to many thousands of pages . . . The briefs ran to hundreds of pages. The lawyers' fees were appropriately large. And all of this was merely preliminary. It was estimated that the full withdrawal proceeding would be far more massive and expensive, and would take a couple of years to complete . . . After all that effort the decision on withdrawal, like the decision on suspension, would turn on imponderable trade-offs.[104]

There is no easy answer to the question of how benefits are to be measured, proved, and weighed against risks. Sometimes administrators argue that congressional statutes forbid or should forbid them to take benefits into account at all. Yet most such statutes—food additive statutes, for example—speak in terms of "safety." To determine whether a risk of a certain degree is safe requires some consideration of the circumstances, the alternatives, and the benefits at stake. Where Congress has enacted language, as in the Delaney Amendment, that rules out all considerations other than risk of cancer, regulation may produce absurd results. The Delaney Amendment may forbid the addition of even one molecule of a substance to food if any dose of that substance (even a very high one) leads any test animal to develop cancer. Thus, because a few molecules of packaging material can migrate into packaged food, it may ban a plastic drink bottle that arguably would kill *almost* no one by inducing cancer and would lead producers to switch to glass bottles which can injure thousands.[105]

Other times regulators seek to limit the types of benefits that will be considered. In evaluating drug safety, for example, the agency looks at therapeutic risks and benefits to a particular patient population. A drug that poisons may be considered safe for treatment of cancer. To limit benefit consideration to health benefits, however, does not necessarily ease the agencies' task. Health benefits are sometimes fairly difficult to measure, as when one seeks to measure the risks of alternatives, whereas economic benefits are sometimes easy to measure, as when there is a well-developed market for the product.[106] Moreover, it may be extremely difficult to make health risks commensurable, as when different groups, time periods, and types of activities are affected. Health risks can be made commensurable with economic benefits only where well-developed markets for risk are involved.

The agency is left with the task of fashioning evidentiary rules governing burdens of proof, determining what type of benefits it will consider, what evidence is relevant, and when evidence becomes cumulative. This task is similar to that engaged in by courts in antitrust cases to make those cases manageable.[107] The task is difficult; sometimes it works moderately well, but it is normally time-consuming and unwieldy.

Varying Standards of Selection

When systems of individualized screening have been introduced, a double standard is typically applied. New items are subjected to more rigorous standards than those already on the market. In trying to develop tests that will screen out incompetent lawyers or doctors currently practicing, it is more difficult to remove those who have already practiced than to refuse admission to those applying. Similarly, in the case of drugs or food additives, the agency can solve many administrative problems by imposing a heavy burden of proof upon those who would introduce a new product. The new food additive manufacturer is required to submit his product to rigorous double-blind testings. The new drug manufacturer must submit his product to a rigorous series of tests and experiments for both safety and effectiveness.[108] Through strict burden-of-proof requirements the agency can approach near-perfect safety, though it may vastly reduce the number of new entities introduced (and may risk depriving consumers of valuable new products in the process). The agency rarely applies such strict requirements to drugs or additives already on the market. When the NAS advisory committees scrutinized existing drugs for effectiveness, they allowed many to remain despite the absence of double-blind tests.[109] When the FASEB panels reviewed food additives, many were allowed to remain despite the absence of testing as thorough as that which the FDA required of new additives.

To treat existing and new items differently may be rational, for many products not yet on the market may be less safe than a marketed product in one important sense: in the absence of the marketed product, consumers will switch in an undetermined way to alternatives, many of which are risky;[110] in the absence of the new product, they will continue with the products they are using. Thus, to remove a marketed product involves the creation of new risks that refusal to admit a new product does not. Of course, precisely the converse claim can be made of the unknown benefits that a new product might bring. Yet insofar as individuals or agencies are risk-averse, or insofar as they act on the maxim "First, cause no harm," the fear of added risk is more powerful.

There are other reasons that may make an agency reluctant to apply its new-product standards to existing products. The removal of existing products directly injures those who have relied upon them—those who use or make them. These people will recognize their injury, defending the legitimacy of their claim and organizing to protect it. In this case the agency may fear stronger legal or political opposition than it would when seeking to keep out a new substance, upon which there has been no reliance and whose potential beneficiaries may not recognize or do not feel their potential loss.

The result—particularly if the agency's statutory mandate does not explicitly provide for different treatment—is that much will depend upon which marketed substances are selected for testings and how the selection is made. In the case of the 63,000 chemicals in common use, the National Cancer Institute delegated to a working subcommittee the job of selecting the 100 or so that it had funds to test each year. This working group tried to identify those that were potentially most risky. Selection was influenced by a second panel of consumer, labor, and academic representatives, who argued for selection on the basis of the extent to which use was widespread. The final selections were the result of compromises among the different interest groups represented.[111]

Moreover, when substances in widespread use are subjected to strict testing requirements, a political reaction can lead Congress to pass special legislation to deal with a substance, like saccharin, on an individual basis. Yet Congress cannot readily screen thousands of individual substances.[112] At the same time, the agency will remain reluctant to relax its standards for new products; to do so would deprive it of the administrative advantages of burden-of-proof rules that shift the testing burden to manufacturers. At the same time, imposing those same burdens on manufacturers of saccharin, vitamins, aspirin, phenobarbital, and other chemicals is unrealistic. The agency is likely to retain an unofficial double standard, accepting the criticism of irrationality that will arise from time to time.[113]

Conclusion

Many of the problems of individualized screening grow out of the fact that neither science nor professional training nor common sense is likely to provide administrable, accurate tests for the regulator to use. The inability of scientists to develop such tests is not so surprising, once one understands that science and scientists seek to develop *general* laws—laws that hold, *other things being equal*. Indeed, the work of the scientist is judged in part according to his ability to deal fruitfully and precisely with a few variables, holding others constant. What the regulator must know, on the other hand, is how *specific* substances will perform in the real world, where *other things are not equal and where nothing is constant*. Those whose work is judged by its ability to take all into account and who recommend policy judgments based on likely effects in the world—administrators, lawyers, politicians—do not have the skills to devise the precise scientific tests needed to screen accurately.

As the regulator becomes ever more interested in fine-tuning the screening process (and as he seeks to uncover ever smaller risks), he faces serious problems in measuring risk and assessing benefits. He cannot rely fully upon expert committees to substitute their judgment for his. He is likely to make scientifically irrational distinctions between, say, old and new substances. The upshot has been a variety of suggestions to use less restrictive devices. For example, clear disclosure in the form of labeling may be preferable to banning a substance where the risks are not serious or where benefits are potentially great.[114] This, along with increased reliance upon burden-of-proof rules, can help produce more rational and administrable processes. But one can determine the comparative advantages of major alternatives to classical regulation only after considering the advantages and defects of these alternatives.

8
Alternatives to Classical Regulation

We have thus far considered six classical modes of regulation, focusing systematically upon typical problems that arise as each is applied. At this point, it may seem that classical regulation is simply undesirable and should be abandoned. To think that, however, would be to forget that regulation is often instituted to deal with genuine problems of an unregulated marketplace. It cannot be abandoned without a close consideration of the alternatives.

These alternatives will sometimes prove appropriate *substitutes* for classical regulation; sometimes they will prove useful *supplements* to regulation as applied in particular areas, allowing relaxation of some of its strictures. The description given here is not sufficiently detailed to enable readers to develop a definitive gauge as to when an alternative regime is desirable. Yet it will help readers remain aware of the types of alternatives available as they seek to evaluate the usefulness of classical regulation in a particular instance. The first alternative—antitrust—typically accompanies the *absence* of regulation. The next five alternatives—disclosure, taxes, marketable rights, disability rules, and bargaining—may be thought of as generally less restrictive ways of achieving regulation's ends. The final alternative regime—nationalization—usually involves a larger governmental presence than does regulation.

Unregulated Markets Policed by Antitrust

In deciding whether to regulate, one should compare the likely defects of the unregulated market with the potential effectiveness (and the likely defects) of classical regulation. But in doing so, one should recognize that unregulated markets are subject to the antitrust laws—a form of governmental intervention designed to maintain a workably competitive marketplace.

Although some critics claim that antitrust is another form of governmental regulation,[1] in principle the antitrust laws differ from classical regulation both in their aims and in their methods. The antitrust laws seek to create or maintain the *conditions* of a competitive marketplace rather than replicate the *results* of competition or correct for the defects of competitive markets. In doing so, they act negatively, through a few highly general provisions *prohibiting* certain forms of private conduct. They do not affirmatively order firms to behave in specified ways; for the most part, they tell private firms what not to do. They are enforced through adjudicatory proceedings in court (or before the Federal Trade Commission). Only rarely do the antitrust enforcement agencies create the detailed web of affirmative legal obligations that characterizes classical regulation.[2] When critics contrast regulated with unregulated marketplaces, they typically think of "workably competitive" markets—markets that are free of private restraint as well as of governmental regulation. If so, they are considering markets policed by antitrust. For these reasons, antitrust is more accurately contrasted with, rather than viewed as another form of, governmental regulation.

The antitrust laws. Although antitrust laws are extremely complex in their application, their essence and objectives can be described very simply. Essentially, the antitrust laws' broadly phrased prohibitions forbid agreements "in restraint of trade,"[3] "attempts to monopolize,"[4] "monopolization,"[5] and mergers that may "lessen competition substantially."[6] The first two prohibitions police anticompetitive market *conduct*—agreements among firms or actions of individual firms that may prevent or inhibit competition in a particular market. The third and fourth prohibitions are aimed at anticompetitive market *structures,* in which one firm or a handful of firms, instead of many competing firms, supply an industry's entire output. The law against monopolization allows the courts to restore competition where there is an existing monopoly— say, by breaking apart a firm with monopoly power into several smaller competing firms, thereby restoring competition. The merger law seeks to prevent a presently competitive marketplace from becoming uncompetitive in the future through mergers that reduce the number of competitors and increase concentration within the marketplace.

The basic principle used in applying these prohibitions is the "rule of reason."[7] Essentially, the courts have realized that some agreements or conduct that injure competition or restrain trade may also be commercially necessary or desirable. A partnership agreement restrains trade between the partners but allows them to compete more effectively against others. Similarly, a firm may obtain a monopoly by selling a better product. Should it be discouraged from doing so? Mergers that increase concentration may also allow firms to produce more efficiently. The "rule of reason" allows the courts to weigh the anticompetitive harms of the practice under attack against the procompetitive justifications, condemning the practice only if, on balance, it produces significant injury.

When the rule of reason is applied to agreements, for example, the courts ask several questions. First, does the agreement tend to limit competition, and in what respects? Second, does the agreement nonetheless achieve certain legitimate commercial objectives? Third, is the agreement needed to achieve those objectives or is there a less restrictive way of doing so? Suppose a court is considering an agreement among bread manufacturers not to sell bread more than one day old. The answer to the first question is yes, for the agreement limits the ability of potential buyers and sellers of day-old bread to strike a bargain. The answer to the second question may also be yes, for the agreement helps prevent consumers from being deceived by receiving old bread instead of fresh bread. But the answer to the third question is no, for a date stamped on the label prevents consumer deception, and in a less restrictive manner. Thus, the agreement is unlawful, for it is unreasonable.

The basic principle embodied in the rule of reason is not always applied as directly in other areas of the antitrust law as it is in the above example, but its influence is nonetheless continuously felt. Certain sorts of agreements, such as price fixing, market division, boycotts, and tying arrangements, are usually considered unlawful "per se"—the court will condemn them without examining their justifications. Yet, these per se categories have been developed for administrative reasons and their boundaries have been drawn so as to include just those agreements with a high potential for harm and low probability of countervailing justification. The occasional justified agreement is sacrificed to the need for clear lines and simplified court proceedings. Similarly, the courts do not weigh the "good" versus the "bad" characteristics of individual monopolies. Yet a series of exceptions has developed for patent monopolies, natural monopolies, and monopolies based on skill, foresight, and industry. The exceptions reflect the reasonableness of allowing monopolies in certain circumstances, particularly those in which monopoly is needed to achieve efficiency—one of the major objectives of the competitive process. In the case of mergers, courts and enforcement agencies have struggled to draw lines that separate beneficial mergers (those likely to improve efficiency) from harmful mergers (those likely to produce increased concentration without corresponding benefits). They have developed rather strict rules against "horizontal" mergers (between direct competitors), less restrictive rules against "vertical" mergers (between customer and supplier), and still more liberal rules governing conglomerate mergers (all others).[8]

In sum, the antitrust laws rest upon the assumption that a workably competitive marketplace will achieve a more efficient allocation of resources, greater efficiency in production, and increased innovation. They seek to achieve these ends by removing private impediments to workable competition. Where this assumption holds true, antitrust would ordinarily seem the appropriate form for government intervention to take. Where the assumption fails, one finds the demand for other modes of governmental intervention, such as classical regulation. Viewed in this way, regulation is an alternative to antitrust, necessary when antitrust cannot successfully maintain a workably competitive marketplace or when such a marketplace is inadequate due to some other serious defect.[9]

Antitrust and regulation. Few of the market defects discussed in Chapter 1 are properly described as defects in the competitive process or in terms of noncompetitive market structure. For example, well-functioning competitive markets, subject to changing economic conditions, can generate rents. Or they can suffer from the existence of spillover costs. Problems of inadequate information or moral hazard may also coexist with a workably competitive market structure. Antitrust is not ordinarily an effective weapon for dealing with these problems. Nor is it an effective way to control the market power of a natural monopolist. If the antitrust laws were used to create, say, several firms where one natural monopoly now exists, each new smaller firm would have higher unit costs than the older, larger firm and the price of the product would rise. Moreover, any such market structure would be unstable, for a small marketing advantage by one firm would give that firm a cost advantage, allowing it to lower its prices and attract more customers until the natural monopoly was reestablished. There is no stable, competitive market structure in such an industry. Application of the antitrust laws cannot create one. Similarly, antitrust cannot deal with rationalization problems, where firms are too small, not too large. Finally, unequal bargaining power has necessitated exemptions from the antitrust laws—to allow laborers, fishermen, or farmers to agree and to bargain jointly when they sell to large buyers.

Antitrust is more likely to prove an effective substitute for regulation when the market defect is the risk of predatory pricing. Predatory pricing is a typical example of anticompetitive market behavior. As such, the antitrust laws prohibit it. To determine when a price below cost is predatory, the court must look at its anticompetitive tendencies and its procompetitive justification. Thus, a predatory price is not just a price that injures competition—any low price will do that. Rather, it is a price set so low that the firm loses money in the short run, while it drives its competitors out of business. Then the firm raises its prices to recoup its losses and more, before new firms, attracted by the high prices, enter the industry. Such a price brings the consumer no benefit and injures the competitive process.

The major problem facing antitrust enforcement is to determine precisely when a low price is unreasonably low and therefore predatory. What test of predatory pricing should be used? For the most part, the debate concerns a firm's average costs and its incremental costs. Can a price that exceeds average cost ever be predatory? Some believe so. They argue that a firm such as IBM might forgo an opportunity to make 20 percent profit on line A, and instead produce more of line B, on which it lowers price and earns only 10 percent profit. There is no good reason why IBM would do this, unless it hoped that the lower price would drive its competitors from the market so that it could then raise prices and earn still higher profits. Others reply that a price above average cost should never be considered predatory. Though price cutting always injures competitors, it is also an essential part of the competitive process. It is the object of the antitrust laws to encourage just such price cutting. It is too difficult to determine the precise intent of a firm that cuts prices to a level where it still earns profits. If disgruntled competitors can sue and collect damages when a firm cuts its prices to a level where it is still earning profits, there will be too many such suits, and price competition will be unduly inhibited.

Should prices below average costs but above incremental costs be considered predatory? Since sales are profitable for a firm as long as the revenues they generate exceed their incremental costs, the arguments are the same as those given above.

Prices below incremental costs are ordinarily considered predatory, for they *must* be unprofitable. The firm *must* be losing money on each sale and it *must* intend to raise prices (or lower costs) at a later date. Discouragement of such pricing seems desirable. Yet even here one can ask whether firms should not be allowed to price below incremental costs temporarily when, say, they are promoting a new product or they expect costs to fall.[10]

Though courts and scholars have differed about the proper way to determine when a price is predatory, the issues are the same whether a court or an agency is determining the matter. The CAB and ICC are no better able to determine when a price is predatory than are the Federal Trade Commission and the courts. The issues just described do not suggest a need for regulation. The fact that antitrust courts and agencies can as easily deal with the issue of predatory pricing as other regulatory agencies suggests that the threat of predatory pricing is not a market failure, calling for regulation. Rather, it is an instance of private anticompetitive behavior with which the antitrust laws are designed to deal.

In the area of monopoly and oligopoly some might argue that there should be more regulation and less antitrust. Although the antitrust laws are reasonably effective in dealing with anticompetitive conduct and in preventing mergers, they are less effective in correcting anticompetitive market structures—monopolies and oligopolies. Monopoly cases, for example, typically take years to resolve.[11] The parties argue whether the defendant in fact possesses monopoly power and whether he has achieved that power through illegitimate exclusionary conduct. Enormous amounts of documentary and economic evidence are produced, and the cases remain in the courts for a decade or more.[12] Moreover, the law condemns only monopolies that rest upon exclusionary conduct. It is feared that to condemn all (nonnatural) monopolies might discourage firms from competing, because the winner of the competitive game would then lose the prize.[13] Thus, the "honest" monopolist may continue to exert economic power in the marketplace. Finally, and most important, the law does not attack existing oligopolies—industries in which a handful of firms dominate the market, and which together may exert as much power as a monopolist. Yet if the law were interpreted to attack oligopolists, it might severely interfere with the incentive of firms to outcompete each other, or it would risk being ineffective. For these reasons, it has occasionally been proposed to regulate the prices of ordinary monopolies and oligopolies.[14] Although the choice—regulation or antitrust—in the area is a close one, the problems of regulation have been thought sufficiently great to warrant reliance upon antitrust instead.

Finally, to some extent antitrust and regulation converge. Courts considering antitrust and regulatory matters must deal with such questions as: To what extent should ordinary principles of merger law apply to mergers in the regulated trucking or airline industries? To what extent should such industries be exempt from the scope of the antitrust laws? To what extent should antitrust principles apply to competitively structured portions of industries that are in part naturally monopolized? Should, for example, one portion of the telephone communications industry be regulated as a natural monopoly, while other portions are fully competitive and subject to antitrust?

These questions are highly complex and require detailed analysis in individual cases. The courts have tended to interpret narrowly those statutes that restrict the application of the antitrust laws.[15] Thus, the courts apply those laws to regulated industries unless Congress specifically exempts the industries or unless such an exemption *must* be implied to make the regulatory scheme work. The fact that one portion of an industry is regulated, however, can in certain circumstances make it extremely difficult to determine the extent to which competition is appropriate in other related portions. This issue will be explored in Chapter 15. Here, one should only conclude that antitrust itself is not a direct substitute for regulation, with one exception: it can deal with predatory pricing and thereby undercuts the excessive competition rationale. Rather, it is the unregulated market which is often the alternative to regulation. The function of antitrust is to make that unregulated market a competitive one.

Disclosure

Regulation that requires disclosure of certain information is so common today that it may be regarded as another form of classical regulation. It is presented here as an alternative regime, however, because it does not regulate production processes, output, price, or allocation of products. Nor does it restrict individual choice as much as do the other classical forms of regulation. Moreover, since freely functioning markets require adequate information— which disclosure helps provide—disclosure, like antitrust, can be viewed as augmenting the preconditions of a competitive marketplace rather than substituting regulation for competition.

Not all disclosure is designed to make competitive markets function more effectively. Sometimes its object is to outlaw particular conduct by bringing legal or moral pressure to bear upon those engaging in it. Thus, federal ''gambler registration'' measures helped enforce state gambling laws.[16] The Bank Secrecy Act, requiring the disclosure of large currency transactions, helps investigators uncover violations of tax and narcotics laws.[17] And the Home Mortgage Disclosure Act, requiring disclosure of the geographic sources of a bank's deposits and geographic distribution of its loans, is designed to discourage banks from refusing to lend to particular neighborhoods or communities.[18]

Disclosure also, by itself, can change the underlying substantive law. The Federal Trade Commission requires that sellers print on any credit contract a legend stating that the buyer can exercise against a third party (buying the contract) whatever claims or defense the buyer has against the original seller. The FTC's object is not to disclose information, but rather to defeat the "holder in due course" rule, which allowed sellers to transfer credit contracts to others (say, banks) which would then collect the debt free of the debtor's claim that the merchandise was defective.[19] Similarly, the Uniform Commercial Code, in providing for the public notification of liens, creates a system that determines priorities of creditors in bankruptcy.[20] Its object is to affect the underlying substantive law, not simply to improve the information flow among buyers and sellers.

When used for economic purposes, however, disclosure typically aims to help buyers and sellers make more informed choices. The federal securities laws, for example, require sellers of securities to publish prospectuses providing potential investors with vast amounts of information.[21] Labeling acts require manufacturers to tell buyers what substances are contained in packaged foods and drugs, and their likely effects.[22] Truth-in-lending statutes require explanations about the true rate of interest.[23] All are designed to facilitate comparison by purchasers and to prevent the purchasing of unwanted products. When the regulator enforces these statutes, he typically must set standards defining what precisely is to be disclosed, where, and how. He must decide how those standards will be enforced. In setting standards, he must deal with those very problems of information sources, enforcement, anticompetitive effects, and judicial review that plague other forms of standard setting.

Consider, for example, the problems faced by NHTSA in deciding what combination of stopping distance, treadwear, and blowout resistance characteristics for auto tires would be disclosed.[24] The agency had great difficulty gathering the information needed to develop a meaningful rating system. Developing a fair testing system for enforcement purposes was difficult. The rating system, some feared, would unfairly favor certain firms over others, and preparing the necessary support to survive judicial review was time-consuming. The whole process took eight years.[25]

In other instances, the major problems feared by regulators will be those that characterize the process of individualized screening. It may be difficult to determine precisely which characteristics of a drug should be described upon the bottle's label. Or it may be uncertain whether a prospectus adequately describes the risks that an investor will encounter—a matter that can be determined only after lengthy staff investigation.

Despite the similarity of problems faced by the regulator implementing disclosure and these other forms of classical regulation, there remains one important difference. Ordinary standards governing primary conduct ofttimes forbid or dictate the type of product that must be sold or the process that must be used. As such, they interfere with consumer choice and impede producer flexibility. To the extent that those standards deviate from the policy planner's ideal (as they inevitably do), the restrictions on choice and conduct are clearly undesirable. Standards governing disclosure, however, do not restrict conduct beyond requiring that certain information be provided. The freedom of action that disclosure allows vastly reduces the cost of deviations from the policy planner's ideal. At worst, too much information or the wrong information has been called for. It does not stop buyers from obtaining products or producers from making them. Federal Securities laws, in principle, allow any security to be sold, provided that it is described accurately. State blue-sky laws, in contrast, prohibit the sale of very risky securities, thus preventing willing buyers and sellers of such securities from getting together.[26]

For these reasons, disclosure regulation does not require regulators to fine-tune standards as precisely. The regulators need less information from industry, there are fewer enforcement problems, there is less risk of anticompetitive harm, and there is greater probability of surviving judicial review. Although NHTSA faced many problems in trying to set tire disclosure standards, its problems would have been still worse had it sought to set ordinary standards governing the types of tires that could or could not be manufactured. Similarly, those who work in the securities industries seem to feel that the SEC's efforts to police stock fraud by administering disclosure standards are more successful and more efficient than state efforts to do so through blue-sky laws, which often set substantive standards.[27]

Despite this major advantage, disclosure will not work unless the information is transmitted to the buyer in a simple and meaningful way. Efforts to regulate drugs and food additives often lead to bitter arguments about the risks disclosed on the label. Those who favor warnings argue in favor of consumer choice and claim that warnings are adequate to overcome the informational defects in the marketplace that produced a demand for regulation. Those who favor banning a substance often argue that there is no way to convey a meaningful warning. Consumers do not know how to react to a label that says "Saccharin may cause cancer." Many will feel that if saccharin were truly dangerous the government would ban it, and they will ignore the warning. Others may refuse to touch anything that bears such a label. In neither case is the choice based upon a meaningful assessment of risk. Yet a label that said "One bottle of saccharin increases risk of bladder cancer in males by one in six thousand" would be no more helpful. Few persons would read it. Fewer would understand it. Hardly anyone would know how to use this information to make a meaningful choice. Suggestions to overcome this problem include developing a sign or mark to be placed upon every food with slight cancer risk along with an informational campaign that would warn people not to eat too much of several such foods. Whether this program would prove practical is unknown.

Yet it illustrates the difficulty of communicating through disclosure in many instances.

A second weakness of disclosure regulation arises when the information disclosed has little practical effect on choice. Often proponents of such regulation feel that certain particular items of information ought to be important to buyers but in fact they are not. Truth-in-lending legislation[28] provides a practical example. The legislation requires anyone providing consumer credit to disclose the true annual rate of interest. The legislation has led to many lawsuits, perhaps because it provides automatic penalties paid to plaintiffs, plus attorney's fees, when violations are shown. Yet there is little indication that it has changed consumer behavior. Financing schemes for consumer purchases with very high annual interest rates are still common, perhaps because the availability of short-term credit for small purchases is important to consumers but the precise interest rate is not. Similarly, the vast amount of information contained in securities prospectuses has been characterized as useless for the small investor. He is unlikely to wade through the material or to use it in making investment decisions.

Thus, disclosure is likely to be effective only where the public can understand the information disclosed, where it is free to choose on the basis of that information, and where it believes the information is materially relevant to the choice. Where these conditions exist, disclosure standards offer a less restrictive means to obtain a regulatory end than do standards governing primary conduct or outright banning of a substance.

Taxes

Taxation ordinarily seeks to raise revenue or to encourage conduct through special deductions or credits.[29] So far, taxes have only rarely been used specifically to substitute for regulation. Taxation should be considered where regulation is intended to transfer income, such as when cost-of-service ratemaking is used to control rents or windfall profits earned by those who control scarce, low-cost sources of oil, natural gas, or housing. Moreover, taxes might deter socially undesirable conduct, such as pollution. Taxation might thereby supplement, or substitute for, classical standard setting.

In the income-transfer area, taxes avoid the major defects of cost-of-service ratemaking. They bring about prices that equate demand with supply and thus avoid shortages. As applied to the conduct-guiding area, taxes have several characteristics that may prove advantageous. The very fact that they do not prohibit an activity, or suppress a product totally, means that those with special needs and willingness to pay may obtain it. Taxes thus lessen the risk, present with standard setting, of working serious harm in an unknown special case. Taxes involve the regulator less directly with the firms related, thus mitigating the protectionist instinct present in much classical regulation. And perhaps most important, taxes, unlike classical standards, provide incentive for beneficial technological change and innovation. While standards can set an absolute level of sulfur emissions, for example, they cannot readily provide an incentive to emit still less.

Substituting taxes for classical regulation nonetheless introduces difficult problems. Using an excise tax instead of cost-of-service ratemaking to capture excess profits requires the administrator to specify the bounds of the tax. If the upper bound is based on production costs, these costs must be determined. If the upper bound is the free market price, then the regulator must decide which market price to use. Employing a tax instead of standard setting to control spillovers requires the administrator to determine both the level of the tax and the amount of "taxable conduct."[30]

Regardless of the purpose of the tax, it must be decided how the proceeds will be spent, which committee of Congress will have legislative jurisdiction, and which agency will have administrative jurisdiction over the tax. Moreover, it should be recognized that the congressional committees are used to dealing with macroeconomic issues and may be unfamiliar with the microeconomic objectives at which a regulatory tax is aimed. This will aggravate the problem of making the tax politically acceptable. Despite these difficulties, the problems raised by taxation may be significantly less serious than those of the regulatory system it would replace. The very fact that these problems are different from those accompanying classical regulation suggests that a tax regime must be considered as a possible alternative.

Some of the virtues and vices of a regulatory tax can be shown by considering the regulation of oil prices.[31] Doing so will illustrate the application of taxes to problems of rent control or excess profits. Chapter 14 will consider the application of taxes to a spillover problem—environmental pollution.

Oil price regulation was initiated to control rents and large windfall profits. The regulatory method used was a variation of historically based pricing. Domestic crude production was divided into tiers—old oil and new oil—and a price ceiling ($5.68 and $12.17 respectively in 1978) was set on each. The ceiling was based upon very rough estimates of production costs.

Potential shortages were avoided by use of an ingenious program that distributed entitlements to refine old, cheap oil. The program allocated the cheap oil "fairly" among refiners. Each refiner received the right to process an amount of old oil in proportion to the total amount of oil he refined. The government determined monthly the total amount of oil refined in the United States and the proportion of that oil accounted for by old, cheap crude. Each refiner then received a number of entitlement tickets roughly equal to that proportion of his total throughput. Thus, if 23 percent of all oil refined was old, a refiner with a throughput of 1,000 barrels received 230 tickets. If he refined 2,000 barrels, he received 460 tickets. It was unlawful to refine old oil without an entitlement. A refiner with extra (more than 23 percent) supplies of old oil had to buy entitlements from refiners with extra tickets (those using less than

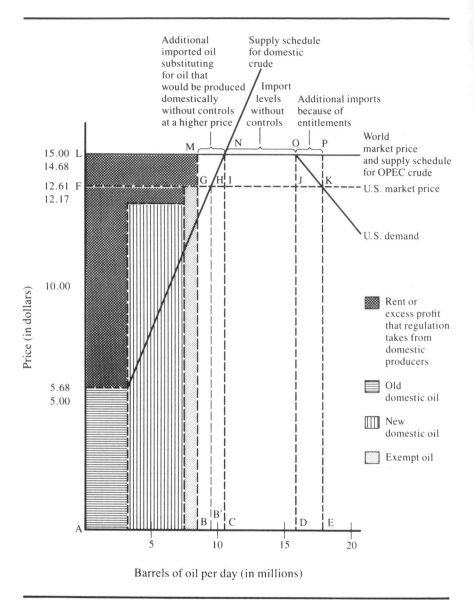

Figure 1. The effects of oil regulation.

Note: This graph shows how oil regulation leads to an increased demand for foreign imports because of its effect both on domestic supply and on domestic demand. Using 1979 prices as illustrative, it assumes a world market price of $14.68, which also represents the supply schedule for imported oil. The supply schedule for domestic crude oil is drawn to show the amounts that (illustratively) would be produced at different prices without domestic controls. Controls, as stated in the text, are assumed to keep the domestic price at $12.61. Producers are allowed to sell old

23 percent old oil). The price paid equaled the difference between the world market price and the old-oil price, or about $9.00 per ticket. Each refiner in effect received the value of having 23 percent of his throughput made up of old, cheap oil, because those with too many tickets sold them to those with too few.

The effect of this system was to lower the cost of imports to the refiner and to lower domestic market prices. The refiner had to pay about $14.50 for a barrel of imported oil. Yet he received 23 percent of an entitlement ticket (worth about $2.25) when he imported an extra barrel. Hence, the barrel actually cost him slightly more than $12.00. He received the $2.25 when he sold the .23 entitlement to a refiner with an extra .23 barrel of old oil. It represented the potential windfall profit available from the sale of that .23 barrel. Thus, part of the windfall profit was used to subsidize the cost of the import. Under this system, oil will continue to be imported to satisfy demand at prices lower than the world market price so long as rents are available to pay the cost. In other words, there will be (and has been) no perceived shortage because the rents are used in part to pay for the import of sufficient foreign crude to satisfy all demand (see Figure 1).

Although oil regulation avoided the shortage problem, no one could say that it was successful. The rents were transferred not only to consumers but also to the sellers. And the lower price encouraged increased importation of oil. The problems of classical regulation were avoided, but at the price of partial failure to achieve the system's major objective: the transfer of windfall profits to the consumer.

In principle, a tax system might accomplish the ends of regulation more directly. It would tax away the producer's excess profit and redistribute it to the consumer. The producer would sell the product to the consumer at a world market price and would pay a tax on sales of older, less costly units, but he would pay no tax on sales of newer, high-cost units.

Such a tax system arguably would overcome two problems that plague classical regulation. First, a system of regulation that sets a tiered price must make

---

domestic oil for $5.68 and new domestic oil for $12.17, and exempt domestic oil sells at the "free" domestic price of $12.61. Without controls, the domestic price of crude would rise to the world price ($14.68) and amount AC would be elicited domestically. With controls, the domestic price is $12.61 and amount AB is elicited. Part of the decline in domestic supply is caused by the lower price (amount B'C) and part is caused by the regulatory rules, which, for reasons described in the text, inevitably lead to some misclassification (amount BB'). The fact that the domestic price for crude as seen by domestic consumers is $12.61 instead of $14.68 also leads to an increase in domestic demand for crude (DE). The increase in demand is satisfied (through the mechanism described in the text) by an increase in imports; the decrease in domestic supply is made up for by another increase in imports. Thus, controls lead to an increase in imports by an amount equal to BC plus DE. Controls also capture a considerable amount of the rent that would otherwise be earned by domestic producers of old domestic, and new domestic, oil. Of course, some of that rent (amounts MNIG and OPKJ) is transferred to OPEC producers through the mechanism described in the text, because of the additional demand for OPEC oil.

certain that the high-tier price is high enough to elicit new supply. The tax system need not be as concerned. Since the price of the high-cost product would not be controlled, the producer would have a strong market incentive to find and to sell it. Second, a regulatory system must determine how to allocate the portion of the product that is subject to the low-tier price. Everyone will want it, but there is too little to go around. The tax system again is less concerned with this problem. Since the customer would have to pay a world price whether he bought old or new units, the market would allocate the product by giving it to whoever would pay the most.[32] Thus, there would be no need for regulatory allocation. Of course, if the tax is based on profits—if it is, in effect, an excess profits tax—the authorities must face the difficult problem of determining what profit is normal and what is excess. But this problem can be mitigated by setting an excise tax at a level equal to the difference between cost and world market price.

The Carter administration chose this approach in its proposal for a wellhead tax on oil. It categorized oil according to cost, set a tax equal to the difference between such cost and the world market price, and allowed the resale price to rise to that level. When a tax system is used to control rents, however, the following problems arise.

Determining the upper bound of the tax. In principle, the upper bound of the tax is the free-market price of the product. Yet that bound must be fixed and determinable for purposes of calculation, while free-market prices fluctuate. Thus the tax authority must both set an initial upper bound and decide when and how to change that bound as market prices fluctuate.

Setting the bound initially is not as easy as the instruction "Look to the free-market price" implies. The price of the new oil or gas is not controlled, and so the administrator can find a free-market price. However, since crude oil and natural gas and oil are not perfectly homogeneous products, the administrator will be faced with several prices. He is then faced with the problem of choosing the appropriate price from which to calculate the tax. In the case of oil, for example, there are several grades of crude. Selling prices differ, depending upon distance from a seaport. Further, crude prices fluctuate according to the time of year, availability of tankers, and so on. The fact that refiners are often integrated with producers creates uncertainty as to whether the market price of crude can be manipulated. In the case of natural gas, free-market prices would also vary, depending upon product quality and location. At best, the upper bound would require categorization (several upper bounds), calculation (of numerous associated costs), and estimation of a final set of rough approximations. These problems may not be overly severe where the taxed product, like crude oil or natural gas, is reasonably homogeneous and its world price is capable of calculation. The problem would be very severe with a nonhomogeneous product, such as housing, where the administrator would have to calculate market prices for thousands or millions of individual units, each of which has some claim to uniqueness. (This administrative difficulty would be comparable to that involved in fairly assessing property taxes.)

The need for flexibility primarily depends upon the likelihood of decline in the free-market price. If market price increases but the tax does not, the producers retain some of the windfall profits that the system sought to capture. If market prices decline, however, producers will be unable to sell existing low-cost stocks unless the tax is reduced. When prices fluctuate seasonally, with local shortages, temporary oversupply, and so on, the administrator must decide whether the fluctuation is temporary or whether it is serious enough to warrant a change in the tax rate. The more the statute confines the administrator's discretion and the more important certainty of the tax level is to the industry, the less likely that the administrator can adjust to fluctuations. And the less the administrator's flexibility, the greater the likelihood that the tax will inhibit the sale of the older, cheaper product.

Determining the lower bound. A tax that would capture all windfalls must equal the difference between the cost of the older, cheaper product and the free-market price (which reflects the cost of the newer, higher-cost product). The administrator must determine the lower bound of the tax by determining the cost of the older product.[33] The only feasible way to do so is to determine categories that correspond roughly to cost and impose a price ceiling upon each. The price ceiling sets the lower bound for purposes of calculating the tax.

This cost-determining process produces the problems inherent in cost-of-service ratemaking. After drawing rough categories, the administrator must determine the approximate costs of producing the oil or natural gas that falls into each. To do so accurately would involve allocating joint costs, setting a fair rate of return on investment, and determining the accuracy of historical cost information submitted by hundreds or thousands of producers. Thus, the wellhead tax proposal takes the only path that is administratively feasible: it creates a few very general categories and imposes judgmentally determined cost figures to determine a lower bound.

The rough nature of the categorization and cost-determining process inevitably will result in some miscategorization, which may discourage further production. As soon as one defines "old oil" or "old gas" for example, one must decide how to categorize new product from old wells and new wells in old fields. Ultimately, the legislature or the administrator will make rough judgmental decisions—such as "Any well drilled within two miles of an existing well produces old oil." Having done so, the administrator will have inevitably included some high-cost oil or gas in his low-cost categories. Oil or gas, for example, that is expensive to produce and is within 2.5 miles of an existing well will never be produced. Efforts to ameliorate this problem through special exceptions can create an extremely complex set of regulations.

These problems do not necessarily make the tax unworkable, provided the product is relatively homogeneous and there are a few likely cost categories. In such cases the consequences of administrative mistakes may be less serious under a tax than under a classical regulatory system. A cost or categorization mistake in the former case results in a failure to capture all rents or in a disincentive to produce a small amount of product. Thus, categories can be drawn roughly. A mistake in the regulatory case—at least in setting the price of new product—may seriously inhibit the production of all new product. Moreover, as previously mentioned, the tax system at least resolves the problem of allocating the older, cheaper product—and this is no small advantage.

Collection and enforcement. The windfall profits tax presents the same collection and enforcement problems presented by other excise taxes. The persons upon whom the tax is assessed are, in the case of oil, the producers, who are most directly aware of the source of the oil, the appropriate tax category, and the amount of the tax. Obviously, the more categories, the more difficult it is to administer the enforcement system. Moreover, the sheer amount involved may create administrative problems. For example, the crude oil tax was to have generated about $15 billion annually in gross collections, while all other excise taxes combined generated less than $20 billion.[34]

Disposing of the proceeds. The object of the tax is to transfer the producers' windfall profits to a "worthier cause." In principle, it is not important whether all consumers or all taxpayers receive the tax revenue or whether it is used to defray governmental expenditures. In practice, its distribution matters a great deal to potential recipients. The very fact that there is, ex ante, no logical set of principles to guide distribution of the proceeds opens the door to political pressure. Oil companies argue that the wellhead tax proceeds should be returned to them as an incentive to search for new oil (though to provide such an incentive, the proceeds would have to be returned in proportion to *new* exploration efforts). Those interested in energy programs argue that the proceeds should be earmarked for such programs. Consumers and taxpayers argue that such revenue should be rebated through the tax system.

A rebate raises problems of practicability and fairness. As a practical matter, a method must be found to rebate the tax to those who do not pay taxes. The social security and welfare administrative apparatuses might be used, and additional rebates can be offered (on application) to those who do not receive them elsewhere. But the small amounts involved will make the administrative apparatus expensive to use for those who do not pay taxes. As a matter of fairness, it is difficult to determine how large a rebate each taxpayer should receive. To allow a rebate in proportion to the amount of the taxed product a taxpayer uses may appear fair, but it would defeat the purpose of the tax, for it is equivalent to lowering the price of the product. Yet to provide each taxpayer with equal payment seems unfair, for why should coal users as well as oil users receive the tax rebate? Any eventual division will appear arbitrary.

Acceptability. Despite its advantages, the public may be reluctant to accept a tax system as a substitute for classical regulation. Its use for this purpose is unfamiliar. In addition, as experience with oil and natural gas demonstrates, the political demand for regulation is in large part due to public dismay at large price increases accompanied by large producer profits. Although the profits may provide the excuse for governmental action, it is the price increase which the public feels directly. A tax does not prevent prices from rising; regulation does (at least initially). Thus, unless the public has been educated through experience (as in the case of natural gas), it may be far more difficult to obtain support for the tax than for regulation, whatever the latter's defects.

Legislative jurisdiction. A shift from reliance upon regulation to reliance upon a tax also means a shift in the congressional committees that have jurisdiction over the issue. The committees now most directly concerned with energy, or pollution, or other substantive areas would lose jurisdiction to the tax committees. The tax committees are likely to be less familiar with the particular area regulated, such as gas or oil, and more interested in the general macroeconomic effects of taxes. Indeed, it may be humanly impossible for the eighteen members of the Senate Finance Committee and the thirty-seven members of the House Ways and Means Committee to become experts in employment, commerce, shipping, the environment, energy, and the other areas in which taxes may be used for substantive policy ends.[35] Thus, they are less likely to be able to work out the legislative fine tuning needed for this type of tax. At the same time, they may be quite sensitive to the political claims of those interested in revenue division—or the claims of those wanting special exemption. The result is increased risk that such a tax will be deflected from its basic aim. Moreover, the congressional committees with jurisdiction over the regulatory system are likely to oppose the use of a tax because of the loss of jurisdictional authority it entails.

The Creation of Marketable Property Rights

In applying taxation to the spillover problem, it is often difficult to determine the proper tax to achieve the desired results. A tax on pollution, for example, will lead some firms to install antipollution equipment, while others will continue to pollute and pay the tax. In principle, it is easy to say that firms will install equipment until its cost at the margin exceeds the tax rate. But in practice a regulator cannot know how much smoke will continue to be emitted, for neither he nor anyone else is likely to have the relevant cost and quantity information.

This problem can be partially overcome by a related system of market-based incentives: a limited number of rights to engage in the conduct (such as polluting) are established, and these are then bought and sold in a market. Eventually those willing to pay the most for the privilege of polluting, usually those for whom the costs of avoiding or limiting the conduct would be the greatest, will buy up the rights. Since the number of rights is limited, the regulator knows in advance how much pollution will be emitted. He does not know in advance, however, what price firms will pay for the rights. He does not know the price at which firms will find it cheaper to install control equipment than to buy rights to pollute, and, unlike a tax system, a system of marketable rights does not permit estimation of the pollution control costs imposed upon the firms. The virtues and drawbacks of marketable rights are thus different from those of taxes.

The use of taxes and marketable rights to control pollution will be discussed in detail in Chapter 14. The use of marketable rights as a substitute for regulation, however, is by no means limited to environmental regulation or even to spillovers. They may be used to allocate whenever there is a shortage, where (perhaps because of regulation) no market presently exists, or when it is not necessary that allocation of the rights be determined on a public interest or other nonmonetary basis. Proposals to create marketable rights in airplane arrival gates at airports illustrates the system's use and also problems that can arise when regulators, whether environmental, airline, or other, try to create them.[36]

With four exceptions airports throughout the United States have enough gates to handle arriving and departing airplanes. However, at LaGuardia and Kennedy (New York), National Airport (Washington) and O'Hare (Chicago) traffic is so great that gates (or "slots") must be allocated. National Airport, for example, allocates sixty slots—forty to certificated air carriers, eight to small commuter carriers, and twelve to general aviation (private planes).

The present method of allocating slots among the certificated carriers consists of bargaining. The Air Transport Association, the main airline industry trade association, sponsors meetings twice a year, at which the carriers agree upon specific allocations. Their agreement is exempted from the antitrust laws.[37] Under their own rules, they must unanimously agree to the allocation and they must provide a slot for any airline wishing to serve an airport. These two conditions are likely to become more difficult to meet, for recent legislation has made it far easier for firms to enter the airline industry and to serve new markets. In the near future there will be too few slots to go around.[38]

One possible solution is functionally equivalent to a tax. The airport could ration the slots by raising landing fees. These fees might differ, depending upon time of day or season of the year, to reflect the degree of crowding. This approach embodies several of the difficulties present when taxes are applied to spillovers. But its major problem is that the regulator does not know what fee to set to assure that the demand and supply of slots are equal. The fee would require continuous readjustment to prevent crowding, or empty gates. Since economic conditions change continuously, a stable equilibrium might never be found.

The Civil Aeronautics Board is attempting to develop a plan under which slots are sold to the highest bidder. Slotholders could then freely resell the slot. Eventually the slots would end up in the hands of those willing to pay the most—presumably those to whom they were most valuable. Since the number of rights would be fixed, the problem of empty or crowded gates would be solved, though the ultimate price of the rights would be unknown in advance.

In developing its system, the CAB has encountered several problems. First, how is the system to be administered? In particular, what is the "right" being sold? Should it consist of an hour of gate time? An hour (say 3 to 4 P.M.) for one month? For six months? Several hours per day per gate for one month? For one year? The smaller the division of the rights, the more complex the auction. The larger the division, the greater the risk that those needing a small slot will not get it. Should the rights be auctioned initially through sealed bids or in an open meeting? How are the interested parties to keep track of the bidding? Will resales be worked out privately or must they take place in an open market? With the aid of computers, the CAB believes that rights could be kept "small" and that prices could be publicized to potential bidders quickly. The market could resemble that for the auction of Treasury bills.

Second, there is a risk that bidding firms will engage in strategic bidding behavior with anticompetitive consequences. There are ten major domestic trunk carriers and about half as many smaller regional carriers. At any one airport there may be fewer than a dozen firms bidding. Are there enough firms likely to bid to assure competitive bidding or could a few firms tacitly collude to keep prices low? Might they act like oligopolists setting prices, considering rivals' retaliatory actions, and, hence hesitating to compete? The antitrust laws cannot effectively deal with tacit collusion or oligopolistic behavior—the behavior of several firms in a concentrated industry that do not agree to certain anticompetitive behavior but over time informally take actions with the same effect.

Moreover, might large airlines behave in a predatory manner, buying up unneeded slots in order to prevent smaller rivals from entering the market? In principle, predatory buying presents problems similar to those of predatory pricing. The antitrust laws could be used to see that a firm does not bid more for a slot than it is incrementally worth. Moreover, the antitrust laws may require firms that control a bottleneck, such as a bridge or airport gates, to give competitors reasonable access. Yet applying the antitrust laws would raise difficult factual issues. Is a bid that excludes a smaller firm predatory? When might a purchase of a right from a small competitor lessen competition substantially? Could a large firm buy all of a smaller firm's slots at, say, National Airport and thus limit the number of firms competing there? Balancing the need for transferable rights against the risk of excluding smaller competitors will obviously be difficult.

Third, it is difficult to fix an initial allocation of rights. If rights are auctioned off, the commercial airlines will find they must pay a substantial additional sum of money to maintain their existing route networks. Smaller lines may find it difficult to raise the money needed for the purchase. Even if the gates are allocated to those firms to which they are most valuable, the extra cost reduces the amount of funds available for other needed investments, such as new airplanes. Alternatively, grandfathering slots gives existing firms a large windfall. Firms seeking to enter the market will have an additional large capital cost that the present firms need not bear.[39]

Fourth, the administrator must solve certain other practical problems similar to those created by a tax. What is to be done with proceeds of the sales? Should they somehow be returned to air travelers (say, through reductions of the tax on tickets) in order to prevent total air travel costs from rising? Which agency will administer the system? Does it possess the necessary expertise? Which committees of Congress must authorize the system? Will the question of revenue allocation lead to political difficulties as the measure proceeds through Congress?

The marketable rights approach, despite its difficulties, may be preferable to alternative allocation methods. Moreover, it offers an alternative superior in many respects to environmental taxes, though, as will be seen in Chapter 14, many of the same problems mentioned here reemerge when the system is applied to environmental pollution.

Changes in Liability Rules

Scholars have sometimes advocated reliance upon (or changing) the law of torts to mitigate the harm caused by several market defects. For many years, the only effective course of action open to pollution victims was to sue the polluter for "trespass" or "nuisance." These suits, asking for an injunction or damages, discouraged or prevented pollution to a limited degree. Similarly, tort law has been used to prevent or discourage accident-causing activity. In both cases, market defects arguably are present. Pollution often represents a spillover cost of producing a product. Accidents also impose spillover costs. A power lawnmower may injure not only its purchaser, but also innocent bystanders, the victim's family, and the general public which pays for his medical care. Accidents may also result in part from informational defects. If the buyer of the lawnmower does not understand the risk he runs in purchasing it, he may not buy a higher-priced, safer product. Is it possible to mitigate these problems by changing the law of torts? By creating class actions, for example, or by liberalizing standing rules to allow more pollution victims to sue? Will the number of accidents or their costs decline if producers are held strictly liable for the accidents caused by their products instead of being held liable only for negligence?

The accident problem illustrates the potential uses and pitfalls of changing liability rules. In principle, consumers are willing to take some risk. How safe the product ought to be depends upon the amount of harm its users are likely to suffer, and upon the cost of reducing that harm by making the product safer. Ideally, if all potential victims know the precise risks of harm from using a product and the precise costs of making the use of that product safer, they might bargain with producers (for example, by purchasing safer products and thus forcing manufacturers of more hazardous products to improve the safety of their products or risk going out of business).[40] Ideally, such a bargaining process would result in production of goods exhibiting just the right amount of safety characteristics.[41] Yet, arguably, buyers do not have adequate information about safety and may be unable to understand the information they are given. Indeed, the government for paternalistic reasons may wish to require more safety than users would otherwise purchase. Thus, power lawnmower buyers may not shop around sufficiently to find safer mowers, and producers may make mowers that are less safe than is desirable. At this point, one might ask whether rearranging liability rules will reduce the cost of accidents by encouraging manufacturers to make safer products.

In the past few years the law governing product liability has indeed changed. Previously, producers were liable only for accidents caused by their negligence. Now they are "strictly liable" for any accident caused by a defect in the product, whether or not it was negligently produced.[42] The change has helped overcome the market defects. Previously, buyers of dangerous products may have been unaware of the risk or had inadequate opportunity to buy, say, power lawnmowers that were safer but slightly more expensive.[43] If so, the lawnmower producer had no direct financial incentive to look for ways to make the mower safer. A shift to strict liability forces the manufacturer to pay compensation for many more of the accidents caused by the mower. Moreover, the larger the number of accidents, the more he must raise the price of the mower, deterring purchases of a dangerous product. Where insurance companies charge lower premiums to manufacturers with better safety records, each firm will also find that increased safety saves it premium money and thereby may allow it to charge lower prices, giving the safer machine a competitive edge.

Calabresi and Melamud[44] suggest that to structure liability rules one should begin by using the following principle: when it is uncertain whether a benefit (such as a lawnmower with a certain risk) is worth the potential costs (such as the harm of related accidents), one should construct liability rules such that the costs (of the harm) are placed on the party best able to weigh the costs against the benefits. This principle is likely to place costs upon the party best able to avoid them, or, where this is unknown, on the party best able to induce others to act more safely. This principle seems to argue for making the lawnmower manufacturer strictly liable if he is best able to weigh the benefits, risks, and avoidance costs involved. Similarly, in the case of pollution, the rule would place liability on the factory owner, for he is in the best position to determine whether it is more efficient to curtail pollution or to compensate the victims of his noisome emissions.

The decision to shift liability rules is difficult to make in practice. First, all liability rules embody a complex system of incentives. It is difficult to obtain enough empirical information to know just how the incentives created by a new rule will work. Take even the simple case of lawnmower accidents. Assume that there are "too many" accidents and that their costs or number would be reduced if all concerned knew the true risks and were free to bargain with one another. Still, accidents result from the production of lawnmowers and the use of lawnmowers in certain (possibly negligent) ways. A system under which manufacturers pay only for their own obvious negligence does not encourage them to make safer products, but a system under which manufacturers are strictly liable will require them to pay for some accidents that could have been avoided if users had been more careful. This system does not encourage consumers to use products in safer ways. Even without strict liability, if the major cause of accidents is unsafe lawnmowers, users could compel manufacturers to provide more safety by shopping for safer products. In practice, such shopping around may be unlikely to occur for reasons discussed above, and a shift to strict liability will substitute for the inability of users to bargain for safer mowers. But that shift then leaves it to producers to "shop" for buyers who will use their product safely. It is highly unlikely that there is any practical way for producers to restrict their sales to prudent users or to encourage them to use lawnmowers more safely. Thus, some have argued that the result of a shift in liability rules may be safer products but *more* accidents (as users become more careless).[45] Ultimately, the issue turns on the predicted empirical effects of changing incentives—in areas where empirical predictions are difficult to make.[46]

Second, the court system itself functions imperfectly. Many injured persons may be unaware of their rights or reluctant to sue for other reasons. Or they may find it too expensive to sue. The courts are plagued by delay, with plaintiffs often waiting years for trial. Moreover, the damage verdict may bear little relation to the actual harm—juries may be swayed by sympathy for a plaintiff or they may feel that a defendant has a deep pocket. The resulting award may exceed any compensation for which the victim would have been willing to insure before the accident. At a minimum, verdicts will differ widely in amount from one court and case to another. Further, the courts will have to draw fine legal lines: What is a product "defect"? When is a plaintiff himself "negligent"? When did a product "cause" an accident? Did the producer's smoke "cause" the plaintiff's suffering? How much smoke came from adjoining plants? What exactly was the extent of the injury to the plaintiff? The results, directly affecting a producer's or user's duty of care, will also vary from one court or region to another, and can result in an ever-changing standard of liability.

Also, the common law, as administered by the courts, may reflect certain noneconomic or moral factors that will make it difficult to use shifts in common-law liability to achieve basically economic ends. No rearrangement of property rights that makes a drug manufacturer liable for *failure* to produce a drug, for example, is likely to prove acceptable. Some have argued for the existence of other moral constraints as well.[47]

Third, the shift of liability rules will affect the relative wealth of the parties.

If, for example, liability rules are changed so that airports emitting noise must pay those living nearby, the value of homes in the nearby area will rise and the wealth of those who must pay increased airfares (which pay the cost of compensating the homeowners) will fall.[48] Similarly, a system that shifts the allocation of rights between firms emitting smoke and nearby residents or between manufacturers and accident victims affects the income or wealth of the parties. This shift will affect the desirability of the change and certainly will determine the strength of support for or opposition to it.

Fourth, the process of changing a liability rule may have other, broad social consequences that affect its desirability. For example, if appellate courts change the rule, will they do so prospectively or retroactively? What is the precedental effect of their decision on the general power of the courts to change prior case law? How does this precedent affect the relation between courts and legislatures? If new rights are suddenly created, but the courts lack the resources to enforce them or to satisfy them, what are the consequences? Will the public lose faith in the courts? Will Congress be forced to double or triple the number of federal judges? Such questions can be multiplied. But they are clearly relevant to a decision to overcome a market defect through shifts in liability rules.[49]

As indicated in Chapter 1, reliance upon court-enforced liability rules has not proven adequate to deal with the problem of pollution. Determining the extent of the damage and providing a standard of conduct for manufacturers, developing criteria that might apply uniformly and independent of the court, overcoming the problem of inadequate access to the court—all have made recourse to some form of administrative process seem desirable. The efforts to change liability rules governing accidents have proved more successful. Thus, the changing of liability rules remains, in some instances, a possible substitute for (or supplement to) a classical system of regulation.

Bargaining

Bargaining[50] among groups affected by regulation, as a method of dealing with regulatory problems, can have certain advantages. First, compared with standard setting, it can offer participating groups a greater opportunity to maximize the benefits that each receives. Members of all participating groups may be better off in part because the process requires the members of each group to order their own priorities. This internal ordering is important, for the individual members of each group, whether a union, a firm, or some other organization, have different needs and objectives. The need to come to the bargaining table with a list of demands ranked in order of priority forces each group to consider not only whether it wants a specific objective—say, a health benefit—but also how much it wants the benefit in comparison to other objectives, such as higher pay or longer vacations. Different opinions must be reconciled. Then, at the bargaining table, each group will give up what it values less in order to gain what it values more. The process of internally trading off objectives to arrive at a consensus and then explicitly trading at the bargaining table produces a result that may satisfy those involved more than would an exogenously imposed standard. The standard reflects in part an agency's efforts to guess the true priorities of the parties from the adversary pose each strikes at a hearing. The standard setter cannot know whether all concerned would have substituted a different standard at the eleventh hour, had they been free to do so.

Second, bargaining can adapt readily to the need for decentralized decision making. Bargainers can negotiate one set of issues at the industry level, while other issues are sent to local plants for resolution. In the construction industry, for example, firms and unions can decide issues of pensions, apprenticeships, or work seasonality on an industry basis. They can decide wage issues firm by firm. If necessary, they could negotiate certain working conditions plant by plant, or site by site. Moreover, workplace rules, seniority systems, and transfer systems not only can be developed locally, within the context of a broader industry-wide agreement, but the resulting rules and contract provisions can be enforced locally through grievance systems, with arbitration based upon the expectations and practices of workers and employers in the individual plant.

This ability of a bargaining system to produce decentralized decision making, to respond flexibly to differing local needs, and to bring about decentralized administration of the resulting agreements contrasts strongly with classical regulatory systems, where rules tend to be broad, uniform, and resistant to change.

Third, bargaining minimizes enforcement problems, because it produces consensus. Affected parties are more likely to know what the rules are, because they (or their representatives) have participated in their formulation. They are more likely to find the rules acceptable and to comply with them voluntarily. They are less likely to seek continuous change, fighting the rules in court proceedings and continuously asking the agency for their revision. Moreover, the rules are more likely to prove workable in practice, for those with information about, experience in, and an instinctive feel for the problems and the situation determine the outcome.

Despite these strengths, the bargaining process has several weaknesses that may make it an unsuitable substitute for a regulatory system. First, there must be some device to force the parties to reach agreement. That device may affect the bargaining strengths of the parties and thus determine the outcome, and its use may impose costs when agreement is not reached. Collective bargaining works in labor negotiations primarily due to the threat of a strike. Indeed, in difficult wage negotiations agreement is often not reached until the very last moment—when there is no alternative other than compromise or strike. If each party calculates that its likely loss through strike exceeds the likely gain, they will reach agreement.

The strike weapon when used, however, means that production time is lost, third parties may be seriously injured, and economic hardship is likely to result.

Any system that employs a strike as a weapon foresees its use. Indeed, it may be used simply to show that the threat it poses is credible. At the same time, if the employer is too weak to weather a strike, or if the union is not strong enough ever to engage in one, bargaining may amount to little more than unilateral imposition of terms by one party on another. Efforts to even the balance by adjusting the weapon through rules that limit or condition its use require the government to determine what the right degree of bargaining power is and to predict what conditions will achieve this balance. As experience with the NLRB attests, this regulatory activity can become complicated. Of course, strikes are not the only possible forcing mechanism. A regulatory agency might, for example, impose its own judgment if the parties do not reach agreement. But the development of a fair and adequate forcing mechanism remains a difficult problem.

Second, bargaining is not likely to work where the parties cannot organize or where one side is far weaker than the other. In this case, an effort to bargain again amounts to unilateral imposition of terms by one group upon the other. The laws governing labor relations seek to create the conditions for union organization so that bargaining is possible. Similarly, laws granting an exemption from the antitrust laws[51] for fishermen's and farmers' cooperatives are designed to allow the fishermen and farmers to organize and bargain collectively, which in turn allows the weaker group to bargain effectively with the stronger. Still, permitting the development of such groups affects both their strength and the subsequent substantive outcome. When the desired substantive outcome is known in advance, it may be simpler to achieve it through standards or other forms of regulation than to do so indirectly by bargaining.

Third, bargaining may benefit the participating parties but injure others who are not represented. Workers and managers alike, for example, might want higher prices that bring about both higher wages and profits, but at the expense of the consumer. A strike, during which both workers and managers may be compensated through strike funds or strike insurance, can harm the public more than it harms the participants. In fact, the bargaining itself could involve allocating costs that will be paid by, or imposed directly upon, third parties.

In sum, bargaining may work well when the strength of the parties is roughly equivalent; when decentralization, compromise, and the ranking of priorities is important; when the effect upon nonrepresented parties is not significant; and when agreement itself and not its precise substantive details is of particular importance. Where these conditions hold, bargaining may constitute a sensible substitute for classical regulation. At a minimum, it could profitably be used to supplement such a system.

Dunlop, for example, has written of his experience as secretary of labor in administering Section 13(c) of the Urban Mass Transportation Act.[52] Under the act, municipalities could take over private transportation firms, but had to obtain certification from the secretary of labor that the firms' employees would not be adversely affected. This requirement meant that the town had to compensate employees it wanted to lay off. But how should it and the Labor Department determine the proper level of equitable compensation? Rather than try to set standards itself, the Labor Department brought together union and transportation authority representatives and had them bargain a three-year agreement upon standards that would apply in individual cases. The department provided technical assistance (and presumably would have imposed its own standards had the process broken down). Bargaining, in this instance, according to Dunlop, proved a far speedier and more effective method of producing standards than classical standard setting.

Increased use of the bargaining process has also been suggested as a means of improving the Occupational Safety and Health Administration. Since its inception in the early 1970s, OSHA has relied almost exclusively upon standard setting to produce safer workplaces. Its efforts have been severely criticized, both as requiring excessive expenditure by industry and as being ineffective in protecting workers.[53] Statistical evidence does not show that OSHA has had a significant effect on safety so far.[54] Indeed, the existence of 5 million workplaces in the United States, with highly varying conditions, obviously makes it difficult for OSHA to obtain sufficient information to develop sufficiently flexible standards, or to consider the effects of its rules on the competitive positions of affected firms. Given the twelve hundred inspectors it employs, it can police less than 2 percent of those workplaces annually.[55] OSHA must work within closely defined legal rules designed to protect individuals from arbitrary governmental action. And since rulemaking and enforcement proceedings require substantial periods of time, it is not surprising to find that OSHA has created few new rules since its inception. Initially it mistakenly adopted several thousand existing state and local safety requirements without adequate review, thus creating a set of absurd requirements (such as ''No ice in drinking water'') which opened it to serious political criticism.[56]

Some students of the subject have contrasted OSHA's approach with the speedier, more effective method of policing workplace safety in Sweden.[57] Swedish procedure is far less formal. When ASU, the Swedish safety agency, considers promulgating a safety rule, it convenes a committee composed of labor, business, and agency representatives to consider the matter. The labor representative comes from LO, Sweden's central organization of blue-collar workers, and the business representative from SAF, the leading employers' association, which negotiates nationwide collective bargaining agreements. Both organizations employ full time OSH (occupational safety and health) experts. The committee sends out standard proposals in draft form to local unions for comment. Committee meetings are informal and no transcript is kept. ASU decides who will be represented and the number of persons involved is small. ASU has the ultimate decision-making power if agreement is not reached. There are no lengthy legal formalities. Standards are promulgated quietly—in days or weeks rather than months or years. And American observers report favorably on the results of the process.[58]

How well a similar bargaining process would work in the United States is debatable. American legal traditions are different. It may be difficult to avoid formal legal requirements. Moreover, those that suffer most from inadequate workplace safety are usually unorganized workers who cannot bargain. For various reasons, it may be difficult for union leaders to bargain for adequate safety.[59] Nor is there a single trade association or union organization that can adequately represent all management or labor.[60]

Moreover, insofar as accidents reflect an inadequate understanding of risks by workers, unequal bargaining power, or unconcern for accident costs borne by others, bargaining will not produce sufficient accident protection. Finally, one might ask whether the presence of an OSHA representative at a bargaining session would be sufficient to produce agreement. Would representatives turn the problem over to OSHA rather than agree upon less strict standards than OSHA would impose?

Despite uncertainties surrounding the use of bargaining in an American context, it has been proposed and tried as a supplement to the present system. Some labor contracts contain elaborately worked out OSH provisions.[61] Dunlop, when secretary of labor, sought (without success) to induce negotiation to determine the contents of a safety standard governing coke-oven emissions.[62] A recent study by the Department of Labor and the Council of Economic Advisors suggested certain exemptions from standards where firms or industries made (effective) use of the bargaining process.[63]

The major advantage that the Department of Labor saw in such a system was its flexibility. OSHA standards tend to govern the physical characteristics of the workplace. However, in many instances the major causes of industrial accidents are not permanent physical characteristics, but carelessness or other nonpermanent features of the workplace. A safety officer or education program might reduce accidents far more than, say, adding guardrails to machines. Yet that type of feature is more easily bargained for than created through rule. Similarly, enforcement problems might be eased to the extent that joint worker-management committees could develop and administer plant-specific rules.

Of course, the parties directly affected may agree only about worst cases—the most obvious examples of the evil at which the regulatory program is aimed. Obtaining agreement about how to proceed against lesser evils may be more difficult. As one abandons the goals of perfect regulation and recognizes the serious problems embedded in classical regulation, the use of bargaining becomes a more attractive alternative.

Nationalization

Nationalization as an alternative to regulation is less popular in the United States than elsewhere in the world. In principle, it might be used to deal with the natural monopoly. It might help to internalize spillover costs as well. During the 1920s and 1930s, welfare economists demonstrated that nationalizing an industry would not necessarily distort the workings of a free-enterprise system.[64] It need not misallocate resources. On the contrary, the government could instruct the managers of the firm to set prices equal to marginal costs. Thus, the nationalized firm's prices would replicate those set by firms operating under competitive conditions.[65] If the firm's costs declined (as in Hotelling's bridge example), the government might provide some of the funds needed for initial investment at low, subsidized interest rates. The firm could then charge a price closer to marginal costs than could a privately owned monopolist, which must earn a reasonable return for its investors. Even if the nationalized firm must earn a comparable return, the managers are more likely to find an economically proper set of prices (using Ramsey pricing, for example) than are regulated managers whose incentives are distorted by the adversary relationship between regulator and private firm.[66] Indeed, economists in England and France have produced a detailed set of pricing rules that have allowed their nationally owned electricity companies to implement "marginal cost pricing in practice."[67] Moreover, in principle, the government might instruct its managers to take proper account of pollution and other spillover costs when they price their product or seek to build a new plant.[68]

Those who oppose nationalization tend to base their arguments more upon political than upon economic grounds. Nonetheless, their objections are weighty. First, they fear that staffing in a nationalized firm would reflect political rather than managerial considerations. One again recalls Ambrose Bierce's definition of a lighthouse as a "tall building on the seashore in which the government maintains a lamp and the friend of a politician."[69] Second, critics argue that a nationalized firm lacks adequate power to resist union wage demands. While a private firm can use the threat of bankruptcy or the need to secure regulatory approval as a bargaining weapon, the public firm cannot. Its union's expectations may be raised by the perception of a large public purse into which the firm can dip.[70] Thus, nationalization may add to inflationary wage pressure, though the evidence on the subject (from England, for example) is indeterminate.[71]

Moreover, the staff of the nationalized firm or the government that controls it may view nationalization as an instrument for carrying out a wide variety of desirable social objectives, and their efforts to achieve those objectives may yield price and investment decisions that are economically unreasonable. The Central Electricity Generating Board in England, for instance, found that it was not allowed to raise prices during serious inflation because it had to set an example for others. The results were uneconomically low prices, distortion in demand, and large electricity subsidies.[72] The government could not have used the industry in this way had it rested in private hands. Similarly, British and French national airlines were forced to buy the Concorde for reasons of national prestige, despite the fact that doing so was economically unsound.[73]

Further, the fact that a nationalized industry is public rather than private may carry with it legal consequences that in turn have economic consequences. The most obvious of these in the United States is that public authorities can raise money by issuing bonds with interest exempt from federal taxes. Tax-free bonds bear lower interest charges. Thus, government-owned electricity companies can raise money at savings of up to 50 percent compared with private firms—a fact that has led privately owned firms to complain of unfair competition and that may inefficiently encourage the use of electricity when it is becoming economically more costly to produce.

Finally, some people fear that large state-owned enterprises with some access to public funds will exercise too much power free of effective checks from public regulatory bodies, private competitors, or consumers. If nationalized firms by virtue of their ownership are treated more leniently by other regulatory bodies, treated less suspiciously by the public, or exempted from other rules and regulations the result may be less attention to important public concerns. For example, managers, anxious to see their firms function efficiently, may take inadequate account of environmental pollution, whether or not their firm is nationalized. Indeed, studies of the structure of American industry have shown that firms owned by the government are no more sensitive to the environment than are other firms.[74] If such a firm were freed from environmental regulation by virtue of its public ownership, the result would be more pollution. Publicly owned firms may also find it easier to exclude competitors. Publicly owned corporations might obtain authority to exercise the power of eminent domain. In New York State, public housing authorities were able to raise money while providing investors with far less protection than would have been required of a private firm in comparable circumstances.[75] The most extreme case cited is that of Pertamina, Indonesia's government-owned oil company, which became a small state itself, with its own private army.[76]

Experience with government ownership within the United States has not been studied systematically to the point where firm conclusions are possible. In part, this may be due to the many different forms that such ownership may take, ranging from partial stock ownership by the government, to government members of a board of directors, to operation by an autonomous government authority, to direct incorporation into a government bureau or department.[77] Some managerial incentives remain the same as in private firms, regardless of the form. Even government bureaus often behave like rivalrous private firms, with their own institutional interest rather than the public interest in mind.[78] Other incentives and behavior will vary, depending on the actual form of governmental participation. In part, the lack of systematic study may reflect the relative unpopularity in the United States of nationalization as a solution to regulatory problems. Regardless, nationalization or direct participation of government in the management of an enterprise should be kept in mind as a possible, though only cursorily explored, alternative to classical regulation.

9

General Guidelines for Policy Makers

Part I of this book has set out a framework for the analysis of regulation. That framework consists of three lists, or sets of considerations: typical market defects thought to call for regulation, six typical modes of regulation, and alternative regimes. The role of these lists is primarily suggestive. They suggest to the administrator of existing programs the extent to which the problems he encounters are endemic to the system; they may help him focus his aims and consider the value of alternative approaches.

As a more general matter, the discussion suggests certain rules of thumb usefully applied to classical regulation. First and most obviously, *modesty* is desirable in one's approach to regulation. It should be painfully apparent that whatever problems one has with an unregulated status quo, the regulatory alternatives will also prove difficult. Before advocating the use of regulation, one must be quite clear that the unregulated market possesses serious defects for which regulation offers a cure.

Beyond this, however, the discussion strongly suggests that regulators ought to *aim at worst cases* and that, in attacking such cases, they should strive for *simplicity*. Efforts to cure every minor defect, to close every conceivable loophole, are ultimately counterproductive. Recall the effort to screen out dangerous or defective ingredients, substances, or products discussed in Chapter 7. As long as the agency focused upon major dangers with greater risks, there was no reason in principle why it should fail. Once it focused on ingredients with very small risks and unknown effects, however, it risked failure, particularly since regulatory action in such a case might injure the very people the program was designed to protect. Thus, to ban saccharin might save a handful of people from death through bladder cancer, but it might condemn others to death from diseases associated with obesity. When small risks were at issue, given the difficulties inherent in the screening process, it was impossible for the agency to know the ultimate effect of its action. Despite arguments by some food safety experts that banning was the "conservative" or "safe" thing to do, in reality there was no conservative position. Regulation of this type was simply not capable of dealing with the problem of marginal risks.

Similarly, environmental administrators and antipollution programs may find it possible to remove as much as 90 percent of a river's industrial effluent or 90 percent of the sulfur dioxide in the air, but when they seek to remove the final 10 percent of the pollutant they face mounting difficulties. At that point costs begin to rise, the agency meets strong resistance from the firms involved, and enforcement problems may become so serious that the program ends up being less effective than if the agency had begun with a more modest goal. As our discussion of bumper standards suggests, NHTSA might have produced enforceable standards far sooner, had it initially aimed at a goal that would have allowed some dents. Instead, it aimed for perfection—the dent-free bumper—and there was, as a result, a long delay before *any* standard could take effect.

We have also seen how regulatory efforts at detailed precision can prove wasteful or even counterproductive. The utility regulator, engaged in cost-of-service ratemaking, cannot find the cost of capital, the appropriate revenue requirement, or the "correct" price, except very approximately. An allowed rate of return that is below the cost of capital (or a price that is too low) does not necessarily help consumers at the expense of the company, for it simply increases the risk of investing in the firm, raising future capital costs and thereby ultimately increasing consumer prices. Since efforts at precision are at least as likely to yield prices that are further from (higher or lower than) the mark as they are to yield prices that are closer to it, they are as likely to hurt consumers as to help them.

In other words, increased efforts to fine-tune regulation often will not yield improved results. Regulators of great intelligence, with genuine good will, working extremely hard, are nonetheless unlikely to deal effectively with borderline cases. The defects and difficulties inherent in the system make regulation a crude weapon of governmental intervention—a blunderbuss, not a rifle. These defects are embedded in the process to such an extent that they cannot readily be changed.

Another general conclusion is that classical regulation ought to be looked upon as a weapon of last resort. The problems accompanying classical regulation would seem sufficiently serious to warrant adopting a "least restrictive alternative" approach to regulation. Such an approach would view regulation through a procompetitive lens. It would urge reliance upon an unregulated market in the absence of a significant market defect. Then, when the harm produced by the unregulated market is serious, it would suggest first examining incentive-based intervention, such as taxes or marketable rights, or disclosure regulation, bargaining, or other less restrictive forms of interventions before turning to classical regulation itself. It would urge the adoption of classical regulatory methods only where less restrictive methods will not work.

Our discussion does not prove the validity of this approach, but it supports its adoption when combined with a recognition of the virtues of the competitive marketplace—virtues that have been discussed fully elsewhere.[1] In summary form, they include the market's tendency to minimize economic waste by allowing for continuous individual balancing of economic costs and benefits by consumers and producers, the carrot-and-stick incentive the market provides for greater efficiency in production methods, and the incentives it provides for innovation and the channeling of innovation into socially desirable directions. In achieving these ends, competitive markets reduce the need for the central collection of information.[2] Price signals allow producers and consumers to adapt quickly to change. The impersonality of the decision-making process in competitive markets prevents those injured in the process (because, for example, their goods are no longer in demand) from obstructing change. To these advantages may be added a competitive market's tendency to decentralize power and to make decisions that are "fair" in the sense of being impersonal.[3] Finally, as Schultze has noted, "relationships in the market are a form of anonymous consent arrangement . . . [minimizing] the need for coercion as a means of organizing society."[4] Incentive systems preserve many of these virtues, while classical regulatory systems do not. Thus, one should hesitate to adopt a classical regulatory system and to risk losing advantages of the competitive marketplace, unless one has the compensating certainty that the regulatory system can successfully achieve its aims.

At the same time, there are some less restrictive approaches that offer ways of dealing with market defects without losing so many advantages of the competitive marketplace. Bargaining, for example, can provide a practical method for identifying market defects and obtaining effective cooperation in dealing with them. Disclosure often provides a sensible middle path between banning an ingredient with a small risk and doing nothing about it. Taxes, marketable rights, and similar incentive-based approaches often provide practical methods for reconciling the need for simple regulatory rules with the diversity and complexity of the industrial world. Thus, together with a recognition of the advantages of competitive markets, our discussion supports a "least restrictive alternative" attitude toward the regulatory process.

Part I may also prove useful to the administrator of a new regulatory program or to those who propose such a program, for it will alert them to problems they are likely to encounter and may guide them toward alternative solutions. How this might occur can be seen by considering briefly a simplified example concerning the control of medical costs. Regulation has been advocated to control these costs because the unregulated market has been deemed inadequate. Indeed, one can readily identify this market defect as a moral hazard. The person using the medical service does not pay the bill. Neither he, nor the doctor, nor the hospital may have sufficient incentive to hold down costs. The Carter administration therefore proposed a regulatory program that would hold hospital prices to historical costs plus a percentage fixed by statutory formula.[5]

Those considering such a program should be aware that any such historical system of price setting evolves toward cost-of-service ratemaking, as the need for exceptions forces consideration of individual cases. The case of hospitals would seem to be no different. There is an obvious need for exceptions for new units, for units with special historical need, for unusually costly items required by the nature of the service or by the needs of the users, and for unusually high costs brought about by an inability to stop wage increases. Given the ability of hospitals to appeal directly to legislatures, the regulator will find it difficult indeed to ignore justifiable claims for exception.

If the historical system evolves as we have described, the resulting cost-of-service ratemaking will bring with it the classical set of problems accompanying that regime. These include problems associated with the test year, with inadequate incentives for efficient production, and with rate structure. Since those creating medical regulatory programs seek to improve production efficiency, knowledge that cost-of-service ratemaking is unlikely to promote efficiency—in fact, its failure to do so is perhaps its greatest single weakness—may lead them to question the regulatory scheme.

A different plan would control medical costs directly. It would impose a limit on the capital expenditures that a hospital can make by requiring each hospital to obtain a "certificate of need" before making any such expenditures.[6] We have seen the sorts of problems that this plan will raise. The regulator will face an allocation problem—at least if the number of certificates is limited and must be allocated to hospitals with excess demand for them. The regulator will be limited in his responses to the allocation problem. He may try to find criteria that automatically and objectively select applicants for certificates—for example, by allowing hospitals to maintain what they presently operate, categorizing and allocating through some form of quota or distributing certificates among competitor hospitals "equally." That is to say, he may try standard setting. But it is unlikely that there exists any set of standards that can obviate the need for numerous special exceptions, particularly if a meaningful limit is placed on total hospital expenditure within a given geographic area.

Thus, the regulator will be pushed toward public interest allocation. He is likely to end up with too many standards relevant to his decision, with no clear way to balance among them, and he will become involved in lengthy, unmanageable proceedings leading to inconsistent decisions. To avoid these problems, which are typically associated with public interest allocation, he may allow existing hospitals to negotiate the allocation of the certificate-of-need entitlement among themselves (as is the case in some cities where a certificate-of-need program is being administered).[7] Such negotiation may work to the disadvantage of outsiders, may not be totally rational, and may reflect political considerations. But the fact that it obtains consensus among those directly affected, that knowledgeable parties make the allocation decision, and that the worst cases of waste are likely to be stopped may make this bargaining solution preferable to any form of classical regulation.

This example makes clear the suggestive role of our analysis. It does not prove whether government intervention in a particular case is warranted, nor does it prove what form that intervention should take. Rather, it suggests lines of inquiry, presumptions, and relevant facts. It allows the policy maker, in an individual case, to investigate the facts in depth with the framework to guide him. He can thus more easily weigh the policy alternatives and select governmental interventions (or possible noninterventions) best suited to the case at hand.

II

Appropriate Solutions

10
Match and Mismatch

The remainder of this book will seek to draw from Part I some general guidance for approaching the issue of regulatory reform. Our examination of market defects, classical modes of regulation, and alternative regimes suggests that regulatory failure sometimes means a failure to correctly match the tool to the problem at hand. Classical regulation may represent the wrong governmental response to the perceived market defect. If so, regulatory reform would consist not of procedural or structural changes within the agency, but rather of a detailed examination of a particular program with an eye toward radical substantive change—a change in the use of classical regulation itself. Recently, such major changes in regulatory programs—in airlines, trucking, and natural gas—indicate the gradual acceptance of this point of view. In the remainder of the book, we will use these and other examples to explore this mismatch thesis, drawing to some extent upon my personal involvement in the reform process, particularly in the case of airlines.

What sorts of matches of regulatory ends and means—or, conversely, what sort of mismatches—does our analysis so far suggest? The matches that it indicates are of less practical value than the mismatches. And they are highly tentative. Table 3 suggests several modes that a policy maker might be drawn to consider. The matches are not definitive, yet it may still be useful to review the considerations that lead to the formulation of the chart.

Natural monopoly. A serious natural monopoly problem cannot be left to the unregulated marketplace or to the antitrust laws for correction. Traditional cost-of-service ratemaking, although incapable of precision, can keep prices down, equating them very roughly with costs and eliminating some potential monopoly profit. Nationalization, in principle, can achieve a similar result, provided the government gives its administrators proper pricing instructions. However, nationalization is politically unpopular in the United States, in part because the electorate fears that the firm would become too susceptible to political pressures. Taxes might be used to capture some of an unregulated monopolist's profits, yet a tax will not deal effectively with the social objectives

Table 3. Matches of regulatory ends and means.

Problem	Tentative solution
Natural monopoly	Cost-of-service ratemaking; nationalization
Rent control (excess profits)	Taxes; deregulation
Spillovers	Marketable rights; bargaining standards
Excessive competition	Deregulation; antitrust
Inadequate information	Disclosure; screening; standard setting; bargaining
Other (moral hazard, unequal bargaining power, paternalism)	Incentive-based regulation; standards

of control. It is difficult to design a tax that would capture monopoly profits. It is similarly difficult to see how one might design a bargaining system that adequately represented consumers. At first blush, cost-of-service ratemaking seems a plausible approach—a conclusion that a more detailed discussion in Chapter 15 will reinforce.

Excess profits or rent control. A problem of excess profits or excess rents— if serious enough to demand intervention—cannot be dealt with by an unregulated market, because it reflects the proper functioning of a competitive marketplace. Since the object of governmental intervention here is to transfer income from producers to others, a tax would seem most likely to work. Of course, a tax has the drawbacks we have discussed, but the alternative relevant forms of governmental intervention are more seriously flawed. There is no obvious way for consumers, as a group, to bargain for a share of the rents. Nationalization could capture the rents for the public, but a rent problem is temporary, and does not call for so drastic a remedy, which would persist long after the rents have disappeared. As will be shown in Chapter 13, cost-of-service ratemaking when applied to rent control creates problems that are likely to prove more serious than those it cures.

Spillovers. A spillover cost problem results when the price of a product does not adequately reflect all the costs that its creation imposes. Thus, its solution rarely involves suppressing the product entirely. Rather, it requires more accurate balancing by producers and consumers in choosing among products and production processes (say, among polluting and nonpolluting processes or between products that create pollution and those that do not). It also requires increased incentives for consumers to avoid products that create the cost and for producers to look for methods to reduce those costs. Taxes automatically allow that type of balancing and create that type of incentive. Insofar as large numbers of products and production processes are involved, proper solutions are likely to vary among products. If a large number of enterprises are involved, simplicity is necessary to help enforcement. These factors also argue in favor of taxes, for taxes offer comparative simplicity in design yet allow variation and flexibility in result. A system of marketable rights has many of the same advantages, allowing a balancing of choice, providing incentives, and allowing variation in results.

Whether bargaining or changes in liability rules can be used to deal with spillovers depends upon whether the disadvantages of those modes are great, given the features of the individual case. In the case of pollution, for example, organizing the affected groups is too difficult to make bargaining feasible, and it is impractical to rely upon courts to enforce reformulated rules of liability.

Standard setting is frequently used to deal with spillovers, but, as we have noted, it is extremely difficult to develop a system of standards with the virtues of flexibility, incentive, and simplicity enjoyed by taxes. In some instances, where the defects of tax or liability systems are great, standard setting may be the only weapon available. But where the need for balancing and incentives is combined with a need for evaluation in result and simplicity of rule, incentive-based systems are more likely to prove appropriate. This subject will be pursued at greater length in Chapter 14, where the merits of the two systems will be examined in the context of environmental pollution.

Excessive competition. Excessive competition does not provide an adequate justification for regulation. Insofar as it represents a market defect, it consists of predatory pricing. The antitrust laws provide an adequate remedy. Thus, regulation is likely to bring numerous regulatory problems without compensating benefits—a matter that will be discussed further in Chapters 11 and 12.

Inadequate information. Disclosure provides an obvious remedy to problems of inadequate information. Indeed, labeling is often suggested as a practical alternative to the regulation of an ingredient that is useful but also risky. Yet labeling may prove inadequate. It may be impossible, for example, to convey to a workman the particular dangers of a workplace. Or consumers may be puzzled about the meaning of signs saying "Saccharin may cause cancer" and therefore ignore them. (Some may reason that if the product were truly dangerous, it would be banned.) Thus, other forms of intervention are sometimes necessary, including classical regulation (screening and standards) where disclosure does not work.

Other instances. We have not specifically suggested which forms of intervention are likely to fit the problems of moral hazard, scarcity, unequal bargaining power, and paternalism. One might associate paternalism with standard setting, scarcity with allocation, unequal bargaining power with exemptions from the antitrust laws, and moral hazard with classical regulation, but these associations arise more from historical practice than from any system of analysis. Indeed, one suspects that in several of these areas, more incentive-based systems could be used profitably.

In sum, a few rough associations can be worked out in the form of matches. These are useful, however, only to provide a first impression. They limit only slightly the class of potentially usable weapons. Which weapon fits which problem can be determined precisely only by taking the particular example through a more detailed analysis, as will be done in later chapters.

The analysis presented in Part I may be somewhat more useful for regulatory reform purposes when put to the converse task of identifying mismatches or areas where the wrong regulatory tools are likely being used. We will illustrate how this has been or might be done, identifying areas where classical regulation can cause unusually severe anticompetitive harm and where alternatives are possible.

We already know that classical regulation can cause various sorts of anticompetitive harm. Virtually every form of classical regulation tends to *raise barriers to entry* into the regulated industry. Cost-of-service ratemaking is almost always accompanied by rules or laws that require a commission to allow new firms to enter the industry only if it serves the "public convenience and necessity." Thus, regulation significantly raised entry barriers into the airlines and trucking industries. Standard setting also raises entry barriers. Since standards are written with existing firms in mind, they may exclude or hinder potential competitors. The standard itself may increase costs; standards may provide inadequate incentive for firms to meet their health, environmental, or safety objectives in nonconforming ways. Thus, standard-setting may slow technological change and may protect existing firms from competition. Allocation systems also tend to favor the status quo insofar as allocators follow historical patterns of distribution. New firms needing a commodity in scarce supply tend to be at a disadvantage compared with their established competitors. Oil allocation, for example, makes it more difficult to enter retail distribution. New firms seeking natural gas cannot readily obtain it.

In place of impersonal market forces that can drive an inefficient or unresponsive firm into bankruptcy, classical regulation substitutes responsible human beings who can save individual regulated firms from failure. Indeed, regulators are often blamed by the relevant industry, the unions, and the general public if a regulated firm fails, while regulatory decisions that seek to preserve the historical market shares of regulated firms and to protect them from new competition either pass unnoticed or are praised by the public as fair. Thus, in the airline and trucking industries regulation led to relatively stable market shares, to protection of inefficient firms, and to the merger of weaker firms into stronger ones as an alternative to bankruptcy. Similarly, variations in standards that take account of variations in technology and costs among existing firms will help to protect those firms from failure.

Finally, particular anticompetitive harms may arise that are specific to one form of regulation. When cost-of-service ratemaking, for example, is imposed upon an industry that is structurally capable of supporting competition, the firms in that industry may substitute competition in service for competition in price. That is to say, since the need to obtain regulatory approval inhibits firms from competing vigorously in price, they will improve product quality to attract customers. This can cause harm when it means that the customer is prevented from choosing an inferior product at a significantly lower price.

Using our analysis in Part I to identify a mismatch, then, involves finding an area where the regulatory process is particularly likely to cause significant anticompetitive harm. It also involves finding an area where the rationale for regulation, judged by empirical fact, is not compelling, or where there are apparently less restrictive or more incentive-based forms of governmental intervention that can obtain regulation's purported objectives.

There are at least three maxims that can help identify areas where mismatches are likely to be found.

Classical regulation should not be used to control excessive competition. Deregulation and reliance upon antitrust are more suitable. The analysis upon which this conclusion rests is provided in Chapters 11 and 12, using airlines and trucks as examples. Essentially, the use of classical regulation creates anticompetitive harms, inhibiting price competition that would otherwise prove possible and protecting existing firms by restricting the entry of new ones. At the same time, the justification for regulation is weak. Insofar as excessive competition reflects a fear of predatory pricing, the antitrust laws provide adequate protection. The extent of the harm that classical regulation is likely to cause and the existence of a practical alternative, as will be seen, makes this sort of case a prime candidate for reform.

Classical regulation should ordinarily not be used for purposes of rent control. Taxes or deregulation offer preferable alternatives. Chapter 13 illustrates this maxim by focusing on the effort to regulate natural gas. It demonstrates that cost-of-service ratemaking is unable to transfer rents without creating serious shortages—shortages that allocation procedures cannot handle adequately. Taxes, despite their problems, are likely to transfer rents more effectively. If taxes prove impractical, the effort to regulate classically will tend (except in an unusual case) to cause more harm than benefit.

Classical regulation is not able to deal comprehensively with spillover problems. Taxes, marketable rights, and even bargaining are likely to prove useful as substitutes or supplements. Chapter 14 illustrates this maxim by focusing upon the problem of environmental pollution. It shows how standard setting is particularly prone to the problems described in Chapter 6—at least when there is a need for balancing, incentives, variation in outcome, and simplicity of rule. The use of standards in the pollution area may prove anticompetitive and not very effective, while greater reliance upon incentive-based solutions seem more promising.

Chapter 15 illustrates another maxim, but applied to a match, not a mismatch. It is designed to show the additional complexity of achieving reform when one deals with a basic match: cost-of-service ratemaking as applied to natural monopoly.

Examining particular programs will help illustrate the value of a particular approach to reform: identify a program that likely embodies a mismatch; analyze that program in depth; and then change the underlying statute or practices of the agency. We will suggest how certain mismatches or candidates for reform have been or might be identified. Finally, in Part III we will illustrate how reform can be carried out once a particular candidate has been identified.

11

Mismatch: Excessive Competition and Airline Regulation

The clearest examples of a mismatch arise when classical price and entry regulation is applied to a structurally competitive industry. In such cases, one should consider abolishing regulation and relying instead upon an unregulated market policed by antitrust. Three arguments support this conclusion. First, application of classical price and entry regulation is likely to produce unnecessary anticompetitive harms. In particular, cost-of-service ratemaking inhibits price cutting and price competition. Firms in a competitive industry subject to cost-of-service ratemaking may compete by providing consumers with more service or quality than they want, and eventually charging a higher price for doing so. Second, regulators find it particularly difficult to apply cost-of-service ratemaking to an industry with many firms. Third, the underlying rationale for price regulation in such industries is ordinarily weak. The commonly given justification—excessive competition—is an empty box. Insofar as one legitimately fears predatory pricing, alternatives to regulation, such as the antitrust laws, are available.

Airline regulation is the best-documented example of this type of mismatch. Prior to 1974 this competitively structured industry was regulated in a classical manner by the Civil Aeronautics Board. A detailed investigation by the U.S. Senate Subcommittee on Administrative Practice and Procedure, chaired by Edward Kennedy, demonstrated that regulation was responsible for excessive service and for prices that were too high.[1] It also showed how the regulatory form itself, not the ineptitude or malevolence of the regulators, was responsible for the problem.

It is worth examining the state of the industry and related regulation as of 1975, for it is the one instance that has been studied in sufficient depth to demonstrate—not just to suggest—a mismatch. Following Senator Kennedy's study, the industry was effectively deregulated by the CAB, which adopted less restrictive rules, and then by Congress, which enacted a new law.[2] Experience since the passage of that law suggests that the diagnosis of a mismatch is correct, because prices in real terms have fallen despite rising fuel costs and the industry's profitability has not been significantly affected. An examination of the details of airline regulation prior to 1975 shows why classical regulation was inappropriate and supports a general presumption against regulating structurally competitive industries.

The Industry

In 1974 ten major trunk airlines provided more than 90 percent of scheduled airline service in the United States. Nine "local-service carriers" provided about 8 percent. Intrastate carriers providing scheduled service wholly within California, Texas, and several other states were not regulated by the CAB, nor were commuter carriers operating small airplanes. Eight supplemental carriers provided only charter service.

The industry had grown enormously since 1938 when CAB regulation began. The number of revenue passenger-miles flown per year had increased from 476 million to 120 billion, while investment had increased from $30 million to more than $8 billion. The nature of the industry had also changed. Prior to the 1950s it had been highly subsidized. Since the 1960s, however, the major trunk carriers had received no significant subsidy.

There are three characteristics of the industry that make it an inappropriate subject of classical cost-of-service ratemaking. First, the industry is highly *competitive*. Its structure is not that of a natural monopoly, for it can support several, perhaps many, firms of efficient size. There are no huge economies of scale. Thus, smaller airlines such as Northwest and Continental operated profitably next to such giants as TWA. Entry into the industry, while expensive, is made easier by the ability of new firms to lease airplanes, and entry into new routes by firms already in the industry is cheap. The industry's performance also suggested a high degree of competition among the firms within it. Domestic trunk carriers' profits were low; indeed, between 1960 and 1975 they ranged from a high of 12.2 percent to a loss of 4.4 percent, and topped 10 percent in only five of the fifteen years.[3] Moreover, where carriers were free to compete (in service), they competed vigorously. This competition took the form not simply of better meals or other frills, but of better scheduling, more flights, and less crowded planes. In the late 1960s and early 1970s, when the airlines received delivery of the many large new aircraft that they had previously ordered, scheduling competition was so severe that planes flew across country more than 60 percent empty. (In 1971 transcontinental "load factors" averaged 39 percent.)[4] The CAB found it impossible to convince the domestic carriers to agree to compete less by limiting the number of flights. In California and Texas, where airlines were not regulated and were free to cut prices as well as engage in service competition, significant price competition generally existed.

Second, the industry is highly *volatile*. Demand for air travel is cyclical because it is strongly affected by changes in disposable personal income. Costs per passenger are very sensitive to the number of persons flying, because increased demand for flights tends to fill planes and full planes cost far less to fly per passenger than half-empty ones. Hence, profits vary enormously with economic fluctuations.

Third, the industry cost structure is highly *complex*. In 1974 the ten major scheduled air carriers served about 430 cities. Mathematical permutations show more than 90,000 possible city-pair combinations and, of these, more than 58,000 received certificated carrier-scheduled services.

The largest 145 markets accounted for about 40 percent of all service, and the largest 908 for about 70 percent of all passenger-miles flown.[5] The cost of serving city pairs varied not only with distance but also with air and ground congestion, type of service and equipment, time of day, amount of traffic, and the relation of the particular city pair to the network of routes flown by the particular airline. Thus, each airline's total costs differed according to its efficiency, types of equipment, labor contracts, configuration of routes, and so on. And within each airline's system, the cost of flying even routes of the same length differed, depending upon the factors listed above.

These three factors —competitiveness, volatility, and complexity—distinguish the airline industry from a single-firm natural monopoly such as electricity generation, and make it far more difficult to regulate.

Regulation

The Civil Aeronautics Board regulated the prices charged by the interstate scheduled carriers as well as entry into the industry. It did not regulate safety, which is the domain of the Federal Aviation Administration. The statutes that it administered were typical of many others: they were modeled after those of the Interstate Commerce Act of 1887, which in turn were copied from the British Railway Act of 1845. These provisions, now regarded as creating classical price and entry regulation, included: (1) a requirement that the CAB allow a firm to enter the industry to provide service if the "applicant is fit, willing, and able to perform such transportation properly . . . and . . . such transportation is required by the public convenience and necessity,"[6] and (2) a requirement that rates and practices be neither too high nor too low, but that they be just, reasonable, and nondiscriminatory.

The statutory goals, which specified guidelines for the CAB's exercise of its rate and entry powers, were vague and somewhat contradictory. Taken together, the statutory provisions seemed to have the twin objectives of promoting the growth of aviation while maintaining fares sufficiently low to allow the public access to air travel. Thus, the board in setting rates was to consider the effect of rates on the movement of traffic; the need for adequate and efficient transport at the lowest cost consistent with furnishing service; the inherent advantages of air transport; and the need of each carrier for revenue sufficient to enable it, under honest, economical, and efficient management, to provide adequate and efficient service. At the same time, the board, in carrying out all its duties, was also to encourage the development of the air transportation system adapted to the present and future needs of commerce; to see that the carriers provided adequate, economical, and efficient service at reasonable charges without unjust discrimination; to promote safety; to encourage sound economic conditions in the industry; to encourage competition to the extent necessary to assure development of an air transport system; and so forth.

The CAB also possessed certain other powers, such as the power to grant antitrust immunity to agreements among carriers, and the power to approve or to disapprove mergers, to grant or to withhold subsidy, to formulate and to enforce regulations involving such subjects as baggage liability, depreciation, and smoking.[7]

The problems that led to the creation of the Civil Aeronautics Board in 1938 were quite different from those facing the board and the industry in 1974. Before 1934 the United States Postal Service administered a subsidy and in doing so exerted considerable control over which airlines flew over which routes. Dissatisfaction with this system, and charges of impropriety, led Congress between 1934 and 1938 to try alternatives, including the grant of regulatory power to the ICC. When power was vested in the CAB in 1938, the board's main job was administering a subsidy; control of rates was secondary. Beginning in the 1950s, however, the relative importance of the two jobs was reversed.[8]

Harmful Effects of Regulation

To determine the effects of classical price and entry regulation in the airline industry, it is best to focus on regulation prior to 1976, when the current reform movement began. The Senate study revealed four serious defects, relating to rates, routes, efficiency, and agency procedures.

Rates. Regulation led to high prices and overcapacity. Because the airline industry was highly competitive and because the CAB prevented price competition, the airlines channeled their competitive energies into providing more and costlier service—more flights, more planes, and more frills—to the point where travelers were offered frequent scheduling as well as in-flight gourmet meals and Polynesian pubs. Yet the planes themselves flew more than half-empty.

These facts suggested that fares were too high. But it was difficult to say to what extent they were too high, for two reasons. First, adding passengers to half-empty planes would cut costs per passenger dramatically, because the additional cost of carrying a passenger on an existing flight is low (the airlines used "10 percent of the fare" as a rule of thumb). Thus, the extent to which fares might be lowered depended upon the extent to which planes could be filled. Second, extra passengers needed to fill planes could be obtained in two ways: by cutting the number of flights so that more passengers could be crowded onto each remaining flight, or by cutting fares so that more passengers might be induced to fly. The former method of filling planes meant inconvenience—fewer flights and more crowding. More crowded airplanes might lower costs and hence lower fares, but this added inconvenience must be subtracted from the lower fare before one can say that the fare-saving itself produced a net benefit for the traveler. The second factor tended to offset the first, for the lower fare would also bring increased demand, which would help fill planes without requiring a cut in the number of flights. It was difficult to measure the extent to which this would happen, because it depends upon demand elasticity which is extremely hard to estimate.

Despite these uncertainties, there was strong evidence that fares were too high. For one thing, comparing the fare level with what might have been charged with fuller planes showed a great difference. Lockheed estimated that by using an all-coach seating configuration (330 seats in an L-1101) and filling the plane to 70 percent of capacity, a transcontinental flight could be operated profitably at a fare of $90 one way. Boeing estimated that with a similar seating configuration and load factor, a B-747 could fly across the country for about the same fare. At that time (1975) the airlines were charging $175 for a one-way transcontinental ticket (and discount fares were being phased out). Calculations made with Boeing and Lockheed figures showed possible savings of 50 percent or more through fuller planes (see Tables 4 and 5).

Similarly, a comparison of fares in California and Texas, where economic regulation existed to only a limited extent (none in California before 1967), suggested that fares could be lowered substantially by increasing the number of seats in the plane and filling more of them. Thus, in 1975, for example, the 456-mile, one-hour-five-minute flight from San Diego to San Francisco cost $26.21, while the 399-mile, one-hour-seven-minute flight from Boston to Washington cost $41.67. Information from American Airlines and PSA, the California intrastate carrier, showed that most of the fare difference was due to the average number of passengers carried on each flight. Thus, PSA put 158 seats in a Boeing 727-200 jet aircraft and filled their planes approximately 60 percent full. American put 121 seats in the same plane and filled their fleet on average 55 percent full. When flying PSA, 95 passengers shared the costs that American's passengers had to share among only 66. American's data showed that if it had put 158 seats in its 727-200s and filled its Boston-Washington flights 60 percent full, it could have covered its $2,876 one-way cost by charging each of its 95 passengers $32 rather than $42 per trip (and other factors such as supplying turnaround service could have reduced the price still further).[9] Work by independent economists using econometric models based on information from many airlines confirmed those rough estimates.

Whether the high fares constituted a problem depends upon whether travelers preferred them—and the frequent scheduling they allowed—to lower fares and a different level of service. Of course, whether lower fares required a

Table 4. Estimated total operating cost (TOC) at various seating configurations, load factors, and mileages: Boeing Aircraft.

Boeing 747-100

Flight distance and load factor	386 available seats (mixed) 9-abreast			433 available seats (mixed) 10-abreast				500 available seats (all economy)			
	Number of passengers	TOC (in millions of dollars)	TOC (cents per passenger-mile)	Number of passengers	TOC (in millions of dollars)	TOC (cents per passenger-mile)	Regulated CAB-formula fare	Number of passengers	TOC (in millions of dollars)	TOC (cents per passenger-mile)	Staff calculation of possible one-way fare
500:											
50 percent	193.0	14.75	7.6	216.5	15.49	7.2	52.80	250	16.54	6.7	36.85
60 percent	231.6	15.96	6.9	259.8	16.84	6.5	52.80	300	17.71	5.9	32.45
70 percent	270.2	17.17	6.4	303.1	18.20	6.0	52.80	350	19.67	5.6	30.80
1,200:											
50 percent	193.0	9.68	5.0	216.5	10.07	4.7	85.13	250	10.64	4.3	56.76
60 percent	231.6	10.33	4.5	259.8	10.80	4.2	85.13	300	11.47	3.8	50.16
70 percent	270.2	10.98	4.1	303.1	11.52	3.8	85.13	350	12.31	3.5	46.20
2,500:											
50 percent	193.0	7.80	4.0	216.5	8.04	3.5	156.60	250	8.40	3.4	93.50
60 percent	231.6	8.20	3.5	259.8	8.49	3.3	156.60	300	8.91	3.0	82.50
70 percent	270.2	8.60	3.2	303.1	8.94	3.0	156.60	350	9.54	2.7	74.25

Boeing 727-200

Flight distance and load factor	134 available seats (mixed)			155 available seats (all economy)			
	Number of passengers	TOC (in millions of dollars)	TOC (cents per passenger-mile)	Number of passengers	TOC (in millions of dollars)	TOC (cents per passenger-mile)	Staff calculation of possible one-way fare
500:							
50 percent	67.0	5.48	8.2	77.5	5.81	7.5	41.25
60 percent	80.4	5.90	7.3	93.0	6.29	6.8	37.40
70 percent	93.8	6.32	6.7	108.5	6.78	6.3	34.65
1,200:							
50 percent	67.0	3.84	5.7	77.5	4.07	5.2	68.64
60 percent	80.4	4.06	5.1	93.0	4.28	4.6	60.72
70 percent	93.8	4.29	4.6	108.5	4.53	4.2	55.44
2,500:							
50 percent	67.0	3.09	4.6	77.5	3.11	4.0	110.00
60 percent	80.4	3.22	4.0	93.0	3.?7		

Flight distance and load factor	103 available seats (mixed)			117 available seats (all economy)		
	Number of passengers	TOC (in millions of dollars)	TOC (cents per passenger-mile)	Number of passengers	TOC (in millions of dollars)	TOC (cents per passenger-mile)
500:						
50 percent	51.5	4.71	9.2	58.5	4.93	8.4
60 percent	61.8	5.03	8.2	70.2	5.30	7.6
70 percent	72.1	5.36	7.4	81.9	5.66	6.9
1,200:						
50 percent	51.5	3.35	6.6	58.5	3.50	6.0
60 percent	61.8	3.57	5.8	70.2	3.71	5.3
70 percent	72.1	3.75	5.2	81.9	3.90	4.8
2,500:						
50 percent	51.5	2.77	5.4	58.5	2.82	4.8
60 percent	61.8	2.86	4.6	70.2	2.95	4.2
70 percent	72.1	2.97	4.1	81.9	3.07	3.8

Boeing 737-200

Flight distance and load factor	102 available seats (mixed)			115 available seats (all economy)		
	Number of passengers	TOC (in millions of dollars)	TOC (cents per passenger-mile)	Number of passengers	TOC (in millions of dollars)	TOC (cents per passenger-mile)
500:						
50 percent	51.0	4.00	7.8	57.5	4.20	7.3
60 percent	61.2	4.32	7.1	69.0	4.56	6.6
70 percent	71.4	4.63	6.5	80.5	4.92	6.1
1,200:						
50 percent	51.0	2.76	5.4	57.5	2.86	5.0
60 percent	61.2	2.92	4.8	69.0	3.05	4.4
70 percent	71.4	3.09	4.3	80.5	3.24	4.0

Source: U.S. Senate Committee on the Judiciary, Sub-committee on Administrative Practice and Procedure, *Civil Aeronautics Board Practices and Procedures,* Sub-committee Report, 94th Cong., 1st Sess. (1975), at 56–57.

Table 5. Estimated total operating cost (TOC) at various seating configurations, load factors, an⁣ mileages: Lockheed Aircraft, L-1011-1 domestic passenger service, no cargo (in 1970 dollars).ᵃ

Flight distance (in statute miles)	Load factor (in percent)	Number of passengers	TOC per airport-mile	TOC per passenger-mile	Staff calculation of possible one-way fare[b]	Regulate CAB-form fare (in dollars)
256 available seats (20/80 mixed class):						
500	50	128	11.48	8.97	49.30	52.80[c]
	60	154	12.25	7.95	43.72	52.80[c]
	70	179	13.05	7.29	40.09	52.80[c]
1,200	50	128	7.59	5.93	78.27	85.13[d]
	60	154	8.04	5.22	68.90	85.13[d]
	70	179	8.49	4.74	62.56	85.13[d]
2,500	50	128	6.16	4.81	132.27	156.60[e]
	60	154	6.50	4.22	116.05	156.60[e]
	70	179	6.83	3.82	105.05	156.60[e]
330 available seats (all economy):						
500	50	165	12.50	7.58	41.87	52.80[c]
	60	198	13.48	6.81	37.45	52.80[c]
	70	231	14.43	6.25	34.37	52.80[c]
1,200	50	165	8.20	4.97	65.60	85.13[d]
	60	198	8.74	4.41	58.21	85.13[d]
	70	231	9.29	4.02	53.06	85.13[d]
2,500	50	165	6.62	4.01	110.27	156.60[e]
	60	198	7.02	3.55	97.62	156.60[e]
	70	231	7.42	3.21	88.27	156.60[e]

Source: U.S. Senate Committee on the Judiciary, Subcommittee on Administrative Practice and Procedure, *Civi⁣ Aeronautics Board Practices and Procedures,* Subcommittee Report, 94th Cong., 1st Sess. (1975), at 54.

a. Fares have been calculated by adding onto a fare calculated on the basis of total operating costs an additional 15 percent to represent such nonoperating items as return on investment.

b. Indicates calculations performed by the subcommittee. All other figures and calculations performed by Lockheed Aircraft Corp.

c. CAB Order 74-12-109 (13.85 plus [500 × 7.79 cents per mile]).

d. Id. (13.85 plus [1,200 × 5.94 cents per mile]).

e. Id. (13.85 plus [2,500 × 5.71 cents per mile]).

significant reduction in the number of scheduled flights depends upon how much extra demand for air travel the lower fares will generate. Texas' and California's experience suggested that demand for air travel is highly elastic and the lower prices will result in a great increase in demand. In the triangle of San Antonio, Dallas/Fort Worth, and Houston, for example, traffic had declined slightly prior to 1971. Then Southwest Airlines, an intrastate carrier unregulated by the CAB, entered the market with fares about 50 percent below those of its competitors; total air traffic on those routes increased 100–150 percent between 1971 and 1975. Similar increases occurred in the Harlingen Valley when Southwest entered the market, and in California when PSA (an unregulated intrastate carrier) entered a new market with significantly lower prices.[10]

In any event, even if demand had been less elastic,[11] the price/service trade-off did not reflect what most travelers wanted. One economist calculated that in 1969 the fare/service combination was likely to have suited only those whose waiting time was particularly valuable—such as business travelers whose time was worth $60,000 per year or more. Assuming that waiting time was worth $10 per hour (an assumption used by the industry trade association) travelers paid about half a billion dollars more than necessary in 1969.[12] Moreover, whenever passengers had the choice of lower fares and fuller planes or better schedules but more expensive flights, they tended to choose the former. In California, PSA (which offered low-fare, full-plane service) prospered, while its competitors went bankrupt. In Europe, where charter flights were less restricted (though regular fares were higher) than in the United States, charters carried considerably more passengers.

In sum, fares prior to 1975 seemed too high—higher than appropriate for the level of service demanded. Depending upon assumptions governing demand elasticity and value of waiting time, the problem amounted to overcharges of between $.5 billion and $3.5 billion annually.[13]

Routes. Regulation effectively closed the industry to newcomers and effectively guaranteed relatively stable market shares to firms already in the industry. True, the statute instructed the CAB to allow a firm to offer air service if it was "fit, willing, and able" to do so and if its service was "required by the public convenience and necessity." It also required the board to hold a public hearing on any application and to "dispose of such application as speedily as possible." Given this statute, the CAB denied that it had any policy that precluded entry of a new carrier. But the Senate investigation showed the contrary. Between 1950 and 1974, for example, the board had received seventy-nine applications from companies wishing to enter the domestic scheduled airline industry; it granted none. Indeed, since 1960 only four (of thirty-two) such applications had been granted a hearing. Since 1965, less than 10 percent of all applications by existing airlines to serve new routes had been granted and between 1969 and 1974 fewer than 4 percent had been granted.

Overall, entry into the industry since 1938 had been limited to: (1) the eight supplemental carriers that provided charter service and that were descended from a group of nonscheduled carriers allowed into the industry at the behest of Congress just after World War II; (2) the nineteen local-service carriers admitted to the industry just after World War II; and (3) commuter carriers, which operated small airplanes over short routes. But when it came to the domestic trunk carriers (which accounted for more than 90 percent of all traffic and revenue), entry into the industry was effectively blocked.

At the same time, market shares of the major firms remained remarkably stable. In 1938 the four largest domestic carriers—United, American, Eastern, and TWA—accounted for about 82.5 percent of all revenue passenger-miles flown domestically. In 1950 they accounted for 68.9 percent and in 1972 the figure was 60 percent. While their combined share fell 20 percentage points, the industry itself expanded by 238 times (that is, increased by 23,800 percentage points). United, the largest airline, accounted for 22.9 percent of the market in 1938; in 1972, after merging with Capital Airlines, it accounted for 22.0 percent.

This stability of market shares also reflected in part the CAB's policy of preventing airline bankruptcies by allowing mergers. Of the sixteen trunk carriers in business in 1938, ten remained in 1975; of the nineteen local-service carriers allowed to enter the industry after World War II, only nine remained. The smaller, weaker firms were merged into larger, stronger ones. Stability of market share also reflected the board's tendency to award better routes to weaker firms, thus using route awards as a handicap system to counteract any advantage gained competitively by stronger lines.

Efficiency. The efficiency with which the airlines conducted their business varied considerably from one firm to another. Efficiency is difficult to measure because a variety of figures can be used—such as seat miles flown per employee, average hours an aircraft is used per day, total expenses per ton-mile—and such figures depend in part on the nature of the route system the particular airline must fly. Yet all such measures, as well as other measures devised by economists to take route differences into account, showed large variation (see Table 6).

While variations in efficiency among firms are common in an unregulated, competitive market, the fear that a more efficient firm will cut prices and take business from the higher-cost, less efficient firm provides a strong incentive for peak efficiency. The CAB's pricing policy and its tendency to keep market shares stable weakened this incentive. At the same time, the CAB could not directly supervise the business practices of the firms. While some incentives to perform more efficiently remained (because greater profit could be earned), the weakening of the incentive structure tended to bring about higher costs of performance.

Agency procedures. The procedures that the CAB followed were shown to have violated accepted administrative norms of efficiency, fairness, or propriety. For example:

1. Route applications were subject to serious delay. As of January 1975, 40 percent of all applications had been pending more than two years, 28 percent more than five years, and 8 percent more than nine years.[14]

2. The board's standards for determining *when* new route authority was to

Table 6. Carrier efficiency (1972).

Carrier	Employees	Total operating expenses (millions of dollars)	Available ton-miles (millions)	Available seat-miles (millions)	Expenses per available ton-mile (cents)	Available seat-miles per employee	Aircraft utilization per day
American	34,465	1,309.6	5,502.5	33,033.2	23.8	958,455	7:45
Braniff	8,441	340.7	1,059.8	7,705.4	31.8	912,860	7:57
Continental	9,163	329.4	1,832.1	10,707.4	18.0	1,168,548	8:56
Delta/Northeast[a]	26,696	863.8	3,710.1	26,986.9	23.3	1,010,895	8:34
Eastern	33,157	1,107.8	3,219.5	23,404.3	34.4	705,861	8:04
National	7,625	324.0	1,438.2	10,547.2	22.5	1,383,239	7:35
Northwest	9,118	377.4	1,553.7	9,939.7	24.3	1,090,121	4:49
Trans World	32,680	1,339.3	4,018.8	26,089.9	33.3	798,344	7:15
United	48,690	1,638.1	7,487.5	49,359.1	21.9	1,013,743	6:54
Western	9,517	342.1	1,241.0	9,610.0	27.6	1,009,775	7:51

Source: U.S. Senate Committee on the Judiciary, Subcommittee on Administrative Practice and Procedure, Civil Aeronautics Board Practices and Procedures, Subcommittee Report, 94th Cong., 1st Sess. (1975), at 126–127. Data compiled by the CAB.
a. Delta and Northeast merged in 1972. Data are sums for the two airlines, and may not be accurate.

be awarded were obscure; its determination of *which* applicant airline would be awarded such authority was characterized by a CAB study as "random"—a conclusion confirmed by outside observers.[15]

3. The board developed a procedure for awarding routes that effectively immunized its actions from judicial review: no applicant could receive a route award without a hearing, yet the board would refuse to grant a hearing unless it first approved a preliminary "motion for an expedited hearing." It would grant this motion only if it intended to make a route award; otherwise it would deny it. The application would then remain on its docket for three years, after which it would be dismissed as "stale." In this way, World Airways' application to fly from Los Angeles to New York for $75 was denied an expedited hearing, remained on the docket for three years, and was then dismissed as stale. It was difficult for a carrier to obtain judicial review of these board actions, because its application had not been officially denied. It appeared to the courts that the board's action had been procedural; if a carrier had won in court, the appropriate remedy would have been to remand the case to the CAB for a hearing, where the carrier would have had to renew its route requirement before a board unwilling to grant it.[16]

4. Between 1969 and 1974 the CAB administered a policy known as the "route moratorium," under which it refused to hear applications (by existing airlines) for new routes. The policy was developed as follows.

In 1969 and 1970 the CAB chairman and several other board members became concerned about the problem of overcapacity in the industry. Several carrier representatives discussed the problem with them during informal private meetings and suggested a route moratorium.

The chairman then gave a set of public speeches at which he announced that the board would set down few, if any, route applications for hearing.

The board staff, understanding the new policy as a result of reading the speeches or through discussions between the chairman and his top staff, simply refrained from setting cases for hearing. In other instances, cases already set for hearing were withdrawn from the hearing docket. For example, one administrative law judge wrote to the board chairman that "the following cases, which have been set for hearing by Board order, have not been noticed for a conference and hearing . . . pursuant to informal instructions of the Chairman's office in connection with the unofficial route moratorium."[17]

This method of determining major route policy violates accepted norms of administrative behavior. The failure to grant hearings on applications was probably unlawful under the governing statute, which required that cases be set for hearing and also required a "speedy disposition." In addition, to make so major a policy change without prior public hearing is itself undesirable. The carriers, government agencies, and consumer groups were either divided about or opposed to the route moratorium, but they had no opportunity to present their views to the board and there was no open debate. Board members themselves opposed certain aspects of the policy and expressed surprise that a chairman would remove cases from a hearing docket without formal board approval. Further, without a formal policy-making decision, no one could challenge the board's policy in court. As long as the board denied the existence of the policy, it was difficult for an individual firm to show that *its* denial of a hearing flowed from the policy change and not, as the board claimed, from lack of time to hear the case. The combination of, first, determining the merits of a case on a procedural motion for expedited hearing; second, a refusal to hold hearings on whether it should adopt a route moratorium; and, third, its claim that a failure to grant hearings simply reflected its ordering of business on its own docket destroyed the incentive of applicants to seek judicial review.

5. The large number of private meetings between board members and industry groups—769 in 1974—was of doubtful propriety.[18]

6. Between 1971 and 1975 the board encouraged the airlines to make agreements to limit the number of flights that each would provide on particular routes. The object was to increase airline profits—which had fallen to very low levels—by limiting service competition. These "capacity-restricting" agreements required CAB approval, for without it the airlines would have been subject to attack under the antitrust laws. The board granted its approval to several such agreements, which were renewed from time to time. Between 1971 and 1973 the board referred to these agreements as "capacity-reduction agreements." Between 1973 and 1975 the board referred to them as "fuel-saving agreements." The effect of the capacity-restricting agreements was to curtail service severely on major routes. They also raised airline profits. They did not, however, lead to lower fares. Thus, travelers could legitimately complain that on restricted routes they paid high fares but received the level of service (fewer flights and fuller planes) that ought to have been associated with low fares.

The board instituted and enforced its capacity-restriction policy without prior hearings. In fact, it began hearings two years after instituting its policy. In 1975, after the hearing, the board decided that the agreements were unlawful. Thus, for four years unlawful agreements remained in effect, despite the fact that, legality aside, their wisdom was highly debatable and that major carriers, government departments, and local organizations were anxious to debate their merits.[19]

Mismatch as Cause

It is apparent that airline regulation, as seen in 1975, was not working well. To some extent, one might blame inadequate personnel or inadequate procedures for the problem. A major part of the blame, however, lies in the regulatory process itself, or, rather, in the effort to use that process to deal with a problem for which it is ill-suited. Our purpose here is to demonstrate, in the one completed case study available, how this fundamental mismatch was responsible for the failure of airline regulation—how most of the problems just documented arise, plausibly if not inevitably, from the effort to apply classical regulation to a highly competitive, volatile, and complex industry.

Price Regulation

The problem of high fares was essentially a problem of low load factors, which reflected excessive scheduling, which in turn resulted from CAB action that inhibited price competition. But how and why, one might ask, did the board stop price competition? After all, the statute did not forbid an airline to cut its fares.

The procedures that typically accompany cost-of-service ratemaking provide an initial explanation. For one thing, carriers must file tariffs, and rate changes must be announced in tariff filings thirty days before they take effect. The filing of proposed fare cuts alerts competitors, who immediately announce similar cuts; the filing of proposed increases allows a firm to "test the waters"— to see if competitors will go along. In other words, the publicity requirement was thought to promote interdependent pricing behavior. For another thing, the filing of a proposed fare cut allowed a competitor to challenge the proposal as unreasonably low, discriminatorily preferential, prejudicial, or unfairly competitive. The board had to suspend the tariff if the challenge was plausible. Given the vagueness of the standards and the inventiveness of the legal profession, most challenges raised litigable issues. The board was thus likely to suspend a fare-cutting tariff, costing the carrier whatever money it had spent promoting its new fare and forcing it into expensive litigation. Fear of challenge, suspension, and litigation thus tended to keep carriers from proposing fare cuts in the first place.

There was, however, a deeper explanation. Consider the choices facing the board as it tried to apply cost-of-service ratemaking principles to the airline industry. The board had three basic alternatives.

First, it might have applied cost-of-service ratemaking principles on a firm-by-firm, issue-by-issue basis, using formal ratemaking to resolve each rate-policy problem. But the complexity of the costs, routes, and fares involved, together with the ever-changing economic environment, made this alternative administratively unworkable. One need only note the difficulties that arise in applying the system to a comparatively stable, noncompetitive industry such as electricity production to reach this conclusion.

Second, the board was therefore tempted to substitute a negotiation for classical regulatory hearing procedures. By staying in close contact with industry members, the board's staff could learn about industry problems, become familiar with industry predictions of costs and revenues, and thus more easily formulate appropriate rate policies while informally forcing industry members to accept them.

The board handled major pricing issues in this way during most of the 1960s. Board members and carrier representatives would talk to one another directly or would use the board staff to communicate views and positions. In fact, "particular carriers" and occasionally the industry trade association, the ATA, "would come in and have private meetings with the entire Board." They "made a pitch and discussed their problems and aspirations."[20]

Although these informal proceedings allowed the CAB to adjust its rate policy rapidly to changing economic conditions, from an administrative point of view the procedure was unfair. Many affected parties, such as shippers and travelers, neither knew the facts and arguments underlying a board change of position nor were allowed the opportunity to comment upon or refute them. Two board members insisted that the practice be modified and in *Moss* v. *Civil Aeronautics Board*[21] the Court of Appeals held it unlawful.

Third, the only remaining alternative was for the board to develop a set of rules and regulations that would work *automatically* without elaborate individualized hearings, to adjust rates to the industry's economic condition as it changed in response to the general condition of the economy. This was precisely what the board did in the late 1960s when it launched the Domestic Passenger Fare Investigation (DPFI).

As a result of that investigation, the board developed a set of rules governing fares that worked almost automatically. The DPFI system represented an effort to apply cost-of-service ratemaking to the airline industry by modifying the classical system in two important ways. Rather than determining costs firm by firm, the CAB determined costs for the industry as a whole; its "revenue requirement" was an *industry* requirement, not a firm requirement, and fares were set at a level predicted to generate revenues equal to that requirement for the entire industry. In addition, the board set fare levels that would earn the industry profits only if it met a "load factor standard"—that is, only if planes were filled to 55 percent of capacity on average.

The DPFI standards represent an interesting effort to modify classical cost-of-service ratemaking principles in order to deal with a structurally competitive industry. The system worked as follows.

1. Every three months domestic airlines submitted cost and revenue figures to the board.

2. The board "adjusted" twelve-month cost/revenue figures: it applied the "55 percent load factor" by subtracting any costs associated with carrying any extra empty seats; it made a similar adjustment to penalize airlines for flying too few seats or for charging too many discount fares; and it made another adjustment to reflect inflation.

3. It subtracted adjusted costs from adjusted profits, and if the remainder was less than 12 percent of the industry's rate base it allowed a fare increase.

4. In the same way, it calculated the fare increase needed to obtain the allowed revenue requirement, assuming that the elasticity of demand was .7. Having determined the percentage fare increase allowable for the industry as a whole, it allowed each firm in the industry to file for and to obtain an increase equal to that percent.

5. The board's fare structure rules required the charging of "equal fares for equal miles." They also required the calculation of fares by setting a fixed terminal charge, and a mileage charge which declined for longer trips. The fixed charge added to the mileage charge meant that the fare per mile fell as the length of the trip increased.

Since industry accounts were submitted to the board every three months and the fare level could be readily calculated from the rules, there was little need for hearings. There were few facts or policies to contest, because the rules worked automatically. The rules themselves were set after elaborate hearings, which lasted several years. Thus, the board seemed to have solved its legal and administrative problems. It found a system that was procedurally fair and yet administratively workable. It is not surprising that in the Washington legal community in the early 1970s the CAB was viewed as a well-functioning administrative agency.

This same system, however, aggravated the board's economic problem. It made it more difficult for airlines to charge lower prices and to offer full plane service. Airlines were effectively prevented from charging lower fares than DPFI standards dictated, because the board would suspend filings containing departures from those standards. The fare structure rules—which the board insisted were necessary to make its system administratively workable—prevented selective price cuts. A carrier could not charge lower prices on some routes without changing the fare relationship dictated by the fare structure standards. And if airlines were not allowed to cut prices selectively, they were unlikely to try to cut them at all. (In fact, the DPFI rules effectively ruled out across-the-board fare cuts as well.) Finally, the profit standard of 12 percent and the demand elasticity figure of .7 were highly inexact. Efforts to measure demand elasticity in this area produce, at best, educated guesses, and the increase in air travel once fares were cut shows that .7 was overly conservative. Similarly, "scientific" estimates of a reasonable profit were probably on the high side. This overestimate results from measuring the rate of return during a period of stock market boom and using the returns actually received as a basis for predicting what shareholders will insist upon to hold shares in the future. The fact that airlines obtained capital while consistently earning less than the 12 percent overall (or 20 percent on equity) return allowed suggests that the figure was too high.

The existence of rigid pricing rules, which effectively halted efforts to charge lower prices, explains the persistent tendency of airlines to substitute service competition for price competition. Yet given one simple fact—the fact that the statute ordered the board to set reasonable prices—its decision to use modified cost-of-service ratemaking principles is understandable. Once it sought to do so, the subsequent evolution to a system that stopped price competition became a likely result.

Route Awards

The problems that the CAB encountered in its route-award activities arose from its efforts to follow a system of public interest allocation. They typify those described in Chapter 4. Before turning to these problems, however, it is interesting to note how a major substantive problem of airline regulation—the fact that the CAB barred new entry and kept market shares stable—also flowed in part from the process of regulation itself.

One way in which regulation tended to bring about closed entry and stable market shares stemmed from the fact that any regulator would hesitate to adopt policies that would threaten a regulated firm with bankruptcy. Unlike an impersonal, competitive market, the regulator knows and inevitably feels responsible for the firms he regulates. The perceived identity of an injured firm may lead a regulator to be criticized politically if he allows a bankruptcy, but a decision that helps preserve firms will be viewed as fair. Thus, the regulator has a strong motive for not allowing too much competition. This tendency was aggravated by the CAB's rate rules (which in turn arose out of the effort to apply cost-of-service ratemaking to a competitively structured industry). At first, profit standards that exceeded the profits actually earned year after year led the CAB to believe that the industry was "sick" or suffered a "surfeit" of competition, or, at any rate, needed no more of it. Indeed, once the CAB set to work to formalize its route-award standards, it proposed criteria that would have been still more stringent, effectively stopping *all* new entry—even entry into new routes by existing airlines seeking expansion. The standards and their tendency to overstate the profit problem resulted in part from the system itself.

Second, the "equal fares for equal miles" rule—which may have been administratively necessary—forced the CAB to equalize market shares. Since costs are a function of many factors—such as congestion, number of passengers, weather, flight time, aircraft type—and not just distance, the rule produced equal fares for routes with very different costs. It also produced a wide variation in profits, depending upon the competition along each route. Thus, airline profitability depended upon route configuration, and not those aspects of its performance within its control. The board consequently awarded new routes so as to balance the advantages or disadvantages it had created through its prior route awards and its "equal fares" rule. In other words, the board used the route-award process combined with the fare rules paternalistically to provide "handicaps" or "rewards." Doing so prevented the award of routes to newcomers wishing to fly them.

The more interesting effects of regulation, however, are the procedural defects of airline route regulation. It is interesting to see how they arose out of the regulatory process itself. Consider how the CAB's route-award problems resembled those of the FCC discussed in Chapter 5.

1. The board's basic problem was to award a scarce commodity (though the scarcity was artificially created by regulatory policy). The board would not

award routes to all who wanted them; thus, it had to distinguish among competing applicants, and it had to do so without a lottery or an auction.

2. The board combined the question of *what* to award with the question of *who* would receive it, for whether a particular applicant should receive a particular new route depended in large part upon the shape of its existing route network. Thus, an award to a particular firm in Proceeding 1 would affect both what new routes the board would award in Proceeding 2 and which firms would receive them. To award Delta nonstop Miami–Los Angeles authority in Proceeding 1 would affect both the question of whether new nonstop Miami-Houston authority ought to be created, as well as who should receive it if it were created. For this reason, the board consolidated several route applications into a single proceeding for joint hearing. It had to try to draw new route maps and award new authority for an entire region in a single proceeding.

This interrelationship between what to award and who to award it to made it difficult for the CAB to create clear standards for deciding the "what" question (whether to award new authority and where). The board claimed that it used fixed standards to answer that question. It would allow new service if and only if the market were large enough to support additional service *and* existing service was deficient. Yet the interrelationship of the "what" and "who" questions meant, as the board's route study pointed out, that "factors of carrier selection overlap in part the question of need."[22] The interrelationship also meant complex proceedings lasting several years, without fixed criteria for determining relevant issues or how they should be decided.

3. The selection process itself suffered from a lack of coherent standards to be consistently applied. The board described its selection criteria as follows: "In no event would we select a carrier to serve a particular market unless we were convinced that it could render effective services, responsive to the needs of the traveling public in that market. Additional factors are (1) the ability to provide benefits to beyond-segment traffic; (2) route integration; (3) identity at the points involved; (4) historic participation in the traffic; (5) diversion; (6) need for strengthening; and (7) other similar factors."[23]

Again, the board's problem was similar to that of the FCC. It had not too few standards, but too many. How could it evaluate applicants within any particular category? It might have ranked applicants in terms of "route integration"—whether the route at issue would produce a more coherent route system in the hands of a particular applicant. But route integration is not a factor that is easily measured, nor are different degrees of integration readily weighed one against the other. Nor could the board readily weigh integration against traffic diversion. How could it compare objectively the need for strengthening an airline with the benefits for beyond-segment traffic? In any case, is not "diversion" the polar opposite of "responsiveness to the needs of the traveling public"? (The more "responsive" the new carrier is to demand, the more business it will divert from existing carriers.) Finally, how do these criteria relate to the CAB's overall mission—to provide the public with adequate, safe air travel at low cost? The pre-1976 board did not consider a carrier's offer of a lower fare as a significant factor in its favor.

It was possible to infer from the board's decisions that certain factors were more important than others. It placed considerable weight, for example, on "beyond-area" benefits. But there was such variation among decisions that the board's own staff concluded that major awards were "random as to carrier selection."[24] Outside experts concluded that the board's choice of carrier did not emerge from the consistent application of comprehensible standards.[25] This is not surprising, since the CAB could not use a competitive marketplace, a lottery, or an auction to award routes. How, then, could it develop a consistent set of standards that would produce lower price and better product? As in the case of television licensing, it is difficult to suggest any set of standards that would avoid this basic difficulty.

4. Route proceedings became lengthy and difficult to manage. The range of relevant issues was broad and impossible to define narrowly. The CAB administrative law judges, like those of the FCC, had to decide relevant issues on a case-by-case basis. Each party argued that the case should turn upon those issues where it could make the most favorable showing. The number of parties in each proceeding was large. Each party produced a host of witnesses, ranging from mayors to labor leaders to community business executives. Each witness would describe in detail advantages to the local community if the board allowed new service and awarded the route to the witnesses' favorite airline. Economists and expert consultants would testify about probable diversion of traffic. Since diversion turned upon unknowable demand elasticities, that issue in itself led to time-consuming debate. The economists could also testify about integration benefits. The evidence was difficult to evaluate, because the board (like the FCC), in determining the type of service, the amount of service, and the benefits that arise had to rely upon the promises of the parties. Further, the parties had every incentive not only to exaggerate benefits, but also to discuss many factors and to cumulate evidence relevant to each factor, because no applicant could be certain about what might tip the balance in a close case. In sum, the manageability problems described in Chapter 5 were present here. This is not surprising, since the CAB's allocation problem was very similar to that of the FCC.[26]

5. The consistency problem arises in CAB route cases as it did in FCC licensing cases. In *Continental Airlines* v. *CAB*,[27] for example, the court compared the board's decision awarding Delta authority to fly between Dallas and Phoenix with its decision awarding Delta Houston-Miami authority. In the first case Continental had offered to fly two flights per day between Dallas and Phoenix, with turnaround service. Delta had offered five flights per day at a higher fare, and showed that those flights would help many passengers coming from or going to areas beyond (east of) Dallas on Delta planes. Continental argued that Delta's greater frequency of service and greater beyond-segment benefits were offset by the fact that Continental already served both airports

whereas Delta did not. Delta received the award. In the second case, by coincidence, the circumstances were almost exactly reversed. Delta offered two flights between Houston and Miami, while Continental offered five; Continental showed much greater beyond-segment benefits; Delta argued that Continental's greater frequency of service and beyond-segment benefits were outweighed by the fact that Delta already served both airports while Continental served only one. A hearing examiner awarded the route to Continental. The CAB reversed the decision and awarded the route to Delta, arguing that Delta had not recently been awarded many routes and it needed strengthening. The board wrote: "Since the balance of other factors in the Houston-Miami market is quite close—Continental's greater beyond-segment benefits are balanced by Delta's greater identity [the fact that it did business at both terminals]—we find that considerations of the overall balance of awards militate decisively in favor of an award to Delta here." The D.C. Circuit could not understand how the board could find that the identity and beyond-area benefits "balanced" each other in the Miami case, yet solidly favored Delta in the Phoenix case. It reversed on grounds of inconsistency and remanded to the board.

These cases suggest not only that inconsistent CAB policies exist, but also that inconsistency cannot be dealt with readily by the courts. The board might have avoided court reversal simply by omitting the word "balanced" in its opinion. Indeed, the board's counsel argued that the decision meant only that the need to preserve carrier balance outweighed Continental's advantages. Had the board's opinion-writing staff stated this explicitly (and the word "balanced" was probably that of the staff, not of any board member), its decision would not have been reversible. Moreover, the inconsistency here was flagged for the court by the extraordinary coincidence that the two cases were near mirror images of each other and arose at almost precisely the same time. Thus, one is left with the strong suspicion that there are many other unprovable instances of inconsistency.

6. Again like FCC regulation, the airline regulatory process led to fear of corruption. Commodities (routes) worth millions of dollars were awarded through a process highly dependent upon subjective judgment. Thus, there was considerable public concern when the Senate hearings revealed that board members had held 769 private meetings with industry representatives in 1974, that they had flown on "inaugural flights" at airline expense, and that the board's chairman had spent golfing vacations in Bermuda with airline presidents as the guest of Boeing. Similarly, the airlines were found to have illegally contributed corporate funds to political campaigns. And the Senate subcommittee found strong evidence that investigations of illegal corporate giving had been improperly suppressed by the board.[28]

Given the CAB's task (awarding valuable routes on nonmarket criteria) and the regulatory technique available (public interest allocation), it is not surprising that the investigating committee found not only suspicion of impropriety, but evidence of corruption itself.

To avoid the problems of public interest allocation, the board need not have abandoned all allocation. It might, for example, have awarded route authority to those applicants promising the lowest fares or the best service/fare combination. This approach offers more definite standards, but it also would have left much of the selection process to the market to judge what is "best." To abandon the complex standards actually used would suggest board abandonment of classical regulation itself. The board was reluctant to follow that path.

The difficulty of developing a coherent set of route standards helps explain several other procedural defects that the Senate subcommittee criticized. Given the extraordinary complexity and length of a route case and the lack of clear standards, the CAB was tempted to cast the route-award decision in a procedural mold. By casting its decisions in the form of "denial of a motion to expedite a hearing," the board did not have to apply precise, stringent route-award standards, and the courts were less likely to reverse (for an agency has discretionary control over its own docket). The proceeding could be shortened, and outside commentators were less likely to understand, and hence to criticize, what was taking place. Once the board and its staff became used to seeing substantive route decisions transformed into purely procedural ones, they saw nothing improper about casting a still more important substantive decision— that of the route moratorium—into the same procedural mold (where it, too, was protected from judicial review).

Thus, the CAB's procedural problems stemmed in part from the difficulty of finding a manageable set of route-award standards—a difficulty endemic to public interest allocation. Coherent, consistent standards were virtually impossible as long as the board pursued a restrictive route policy. Yet the tendency to administer just such a policy arose naturally (but not inevitably) out of classical regulation itself.

Efficiency

The difficulties of supervising the efficiency of utilities, described in Chapter 3, also help explain why the CAB was unable to supervise the efficiency of the airlines directly. An added explanation arises out of the board's rate-setting and route-award policies. Its fare-setting rules required the charging of "equal fares for equal miles." This prompted considerable variation in the profitability of equidistant flights, which depended upon actual costs and the competitiveness of the route segment. Its route-award policy used this variation as a form of handicapping: some routes that were considered "plums" and some routes that were considered "dogs" were deliberately awarded in ways designed to stabilize market shares.

The existence of route "plums" or "dogs," however, makes it difficult to determine which firms are inefficient. The profitability of a firm was highly dependent on its route structure; the effect of route structure on costs was difficult to measure; hence, the responsibility of management for high costs was difficult to assess. Though "the least efficient carrier had a management 13 times the size of the most efficient, and paid its managers an average of 63 percent higher salary,"[29] the causal relationships are uncertain. It may be the fault of management or it may reflect the comparative distribution of good and bad routes. Moreover, the use of routes to handicap airlines inevitably made the board reluctant to allow the more efficient firms to take business from the less efficient. To the extent that that was allowed to occur, "plums" would cease to be "plums" and route-award policy would cease to be so effective a stabilizing weapon. Thus, these policies offer partial explanation of why the board sought to inhibit competition on many routes. Insofar as it succeeded in doing so (often it could inhibit service competition), it removed the threat of losing customers as a driving force for greater efficiency. That is to say, firms on certain routes were able to relax—to opt for the easy life of the protected firm, instead of competing vigorously.

The Effort to Regulate Schedules

The CAB's efforts to deal with the problem of overcapacity in the early 1970s reflect the classical regulatory approach to a regulatory problem: the agency sought to cure a problem caused by regulation by introducing still more comprehensive regulation. After deciding that the airlines were overscheduling (flying too many, too empty airplanes), the board sought to regulate schedules itself. It sought to "perfect the cartel" by controlling airline service as well as price. It hoped to force the airlines to provide a level of service that consumers wanted (fuller planes and fewer flights). Then, once costs fell, it could require the airlines to lower their fares. This strategy did not work, however, but not because of any mistake in economic principle.[30] Rather, it failed because of the regulatory problems that typically accompany standard setting—problems that were aggravated by certain special features of the airlines industry (a high degree of competitiveness) and the lack of legal authority allowing the CAB to control all schedules.

To set capacity standards, the board first had to determine an appropriate level of service. But the service/fare combination desired on one route was not necessarily that preferred on others. Indeed, the preferred combination depended upon whether travel was primarily for business or pleasure, the length of the trip, the type of destination, and so forth. The board dealt with this problem by refusing to set standards itself. Instead, it allowed and encouraged the carriers to agree upon what level of service to offer.[31] The schedules set by carrier agreement, however, did not necessarily approximate those desired by travelers, because the carriers sought to maximize profits, not to replicate a competitive level of price and service. Thus, it is not surprising that *on routes subject to capacity-restricting agreements,* profits more than doubled, but travelers and cities dependent on air travel (such as Las Vegas) complained bitterly of inadequate service.

Second, the board found that it could not enforce the agreements. For one thing, it could not entice all carriers to enter into them. Thus, many routes were not subject to the agreements and the carriers accused one another of cheating by transferring aircraft from restricted routes to unrestricted routes. Although the board's rules forbade this, it was impossible to ascertain whether such transfers actually took place. American Airlines, for example increased its Chicago-Dallas frequencies from six to ten trips per day in June 1974. It was accused of transferring aircraft, but it replied that the increase was needed to meet new competition from Braniff and would have taken place in the absence of any capacity-restricting agreement. The board agreed, but its opinion reveals that the decision turned on which party had the burden of proof. Eastern conceded that airplane capacity exceeding that fixed by the agreements became an undifferentiated part of the fleet and was assigned wherever it was needed. "With the possible exception of the scheduling carrier itself, no outsider can trace and sort out the fixed capacity from among the thousands of scheduling incidents of the operations of a large fleet of aircraft."[32] The enforcement problem was exacerbated by the fact that some airlines remained outside the agreements.

Third, the relationship of the fare setting rules to the capacity-restricting agreements doomed the effort. Insofar as airlines transferred aircraft to nonrestricted routes, the reduction in competition on some routes was offset by an increase in competition elsewhere. The transferring airline may have benefited, but its increased profits were offset by losses elsewhere in the industry. Thus, *industry* profits—the basis for setting fares—showed no significant change. Moreover, even had the extra capacity been removed from service—by, say, grounding planes—the planes would have remained in the rate base, and fares would have reflected this fact. Finally, even had capacity restrictions led to cost savings, given rules forbidding price competition, the airlines would have had an incentive to increase costs in other ways—through flying more complex equipment or awarding executives higher salaries. Thus, it is not surprising that despite the fuller planes and less frequent schedules on many routes, fares did not fall, and travelers on restricted routes received poorer service without corresponding fare reductions.

In sum, the CAB's most serious problems, as documented by the Senate subcommittee, flowed directly from the specific defects inherent in any classical regulatory system, described in several chapters in Part I—as aggravated by the effort to apply those systems to a highly competitive, volatile, and complex industry.

An Alternative to Classical Regulation

Economic regulation of the airlines industry was thought to be necessary to prevent excessive or destructive competition, but the claim did not justify regulation. The antitrust laws were sufficient to cope with the problem. There is no need to repeat Chapter 1's discussion of "excessive competition" here, except to point out two potentially special features of airline regulation.

First, the excessive competition rationale was plausible in 1938, when airline regulation began. At that time the government sought to promote the airline industry by providing a large subsidy. Cost-of-service ratemaking and severe entry limitations made sense in that context. Many firms sought the subsidy. Moreover, each had an incentive to cut its prices below its cost, making up the difference out of subsidy, in order to increase the size of its system. Yet once the subsidy ceased to play an important role in the industry—beginning in the 1950s when it became subsidy-free—the need for classical regulation ceased. Only its problems remained.

Second, some have argued that the industry is unusually susceptible to predatory pricing. Service or scheduling competition, for example, led certain academics to postulate the existence of an S-curve. The curve showed that a carrier, by increasing the number of its flights in a market, would win more than a proportional share of that market from its competitors; by cutting its capacity, it would lose more than a proportional share. Hence, it was argued, the carriers would fight to avoid any loss in market share and would engage in "ruinous" scheduling competition.[33]

The S-curve argument was probably invalid as an empirical matter.[34] But in any case it showed no market imperfection. It simply illustrated one reason (among others) why a carrier would hesitate to withdraw from a market as long as incremental capacity earns enough revenue to cover incremental costs. If the industry suffers from overcapacity—as did the airline industry in the early 1970s—firms may increase scheduling to the point where overall industry profits are diminished. Had those firms not been prevented from cutting prices, they would have cut prices to the level of incremental costs, and until demand increased or capacity left the industry, the industry as a whole would have lost money. Instead it brought about the same result through increased scheduling competition. This behavior is perfectly consistent with a normally functioning competitive industry.

The concern with destructive competition in the airline industry thus came down to concern about predatory pricing. But, as we have suggested, the antitrust laws are capable of dealing with this problem. At the same time, many of the serious problems discussed above grow out of, or are connected with, the use of regulation itself.

Conclusion

This analysis is designed to show why and how airline regulation constituted a mismatch. The regulatory system brought with it the particular serious and typical problems described in Part I of this book. They were aggravated through the application of classical regulation to a competitively structured industry. The ostensible objective of regulation could be met through reliance upon other weapons—here antitrust. Thus, since a mismatch appeared to exist, a major change away from reliance upon regulation was likely to do considerable good.

For change to be accomplished, however, it was necessary to investigate the industry and its regulation in detail, to ascertain the true extent of the problem and to raise the level of public interest in the question to the point where it became politically visible. How this was done will be described in Chapter 16. Since that change was brought about and since deregulation began to take effect, increased price competition has led to a decline of 10 percent in the real average domestic ticket price, increased industry profits, and greatly increased demand for travel. These facts bear out the initial mismatch assessment.

12

Mismatch: Excessive Competition and the Trucking Industry

Trucking provides a second example of the principle that classical regulation cannot deal with the problem of destructive competition.[1] Classical regulation causes harm when applied to a structurally competitive industry. Judging from the evidence presented in a recent congressional investigation of trucking, the industry is a strong candidate for reform. In fact, since 1979 both Congress and the ICC have taken major steps in the direction of the procompetitive reforms recommended. Thus, our description of agency and industry behavior applies prior to 1979. The analysis remains highly relevant, however, for the new legislation gives considerable discretion to the ICC to move toward or away from a procompetitive system.

Trucking regulation presents problems very similar to those of airline regulation. The industry is structurally competitive. Classical regulation takes the form of price and entry controls, which make it difficult for firms to engage in price competition or to enter the industry. The results are predictable. Prices are higher than necessary; market shares are fairly stable and protected from competition; pricing rules make administrative but not economic sense; and there is considerable inefficiency and waste. At the same time, the arguments used to justify regulation, when it began in 1935, are no longer convincing. Deregulation with reliance upon the antitrust laws seems superior.

The case made for these propositions is strong enough to shift the burden of persuasion to those who defend the regulatory status quo.

The Industry and Regulation

The total value of motor carrier service was estimated in 1976 to be \$110 billion, or about 6 percent of the gross national product.[2] Most of this, however, consisted of firms doing their own haulage or otherwise exempt from Interstate Commerce Commission regulation. Of the smaller, regulated portion, regulation affects most significantly less-than-truckload (LTL) carriage by general-commodity carriers.

Because accurate statistics are difficult to obtain and various classifications of firms in the industry are used for different purposes, it is important to understand the basis for the division of the industry. First, goods accounting for about 40 percent of all intercity truck ton-miles are moved by private carriage.[3] These firms can carry only their own goods and not the goods of others. The remaining shipments, accounting for about 60 percent of all interstate truck ton-miles, move in "for-hire" vehicles.

Second, about 20 percent of all intercity truck ton-miles are accounted for by for-hire carriers that are exempt from ICC regulation.[4] These include trucks used for transporting agricultural commodities, carrying goods within special commercial zones around cities, and carrying goods intrastate. Many of these carriers are small, one-man operations.

Third, the remaining 40 percent of intercity truck ton-miles are accounted for by ICC-regulated carriers. A few of these are "contract carriers," which sign contracts with a limited number of shippers (prior to 1978 fewer than eight) to perform specialized services.[5] They do not hire themselves out to the general public as "common carriers." All other ICC-regulated carriers are common carriers. Some of these are "special-commodity" carriers, hauling motor vehicles, petroleum products, refrigerated items, or certain other specialized goods. These special-commodity carriers account for nearly 40 percent of the revenues of the ICC-regulated carriers.[6] The largest class of ICC-regulated carriers—general-freight carriers—account for nearly 60 percent of the revenues of all ICC-regulated carriers.[7] They specialize in LTL shipments, making multiple deliveries along regular routes, picking up and dropping off less than the entire truckload.[8]

Although the general-freight carrier specializing in LTL service accounts for only 20–25 percent of the entire industry, for purposes of regulatory reform it is the most important. All other segments of the industry almost always carry full truckloads for individual shippers.[9] This fact means that rates cannot rise too far, because if they do, the shipper may shift from, say, a specialized carrier to a contract carrier or may perform his own carriage free of regulation. As a result, rates for full truckloads tend to be less heavily regulated.[10] Those who ship LTL amounts, however, cannot readily turn to other forms of carriage. They must rely upon ICC-regulated shippers. And the ICC tends to regulate general-freight carriers and LTL shipments most heavily. Our analysis will focus primarily upon general-freight carriers hauling LTL shipments.

The reader should keep in mind that there is a totally different classification of the industry under which the ICC groups together *all* regulated carriers (contract carriers, special-commodity carriers, and general-freight carriers) and divides them by size. In 1977 the 1,052 Class I carriers (annual revenues exceeding $3 million) had total revenues of $24 billion. The 3,101 Class II carriers (revenues between $500,000 and $3 million) had total revenues of $4 billion.

The 12,453 Class III carriers (revenues less than $500,000) had total revenues of $3 billion.[11]

The most important characteristic of the trucking industry—and its general-freight LTL sector—is that it is structurally competitive. That is to say, markets within the industry are capable of supporting a sufficient number of competing firms to prevent any one firm from raising its prices well above costs. If any firm seeks to do so, other firms already in the market or new firms that enter the market will charge lower prices and take away its business. The competitive market process would keep prices near cost in the absence of regulation.

The evidence that LTL[12] markets are structurally competitive flows from the fact that there are no significant economies of scale in the trucking industry and that barriers to entry are reasonably low. Most industry costs are variable, consisting of trucks and drivers,[13] neither of which is expensive. Larger firms may have some cost advantages over the "mom and pop" trucker, in that repair[14] and administrative[15] costs fall as fleets increase in size and the larger firms can consolidate shipments more easily at terminals than can smaller firms.[16] The extent to which these cost savings give advantages to larger firms is debatable. The industry as a whole is unconcentrated, with the largest four firms accounting for 12 percent of all revenues and the largest ten for 20 percent.[17] Economists who have studied the matter have concluded that economies of scale are not important enough to make the industry uncompetitive[18] (though some disagree).[19] In any event, even if the ability to consolidate shipments gives larger firms a cost advantage on certain routes or in certain areas, such firms would not be able to raise prices much above cost or their customers would be sought by other firms doing business nearby. It would be comparatively easy for firms on nearby routes to extend their operations or for large national firms to enter new territories. People not now in the business also could enter, but there are already 15,000 truckers in the industry ready to take advantage of any such business opportunities.

The comparative ease with which firms can expand or switch from one route to another is important, because the number of firms that can economically serve any individual route is limited. The greater the extent to which trucks are full when they drive, on average, the lower their costs. The number of firms that operate will then depend on the amount of shipments available and the extent to which pickup and delivery schedules can be arranged to ensure that trucks are reasonably full. In this sense, trucking resembles airline passenger service. There is a network of routes; shipments or passengers may be "interlined"; there may be a trade-off between more frequent schedules and lower-priced service; and few firms operate on any particular route. Yet, as with airlines, the ease of expansion means that firms could not readily raise price in the absence of competition, indicating that essentially the industry is structured competitively.

Regulation of prices. The Interstate Commerce Act gives the ICC power to set both maximum and minimum general freight rates and to ensure rates that are just and reasonable and neither discriminatory nor preferential.[20] In practice, the ICC has delegated the ratemaking power to rate bureaus, which are associations of private carriers operating under a grant of antitrust immunity provided by the Reed-Bulwinkle Act.[21] There are ten major regional motor-carrier rate bureaus.[22] Nearly all general-freight carriers within a region belong to a bureau. Each bureau has rate committees, which pass upon rate changes proposed by any member. The bureau then files any approved rate with the ICC. The ICC normally approves filed rates. In fact, it approves them automatically unless they are protested by a shipper or competitor.[23]

Essentially, the process resembles ratefixing by a cartel, with the ICC empowered to determine whether the cartel-set rate is reasonable. Some competitive check on LTL rates is provided, however, by the fact that any firm can file an "independent"[24] rate action; it need not accept the rate filed on behalf of the bureau. Indeed, about 30 percent of all rates represent independent filings, and the ICC accepts 95 percent of all independent filings made.[25]

The check on price provided by the possibility of independent filing, however, does not seem great. Many such filings concern administrative, special, or trivial matters that have little competitive impact. They may represent special adjustments after a general rate increase, or they may represent requests for rate increases. They are usually accepted automatically. Independent rates that affect competitors will be "protested" before the commission by competitors, however, and protested rates are not likely to be accepted. One study found that 80 percent of protested rates are withdrawn.[26] Another found that only one third of protested independent actions take effect.[27] A sampling of general-freight carriers showed that no carrier moved more than a few of its LTL shipments under independently filed rates.[28]

There are several reasons why rate bureaus are able to hold their members together—to act effectively as a rate cartel and to discourage independent actions and rate cutting. First, the ICC restricts entry into the industry and into individual markets. Thus, existing firms need not fear that their rates will be undercut by new rivals. Second, many individual routes are served by only a few firms, and there are only a few major competitors on many high-volume routes.[29] These carriers may act interdependently, each realizing that a price cut would simply invite retaliatory responses from its few major rivals. Third, the ICC rate-setting process may also inhibit competitive responses, even though such potentially competitive routes as New York–Boston are served by 92 competing carriers.[30] The "protest" system makes rate cutting difficult, because protested rates are suspended and small firms do not have the resources to win the legal battle before the ICC. Moreover, the filing system gives competing firms notice of the rate cut, making it impossible for a maverick to capture business through secret price cutting.[31]

In sum, although the system is complex in detail, in broad outline it is simple. The ICC allows combinations of private carriers to propose rates, which it reviews for reasonableness. Individual price cutting is discouraged. The result is regulatory rate review of cartel-proposed prices.

The regulation of entry. An applicant for a new common-carrier route must show that he is "fit, willing, and able to perform the service proposed" and that the service "is required by the present or future public convenience and necessity."[32] The ICC has interpreted the statute to mean in part that an applicant for new service must show that the area cannot be served as well by existing carriers. The burden of proof is on new applicants.[33] Shipper dissatisfaction with existing rates or service is not necessarily enough to show inadequacy.[34] Moreover, the LTL applicant, to be efficient, must apply to serve a network of related routes. To prevail, he must show that service is inadequate on most of the network.[35] It is extremely difficult to meet these standards of proof. Since LTL service is now provided to virtually every point in the country, an applicant for new LTL service will be met with protests by existing truckers claiming that their service is, or can be made, adequate. The applicant is unlikely to win.

As a result of these strict requirements, almost all entry applications before the ICC have been for irregular routes or special-commodity service, where protests are far less likely. In 1977 only 6 percent of all entry applications were for general-freight carriage (including general-freight truckload). And a large number of these applications were denied.[36] Firms currently in the industry are almost all descended from the 28,000 carriers[37] that received grandfather authority when the Motor Carrier Act took effect in 1935.[38] Many of these firms have merged with others, for the ICC has administered a liberal merger policy[39] to the point where the number of firms in the industry has dropped to 15,000. The American Trucking Association (ATA) summed up the ICC's entry and merger policy when it wrote, "Virtually the only way . . . to obtain additional operating authorities is to buy them from other carriers."[40]

The ICC's entry policy differs from that pursued by the CAB in one important way. For many years it was comparatively easy for an airline already in the industry to obtain permission to serve new routes. It was not easy for a trucking firm engaged in LTL carriage to obtain permission to enter new territories. It expanded primarily by acquiring rights of existing truckers, thus replacing one firm with another. As a result, some trucking routes became highly concentrated. One can see the effect of this policy by comparing concentration on trucking routes east of the Mississippi, where there were many grandfathered competitors, with that on routes west of the Mississippi, where entry depended on ICC approval. High-volume traffic lanes east of the Mississippi each support twenty or thirty competitors, with the top four firms accounting for 50–60 percent of the business. Those west of the Mississippi tend to be served by a dozen carriers, with the top four firms generally accounting for 90 percent of the business.[41] Moreover, trucking firms in concentrated markets have feared entry even less than did airlines. For this reason, on some of those routes trucks, unlike airlines, have not engaged extensively in service competition. To a greater extent than airlines, high prices led not to more service but to higher profits.

The Effects of Regulation

The description of the industry and related regulation suggests that, at bottom, trucking and airlines present similar cases. In both instances classical regulation—price and entry controls—are applied to a structurally competitive industry. One should expect to see similar results: high prices, stability of market shares, pricing rules that make administrative but not economic sense, and inefficiency. There is evidence bearing out each of these predictions. The major difference between the two is the fact that existing airlines competed vigorously with each other. Regulatory rules that inhibited airline price competition led to increased service competition, so that price increases were followed by cost increases and profits stayed low. In the case of trucking, strict ICC entry policy insulated firms in some markets from nearly all competition. In such markets high prices will not necessarily mean more service, but will instead mean higher profits.

Prices. Higher than competitive prices should be reflected in abnormally high profits, unnecessarily high costs, or both. There is some evidence of both of these tendencies. First, and most important, truckers' certificates of operating authorities have become valuable and can be sold at high prices. If firms in the industry earned only normal profits, licenses to enter would normally be valueless, for investors could, in general, earn as much investing elsewhere. When expected profits are unusually high, however, the right to enter can be sold at a premium. In fact, the premium will be just high enough so that the return earned by the investor after paying the premium will roughly equal what he could earn investing elsewhere. The premium will equal the discounted value of the expected excess return.

The premiums paid for trucking licenses have been high enough for long enough to suggest that revenues are excessive. In 1972 the American Trucking Association stated that "recent acquisitions in the motor carrier industry indicate that amounts paid for operating authorities are approximately 15% to 20% of the annual revenues produced by those authorities."[42] The Council on Wage and Price Stability estimated the value of operating authorities at $3–4 billion in 1974,[43] while Moore estimated the rents (excess profits) generated by certificates in 1972 at $1.5–2 billion.[44] Since other portions of the industry were more competitive, most of these rents flow to general-freight LTL carriers. Were firms free to enter the industry, these operating rights would not be particularly valuable and revenues would not have to be high enough to earn a return on that investment.

Second, efforts to measure rates of return directly also suggest the existence of excess profits. Profit rates are difficult to compare because different industries bear different degrees of risk, and special circumstances can make comparisons at any given time misleading. Nonetheless, an examination of the profits of major firms in the trucking industry over a five-year period, prepared by *Forbes* magazine, shows that those profits are high (see Table 7).

A more careful comparison of profit rates made by Blumenthal shows that large general-freight carriers consistently earn higher returns on equity than the average manufacturer, once one excludes "intangibles"—namely, the investment in operating rights.[45] The large, publicly traded carriers account for about half of all general-freight coverage. The smallest carriers with low returns account for less than 10 percent[46] (see Table 8).

Third, there is some indication that service competition is excessive. If rates are fixed, insofar as truckers compete to provide better service they will provide more frequent service, but they will drive trucks that are inefficiently empty. There will be fewer trucks carrying full loads and more unnecessary miles will be traveled. Direct restrictions imposed by the ICC can also force truckers to drive empty backhauls, because their certificates may allow them to carry goods only from point A to point B, but not from B to A.

Regardless of the cause, one study found that regulated general-freight vans return empty 38 percent of the time.[47] Another estimated that without regulatory restrictions, general-freight LTL carriers would increase their load factors by 10 percent.[48] A third study estimated that without ICC restrictions, motor freight rates would fall 6–15 percent.[49] At the same time, shipper surveys suggest that they are generally pleased with the level of service, but many would be willing to accept somewhat less frequent service if rates were significantly lower.[50]

Fourth, comparisons with deregulated trucking in the United States and abroad suggest that deregulation means lower prices. When poultry and frozen fruits and vegetables were reclassified as exempt commodities in the 1950s, rates fell over a five-year period by an average of 33 percent for poultry and 19 percent for frozen foods.[51] A study of trucking in New Jersey, where in-

Table 7. Profits of major firms over a five-year period.

	Return on total investment (percent)	Return on equity (percent)
Major trucking firms	13.4	21.2
Airlines	4.3	7.9
Railroads	5.4	8.0
All industries	9.7	12.9

Source: Forbes, January 9, 1978, at 139.

Table 8. After-tax return on equity among firms in the trucking industry (in percent).

	1977	1976	1975	1974
All manufacturers	14.2	15.0	12.6	15.4
All general-freight (GF) carriers	16.4	12.9	9.7	14.1
Excluding intangibles	18.8	14.7	11.0	16.1
GF carriers, $5–1 million	17.2	4.3	—	—
Excluding intangibles	19.4	5.0	—	—
GF carriers, $1–5 million	15.4	11.5	—	—
Excluding intangibles	17.5	13.1	—	—
GF carriers, $5–10 million	11.1	10.0	—	—
Excluding intangibles	12.3	11.0	—	—
GF carriers, >$10 million[a]	16.7	13.2	—	—
Excluding intangibles	19.2	15.1	—	—
Large, interregional GF carriers[b]	21.1	16.7	—	—
Excluding intangibles	23.9	18.7	—	—
Large, publicly traded GF carriers[c]	16.5	16.2	11.0	14.0
Excluding intangibles	19.5	18.9	13.0	16.7

Source: All manufacturers, 1977: *General Increase, SMCRC*, I. & S. M-29772 (ICC, November 28, 1978). All manufacturers, 1974–76; *Forbes*, January 9, 1978, at 139. Trucking industry data: American Trucking Association, *1978 Financial Analysis of the Motor Carrier Industry* (1979).
   a. 1977 annual revenues averaged $255.6 million
   b. 1977 annual revenues averaged $198.6 million.
   c. 1977 annual revenues averaged $67.3 million.
Note: A dash indicates that data are not available.

trastate shipments are not regulated, found that intrastate rates were generally 10–13 percent below the interstate tariff for comparable shipments.[52] In Great Britain, which regulated entry but not rates, deregulation led to a 10 percent rate decline.[53] Relaxation of rate restrictions in West Germany[54] and deregulation in Australia[55] were followed by rate declines. Studies based on regulation in Canada suggest that without regulation, rates would decline 7–18 percent.[56]

None of these studies presents a totally comparable experience. The agricultural studies are outdated; the mix of short and long hauls in other countries differs from that found in the United States; and regulation elsewhere is not quite the same. The studies also have critics who argue that they are technically flawed.[57] Nonetheless, when taken together they make a case for the claim that regulation of trucks and airlines has similar effects: cost-of-service ratemaking cannot control prices in a structurally competitive industry. Regulators search for ways to administer pricing rules and achieve price stability at the expense of price competition. And once price competition disappears, prices rise higher than competition would allow.

Stability. The extent to which ICC regulation has protected the market shares of individual firms and limited the risk of bankruptcy is debatable. On the one hand, the strict entry policy has undoubtedly protected many firms against the threat of new competition. The low degree of concentration east of the Mississippi contrasted with high concentration on comparable routes west of the river suggests that firms might enter western markets were they free to do so. Since the difference in concentration also reflects the fact that more carriers in the east have grandfathered licenses, it suggests that firms, once established, tend to remain in business. Moreover, the ICC's practice of allowing transfer of existing route authority, but not granting new authority, makes firms less likely to want to enter the industry. A new firm must provide better service or lower prices to attract business. But ICC route policy makes it difficult for potential entrants to offer innovative service: the new firm cannot look for shortcuts or rearrange its route system; it must follow the route from point A to B to C, as spelled out in the certificate. At the same time, ICC rate policy inhibits rate cutting by the new firm.

On the other hand, many thousands of carriers have gone out of business since 1935. About 28,000 carriers received grandfathered authority. Today, that number has diminished to about 15,000. Yet the number of firms that disappeared through bankruptcy may be fairly small. The ICC has allowed mergers rather freely. In the late 1970s, mergers were taking place at a rate of well over 300 per year. And many of the large national trucking firms have grown through merger with smaller regional carriers.[58] In fact, bankruptcy when it occurs has not proved enormously harmful to truck owners. Their primary assets are trucks and trailers, which are liquid, and operating rights, which, due to regulation, normally sell at prices well above their book value.[59]

Economically unreasonable regulatory rules. The ICC must apply a regulatory system designed to measure the reasonableness of rates to a highly complex trucking system with 15,000 carriers, 25,000 commodities, and hundreds of thousands of possible routes. In 1977 there were 360,000 tariffs filed at the ICC. The ICC's chairman has stated that 5,000 pages of tariffs containing several million rates are filed at the commission each day.[60] The need for administrative workability has led the ICC to rely upon rate bureaus and a set of simplified rules for judging the reasonableness of the bureaus' proposals. Those rules, derived from cost-of-service ratemaking principles, help produce a workable system but, not surprisingly, produce many economically irrational results as well.

Cost-of-service ratemaking has two major parts: determining the revenue requirement and determining the rate structure, or the set of individual prices designed to yield that requirement. The ICC determines the revenue requirement when the industry (or a major segment of it) asks for a rate increase. Such increases take the form of across-the-board percent increases.

The ICC, like many other regulatory agencies, determines whether a rate increase is justified primarily by looking to see whether industry profits were adequate. Unlike most other agencies, however, for many years prior to the 1970s the ICC measured profits by return on revenues, not investment. It presumed that a fair profit meant an operating ratio of 93 percent—that is to say, costs had to equal 93 percent of revenues.[61] When costs rose above that percentage, the ICC allowed a rate increase. One major defect of this approach is that the industry has a strong incentive to increase its costs. A firm with $50 of investment and $100 in sales, allowed $7 in profit under the ICC's rules, would earn a 14 percent return on its investment. If its costs double and it is allowed $14 (on $200 of sales), its return on its $50 investment increases to 28 percent. Increased costs mean increased profits. The result is that the industry could earn increased returns on a constant investment by granting industry-wide wage increases. These would be followed by price increases that *increase* industry profits. Some ICC critics have argued that the system in the past led to vast increases in trucking wages at the expense of the shippers and the public.[62] About ten years ago, the ICC changed the system. The commission now judges the reasonableness of profits as a percent of investment, not of revenues.[63] Though it has expressed some willingness to pass-through wage increases in the form of price increases,[64] such a pass-through would keep truckers' profits constant, not increase them. Thus, the truckers at least have lost their incentive to encourage wage increases.

The major part of the ICC's rate-setting job has been passing upon the validity of individual tariffs—a job that has required the ICC to develop standards for a proper rate structure. In doing so, the ICC allowed the truckers to copy the system used by the railroads—a system based upon "value-of-service" pricing.[65] From an administrative point of view, the system was already in existence and the ICC had experience using it. Moreover, the system classified commodities in the same way for both trucking and rail transport, thus tending to minimize competition between them.

The "class rate" lies at the heart of the system. The National Motor Freight Classification assigns approximately 25,000 commodities to 23 classes. The standards used for classifying include both cost- and demand-related factors.[66] Each class is given an index number from 35 to 500, with 100 as the reference point. This number gives the class a constant relationship to all other classes. A tariff also develops a series of "rate-basis numbers"—basically a mileage scale occasionally modified to reflect special transportation characteristics such as mountainous terrain. A shipper looks up a rate on a tariff table. He determines the class-rating number from the commodity classification table and the rate-basis number from a list of origin and destination points. He then refers to a table, or "class tariff," which has class ratings on one axis and rate-basis numbers on the others. The cell that he locates will have the rate in cents per hundredweight (it may have several rates, for different weight categories).[67]

The system is sufficiently complex so that once it is in place, administrators will change the numbers in the cells—or their relation to one another—only very reluctantly. The most important question, however, is how those numbers were derived. The ICC says that it uses both relative cost and relative value considerations. The cost-related factors include weight density, liability to damage, likelihood of causing damage, perishability, liability to fire or explosion, likelihood of theft, difficulty of loading, attention needed, stowability, unusual weight or length. The values related to class include "value per pound in comparison with other articles," "trade conditions," and "competition with other commodities transported."[68]

Insofar as value of service plays an important role in setting class rates, the ICC seeks to use Ramsey pricing, which we discussed in Chapter 2. Its rate structure sets relative rates inversely in relation to elasticity of demand. It sets higher charges where shippers are more likely to pay than to stop shipping. The higher the products' value in relation to transportation costs and the less the shipper must worry about small price differences destroying his sales, the more likely he will pay higher transport costs.[69]

This rate structure makes sense where a regulator sets rates for a natural monopoly. These prices must be set above incremental costs in order to recover the cost of initial large, fixed investment, such as the cost of building a bridge. Ramsey pricing, which discriminates in price among users by charging more to those for whom the service is worth more, will extract the extra revenue needed, without unduly disturbing the pattern of bridge use.

But why is Ramsey pricing, or value-of-service pricing, valid in the case of trucking? Is it possible that its use came about through blind copying of the system that the ICC used to set railroad rates? If so, its appearance is something of a bad joke, for there is no reason to adopt such a rate structure in the absence of a natural monopoly. In a competitively structured industry such as trucking, competition would bring rates close to the incremental cost of providing service. Valuable items would not necessarily be transported at higher rates than less valuable items. Yet overhead costs would be covered out of the revenues received. The cost and price of carrying gold under competitive conditions might be less per pound than carrying soap. Imposition of a Ramsey-type value-of-service rate structure produces a pattern of rates very different from one that would exist were competition allowed. It may also distort service, for truckers will seek to carry as many high-value, high-rate shipments as possible and will avoid low-value, low-rate products.

Of course, the truckers themselves favor a value-of-service approach, because it tends to increase revenues. A profit-maximizing monopolist would charge shippers of gold more per pound than shippers of soap. If the ICC can effectively prevent price competition among truckers for the higher-priced shipments, the industry as a whole will make more money.

The ICC's class rates embody many of the cost elements that would also be reflected in competitively set prices. But some of the cost elements are less important than the rate system suggests. For example, rates vary significantly with the weight of the shipment, but weight may be only a minor factor in the cost of many shipments. Moreover, the rate system omits several types of cost that are important and would likely be reflected in rates, were they set competitively. For one thing, the number of pieces in a shipment is the greatest source of variation in terminal costs. Ten 30-pound boxes are far more expensive to handle than one 300-pound box. Further, if a carrier receives two shipments at a single stop it undergoes far less expense than if it must make two stops, one for each shipment. Shippers with crowded facilities, inadequate loading-dock staff, and locations far from major highways are more expensive to serve. Finally, and most important, a trucker that has more capacity available in one direction than another has lower costs where the extra capacity is available (the backhaul). Under a competitive system, he would charge lower rates on the backhaul in order to attract shipments for a trip that he *must* make back to his point of origin. Class rates do not consider the existence of backhauls or the other cost considerations mentioned above. To the extent that a competitive system would reflect these costs differences, class rates produce economic distortion.

Class rates are important to the evaluation of ICC trucking regulation because 95 percent of all LTL shipments move on class-rate tariffs.[70] The ICC, however, also sets commodity rates, for specific point-to-point movements of commodities,[71] and "exception rates" for special circumstances.[72] The commodity and exception rates are likely to be lower than class rates; they are more likely to reflect competitive conditions, and most truckload traffic and many heavy LTL shipments[73] move on them.

Commodity rates, too, however, are likely to deviate from rates that would be generated by a competitive market. In judging the lawfulness of a proposed commodity rate, the ICC normally insists that it cover the carrier's fully allocated cost. A carrier can cut its rates to its variable costs only by showing the existence of "special competitive circumstances," such as imbalanced traffic flows or competition from unregulated transport.[74] The difficulty of demonstrating these circumstances to the ICC's satisfaction means that it is difficult for a trucker to cut rates to fill up an empty backhaul. This makes it impossible for the trucker to reflect the lower costs of doing business with a particular shipper, to reflect any other special conditions that would lead to lower rates under competitive circumstances, or simply to compete by attracting business from another firm.

It is understandable why an ICC intent on regulating prices would discourage rates that equal variable costs, for if the ICC allowed such rates, truckers could effectively charge virtually any price. A general-freight trucker carriers various shipments of commodities on a single trip from point A to point B and then other shipments back to A. In logic, any one of these shipments might be considered the "last" or "incremental" shipment and a very low rate could be charged for it. Any of the others could be considered the "first" or "basic" shipment and charged a rate covering up to the whole cost of the trip. The only way to determine whether rates were too high or too low would be to compare the total cost of the round trip with total revenue to see if they matched. But the ICC could not do this administratively, as this would involve overseeing individually varying rates, varying costs, and millions of journeys.

The ICC, then, has adopted a set of pricing rules that lead to prices quite different from those that would be set under competitive conditions. These rules bring about prices that often do not reflect costs and that create economic distortion. Given the need for an administratively workable system, however, it is difficult to see how the ICC could do much better, unless it were willing to abandon regulation of prices and rely instead upon prices set through competition and the free marketplace.

Inefficiencies. The major inefficiencies arising from the need for specific pricing rules and a restrictive entry policy have been discussed above. In addition, the ICC's route and entry policies lead directly to inefficiency by restricting the services that carriers can offer. Thus, empty backhauls are caused not only by a rate policy that inhibits price cutting, but also by route certificates that give a carrier only one-way authority, requiring it to return empty.[75] Certificates may also prescribe specific routes that carriers must follow. These routes can be created by a carrier combining separate authority acquired from other carriers. They may be circuitous, sometimes requiring the carrier to travel 30–40 percent farther,[76] possibly over secondary roads rather than primary highways. Until recently the ICC usually denied petitions by carriers to reduce the circuitousness of routes. Similarly, certificates may limit the commodities that a carrier can transport between two points. This means that a truck must remain idle, rather than carry commodites for which it is not certificated.[77]

At bottom, however, the inefficiency is created by a system that depends upon trucker "cartels" to set rates and upon classical regulatory pricing rules to judge the reasonableness of those rates. The system provides incentives to substitute service competition for price competition and to increase costs. It allows the setting of prices that will provide many firms with higher than competitive profits and it inhibits pricing flexibility and prevents the setting of rates that reflect competitive pressures. Yet this system, or something like it, seems inevitable once one decides to try to regulate the prices of such a complex, competitively structured industry. There is no way to do so without administrable pricing rules, and those rules will automatically produce prices that are too high in some cases and possibly too low in others. Trucking, like airlines, illustrates how classical cost-of-service ratemaking simply does not suit a competitively structured industry.

Alternatives to Classical Regulation

The application of classical regulation to the trucking industry raises several difficulties reminiscent of airline regulation. Similarly, the rationales for trucking regulation appear weak. Changing circumstances have made several of the reasons advanced in support of regulation in 1935 irrelevant today. The major justification—excessive competition—is, as previously discussed, "an empty box." Insofar as there is a problem of excessive competition, antitrust provides a more suitable remedy than classical regulation.

The original justifications. Federal regulation of the trucking industry began in 1935 with the enactment of the Motor Carrier Act, which gave the ICC rate and entry authority.[78] The act became law at the urging of President Roosevelt and Federal Coordinator of Transportation Joseph Eastman, at a time when the administration believed that eliminating (or moderating) competition would stabilize industry and end the Depression.[79] The act had three major objectives.

First, the railroads during the previous decade had argued that it was unfair to regulate them while leaving trucking unregulated. They claimed that the truckers would skim the markets' cream by attracting the railroad's most lucrative business while regulation prevented the railroads from retaliating by lowering their own rates.[80]

Second, proponents of regulation in 1935 argued for increased coordination among transportation modes. They feared that the truckers would drive the railroads into bankruptcy. Alternatively, they feared that if the railroads were free to compete, they would use their superior economic power to destroy the trucking industry. They concluded that only an administrative regulatory system could properly "coordinate" the two modes, directing each to its "proper" sphere of business.[81]

Third, during the Depression many truckers went bankrupt and there was considerable industry overcapacity. Proponents of regulation argued that these facts demonstrated a need to protect truckers from predatory pricing, to exclude fly-by-night operators, and to maintain employment and stability by stopping excessive competition.[82]

Whatever the need for intermodal coordination in 1935, or for protecting railroad revenues, one now rarely hears these arguments advanced as justifications for trucking regulation. Indeed, there is little evidence that the ICC has consciously protected railroad revenues, for few trucking cases have raised that issue.[83] Indeed, in 1958 Congress passed a new transportation law, which stated that the "rates of a carrier shall not be held up to a particular level to protect the traffic of any other mode of transportation" (though it generated controversy by adding the exception: "giving due consideration to the objectives of the national transportation policy").[84] Since 1958 the railroads have urged the ICC to allow them greater freedom to cut rates (so as to compete more strongly against barges). And in 1976, at the railroads' urging, Congress passed a law stating that "no rate of a common carrier by railroad shall be held up to a particular level to protect the traffic of any other carrier or mode" (though again it added: "unless the Commission finds that such rate reduces or would reduce the going concern value of the carrier charging the rate").[85] The railroads have argued for this freedom for themselves and they do not oppose others having the same freedom.

A "depression cartel," as described in Chapter 1, might be justified for an industry with high fixed costs and low variable costs, subject to large fluctuations in demand for its product. Regulation of such an industry would seek to prevent capacity from being forced from the industry during downswings, leading to heavy start-up costs in the upswings.

Trucking, however, does not have high fixed costs and low variable costs. On the contrary, most trucking costs are variable.[86] The truck itself is inexpensive compared to plant costs in other industries, particularly industries such as steel or copper where the depression cartel argument is typically made. Trucks can readily enter and leave the industry. They can be stored or sold in a second-hand market. Terminals are more expensive and cannot readily be brought into and out of the industry. Yet if deregulation is accompanied by more price competition and less service competition, trucks will travel fuller, there will be greater need for temporary storage of shipments, and there will be greater demand for terminals. Moreover, the trucking industry is not characterized by sharp cyclical fluctuations in demand. Tonnage fluctuation over the course of a year is small. Even during recessions, demand for trucking services has fallen only slightly.[87]

The "excessive competition" argument may refer to the risk of predatory pricing. However, predatory pricing makes sense for a firm only if (1) it believes it is so much stronger than its competitors that it can outlast them while incurring losses, and (2) entry barriers are high enough so that the predator can raise its prices and recoup its losses before other firms, attracted by the high profits, try to enter.

Trucking, however, does not typically create high entry barriers. The barriers to entering truckload trucking are very low indeed. Barriers in the LTL sector are higher, because new firms must develop terminals and a route network. Yet these barriers are not formidable for firms already in the industry. A firm seeking to recoup losses by charging excessive prices must worry that other national or regional LTL carriers will expand their operations and take away its customers. In other words, a firm will not be able to charge prices well above the competitive levels and will think twice before pricing predatorily. The predatory pricing problem should be no greater than in other industries, where it is controlled through application of the antitrust laws.

During the 1930s, economic conditions were different. The Great Depression involved an unusually serious downturn in demand for trucking services. Moreover, bankruptcies led to a glut in the market for second-hand trucks. Thus, industry capacity could not be reduced in the short run. Further, over 80 percent of trucking firms at that time were composed of single-owner operators. Fewer than one half of one percent had more than ten vehicles.[88] One-man firms, without knowledge of industry costs, may have engaged in self-defeating price cutting until forced into bankruptcy. Today, the level of industry sophistication is greater. Studies of *un*regulated, exempt trucking show that neither entry nor exit is more difficult or more frequent there than in other unregulated industries with low capital requirements, such as dry cleaning or restaurants.[89]

Experience abroad tends to confirm the absence of any special problem of excessive competition. The trucking industries in Australia and Britain remained stable when regulation was relaxed.[90] Studies of exempt agricultural commodity carriers found that "exempt rates, although lower than regulated rates, are sufficient to cover the total cost of carriage in the long run."[91] Exemption has not led to substantial instability of firms.[92] In fact, the Department of Agriculture, farmers, and growers have consistently supported the exemption of agricultural trucking from regulation. They would not support the exemption if it produced industry instability.

Other justifications. Trucking deregulation is currently a subject of study within Congress and the Executive Branch. A new trucking law will allow the ICC to relax regulation significantly. In response to advocates of deregulation, the American Trucking Association and others raised a number of objections.[93] For the most part, they resemble those that the airlines raised against airline deregulation. Some of them seem empirically implausible. For example, the ATA suggests that the system of shipping thousands of commodities to tens of thousands of cities is so complex that deregulation would lead to an impenetrable matrix of several million different rates.[94] The very virtue of a competitive system, however, lies in its ability to create, for millions or tens of millions of transactions, prices that approximate cost. In highly complex industries, product or service classifications are used, which may change gradually over time. Price information is collected and distributed in readily usable tables, which are updated regularly. Thus, hardware stores, department stores, credit card banking systems, trucking in Britain, and now the airlines all manage to create and to change prices without complaint from their customers about inadequate or unusable price information.

A more serious argument is based on the fact that the present regulatory system may have created prices under which some shipments subsidize others. The American Trucking Association claims that large shipments subsidize small shipments and that service to large towns subsidizes service to small communities.

Each of these claims is disputed. A number of studies suggest, for example, that small LTL shipments of less than 500 pounds are charged less than it costs to ship them, while larger shipments are charged more.[95] Yet there are carriers that specialize in small shipments and operate profitably. Moreover, many carriers opposed before the ICC the request by United Parcel Service to carry shipments up to 300 pounds.[96] The economic debate over whether small shipments are subsidized is relevant not because it is socially desirable to subsidize small shipments, but because many individual shippers may have built plants or made investments in reliance upon a rate structure that favored them. They may have a claim to relief based on that reliance. The more such shippers there are, the more political influence they can wield against deregulation. At this point, one must conclude that the extent of this reliance and its importance has not been shown.

The most important argument of this sort is the ATA's claim that deregulation, which would allow truckers to abandon unprofitable services, would mean the end of trucking service to thousands of small communities. The ATA provided evidence in the form of a survey that supports this contention.[97] On the other hand, there is considerable evidence to the contrary. As a practical matter, truckers have long been free to abandon unprofitable service. Surveys show that many trucking lines do not serve all towns listed in their certificates,[98] yet the ICC has been unable to find any trucker whose certificate was revoked for this reason.[99] Moreover, operating rights to small communities trade at substantial prices.[100] Thus, some truckers must believe that the right to serve those communities is quite profitable. Further, several studies have found that carriers specializing in service to small communities are profitable,[101] that at least one carrier would continue to serve each isolated community after deregulation,[102] and that the average community of 10,000–25,000 people is served by several carriers who consider the market desirable.[103] A similar problem was met in the case of airline deregulation by a special subsidy administered to guarantee continued service to small communities.

The problem of small-community service illustrates the arguments raised against deregulation. They do not raise objections to deregulation in principle. They provide no convincing rationale for regulation. They do not demonstrate market defects that regulation is required to overcome. Rather, they constitute a set of practical arguments in favor of the status quo. The deregulator, like any proponent of change, must show that the beneficial consequences of change are likely to overcome its practical drawbacks.

Conclusion

We have discussed trucking in detail in order to further illustrate a basic point, brought out in the discussion of airline regulation. That point is that classical price and entry regulation is particularly unsuited to a competitively structured industry. Moreover, when it is applied to such an industry, there are likely to be certain predictable effects: higher than competitive prices, a stable industry structure, uneconomic pricing rules, and inefficiency. At the same time, there is unlikely to be any strong economic justification for price and entry regulation. The problem of predatory pricing, if it exists, can be dealt with by the antitrust laws. These considerations make trucking a leading candidate for regulatory reform. The facts discussed here do not *prove* the case for regulatory reform, for many of the studies are controverted. Opponents raise important practical objections and argue that the harms of change are not worth the benefits. However, the facts do suggest that trucking regulation is in all likelihood fit for reform, that Congress was correct in recently enacting a law that makes reform likely, and that the ICC and Congress should continue to move toward the deregulation of the trucking industry.

13
Mismatch: Rent Control and Natural Gas Field Prices

This chapter will describe a second type of fundamental mismatch, one that arises when traditional cost-of-service ratemaking is applied to a rent control problem. Classical regulation cannot deal effectively with rent control; taxes or deregulation is ordinarily preferable. Our example here will be the regulation of the field price of natural gas. We will see that the system of regulation itself was responsible for serious problems of inefficiency and shortage—that these problems were caused by a basic mismatch.

The object of rent control, as described in Chapter 1, is to capture windfall profits earned by producers and transfer them to consumers. The windfalls are earned by the sales of existing or older stocks of a commodity that now costs more to produce. Cost-of-service ratemaking seeks to transfer these windfalls to consumers by holding the price of old and new units down to their respective costs. Since uniformly low prices yield no new production, while uniformly high prices would not capture the windfalls, ratemakers typically set tiered prices, setting lower or high prices depending upon costs of production in individual cost categories.

To use cost-of-service ratemaking in this way, regulators must decide: (1) when the high tier price is high enough to elicit sufficient new production, and (2) who will obtain the low-priced product. All users want it, but cannot be allowed to bid for it, as prices would then simply rise to the high level. How then can it be allocated? The first of these decisions is, as a practical matter, difficult to make, given continuously rising costs of production. The second is virtually incapable of satisfactory solution.

The history of natural gas field price regulation provides an excellent illustration of these principles. As is true of airline regulation, the effects of natural gas regulation have been studied in detail and the law has recently been amended to end regulation by 1985.[1]

Regulation began in 1954 but did not take effect until the 1960s. It helped cause a serious shortage which consumers felt directly in the mid-1970s. Regulators then took steps to mitigate the shortage by raising interstate price ceilings in 1976, 1977, and 1978. In 1978 Congress passed legislation foreseeing the end of regulation. Thus, an examination of natural gas regulation from the early 1960s to the mid-1970s reveals the flaws of applying a classical regulatory system to rent control and indicates why both Congress and the regulators felt it necessary to relax the system's price constraints.

The Industry

The natural gas industry can be readily divided into three parts.

Exploration and production. Gas producers must initially explore to uncover supplies of natural gas. Traditionally, this predominantly involved drilling in fields in Alaska, Texas, Oklahoma, Louisiana, and offshore in the Gulf of Mexico. Before World War II gas was produced mainly as a by-product of the search for oil. But in recent years increased demand for gas and increased technical skills has led producers to develop new drilling methods, such that presently less than 25 percent of U.S. gas reserves reflect the results of a search for oil.[2] The major costs of production are still accounted for by exploration and drilling; extraction costs are comparatively low.[3]

The largest natural gas producers are major integrated oil companies. Moreover, the twenty largest natural gas producers account for most industry sales. They accounted for 70 percent of all sales to interstate pipelines in 1971 (and they hold almost all offshore drilling leases).[4] On the other hand, thousands of small, independent gas producers coexisted with the majors.[5] In fact, in 1974 the independent producers drilled 86 percent of all new gas wells and discovered 70 percent of new potential reserves.[6]

Transmission. During the 1960s and early 1970s, the producers sold gas (typically under long-term, 20-year contracts) to pipeline companies, which transported it from the field to cities located throughout the country. Most gas was transported interstate. Twenty-two large interstate companies transported 71 percent of all the gas shipped interstate.[7] Most other gas was sold to local distributing companies and directly to industry (often under "interruptible" contracts). The proportion of industrial sales and of local distributor sales varied considerably from one pipeline to another.

Distribution to consumers. Gas was distributed by 1,500 local retail distributing companies.[8] They supplied gas directly to homes, as well as to industrial and commercial users (many of which also bought gas under interruptible contracts).[9]

Of these three major parts, the producing segment of the industry was structured competitively. The market shares of the major firms, measured field by field, indicated that market concentration was "lower than that in 75 to 85 percent of industries in manufactured products."[10] Moreover, an examination of new gas sales year by year showed considerable volatility in a firm's market position. Finally, entry barriers were fairly low.[11] There were no major economies of scale in gas production. The major entry barrier consisted of the need to sustain dry-hole losses or other exploration costs. Thousands of small producers found it possible to surmount this obstacle.[12] Although the conclusion is disputed by some, the consensus of those economists who have studied the matter was that the industry was workably competitive.[13]

The transmission segment of the industry, however, had elements of both monopoly and monopsony. Frequently a city was served by only one interstate pipeline. Moreover, on the buying side of the market, a natural gas field might be served by only two or three pipelines (viewed nationally, the top eight pipelines accounted for 58 percent of all purchases).[14]

Distribution companies, for the most part, were natural monopolies, as economies of scale made it inefficient to have more than one such firm per city.

Natural gas had a wide variety of users and uses. The largest use was industrial, which accounted for 64 percent of gas consumption.[15] Of this amount, about one third (or about one fifth of total consumption) was accounted for by electricity generation.[16] Electric utilities turned to gas to operate boilers primarily because it was cheap and nonpolluting. The remaining industrial users consisted of about 210,000 firms, many of which produced chemicals, primary metals, petroleum, stone, clay, glass, and food.[17] The gas was used to run boilers, for space heating, for processing directly, or as raw material. It has been estimated that natural gas was used in about 25,000 different industrial applications.[18]

The second largest market for natural gas was residential, which accounted for 24 percent of all consumption.[19] About 70 percent of this amount was used for space heating, 20 percent was burned to heat hot water, and 10 percent was used to operate stoves and appliances.[20]

The commercial market for natural gas accounted for approximately 11 percent of consumption. More than half of this amount was used for space heating. Water heating accounted for 25 percent and stoves and appliances[21] accounted for the rest.[22]

In sum, natural gas production was probably a workably competitive industry; its transmission was probably not a workably competitive industry; and it was consumed by thousands of different industrial customers with a vast range of costs. These characteristics made the application of classical regulation to the industry particularly difficult.

Regulation

The Natural Gas Act[23] gave the Federal Power Commission authority to regulate the price of natural gas that was sold interstate *and* for resale. The act was designed to overcome the fact that state regulators, with power to control local distributing companies, lacked the legal authority to regulate the prices at which large interstate pipelines (with monopoly power) sold to them.

In 1954, somewhat to the FPC's surprise, the Supreme Court held in *Phillips Petroleum Co.* v. *Wisconsin*[24] that the act also gave the commission authority to regulate the prices at which field producers sold gas to the pipelines. A move to enact legislation to remove this power was defeated and the commission began to regulate.

Initially, the FPC seemed uncertain about the precise justification for its new authority. Some thought it was seeking to control monopoly power and pointed to the rapid rise in gas field prices between 1950 and 1958 as evidence that producers possessed such monopoly power.[25] Economic studies of the markets for new contracts during that period, however, show that anticompetitive producer behavior did not cause the price increase. Rather, during the 1950s many fields previously served by only one pipeline began to receive service from two or three. Increased competition among pipelines raised prices from a previously depressed (monopsonistic) level and accounted for much of the price increase.[26] At the same time, the cost of finding and developing gas reserves increased significantly.[27] Hence, neither the price increase nor the structure of producer markets suggested that producers possessed monopoly power, or that any such rationale underlay the need for regulation.

Later, proponents of regulation argued that regulation was needed to control excess producer rents. There were several reasons for believing that gas producers earned unusually large rents. First, gas is a wasting (nonrenewable) resource, and its presence in the ground is uncertain until exploration and development are complete. At that point, the value (or the price) of gas is determined largely by the incremental cost of additional exploration and development.[28] The difference between that incremental cost and the actual costs of many "lucky" producers will be reflected in the rent that they will receive. Second, as natural gas has become harder to find, the costs of finding and extracting it have increased considerably. Those producers who possessed an existing stock of gas found it more valuable because there was not enough old, cheap gas to go around and it could therefore be sold at the same price as the more expensive new (incremental) gas. Finally, these effects were aggravated by the existence of "most favored nation" clauses in existing long-term contracts, which allowed producers to increase the price of all gas, though the increase was made possible by the increased cost of new gas alone.

In other words, though the FPC believed for some time that it was trying to control the producers' monopoly power, it was in fact trying to administer a system of rent control. Regardless, it had only one weapon to use: classical cost-of-service ratemaking. The commission first tried to apply that system on a straightforward case-by-case basis. It then switched to an areawide system setting maximum rates for each field. Though the latter method was administratively workable (while the former was not), neither method was able to avoid seriously adverse side-effects—adverse effects that are inevitable once an agency seeks to use cost-of-service ratemaking to deal with a rent control problem.

Adverse Effects

The major adverse effect of regulation was to cause—or at least to aggravate—a serious natural gas shortage. Moreover, once the shortage was created, it was necessary to develop another system of regulatory allocation. The FPC was inevitably forced to fall back upon a public interest allocation system (described in Chapter 4), with its attendant vices.

Four points about the natural gas shortage should be kept in mind. First, until the 1978 deregulation legislation and major increases in regulatory price ceilings in the late 1970s, the shortage was serious. In the winter of 1976–77 there was a curtailment of supply of approximately 20 percent.[29] This curtailment was spread unevenly throughout the country with some states forced to cut back on consumption by up to 50 percent, while others, in the Northeast, for example, were relatively unaffected. The loss of gas meant the curtailment of industrial production and the loss of hundreds of thousands (some have estimated millions) of jobs.

Some notion of the extent of the problem through 1974 may be obtained from Tables 9 and 10. The 4.0 trillion cubic feet shown in Table 9 as the expected curtailment amounts to 20 percent of the 20 trillion cubic feet needed to satisfy demand. Table 10 illustrates the differential effect of these curtailments among the states. The need for curtailment depended upon which pipe-

Table 9. Curtailment trends.

Year (April–March)	Annual firm[a] curtailments (in trillions of cubic feet)	Heating season (Nov.–Mar.) curtailments (in trillions of cubic feet)
1970–71	0.1	0.1
1971–72	0.5	0.2
1972–73	1.1	0.5
1973–74	1.6	0.6
1974–75	2.0	1.0
1975–76 (expected)	2.9	1.3
1976–77 (forecast)	4.0	about 1.9

Source: Federal Energy Administration, "The Natural Gas Shortage: A Preliminary Report" (August 1975).
a. Pipeline-to-pipeline curtailments not included in 1974–76 data.

Table 10. Economic impact in 1975–76 in most affected states.

State	Projected reduction as % of 1974–75 deliveries	Reduction as % of 1973 industrial gas consumption	State employment in gas-using industry	
			As % of total employment	In thousands
New Jersey	8	41	32	717
Maryland	19	60	20	202
Virginia	20	50	9	116
North Carolina	29	41	33	552
South Carolina	12	20	29	227
Pennsylvania	8	17	23	854
Ohio	9	22	29	996
New York	(1)	(3)	21	1,249
Kentucky	4	11	28	196
West Virginia	18	26	19	77
Delaware	16	33	7	11
Missouri	10	31	18	249
Iowa	5	11	14	101
California	4	10	18	972

Source: Federal Energy Administration, "The Natural Gas Shortage: A Preliminary Report" (August 1975).
Note: Parentheses indicate an increase.

line served a particular state and the security of that pipeline's sources of supply. Transcontinental Gas Pipeline, for example, the sole supplier of North and South Carolina, projected a 40 percent deficiency for the winter of 1975–76,[30] while pipelines serving Massachusetts found little need to curtail.

Second, the shortage was not simply a shortage in existing production. Several years before the public noticed any shortage in current supply, there was an obvious and growing shortage of reserves. Between 1947 and 1954, when FPC regulation of producers began, pipelines, when buying gas under long-term contracts, bought reserves equal to 20 times yearly production—enough to provide a 20-year backlog of supply.[31] After regulation began, the FPC required that any new production sold to interstate pipelines have 20 years of reserve backing. Beginning in 1964, however, reserve capacity began to decline.[32] Between 1968 and 1975, the interstate reserves-to-production ratio fell from 16.8 to 9.3 years.[33] The fact that reserves gradually and continuously declined suggests that the shortage was not (as some have claimed) contrived by producers who "withheld" gas from the market in order to force decontrol. While some withholding could be rational for producers who anticipate an imminent end to controls, it is not rational to withhold gas for 8–12 years. Yet the shortage existed for at least that long a time. That is to say, since 1964 or 1965 producers supplied less than the amounts demanded.[34] But this fact was disguised until the early 1970s by the depletion of existing reserves.[35]

Third, the shortage was in part accounted for by the fact that interstate prices were regulated while intrastate prices were not.[36] Thus, producers tried to sell their gas intrastate[37] and many industrial consumers moved to the producing states in order to take advantage of the fuel's availability. Before 1976 prices for *intra*state natural gas were over $1.75 per thousand cubic feet (mcf), while *inter*state, prices were under 51 cents per mcf. Total U.S. production dropped from a peak of 22.5 trillions of cubic feet (tcf) in 1973 to 21.2 tcf in 1974, while production in the interstate market declined from its peak of 14.2 tcf (1972) to 12.9 tcf[38] in 1974. As one can see from Table 11, considerable additions to reserves between 1970 and 1976 were almost exclusively *intra*state. (In 1976, the FPC dramatically increased the interstate price ceiling to $1.42 per mcf and additions to the interstate market increased.)

Fourth, the shortage had two causes. The first cause was a low interstate ceiling price that discouraged producers from searching for gas. During the early 1960s the commission set provisional price ceilings of 16–18 cents per mcf. When the commission later collected cost information to set permanent price ceilings, it found that the costs of existing producers were equal to or less than this provisional ceiling. The commission believed that this fact proved that production costs were less than 16–18 cents per mcf. In fact, this was illusory, because firms with higher costs simply did not answer the FPC's questionnaire. They had long since left the industry.[39]

The extent to which higher prices would elicit additional supply is a technical question that depends upon geological estimates of availability as well as economic cost estimates. Greater supply would certainly be forthcoming at higher prices, but *how much* additional supply is a moot point.

A second and different cause of the shortage concerns the allocation of existing supply. Regulation led to old gas prices considerably below the cost of producing new gas. By definition, demand for the old gas exceeded supply, and its price was not allowed to rise in order to determine who would receive it. Thus, there was a shortage of older, cheaper gas, which had to be alleviated through some system of allocation. This aspect of the shortage existed independently of the high-price problem and had nothing to do with the issue of whether higher prices would increase new gas supplies.

The shortage had other adverse effects. Industry moved south to obtain fuel. Gas supplies were curtailed in a pattern that, from a rational point of view, is random. Because firms could not count on gas availability regardless of their willingness to pay, many incurred large conversion costs. Curtailment decisions spawned a host of lawsuits. And the allocation process itself involved lengthy and complex administrative proceedings.

Table 11. State net reserve additions, interstate versus intrastate, excluding Alaska and Hawaii.

Year	Total net AGA reserve additions in trillions of cubic feet (tcf)	Net interstate reserve additions		Inferred intrastate reserve additions[a]	
		Tcf	Percent	Tcf	Percent
1965	21.2	13.3	63	7.9	37
1966	19.2	14.2	74	5.0	26
1967	21.1	14.8	70	6.3	30
1968	12.0	9.5	79	2.5	21
1969	8.3	6.1	73	2.2	27
1970	11.1	0.0	0	11.1	100
1971	9.4	2.0	21	7.4	79
1972	9.4	(0.2)	0	9.6	100
1973	6.5	1.1	17	5.4	83
1974	8.3	(1.0)	0	9.3	100
1975	10.5[b]	(1.7)[d]		12.2	100
1976	7.6[c]	2.9[d]		4.7	62
1977	12.0[c]	8.6[e]		3.4	28

Source: Federal Power Commission, Bureau of Natural Gas, *A Realistic View of U.S. Natural Gas Supply,* Staff Report, December 1974, at 17.

a. Derived by assuming that intrastate reserve additions are equal to the difference between total American Gas Association reserve additions and the reserve additions committed to the interstate market.

b. American Gas Association, *Gas Facts,* 1976.

c. American Public Gas Association, cited by Bureau of National Affairs, *Energy Users' Report,* 258:8 (July 20, 1978).

d. Federal Energy Regulatory Commission, *Gas Supplies of Interstate Natural Gas Pipeline Companies,* 1976.

e. Federal Energy Regulatory Commission, preliminary staff report released June 21, 1978, cited by Bureau of National Affairs, *Energy Users' Report,* 254:6 (June 22, 1978).

Note: Parentheses indicate a decrease.

The Mismatch and the Shortage

The natural gas shortage and the accompanying dislocations partly resulted from regulation itself—or the use of classical regulation where it is ill-suited. The gap between supply and demand, the sudden shortage, the difficulty of adjustment, and the inefficient allocation among potential customers all flowed from a regulatory mismatch. Those familiar with the regulatory process and the nature of the problem could have predicted (and did predict) almost precisely what would occur. Perhaps policy makers, had they been familiar with such predictions and their bases, would have changed their minds about how to proceed.

To see how the problems of gas regulation flowed from the classical regulatory system, consider the FPC's regulatory efforts. After the 1954 *Phillips* decision, the commission, faced for the first time with the need to regulate producers, turned to the ordinary system available to regulate price: classical cost-of-service ratemaking.

Firm-by-Firm Cost-of-Service Ratemaking

The commission first attempted to apply cost-of-service ratemaking on a firm-by-firm basis. It failed to do so successfully, however, for several reasons.

First, cost-of-service ratemaking is able to determine producer costs and hold price to that level when only a few firms are involved. But the commission found that it had to deal with thousands of producers. In 1954 there were more than 4,500 gas producers. By 1962 they had submitted more than 2,900 applications for increased prices.[40] Moreover, producers typically had different cost structures, depending in part upon the extent to which their exploration and production involved oil as well as gas. Separating joint oil and gas costs and determining a fair return on investment were time-consuming. The first producer rate case undertaken, the *Phillips* case itself, took 82 hearing days, with testimony filling 10,620 pages and a record that included 235 exhibits. By 1960 the commission had completed only ten cases.[41] The commission's backlog led Landis in his report to President Kennedy to conclude that "the Federal Power Commission without question represents the outstanding example in the federal government of the breakdown of the administrative process."[42]

Second, cost-of-service ratemaking assumes that detailed, accurate information about producer costs can be obtained from accounting records and that the cost of capital can be determined from these records with reasonable accuracy. The commission found, however, that in this instance the problems of separating joint costs and determining the cost of capital, as described in Chapter 2, invalidated both of these assumptions.

Gas costs were difficult to specify because in 1954 gas was frequently produced together with oil. Exploration yielded some gas wells, some oil wells, some wells producing both, and many dry holes. Extraction yielded gas together with petroleum liquids, and refining or processing gas also yielded salable liquids. How should the costs of producing these products be allocated between the gas and the liquids? For that matter how should the costs of dry holes be allocated—as a "failure to produce gas," "oil," or both?

As pointed out in Chapter 2, joint costs pose a problem *only* under regulation. In competitive markets producers would recover incremental joint costs from the sale of gas and oil, with the relative amounts received from sales of each varying from firm to firm. Assume, for example, that to find and to produce a certain volume of gas and oil from an incremental well costs a certain producer $100,000. Assume further that, of this cost, $70,000 is joint, $20,000 represents the ascertainable separate cost of extracting oil, and $10,000 the separate cost of extracting gas. The producer will develop the well and sell both gas and oil, provided he can sell the oil for at least $20,000, the gas for at least $10,000, and the two together for at least $100,000. But he will not care whether the extra $70,000 comes from gas sales, oil sales, or a combination of the two. The source of the $70,000 will depend upon the relative strength of the demands of gas buyers and oil buyers for the producer's supplies—a factor that will depend upon supply and demand in each industry.[43]

If a regulatory agency controlled *both* gas and oil, it might try to replicate these competitive market results simply by requiring that the combined revenues from the sale of the two products equal their combined costs. Any combination of prices that would do no more than return costs (including capital costs) would meet this requirement. Thus, in the example, the agency would allow the producer to recover $100,000, permitting him to set whatever combination of prices was necessary to obtain this revenue. Similarly, the agency would allow the owner of an inframarginal well (a well with lower costs) with joint costs of $40,000, separate gas costs of $5,000, and separate oil costs of $10,000 to set whatever prices would yield him $55,000. Thus, he would be prevented from earning any excess profit.

The FPC, however, had authority to regulate natural gas, not oil. Thus, to eliminate excess returns, it would have had to find the exact cost of one of two joint products—a task that was logically impossible—or to regulate indirectly the earnings on the unregulated sales of liquids—a task that was legally impossible. Of course, the commission might still have tried to replicate competitive market conditions. It might, for example, have required producers to submit prices that covered the costs of producing gas only, but which included (1) the separate gas costs and (2) such joint costs as could not be recovered from oil sales. (Thus, the firm in the first example would set gas prices that would recover $10,000 plus whatever part of the $70,000 joint costs could not be recovered from oil sales.) But the producer is unlikely to know the amount of joint cost recoverable from oil sales—particularly when oil prices fluctuate. Moreover, the producer might lower oil prices deliberately in order to obtain commission approval to raise gas prices, in hope of later raising oil prices.[44]

In fact, the commission tried to allocate joint costs by using a number of accounting methods, which, for example, allocated costs among gas and oil in proportion to comparative Btu heat content. These methods had little to do with economic reality. All of them allocated *more* joint costs to gas than producers actually recovered from gas sales. Thus, the commission, in the ten cases it completed, held, contrary to every public expectation, that gas prices were too *low*—that the proposed prices would not generate enough revenue to cover gas costs. This result was interpreted as evidence that the commission failed to protect the public interest. An understanding of the joint cost problem, however, makes it likely that the problem, not the commission, was at fault.

The FPC faced a similarly difficult problem in trying to determine a fair rate of return. The ordinary difficulties, described in Chapter 2, were aggravated in the case of natural gas by the nature of the product and the industry. How was the commission to choose "comparable industries"—industries with "comparable risk"—for comparison? Natural gas production is riskier than running an electricity company, but is it as risky as mining copper? How could the commission apply a "discounted cash flow" model based upon share prices to determine the cost of capital? Few producers sold shares on exchanges and those that did produced both gas and oil. Nor did producers issue significant amounts of debt securities. Risks varied greatly among producers. Thus, to determine capital costs required subjective decisions about thousands of individual producers. And the problem was the more serious in that capital costs accounted for the majority of total gas production costs.

In sum, the administrative problems were aggravated by the large number of producers, an intractable joint cost problem, and a difficult capital cost ascertainment problem. This doomed to failure the FPC's efforts to apply cost-of-service ratemaking on a firm-by-firm basis.

Areawide Cost-of-Service Ratemaking

The commission, faced with an unworkable individual-firm approach, decided in 1960 to set rates on an areawide basis. Gas-producing regions were divided into five geographical areas,[45] interim ceiling prices were set for each, and hearings were begun to determine final reasonable prices in each area. By this time, the commission had also determined that it was faced with a rent control problem, not a monopoly power problem. And it approached the problem by trying to develop a tiered pricing system. It set different prices for different vintages of production, depending upon whether gas was old or new and whether it was produced in conjunction with oil or separately. By allowing higher prices for gas with progressively higher costs, the tiered system would transfer rents to consumers by keeping down the price of low-cost, older gas. It would not discourage production, for producers would obtain higher prices for new gas. It thus sought a middle path between uniformly low prices (which would inevitably discourage production) and uniformly high prices (which would leave the producers with all the rents).

As discussed above, tiered pricing regulation to control rents must deal with two serious problems: (1) How will the regulator determine the "high" price? How does one know that it is high enough to elicit new supply? (2) Who obtains the low-priced product? All users want it, but users cannot be allowed to bid for it because prices would then simply rise to the high level. How is the low-priced product to be allocated?

The commission did not deal with either of these problems successfully. In the late 1960s it set final "high" prices which were well below the costs of producing new natural gas. In fact, its permanent price ceilings for new gas roughly equaled the interim price ceiling that the commission had set in the early 1960s.[46]

Four factors led the commission to set a "high" price ceiling that was too low. First, the interim price ceilings themselves led to a low final price ceiling. A producer unable to sell gas for more than an interim ceiling price would have developed only those reserves with incremental costs below that ceiling. A producer with higher costs would have left the business. Only producers with cheap, lucky finds would remain. Thus, it is not surprising that when the FPC surveyed producer costs several years after interim price ceilings had been set, it found that average costs of new gas were below the interim ceiling level. The interim ceiling prevented the commission from finding out, via survey, the true incremental costs of new reserves.

Second, in order to allow development of new gas supplies, the "high" price must cover incremental exploration and extraction costs over a *future* period. The commission, however, set prices in part by *averaging* recent *past* incremental costs in the producing region. By averaging costs of unusually lucky or skillful producers in with the others, the commission understated the true incremental costs of new production.

Third, in determining its ceiling price, the commission added an 8 percent "growth allowance" to costs in order to consider the fact that new gas might become more expensive to produce in the future.[47] The commission reached this 8 percent figure not by estimating probable costs, but by compromising customer and producer estimates of a proper growth allowance. Given the speculative nature of the inquiry—the extent to which gas production costs would likely increase over several years—it was reasonable for the commission judgmentally to select a compromise figure instead of trying to determine a figure technically. However, the result understated the increase in costs.

Fourth, both producer and customer estimates of probable future production costs were, in fact, far too low. Yet it was administratively difficult for the commission to reopen the proceeding and recalculate costs even after the error became evident. The *Permian Basin* proceedings, for example, had lasted for eight years, involving hundreds of witnesses and exhibits. Moreover, there was strong customer opposition to price increases, and evidentiary hearings would have been required. Thus, the "high" price ceiling remained too low until so severe a shortage developed that the misallocative effect of the low price became obvious to almost everyone.

To some extent these failings grew out of the process itself. The large number of firms, the uncertainties of exploration, and the difficulties of accurate cost determination made compromise inevitable and reopening the proceedings difficult. Yet to some extent, the commission *and* the parties simply misestimated future costs—a failing that cannot be blamed upon the regulatory system.

Blame for the second cause of the shortage—the inability to allocate the limited supply of inexpensive old gas—*can* be placed entirely upon regulation, for regulation can cause that problem (by keeping prices low) but it cannot solve it.

Initially the commission rationed old gas on a historical basis, by refusing to allow new pipeline construction that might divert reserves from the customers that a particular field had historically served. The commission also refused to allow interstate gas shipments to utility companies for use as boiler fuel—a use that the commision considered "inferior." But the commission was legally unable to control the shipment of intrastate gas as well as gas that was sold directly to a producer's industrial customers. Thus, certain customers were legally free to bid for older, cheaper gas.

The commission was able to allocate the older, cheaper gas successfully for many years by allowing the pipelines, which bought gas from several producers, to average all gas costs and resell their gas at a single price. New gas costs were "rolled-in" with old. Thus, a buyer might find, for example, that a pipeline charged transportation costs plus 18 cents per mcf for gas, some of which cost the pipeline 15 cents and the remainder of which cost it 20 cents.

The rolling-in of old gas and new prices had two adverse effects. First, gas from different pipelines had different costs, depending on the historical pattern of the pipeline's gas purchases. This encouraged industry to locate along pipelines where the cheapest gas—overall—was available. This relocation was wasteful insofar as the new gas that the pipeline disgorged was as costly as new gas transported by any other pipeline. The new gas used to supply a new industrial customer, for example, cost the pipeline 20 cents per mcf, regardless of which pipeline served the customer. The customer, however, when faced with a rolled-in price of, say, 15 cents from pipeline A and 18 cents from B, will move to A—though the move simply wastes resources.

Second, the rolling-in of gas vintages disguised the shortage. Markets cleared because an ultimate customer, paying an average price of, say, 18 cents per mcf, paid 2 cents more than the cost of old (say, 16-cent) gas. This extra 2 cents allowed the pipeline to recover the cost of 20-cent gas, which it also sold for 18 cents. The rent from the sale of the older, cheaper gas was thus used to finance the production of more expensive gas. This system, by holding the price of new gas below its cost, encouraged customers to demand new natural gas, despite the possibility that they might have used other fuels that in terms of real resources were less costly to produce.

The charging of a price that equaled average cost—the rolling-in of rents—disguised the shortage as long as each pipeline collected enough extra profit on the sale of old gas to cover its potential losses on its sales of new gas. In practice the cost of new gas rose rapidly, the reserves of older, low-cost gas ran down rapidly, the price of new (interstate) gas to the *pipeline* was held below production cost, and intrastate buyers were allowed to pay unregulated prices. The amount of gas available to interstate markets therefore soon fell below the amount demanded, and serious shortages developed, not just in reserves but also in production.

The shortage did not arise out of incompetent or malevolent application of a regulatory system. Rather, it was prompted by the regulatory system itself. The application of cost-of-service ratemaking to a rent control problem will produce prices equal to production cost of low-cost as well as high-cost units— and will inevitably lead to a shortage of the low-cost items. Cost-of-service ratemaking does not and cannot provide for the allocation of the commodity in short supply. Although charging average price could work in the short run (as illustrated by our earlier discussion of oil allocation), it had seriously adverse side-effects, such as overstimulating demand and randomly redistributing rents. And once the agency was forced to consider who should receive the cheap product, the agency had to turn to some other system of allocation.

The Mismatch and Natural Gas Allocation

Once gas reserves ran down to the point where there was a shortage in current production of gas, the FPC had to decide how to allocate the insufficient supply. The commission could not auction the supply to the highest bidder, for to do so would have created a free market in natural gas, allowing gas producers to retain all the economic rent. Rather, it had to turn to regulatory mechanisms to do the allocating.

There are, as we showed in Part I, a limited number of regulatory solutions. The FPC considered two of them—standard setting and public interest allocation—and tried both systems. It first tried to set rules, and then turned to an ad hoc adjudicatory approach. The problems noted in Chapters 5 and 6 in connection with standard setting and with public interest allocation haunted the commission's efforts, and eventually prevented it from achieving satisfactory results.

Standard Setting

In 1970 pipeline companies began to see the need to curtail deliveries during the next winter, when demand for gas would be at a peak. In October 1970 United Gas Pipeline Company developed a plan to curtail its deliveries to certain customers, and it petitioned the commission for a declaratory order that its plan was consistent with its contractual obligations. United hoped that an FPC order would immunize it from customer suits for breach of contract.[48]

In April 1971 the commission issued Order 431[49] which specified acceptable curtailment procedures. It stated that each pipeline should develop its own curtailment plan and that, in general, pipelines should curtail interruptible service first, and large boiler-fuel use (where alternative fuels were available) next, before interrupting other types of service.[50]

In October 1971 the FPC approved a United plan embodying these priorities.[51] In 1972 it rejected an El Paso plan, which would have curtailed all customers outside California before any customer within California. In its place, the commission substituted its own plan which detailed five priorities for curtailment (in reverse order of curtailment):[52] (1) residential, small commercial, and residential needs associated with industrial requirements; (2) large commercial and industrial requirements for plant protection, feedstock, and process needs; (3) all industrial requirements not mentioned elsewhere; (4) industrial requirements for boiler fuel of less than 3,000 mcf per day but more than 1,500 mcf per day where alternative fuel capability was not present; (5) large-volume industrial (more than 3,000 mcf per day) boiler fuel where existing alternative fuel capability was present.

In January 1973 the FPC issued Order 467[53]—a statement of policy that sought to give guidance to the pipelines. It set eight priorities of service categories which the commission believed were "generally applicable industry-wide" and could be used for establishing curtailment plans on any interstate pipeline system. They were the five above with these lower-priority additions: (6) interruptible requirements of less than 1,500 mcf per day; (7) interruptible requirements of 1,500–3,000 mcf per day; and (8) interruptible requirements of more than 3,000 mcf per day. Thus, the first customers curtailed would be large interruptible customers and the last would be small residential or commercial customers.

These standards were revised a final time when a ninth category (first to be curtailed) was added (in Order 467B). These were interruptible sales of more than 10,000 mcf per day where alternate fuel capability could meet the requirements. At the same time, "pipeline customer storage injection requirements" were added to category 2.[54] Essentially, curtailments were to take place first where alternative fuel capability existed (for interruptible customers and then for boiler-fuel customers), and, second, whether or not alternative fuel was available (for industry, then for commercial use and special industrial use, and then for residences).

While these rules are fairly clear, the priorities did not necessarily correspond to any reasonable view of social priorities. One might conclude as a general matter that residential uses are more important than commercial uses and industrial uses more important than boiler-fuel uses, and that interruptible sales were least important. But there were far too many exceptions to warrant applying any such general system of priorities throughout the industry.

Interruptible sales, for example, often reflect the need to balance loads on particular pipelines. Since the pipeline would be stretched beyond capacity on only 10–15 of the coldest winter days, the pipeline company would try to obtain industrial customers willing to interrupt service during those few days. It thus could build the pipeline with a smaller peak capacity and the pipeline would be used more fully the remaining 350 days of the year. Interruptible customers could store enough gas to take them through the interrupted two weeks. They could schedule maintenance for that period, or they could obtain alternative fuels temporarily. Thus, the fact that customers signed interruptible contracts (and could withstand two weeks of curtailment) did not mean that they had less need for gas (or that they found it easier to obtain alternative fuels) than other customers who had firm contracts. It did not mean that they could withstand loss of service for months instead of weeks, or that their use of gas was less important socially. Indeed, in 1974 Piedmont Natural Gas Company was serving twenty hospitals under interruptible contracts.[55]

It was still more difficult to say whether, or when, boiler-fuel users needed gas more than, say, industrial users. In some instances boiler fuel may have constituted a far more important end use than an industrial use such as fabric finishing. It depended upon what the boiler was used for and the availability of alternative fuels.

The problem could not be solved readily by looking to alternative fuel availability, for alternative fuels were always available at a price. The question was a practical one: At what cost in capital outlay, added operating expenses, and lost production during conversion could conversion be feasible? How much of a decline in output or deterioration in product quality would render it infeasible? The cost of conversion varied considerably within each of the FPC's categories. About 60 percent of all existing boilers, for example (accounting for about 8 percent of all natural gas use annually), were equipped to run on fuel oil, but 40 percent were not.[56] Conversion to fuel oil was not expensive, but fuel oil was itself scarce. Moreover, was it desirable to increase dependence on imported oil? Was it sensible to require conversion to oil, when reconversion to coal might soon be necessary? Most (nonutility) industrial boilers were not equipped to take alternate fuels; the costs of conversion varied; and the costs of converting small commercial or residential users were highest. Thus, even if these figures suggest that as a *general* matter the FPC's categories made sense, they also suggest that in many particular cases they did not. And it is difficult to know in advance which cases are which, because actual conversion costs and associated costs cannot be known except by examining costs plant by plant or firm by firm. Moreover, to look only at conversion costs is to leave out the competitive impact on particular industries arising from even a small cost increase—an important factor, because saving production or jobs may be more important than heating small commercial establishments.

In trying to develop and apply its rules, the FPC faced the very difficulties described in Chapter 5 as typically plaguing standard setting. Most serious of these was lack of *information*. There were 210,000 industrial nonutility gas users, and each has different costs associated with gas use. Moreover, natural gas had more than 25,000 different industrial uses,[57] and each involved different costs in individual firms. Yet to know the effects of curtailment, the FPC needed to have at least a rough idea of the costs associated with natural gas in interruptible boiler-fuel, industrial, and commercial uses.

The information problem was aggravated by the fact that pipelines served distributors who did not know the precise use to which their customers put gas. The pipelines had to rely upon distributors for this information. The distributors in turn had to rely upon information supplied by their customers. Thus, the FPC relied upon gas customers to assign themselves into different curtailment categories. And given the difficulty of defining the end uses with precision, a customer could upgrade its category. Prior to the determination of the curtailment categories, the FPC distributed a questionnaire that asked customers to indicate whether they received "firm" or "interruptible" service. After Order 467B appeared, and customers saw the relevance of their answers to curtailment, many sent in revised answers leading to more than 50 billion mcf of delivery being reclassified from "interruptible" to "firm." This information problem was exacerbated by the difficulty of distinguishing precisely between an "industrial" and a "commercial" establishment or between a "process" and a "nonprocess" use of gas.[58]

Enforcement problems arose out of the difficulty of verifying the information provided by customers, distributing companies, and pipelines. They were further complicated by the fact that the FPC lacked authority over distributing companies. It could determine how much gas the interstate pipeline was to give the distributor, and it could base this amount on the types of use to which the distributor's customers put the gas, but it could not force the distributor to follow the FPC's end-use plan. Finally, FPC enforcement had to consider the physical difficulty of disconnecting gas lines. If gas is curtailed to a customer, the physical gas connection must be closed and the pilot light extinguished. When gas delivery is resumed, unless the pilot light is relit, there may be an explosion. The need to supervise closely these physical connections made curtailment of deliveries to residences or small commercial establishments impractical or dangerous. Although the FPC might have tried financial penalties to force home customers to reduce their use (for example, penalty surcharges for use exceeding a specified amount), it could not predict how much of a reduction this would bring about, nor could the penalties be easily enforced. Thus, the FPC placed at the top of the curtailment list the largest industrial customers, whose compliance was easier to ensure.

The *anticompetitive impact* of curtailment rules was also potentially serious. Fuel costs vary considerably among competitors according to the fuel used, and, in the case of gas, depending upon the pipeline that serves the firm and upon the availability of alternative fuels. The effect of any given cost increase on output, employment, and profits depends upon the state of competition, the nature of competitors' costs, and the sensitivity of demand to price changes. Thus, the fact that a firm might switch to an alternative fuel at low cost may not keep that firm in business if it faces stiff competition from other firms that need not switch. This type of consequence militated in favor of numerous exceptions from the end-use standards.

Judicial review of the FPC's standards would have posed a serious problem had the FPC given the standards the status of formal rules, for there was little evidence to support the distinctions made. In fact, the commission referred to Order 467 as a "statement of policy." It then asked individual pipelines to develop curtailment plans, and it sought to use its statement of policy as a basis for approving or disapproving specific curtailment plans. In two instances courts reversed an FPC decision for lack of substantial evidence supporting the statement's distinctions.[59] Other cases suggested that the commission could rely on the statement as a basis for approving individual plans, provided that the record of the commission's consideration of the *individual* plan itself contained enough evidence to support the commission's decision.[60]

In sum, the standard-setting process did not lead to a sensible method for allocating scarce gas.

Public Interest Allocation

The difficulty of creating rules that would automatically and sensibly allocate the natural gas available led the FPC to turn to a form of public interest allocation. Soon after the promulgation of Order 467B, it established procedures for making exceptions. The pipeline's curtailment plan was to be sufficiently flexible to permit pipeline companies to respond to emergency situations (including environmental emergencies) during curtailment periods. Order 467A allowed users needing this relief to obtain it directly from the pipeline. Otherwise a pipeline, distributor, or regulatory commission could petition the FPC directly for extraordinary relief. The petitioner had to prove special circumstances that justified exemption from the curtailment plan.

The extraordinary relief proceeding bore many of the characteristics of public interest allocation. The factors used in reaching a decision were many but conflicting. After examining the FPC's decisions, Willrich noted[61] that the following factors were important to the granting of extraordinary relief: (1) extent of unemployment that would result if the petitioner were curtailed according to the plan; (2) type of end use for which relief is requested (the lower the end use on the 467B scale, the less likely it was that relief would be granted); (3) availability of alternative fuel and cost of conversion; (4) end product of customer's gas use; and (5) effect of relief on other customers. The relief proceedings based on these criteria worked fairly well in 1973 and 1974, when the production shortage was slight. But in 1974–75 the number of petitions increased to 100, and promised to increase further. In the summer of 1975 the commission sought to devise a method for consolidating petitions to prevent a breakdown of the administrative process.[62]

The FPC was unable to devise a satisfactory method for dealing with exceptions. This fact should not be surprising, for its efforts to examine the needs of particular customers produced the same major problems previously described as existing whenever an agency uses public interest allocation. The number of criteria, considerations, and factors proliferated. All the factors mentioned were important, but there was no clear method to measure these factors or to decide their comparative importance. The number of parties presenting claims was large. Each tried to induce the use of criteria favorable to its cause. Proceedings became lengthy and complicated. (The hearing transcript for Columbia Gas pipeline's curtailment plan covered 13,000 pages and the hearing lasted over a year.) The results did not strike observers as particularly fair, and the party that obtained the most gas may have been the party with the better lawyers rather than the greater need. In sum, one sees here a reappearance of the problems faced by the CAB and FCC in allocating a product through individual hearings without reliance on a market.

Negotiation

The difficulties of standard setting and public interest allocation led the FPC to rely in part upon negotiation and bargaining among pipelines and their customers. The FPC encouraged agreed-upon curtailment plans. Yet negotiated plans, too, had serious drawbacks, of the sort described in Chapter 8. First, many of those affected by the plan were not represented at the bargaining table. Pipelines met with large industrial customers and distributing companies. They did not meet with individual consumers, small commercial establishments, or any firm or individual not currently receiving natural gas.

Second, mutually satisfactory negotiated solutions did not necessarily send gas to where it was most valuable. Pipelines' preferences depended upon their own regulated rate structure. If a pipeline was filled at peak periods, it would favor off-peak customers. But if it was not filled at peak, it would favor peak customers who could be charged higher transportation rates. The bargaining power of consumer groups depended as much upon their ability to secure political support as upon their economic need. And every customer had the potential ability to make a complaint to the FPC if not satisfied. Thus, allocation was more likely to reflect a principle of "treat all alike"—reducing all customers the same pro rata amount—than to reflect the different value of gas to different customers.

Finally, the FPC decided to retreat to the rules set out in Order 467 and simply overlook the need for exceptions. This approach solved the administrative problem, but at the price of allocating gas in what was an economically arbitrary way.

Alternatives

The natural gas example illustrates the likely consequences of dealing with a rent control problem through classical regulation. Tiered cost-of-service rate-making must solve two problems: the "high price/new supply" problem and the "low price/allocation" problem. It failed to solve the first of these in large part because of the unascertainable and unknowable nature of future natural gas costs. It failed to solve the second simply because there is no solution. The commission could only (1) run down existing reserves, or (2) use "rolled-in/average cost'' pricing, or (3) use classical regulatory allocation techniques. Each method had serious drawbacks, which exacerbated the gas shortage and its adverse effects.

The resulting shortage and the FPC's inability to deal with it led to a retreat from regulation. In 1976 the commission trebled the ceiling price of gas (to $1.42 per mcf). In 1978 a new law raised the ceiling price of new natural gas still further. The commission allowed imports from Canada and Mexico at prices ($2.00–2.25 per mcf) fairly close to the new domestic high price. Finally, the new law effectively deregulated natural gas as of 1985.[63] Though the rapid increase in all energy prices since 1974 and the uncertainties about future supply make it difficult to trace cause and effect, the effect of the substantial increase in gas prices was quite predictable. The narrowing of the gap in price between intrastate and interstate gas led to an increased flow from the former market into the latter. Imports from Canada and Mexico increased to the point where they account for about 5 percent of the American market; they are predicted to account for 20–25 percent by 1985.[64] Many industrial users switched to oil after experiencing the curtailments of the mid-1970s, and in 1977 gas sales to industry fell 9 percent below those of 1976.[65] Conservation efforts by home users since 1974 led to a 13 percent drop in sales of gas for heating homes.[66] Thus, the increase in supply and fall in demand has at least temporarily ended the shortage. Yet in doing so, the retreat from regulation has also meant the end of the effort to redistribute the rents or excess profits created by the increase in the cost of new supply. The 1978 Energy Act seeks to prevent producers from capturing all the rent by raising prices gradually. However, the act legislates a set of price schedules with more than twenty different gas categories and prices. It creates so complex a system that one suspects it will create an essentially random distribution of rents between now and 1985.

The rationale for regulation, however—the desire to transfer rents or windfall profits from producers to consumers—is plausible. Unlike excessive competition, it does not describe an ''empty box.'' And there is an alternative, less restrictive mode of governmental intervention, which in all likelihood could have done the regulatory job better: Congress might have imposed a tax that would have transferred the excess producer profits to consumers. This would have accomplished Congress' major regulatory objective without the severe problems endemic to classical regulation.

Of course, as previously pointed out, a tax system raises problems of its own. The amount of the tax is difficult (but not impossible) to calculate. The Carter administration's initial oil wellhead tax plan, for example, categorized oil roughly according to cost, allowed the price of the newest, most expensive oil to rise to free market levels, and in each other category set the tax equal to the difference between ''cost'' and the free-market price.[67] By requiring the regulator to categorize old gas or cheap gas according to cost, this system risks the erroneous placement of expensive gas into a cheap-gas category. It requires the producer to determine which free-market price of the several available (varying with product quality and place at which gas is sold) is to be used for tax purposes. The tax system also raises political problems, such as how the tax revenues would be allocated. Moreover, the tax system would end as the older, cheaper gas is used up.

None of these problems, however, is likely to prove as harmful as the misallocation brought about by cost-of-service ratemaking. Indeed, the automatic termination is desirable, for the tax would end at the very moment that the rationale for its imposition disappeared. Our discussion of the tax alternative in Chapter 8 suggests that application here might have proved practical and that it certainly would have been less harmful than classical regulation.[68]

Conclusion

Classical regulation seems particularly ill-suited to deal with rent control problems. The history of natural gas regulation illustrates the difficulties that created a mismatch. These are serious enough to raise doubts about whether consumers themselves have, on balance, been helped or harmed by natural gas regulation. One cannot prove that the effort to regulate was unfounded, for there was a legitimate problem that arguably warranted a governmental solution. Yet even if one accepts that argument, there was an alternative untried weapon available. A tax system may well have been more effective. Were the nation again to embark upon an effort to control rents in the energy industries, its policy makers ought to explore the tax alternative with greater care.

14

Partial Mismatch: Spillovers and Environmental Pollution

The analysis in Part I suggests that greater reliance should be placed upon less restrictive regimes as a means for dealing with spillover problems. The classical approach to the spillover problem—standard setting—is difficult to administer, can cause serious anticompetitive harm, and ofttimes freezes existing technology. The likelihood that these harms will occur is increased by the number of factors that must be controlled and the inherent technological complexity of the problem. Thus, where complex spillovers are present, one may find the standard-setting problems severe. At the same time, substitution of less restrictive regimes of intervention may be feasible. Of course, any actual regulatory program may involve a mix of standards and incentive-based elements. But emphasizing the latter rather than the former is likely to prove a more effective method for dealing with the problem.

The government's effort to control air and water pollution is an excellent example of a case in which increased emphasis upon less restrictive regimes is likely to prove more effective.[1] First, governmental intervention is warranted. As previously discussed, the essential problem is that the price of a product made by means of a polluting process does not reflect the harm that the resulting pollution causes. The producer has little reason to install expensive equipment to prevent pollution of the air or water. On the contrary, if he installs such equipment and his competitors do not, their prices will be lower and he will lose sales and profits. If left alone, these incentives bring about serious problems.[2]

Second, the problem is technologically complex. The major elements of air pollution are sulfur dioxide (SO_2), carbon monoxide (CO), nitrous oxides (NOx), hydrocarbons (HC), and suspended particulates. These are primarily produced by automobiles, power plants that burn fossil fuels, and other large industrial facilities that emit smoke and fumes. Most water pollution is caused by chemicals and other material that use up the dissolved oxygen in lakes and streams (making the water unfit for aquatic life, drinking, or swimming) or that encourage the growth of undesirable plant life, such as algae. The polluting tendency of many of these effluents is measured by "biological oxygen demand" (BOD) to reflect the reduction in dissolved oxygen in the water available for other uses.[3] The relationship of an *emission* to pollution itself is complicated and varies over time and location. Whether, for example, a pound of SO_2 emitted from a smokestack pollutes or causes harm depends upon the wind, the temperature, the amount of SO_2 in the air already, the time of day, and so on. Similarly, the polluting effect of an additional pound of BOD depends upon the amount of pollutant already in the water, how soon the water can "recover," and how quickly the water can obtain additional oxygen, which depends upon the rate of flow, exposed water surface, and so on. Given the considerable number of pollutants, of processes that can pollute, and of deleterious effects produced it is not surprising that there are many techniques for controlling pollution. These processes have uncertain effects and their cost-effectiveness will differ significantly depending upon the individual plant, location, time, and a host of other factors.[4]

Third, the number of individual sources that emit pollutants is vast. A rough estimate of major air pollution sources includes 138 million automobiles (with 100 million separate owners); 20,000 major stationary sources, each capable of emitting over 100 tons of pollutant per year; 180,000 other stationary sources; and millions of space-heating systems contribute a small but significant amount of pollution.[5] Most water pollution comes from storm runoffs, municipal sewer systems, and industrial sources. There are at least 40,000–55,000 significant individual sources.[6]

Fourth, efforts to control pollution so far have relied almost exclusively upon classical standard setting. Two different varieties of standards have been used. The Clean Air Act of 1970 provides for an "ambient" standard system, under which federal regulators set standards of air quality governing particular regions of the country. Local regulators are required to tell individual polluters what to do in order to achieve the region's overall ambient goal.[7] Thus, an ambient standard for New York City might consist of an annual mean concentration of 0.02 parts of SO_2 per million parts of air.[8] The local authority would then devise a plan (a State Implementation Plan, or SIP) that would require firms (or drivers) emitting SO_2 to take specific actions so that the ambient standard could be met. Under the "emissions" standard system, the federal regulators impose an emissions limitation directly on polluters. The Clean Air Act provided specific emissions standards for automobiles, and required the Environmental Protection Agency to set emissions standards for new firms and particularly dangerous substances. Under the 1972 Federal Water Pollution Control Act, the EPA must set effluent standards that require all effluent sources to use the "best practicable control technology" by 1977 and the "best available technology" by 1983.[9] Moreover, firms and municipal waste dischargers must comply with these standards to receive a permit needed to discharge any effluent whatsoever.

Fifth, the standard-setting effort to control pollution has been severely criticized as expensive, wasteful, and ineffective. A recent study of the Clean Air Act commissioned by the Senate Government Operations Committee found modest improvement in the ambient air quality. The pollutant content of the air, which had risen steadily until 1970, had been reduced by 1974 so that, as a percentage of the 1970 level, particulate content was 71 percent as high; CO, 88 percent; SO_2, 92 percent; and HC, 94 percent. (NOx alone had risen to 110 percent of the 1970 level.) The study found, however, that most of the improvement was due to the substitution of oil for coal as boiler fuel, and the use of lower-sulfur coal.[10] Although auto pollution appears to have improved since 1970, the degree of improvement is debatable, because stringent pollution standards have been relaxed by Congress. In addition, pollution testing suggests that new cars complying with strict standards quickly fall out of compliance as they get older.[11] The Senate study found evidence of improvement in water pollution, though it doubted that water quality would approach the goals set in the federal act.[12]

Finally, for some time economists and others have advocated the use of charges, taxes, and marketable rights as a more effective and efficient method for dealing with the pollution problem. Other countries have begun to experiment with such systems.

Given these characteristics, the pollution problem provides a good example of an important, complex spillover problem, where standard setting has been relied upon heavily, where only moderate progress has been made, and where other approaches to the problem might be tried. Thus, a brief discussion of the major problems of standard setting in the pollution area, as well as those of the less restrictive alternatives suggested, will illustrate the more obvious virtues and vices of a shift in the latter direction. It will also indicate that this area is a major candidate for reform, and that an effort should be made to see whether a major shift should take place and to work out its details.

The Problems of Standard Setting

The major dilemma confronting those creating or administering antipollution standards is whether to make them simple and widely applicable or to create particularized standards that are finely tailored to individual areas, firms, and pollutants. Administrative considerations favor the former direction; powerful technical and economic factors require the latter.

The impracticality of simple uniform standards can be easily seen. First, as previously mentioned, the relationship between a pound of discharge or emission (of, say, SO_2 or BOD) and a given amount of pollutant damage (pollution)[13] is quite complex. It depends upon natural factors such as seasons, temperature variations, rates of water or air flow, preexisting purity of air or water, and synergistic effects, such as whether SO_2 and dust are present together.[14]

Thus, to limit emissions everywhere by a given amount would produce varying effects on the resulting distribution of pollution.

Second, emission or effluent control technology is characterized by rising incremental costs. The more emissions are reduced, the more expensive it becomes to remove an additional pound of discharge. To remove an extra pound of BOD discharged by a meat processing plant might cost 6 cents if 30 percent of its discharge has already been removed, 60 cents if 90 percent has been removed, and 90 cents if 95 percent has been removed.[15] Economic estimates of the resource costs involved, although rough, suggest that this problem is serious. A typical study by the EPA estimated it would cost $61 billion to eliminate 85–90 percent of effluents from the nation's water supply over ten years. Elimination of all effluents might cost an additional $200 billion.[16] While technological changes make numerical estimates uncertain, such dramatic increases in the cost of removal, as the standard of air or water purity moves from 85 percent to 95 percent to 99 percent, characterize both air and water pollution control technologies.[17]

Third, the cost of removing a given pound of effluent varies considerably, depending on the nature of the source—whether it is a car or a plant, whether it manufactures plastics or sugar. To remove an additional pound of BOD from the discharge of a beet sugar refinery costs about 5 cents (with 90 percent already removed); to remove a pound of BOD from a petroleum refinery's discharge (with 90 percent already removed) would cost about 22 cents.[18]

The combination of (1) the complex relation between emission removal and pollution reduction, (2) marginal costs that rise significantly, and (3) significant variation in removal costs from source to source spells disaster for simple uniform emissions standards. A simple uniform emission standard applied across a given region not only will produce varying results from place to place, but also may not reflect the desires of those in the region. Parks and open spaces may end up too dirty. Some industrial regions will also remain too dirty while others become cleaner than necessary to satisfy most of those affected.[19] Rising marginal costs make "total cleanup" standards impractical. If voters or consumers are forced to focus on the enormous cost and comparatively small benefit of moving from 95 percent to 99 percent removal, they are likely to disavow the program. At the same time, the variation in cost from source to source makes uniform, simple emissions standards wasteful. Estimates of the waste involved suggest that it is large. Studies of the Delaware Basin estimate that by reducing effluent where it was cheapest to do so instead of applying simple, uniform standards to all polluters would have yielded the same degree of cleanup at one third to one tenth the cost.[20] Similarly, a cost-minimizing approach to sulfur emissions might reduce cleanup costs by 35–40 percent.[21] As Stewart and Krier noted, "There has been no detailed study of the economic waste generated by the use of uniform effluent limitations, but the figure would run into many billions of dollars."[22]

For these reasons, in part, emissions standards that were initially simple and nonparticularized have tended to become particularized and complex as they have been administered. The Water Pollution Act, for example, provides a definite uniform standard: each firm is to use the "best practicable control technology" by 1977 and the "best available technology economically achievable" by 1983. Yet the statute leaves to the administrator the definition and application of these terms.[23] The EPA has examined the economic circumstances of the particular industry and firm, tailoring its standards to prevent obvious waste.

Similarly, states, in drawing up plans to achieve their ambient air quality goals, have considered adoption of simple emissions standards—for example, all sources in a state or region must reduce their SO_2 emissions by 90 percent. But they have then been faced with the resulting waste caused by selective enforcement of such a crude standard. Pursuing large firms, for example, while ignoring small ones, or entering into consent decrees with "compliance schedules" that effectively allow variation from industry to industry or firm to firm, ultimately proves a grossly inefficient way of reducing pollution.[24]

The one instance in which Congress imposed a strict uniform emissions limitation—on new cars—has not proved a great success. Congress required manufacturers to reduce emissions of HC, CO, and NOx to about 10 percent of 1970 levels by 1975–76. Since Congress could effectively regulate only one source of air pollution (new cars), the standards had to be strict to bring about significantly cleaner air. Yet their very stringency impeded their effectiveness. The auto companies claimed they could not be met. The standards were then relaxed, so that the actual standards for 1978–79 were closer to a 50 percent than to a 90 percent reduction. Moreover, controls on new cars soon deteriorated, lessening the standard's practical impact. Cost/benefit studies of the standard's effect found that the undoubted benefit of reduced pollution could be offset by the standards' large costs.[25]

Congress and administrators have been driven toward the creation of particularized standards, due to the nature of the problem and the desire to avoid waste. Yet the problems besetting standard setting, as described in Chapter 5, are particularly acute with particularized pollution standards—a fact that tends to push administrators in the opposite direction.

Information. The problem of obtaining enough information to set detailed standards is severe. In principle, different areas or bodies of water might appropriately tolerate different amounts of pollution. Yet how is one to determine what level is appropriate for each location? Efforts to assign value to the pollution-free quality of air or water, by noting differences in land values or wage rates in polluted and unpolluted areas, are notoriously unconvincing, and produce widely varying results.[26] Nor is there any practical way to place a specific value on aesthetic or health benefits, particularly when preferences may change rapidly over time.[27] Similarly, it is easier to observe that complex cumulative or synergistic factors determine how much pollution a given pound of effluent will yield than to predict even vaguely *how much* pollution a particular discharge at a particular time or place will cause. Complicated computer models of air basins and water basins have been developed. Yet these models must themselves embody so many simplifying assumptions that they work imperfectly in practice.[28] The director of Connecticut's environmental program pointed out two reasons why simplification is essential. First, data on short term emission cannot be gathered quickly enough to make the results timely; terrain is typically too complex, and so the model only distantly reflects the real world. Second, determining the emission level of any single source will affect the appropriate emission level for every other source. In principle, one would need to model a number of scenarios equal to the factorial of all sources—a number in the tens of millions for any one state—in order to determine the individual source standards that would yield an acceptable level of pollution.[29] Yet modeling even one scenario for a state the size of Connecticut can cost up to $5,000.[30] Obviously, basin models will be simplified. As they pass through the administrative process, they become distorted for political reasons as well.

Moreover, one cannot use a computer model to develop particularized standards unless the administrator has fairly good information concerning abatement costs. Yet as Kneese and Schultze point out, "There are up to 55,000 major sources of industrial water pollution alone. A regulatory agency cannot know the costs, the technological opportunities, the alternative raw materials, and the kinds of products available for every firm in every industry. Even if it could determine the appropriate reduction standards for each firm, it would have to revise them frequently to accommodate changing costs and markets, new technologies, and economic growth."[31] Dewees noted that engineering estimates of the equipment cost at a particular plant are "difficult to generalize . . . to an industry that includes new and old firms using a variety of production technology and having a wide range of output rates."[32] Econometric studies consider these factors but typically suffer from inadequate cost data. Nor can studies determine the likelihood of cost-saving technological change or the effects on product demand, output, and subsequent cost of the pollution abatement.

Were it practical to gather and use cost information, the agency would nonetheless find that most of the information was in the hands of the firms it seeks to regulate. Prior to 1970, environmental administrators found it difficult to enforce even weak environmental standards because they could not force waste dischargers to divulge information. Firms have every incentive to overstate abatement costs. Given the range of judgmental issues in predicting future cost changes, the agency administrator is likely to distrust the accuracy of the information provided.

Faced with these difficulties, it is no wonder that administrators have been reluctant to promulgate standards directly tied to individual plant costs. To do so not only necessitates plant-by-plant examination of costs, but requires the administrator to know nearly as much about each plant as its manager. Thorough study of the effort to develop detailed information and to set particularized standards in the Delaware Basin suggests that the effort was far from successful, with less pollution reduction and higher costs than necessary.[33] Thus, the difficulties of developing detailed information have led many state administrators to set highly general standards (such as a requirement that a plant take "suitable" measures to reduce emissions) or nonparticularized standards (requiring every firm, for example, to reduce SO_2 emissions by 90 percent) and then to rely on the enforcement process to bring about necessary modifications in individual cases.[34]

Enforcement. The problems of enforcing highly particularized standards are also severe. First, the individual firm has little incentive to comply with general ambient standards or generalized exhortations to "reduce pollution" where it is uncertain precisely what it is supposed to do. Even if it wants to control emissions voluntarily, it must worry whether its competitors will prove equally public-spirited. An air polluter is likely to await discussions with state environmental officials, who will issue a permit for each major source, describing what it must do to bring itself into compliance with the "state implementation plan."[35] Similarly, a water polluter may await negotiations with EPA officials, who will seek to determine what precisely constitutes the "best practicable" pollution control technique, given the firm's production processes and economic circumstances.[36] Negotiation with 35,000 water pollution sources,[37] or with 200–1,500 major stationary air pollution sources (let alone the tens of thousands of minor sources), is obviously difficult or impossible. Most state agencies have 15–200 inspectors available for granting permits and making inspections.[38] The upshot is that enforcement agencies will focus on the largest sources. The others have little incentive to reduce emissions and even the largest sources will await the outcome of individual proceedings. The incentive to comply voluntarily—which EPA officials have described as essential to the working of the system[39]—is much diminished.

The incentive to comply voluntarily is diminished by several other factors as well. First, it is difficult to determine whether a firm is in compliance—even where there is a highly particularized standard. Second, the uncertainty of punishment for noncompliance can lead firms to violate the statute where the expected value of the fine is less than the cost of compliance. While it is fairly easy for an inspector to determine whether a firm has installed promised anti-pollution equipment, he cannot readily assess whether the equipment is operating properly. Emissions tests may cost $2,000 per smokestack—$10,000 for a typical plant. And unlawful emissions may result from leaky fuel or storage tanks, not just smokestacks. Some emissions, such as SO_2, are best checked by examining the fuel burned, not the smoke. The sulfur content of coal, moreover, is highly variable, and the sulfur content of a plant's coal supply may vary from week to week depending upon the mix received from suppliers.

If a violation is detected, the firm may bargain for a reduced penalty by threatening to force the agency to bring a court action. The threat is serious, for the agency knows that the firm is likely to argue (1) that it was in compliance, (2) that the individual permit requirements were unreasonable, (3) that the general regulations and standards are unreasonable, and (4) that it needs more time.[40] Given the informational difficulties facing the agency, the firm may well win. Even if it loses, the court will wish to work out a reasonable compliance schedule. Only repeat violators are likely to be penalized severely. A large violation may well receive no greater penality than a small one, and firms will have little incentive to comply with particularized standards.[41] They lose little—and may even gain—by waiting for court-imposed compliance schedules[42] and by using this threat as a weapon to obtain more relaxed requirements from the agency.

It is tempting to think that the enforcement agencies can escape these enforcement problems and secure widespread compliance through the threat of severe sanctions and the promulgation of rigorous, simple, nonparticularized standards. Unfortunately, this is wrong. The oversimplifications and waste inherent in the nonparticularized approach make courts and regulators reluctant to enforce such standards. In practice, they search for ways to avoid doing so. Even if they do not *voluntarily* avoid strict enforcement of simple standards, they tend to be forced to do so by political pressures that temper the rigors of simple rules in a highly ad hoc manner. The net result is an enforcement system that looks strict on paper, but is much less effective in practice.

The emissions standards for automobile manufacturers mandated by the Clean Air Act of 1970 provide the clearest example of the way in which political considerations can cause strict uniform standards to fail in practice. As previously pointed out, the required emissions reduction—90 percent within five years—was not met. In 1973 Congress extended the deadline to 1975, and in 1977 again extended it to 1981. Congress had little choice, since the companies plausibly claimed that the standards simply could not be met—and neither environmentalists nor the EPA could prove the contrary. The enforcement sanction—closing down the noncomplying firms—would, in the case of the Ford Motor Company alone, have meant a GNP reduction of $17 billion, increased unemployment of 800,000 workers, and a loss of $5 billion in government tax receipts.[43] As long as politically responsive bodies such as Congress are functioning, the environmental agency's sanctions in such an instance are unlikely to pose a credible threat.

An individual state's experience in developing an implementation plan illustrates a similar process. Political pressures often initially led officials to adopt rigorous, simple, nonparticularized standards.[44] Yet the practical consequences of those standards soon led to the adoption of a more particularized approach. Thus, the Los Angeles Air Pollution Control District, under strong political pressure to "do something" about smog, adopted a flat quantity restriction on NOx omissions from any source, regardless of size. As the effects of the regulation became apparent, the agency rewrote and relaxed the requirement. Similarly, Roberts and Farrell found the political process, which prevents nonparticularized standards from being enforced in practice, at work in Florida, Georgia, South Carolina, North Carolina, and Massachusetts.[45] Essentially, politically responsible bodies find the simple standard unreasonable when applied in a particular case—a case where political pressures, as well, favor noncompliance.

Even the Connecticut enforcement plan—an ingenious scheme that tailors the noncompliance penalty to the amount of money the violator saved through noncompliance—is unable to avoid major enforcement problems. Under the plan, the fine equals the cost of installing and operating the antipollution equipment, plus interest. These complex plant-by-plant calculations have been reduced to a set of fairly accurate, easily administrable rules. As a result, the violator loses much of his incentive to avoid compliance. Moreover, partial compliance will prove cheaper for him than noncompliance, since this cost is subtracted from the eventual fine.[46] Yet the plan changes only one factor that encourages noncompliance: it removes some of the firm's economic incentive to disobey an enforcement agency's order. It does not make the problems of drawing up such an individualized order any easier. Nor does it make it easier for the agency to determine whether the firm is in compliance. The firm also can still attack the order as unreasonable and seek to convince a judge to adopt a more lenient compliance schedule.

It is not surprising then, that enforcement of pollution standards has proved difficult to achieve in practice. The EPA has exempted whole valleys from its water pollution standards. Reports by the Council on Environmental Quality (CEQ) note that in 1974, 111 out of 198 Air Quality Control Regions had monitoring sites showing noncompliance (over half were out of compliance in 1977). About a third of the population, according to the CEQ, lived in noncompliance areas, and many major cities were predicted to be out of compliance with ambient standards.[47] Mills and White observe that even new automobiles in compliance with relaxed standards soon fall out of compliance as their control equipment ceases functioning.[48] The Senate study noted that of 33 enforcement actions brought by the EPA in the iron and steel industries, "the result was about half promises to comply and about half delaying actions." The result of the remaining 1,000 EPA enforcement actions brought in 1974 was unknown.

Anticompetitive effects. The lack of systematic study makes it difficult to assess the anticompetitive effects of environmental standard setting. However, there is reason to believe that they have had significant anticompetitive consequences. Requiring installation of antipollution equipment impedes entry into an industry by raising the cost of building a new plant. But that consequence is an acceptable part of the cost of clean air or water. More serious are those anticompetitive effects that appear to be avoidable.

First, the introduction of specific emission standards may freeze antipollution technology. Dewees argues that very different auto technologies—stratified charge or diesel engine technologies—would more cheaply and more effectively abate air pollution. Yet by enacting and gradually tightening specific emissions limitations, the auto companies have been encouraged to make incremental changes in their current engines, rather than to risk radically new techniques.[49] The threat of overly strict standards, followed by their relaxation, discouraged long-run research into these alternatives. Further, the technology chosen requires significant maintenance, guaranteed by a warranty, which manufacturers honor at their own repair shops. Insofar as car owners seek to repair this equipment, independent repair shops are placed at a disadvantage.[50]

Second, uniform general standards tend to place small firms at a disadvantage. A small widget company finds antipollution equipment more expensive to buy per widget of output than a large widget company, because the equipment itself benefits from economies of scale. This fact makes it difficult for small firms to stay in the industry and particularly difficult for new, small firms to enter. By increasing the required size for a new entrant, these standards impede new entry. Yet this anticompetitive effect may be unnecessary, because it may be possible, and even cheaper or more effective, to allow smaller firms to release more emissions while requiring larger firms to emit less. Of course, enforcement agencies take the plight of the small *existing* firm into account when they create particularized standards or enforcement schedules. However, they are less likely to consider the need to facilitate new entry into an industry. Moreover, insofar as agencies work out individualized compliance schedules with particular firms, they create different per-unit cleanup costs across firms in the same industry. Some firms will benefit, others will be hurt. The distribution of competitive advantages and disadvantages is random and bears no rational relation to the firms' comparative prices, product quality, or actual effects on the environment.

Finally, enforcement agencies may simply prohibit new entry into regions that do not meet ambient (air quality) standards—which includes a large portion of the country. In many areas, agencies have made new entry in noncompliance regions extremely difficult.[51] To the extent that this occurs, they protect existing firms from new competition. Indeed, they may even stimulate noncompliance if firms know that protection is the likely result.

Judicial review. Many of the problems of judicial review have been discussed as enforcement problems.[52] Given the vast number of complicated decisions that the agency must make—usually with inadequate information—numerous grounds exist for challenging individual orders as unreasonable. Potential plaintiffs can use this fact when bargaining with the agency. Moreover, judicial challenges are numerous. The Senate study described the state of legal challenges to one portion of the EPA's work—the setting of effluent guidelines—as follows: "As of late 1975, 250 lawsuits challenging effluent guidelines had been consolidated to 21 proceedings. Only one of these had been decided on its merits, and that one resulted in the Court instructing EPA to reconsider most of the standards in the Corn Wet Milling Subcategory. On March 10, 1976, . . . [the appeals court] remanded to EPA effluent limitations for 11 of the 22 subcategories in the inorganic chemical category, and most of the limitations in the plastics and synthetics and in the leather tanning and finishing categories.''[53] These represent only a small portion of the guidelines staff's work and of the potential number of cases seeking judicial review.

In sum, the standard-setting system appears to suffer significantly from the defects described earlier—defects that are typical of the standard-setting process. As a result of those defects, the actual environmental regulation system is made up of a combination of nonparticularized and particularized standards. The statutes themselves mandate sometimes the former and sometimes the latter. Enforcement agencies are under strong administrative pressures to promulgate nonparticularized standards. Nonetheless, the need to make the standards workable and enforceable leads the agencies frequently to tailor them to the needs of individual firms. In any event, neither the broad administratively simple standard nor the particularized standard works very well. The former tends to require the continuous granting of exceptions—if it is enforced at all. The latter is too difficult to develop and to enforce. The result is a system that appears coherent, but that is nonuniform, perhaps random, in its effects. And despite some improvement in the quality of the environment, most observers suggest that the system is significantly less effective than it might be.

Incentive Based Systems: Taxes and Marketable Rights

In Principle

Given the difficulties with standard setting, many economists have urged the use of taxes or other incentive-based systems to deal with spillover problems. ''Since the price of product A does not reflect an important social cost that it imposes (in this case pollution), why,'' the economist asks, ''not simply raise A's price through a tax to reflect the harm?'' ''But wait,'' the classical regulator replies, ''no one knows *how much* to raise the price. It is no easier to decide the amount of tax than to decide how much smoke the maker of product A should be allowed to emit. So why not just tackle the problem through standards?''

The regulator's response is correct, but it misses the point. The main theoretical advantages of incentive-based systems, such as fines, in dealing with complex spillover problems have nothing to do with their ability to measure harm. Rather, the true virtue of a tax, fee, or similar system lies in its power to provide incentives to direct behavior in a socially desirable direction, without freezing current technology and while preserving a degree of individual choice. Several factors suggest the suitability of such a system to the environmental spillover problem.

First, the solution to this type of problem is not an outright ban on production of polluting products and use of polluting processing. Rather, the regulator must seek (1) a better balance between two competing objectives—clean environment and industrial production—which are in part mutually exclusive but both of which are desired, and (2) increased encouragement to shift to, or to develop, production processes that allow more of both. In other words, the solution requires *balancing* among goods. It requires *incentives* (1) to consumers to shift away from using pollution-causing products whose prices do not reflect social costs, and (2) to producers to shift to or to develop pollution-free production processes which would reduce the *total* social cost of producing the good. Relative prices perform just such functions throughout the economy. In this case, putting a price tag upon pollution would allow buyers to balance the competing environmental and industrial goods. And it would provide incentives in the right direction. Whatever the problems of determining how much the price of polluting products or processes should be raised, the use of increased price allows those with a·special need for the polluting item to obtain it (thus permitting continuous individual balancing), and provides a continuing incentive for manufacturers to find less polluting production methods.[54]

Second, proper solutions are likely to vary enormously across thousands of products, processes, and geographical locations. A method that allows for this variation is essential. Raising price, and hence allowing the use of those productive processes for which consumers are still willing to pay, can deal to some extent with the need for flexibility (though it does not suggest how to decide the extent to which prices should rise).[55]

Third, the existence of a large number of point sources suggests the desirability, from an enforcement point of view, of a fairly simple rule. A tax system offers the prospect of a solution that is fairly simple in application, yet can produce variation and flexibility in results.[56]

In sum, the need is to find a system that can *balance (optimize) the extent to which resources are put to conflicting uses, provide proper incentives, produce flexible results, and deal with a large number of enterprises.* All of these point toward the use of a tax or similar incentive-based system. The most promising market-based alternative to a tax would be to allocate pollution under a system of marketable rights, as described earlier. Under this approach, the agency would set an absolute limit on the amount of emissions to be allowed in a given region. It then would issue salable rights, in denominations of say, 100 pounds of BOD, totaling the specified maximum amount of pollution. These rights could be freely exchanged in the marketplace. They would eventually end up in the hands of those[57] who find it most expensive to eliminate polluting emissions. Those who can eliminate emissions most cheaply would be the first to do so. Individual firms would ultimately produce differing amounts of pollution, yet the outcome would be economically efficient and would achieve the socially desired result. In this sense, the system resembles a tax or fine.[58]

The EPA is already experimenting with a similar system: the "bubble." Instead of a rule limiting the amount of emissions from each of a factory's smokestacks, the EPA places an imaginary bubble over the factory in the form of a rule stating the *total* amount of pollution the factory can emit, leaving it to the owner to decide how much pollutant each stack will emit. The owner will curtail emissions more from those stacks where curtailment is cheaper, and less from those where curtailment is more expensive; thus, the same level of curtailment is brought about more efficiently. In essence, a system of marketable rights allows the EPA to place a bubble over an entire city or region. The tradeable rights are a means to assure that, within the bubble, those who emit the allowed pollutant are just those for whom curtailment would be most expensive.

While both taxes and marketable rights promote efficiency (by encouraging those for whom it is cheapest to curtail pollution to do so first), these systems may produce quite different results in a world of uncertainty. An administrator operating a tax system, and firms operating within it, know fairly well what ceiling the system has placed on their costs. They will have to pay the tax multiplied by their actual emissions. Insofar as they curtail emissions, they will pay less. Yet without knowing the individual cost schedules, technology, and demand facing every firm, no one can be certain in advance to what extent firms will curtail emissions or choose to pay the tax. The cost ceiling is known; the future pollution level is not.

An administrator of a marketable rights system faces a converse problem. Since the number of rights is within his control, he knows fairly well the maximum emissions that will be produced. He cannot know, however (without detailed cost information about each firm), how much firms will have to pay to achieve that emissions level. He cannot know in advance the price that the marketable right will fetch at auction. The pollution level is known; the future cost of achieving it is not.

For this reason, advocates of market-based systems claim that the choice between taxes and marketable rights depends upon one's estimates about the way in which emissions and abatement costs are related to the damage caused by pollution.[59] If one believes that pollution harm increases gradually as emissions increase but that abatement costs take a radical jump upward at a certain abatement level, one might favor a tax, since a small mistake in tax level would not lead to an enormous increase in pollution or impose enormous unknown costs. A small mistake in the number of authorized marketable rights, however, might cause substantial cost increases by passing the "high abatement cost" threshold with little compensating benefit in the form of reduced pollution. On the other hand, if one believes that pollution's harm increases suddenly and dramatically as a threshold level is passed but that abatement costs rise gradually, one might favor marketable rights. It would be important to guarantee that the threshold pollution level not be reached, while a mistaken estimate of the cost of reducing pollution to that level would not be enormously important.

Thus, in principle, the preference for a particular system should vary depending upon the estimated cleanup costs. The Senate committee studying regulatory reform tended to favor a tax.[60] Yet in practice, technical features may be less important than political factors, such as whether it is more important to protect consumers against unknown pollution levels or industry against unknown cost levels.

Although the systems vary in their ability to achieve desirable results, they generate similar enforcement problems. Compared to standards, they have one major advantage and one major disadvantage. The major advantage of both is that the regulated firms' incentive to fight the regulators' action is diminished in two respects. The uniform rule implicit in both these systems means that the firm knows what it is supposed to do in advance. It cannot pretend that action must await individual negotiation with an administrator. Moreover, if a firm challenges the regulator's actions, a victory is likely to mean only a diminished tax or a smaller payment. It is not likely to excuse the firm totally from previous noncompliance. Thus, legal victory for the polluter is less likely to halt antipollution enforcement, and much of the advantage that the polluter derives from delay is reduced.

As will be discussed below, a major enforcement disadvantage lies in the increased difficulty of monitoring. The use of a marketable rights or tax system allows some firms to continue to use older technology, so that inspectors, noting that a firm has not installed a scrubber (a device for filtering pollutants), cannot be certain whether or not the firm has violated the law. A standard that required the firm to install scrubbers might be easier to check for noncompliance.

A system of marketable rights raises one additional enforcement problem: the administrator must prevent a firm or group of firms from obtaining control of marketable rights in order to use them for anticompetitive purposes. By monopolizing the supply, they could prevent new firms from entering the industry.[61] In principle, this problem is no different from any other instance in which a firm or group of firms monopolizes a scarce resource.[62] If they do so without a legitimate business objective, they may be accused of violating Section 2 of the Sherman Act. Alcoa Aluminum, for example, was accused of having bought up more bauxite than it needed in order to keep new firms out of the market.[63] An antitrust action may be required to force monopolizing firms to sell their rights to a new competitor on reasonable terms, just as one was required to force a group of railroads that owned a bridge into St. Louis to permit their competitors to use the bridge as well.[64] As a practical matter, it may be difficult for either antitrust officials or environmental administrators to know whether high bids for marketable rights reflect concern for the environment, a present industrial need, the need for future expansion, a desire to preserve the possibility for such expansion, or an effort to protect an existing market from new competitors.

In terms of flexibility, incentive-based systems share two important features. Both provide a continuous incentive to develop and to adopt technology and production methods that yield less pollution. In both instances, such methods save the firm money. Moreover, both systems adapt automatically to changes in the relative costs of pollution-related production factors. If, for example, low-sulfur coal becomes cheaper, the individual firm saves money by using more of it. Under standard-setting systems, it does not.

On the other hand, a system of marketable rights might be more difficult to modify than a system of taxes. Once the rights are issued, administrative intervention to increase or diminish the number available will have profound effects on the value of rights already held.[65] Such manipulation of a market in property rights is more likely to be perceived as fundamentally unfair than a change in the level of taxes. A tax system could allow administrators to change tax levels, adjusting them to reduce pollution or to reduce costs. Furthermore, administrators could create complex taxes that allow for the fact that the damaging effects of emissions vary with such factors as the time of day, season of the year, and terrain.[66] Yet too much flexibility in a tax system is likely to cause trouble. Firms will complain of inability to plan. Special interests will plead for special tax breaks. Congressional committees will be reluctant to delegate to administrators the power to set tax levels.[67] If both systems, as developed, prove inflexible, marketable rights will impede economic growth, by making new entry into a region possible only by forgoing some existing economic activity. A tax system allows such growth, because increases in demand will make firms more willing to pay the tax. To the extent this occurs, the system will prove less effective in stopping pollution. On the other hand, a system of rights, set pollutant by pollutant, may inhibit, say, auto manufacturers from adopting technology that reduces SO_2 greatly, but produces a small increase in NOx. A tax system, by specifying the additional NOx cost, may make it easier for those manufacturers to do so.[68]

In principle, both systems enjoy theoretical advantages compared with standard setting. They are likely to prove more efficient and effective in stopping pollution. They may prove as easy to enhance. They may be more flexible. Their effects in each of these areas differ somewhat. However, before concluding that the present system should be abandoned in their favor, these pros and cons should be explored with somewhat greater specificity.[69]

A More Practical Comparison

Incentive-based systems themselves face the typical and serious problems described in Part I. Before concluding that such systems are likely to be superior to standard setting, their defects should be examined and compared with those of standard setting. Only then can one understand both the basic strength of the market-based systems and the detailed work and compromise that movement in that direction would require. Before deciding to adopt any such system, one must consider five objections.

Is it possible to develop an efficient system of incentives? To understand the virtues of fines, taxes, or marketable rights, one must understand what they will *not* do. First, it is difficult, if not impossible, to measure the amount of harm that pollution causes. Neither an administrator nor a legislator is likely to set a tax that even roughly approximates the dollar cost of additional units of pollution. Nor are marketable rights likely to be set at the "optimal" level, where marginal harm from pollution equals the marginal cost of abatement. Of course, standards are no better than fees or taxes in this regard.

Second, incentive-based systems are not likely to deal effectively with the complex relations between emission levels and pollution. The polluting effect of a given emission depends upon weather, season, air and water flow, and a host of other factors. A tax on emissions, for example (or marketable rights to emit), does not consider these factors and could make matters worse. (A 15-cent-per-pound BOD tax may lead a firm at a river's mouth to pay 14 cents for abatement. A different firm at the river's source, emitting the same amount of pollutants, may pay the tax rather than adopt a 16 cent abatement alternative. Yet the pound of discharge at the river's mouth may be a far less serious problem than at its source.) In principle, one could adopt complex taxes or rights systems that would take these factors into account. Yet in practice, non-uniformity, particularizing, and continuous change would make the schemes too complex. It would lead to charges of favoritism or corruption. It would make it difficult for firms to plan. Further, one suspects that Congress or the public may be more willing to tolerate individualized standard setting than in-dividualized tax assessment. A proposal for a charge on SO_2 emissions, for example, was defeated in Congress in part because the copper smelting industry argued that it would no longer be able to compete with foreign producers.[70] In effect, it wanted an exception. Of course, precisely the same issue arose under a standard system, but presumably the industry believed that it would be easier to obtain an exception from a standard than an exception in a tax rate. This "political" fact may make taxes in practice less flexible than standards.

In these respects, then, incentive systems seem no better than standard set-ting. On the other hand, neither do they seem worse than the actual standard-setting system in practice. Rather, these facts suggest the complexity of pollu-tion problems and why some combination of standards, subsidies (for, say, effluent treatment), and incentives is likely to be necessary.

In any event, advocates of incentive systems do not rest their claims of superiority on an ability to deal with the problems just mentioned. Rather, they claim that taxes or marketable rights are not significantly worse than standards in this regard and that they are likely to be significantly more effective and efficient in several other respects. They provide a continuous incentive for firms to decrease effluents or emissions and to adopt ever more effective tech-nology. They lead firms to curtail discharges in rank order, with the firms able to curtail most cheaply doing so first. They discourage consumption of products made by pollution-causing processes. Finally, they provide increased incentive for firms to comply.

In each of these respects, advocates of incentives provide empirical estimates suggesting that the potential benefits are significant. Schultze, for example, points out that technological change increases productivity to the point where labor costs are halved every twenty-five years.[71] With an effluent fee, firms see pollution reduction—below the level set by any standard—as a way to save money. Thus, they will look for technological change aimed at reducing pollution costs. Similarly, auto emissions standards, it is claimed, encouraged the auto manufacturer to adopt an unnecessarily expensive catalytic converter technology, in part because only that technology was likely to reduce NOx emissions to desired levels. A tax, on the other hand, would have allowed the firms to postpone compliance—though at a high financial cost in tax payments—and then to develop diesel and other technologies, which would not have met standards in the short run (and would initially have emitted too much NOx) but which, in the longer run, would have meant less pollution at far lower costs. Indeed, according to some economic estimates, diesel or stratified engines would have saved billions of dollars.[72]

As previously mentioned, it is possible to save enormous amounts of money through the simple expedient of having those firms for whom abatement is cheapest do most of the cleanup. The National Academy of Sciences predicted that abandoning uniform effluent standards and concentrating abatement where it is least costly would "save 40% of the capital costs required to meet the 1977 standards and 30 to 35% of the total capital costs required to meet the 1983 standards."[73] Schultze has reported the results of numerous studies suggesting similar cost savings—indeed, one study suggested that cost-minimizing programs might achieve the same environmental objectives at only 10 percent of the costs of uniform cutback.[74] The Senate study reached roughly similar conclusions.[75]

Of course, these studies may overstate the benefits, since they compare an ideal least-cost cleanup method with a standard that *uniformly* rolls back effluent or emissions levels. In fact, any actual tax or rights system will not be ideal. As previously noted, the actual standard setting system is highly particularized, despite the fact that the rules often *appear* to require uniform rollbacks.[76] Nonetheless, the actual standard-setting system does not impose the strictest rules on those who can abate the most cheaply. Rather, for enforcement reasons, administrators tend to focus on larger firms. Depending on the industry, these may or may not be those whose abatement is cheapest. The results of the individual negotiating process, from a cost point of view, may be random. Thus, it is not surprising that the detailed study of actual practice in the Delaware Basin found hundreds of millions of dollars spent to achieve negligible pollution control benefits.[77]

Finally, the price-raising effect of both taxes and marketable rights will encourage consumers to switch to products that pollute less. The production of bleached household paper products produces ten times the amount of pollution as unbleached paper. A very small price increase might induce consumers to switch from the former to the latter. This would prove far more effective than rules requiring the introduction of expensive abatement technology in the paper industry.[78]

Despite the difficulties of determining the "right" level for charges, even the most crudely designed incentive systems might be more effective than a system that relies totally on standards. European experience suggests that this is so. In the Ruhr Valley, for example, the "damage measurement" problem that faces incentive systems is divided into two parts—how the relative damages of different pollutants are to be measured, and how the baseline effluent charges are to be set. The relative damages caused by different pollutants are fairly easy to measure. A toxicity index is established by measuring the relative effect on test fish, and charges are scaled accordingly. Thus, the charge per pound of mercury is thousands of times higher than the charge per pound of BOD. Ad hoc adjustments are made for pollutants that do not kill but, say, have a bad taste.[79]

Determining baseline damages—that is, setting the baseline effluent charge—is more difficult. One might estimate aggregate damage for a region by looking at factors such as the total value of crops lost, medical costs, and productivity lost, with arbitrary amounts set for such items as lives lost and inability to swim in polluted water. This estimate could be divided by existing units of effluent to determine a baseline charge. This charge would be highly arbitrary, since the estimate would be extraordinarily crude, and even at its most conservative it may be higher than any politically acceptable amount. (Fees in Germany and the very low fees used in France since 1964 may well reflect what is politically acceptable.) Nonetheless, the considerations advanced so far—and French experience—suggest that even politically acceptable lower-than-reasonable damage estimates, when translated into a charge, may prove more effective at stopping pollution than standards that on paper appear to be far tougher. Indeed, an official of the Organization for European Cooperation and Development (OECD) estimated that where these low charges have been used, pollution has been cut in half—an estimate that compares favorably with results in the United States.[80]

Detailed charge or fee systems have been put into effect in several European countries, and others have been designed by economists for possible implementation in the United States.[81] Moreover, the EPA's present tendency to allow new firms to enter an area by cleaning up pollution caused by existing firms contains the germ of a system of marketable rights.[82] In effect, the new firm buys rights to pollute from existing firms. At present, however, the restrictions on purchase are too severe to create an open market in pollution rights. Such a market appears practical and could emerge out of the present system.[83]

Are incentive-based systems more difficult to enforce than present standards? It is sometimes argued that tax or other incentive-based systems would be difficult to enforce. Those who make this argument tend to focus on one aspect of the enforcement problem—determining whether a firm is in compliance. They suggest that an inspector might determine compliance with a regulation by simply noting whether a firm has installed specified abatement equipment, whereas to determine compliance with a tax requirement he would have to measure the *amount* of emission—a far more difficult task.[84]

In fact, determining compliance with standards is a more difficult task than this argument suggests. Abatement depends not simply upon installing the proper equipment, but also upon operating it properly. An electrostatic precipitator on a coal-fired plant, for example, without adequate maintenance or with the wrong sort of fuel, might function at 70–80 percent of its capacity.[85] Since operating costs of major abatement equipment range from 25–60 percent of annual capital cost,[86] firms have financial incentives to limit their use of the equipment once installed. Inspection staffs are typically too small to permit more than a handful of visits each year, even to likely violators. Massachusetts inspectors simply look for dark plumes of smoke. In other states, inspectors rarely visit any but the most likely violators. To determine whether a firm is in violation, these inspectors must determine whether the emissions level is *too high*—not simply whether the plant has proper equipment installed.

The fact that monitoring equipment is expensive—perhaps costing $10,000–52,000 for a large air pollution source and $5,000–15,000 for a major water pollution source[87]—does not automatically demonstrate the superiority of a standard system. In *either* system inspectors must use rough sampling methods to determine the extent of compliance. Indeed, the standard-enforcement method generally cited as most effective—the Connecticut plan—gears the amount of the penalty to the *degree* of noncompliance by the firm.

In Germany, where fees are used, enforcement seems reasonably effective although it is based upon reports by dischargers themselves followed up by random checks.[88] Nor does enforcement seem to be a major problem in France, though only the very largest (2–3 percent) of all polluters are monitored continuously. The others are simply assessed a flat fee based on plant design and annual output. These two factors allow for a reasonably accurate and simple calculation of the amount of effluent. If a plant changes its production processes, installs control equipment, or changes output, it can apply for an adjustment.

The French system also provides that if a firm is found in violation, it must pay a penalty as well as the costs of the investigation. Thus, violators run a considerable risk if they are caught, and the harder they are to catch, the more they will pay. Similarly, the government is not discouraged from pursuing the short-term, large-scale violator (say, a one-time mercury dumper). In fact, in France administrative costs may have amounted to no more than an estimated 5 percent of the revenues earned through effluent charges.[89]

Even if it is somewhat easier to check compliance under a standards system, there are other, equally important aspects of the compliance problem, in which incentive schemes enjoy the advantage. First, as previously mentioned, the fact that individual firms know precisely what they are to do—reduce effluents or emissions, pay a tax, or buy marketable rights—makes it more likely that they will comply voluntarily. They will not have available the excuse that they must await the negotiation of a compliance schedule with an administrator. Second, the fact that violation, when proved, is likely to result only in an additional money payment—related to the tax or marketable right cost avoided—makes a decision to contest the agency in court more costly to the violator. He cannot escape *all* costs by winning. At the same time, the courts are less likely to set aside the regulator's actions as "unreasonable" or "requiring the impossible." The choice for the court does not become one of "allow pollution" or "force the firm to close down."[90] This latter advantage is similar to that of the Connecticut enforcement plan.

The most serious enforcement objection to incentive-based systems is not that they will prove ineffective in practice but that they will prove *too* effective. Certain comments by EPA officials suggest that the following type of argument may be at the back of their minds: "The current system of selective enforcement works because administrators leave smaller firms free to do what they want, to violate standards if necessary, while they concentrate on larger firms, extracting through negotiation as strong a set of abatement promises as possible. A tax system (or marketable rights) would treat all firms equally in proportion to emissions. Smaller firms would be affected (unless the tax is too small to be effective). They will insist upon special treatment or they may go out of business. In either case, the enforcement system will be discredited."[91]

The difficulty with this argument rests in part upon the morality of its hidden premise—that the present system works because it treats similar firms differently, distributing cost advantages and disadvantages among firms within an industry on a political basis, and randomly enforcing the law. The argument also lacks conviction because certain of its premises are unproven. That such enforcement methods are needed is unclear. The extent to which a charge system would become riddled with exceptions is unknown. The Internal Revenue Code could be cited to support either side in the debate. Finally, European experience suggests that, as a practical matter, charges have made the system more, not less, effective.[92]

Are incentive systems politically acceptable? When taxes and marketable rights have been debated in political forums, their opponents have raised three objections designed to suggest that they are unacceptable to the general public. First, some environmentalists initially claimed that a tax provided a "license to pollute."[93] This argument reflected the view that strict rules requiring "zero discharge" would force firms to develop abatement technology. The Clean Air Act embodied this philosophy in its technology-forcing auto emissions standards. The argument is less forceful now, however, since many environmentalists now believe that standards that are too strict are ineffective, for they will not be enforced. The Clean Air Act has been amended and numerous exceptions are provided for firms unable to meet strict standards and deadlines. Thus, there may be greater willingness now than there was ten years ago to accept taxes for their deterrent and incentive effects, recognizing that the choice they

offer the firm—to pay rather than to abate—is helpful from an environmenta:
as well as an industrial point of view.[94]

Second, a more topical claim is that a tax requires the firms to pay twice.
They must pay for their abatement technology and also pay for the emissions
that they are unable to abate. A system of marketable rights has the same
effect, for a firm must pay to abate some emissions and then purchase rights to
discharge those emissions that it has not abated. Industry spokesmen have argued that this system is unfair and that it will raise prices unnecessarily.[95]
Indeed, industry argued that a 20-cent-per-pound sulfur tax would raise prices
by $1.7 billion over and above the cost of abatement technology. Copper smelt-
ers claimed that in addition to the $500 million they would have to invest in
abatement equipment, a 20-cent tax would mean that they would have to pay
$60 million as the tax on emissions that could not be abated.[96] There was no
need, they claimed, to raise prices by this additional amount.

One might reply by noting that there is no double payment, for neither
producers nor consumers pay twice. The tax payment reflects the loss that pollution imposes upon others. Insofar as it discourages use of the product, it is
desirable. This theoretical argument may not carry the day, however, with
those who notice rising prices. Nor are they likely to be satisfied by the claim
that the tax's revenues could be returned to the consumer or taxpayer. The
latter is likely to be skeptical that he will ever see them again. Rather, the
strongest reply is to note the fallacy in the copper smelter's claim: it implicitly
compares "perfect" regulation—a set of standards that requires the "right"
firms to use the "right" equipment—with a system of taxes. Indeed, if a regulator could produce the optimal set of standards, a tax would be unnecessary.
If, however, one compares the actual standard-setting process with an incentive
system, because of increased efficiency that market-based systems encourage,
total costs in terms of resources expended may well fall, not rise. Indeed, the
savings may be sufficiently great so that the total spent by industry, for both
abatement equipment and the tax, is less than before.

Third, taxes and marketable rights make the costs of both pollution and its
abatement more dramatically visible. This very visibility may diminish support
for antipollution efforts. In part, the reaction against a visible tax system may
be rational. A consumer may accept the fact that a tax or marketable rights
system will stop waste by using fewer resources to achieve the same abatement,
but he might also believe that total costs to him—efficient abatement costs plus
tax costs—are greater than he paid before.[97] The fact that the tax revenue can
be spent on good causes instead of unnecessary abatement equipment may be
a matter of indifference to him. Moreover, higher prices trigger cost-of-living
adjustment clauses in wage contracts and thus feed inflation.

More likely, however, the reaction against visible costs is largely emotional.
Opinion polls suggest that the public strongly supports pollution control but
even more strongly believes that industry should pay the cost of abatement.
The fact that abatement costs are mostly passed on in the form of higher prices

is only gradually becoming apparent. To the extent that there is an emotional reaction against the visible (as opposed to the invisible) price, legislators will hesitate to enact incentive-based systems.

The best way to deal with this problem may be, as in France, to start with a tax set at a very low level that supplements the existing system. French experience suggests that even small taxes are effective in comparison to standard setting. Once introduced, a tax that worked might gradually be raised. Similarly, marketable rights can be—and are being—introduced as adjuncts to the present system. Such rights are designed to ease entry by new firms into a region that does not meet ambient pollution standards.

How should the tax proceeds be disposed of? One of the most difficult practical problems of an incentive system is determining how to dispose of the funds collected. They can be earmarked for some general good purpose, they can be rebated to those who pay them, or they can be added to the general revenue of the government. In principle, the tax revenues should be given to those who suffer from the pollution still produced. Thus, those who pay higher prices to use pollution-causing products would compensate those who suffer from the pollution.[98] In practice, however, such compensation schemes are difficult to work out.

Any effort to earmark funds will force legislators to deal with advocates of many different special programs. Rebates face the difficulty of developing an administrative rebate mechanism. If the rebate is geared directly to use of the polluting product, such as automobiles or bleached household paper, it undercuts a major tax objective by encouraging that product's consumption. The safest course of action may be to send the revenues to the federal Treasury, to be added to general funds.[99] But then the legislator has exposed himself to the charge of having voted for a general tax increase, which is not likely to make him popular with his constituents. These problems can, of course, be worked out, but they help explain the political unpopularity of tax proposals.

Marketable rights do not present a revenue disposal problem, but they produce a converse problem when rights are initially given out. Should existing firms be given an initial allocation? Not to do so will raise their costs undoubtedly and may bankrupt many existing firms.[100] To give rights to existing firms rewards pollution and presents complicated allocational questions, but it does not force any existing firm into bankruptcy.[101] The EPA's administration has apparently chosen this latter alternative.

Which legislative and administrative bodies will create and administer the system? To enact legislation that changes a standard-setting regulatory system to a system that relies heavily upon taxes or fees does not raise serious legal problems. However, it would likely mean a change in the congressional committees directly involved in creating and overseeing the program, as well as a possible change in the agency that administers it. Any legislation that creates a tax falls within the jurisdiction of the Senate Finance Committee and the House Ways and Means Committee. Moreover, bills that raise revenue must originate in the House of Representatives.[102]

These requirements cannot be avoided by calling the tax a "fine" or a "civil penalty," for fines and penalties have very different effects than do taxes. A firm is free to pay a tax. It is less likely to wish to pay a fine, for a fine is a sanction designed to deter conduct. Thus, unlike an excise tax, it may not be deductible from the firm's income tax.[103] When the firm engages in the prohibited conduct, its directors may be subject to shareholder suits seeking damages for misconduct.[104] Possibly, the firm could lose government licenses conditioned on good conduct. Thus, a fine may be incapable of achieving the tax's efficiency objective.

The tax might, of course, be called a "fee" charged a polluter for "use" of the pure air or water. This change of name, however, is unlikely to avoid tax committee jurisdiction. In the past, these committees have asserted jurisdictional claims over legislation containing "charges" on the theory that any program that generates significant revenues for the government falls within their purview—though they recognize that the relevant substantive committees of Congress also have concurrent jurisdiction.

Tax committee jurisdiction creates several related problems. The tax committees and their staffs have no particular environmental expertise. They are reluctant to delegate to administrative bodies the power to set rates. And they are used to negotiating special exceptions for groups with claims to special treatment. This could lead to tax rates that do not directly respond to environmental needs. There might be special exceptions that are more closely related to bargaining over provisions in other revenue bills than to the environment. These exceptions, once enacted, could become permanent features of the law. Of course, there is something to be said, for example, for a permanent, fairly low, uniform sulfur tax. Its certainty and inflexibility may help firms plan. Further, certain firms such as copper smelters may have a legitimate claim for an initial exception. Yet to grant them *permanent* tax relief is probably undesirable. If extensive, the exceptions could distort the tax's objective, particularly if they are developed in a committee lacking environmental expertise. Moreover, the tax committees are unlikely to have the time to devote a great deal of effort to such a new and highly complex problem, while the committees substantively charged with environmental responsibility will be reluctant to cede any power and responsibility to other committees.

A related problem may exist at the administrative level. Taxes are traditionally administered by the Internal Revenue Service. The administration of any excise tax is highly complex. It requires establishing rules and regulations, defining precisely who is liable and for what; specifying record-keeping requirements; and setting up exemption procedures, appeals procedures, penalties and the like.[105] The IRS has had experience with just this type of administration, whereas other agencies have not. And the IRS has a reputation for effective enforcement.

To delegate this responsibility to the IRS, however, is to place it in the hands of persons who have no special interest in the environment or training in environmental matters. The IRS would find it particularly difficult to determine individual charges and compliance. The "gas guzzler" tax, however, provides some precedent for having the EPA provide the IRS with sufficient information to determine liability for the tax, while the IRS assesses and collects it.[106] In any event, the IRS, although reluctant to take on a major added responsibility, is likely to administer the tax fairly, but with more of an eye toward increasing governmental revenues than protecting the environment.

The alternative—to grant the EPA full responsibility for assessment and collection of the tax—may be legally possible, particularly if the tax is called an "environmental use charge." But it would require that the EPA develop the same administrative definitional, assessment, collection, record-keeping, and review procedures that the IRS has already developed after years of experience.

These considerations mitigate in favor of a marketable rights approach, though this system too will involve difficult administrative issues. Or they suggest a tax approach that would begin with a simple uniform tax set at a low level, to obviate the need for exceptions as a supplement to the present system; an increased tax rate would be easier to adopt after such an initial experience. They do not pose insuperable objections to the incentive approach. Once one realizes the difficulties that inhibit a system that relies solely upon standards, these problems seem minor by comparison.

Conclusion

A major change from total reliance upon classical standard setting to increased reliance upon incentive mechanisms is *probably* desirable when dealing with a complex spillover problem such as pollution. Given the nature of the standard-setting process, the complex spillover problem, and the incentive-based alternatives, environmental regulation is a candidate for change. To know whether significant improvement is in fact possible requires further exploration. How effective is existing regulation, for example? How clean has the air and water become since 1970? How well do the European incentive systems actually work? How can the practical difficulties with the details of incentive systems be overcome? Enough has been said, however, to suggest that the present system is far from satisfactory, and that incentive-based reform ought to be possible.

15

Problems of a Possible Match: Natural Monopoly and Telecommunications

The previous four chapters have developed a few simple rules for identifying a likely mismatch of regulatory problem and the weapon used to attack it. More rules, in turn, may help identify easy targets for regulatory reform—other areas where major change of emphasis on a classical regulatory tool will likely prove beneficial. This chapter provides something of a counterbalance, for it suggests that "deregulation" or even "less restrictive regulation" is not the answer to every problem, even when classical rate and entry regulation is at issue. Rather, where natural monopoly is at issue, regulation remains appropriate. And in such cases line-drawing questions of how far regulation should extend will exist. Part I provides no obvious key to how they should be answered. Rather, the appropriateness of classical regulation in one area is highly relevant to the appropriateness of regulation in related areas. It affects the nature of the argument. Part I can, at best, help provide a framework for analysis.

The extent to which new competition should be allowed in longline telecommunications—a matter currently being considered by Congress and by the Federal Communications Commission—illustrates these points. Once one admits the legitimacy of classical regulations in one major area (here local telephone service), one can no longer simply refer to fairly straightforward indicia such as market structure to determine the nature or amount of regulation in related areas—for example, long-distance service.

Before analyzing the problem, one must begin by accepting the match of cost-of-service ratemaking and natural monopoly. While not strictly provable, it is at least plausible to believe that cost-of-service ratemaking is reasonably well suited to the natural monopoly problem. Classical cost-of-service ratemaking is fairly capable of dealing with a single large firm with costs and demands that stay fairly constant. Its problems there, while serious, are less imposing than when the system is applied to markets with many firms with fluctuating costs and demand. In the former case, the system can hold prices somewhere near cost, offer some incentive for efficiency, and provide some guarantee of fair dealing for the customer.

More important, there is no obvious alternative regime that offers promise of significant improvement. Unregulated markets could allow the single natural monopolist to raise prices well above costs. An examination of electricity prices during the 1960s led some economists to question this statement on empirical grounds—to wonder whether classical regulation had in fact held regulated prices down near costs.[1] But experience with natural gas in the 1960s, and with electricity in the 1970s, indicates that classical regulation can indeed keep prices down—though, as we have seen, this effect is not always desirable.[2] In any case, the pressing need for telephone service and electricity allows a reasonable fear that without regulation, or the threat of it,[3] unregulated prices would significantly exceed regulated prices.

One must note, however, that some economists have proposed as an alternative to regulation in this area that a natural monopoly be made *competitive* by allowing firms to bid for a franchise and allowing the winner to serve the franchised area. The franchise would be awarded to the firm promising to charge customers the lowest prices or offer the best service.[4] The difficulties with this system lie not in theory but in practice. During the late nineteenth century municipal authorities, awarding such franchises to electricity and telephone companies, found it virtually impossible to hold the companies' rates down to those promised in the franchise contract, because changing costs and economic conditions always made arguments for contract rate revision plausible. And, in any event, the contract rate sometimes turned out to be far too high. The result was fluctuating prices, high profits, endless arguments about the service terms of the contract, and claims of local corruption.[5]

Others have suggested combining deregulation with a *tax* on excess profits. This system would require a careful definition of "excess." The tax authorities would find themselves plagued with "reasonable rate of return" problems. Moreover, the tax would not encourage the firm to expand its output. On the contrary, any tax of less than 100 percent on the excess could lead a firm to increase its prices above and restrict its output below a competitive level. *Nationalization* has severe drawbacks, as we have seen, and, in any event, while accepted in Europe, it is politically unpopular here. Thus, one must be pessimistic about the likelihood that an alternative regime can effectively supplant classical regulation in this area.

This is not to say that all natural monopolies must be regulated. Competitive pressures from other industries may help keep the prices of a natural monopolist near its costs. The oil industry, for example, may provide some competition for the monopolist gas distributor. Indeed, before regulating one should estimate the extent of the monopolist's power. How large is the industry? How far above cost can the monopolist raise price? The answers depend upon the ease with which new producers may provide substitutes (or enter) as the monopolist raises price above cost and the ease with which consumers may turn to substitute goods. Moreover, because regulation, once in place, is hard to dismantle, one would like to know whether future technological change is likely to transform an industry that is now a natural monopoly, making it structurally suited to competition.[6] The logic of the inquiry is clear and simple, but the making of empirical estimates is difficult. In any event, if, after such an inquiry, one believes that a producer is a natural monopolist and possesses *considerable* power to raise price above cost, then it is reasonable to accept cost-of-service ratemaking as the regime most likely to deal with the problem.

We will not examine here these empirical questions related to natural monopoly. Rather, we will turn to an analytically difficult but related question: whether, once a firm is regulated as a natural monopolist, it should also be regulated when it produces other goods and services jointly with the monopoly product. More specifically, should the regulator allow new firms to enter and to compete with the monopolist in the production of these other, related goods or services which may not be naturally monopolizable?

The issue is an important one because, in the recent enthusiasm for deregulation, many have advocated an end to regulation of prices and entry across the board—or at least unless it can be proved that the market in question is a significant natural monopoly. Thus, they would allow entry into any related market that is not itself characterizable as a natural monopoly. Moreover, many regulated firms are complex entities selling many different services in many different markets. Some of these related markets may be natural monopolies, others may be capable of supporting competition, and still others may be the subject of argument about whether competition is or is not possible.

The issue is timely, for the Federal Communications Commission, the Department of Justice, and Congress have all been considering the extent to which the communications services provided by the American Telephone and Telegraph Company (AT&T) ought to be regulated.

An analysis of the issue, along the lines set out in Part I, suggests that it is more difficult to resolve than some of the enthusiasts for deregulation will admit. Regulation of a product that shares significant production costs with a naturally monopolized product is *not* an obvious mismatch. The existence of joint costs, natural monopoly, and regulation makes it impossible to answer the competition/regulation question by simply analyzing market structure. An analysis of the FCC's efforts to introduce competition into longline telecommunications markets[7] can show why it is difficult to decide whether to allow competitors to enter such a market and on what terms.

The longline issue is but one of several government efforts to make the telephone industry more competitive.[8] In 1968 the FCC held that AT&T must permit subscribers to buy terminal equipment from competitors of AT&T's manufacturing subsidiary, Western Electric, and to attach the equipment to AT&T's lines.[9] The Department of Justice has brought an antitrust suit aimed at breaking Western Electric apart from AT&T and splitting it into several pieces in order to obtain more competition in the manufacturing of telephone equipment. Members of Congress have sponsored legislation that favors competition and would replace the original communications act.[10] Unlike the manufacturing and sale of telephones and telephone equipment, however, longline involves a service that is not readily separable from the rest of AT&T's business. Longline telephone service and local telephone service are at the heart of that business and share many costs. Moreover, local telephone service is thought to be a natural monopoly. The analysis of whether regulation or competition is appropriate in this area (related to natural monopoly through joint costs) will show that there is no fundamental mismatch; this means that neither regulation nor deregulation offers an obvious solution to the problem.

The basic issue before the FCC and Congress is whether to allow new firms to compete with AT&T in the business of providing longline telecommunications service. This issue is difficult to decide for three related reasons. First, there is uncertainty as to whether longline service is or is not a natural monopoly, and whether, if it is, it will continue to be. Second, longline and local service share many costs. Third, local service is a regulated natural monopoly. The first of these facts means that a decision to *exclude* competitors will prove harmful, if longline markets can in fact efficiently support several competitors. The second of these facts means that a decision to allow new entry may lead AT&T to cut its prices so low that the new firms are driven out of business. And the third fact means that the regulator is unlikely to know whether AT&T is behaving predatorily or honestly in doing so. Should the regulatory agency allow new firms into the market and forbid AT&T to cut its prices? Then it may be protecting inefficient firms. Should it allow new firms into the market and permit AT&T to cut its prices? Then it may be allowing predatory behavior that drives efficient firms from the market. Should it prevent new firms from entering the market? Then it may be unnecessarily protecting AT&T from legitimate competition.

The Characteristics of the Longline Problem

To understand the argument about competition in longline service, one must understand the industry and the extent to which it has the characteristics of a natural monopoly. One must also understand the major difficulty the industry presents to the cost-of-service ratemaker: this difficulty lies *not* in determining the revenue requirement, but in designing a rate structure that will yield that requirement. The presence of joint costs has made the latter task nearly impossible. Hence, not surprisingly, the regulators looked to competition as offering a way out of their regulatory dilemma.

To understand the rate structure problem it is well to review the bridge/ferry boat problem discussed in Chapter 2. The bridge was a natural monopoly. It cost $25 million to build, but the incremental cost of crossing it—the wear and tear—amounted to far less. What toll should the bridge authority charge? We found that it is wasteful to charge bridge users more than the incremental costs that their use of the bridge imposes. Otherwise some will not use the bridge and will stay home, which is a pity in that the economy could provide what they want (bridge crossing) through the use of additional resources that cost *less* than they are willing to pay. Some who wish to use the bridge may spend their money on other items instead—an even greater pity in that those items may cost the economy *more* (in terms of additional resources) to produce than the extra bridge crossings, but they may satisfy the frustrated bridge user less. To deal with these problems, some economists have suggested that bridge tolls reflect a division of fixed costs that increases charges most for those who are likely to mind the least. Those whom a higher price (higher than incremental cost) would most discourage from bridge use would be charged the lowest prices. This form of price discrimination—known as Ramsey pricing—is aimed at keeping the pattern of bridge use as close as possible to what it would be in the absence of a need to recover nonrepeatable fixed costs from bridge users. Of course, it is difficult to determine in practice just how different classes of potential users will react to changes in tolls, and as long as they have few alternative ways to cross the river, there may be a wide range within which different divisions among different classes (or even uniform tolls) make little difference.

But what happens if a new competitor threatens to take away some of the bridge's customers? To be more specific, assume that the bridge authority charges all vehicles a toll of 75 cents. This price covers the 50-cent incremental (repair, maintenance) costs incurred and contributes 25 cents to capital costs, which, when cumulated, is sufficient to pay interest plus debt retirement. Now suppose a ferry boat begins to take passengers across for a fee of 60 cents, which covers its total costs. Many travelers will desert the bridge. What should the regulator do?

There are two traditional regulatory responses. First, the regulator may simply ban the ferry boat. He would reason that the cost to the economy of carrying passengers across the river by ferry (in the example, 60 cents per passenger) is greater than the *incremental* cost of carrying them by bridge. Only the need for capturing the bridge's fixed costs leads to a different set of relative prices. Hence, to allow the ferry to compete would be wasteful.

Second, the regulator may allow the ferry to enter. He may be uncertain about relative incremental costs. Can he be so sure that the total cost of bringing a ferry boat to the river and running it is *less* than the *incremental* cost of bridge crossings? Maybe it really only costs 40 cents per passenger to run the ferry boat. What does the regulator know about ferries? And what is the true incremental cost of bridge crossing? After all, the parties in his proceeding will present him with a complex set of cost figures, each of which supports their separate positions. Thus, the regulator may decide to allow the ferry boat to enter the market, while simultaneously allowing the bridge authority to cut its prices to incremental cost. Then, if it is in fact less costly to carry those potential passengers by bridge, the ferry will be driven out of business.

It should be noted that the bridge authority is likely to cut prices *only* for those travelers who would otherwise go by boat. Thus, if the boat will take cars but not trucks, car tolls will be cut and truck tolls raised to make up the difference. The truck owners will complain, but they are better off than if car tolls remained high, for then car owners would all take the ferry, desert the bridge, and leave the truck owners to pay *all* the fixed costs through *still higher* tolls. The result is a simple example of Ramsey pricing.

The problem can become somewhat more complicated when the bridge has several types of customers and the ferry boat can provide for some of them. Suppose that pedestrians, cyclists, cars, and trucks all use the bridge. Will a higher toll for bicycles lead some cyclists to walk? Suppose that the ferry boat can take pedestrians, cyclists, and cars, but no trucks. Will there be enough truck traffic to cover the bridge's fixed costs? If the bridge is allowed to cut its toll in response to the ferry, might it cut its toll below its incremental cost—say, as a device to increase its traffic to the point where the regulator will allow it to add a deck?

Should the regulator allow the ferry to enter or not? Should it allow the bridge to respond with price cuts or not? This is essentially the FCC's problem. Economists have tended to think that the regulator ought to allow the new firm to enter in these circumstances and also allow the regulated firm to cut its prices in response down to the level of incremental costs.[11] But, as will become apparent, a regulator may find it difficult, as a practical matter, to follow this advice. The way in which the bridge analogy fits the longline problem will also become apparent.

The Industry and the Service

The domestic telecommunications industry consists almost entirely of the Bell System, the largest nonfinancial corporation in the world. At the center of the system is AT&T, which manages the long-distance network through its longline department and owns a controlling interest in 21 of the 23 Bell Operating Companies (BOCs) that provide intrastate service to much of the nation. (These companies provide some interstate service as well; in addition, approximately 1,800 independent telephone companies tie into the Bell network and serve the regions that the BOCs do not reach.) AT&T also owns Western Electric, the largest manufacturer of telecommunication equipment, and, along with Western Electric, it owns Bell Laboratories, a research and development laboratory. The Bell System has net assets worth about $100 billion and annual revenues of about $40 billion.[12] It employs approximately one million people, operates about 82 percent of the 150 million telephones used for local and long-distance service, and accounts for about 84 percent of domestic telephone operating revenues. In addition, it devotes considerable resources to communications technology: in 1974, for example, nearly $760 million was spent on basic research and development.[13]

AT&T essentially provides telephone service (and data transmission service) both locally and long distance. For local service, subscribers need a telephone, which is connected by wire to a central office. The office contains an exchange, which switches calls, connecting subscribers with one another. It also provides operators for assistance, billing devices, and various other services. The cost of the telephone and loop from a home or business to the central office does not vary with intensity of use. These items are therefore classified as "usage-insensitive" plant. The other items are "usage-sensitive."

Long-distance service requires the elements mentioned above, plus "long lines" capable of carrying the call over long distances. These lines may consist of cables, microwaves beamed between towers, or waves sent via satellite. Long-distance service may also require additional operators, additional repair personnel, additional billing equipment, and more complex switching equipment. Of the Bell System's operating revenues—over $20 billion in 1976— about half comes from local service and half from long-distance service.[14]

AT&T's long-distance service may be divided into three types, depending in part upon the method used to charge for a call. Long-distance revenues are generated primarily by the sale of message toll service (MTS), which is regular long-distance service. AT&T also sells wide-area telephone service (WATS), which for a fixed monthly fee allows a subscriber to dial anywhere within a given region without additional charges. Both services allow subscribers to use the telephones, local loops, long lines, and switching systems to reach any other subscriber within the system. The third type of service may be described as the provision of "specialized communications," and, in particular, "private-line" service. A private line consists basically of an open line between two fixed points—say, between an office in New York and one in Los Angeles. For a fee, a subscriber, such as North American Rockwell, can buy an open line, which it can then connect to its office exchange system at each end. A person in any of its New York offices could thereby dial directly to anyone in any of its Los Angeles offices. From a technical point of view, either end of the open line could as easily be connected to the Los Angeles local switching system, and connections to all other local systems could also be provided. The more switching that is provided, the more the service, from the subscriber's point of view, resembles what he receives with message toll service or WATS service; the fewer the connections he can make at the other end, the more the service seems special, or restricted, or private line. All these services can be used to transmit voice or data or other messages (though private-line service is often used by large firms particularly to transmit data, bunched messages, or even television signals).

Natural monopoly. Local telephone service seems to be generally accepted as a natural monopoly. Local regulators at the turn of the century recognized that it would be inefficient to have more than one firm offer local service, given the resulting duplication of facilities. And this view was reflected in the Communications Act which instituted federal regulation in 1934. Local service still requires local exchanges and local loops, which consist of cables under the streets or wires strung on telephone polls. The inconvenience and unnecessary duplication involved in having several sets of wires, extra poles, several competing local exchanges, or several telephones in each house leads most observers to continue to characterize local service as "an undisputed natural monopoly."[15] While it has been argued that technological developments such as optic fiber transmission or mobile land telephone service may make competition possible in the future, or may allow firms to bypass local exchanges when they offer long-distance service, these developments seem speculative enough that new firms have not asked to enter the local business.[16]

The more debatable question is whether long-distance communications is a natural monopoly. A number of studies have claimed that it is.[17] These studies have been criticized by researchers who have reached somewhat different conclusions.[18]

Those who argue that there *are* important economies of scale point to two important facts. First, throughout the century, as demand has grown, costs have declined because AT&T has introduced new types of technology. As coaxial cable succeeded ordinary cable and microwave and satellites succeeded coaxial cable, costs fell dramatically. For the future, Bell Labs has developed a new technology called wave guide and is working on a laser technology; these are expected to cut costs still further. They are impractical, however, without demand for transmissions of about 250,000 circuits over a particular route—a demand many times that currently experienced over even very crowded routes. AT&T argues that if competitors are allowed to enter, it will be more difficult to offer wave guide transmission when adequate demand eventually develops, because demand will be split among several firms.[19]

Second, apart from any economies in transmission, there are efficiencies derived from system planning—what AT&T terms "unified responsibility."[20] Coordinating the network is a complicated process, one that requires a great deal of interaction among the planning, design, and management stages. There must be sufficient backup plant in order to accommodate peak demand. The network must also be able to route calls in a manner that minimizes congestion. It is a common practice to route a call through a distant switching center (from New York to California to Florida, for instance) if the nearest one is operating at full capacity. The entire procedure takes only a matter of seconds. Part of the problem with competition, however, is that new firms violate this "systems approach," which looks "at the network as a whole rather than its piece parts."[21] AT&T argues that competitors prefer to look at pieces (and only the most lucrative ones) because, unlike AT&T, they are under no obligation to serve remote areas. And the fact that different motives guide AT&T and its rivals suggests that it would be both costly and difficult to try to integrate the planning decisions of separate companies.

AT&T's opponents argue that long-distance service is *not* a significant natural monopoly. First, they concede that trunk-line transmission costs have declined rapidly as the scale of service has grown, but they add that on most trunk routes the scale of service is such that there will be no significant additional economies of scale—at least not before demand doubles or trebles. Charles River Associates, for example, in a detailed study of longline telecommunications points out that most long-distance service takes place over routes with 3,000–12,000 circuits (see Figure 2). Microwave technology will be used until a scale of 80,000 circuits is achieved. And it is possible for several different firms to use microwave technology on many routes without raising unit costs of service.[22]

Second, they point out that trunk-line transmission accounts for only about one third the cost of long-distance service. The other elements—switching equipment, land, and buildings—do not involve significant economies of scale.[23]

Third, they note that new competitors can themselves stimulate technological advances, which lower costs.[24] Finally, new competitors need not interfere with "systems" economies; joint planning is possible.

Thus, those favoring new entry attempt to show that even if the new entrants divided the market with AT&T on many specific routes, the result would not necessarily be higher costs. The cost, with existing technology, of serving smaller market shares might rise only slightly if at all. And the spur of competition could lower future costs.

The argument on this point between AT&T and its opponents seems to revolve around the likelihood of developing and adopting new technologies and the possibility of maintaining "system" organizational and planning economies in the presence of competition. These issues are highly controversial and abstract; although economists express judgments about them, their resolution is unlikely to be demonstrable as a matter of fact.[25]

Regulation and Joint Costs

As previously mentioned, regulation of telephone service began when municipalities "sold" franchises to whichever firm promised to charge lower rates or provide better service. When this system failed, in part due to local corruption and the practice of submitting unrealistically low bids followed by efforts to raise price,[26] states began to use rate-setting commissions to control prices.

In the early part of this century these state bodies found it difficult to control telephone company rates for three separate reasons. First, the commissions could not easily value the rate base. And, given a hostile judiciary,[27] the "confiscation doctrine" which allowed judicial redetermination of commission decisions about value, and a rate-setting theory that tried to determine "reproduction" rather than historical costs, commissions tended to accept the phone company's own valuation or to compromise with them to avoid judicial review.[28] The commissions' problem was compounded by the fact that they had no authority outside the state in which they sat. They therefore could not compel AT&T, a New York corporation, to reveal the details of arrangements it

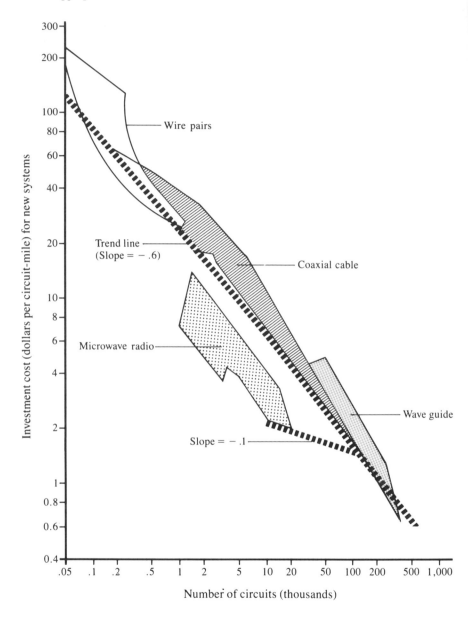

Figure 2. Investment cost for new terrestrial transmission systems. (*Source:* Redrawn from Eugene F. O'Neill, "Radio and Long-Haul Transmission," *Bell Laboratories Record,* January 1975, at 55. Microwave cost extrapolation added by Charles River Associates, "The Economics of Competition in the Telecommunications Industry," Report No. 338, July 1979, ch. 4.)

made with the operating companies. (The most controversial involved the "license contract," a fee paid by the operating company to compensate AT&T for services AT&T provided to its operating subsidiaries. The rate was often contested as excessive, and, until 1926, stood at 4.5 percent of gross operating revenues.)[29]

Second, the state commissions had to allocate joint costs among state users. The problem resembled that of the division of the fixed costs of a bridge among the pedestrians, cyclists, cars, and trucks that use it. That problem was difficult enough as applied to the bridge, for the advice given by economists (namely, allocate costs in proportion to the likelihood that users will continue to cross the bridge) cannot readily be applied when the strength of the users' desires to cross (their elasticity of demand) is unknown. But the problem of telephone service is still *more* difficult, because an extension of service benefits not only the new caller but also those who receive his calls—and also those who *might* call him but never actually do. It is as if the cyclists and pedestrians liked to talk to each other on the bridge and each would pay something to have the others along. Then how should the commission allocate the costs of the bridge, or of an extension of telephone service?

The state commissions faced this problem when service was extended from urban to rural areas. Urban users argued that the new rural users should have to pay at least for their own telephones, the loops to the central exchange, and related switching equipment—just as the urban users had done earlier. But the rural users noted that the lower rural population density meant more telephone poles and wires, and higher costs per phone. They argued that they should not pay higher charges than urban users because connecting them to the system benefited urban users, too—it created a larger system. Moreover it was fair to require urban users to share the cost of extending service to the countryside but *not* vice versa because (1) the urban systems were already in place—the issue was whether to *extend* service to rural areas and how the incremental costs of doing so should be borne; and (2) in any event, providing rural/urban communication links provided a host of social and commercial benefits to the whole country, including city dwellers. Thus, rural users felt that all costs should be averaged among all users.

In response to political and social pressures rather than to economic analysis, state commissions, often over vociferous local objections, began to sanction statewide average pricing rules such as "equal charges for equal miles." Administratively the system had much to recommend it; it was easier to set an average than to determine the fairest way to allocate these joint costs, particularly for regulators with little expertise.[30]

Third, the state regulators had to decide how to allocate costs between intrastate and interstate service. Since some of the same lines, telephones, and other equipment were used to serve each, the joint-cost problem reappeared. Initially, commissions took the approach that was easiest to administer. They assumed that telephones, local loops, and local exchanges were all installed to provide local service. They allocated these costs to local service and sought to recover all of them through local rates. Only additional costs were then allocated to interstate long-distance service (the "board-to-board" principle); they included only the extra cost of long lines, the extra operators used to make long-distance connections, and a portion of usage-sensitive central office costs (such as added billing service) that long-distance service necessitated. AT&T contracted with its own and with independent operating companies to compensate them for these extra operating costs (such as billing and long-distance operators), but it did not compensate them for the use of local plant used to connect the customer with long-distance lines.[31]

AT&T had a strong financial incentive to support board-to-board allocation, for prior to 1934 long-distance rates were not regulated effectively.[32] Thus, to the extent that costs were allocated to local service, its local operating companies could obtain higher local revenues, but their doing so did not force AT&T to lower its long-distance rates. AT&T still had reasons to keep long-distance rates low, to expand demand and to undercut political pressures for nationalization or price regulation. Yet even after the enactment of a weak form of price regulation in 1910, AT&T earned between two and three times as much return on its longline as on its local service. From 1921 to 1925, for example, it earned 7.16 percent on local service investment and 19.21 percent on investment in longlines.[33]

By the 1930s demand for effective regulation increased. Congress responded by enacting the Communications Act of 1934,[34] which gave the Federal Communications Commission the responsibility to regulate interstate phone rates. The FCC then had to grapple with the joint-cost problem.

The FCC did not concern itself directly with the problem of allocating costs *among* various long-distance services. It could avoid that task by focusing its regulatory efforts upon the revenue requirement. What were AT&T's total interstate costs, and what profit should it earn? The FCC determined these matters primarily by negotiation with AT&T, not formal hearings. And after making the global determination—of revenue requirement—the commission basically allowed AT&T to propose the rate structure that would earn it the allowed revenue. The commission did not, and probably could not, determine whether AT&T's proposed structure of rates for different long-distance services represented a reasonable allocation of costs among them. Indeed, since the same long-distance lines supplied many different services, the FCC staff feared that it was within AT&T power to propose virtually any rate structure it wished, and the staff would be unable to challenge it.[35]

The FCC could not avoid the problem of joint costs, however, insofar as the same equipment was used to provide both intrastate and interstate service. Some method of allocating those costs had to be developed in order to determine which costs belonged within the jurisdiction of which regulators. The division took place through negotiations among state and federal regulators, which led to the development of "separations" procedures.

The FCC and state regulators, in allocating costs *between them*, changed from the board-to-board to the station-to-station principle. The latter principle allocated some of the local plant costs to interstate calls. Such an allocation sounds fair,[36] for telephones and local loops are used to supply long-distance as well as local calls. But to determine how much of the local plant costs should be shifted to interstate calls was difficult. As the urban/rural debate revealed, "fairness" does not offer an unambiguous criterion for allocation. Moreover, the effect of the shift in method was to allow a person who made only local calls to escape paying for a portion of his telephone and local loops. (The converse did not occur because *all* subscribers pay a monthly fee for local service, but only those who use long-distance service pay the long-distance charge.) Thus, as Kahn has noted, "If every time an operating company installs a new PBX system something like 20 percent of the capital charges are allocated to interstate services, the charges to the PBX customer need cover only 80 percent of those capital costs . . . The other 20 percent will return to the operating company from its share of interstate revenues."[37] The owner of the PBX may, of course, frequently use it in calling out of state, in which case he will pay its full cost; but he may also use it only for local calls, in which case its cost is paid partly by other users of the interstate system.

The problem of allocation was exacerbated by the fact that separations negotiations among AT&T, the FCC, and the state regulators reflected political and social as well as economic considerations.[38] And as new technology greatly reduced long-distance costs, local regulators sought to allocate more of local plant to long-distance service; by doing so they could hold down local rates without requiring an increase in long-distance rates (in fact, the latter declined).[39]

The result is a separations procedure which, most observers believe, requires long-distance service to contribute more to local plant costs than its proportionate share. In 1967 FCC Commissioner Nicholas Johnson wrote that although "during the time of actual use, subscriber plant is used only four percent of the time for interstate calls, roughly twelve percent of the cost is to be borne by the interstate system."[40] He later added, "Basically, what we are doing is subsidizing the costs of local service with Bell's excess profits from long distance service." In 1977, AT&T paid to the operating companies nearly four billion dollars, as separations compensation for the costs of telephone terminals, local switching equipment, local lines, land, and buildings.[41] This sum, according to AT&T, amounted to about 20 percent of intrastate costs, but that plant is not used twenty percent of the time for long-distance calling.[42] AT&T's analysis of the division of costs and revenues is contained in Figure 3. Some critics dispute the numbers, but virtually all agree that some such pattern of contribution or "cross-subsidy" exists.[43]

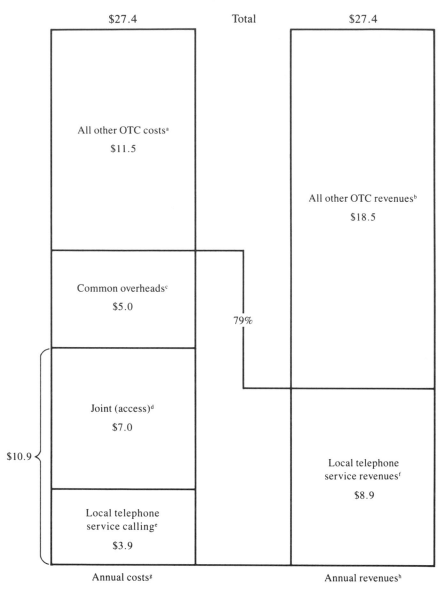

$27.4   Total $27.4

All other OTC costs[a]

$11.5

All other OTC revenues[b]

$18.5

Common overheads[c]

$5.0

79%

Joint (access)[d]

$7.0

$10.9

Local telephone
service revenues[f]

$8.9

Local telephone
service calling[e]

$3.9

Annual costs[g]   Annual revenues[h]

Figure 3. A partitioning of 1975 costs and revenues of AT&T, in billions. (*Source:* AT&T, "Embedded Direct Costs (EDC) Study, 1975," 3rd supp. response to FCC Docket 20003, July 12, 1976, at 6.)

a. All other operating telephone company costs: all traffic-sensitive costs related to usage of the plant provided by the OTC for MTS, WATS, and PLS, as well as costs of producing the Yellow Pages and the costs of vertical services (extensions, PBX, Centrex).

b. All other operating telephone company revenues: all revenues from MTS, WATS, PLS, Yellow Pages, and vertical services (extensions, PBX, Centrex).

c. Common (overhead) costs: general corporate overhead costs related to the provision of all or several of the specific service categories (executive, legal, financial start-up costs, short-run spare capacity).

The Entry of Competition into Long-Distance Telecommunications

The essential elements of the industry and regulation, then, are: (1) AT&T is a huge firm with revenues of billions of dollars; (2) it supplies many different, related communications services characterized by joint costs; (3) local service is in all probability a natural monopoly; long-distance service may also be a natural monopoly, but the issue is debatable; (4) the firm is regulated by both local and national regulators; (5) the regulators allocate some joint costs; the allocation of other joint costs is left up to the company.

This set of circumstances produced a serious problem for the regulators in the mid-1960s, when a new group of firms, MCI and other specialized common carriers, asked the FCC for permission to enter the industry and to compete against AT&T in the provision of long-distance private-line services. Should the FCC allow competition in this segment of the industry?

It was tempting for the FCC to allow this new entry. For one thing, the enormous problem of allocating costs among long-distance services might be alleviated for the regulators if they could rely upon competition rather than regulation to set the price for service. For another, the new competitors might help users by offering private-line long-distance service at lower cost, or they might provide more innovative service. In any event, their presence would put pressure upon AT&T to cut its prices for similar, competing private-line services and hence its costs of providing them. Finally, new entry might provide a practical test of AT&T's claim of large economies of scale in longline telecommunications, because if the competitors could survive despite AT&T price competition, this in itself might show that longline telecommunication was not a natural monopoly.

The FCC, however, initially seemed unaware of the fact that to allow new competition would exacerbate the problems of determining a proper rate structure. Recall the bridge with its clientele of pedestrians, cyclists, cars, and trucks. Ideally, the fixed costs of the bridge should be allocated to each group

---

d. Joint (access) costs: costs associated with the customer's telephone instrument and local loop line to the central office used jointly by interstate and intrastate MTS and local telephone service. Also includes traffic-insensitive portion of local office, especially switching facilities.

e. Local telephone service calling: costs primarily generated by local calling (both business and residence), including the traffic-sensitive local dial equipment, exchange trunking, local tandem and local operator services, and local message-billing expenses.

f. Local telephone service revenues: all revenues of a local nature, including message unit revenues, for both business and residence. The figures used by the FCC ($13.8 billion in 1975) for this category are about 55 percent higher. This large difference would be due entirely to the fact that the FCC includes the so-called vertical services in this category (extensions, PBX, Centrex).

g. Annual (embedded direct) costs: indicates operating costs (and realized return on capital) experienced by Bell telcos, which together are, by definition, equivalent to the revenues realized.

h. Annual revenues: the sum of local and other revenues. The total costs are set equal to total revenues, by definition.

in inverse relation to elasticity of demand (those whom an increased price is most likely to drive away should receive the smallest price increase). In practice, the regulator does not know what the demand elasticities are; thus, he will make some mistakes and some customers will unfortunately not cross the bridge. This problem is exacerbated by the entry of the 60-cent passenger ferry, for the ferry boat may attract many customers from the 75-cent toll bridge. Unless the bridge authority allows the bridge to cut its passenger toll to its incremental cost of 50 cents, the ferry boat will enter and resources are wasted. Indeed, perhaps so many customers will be attracted away that it will be impossible for the bridge to cover its fixed costs, and it will go bankrupt. The authority may have previously struggled with the joint-cost allocation problem, but now the matter is serious. Unless the regulator now makes certain that those costs are allocated in a manner that leaves the bridge free to cut its passenger toll to the *incremental* cost of passenger crossing, the result may be serious economic waste.

Thus, Kahn wrote, "There is a special urgency to the need for bringing rate structures into conformity with the requirements of economic efficiency in communications. As long as the business was essentially monopolistic, the relationship of specific rates to their respective incremental costs could be very loose indeed . . . The industry could also accommodate separations formulae, by which total revenue requirements were allocated between intrastate and interstate services . . . in ways that had only the remotest relationship to incremental costs . . . The entry of competition in recent years . . . has compelled a reexamination of these loose practices."[44]

The issue of entry is complicated still further, however, by the difficulty of measuring incremental costs and by the presence of regulation over a portion of the industry. Suppose, in the bridge example, the authority did not know the bridge's incremental pedestrian cost (and neither perhaps did the bridge). And suppose it suspected that the bridge might seek to charge a price below its incremental costs in order to drive a ferry out of business.

Why might the bridge wish to price at predatory levels below incremental costs? First, there is the traditional possibility described in Chapter 1: the bridge may hope to drive the ferry boat out of business and recoup its losses through higher tolls later. Second, the bridge may be willing to maintain permanently predatory prices and to run losses in order to maintain its market position if it fears that ferry boats, once secured in a corner of the market, will expand through new technology to take over the rest. Third, as discussed in Chapter 2, the bridge may be following Averch and Johnson: it may be willing to charge any price at all for one of its services, believing that it can make up any losses by convincing the regulator to allow it to charge more for the others—so that overall it earns a reasonable return. Fourth, perhaps the bridge was not really necessary. A fleet of ferry boats might do the whole job cheaper than the bridge, but the bridge may enjoy lower incremental costs for each service (given the others) than the ferry boats. If so, and if a new bridge is contemplated, a price equal to incremental costs might be considered predatory or wasteful.

Now, given the possibility of predatory pricing in retaliation, should entry be allowed? And what prices should the bridge be allowed to charge in response? That essentially was the problem faced by the FCC.

The FCC's Response to the Problem

Through 1978 the FCC dealt with the problem without focusing clearly upon it. Its decisions were taken one at a time, each dealing with part of the problem instead of the whole. The FCC first allowed new competitors into a small corner of AT&T's markets—private-line telecommunications. It then hindered AT&T's efforts to respond through lower prices. The courts and the commission together greatly expanded the market area in which the newcomers could compete. The result, according to AT&T, was a serious risk of unnecessary duplication of facilities. How this occurred can best be understood by briefly reviewing several FCC proceedings.[45]

Above 890[46]

Before 1956 the FCC reserved microwave frequencies above 890 megacycles primarily for AT&T, which intended to use them in part to provide private-line telephone service with microwave technology developed in World War II. The FCC would allow other firms to use those bands only if AT&T could not yet provide customers for these facilities.

In 1956 the FCC decided to eliminate these restrictions on private ownership of microwave systems. It felt that companies might prefer to build their own cheaper systems rather than wait for AT&T's higher-quality service. Customer construction and ownership might thus satisfy specialized communications needs. Moreover, competition would promote innovation and provide an outlet for equipment manufacturers other than Western Electric.[47] AT&T argued that new entry would drain its revenues, but the commission replied that AT&T had not proved this.[48] In any event, the market involved was so small that a loss of revenues would not hurt AT&T or its other services.[49]

Above 890 itself had little effect on the industry, but it set the stage for the *MCI* case which was to follow.

MCI[50]

In 1965, Microwave Communications, Inc. (MCI) applied for authority to build $600,000 worth of facilities for limited microwave service connecting Chicago, St. Louis, and nine intermediate points. It proposed to offer private-line services similar to those already offered by AT&T (and Western Union), with subscribers providing the links between their offices and the MCI facility. MCI proposed lower rates than AT&T and Western Union, and unlike them it would allow subscribers to share channels and buy them on a part-time basis.

In 1969 the FCC granted MCI's application. It again stressed the flexibility afforded by competition: "While no new technology is involved in MCI's proposal, it does present a concept of common carrier microwave offerings which differs from those of the established carriers."[51] This factor, more than any price differential, influenced the commission, which felt that the sharing and part-time provisions would increase the efficiency of the subscribers' businesses. And, once again, the FCC rejected the carriers' contention that MCI would adversely affect their revenues.[52]

Although the *MCI* decision strengthened the procompetitive intent of *Above 890* (now a company could lease rather than construct a competitive facility), the FCC carefully noted that the ruling applied only to MCI.[53]

Specialized Common Carriers (SCCs)[54]

Soon after *MCI,* many firms applied to build microwave systems. By June 1970 the commission had received applications by 37 companies to build 1,713 stations (DATRAN requested the largest system, which involved 244 proposed stations serving 35 cities).[55] All these systems would provide specialized common-carrier services, comparable to the transmission of voice and data over private lines.

The FCC decided to adopt a policy favoring new entry into the specialized communications field. It reasoned that new entry meant new services, that it would promote lower prices and increased innovation, and that new entry was unlikely to have any significantly adverse effects on AT&T. In addition, it noted that competition would help the agency (as well as the consumer) by providing a standard for comparing the performances of different companies.[56]

AT&T had argued that new entry would force it to abandon its nationwide average pricing system for message toll service (to prevent businessmen from substituting new MCI-type private-line offerings for AT&T's service system); that it would have to delay the introduction of new long-distance communications techniques with lower unit costs; and that in any event the new services would simply duplicate existing AT&T private-line services.

The FCC's response to these points is important. First, the FCC claimed that the new carriers would serve a "dynamic rapidly growing market," attracting new customers rather than drawing customers from AT&T.[57] Thus, the new firms would be unlikely to drain AT&T's revenues. Moreover, the FCC suggested (but did not specifically state) that the newcomers would be allowed to offer only a limited range of services.

Second, the commission stated that if the new firms competed directly with AT&T, then AT&T could lower its prices to retain customers. It stated: "Where services may be in direct competition, departure from uniform nationwide pricing may be in order, and in such circumstances will not be opposed by the Commission. . . . It is our intention to permit the existing carriers to price their competitive services in a fashion that will realistically and reasonably reflect economic advantages of those carriers. Moreover, we subscribe fully to the views of our staff, endorsed by the Department of Justice, that there should not be any 'protective umbrella' for the new entrants or any artificial bolstering of operations that cannot succeed on their own merits."[58]

Third, the commission indicated that AT&T would have to make its local telephone exchanges available to the new firms "under reasonable terms."[59] To require the new carriers to build their own local links to each local customer would have expensively and needlessly duplicated AT&T's system of local lines.

In essence, the FCC decided that the ferry boat could enter; it would be restricted to a limited market, and the bridge could respond with toll cuts.

AT&T's Competitive Response: Special Rates

For more than ten years after the *SCC* decision, AT&T was able to meet the new entrants by lowering the prices of its own major competitive services. It did so despite the FCC's opposition, for, contrary to its implied position in *SCC,* the FCC rejected or suspended new AT&T tariffs embodying lower rates. But AT&T met each rejection by filing new tariffs and raising procedural objections. Since the FCC could suspend tariffs for only three months[60] when decisions often took years to reach, AT&T was free to put its new rates into effect during that time. And for some time it did so, as follows

Private lines.[61] AT&T's major concern was that it be able to lower its rates to large private-line customers to prevent them from switching to its new competitors. In 1955, even before the *Above 890* decision, AT&T filed tariffs (designed to compete with potential new entry) which offered price discounts to firms buying "multiple private lines."[62] In 1961 the FCC found AT&T's multiple private line tariff unlawful, on the ground that it discriminated unreasonably between small and large buyers of private-line service.[63] The FCC was unwilling to allow AT&T to provide "a like and contemporaneous communications service between the same points at different charges to different users," unless it could demonstrate "convincingly that the circumstances and conditions of the service are substantially dissimilar. Significant differences in a carrier's costs . . . usually constitute differences in conditions sufficient to render the services dissimilar."[64] But AT&T had not shown a cost justification for the discounts.[65]

Thus, the FCC did not come to grips with the main problem: the bridge in competition with the passenger ferry wishes to cut its pedestrian tolls not because it costs less for passengers to cross than bicyclists, but because otherwise they will desert to the ferry boat (a higher incremental cost carrier) and then the bridge will have to raise its charges to all its remaining customers.

TELPAK.[66] In 1961 AT&T filed a new set of tariffs offering discounts to buyers of private line in bulk. In 1964, the FCC considered whether this "TEL-PAK" tariff discriminated unreasonably against small buyers of private-line services.[67] This time, however, the FCC suggested a more logical test of discrimination. It allowed discrimination based on "competitive necessity," provided that the lower rates were "compensatory" and benefited remaining customers by generating revenues that helped cover fixed costs and that would, without the price cut, be lost to AT&T.[68]

These requirements were elaborated in a later and separate portion of the *TELPAK* case. The commission laid down three criteria. The proponent of a discriminatory tariff had to show: "(1) that those benefitting from the discrimination have an alternative of supplying their communications requirement from a substitute source of supply and that they will shift to the substitute source unless the discrimination is maintained; (2) that the discriminatory rate or preference is just sufficient to return the business which would otherwise be lost; and (3) that the discrimination benefits the users of the company's service who are discriminated against, i.e., charges to other users are lower because of the discriminatory rate than they would be without such rates."[69]

Thus, the FCC recognized that if the pedestrians desert the bridge and travel by ferry boat, the remaining bridge customers will have to share among themselves the fixed cost burden that the pedestrians used to shoulder. If more pedestrians can be attracted back—even at a lower toll that contributes only a penny to fixed costs—the other customers are still better off than if the pedestrians desert the bridge and the others must pay that penny themselves.

Despite the soundness of its theory, however, in practice the FCC held against AT&T. By 1964 it had found two portions of the TELPAK tariff unnecessary to meet competition and therefore unlawfully low.[70] It reopened the record to determine whether two other portions (TELEPAK C and D) were compensatory, and continued to collect evidence until 1976. AT&T, meanwhile, continued to charge those rates.

HiLo.[71] In November 1973—after *MCI* and *SCC*—AT&T filed the HiLo tariff covering non-TELPAK private-line services. HiLo departed for the first time from AT&T's nationwide averaging rule of "equal rates for equal miles." Previously, price per mile had declined as distance increased but two private lines of the same length had carried the same price anywhere in the country. The new tariff introduced discrimination between customers in different areas. It distinguished between high-density and low-density routes, charging 85 cents per mile for the former and $2.50 per mile for the latter.[72] The commission suspended the tariff, and, in an interim decision released in 1975, decided that the record was insufficient to permit a finding as to its lawfulness. In 1976 the FCC again found that AT&T had failed to produce sufficient evidence to satisfy its burden of justifying the tariff. It ordered AT&T to file a new one within ninety days.[73]

In April 1976 AT&T complied by filing its Multi-Schedule Private Line

Tariff (MPL), a variant of HiLo. MPL distinguished between "A" rate centers, with large communications traffic, and "B" rate centers, with smaller traffic. Rates differed depending upon whether private-line service ran A to A, A to B, or B to B. (A to A had the lowest rates.) The object of MPL, like that of HiLo, was to charge lower rates in markets where the specialized common carriers connected and offered competition for business. In May 1976 the FCC suspended MPL and reinstated HiLo for three months.[74] These decisions suggest that the FCC had grasped the two basic principles involved: (1) new competition would be allowed, and (2) AT&T would be allowed to respond by cutting its prices to incremental costs. But the FCC was finding it difficult to decide whether a particular proposed price cut *in fact* represented a legitimate competitive response. The FCC had begun to develop costing principles that would help it make this decision. It announced those principles, decided in Docket 18128, at the end of 1976. They superseded and made obsolete the earlier filed AT&T tariffs.

Docket 18128[75]

The FCC soon found that it could not avoid dealing with joint costs by opening markets to new competition. On the contrary, the presence of those competitors forced the commission to face the issue of cost allocation. For one thing, prior to new entry AT&T had spread its fixed costs among its services in an economically haphazard pattern. It charged equal rates for equal miles despite differing costs; it charged residential users considerably lower prices than business users, despite uncertainty about whether their demand was less elastic;[76] and AT&T had itself never fully worked out a system for determining incremental cost. For another thing, AT&T began to cut its prices for competitive services, AT&T's competitors began to complain, and the FCC was forced to consider whether AT&T's prices were too low—discriminatory or predatory. As early as 1965, Western Union, for example, complained that according to AT&T's own cost studies TELPAK was earning a profit of only 0.3 percent, while WATS earned 10.1 percent and AT&T's overall rate of return was 7.5 percent.

Obviously, the profit that a particular service appears to earn depends upon which costs and which revenues are allocated to the service. To decide how this should be done, the FCC consolidated several earlier proceedings into Docket 18128, in which it dealt with the question of how AT&T should allocate joint costs.

The bridge example suggests the difficulty of answering this question: How is one to allocate the fixed bridge costs among the pedestrians, cyclists, cars, and trucks that use it? In fact, the problem is still more complicated than previously suggested because of the presence of significant "cross-elasticity" of demand: the price of one service (say, message toll service) affects the demand for other services (say, WATS). It is as if an increase in the toll for pedestrians led them to buy bicycles and to cycle across the bridge. This fact makes it particularly difficult to divide the fixed costs inversely in proportion to elasticity of demand (Ramsey pricing), for it makes it particularly difficult to determine the pattern of bridge use if a toll is raised or lowered.

Moreover, if pedestrians desert the bridge, say, for the ferry boat, there will be more room on the bridge for cyclists, or a walkway might be removed making more space for cars. And a cut in the car toll might then generate more revenue. This fact makes it difficult to determine the proper toll for pedestrians, for one must take account of the fact that the incremental cost of their using the bridge is not just the extra walkways and the related wear and tear, but that *plus* the revenues from cars and so forth, that the bridge owner forgoes by devoting part of his bridge to pedestrians. (These revenues represent the harm to those bicycles, trucks, and cars that *might* use the bridge were the pedestrians not there but that *now do not* because the bridge serves pedestrians.)

These difficulties plagued the FCC's efforts to determine whether a proposed AT&T price cut would end up with a price that covered at least the incremental cost of the service. At the same time, the FCC felt it had to know whether that cost was covered, for it feared that AT&T, if left on its own, would charge a price *below* the incremental cost of service—a predatory price.

In Docket 18128 the FCC was to decide when the price of a service was below its cost and hence unlawful. It was asked to choose between two methods of determining the cost of a service, both of which should be familiar by now. The first was a "long-run incremental cost" (LRIC) method seeking to identify only the *additional* costs (including any extra plant or other equipment) needed to supply the service (or that would be saved if the service were discontinued). How much would the bridge owner save if pedestrians deserted the bridge and walkways were unnecessary? The second method was a fully distributed cost (FDC) system allocating in some "fair," "equal," or "proportional" way the fixed or joint costs (such as those for telephones, local loops, and cables) among all the services that used them. AT&T's seven-way cost study, submitted to help the FCC make this determination, suggested seven different variations of the FDC theme.

Not all services can be priced at LRIC. The bridge (and AT&T) can recapture fixed costs only if some prices are higher than incremental costs. But LRIC provides an appropriate floor against which to judge whether a price is predatory, when the bridge (or AT&T) responds to new competition by cutting the prices of a service in order to keep its old customers. An FDC floor, on the other hand, runs the risk that higher-cost microwave competitors (ferry) will take customers from a cheaper AT&T service (bridge for pedestrians) by charging for their competing services less than AT&T's FDC, but more than AT&T's LRIC.

But how was the FCC to determine the long-run incremental cost? AT&T suggested that the commission do so by projecting future demand for communications services. It would then estimate the cost of satisfying that demand, first with and then without provision of the service in question. AT&T also noted that a price below LRIC "burdens" other users of the system. If the bridge charges pedestrians, say, 25 cents (less than their 50-cent LRIC), the pedestrians will stay on the bridge, but the other bridge users would have been better off *without* the pedestrians. They now must pay enough to make up for the 25-cent loss the bridge owner incurs every time a pedestrian crosses. On the other hand, a price of 55 cents—above LRIC—benefits the other travelers; they are better off *with* the pedestrians, for now every pedestrian who crosses contributes 5 cents toward fixed costs.

AT&T therefore proposed a "burden test" to see if a price was compensatory. First, the price of the added service must generate revenues sufficient to cover the additional cost of the service. (That cost, for a service using much preexisting equipment, might be very low.) Second, these revenues must not simply be diverted from other services that the same firm provides. It is wasteful to spend $100,000 to build a second deck on the bridge, even if revenues from a 10-cent toll will cover costs, if all the travelers using it would have otherwise used the first deck. Even if drivers had been willing to pay the toll, their demand could have been satisfied without the new expenditure. To solve this problem, AT&T would have added to the "additional costs" of, say, private-line service the additional MTS and WATS revenues that would have been generated without private-line service. In other words, if private-line service uses $200 million in additional equipment and generates $300 million in revenues, its rates are still predatory if its users would spend more than $100 million on MTS or WATS in its absence.

In sum, AT&T proposed that if the total revenues brought in by selling a service at a particular price exceeded (1) "the net *cost savings* to the carrier if the service were not offered," and (2) "the additional revenue that might be generated by shifting to other services if the service in question were not offered,"[77] that service at that price imposed no burden on AT&T's remaining users. The FCC should allow any such price as reasonable (higher than LRIC), because to require a higher price might lead AT&T users to desert AT&T and impose the burden of covering AT&T's fixed costs on its fewer remaining customers. In a nutshell, AT&T was arguing that if the ferry boat enters, AT&T must be allowed to cut its "tolls" to LRIC in response.

The FCC rejected AT&T's approach for two reasons. First, it stated that AT&T would apply LRIC to justify selective price cutting in response to competition and that selective price cuts for private-line service would lead to higher residential (ordinary service) rates. This FCC argument missed the point, however, for residential rates would go up *still more* if AT&T were not allowed to cut its private-line prices to LRIC and customers switched to new microwave competitors.[78] Second, the FCC stated that it had no way to verify the results of any specific LRIC analysis. Here, the FCC was right. LRIC involves forecasting. AT&T, not the FCC, has the expertise to do that forecasting. And given the great uncertainties of predicting demand and of challenging AT&T's demand estimates, the setting of the rate would be in AT&T's hands.[79]

In view of the administrative body's need for certain, verifiable cost figures (compare Chapter 2), it is not surprising that the FCC adopted an FDC costing method. FDC has the virtue of at least appearing to be verifiable. The FCC adopted AT&T's Method Seven, which AT&T had found the least objectionable of all the suggested FDC methods. This method allocated existing plant historically. The cost of each was allocated to the services it was intended to provide when built. However, because it soon proved difficult to decide what service each piece of cable or plant had been intended for, Method Seven soon began to resemble Method One, a system under which plant is allocated among services in proportion to the use each makes of the plant. It was as if the fixed costs of the bridge were allocated to the four classes of users in proportion to the number of crossings made by the members of each class.

The FCC did not close the door on LRIC. It indicated that under "exceptional circumstances," AT&T might depart from the approved methodology.[80] Yet in practice the FCC held that numerous AT&T tariffs were unreasonably low. It set aside AT&T's TELPAK tariffs (on which, according to Method Seven, AT&T earned a 12.6 percent return) as no longer justified by competitive necessity.[81] And AT&T may reasonably have felt that despite the FCC's promise in *SCC* not to protect the new competitors with a price umbrella, the FCC *in practice* was doing just that.

Expanding the Area of Competition

The cases noted so far show that the FCC allowed new competitors into one portion of AT&T's market—the market for private-line services. It then hindered AT&T's efforts to respond by cutting prices. These decisions alone could not cause serious harm, for only one corner of AT&T's business was involved. Even if the ferry boat takes away the pedestrians, the harm to the bridge and to the economy is small, because few pedestrians use the bridge. In a final series of decisions, however, the FCC, in part intentionally and in part inadvertently, greatly expanded the area in which the new firms could compete and the seriousness of the threat to AT&T.

Interconnection.[82] In 1974 the FCC decided that AT&T would have to allow MCI and other specialized common carriers to connect their lines to AT&T's local exchanges. Although the *SCC* case had left the issue open, it was obvious that MCI had to connect its intercity lines to its customers' offices and that the most efficient way to do so was to use AT&T's local lines, which were already in place. The FCC went further, however, and held that MCI could use its link to the local AT&T exchange to offer "foreign exchange" service (FX)—a service that allowed an MCI customer in city A to call city B and use the AT&T exchange in city B to reach any AT&T subscriber there. The FCC wrote that any other interpretation of *SCC* "would be inconsistent with the basic purposes and objectives of the action which we took and with the public interest."[83] But in fact FX significantly expanded the services that MCI could offer—from pure private-line to "partially switched" services. Thus, MCI could begin to compete for ordinary AT&T (MTS) long-distance customers—a fact that it saw as an advantage and that AT&T saw as a serious threat.

Sharing and resale.[84] Prior to 1976 AT&T effectively required each of its private-line customers to lease an entire open line; they were not allowed to resell or to share any portion of that line with others. AT&T's object in preventing sharing and resale was probably price discrimination. It would charge a low price, competitive with MCI, in order to retain large customers who could afford an entire line, but it would charge a higher price (per unit) to smaller customers. If reselling were possible, the former customers might buy lines at bulk rates, divide them, and resell them to the latter. If this process was sufficiently widespread, there would be no way to recover total fixed costs. (It was as if the bridge owner faced competition from a ferry carrying trucks and lowered the truck toll to retain its truck customers; if the bridge owner found that trucks were installing seats and ramps and carrying the pedestrians, cyclists, and cars, he might insist that trucks not carry the others or else pay a higher toll.)

The FCC decided that sharing and resale would have to be allowed. It believed that the result would be lower prices—numerous smaller customers would be able to take advantage of AT&T's low bulk rates. Moreover, it believed that the low rates would facilitate the development and use of new data processing and communications services—the use of computers at long distance by night, for example.[85] It hoped to stimulate a new "highly competitive 'information handling' industry."[86] And it doubted that AT&T would be injured because it believed that "the introduction of new sources of supply and/or service offerings would result . . . in an expansion of market demand."[87]

In fact, the FCC's predictions failed, for AT&T simply canceled the low TELPAK rate. It preferred to offer the low rates to no one rather than to everyone, and it was willing to run the risk of losing large bulk buyers to MCI. The FCC's opinion, however, stands for the principle that MCI will be allowed to share its private-line services; customers could buy, say, three minutes worth of line to city B. MCI service thus came still closer to resembling ordinary AT&T MTS long-distance service.

Execunet.[88] In 1974 MCI, which had previously offered only private-line services, revised its tariffs to allow any customer to call from any telephone in city A to any telephone in any other city that MCI served. Moreover, MCI would charge by the minute. This service, called Execunet, used MCI's long lines and AT&T's local exchanges (to which MCI was connected). The service duplicated AT&T's ordinary long-distance service (MTS). And AT&T feared that MCI might undercut its MTS prices, for, unlike AT&T, MCI's long-distance toll charge did not have to include any of the local plant costs that AT&T had to allocate to its interstate rate base.

AT&T complained to the FCC, which wrote to MCI ordering it to terminate Execunet on the grounds that the carrier was not authorized to provide what was essentially MTS.[89] MCI appealed to the United States Circuit Court of Appeals for the District of Columbia complaining about the FCC's procedures. The FCC ultimately agreed to conduct a more complete investigation.

In 1976 the FCC again found that MCI was not authorized to offer Execunet. Although its *SCC* decision had not stated explicitly that specialized carriers were prohibited from supplying message toll service, the agency explained that "we intended and did open competition only in the limited portion of AT&T's and Western Union's business represented by private-line services."[90] In *SCC* it had focused only on private-line revenues; and MCI, in offering its new service, was taking "a position completely different from that which it had advocated at every previous opportunity."[91]

The FCC defined "private-line" service. Such service must "(a) either originate or terminate at a specific location designated by the customer via a communications channel dedicated to his private use and not used or useable for public communications services; and (b) access only those distant locations (including, if appropriate, distant telephone central offices) specifically designated by the customer to meet his private communications needs."[92] Execunet failed on both counts. A customer could access the service from any telephone, on or off his premises, and he could call any telephone in a number of distant cities. In addition, none of the plant was dedicated to the use of a particular customer during any specified time. Execunet was a toll service and therefore illegal.

The court reversed the FCC and allowed Execunet. Its opinion essentially rested on the theory that once the FCC licensed a firm to provide *any* service, it could provide *every* service (with the same equipment) unless the FCC specifically focused upon, and denied it, the right to do so. The FCC had not specifically investigated whether the public would be harmed by MTS/WATS competition or determined that the "public convenience and necessity" required the limitation.[93] Thus, MCI could compete for AT&T's long-distance customers until the commission explicitly found that a restriction was required. The court admitted that the FCC "did not perhaps intend to open the field of common carriers communications generally," but it believed that the "constant stress on the fact that specialized carriers would provide new, innovative, and hitherto unheard-of communications services clearly indicates that it [the FCC] had no very clear idea of precisely how far or to what services the field should be opened."[94] Moreover, the Communications Act does not itself grant AT&T a monopoly. The FCC might do so, but only for good reason and "one such reason is not simply that AT&T got there first."[95]

In February 1978 the FCC again tried to stop Execunet by ruling that AT&T did not have to interconnect with MCI when it provided this service. The Court of Appeals for the District of Columbia again reversed. And the FCC began a proceeding designed specifically to examine whether or not AT&T should retain a monopoly of long-distance communications service. In the meantime, the SCC's would be allowed to compete.

The Basic Choices

The FCC has now inadvertently created a competitive long-distance communications market. And it now must squarely face the question of whether that competition undesirably threatens to undermine the Bell System and to raise rather than to lower costs. Initially, in allowing the SCCs into *specialized* common-carrier service, the FCC foresaw no real threat to AT&T's revenues. The private-line and other specialized markets amounted to about 3.5–4 percent of AT&T's total revenues.[96] Even in 1975 they accounted for only about $2 billion of AT&T's total $40 billion in revenue.[97] And because AT&T was able to respond through selective price cutting, the SCCs lost money. Indeed, in 1977 they lost $23 million on total revenues of $120 million.[98]

The decisions in *Docket 18128* and *Execunet,* however, have made a difference. The SCCs can now compete for ordinary long-distance MTS customers; AT&T will find it difficult to respond through selective price cutting. Thus, MCI now advertises that "long distance calls cost less when you use MCI with Bell." And it earned its first profit in 1978: $5 million on revenues of $74 million.[99] ITT and IBM are planning to offer intercity communications service—the latter through a domestic satellite system.[100]

The decisions thus far suggest that the FCC, in deciding upon the appropriate role for competition in longline communications, has three basic choices—each of which has drawbacks. It can allow entry and allow AT&T to cut prices in response; it can deny or limit entry; or it can allow entry and inhibit AT&T's price response.

Entry plus price response. To return to our original question, why not simply allow new firms to enter the longline communications business and also allow AT&T to respond by cutting its prices to incremental costs? To do so would provide a practical test of the existence of economies of scale; it would lead to price competition, lower long-distance prices, and possibly bring about less costly service; it would spur innovation and efficiency. Its proponents argue that it might lead to a host of new electronic services, just as the decision to allow competition in the sale of telephones has already broadened the scope of consumer choice.[101] In other words, the traditional arguments for competition—lower prices, more efficient production, greater innovation—seem to favor allowing new entry, without, in the FCC's words, maintaining a "price umbrella" over the heads of the new entrants.

The existence of a natural monopoly in a portion of AT&T's business (local service) combined with the existence of significant joint (local and long-distance) costs, however, produces several nontraditional, contrary considerations. First, there is a theoretical point (drawn from recent literature dealing with the "sustainability" of a natural monopoly).[102] If new entry is allowed into one portion of AT&T's markets, it may not be possible for AT&T to price the remainder of its services so as to cover its fixed costs. If, for example, the ferry boat takes all the cars from the bridge, the bridge may not be able to cover its fixed costs, because the trucks that remain may not be willing or able to pay high enough toll charges to do so. Indeed, the bridge is less likely to be able to cover its fixed charges if the bridge authority refuses to allow it to discriminate in price among its remaining customers, charging, say, cars less than trucks and large trucks more than small ones. And the FCC's decisions prohibiting "sharing and resale" (which inhibit price discrimination between large and small AT&T customers) may have this effect.

Yet it seems empirically unlikely that new entry into longline telecommunication could prevent the Bell System from covering its total costs *provided that* AT&T is allowed to adjust its other rates. More than half its revenues come from local service, which is a natural monopoly, not threatened by new entry. Thus, one suspects that rates could be adjusted so that total costs could be covered even if lower long-distance rates reduced AT&T's long-distance revenues. Indeed, empirical work suggests that this could be done and that the technical conditions for nonsustainability are not met.[103]

Second, predatory pricing presents a more practical difficulty. The regulator might inhibit classical predatory pricing, by a rule that prevented AT&T from raising a low price that drove a competitor from the field unless it could demonstrate "that the disappearance of the competitor is not the reason for the rate increase and that the higher rates are asked for because of other unanticipated changes."[104] Yet even if this rule made predatory pricing unprofitable for an *un*regulated firm (by preventing it from recouping its short-run losses), it would not necessarily discourage the regulated firm. AT&T might be willing to hold competitive long-distance rates below their incremental costs for quite a long time, because the regulator, not knowing that they were predatory, would allow AT&T to recoup its losses through higher residential rates. If AT&T's cost of capital were lower than its allowed rate of return, it would earn more profit by keeping its long-distance costs in its rate base than it would by abandoning long-distance service (see the Averch-Johnson discussion in Chapter 2). But even if this strategy led AT&T only to break even (or produced small losses), AT&T still might be willing to charge prices below incremental costs in order to maintain its control of the telecommunications industry—to prevent new firms from establishing themselves in part of the market and then, through technological development, expanding to threaten AT&T's local monopoly itself.[105] Moreover, regulation may provide AT&T an incentive to provide several joint services, each of which has low incremental costs (given the others) but which, taken together, are produced with unnecessarily expensive technology.[106]

Although there is no evidence that AT&T in fact has priced or would price predatorily in any of these ways, the facts that it has an incentive to do so and that the regulator could not readily determine whether it did so explains the FCC's reluctance to bring down the price umbrella (as demonstrated by Docket 18128).

Third, even without predatory pricing, the removal of the price umbrella would require a restructuring of rates. Rate averaging would disappear; rural rates might increase; and local rates would almost certainly increase. Separations rules would have to be rewritten, and that portion of the local rate base now paid for by long-distance tolls would have to be covered by local charges. This could be done; in fact, Charles River Associates has developed proposals for restructuring rates that would more closely reflect incremental costs and might not impose serious additional burdens upon residential users.[107] Yet the administrative burden of change would be great;[108] reliance by customers and individual expectations of reasonably settled rates would be undermined; and the political opposition to such change is likely to be great.[109] It is understandable why the FCC might be reluctant to remove the price umbrella and radically to changing rate structure, particularly if it believes that AT&T enjoys significant economies of scale in long-distance communications—for then AT&T will simply recapture its competitors' business after changing its rates. The bridge will drive the ferry boat from the market. And the only change will have been a restructuring of rates. Is such a change—albeit in the direction of economically more rational rates—worth the political and social costs involved? Of course, the FCC cannot be certain whether AT&T's long-distance monopoly is in fact "natural," and the FCC's other choices are not necessarily any more desirable.

Deny or limit entry. To deny entry risks depriving the public of the advantages of competition. Advocates of competition, such as Charles River Associates, make a convincing case that the communications industry is undergoing a technological revolution. Electronic advances and the development of computer technology have led to demands for new services, such as processing and transmissions services, and new ways to supply them. They argue that to remove the threat of competitive entry risks slowing down that advance. Moreover, it risks inhibiting the development of technology that would both lower costs and limit economies of scale, making communications markets structurally competitive.[110] Thus, simply retaining the monopoly through legal barriers to entry seems a highly unsatisfactory alternative.

Allow entry and handicap the competitors. The FCC, in practice, seems to be following a third alternative. It will allow entry, but seek to restrict it to a portion of the long-distance market. It will allow AT&T to cut its prices in response, but not allow it to cut those prices to incremental costs. In following this approach, the FCC acts as a handicapper. It will allow competitors to enter but not far enough to hurt AT&T, and it will protect them from AT&T's price responses. One can argue that any resulting inefficiency in private-line service (some amount of higher-cost facilities) is simply a price worth paying in order to obtain new competitors who can put pressure upon AT&T to innovate, to operate more efficiently, and to try to cut its prices. But this approach is dangerous, for the FCC is without standards to determine which competitors to allow to enter where, and how much protection to give them. One is reminded of the CAB's problems in allocating airline routes, acting as a handicapper and trying to treat each airline fairly. The risk in this approach is that it abandons economic criteria, because there are no such criteria that would tell the FCC how to handicap. And once economic criteria are abandoned, there is likely to be no consistent set of principles upon which the FCC can base its handcapping decisions.

Conclusion

The longline communications problem is different from those of airlines, trucking, natural gas, and even environmental pollution in one important respect. In those cases, one could find a plausible mismatch: it looked as if a change of mode would likely lead to a major improvement—a significantly greater likelihood of obtaining the objectives thought to call for regulation. In the case of longline communications, there is much less certainty. One is left with a range of choices, each of which has major drawbacks. Economists may tend to prefer the first—entry plus rate freedom. But they must be willing to run the risk that after radical changes in rate structure, the industry will remain monopolized by AT&T.

The important conclusion for purposes of this book is that the absence of a clear choice flows from the fact that at least one part of AT&T's service—local service—is a natural monopoly; it is regulated, and longline service is connected to it through joint costs. Those facts produce what is essentially a *regulatory* problem. The problem of competition in the production and sale of telephones and equipment is quite different, as long as one believes that there are not significant joint costs of production and service. But where natural monopoly exists and is significant, one can no longer argue that it, or those portions of the industry tied to it through joint costs, are automatically suited to competition. Rather, classical regulation is likely to be appropriate for part of the industry. Those who argue automatically for competitive solutions may be wrong. And detailed analysis is required before one can determine just where and how much regulation is required.

III

Practical Reform

16
From Candidate to Reform

The framework for analysis developed in this book helps identify existing programs that should be considered as potential subjects for individualized reform. It picks out candidates for reform, but it does not demonstrate in any individual case that reform should in fact be made or precisely how it should be carried out.

This chapter is designed to illuminate the process of moving from the stage of candidacy to that of reform. It will focus upon the achievement of airline regulatory reform. The Airline Deregulation Act of 1978[1] ended classical economic regulation of the airline industry by gradually phasing out price and entry controls and eventually abolishing the Civil Aeronautics Board.[2] The initial stages of bringing about that reform will be discussed both because the change represents the first major legislative effort to deregulate an industry[3] and because I can write with first-hand knowledge about some of the initial steps in the reform process.[4] The discussion is inevitably impressionistic and seeks to draw lessons from one instance in which reform was achieved. It is incomplete, viewing reform efforts from the perspective of a congressional committee staff. And it makes no claim about the extent to which those lessons can be generalized. Nonetheless, the discussion casts light on the problem of achieving reform.

The Elements of Implementation

Experience with airline deregulation suggests that identifying a particular regulatory program as a potential candidate for reform is only the first step in bringing about that reform. Certainly by 1975 airline regulation had been sufficiently studied by academics to warrant its recognition as a candidate. Caves[5] identified major anticompetitive harms of airline regulation in 1962, and Douglas and Miller[6] demonstrated how classical regulatory rules led to excessive service competition and undesirably high prices. Levine[7] and then Jordan[8] used experience with unregulated carriers in California to demonstrate that open competition would promote lower fares. These studies identified airline regulation as a likely candidate for reform. Considerable work was needed to achieve it.

The airline experience also suggests that the achievement of reform has three additional aspects. First, to know that change is truly desirable and practical the problem must be investigated further—empirically and in depth. Second, the reformers must produce a concrete alternative to existing regulation and a practical transition plan. Third, they must organize and deal with political factors that ultimately determine whether a new law is passed or a new agency chief is given a reform mandate. These three sets of factors are interrelated.

A detailed inquiry. Detailed empirical investigation of the industry or program in question is necessary for several reasons. First, any actual regulatory program, regardless of its major objectives, may serve a host of subsidiary objectives. Thus, even if the original premise on which airline regulation was based—to prevent destructive competition—is now invalid, it is important to recognize that through the years the regulatory program may have come to serve other desirable social ends. It may, for example, promote service to small communities which, in turn, helps to develop the economies of those communities and the surrounding region. It may help save fuel and thus serve national defense efforts, or it may enable more efficient use of the postal service. One can produce numerous theoretical arguments to justify airline regulation. But only after hearing from the people directly affected can one form an intelligent judgment about the likely magnitude of any such effects and balance them against a similar estimate of harm. For example, if one argues for airline regulation on the grounds that it subsidizes small communities, it is important to know what the extent of the subsidy is likely to be in fact. An empirical effort to determine who is actually being helped or hurt by the program is essential if one is to evaluate the arguments that will be made in their favor and to avoid wasting scarce political resources reforming programs that in practice cause minimal harm.

Second, regardless of the theoretical merits or disadvantages of the program, firms, their customers, their suppliers, and others may have adjusted to the existing system and to the patterns of service that regulation has produced. Unions of airline employees, for example, may have negotiated seniority provisions in their contracts on the assumption that individual firms are not likely to withdraw from service on existing routes. The significance of any such facts is that they indicate reliance that may warrant some protection from change for reasons of fairness, that they signal possible complexity in the likely actual effects of any change in practice, and that they identify groups who will be hurt and who therefore will object to the reform effort. Again, empirical investigation is needed to give the reformers some feeling for whether the benefits of change will outweigh its costs.

Third, empirical investigation is likely to be needed because existing studies, while academically satisfactory, often suffer from inadequate information. Their authors suffer from some of the same problems that plague the regulators when they seek information for purposes of setting standards. Economists may have to rely upon numbers generated in sampling or statistics-collecting processes. These may be out of date or only tangentially related to the facts that the economist wishes to know. Frequently, the most relevant data are held by companies as trade secrets which they are unwilling to supply to academic economists. Firms may respond, however, to a congressional request for information. For example, academic studies showing that cross-country air fares were too high were less convincing to many congressmen than projections by Lockheed and Boeing as to the cost of flying a B-747 cross-country with an all-coach seating configuration filled to 70 percent capacity. The Boeing projections were prepared by a firm with a direct commercial interest in accuracy on the matter, with access to the factual statistical base needed, with ability to make accurate projections, and with an apparent interest in asserting the opposite of what its projection showed (namely, that such lower fares were economically possible). Academic economists, moreover, are more likely to provide detailed studies about the comparative efficiency of policy alternatives than to study the changes in income distribution that reform will produce. An elected official must be concerned with who are the gainers and losers, and what they may gain or lose. Further, since firms tend to focus their work to meet the financial or political demands of the moment, it is highly probable that thorough empirical work on relevant questions will not have been done until a congressional or executive branch investigation forces the private or "nonprofit" experts to turn their time and attention to the issue (and, in some way or other, pays for the results).

Finally, the detailed investigation is itself necessary to convince others that the proponents of reform are serious, thorough, and have made their case. The political strength needed to change an agency's behavior or to enact legislation is unlikely to be generated unless there is widespread conviction that the necessary homework has been done.

Political factors. Once it has been determined that major substantive reform is in fact desirable, a political coalition of sufficient strength to achieve it must be developed. Major change is likely to require direct and continuing activity by major political figures, such as the president (who at a minimum must appoint commissioners favoring the new direction) and leading senators and congressmen. How can they be persuaded to devote the necessary time and effort?

First, the issue must become politically visible. Congressional hearings may accomplish this objective, as can a presidential policy announcement. There must be sufficient activity over a sufficiently long period of time to capture the attention of the press or others, whose interest will, in turn, reinforce and promote that of politicians or administrators who are seeking the change. The process of rendering an issue visible calls the potential benefits of change to the attention of those it is likely to help, so that they ally themselves with those who favor it. Most important, it is a means of forcing those who are acting together to bring about the change to spend the time and effort needed to do so.

Second, as the issue becomes visible it must be characterized in a way that will tend to strengthen the political alliance in its favor. In fact, such a characterization will tend to promote its visibility. Thus airline deregulation was brought to the public's attention through the Ford administration's proposals for airline reform, Senator Kennedy's hearings on the CAB, and support from the CAB itself. The Ford administration first unveiled support of airline deregulation at the Kennedy hearings which, in turn, were designed to depict regulatory reform as an effort to help the consumer and to lessen burdensome regulatory bureaucracy. If the issue is seen as one of "lower prices," "helping the consumer," or "freeing business from the 'dead hand of regulation,' " it can pick up support, time, and effort from many persons who will not interest themselves in "higher airline profits," "more efficient use of aircraft," or "more efficient or effective airline regulatory programs." Thus, political support is, in part, a function of how one sees the issue—how it has been characterized—and that is a matter that is partly, but not wholly, within the control of those who are seeking to bring about reform.

Third, the coalition that will help implement the reform must be formed within the government (in both executive and legislative branches) as well as outside. The Kennedy airline hearings demonstrated that the Departments of Justice and Transportation, the Councils of Economic Advisors and Wage and Price Stability, and a host of other agencies believed that the existing system was wrong, and this had a powerful effect in convincing Congress to try to change the system. It also provided the Senate committee conducting the hearings with information and assistance without which the hearings could not have been nearly as effective.

The coalition of outside forces consists not simply of those with economic interest on one side or the other, but also of those with ideological views that correspond to positions as characterized by the issues used to make reform visible. Thus, consumer groups tended to support airline deregulation but so did many business groups and more conservative senators with ideological preferences for laissez-faire or less government. Similarly, the airline industry and several major unions opposing deregulation sought the support of those politicians whose ideological instincts favored regulation. Characterizing the program in a manner designed to attract ideological support was important to the development of the reform effort.

A practical reform plan. The reformer must develop a practical and fair plan to allow a transition from the regulated regime to the new system. Such a plan serves three functions. First, it demonstrates that the reformer has thought through the problem, to the point where one can see concretely who is likely to be helped or hurt over the next few years. This fact helps overcome a fairly common fear of the unknown. Second, it allows the reformer to ease the adverse effects of sudden change on those who might be hurt. To force those who have relied on the past system to face sudden drastic change without some sort of cushion is often perceived as unfair. Third, from a strictly political viewpoint, a transition plan that cushions adverse effects and that allows those who gain from the change to compensate losers will soften the political opposition and facilitate its passage.

Airline deregulation did not require a complex transition system. Rather the announcement of its consideration together with the several years needed to bring the new system into being—through the appointment of a new CAB chairman and the enactment of new legislation—itself provided gradual change, cushioning the effect of the change and allowing those affected time to adjust.

The way in which these three requirements—the need for a detailed inquiry, for a consideration of political factors, and for a practical reform plan—were implemented as the campaign to bring about airline regulatory reform began is seen in the following discussions of the Kennedy hearings and the Ford administration's actions and proposals.

The Kennedy Hearings

Any effort to accomplish significant change in the mode of regulation is likely to require major political action—which means action by important political personalities. If so, those who wish change must successfully carry out two separate political tasks. First, they must make the issue politically visible. Second, they must gather sufficient political force to secure its enactment. For the most part, academic discussion has focused on the problem of creating political coalitions without considering the related problem of how the issue becomes politically visible. Thus, prior to the Kennedy hearings the conventional wisdom was that those who might lose through deregulation—the airlines, the unions of airline workers, and certain business travelers—would know of their potential losses and strongly oppose change, while the potential gainers, primarily nonbusiness travelers, would neither know nor care enough to overcome their opposition. This analysis proved faulty primarily because it overlooked the potential of the first of the political tasks—making the issue visible—and the effect that accomplishing the first would have upon the second.

The need for political visibility arises out of the fact that "political time"—that is to say, the time and attention of important politicians—is an extremely scarce resource. The number of issues competing for their attention is enormous. To provide an obvious example, a congressman is more likely to vote for a bill if the president himself, say, or some prominent senator (not a staff member) calls him (not a staff member) and requests his support. A personal call is flattering and its recipient knows that the caller realizes that the recipient is being helpful and thus anticipates future reciprocation. Similarly, the greater public attention that an issue enjoys, the more likely the congressman will take the time to learn about its merits; and, without knowledge of the merits of change, there is an instinctive tendency to favor the status quo. This is no more than human nature at work.

The airline issue was ripe for political action after it had become visible. Visibility seemed to depend on several factors. First, what publicity had the issue received? If a given issue is persistently called to the attention of the public, the politician feels he should study it. He will be asked where he stands, and to admit ignorance is to be open to the charge of not doing his job. Moreover, the politician may see direct benefit in becoming involved in a visible issue. He must consider whether and what sort of publicity the issue is likely to bring. In part, this concern is related to his need for reelection. His reelection depends upon his being seen by his constituents as performing effectively. And this perception requires both that he accomplish results and that the press reports his actions to his constituents. In fact, "accomplishment" as perceived by his constituents may be at least as important for attaining reelection and increased political power as is an attractive voting record. "Visibility" is thus closely related to "publicity."

Visibility, however, does not mean *only* publicity. A second factor at work is the thoroughness with which the issue has been studied. Whether a regulatory issue is politically ripe for change depends in part upon whether the opponents of change can raise objections that reasonably evoke questions in the minds of, say, congressmen, about whether serious harm or disaster is possible. Opponents of reform can be relied upon to supply congressmen and others with information sufficient to raise some doubts. Many congressmen will take the path of least resistance and call for further study of the matter. Before pushing ahead to secure reform, one would like to know that one has the answers to these questions, both to know what is right, and because without them the net result is likely to be no more than "further study" of the matter.

Third, for an issue to become politically visible and "live," there must be at least the *potential* for putting together a coalition of political forces sufficient to lead to action. The fact that there is widespread opposition to a measure, or that there is strong opposition among certain groups, is not sufficient to prevent a coalition from developing. Moreover, the process of making the issue visible will itself help to develop and shape the coalition. All that is required is that it not look hopeless as the issue begins to obtain publicity, for few politicians (or others) wish to devote their time and efforts to a hopeless cause.

Once the issue has become visible and live, the political forces that have been generated will tend to determine the outcome. Then the problem is one of maintaining publicity and public pressure, of maintaining the interest and efforts of many different politicians, and of the implementing bargaining and strategy needed to obtain legislation. This second part of the problem will be touched on only briefly here.[9] We shall focus primarily on how airline regulatory reform was made politically visible—the primary objective of the Kennedy hearings.

Preparation

By 1974, when Senator Kennedy began to prepare hearings on airline regulation, the academic work described above had been accomplished. Airline regulation had been severely criticized, much of the detailed groundwork had been laid, and a clear alternative to existing regulation could be formulated. Thus, if a senator chose to go into the arena of regulation at all, airlines became a natural choice.

Yet why might one conduct an investigation in the area of regulatory reform? To some extent it reflected the interest of the subcommittee that Senator Kennedy chaired. The Subcommittee on Administrative Practice and Procedure was looking for a mission in 1974 and arguably had jurisdiction over administrative procedures in this area. Yet there were sound reasons of a less coincidental nature that made airlines a logical candidate for a detailed senatorial investigation. The institutional and political arguments in favor of such an investigation by the subcommittee in 1974 appeared to be the following: (1) The ultimate statute would lead to lower prices, while maintaining the service that travelers desired. (2) The subcommittee would have a coherent mission and a theme for future investigations. The underlying issue in the CAB hearings would be "More competition or more regulation?"—an issue that underlies most of the controversy involving the Interstate Commerce Commission (ICC), the Federal Maritime Commission (FMC), and a host of other agencies. The subcommittee could go from the CAB to some of those others. (3) The subcommittee would develop expertise enabling it to deal with other economic regulatory problems. The framework that the staff would develop would be easily transferred to the ICC, the FMC, and many other areas. This same expertise would make it easier to handle more complicated problems involving such areas as energy shortage and possible nationalization. (4) The subcommittee would be, and would be seen to be, involved in a nonglamorous, detailed, intricate, "good government" job.

The major arguments against CAB hearings appeared to be: (1) The hearings would involve highly complicated issues and extensive, time-consuming preparatory work. (2) They would be unlikely to receive much publicity. As in most regulatory matters, the consumer (the main beneficiary) is not very interested in the issue. On the other hand, the industry would know only too well what was going on. (3) It might be difficult to obtain jurisdiction. (4) Because of the complexity and potential dryness of airline regulation issues, it would be difficult to articulate a clear, simple theme for the hearings. There were some obvious possibilities for themes—for example, "help the consumer," "free the captive agency," and "more competition"—but all of them seemed either insufficiently obvious as products of reform or insufficiently vivid to grab attention.

The driving motive for undertaking the task was one senator's feeling that something could be accomplished—a feeling that arises out of the possession of a framework, the availability of preliminary work, and the existence of a clear, guiding objective.

Once Senator Kennedy decided to hold hearings on Civil Aeronautics Board regulation, preparations for the hearings began. The first step, which began in the spring of 1974, was to draw up a list of issues that the hearings, planned for several months later, would explore. Given the academic work already completed, it was easy to draw up such a list. A memorandum of the Administrative Practice Subcommittee, dated May 1974, arising out of discussions between the staff and Senator Kennedy, described the issues under headings roughly as follows:

Issue 1: Why are fares on unregulated intrastate routes much lower than on apparently comparable, regulated interstate routes? . . .

Issue 2: Does CAB regulation raise prices by forcing the consumer to pay for excess capacity? . . .

Issue 3: Have recent CAB decisions allowing airlines to agree to restrict schedules led to higher fares and worse service as well? . . .

Issue 4: What is the effect of the CAB's action in allowing a "pass-thru" of additional fuel costs? . . .

Issue 5: What are the CAB's restrictions on charters? Why should Freddie Laker not be allowed to provide "airbus" service? . . .

Issue 6: Has the CAB severely restricted entry into the industry? Why? . . .

Issue 7: Are the arguments against increased price competition valid? . . .

    a. Is it true that prices will not fall? . . .

    b. Is it true that the CAB does not now prevent airlines from cutting prices? . . .

    c. Is it true that price competition will prove "destructive"? . . .

    d. Is it true that competition will lead the airlines to discontinue service on "subsidized" routes serving smaller communities?

Other issues also mentioned in the memorandum were overbooking, limitations on lost luggage liability, and first-class fares.

For each of these issues, the memorandum analyzed the arguments, reformulated the questions and suggested how information might be gathered that would help resolve the questions. It also listed the major books and articles in the field, which the subcommittee staff was told to read. The memo structured the hearing along the lines of a judicial inquiry. Thus, the basic question—should more competition be allowed—was broken down into subissues, on each of which evidence was to be accumulated. The purpose was to use the hearing for a comprehensive gathering of information that would allow an informed policy judgment. In short, the memo provided an intellectual structure and organized the task.

The second step in preparation was to commence liaison with allies within the executive branch and elsewhere. These allies and their activities would aid the committee in producing a comprehensive set of hearings. Not only would they mobilize the resources of the executive branch to address the issues, but also they would provide witnesses to testify at the hearings. Thus, in August 1974 the committee counsel spoke at length to John Snow, then in charge of congressional relations in the Department of Transportation, James Miller at the Council of Economic Advisors, George Eads at the Council of Wage and Price Stability, Thomas Kauper and Keith Clearwaters in the Antitrust Division of the Justice Department, and academics such as Michael Levine at the California Institute of Technology and William Jordan at the University of Toronto. All of these people tended to favor airline regulatory reform and had begun a dialogue among themselves over the possibility of an administration reform initiative. Those outside government could supply information and ideas; those within government would supply resources and would help move their own organizations toward a deregulatory position. They would see Senator Kennedy's initiative as a helpful and complementary means of doing so.

The third preparatory step consisted of beginning to collect the necessary information. The committee staff drew up extensive questionnaires to send to the CAB and to the airlines. They had as their object to elicit hard, factual information that could be used in the hearings and as a basis for the later report, and to obtain information that could be used dramatically to illustrate the case. Thus, the subcommittee staff contacted each CAB-regulated airline (and several other, intrastate carriers), informed them of the forthcoming hearings, and sent them one hundred written questions covering information related to company records, studies, policies, proposals, revenues, costs, purchases, training programs, customer policies, and procedures. The questions were not picked at random, but were chosen to elicit information that would cast light on the issues at stake; they were reviewed by Miller, Eads, Snow, Levine, and others with this object in mind. The companies all sent responses—indeed, cartons of material—of which 10–20 percent proved useful.

The CAB officer in charge of congressional relations coordinated an effort within the agency to produce material in response to fifty written questions. The CAB sent certain records of agency decisions of the preceding few years, of procedures the agency used, of meetings and conversations between board members and industry representatives, of studies done for the board, of policies that guided the board in decision making, and of applications for new routes. It also sent a host of factual information on costs and profits. Almost every bit of the material contained in the cartons returned by the board to the subcommittee proved useful. Additional information and assistance were provided by Reuben Robertson and Mimi Cutler of the Aviation Consumer Action Project.

The final preparatory step consisted of organizing the material received and preparing a schedule for the hearings and lists of witnesses. Senator Kennedy decided that the hearings would take place in January, February, and early March 1975. The tentative scheme of organization drawn up would organize the seven days according to subject matter: day 1, overview of the problem; day 2, the unregulated-intrastate versus regulated-interstate example; day 3, the CAB's route policy; day 4, the CAB's consumer policy; day 5, the CAB's rate policy; day 6, questioning the board; and day 7, the capacity-restricting agreements. In essence the intellectual structure of the enterprise controlled the structure of the hearings. The gathering of background facts allowed the issues to be fully focused upon and helped make certain that the relevant questions were asked. That information, together with additional information produced at the hearing, made possible the writing of the comprehensive report that was referred to earlier.[10]

The effectiveness of the preparation—and of the hearings themselves—was largely due to the fact that they were guided by an overall policy direction. The theory that more competition and less regulation were needed was to be tested; it supplied a framework for developing the issues, each of which would help determine whether the theory should be adopted in practice.

The line between testing a hypothesis and prejudging an issue, however, can be a narrow one. Hence, it was important to take steps to see that the hearings were conducted fairly, that all sides of each issue were heard, and that the subcommittee's recommendations were based on the evidence received. First, the subcommittee staff informed all interested parties in advance about the hearings and asked them to submit information. The detailed questionnaire sent to each airline and to the board revealed specifically each subissue that would be considered and suggested what evidence was likely to be relevant on each side. Second, the subcommittee notified each witness well in advance not only what issues would be discussed, but who would testify and what their position would probably be. The staff spoke to representatives of the airlines and their trade associations as well as to the board's critics. Third, representatives of divergent points of view were invited to testify on each issue. Debate and clashing points of view were sought. Representatives of all major airlines testified and were informed in advance about the likely arguments. The board members themselves testified each day but one. The entire board testified for a full day late in the hearings to discuss criticisms previously made against it. Fourth, the report and important intermediate documents (such as conclusions about the relevance of the California experience) were circulated to the industry and to the board; criticisms and corrections were received, and these were incorporated into the final report. Indeed, it was thought that if change was warranted, it was likely to occur only if it appeared that the strongest arguments *against* change had been fully and fairly considered.

The ultimate safeguards for the CAB and the industry (which opposed deregulation) lay in the following facts. First, though the hearings successfully brought the reform issue to the public's attention, they were only the first step. Many further hearings were held by the Senate and House Aviation Committees over the subsequent three years before legislation was passed. The industry and the board had ample opportunity to correct any mistakes or omissions in the subcommittee's hearings or report. Second, the subcommittee stood ready to reach different conclusions, had the evidence turned out differently. There is, of course, no way to prove this statement, for the evidence in fact supported deregulation. It may be relevant, however, to note that initially the subcommittee thought in terms of minor changes that would have introduced a modicum of price competition into the industry. At the beginning of the hearings only Ralph Nader argued for total deregulation. An evaluation of the evidence collected, however, suggested that stronger steps in that direction were called for (as the report suggests), and the subcommittee eventually made recommendations for major change.

The Actual Hearings

The actual hearings served three separate but interrelated functions—as catalyst, as information-gatherer, and as theater. Each of these functions was an essential element in the effort to bring about change.

The hearings as catalyst. The initial function of the Senate hearing was to force several agencies of government to focus upon the problem and provide others with an appropriate forum to express their views. Thus, the Ford administration was generally in favor of deregulation in 1974, but its position had not yet been crystallized into a formal proposal. When the Kennedy staff began to talk to administration officials in August 1974, it was not clear that the administration would soon reach consensus on any particular reform plan. Yet once they knew that hearings would be held in January, they accelerated their timetable to develop such a proposal, for the hearings represented both an opportunity and a possible threat.

The opportunity is obvious: there would be a forum for announcing a major policy initiative. The threat is only slightly more subtle. The committee counsel could tell the Department of Transportation (DOT) that the secretary of transportation would be asked to testify in January. He would be asked to state the administration's position on airline reform. Would he have an answer? What would it be?

The fact that a hearing date was set was sufficient to arm the proponents of reform within the administration with an argument for making a timely, high-level policy decision. But what substantive decision would be made was not obvious. As late as September 1974, the secretary of transportation made a public effort to force air carriers to agree upon minimum charter rates for transatlantic service—a policy directly the opposite of the procompetitive policy that the administration was later to espouse. Reversal of that policy required confrontation within the executive branch and a White House decision. The prospect of the hearings could be used to provoke that decision and to influence its direction.

Announcement of the administration's position was provoked in part by the need to prepare testimony. Arguably, the direction of the decision was influenced to some extent by which people the subcommittee asked to testify and by the informal arrangements made by the subcommittee and its allies within the administration to see that the right people wrote the testimony. To be more specific, it was apparent that John Snow and William A. Kutzke within the DOT understood the subject thoroughly, would favor deregulation, and would urge the department to take a firm position. Another assistant secretary of transportation, Robert Binder, strongly favored the status quo and regulated fares (although he later became a supporter of reform). Thus, it was essential that Snow, not Binder, have primary responsibility for the testimony. Binder was in charge of policy planning; Snow., in charge of congressional relations. It was both desirable and reasonable for Snow, rather than Binder, to deal with the subcommittee staff. His previous involvement and interest made him the logical person for the DOT to put in charge.

Similarly, if a final decision was to be made at the White House it was important that the majority of those at the key White House meetings favor deregulation. This could be influenced in part by whom the subcommittee asked to testify. Thus, when the counsel drew up a tentative list of witnesses for the first day of hearings, it included, in addition to the secretary of transportation, the head of the Antitrust Division, a member of the Council of Economic Advisors, and the staff director of the Council on Wage and Price Stability. In each instance, the agency would be expected to favor procompetitive reform. Moreover, the subcommittee staff spoke to many of the people at each agency in charge of preparing the testimony to make certain they were well informed about the issues and familiar with the relevant previous studies. Finally, there were people at the White House, such as the president's counsel, who were interested in procompetitive airline reform, knew something about the subject, and were willing to help. They, too, would seek responsibility for the subject matter involved, would respond to requests from within the administration to help resolve differences of opinion, and, in doing so, would tend to favor the reform position.

In other words, the scheduled hearings were useful to many within the executive branch and Congress who sought to develop a network of persons favoring reform, who would work on testimony, who were each in a position to influence policy, and who would help one another exert still greater influence upon the process of policy formulation. It was no easy matter to overcome the bureaucratic resistance to major policy change in a limited amount of time. The process was facilitated by the ability of Snow and others to point out to cabinet members and others the obvious advantages of being able to announce a change in January at Senator Kennedy's hearings, and the disadvantages of looking as if their policy were incoherent.

On the first day of the hearings Acting Secretary of Transportation John Barnum announced a major policy initiative on the part of the administration. The present structure of regulation, he said, "is outdated, inequitable, inefficient, uneconomical, and sadly irrational." He went on to describe the administration's proposal for reform of the CAB, calling for airline price competition within a broad "zone of reasonableness," significant relaxation of rules governing entry and exit, and strict limitations on the CAB's authority to grant exemptions from the antitrust laws. In addition to Barnum, Thomas Kauper, head of the Antitrust Division, Lewis Engman, chairman of the Federal Trade Commission, and James Miller, representing the Council of Economic Advisors, testified to the same effect. A clear administration policy had been formulated and forcefully enunciated.

The hearings may have acted as a catalyst for other institutions as well. The individual airlines, forced to develop testimony, began to reassess their positions on CAB regulation. Rather than taking that regulation as a given, they would have to ask themselves how overall regulatory policy and each major aspect of that policy affected their operations. In each instance, the firm would have to make staff studies designed to show how change would affect it. Many airlines had not seriously considered the potential benefits of total freedom to compete on the basis of price, for previously it had not been a real possibility. Other issues had never been considered either. The necessary studies, provoked by the hearings, simply reaffirmed some airlines in their opposition to regulatory change. But in other instances the studies modified instinctive opposition and led some airlines to favor radical departures from the status quo. They led others to dust off proposals for new service—such as World Airways' plan to fly coast-to-coast for $99—bring them up to date, and once again seek to secure CAB approval. Thus, the threat or promise of hearings—the asking of questions and the request for testimony—forced each institution involved to reassess its position, to develop new information, and to put its own bureaucracy to work to develop and assess alternatives. At the same time, the prospect of hearings provided an incentive for consumer groups, such as the Aviation Consumer Action Project, to organize their own resources and information and prepare testimony. The more detailed and serious the hearings appeared to be, the more seriously they were taken, and the greater the likelihood that the relevant groups would undertake work and possibly develop new positions.

The hearings as information-gatherer. The primary function of the hearings was to gather information that would help to write the report. The report did not have to produce empirical information that would definitively resolve every issue, yet it had to be comprehensive. The existing relevant empirical information had to be gathered, and insofar as it was feasible to develop new information that would tend to resolve an issue, that work had to be done. The hearings could lead those in possession of the information to organize and to reveal it, and lead those best able to undertake the new empirical work to do so. The report would help those favoring reform develop a reputation for having dealt thoroughly and fairly with the objections to it—and such a reputation would help convince congressmen without adequate time to read the report to follow its recommendations.

The controversy over the "California experience" provides a concrete example of the way in which the information-gathering process worked. Experience with intrastate carriers in California and Texas appeared to provide strong confirmation for the thesis that competition among carriers brings about significantly lower fares. Open competition was allowed in California until the mid-1960s. And the Texas Aeronautics Commission in the early 1970s allowed a new firm, Southwest Airlines, into the market with freedom to cut fares. The result was fares on non-CAB-regulated intrastate routes only 50–60 percent as high as those on apparently comparable (regulated) interstate routes. For example, in 1974 the traveler flying 338 miles between San Francisco and Los Angeles on Pacific Southwest Airlines (PSA) paid $18.75; the traveler flying the 399 miles between Washington and Boston on CAB-regulated carriers paid $41.67.[11]

The regulated airlines argued that this comparison was misleading. California and Texas were "special cases." The fare differences reflected: (1) weather conditions, (2) greater traffic density, (3) direction of traffic flow, (4) less air and ground congestion, (5) fewer costs from interline connections with other carriers, (6) different aircraft types, (7) less need to provide "through" service, and (8) less need to support other routes in the system.[12]

The subcommittee then tried to examine each of these factors. A check with the Federal Aviation Administration revealed that there were no significant additional costs due to weather differences. An analysis and comparison of a host of different interstate and intrastate routes showed that the same price differences existed for routes of identical traffic density (for example, Los Angeles–Sacramento transporting 915,000 passengers per year, and Boston-Washington transporting 981,000). And by using "block-to-block" (ramp-to-ramp) times for purposes of comparison, one could eliminate the effects of air and ground congestion; again, the price difference stayed the same. The subcommittee requested the Air Transport Association (the major industry trade association) to commission an independent study of the causes of fare differences. That study showed that the host of differences listed by the industry could account for no more than $6 of a price difference that amounted to $20–30 on most routes. The subcommittee went on to request cost information from the airlines as to specific routes. American Airlines submitted detailed information, which showed that their Boston-Washington flight cost $5,752 round trip, based on a Boeing 727-200, with 121 seats, filled on average 55 percent full. PSA, flying the same plane in California, installed 158 seats, filled on average 60 percent full. Thus, if American had carried 95 passengers on average, as did PSA, instead of 66 it could have reduced its fares 30 percent. This fact went far toward showing that the price difference reflected fuller planes, and it helped support the argument that price competition induced the airlines to offer the lower-fare/fuller-plane service that most travelers wanted.[13]

All information was compiled and sent to the airlines with a request for confirmation, refutation, or additional information. The information and the responses allowed the subcommittee to write a section of its report that dealt comprehensively with the California and Texas experience and carefully described the considerable extent to which it offered support for regulatory reform.[14] The net result was that the argument against the use of the California experience simply dropped out of the public debate. As late as the spring of 1975 the chairman of the board of United Airlines, in a letter to *The Wall Street Journal*, had defended vigorously the claim that California was a "special case," listing most of the factors mentioned above. Once the subcommittee's letter with its accompanying information was circulated, however, the carriers stopped making the "special case" argument. Of course, the trained economist might not have needed all that investigation in order to be convinced of the relevance of the California experience. But the airlines themselves (and as a result the informed public) could not be convinced until they were shown that their objections had been considered, treated fairly, and investigated thoroughly. Then, however reluctantly, they were convinced (or at least saw no further advantage in the issue), and the point was established as valid in the public policy debate.

Each of the major objections to reform that the hearings forced to the surface had to be treated similarly. Those objections, raised by the CAB, the airlines, and others, included the following:

1. too much new competition would result in reduced service to smaller communities;
2. less regulation would increase risks to individual firms;
3. increased risk might reduce willingness to invest in new aircraft;
4. existing airport financing arrangements are premised on continuance of the existing system;
5. existing labor arrangements are premised on the continuance of the existing system;
6. less regulation might lead to an industry of only four or five firms;
7. change might mean predatory pricing or destructive competition;
8. competition might destroy the complex national airline network; and
9. competition might make air travel less safe.

The hearings could not systematically prove or disprove all these claims. Rather, they could marshal the existing arguments and information, bring about the necessary additional work, and then suggest a reasonable policy given the state of current information.

The subcommittee's treatment of the "small town" argument illustrates the way in which different types of evidence can be marshaled in support of a conclusion. The argument (in support of regulation) consisted of the claim that airlines earning large profits on popular routes used them to subsidize service to smaller communities. The traditional reply—that it was unfair to charge the cross-country traveler more to subsidize the air travel of others—was unconvincing to those who feared loss of service to their own smaller communities. After looking into the subject, the subcommittee agreed with general academic researchers in reaching a stronger conclusion: the argument was weak because no significant amount of cross-subsidy existed. It then supported the conclusion with three types of evidence.

First, the subcommittee report, drawing on the academic argument of Douglas, Miller, and Eads, claimed that it was illogical to believe that many airlines provided service on routes over which (incremental) costs exceeded (incremental) revenues. For one thing, service competition (especially extra scheduling, which tends to reduce load factors) on heavily traveled, long-distance routes would tend to eat up any extra profit. And transcontinental load factors were indeed lower than average system-wide load factors. In addition, the CAB for some time had allowed the carriers to abandon money-losing service. Why would the carriers not have done so? Further, accounting conventions tended to understate the profitability of short hauls. Finally, commuter carriers already provided service to hundreds of smaller communities and stood ready to pick up service that the trunk lines abandoned.

These arguments, supported with facts, nonetheless proved less convincing than an argument made on the basis of firsthand experience with United Airlines. The committee asked United to determine how many routes it might abandon under deregulation because they were unprofitable in the sense that revenues generated (in 1974) "failed to cover incremental costs." United first wrote that it would consider abandoning as unprofitable 75 of the 327 city pairs that it served. It later revised its estimate to 58. The committee counsel, together with George Eads, then assistant director of the Council on Wage and Price Stability, went to Chicago and spent a day going over a computer printout of United's route system together with United's executives. By the end of the day, there was agreement on several points. The fact that United's accounting system showed these 58 routes as unprofitable did not necessarily mean they were so, or would be abandoned with deregulation. Four of the 58 routes were flown in order to position aircraft; 17 were flown because they generated traffic that flew United to a farther point; these 21 city pairs formed an essential part of a larger route that was profitable overall. Thus, United would classify only 37 routes as actually unprofitable. From these 37 one should subtract 8 more routes each of which was shorter than 60 miles in length, for it was inconceivable that trunk-line service was needed on routes of 24, 30, or 57 miles. (Such segments in fact formed part of a larger "loss route," and these had been double counted.) There remained 29 route segments that might be viewed as beneficiaries of cross-subsidy. These 29 segments averaged 155 miles in length; they accounted together for 130 million revenue passenger-miles, or one half of one percent of United's total domestic revenue passenger-miles. United claimed that it lost $5.5 million serving them. The important point is that if United's cross-subsidy experience was typical and even if commuter airlines did not pick up such abandoned routes, all such service (nationwide) could be retained through a small direct subsidy of $25 million. In other words, direct though impressionistic evidence from the nation's largest airline showed the problem as relatively insignificant.

The third type of evidence consisted of a study prepared by the industry trade association, the Air Transport Association (ATA), on the potential abandonment of small-town service.[15] The ATA had continually made the small-town argument, and the subcommittee had continually urged the ATA to commission a study to investigate the empirical magnitude of the problem. It finally did so, using a Lockheed computer simulation model designed for other purposes. The ATA executives reappeared, with reams of computer printouts in hand, announcing that deregulation would mean an end of service on 373 non-stop route segments. (They also sent copies of these results to each congressman and senator, highlighting the routes in their districts or states that were candidates for abandonment.) Examination of the study by independent economists, the Council of Economic Advisors, and the Council on Wage and Price Stability, however, revealed that it was fatally flawed: it assumed that the entire national airline system was owned by a single monopolist airline with freedom to maximize profits. That is to say, instead of answering the question "How will *competing* airlines respond when given freedom to cut service?" it answered the question "How would a monopolist airline (with resulting profits of around $2 billion) respond when given freedom to cut service?" The academic and governmental experts quickly responded that the study was totally irrelevant, that it was obvious that a monopolist would reduce the level of service well below competitive levels. The ATA could muster no respectable independent support for the conclusions it drew from the study. And the study left the overall impression that the ATA had asked the wrong question because it disliked the answer it got in response to the right one. Thus, the study weakened rather than strengthened the industry's position.

Eventually, consulting firms, at the request of the DOT, made more detailed empirical studies that confirmed the conclusion that the loss of service to small communities would be minimal. Still, perhaps the most convincing point consisted of the subcommittee's ability to state that its staff had met with United's executives and gone over its route system in detail, segment by segment. This fact tended to increase the credibility of the subcommittee and its conclusions, for it suggested a degree of practical knowledge of detail that a more academic study, even if more thorough, often lacks.

In essence, the hearings not only allowed the subcommittee to identify the major issues and points of disagreement, but also allowed it to obtain the information needed to resolve those points in a reasonably convincing way. The information was incorporated into a 250-page report, which was then circulated in draft form to all witnesses, the CAB, every airline, and other interested persons for comment. Detailed comments were received from most, and the report was corrected, amended, and revised to take them into account. The result was a document that was very difficult to attack, that gained a public reputation for being "thorough," "comprehensive," and "responsible." That reputation in turn helped to produce a political attitude that the time had come for change. Whether or not politicians read it, they felt they could rely on it; most of the issues had been dealt with; and change was unlikely to produce disaster. The industry could not point to any major flaws—omitted points or inaccuracies—within the report. This fact helped the airline issue become attractive to politicians, other than those already involved, who wished to be perceived as acting effectively to bring about some type of regulatory reform in the public interest.

It is important to keep in mind, however, that it would have been difficult to manufacture any such reputation or feeling of "ripeness." The reputation had to be based on an underlying truth. The report had to reflect a detailed effort to obtain the facts and to explore the issues fairly.

The hearings as drama. To analogize a legislative hearing to a judicial or administrative fact-finding hearing is to miss an essential difference. The legislative hearing has a very definite political purpose. It has an educational objective, and one of its major goals is to mobilize support for a policy change. The oral hearing itself cannot produce detailed records of factual information. It must make the main points of the argument and do so in a way that is both comprehensible and interesting to the general public.

In other words, the congressional hearing moves on two levels at once: on one level it gathers in written form the masses of dry, detailed fact needed to write a report and develop proposals; but it also moves on a more dramatic and educational oral level, which should illustrate the issues clearly and succinctly to the layman. It can do so only by educating the press, which will report the story. And it can do this only by producing testimony and events that strike journalists as interesting and important. The CAB hearings suggest how these objectives can be satisfied.

First, the structure of the hearings told a story. Each aspect of the overall problem was covered on a different day. Moreover, the way in which it was covered was designed to communicate a message that was not lost on the press or the public. For example, the first day of hearings produced testimony by the secretary of transportation, the assistant attorney general, the chairman of the FTC, members of the Council of Economic Advisors and the Council on Wage and Price Stability, and three leading academic economists—all to the effect that the CAB regulation led to high prices and injured the public. The only persons testifying in support of prior board policies were the industry's trade association representatives. Immediately some dramatic questions were raised. Why was the entire executive branch critical of the CAB? Why did only the industry defend it? Why was there an amicable rather than a hostile relation between the board and the industry? The testimony, given in summary form, began to explain the answers. The economists provided a theoretical explanation. But they were present not so much to provide a theory as to illustrate a fact: namely, that virtually all economists believed that the board's economic regulation was unsound. And the administration critics were there primarily to illustrate the *fact* of criticism. The details of why and how remained to be unfolded.

Similarly, the second day of hearings, focusing on the California and Texas examples, was meant to raise the question "Does CAB regulation keep fares high, not low?" The structure of the day's events was one of dramatic dialogue. Airline economists illustrated, with charts, the fares of PSA, an intrastate carrier not regulated by the CAB, and explained what fares elsewhere might be under a PSA-type cost structure. Senator Kennedy asked representatives of the airlines flying between Boston and Washington to explain why they did not charge similar fares. Why were the routes different? The senator presented them with the subcommittee staff's work suggesting that routes were in fact comparable; he asked them to comment upon it and submit written replies. Representatives of the intrastate airlines stated that they could fly elsewhere just as cheaply if the board would allow them to do so. The CAB chairman was asked why the board took no action on a CAB staff study stating that greater freedom to compete was responsible for lower fares within California. He did not know, but he suggested that the board might change its policy and consider lower-fare applications to fly the Boston-Washington corridor.

The airline deregulation hearings illustrated many characteristics of the congressional hearing in general. The hearing day, while structured to provoke debate and drama, could do so only through the medium of questioning. The senators asked questions that would elucidate the major issues and that would fairly reveal the state of the argument. The questions had to be specific enough to prevent the witness from evading the issue through lengthy dissertation or qualifications or hedging. Thus, an ideal set of questions would allow the witness to display his strong points and respond directly to the strongest points of the other side. To some extent, questions could be thought about in advance and discussed by senators and staff, for most witnesses submitted advance copies of their testimony. Yet to a considerable degree, the senators had to be prepared to improvise and to follow up responses on the day of the hearing itself.

The strongest type of question—which a senator will seek to ask—is colloquially called a "zinger." It (1) makes an important point for one side in the debate, (2) is unanswerable by the opposing witness, and (3) shows that the witness cannot answer satisfactorily only because he is wrong and the other side is right. Moreover, it should be obvious, clear, and easy for a listener who knows nothing about the subject upon hearing the question to understand these three things.

Consider, for example, a question asked during the "intrastate/interstate" day. The ATA expert witness who conducted a study on the comparability of California and interstate routes testified that PSA's costs would increase by $20 million were it subject to requirements applicable to the interstate carriers. After several minutes of facts and figures, this number sounded quite high.

Senator Kennedy then asked: "As I understand this, PSA has about 6½ million passengers, so that $20 million . . . would mean about $3 additional fare per passenger. Yet PSA's fare from San Francisco to Los Angeles is [$18 lower than the interstate fare on comparable routes outside of California and even] $6 lower [than the special fare the CAB allows interstate carriers to fly within California so that they can compete with PSA]. How can you account for the [rest of the fare difference]?"

ATA expert: "I don't have a complete answer to where the differences are, Senator, and there are other differences I have not been able to get any data on . . ."

Senator Kennedy: "Fine. Thank you."

The dramatic point has been made. Not even the ATA's own expert can account for the fare differential in terms of any "special factors."

Similarly, on a broader scale, later in the hearings Senator Kennedy made a devastating impact when he asked the CAB chairman why fares were 40 percent lower in California, or why the CAB had not followed up its own study suggesting that competition was responsible, because the subcommittee and the hearing audience knew that the CAB had no good answers to these questions. Whatever was said in reply would only demonstrate confusion and evasion, making the point dramatically that CAB regulation was illogical or confused, if not pernicious. Consider the point that senators made in asking CAB officials what the board was doing to give people a choice of lower-cost, fuller-plane service. The true answer to this question was nothing, and the more the board members tried to find other answers, the more the unspoken message "nothing" was impressed upon the minds of the listeners.

Finally, consider the effect of detailed questioning of the CAB chairman regarding the way in which rates were set. The CAB's chairman had to turn to a CAB staff member to answer Senator Kennedy's question. The staff member, after what appeared to be considerable evasion, admitted that the CAB's price rules would not allow more efficient firms to cut fares. The net dramatic effect of the interchange was to help erase the impression of a scientific, accurate set of CAB pricing rules and suggest a confusing, complex system that served no apparent public purpose.

After seven days of hearings and questioning, the issues were covered and interested persons were allowed to present their major points. The story—or a synopsis of the story—had been told. Listeners felt that they knew the essence of the argument, and they were prepared to accept a later report that would explore the matter in more detail. Above all, the press was able and willing to communicate the major issues to the public.

The problem of communicating with the public is the problem of the media. If the issue is to become politically visible, journalists must be attracted to the hearings, they must write stories, and the stories must tend to convince the public that reform is possible, and probably desirable. How can this be done when the hearings are trying to tell a complex story about the agency and how it regulates? The problem was well posed by David Burnham, who covered the hearings for *The New York Times:* "What the hearings did was to show the hypocrisy of the CAB. When you sat there and saw how they had run things and what they were doing, it became clear that it was really a fraud. But you had to take about twenty little bits and put them together to see whether the CAB was a fraud. If you only had room in a newspaper story to put these bits together at the beginning, the fraudulent nature of it didn't quite come across. It didn't quite carry. And that is a presentation problem. That's [the committee's job] . . .—to have to present the thing in a way that the public can understand." The problem of attracting journalists to the hearings is not difficult, provided the hearing explores an important topic in some depth with an eye toward change. The staff would explain in detail to journalists (or to anyone else) precisely what it saw as occurring, what it planned, and why. These features made the hearings interesting.

The problem of news stories tended to be solved in several ways. First, there will be good coverage if a major event takes place. Newspapers report events, not opinions. Thus, "Twenty economists criticize CAB" may be interesting, but it is not a story. "Ford administration proposes abolition of CAB" is a page-one news story. The first day of hearings was organized in part to produce that story. The administration produced a new, coherent policy in time for the hearings and announced it there. The next day, on the front page of the *Times,* David Burnham wrote: "Denouncing the impact of the Civil Aeronautics Board as 'inequitable, inefficient, and uneconomical,' the Ford Administration said today that it would introduce legislation aimed at substantially reducing the power of the Board to regulate the airline industry." The article went on to mention Senator Kennedy's hearings, thus calling attention to their existence and suggesting that they constituted some sort of major event.

Second, given the detailed nature of the investigation, unplanned events inevitably occurred at the hearings themselves. Thus, for example, the "route day" focused on a CAB policy of not setting new-route applications for hearing—a policy that was never formally acknowledged by the board and was probably unlawful. After considerable testimony and presentation of evidence by carriers and others that such a policy existed, Acting Chairman Richard O'Melia testified for the board. Under prodding by Senator Kennedy he said that the policy was under reconsideration, finally stating, "In fact, as far as I am concerned, there is no route moratorium as of now." The appearance to the press was that the board had announced a major change, and the next day the *Times* article began: "Three members of the CAB testified today that they would vote to grant hearings to airlines applying for a license to provide new air service in the United States. The testimony by a majority of the board members appeared to signal the end of a never-announced CAB policy that resulted in granting virtually no such licenses in five years."

Third, if the board had in fact been as lax or confused as its critics claimed, an investigation would almost inevitably turn up a number of fairly dramatic instances of unlawful or improper behavior. Thus, for example, after the board had continually denied the existence of the route moratorium, the subcommittee obtained a copy of a memo written by a CAB administrative law judge. The memo listed several cases set for hearing by board order, but added that they had not actually been heard "pursuant to informal instructions of the Chairman's office in connection with the unofficial moratorium on route cases." Under the circumstances, confronting the board with the memo produced a story. *The Washington Post* wrote on its front page: "A Senate subcommittee yesterday produced evidence that the CAB had pursued a deliberate but unannounced policy to severely limit new air route awards by not granting hearings on applications before it . . . Acting CAB Chairman Richard J. O'Melia last week told the Subcommittee that 'there was no board policy stating that there was a moratorium.' Appearing again yesterday, he acknowledged that 'apparently there was a policy.' "

Enough such items appeared to produce a general impression that the board was not an expert group dispassionately applying "scientific" principles of regulation to protect the public interest, but rather a somewhat disorganized group of administrators unable to articulate any coherent, convincing rationale for many of the policies they had followed. The subcommittee also tried to make certain that testimony related to fact, not opinion, because fact can be more easily communicated in a press story. For example, rather than have consumer groups simply complain that the board ignored their problems, the subcommittee asked the board to survey how its Bureau of Enforcement spent its time. The survey showed that it devoted more than 60 percent of its time trying to stop fares that it thought were too low, and about 3 percent of its time investigating consumer complaints, including complaints that fares were too high.

Fifth, one could rely upon the journalists present to write a comprehensive review article once the hearings were completed and the story was told. A second set of comprehensive stories would appear when the draft report was completed, for it would state the subcommittee's tentative conclusions and back them up with data. The previous publicity together with the detail of the hearings and the report produced an impression that action was likely to occur, and made a story that was attractive to the news weeklies. *Business Week,* for example, wrote: "The Report is the greatest in-depth analysis of airline affairs since regulation of the industry began in 1938, and it effectively answers many of the pro-regulation arguments of the airlines and CAB. It provides the economic underpinnings for major change at the CAB.'' A third major set of stories was written when the final report was released several months later. But this time the stories were sparked by a congratulatory letter from President Ford to Senator Kennedy. Cooperation between the subcommittee and the administration had grown and was made easier by the appointment of key officials more favorable to deregulation, such as Paul MacAvoy at the Council of Economic Advisors and John Ely in the Department of Transportation. Still, the spectacle of a Republican president and a Democratic senator working so closely together provoked interest and suggested that change was likely. Of course, the stories themselves were key elements in the bringing about of change, for they produced widespread knowledge of what had occurred and vastly increased the likelihood that politicians not already involved would focus upon the problem and take the necessary steps.

Conclusion

The upshot of the hearings was that the airline regulatory reform issue became politically visible and live. It became "heard of." The administration advanced a reform proposal, Senator Kennedy introduced legislation, and other politicians felt they had to take a position upon or deal with the issue. Moreover, as the issue acquired visibility, it tended to be characterized in certain important ways. It was a "proconsumer" issue; it meant lower fares; it was an "anti-inflation" issue; it was a "major regulatory reform" issue; it was a "less bureaucracy/less regulation/less governmental control" issue. Much of the industry was still against it, and certain unions also opposed it. Yet the unions were likely to understand why senators ordinarily strongly prolabor were in favor of reform, because the unions themselves disliked favoring anticonsumer measures. Of course, one might have characterized airline reform in these ways prior to the hearings; but the point is that the general public now began to make these characterizations as a result of press stories, which in turn reflected events, which made the characterizations natural.

Subsequently President Ford appointed a new chairman of the CAB, John Robson, who began the reform process. Senator Cannon began hearings in his Aviation Subcommittee on specific legislation, which he and Senator Kennedy eventually cosponsored. President Carter, when campaigning, began to adopt the airline issue as his own. It was apparently an issue where one could promise concrete achievement, lower prices, regulatory reform, and less government all in one package. This was apparent because the groundwork had been done. Carter strongly worked for regulatory reform after becoming president and helped achieve enactment of the Kennedy-Cannon Bill by the end of 1978.[16] In the meantime he appointed as new chairman an economist, Alfred E. Kahn, who took steps within the agency effectively to end regulatory control of price

_ entry, and who grew enormously in stature as an outspoken advocate of legislative reform.

All this is not to suggest that once the Kennedy hearings ended, the road to reform was easily traveled. On the contrary, President Ford, President Carter, Senator Kennedy, Senator Cannon, and others continued to work long and hard to attain success. How they did so involves a description of the ordinary legislative and administrative processes as they work to deal with any major political issue—a matter that will not be dealt with here. This chapter has shown simply how the mechanics of a set of hearings can help to elevate one problem to "major issue" status, and thereby to suggest one practical method for bringing about major change in regulatory programs.

17

Generic Approaches to Regulatory Reform

The framework set out in Part I of this book, together with the discussion of the last several chapters, suggests that regulatory reform must proceed step by step, program by program. An agency or program is identified as a likely candidate for reform insofar as the framework identifies a less restrictive method of attacking the problem thought to call for regulation. Then the program is investigated in depth, with the existing system judged against that less restrictive alternative. This method led to reform of airline regulation in the mid-1970s. It is currently being used to reform trucking regulation. It can be applied to many different programs, one after the other. The focus is on the individual program.

The problems surrounding regulation, however, have led many to look for generic solutions. Thus, students of the regulatory process have proposed various changes in agency structure, procedure, personnel selection methods, and systems of accountability that promised improvement.[1] In fact, one might also ask whether there isn't some practical change in the law that would encourage Congress to undertake the step-by-step approach advocated here.

Here we will examine the major *generic* approaches to regulatory reform in light of the preceding discussion of regulation. These include efforts to attract better personnel, to improve agency procedures, to restructure the relationship of the agency to other parts of the government, and to encourage substantive reform. This examination will show that no one approach is likely to cure the problems that produce serious regulatory failure. Some of the proposals, however, are desirable in themselves. Certain procedural changes, for example, may themselves bring about agency decisions that are more fair—a powerful reason for adopting them even if they cannot cure the defects described in this book. Of the approaches considered, the substantive approach seems the most promising. We will conclude with a suggestion for institutionalizing the step-by-step approach advocated here: a proposal that would trigger review of individual programs by the president and by Congress, that would encourage the reviewers to adopt a "procompetitive/less restrictive alternative" outlook, and that would help force congressional action. This last approach has drawbacks and may fail to bring results. Yet of all the generic proposals considered, it seems the one most likely to encourage the government to move in the right direction.

Better Personnel

Critics over the years have explained the failure of regulation by claiming that government has not attracted people best equipped to handle regulatory responsibilities. The notion that agency performance would improve dramatically with better-qualified personnel is seductive, for what organization's performance would not? James Landis, former dean of the Harvard Law School, pointed out in his report to President Kennedy: "The prime key to the improvement of the administrative process is the selection of qualified personnel. Good men make poor laws workable; poor men will wreak havoc with good laws."[2] The Ash Council in 1970 noted that the regulatory agencies had difficulty attracting and retaining "highly qualified personnel."[3] The Senate Commerce Committee complained that many appointments to the Federal Trade Commission and the Federal Communications Commission over a twenty-five-year period "can be explained in terms of powerful political connections and little else."[4] And the Governmental Affairs Committee found that "the preeminent problem with the regulatory appointments process, as it has operated in the past, is that it has not consistently resulted in the selection of people best equipped to handle regulatory responsibilities. For much of the past fifteen years, neither the White House nor the Senate has demonstrated a sustained commitment to high quality regulatory appointments."[5] Occasionally the appointment of a particular person leads to major change. President Carter, for example, appointed Alfred Kahn chairman of the Civil Aeronautics Board in 1977, knowing that Kahn favored deregulation of the airline industry. Kahn, operating within the broad language of the Federal Aviation Act, began to deregulate the airlines administratively. He also worked for and helped secure passage of new deregulating legislation.

Despite the occasional example, efforts to reform agencies by appointing "better people" have been criticized on two grounds: (1) "Better people" is a solution to any institutional problem, but the number of better people is limited. Even if they could be identified and attracted to agency administration, the nation is not necessarily better off than it would be if they administered medical clinics, disarmament conferences, or major corporations. (2) There is no practical proposal for a system more likely to achieve administration by better people. The president does not deliberately appoint poorly qualified people. Rather, the present system leads him to nominate appointees who are neither better nor worse than would be produced by any other selection method.

Some proposals are aimed at *encouraging better people to apply* for agency jobs. The Ash Council, for example, recommended that agency heads have more power and authority. Others have proposed lifetime tenure for commissioners. Still others propose higher salaries. Some have suggested a massive advertising campaign to publicize the jobs, explaining how complex and interesting they are. Common Cause has advocated the creation of a public interest talent bank.

It is difficult to believe, however, that better salaries, status, or publicity will solve the problems of regulation. The salary of the chairman of a regulatory commission is now equal to that of a Cabinet undersecretary, over $60,000. The members of major commissions—the FCC or the Securities and Exchange Commission—enjoy considerable power and prestige. Of course, one way to attract good people into government is to give them an opportunity to make a difference. It helps to have the agency known as an "exciting" one with change taking place. Just this reputation attracted excellent people to the Federal Trade Commission in the early 1970s. Yet it is obviously impossible to institutionalize this type of enticement.

A second type of proposal seeks to encourage the president to *select better people*. Thus, some have argued for a special office in the White House that would develop standards for selection, consult advisory committees, and then select on the basis of competence, experience, and integrity, not politics. Others, including Common Cause and the Senate Governmental Affairs Committee, have argued that Congress or a congressionally created commission or the Senate through its confirmation process should develop similar selection standards and then enforce them through a closer look at the president's nominee. Others seek an "independent" board to evaluate nominees.

One must remain skeptical, however, of the value of such proposals. For one thing, as long as the president appoints and the Senate confirms, the appointment process will remain political. If the politics of the day favor the appointment of an experienced person of great integrity, that is likely to be done, in the presence or in the absence of advisory commissions, standards, and "close looks." If not, it is unlikely that standards and so forth will make much difference. Indeed, the extent to which politicians heed the advice of advisory committees or of various members itself depends upon political factors. And advisory committees, too, can develop politics of their own. It is difficult to find examples of advisory committees or standards improving a basically political selection process.

For another thing, developing a meaningful set of standards is close to impossible. Those suggested tend to be embarrassingly general, such as the suggestion by the Governmental Affairs Committee that "by reason of background, training or experience, the nominee" be "affirmatively qualified for the office to which he or she is nominated." Nor was Common Cause much more specific in suggesting that nominees be honest, administratively competent, committed to the enforcement of major agency policies (was Alfred Kahn?), and believe in the basic principles of regulatory accountability. To become more specific inevitably offends one or another affected group. Drawing up and applying such a list also raises all the problems discussed in Chapter 4. The most likely acceptable standards, such as experience in the field, could weed out those who would make needed changes. Inevitably, in writing job selection standards one ends up with a few obvious variations on the themes of "honesty" and "experience." Further, the commissions, committees, or others called upon to participate or advise must themselves be selected. In a nation without philosopher kings, it is far from obvious that a selection commission will do a better job than a more openly political process. Finally, these proposals, aimed at dishonesty or lack of experience, seem to have little to do with any of the causes of regulatory failure discussed here. More honest or competent regulators would not necessarily bring about the sort of changes suggested. And a standardized selection process might inhibit them.

A third type of proposal focuses upon the *elimination of conflicts of interest.* Popular wisdom identifies a partial cause of regulation's failure with the fact that many regulators have a financial stake in the well-being of the industry or firms that they regulate. This stake may consist of the ownership of stock in companies affected by regulatory action. It may arise out of hoped-for future employment, for many commissioners and agency staff leave the agency for work in regulated industry or law firms or other professional groups that serve industry. Or it may arise out of past associations and loyalties, because staff and commissioners often come from regulated companies or their law firms.[6]

Reformers have typically proposed three types of approach to deal with the conflict-of-interest problem. One proposal would require top executive branch staff to file an annual public financial disclosure statement describing all of their sources of income, including gifts, honoraria, and their net worth including all property, companies, and organizations in which they hold a financial interest. At present, such statements are required only of top officials. Another proposal would require all top officials and employees to divest, unless granted a specific exemption, all financial interests in any company or organization that is affected in any way by any proceeding in which they are likely to participate. Still another proposal would require employees working for the government to sign contracts agreeing that for two years after leaving the government, they will not work, represent, or accept any compensation from any company or organization that was affected by proceedings in which they personally participated.

Why have these suggestions not been welcomed by all those who believe in good government? Some point out that an effort to apply them strictly may make it that much more difficult to attract the highly qualified personnel that reformers typically claim are needed. Will top professionals accept jobs in the government if doing so requires them to sell all their investment, pay the resulting taxes, and reinvest in government securities? Others are concerned about privacy. What are the implications for privacy of working in an office where everyone—and the general public—knows one's net worth from day to day?

The most serious problem these proposals raise, however, concerns the government's need for expertise. The factual information base needed to carry on the many regulatory activities—ranging from determining how pollution controls ought to be implemented to how energy should be allocated—is enormous. Administrators possessing detailed knowledge of the industry—those familiar with its workings, problems, and standards—can often move far more quickly and effectively than those coming fresh to the problem. For example, it took the National Highway Transportation Safety Administration (NHTSA) more than seven years to determine what tire characteristics should appear on a tire's label and how they should be measured. The standard might never have been developed had the job of doing so not been placed in the hands of an agency official who had previously worked for a tire company for thirty-five years. Consider, too, the job of allocating oil discussed in Chapter 5. The Department of Energy had to rely upon executives familiar with the oil industry, though it was later criticized for having done so. Those familiar enough with the industry to possess the necessary qualifications for appointment to many agencies are likely to have had some prior industry connection.

Moreover, if younger employees cannot look for future employment in the regulated industry or the law firms that will serve it, will they seek jobs in regulatory agencies? Must they choose between permanent careers in government and careers totally outside it?

These questions and criticisms suggest that "revolving door" proposals, to be effective, imply a major change in the nature of governmental employment. They move the country in the direction of a more professional, more permanent government career service less open to penetration by temporary appointees from business or the professions. They suggest a civil service more like that of France or Great Britain. Whether such a system is desirable, whether it would be technically ignorant, whether it would prove more skilled and efficient—all are questions that have not been answered but that must be addressed before one can seriously undertake this type of regulatory reform.

In sum, the "better people" proposals seem only to scratch the surface of the regulatory problem. They do not deal with the substantive regulatory problems discussed here. They hint at a possible need for a major change in the nature of the civil service, but the implications of any such far-reaching change go well beyond the problems of regulation.

Procedural Changes

The procedures used to make most agency decisions are those set out in the Administrative Procedure Act (see Appendix 2). Most major agency policies are developed through informal (and sometimes formal) rulemaking. Those policies are applied in individual cases through informal and formal adjudications. Thus, agencies are sometimes likened to "little legislatures" when they create policies through rules, and to "little courts" when they apply those policies to individuals. Critics of the administrative process have often advocated changes in the procedures governing the formulation and application of policy as a means to reform.

Procedural change, however, has several different objectives. Its advocates may want to achieve a fairer process, a more efficient process, or a more legitimate process. Each aim is desirable in itself, but each is related only tangentially, if at all, to the basic problems of regulation described here. The proposals typically advanced as procedural reforms are thus not likely to bring about major improvements (of the sort advocated here) in classical regulation.

Fairness and Efficiency

Procedural change in the past ten to fifteen years has consisted, for the most part, of judicial imposition of increasingly strict formal procedural requirements. The courts, expanding the application of the "due process" clause of the Constitution, have required adjudications to be conducted with increasing legal formality.[7] They have required agencies, when they "legislate" through "informal rulemaking," to conduct their proceedings with greater formality, giving all parties greater opportunity to examine the evidence upon which the agency bases its decision.[8] Congress, too, has been asked to legislate new procedural requirements, which would speed up formal rulemaking while possibly slowing down informal rulemaking. The changes have proved controversial mainly because of the difficulty of determining the "right" degree of procedural formality. The aims of "fairness" and "administrative efficiency" often conflict. Moreover, the subject matter of administrative action is enormously varied. That which appears to suit ratemaking might prove unsuitable for safety standards, and licensing of drugs may require procedures different from allocating oil rights. No one wants totally secretive, arbitrary government, or procedures that prevent action. Within these limits, one can argue about the "right" balance, but the arguments are more likely to affect the form rather than the substance of decision making.

The expansion of due process rights provides a case in point. For the most part, the expansion of those rights has applied to cases involving welfare,[9] public employment,[10] public housing,[11] education,[12] and imprisonment.[13] "Expansion" has meant that agencies when they adjudicate individual cases must use procedures that involve the traditional legal attributes of judicial due process:[14] public notice; an unbiased decision maker; a public record upon which the decision is based; opportunity to present evidence, witnesses, and argument, and to challenge those presented by the opposing side; right to counsel; right to a reasoned decision; and increased judicial review of the decision.[15]

Critics of these procedures tend to concede that they may have led those involved to believe they were treated more fairly.[16] But they are uncertain whether the more elaborate procedures have changed substantive results or have led to more accurate decision making. For example, in 1970 a federal district court required Rhode Island prison officials to use more elaborate due process procedures in prison disciplinary cases. In 1972 the Harvard Center for Criminal Justice studied the effect of the court's order. It concluded that the new procedural requirements changed few results[17] in disciplinary cases. The reasons were simple. Most issues in disciplinary cases came down to the prisoner's word against the guard's. Both before and after the imposition of procedural safeguards, the decision makers tended to take the word of the guard. Further, in most cases, guilt was not the major issue. Punishment was the issue and procedural formality had little effect upon punishment. Studies have also been made of the practical effect of the famous Supreme Court decision requiring more due process in welfare cases. The studies concluded that there has been little improvement in the accuracy of decision making. There are too many cases and too few resources. Alternative methods of achieving accuracy—managerial checks—would, in the view of some critics, work better.[18] Increased procedural protection also has a price. Should more or fewer procedural safeguards be applied to the dismissal of public employees? Those favoring more safeguards point to the injury caused by unjust dismissal. Those favoring the latter argue that inability to fire incompetents has led to inadequate performance by governmental agencies.[19]

More to the point, because it directly concerns policy formulation, is determining the requisite formality for procedures that accompany agency rulemaking. At present, there are two basic procedural models: "formal" rulemaking, which requires the agency to promulgate a rule on the basis of a record created through trial-type procedures, and "informal" rulemaking, which requires the agency only to give notice of a proposed rule and allow comment upon it before the agency makes up its mind. Not surprisingly, critics claim that formal rulemaking is sometimes too cumbersome, while informal rulemaking is sometimes unfair.

In fact, formal rulemaking procedures have worked fairly well in ratemaking cases. But in other areas they have been criticized as too burdensome and time-consuming.[20] The Food and Drug Administration, for example, is required to use formal procedures when it establishes standards for food identity.[21] All sixteen agency proceedings under the statute that took place prior to 1970 lasted longer than two years; two lasted over ten years, including one in which the major issue was whether food labeled "peanut butter" must contain 90 percent or 87 percent peanuts.[22]

But what should be done about these formal procedures? The Administrative Procedures Act currently allows the agency to dispense with cross-examination and oral hearings in "rulemaking or determining claims for money or benefits or applications for initial licenses," provided that "a party will not be prejudiced thereby." Efforts to improve on this language by broadening it run into objections that social security applicants or those whom an agency might find culpable might indeed be prejudiced without a right to cross-examine witnesses. And efforts by Congress to specify just when cross-examination should be used—when an agency makes general policy decisions—have fallen victim to the fact that there are many different sorts of general policy decisions subject to formal rulemaking requirements. Cross-examination of a ratemaking expert, for example, may prove more necessary than cross-examination of a peanut butter expert. Thus, in writing reform legislation, congressional committees have tended to repeat present law by essentially delegating the decision to the agencies.[23]

The more important argument concerns the appropriate formality of informal rulemaking—the more commonly used mode of setting major agency policy. The concept of informal rulemaking has been heralded as "one of the greatest inventions of modern government."[24] Yet to require only that the agency provide notice and accept comments constitutes little check upon its freedom to act. Thus, as agencies have legislated rules of greater and greater significance—affecting health, safety, the environment, and industry—the informality of the procedure has increasingly been criticized as inadequate.

In response, in some cases the courts have required agencies to explain their decisions in greater detail, to show how the decisions were based upon the evidence before them,[25] and to allow the affected parties to see and to respond to the documentary evidence presented. In certain environmental cases they have created a requirement of a "paper hearing." Congress, too, has considered legislation that would force agencies to publicize the data to be used for making their decisions and to allow comments on all significant data before making a final decision. Other proposed legislation would encourage agencies to use more elaborate procedures, including cross-examination, in complex informal rulemaking proceedings.

How far the courts can legally travel down this path[26] and how far Congress ought to go is debatable. Increased formality may mean greater fairness at the cost of speed and flexibility. A public record may offer greater opportunity to present information, but it can also limit what information the agency can consider. Opportunities to participate also mean opportunities to delay. Congress required the Federal Trade Commission, for example, to adopt hybrid rulemaking procedures requiring cross-examination. The result has been lengthy proceedings lasting three to five years[27] without evidence that decisions on the whole have improved.[28]

The dilemma between fairness and efficiency is well illustrated by the decisions of the United States Court of Appeals for the District of Columbia in *Home Box Office* v. *FCC*[29] and *Action for Children's Television* v. *FCC*.[30] The court held that the agency, when engaged in (certain sorts of) informal rulemaking had to base its decision only upon the record before it. Once the agency issued a notice of the proposed rulemaking, it could not obtain information (ex parte) from outside sources without making it available to all parties for comment.[31] This requirement makes proceedings far more fair, for an affected party cannot readily respond to the facts, arguments, and opinions that have been transmitted to an agency unless it knows what they are. Yet the requirement would make it far more difficult for the staff of an agency to formulate a standard. Recall, for example, the efforts of NHTSA's staff to set brake standards. The staff member, who initially knows little about the subject, would have found his assignment virtually impossible if he had been forbidden to talk informally to the Society of Automotive Engineers, to experts in universities, to staff members of auto companies, to public interest lawyers. And they could not have answered frankly if all remarks had been "on the record." If all the staff information comes from lawyers' briefs submitted to the agency, it may be distorted. The staff has no way to check it informally for validity or completeness.

One can argue that if ex parte contacts are allowed, the agency will be at the mercy of those with greater informal access—often the business community. But one can also argue that without an ability to consult informally, at least at the initial stages of a proceeding, the agency staff would be at the mercy of those parties with greatest control of the information and able to pay for expensive legal assistance to digest and present it. Moreover, once a proceeding takes place entirely on the record, one is forced entirely into the back-and-forth adversary mode of legal presentation, which makes it difficult to arrive at an optimum standard. Of course, the agency could avoid these effects of the *Home Box Office* rule by postponing the issuance of a notice of proposed rulemaking until it completed its informal consultations. But by then it is likely to have decided upon the form of the final rule and the affected parties are likely to have had less, not more, influence than at present.

The difficulty of drawing a proper ex parte communications line is exacerbated when one considers proposals that would also prevent the White House from approaching the agency except publicly. Should the head of the Council of Economic Advisors be able to urge an agency head to pay special attention to costs? If he is forced to do so publicly, will he hesitate to describe to the agency how the president actually feels? Is the result likely to be a president less able to control his own appointees and to set uniform policy—increased "Balkanization" of the executive branch?

The difficulty of drawing the proper procedural line, which the ex parte/informal rulemaking controversy illustrates, explains the weakness of the procedural suggestions in the major regulatory reform proposals currently pending in Congress. After several years of study and six volumes of reports[32] the Senate Governmental Affairs Committee limited its major procedural recommendations to easing restrictions on formal rulemaking and giving hearing examiners greater independence when deciding rate cases. The Judiciary Committee sought greater restrictions on informal rulemaking by urging but not requiring agencies to consider using informal public hearings, mediation techniques, paper hearings, or cross-examination in individual proceedings. Both committees considered delegating the job of procedural requirements to experts, perhaps through the administrative conference, in the same way that creating judicial procedures has been delegated to the courts.[33]

Although these procedural proposals can be debated, their impact on substantive policy cannot be great. In fact, informal procedures have had an uneven record in bringing about sound substantive policies. The CAB's anticompetitive rate and route policies were developed and carried out through informal, off-the-record meetings.[34] Yet greater procedural fairness, full public hearings, and scrupulous attention to procedure resulted in still worse CAB policy—the policy of the Domestic Passenger Fare Investigation,[35] which effectively ended all price competition. Similarly, the FPC's natural gas price determinations and the FCC's awarding of television licenses for the most part have been procedurally fair. The very fact that procedures are meant to be "policy neutral" means they are unlikely to cure regulatory problems insofar as the case requires major changes in policy direction.

Legitimacy

Recent procedural changes in the administrative process may also be viewed as an effort to improve the legitimacy of agency decision making by expanding the number of groups and interests represented in the decision making process. The past fifteen years have witnessed major changes in administrative procedure—expanding the opportunity to participate in agency decision making and to seek court review of the results of "legitimate" agency decisions. As Stewart has explained, this expansion responds to an increasingly felt need to "legitimate" agency decision making and meets that need by expanding "public interest representation."[36]

When administrative agencies began to grow in power at the beginning of the twentieth century, the source of their authority was seen to be Congress, and the role of administrative law was to ensure that the agency faithfully carried out its congressional mandate. The agency was a "transmission belt," applying a congressional statute to changing factual circumstances. The basic elements of administrative law included the following:

1. The agency could order private persons to act or to refrain from acting only as authorized by specific laws, through which Congress controlled agency action.
2. The agency had to use procedures that would help it determine that its orders complied with its authorizing legislation (that is, its fact-finding procedures had to be accurate so that it could order people only when the facts fit the legislation's description).

3. Judicial review had to be available to ensure that the agency did not overstep the bounds set out in its legislation.

4. Agency procedures had to facilitate the exercise of this judicial review.[37]

The legitimacy of agency decisions was assured by the facts that (1) they were authorized by Congress, and (2) the agency and the courts followed procedures that kept the agency within the congressionally set bounds.

This procedural model broke down with the New Deal. As congressional delegations were made in broader and broader language, the traditional model could not adequately check the agency's power. When Congress authorized an agency to act "in the public interest," the public could not accept "Congress decided it" as justification for a particular agency decision. At the same time, New Deal supporters felt that judges unduly hampered the administrators. Successful administration was said to be incompatible with legalistic formalities and to involve technical issues beyond the understanding of lay judges. In place of legal procedures and safeguards, defenders of the New Deal agencies relied upon the expert professionalism of administrators. The canons of their professional discipline would keep their actions in check. The legitimacy of their decisions would rest upon their "scientific" correctness.[38]

Since the New Deal and particularly since 1970, public confidence in the scientific accuracy of agency decision making has diminished. Agencies have been attacked as incompetent, "captured" by special interests, or worse.[39] Few students of the subject believed that the CAB's regulation of airline rates or the FCC's awards of television licenses were determined by a professional regulatory discipline. But if agency decisions are not controlled by Congress, if they are not scientifically determined, if agency decision makers are not elected, what right does the agency have to make its policies? What makes the agency's decision legitimate?

In the past decade, the courts and the agencies, as well as Congress, have sought to find a partial answer to the question of legitimacy—and to improve agency decisions—by broadening the degree of participation in agency decision making.[40] Consumer groups, public interest law firms, environmental groups, and others claiming to represent those who cannot readily organize themselves have not only been allowed to appear before agencies but their appearance has been encouraged, sometimes by governmental payment of their costs[41] and by an expansion of their rights to appeal agency decisions to the courts.[42] At the same time, Congress has enacted laws allowing greater access to agency information[43] and forcing the agencies to meet and to make decisions in public.[44] These laws, together with court decisions increasing the formality of informal rulemaking have transformed the decision-making process into an open forum, in which lawyers represent a wide variety of interest groups, including public interest groups, and decisions emerge out of their evidence, argument, and negotiation. The emergence of this "interest representation" model of the administrative process characterizes the procedural change since 1970.

Public interest representation and widespread participation may help legitimate agency decisions. The presence of a representative of senior citizens, for example at an FTC hearing on the eyeglass industry, builds confidence in the decision by a group very likely to buy eyeglasses; they know the FTC will have heard their typical views. It has led to substantively better results. Public interest law firms played a major role in reforming airline and trucking regulation. They have encouraged the development of stronger safety, environmental, and consumer protection regulation. The greater the extent to which agency failure can be explained by the capture of an agency by a special interest, the more likely broadening participation in agency decision making will lead to substantively better agency decisions.

On the other hand, there are several serious difficulties with the interest representation approach that make it less likely to achieve major substantive policy change and that threaten its ability to restore legitimacy to the administrative system.

First, the agency must determine who specifically is to represent unrepresented groups, such as the consumer or the "public." Various public interest law firms, consumer groups, and environmental organizations have developed strong credentials in particular areas. Yet it is unknown whether these credentials will stand the test of time. In the 1930s and 1940s agencies and the public believed that there was no need for such representation, for the agency itself represented the public. A public that has become disenchanted with an agency as its representative, may become equally disenchanted with private groups that claim to represent the public interest. After all, in hearings before the Federal Power Commission on national gas prices, both sides had a legitimate claim to representing the consumer—one stressing lower prices and the other stressing the need to avert a shortage. It becomes more difficult to decide which position a public or consumer representative should take when industry and consumer are not necessarily at odds and when the agency is not necessarily captured by industry—instances that are fairly common.

Second, public interest and consumer representatives are likely to remain underfunded. The Governmental Affairs Committee found that regulated industry participation predominated over public interest group representation by a ratio of about nine to one, in large part because of funds. Some agencies are now able to pay public interest representatives. But funds are limited. Moreover, it is not easy to determine who is the legitimate representative of the consumer or of the public; the agency is often faced with competing claims of several representatives. The only feasible approach is to divide available funds among those with a plausible claim. Yet the more widely a limited amount of funding is dispersed, the less effective each group can be in overcoming the obstacles that called forth the creation of the public interest advocate in the first place; namely, without time, money, and organization, the average citizen or consumer cannot effectively participate in the agency process regardless of his legal right to do so. And does reliance upon the government for funding tend to undercut the group's claim to represent the public?

Third, many agency decisions are (or should be) far more technical and scientific than is likely to be admitted by those who rebelled against the "scientific managerialism" of the 1930s. To have a representative group make these decisions may well result in technically incorrect decisions. Recall, for example, our discussion of whether saccharin is a carcinogen. Saccharin's risk poses a scientific question. There is no clear answer. Yet scientists' estimates, even if subjective and provable through scientific testing, are still likely to be more accurate than the subjective estimates of a lay panel. A decision to ban or to allow saccharin should be reached only after estimating a range of probable deaths (from bladder cancer) if saccharin is allowed and a range of probable deaths (from heart attacks and strokes due to overweight) if it is banned. While scientists may be unwilling or unable to express firm opinions about these probabilities, a person trained in science with some experience with public policy can evaluate the scientific information available, place appropriate weight upon it, and form a subjective judgment within scientifically plausible limits. A representative group of various interests, however, may have members without the requisite background or the funding needed to obtain the requisite information. A group with several such members may find, in part, that it is moved by political considerations, possibly based on preconceptions, toward compromise. And such a compromise is as likely to lead toward a scientifically worse answer as toward a scientifically better one.

Fourth, the fact that public interest representatives do not have financially self-interested clients does not give them total freedom to do what they believe is right. They have financial backers whom they will hesitate to alienate. Moreover, as the participants learn more about the technical matters from the agency or from one another, those representing identifiable clients or firms may find it easier than public interest representatives to compromise. Lawyers representing individual firms can easily discuss the agency proceedings with their clients and seek their agreement to modify their views. Those who represent the public or the consumer, however, may find it more difficult to secure their clients' consent. Suppose, for example, a consumer representative is asked to place a dollar value upon human life. Can he, even if convinced of the need to allow certain risks to exist to secure other benefits, afford to suggest callousness toward injury or death? The legitimacy of many public interest representatives arises out of the fact that the public recognizes them as such after hearing about their activities through the media. Communication to the public through the media is essential. Yet it is difficult to communicate through the media the complex detail involved in scientifically based regulation proceedings. Thus, the advocate may feel pressure to maintain a position that, when communicated through the media, will recognizably fall within the current stereotype of the public interest position. This fact complicates rational decision making on scientific matters.

Fifth, a participatory process can erode consensus and support for the final agency decision. Consider a public interest representative opposing a grant of a nuclear power plant license proceeding. If the license is granted, the representative may not accept the result as legitimate. Indeed, he may not describe his loss as "reasonable" but may view it as an agency mistake, resulting from his opponent's superior financial or informational resources. If so, increased participation in an *adversary* process will not legitimate or win acceptance for an adverse agency decision.

These difficulties do not show that broadened representation before agencies is undesirable or unnecessary. They do suggest that broadened representation does not fairly answer the problem that is most urgent, legitimacy, nor is it likely to satisfy the need for significant substantive reform.

Structural Change

Many critics of the regulatory agencies have argued that restructuring will bring improvement. Two major sorts of structural change are advocated. First, there are *managerial* proposals; these would reorganize, for example, lines of authority and accountability to make the agency a more efficient, responsible managerial unit. Second, there are proposals that would change the relationship between the agencies and other parts of the government to allow *increased supervision* of the agency's substantive performance; these might be viewed as restructuring the checks and balances. Finally, there are a few proposals for new institutions.

Managerial Proposals

The most persistent of the managerial restructuring proposals have been aimed not at all agencies but at the independent agencies. These agencies, such as the ICC, CAB, FTC, and others, are directly responsible neither to the president nor to Congress. The criticisms of independent agency structure usually take the following form: (1) adjudication and management functions should not be combined; (2) multimember boards cannot manage effectively; and (3) independence from the president breeds irresponsibility. In 1937 the President's Committee on Administrative Management observed:

> For the purposes of management, boards and commissions have turned out to be failures. Their mechanism is inevitably slow, cumbersome, wasteful, and ineffective, and does not lend itself readily to cooperation with other agencies. Even strong men on boards find that their individual opinions are watered down in reaching board decisions. When freed from the work of management, boards are, however, extremely useful and necessary for consultation, discussion, and advice; for representation of diverse views and citizen opinion; for quasi-judicial action; and as a repository for corporate powers.

The conspicuously well-managed administrative units in the Government are almost without exception headed by single administrators.[45]

The First Hoover Commission concluded that chairmen are "too frequently merely presiding officers at commission meetings. No one has been responsible for planning and guiding the general program of commission activity."[46] Finding that administration by plural executives was universally regarded as inefficient, the commission noted that it was very difficult for a bureau chief to report to five or more masters. The Second Hoover Commission[47] reached similar conclusions, as did the Landis Report in 1960.[48] As a result of the Landis work, the agencies' structure was somewhat changed. The power of the chairman was increased and his term redefined so that he serves at the pleasure of the president.

The most recent thorough study of agency structure is that of the Ash Council in 1971.[49] The Ash Council recommended that most commissions be headed by a single administrator directly responsible to the president. The council argued that collegial bodies are "inefficient mechanisms for formulating and implementing specific policy in a timely manner." They tend to "overjudicialize" agency procedures. They "are not an efficient form for managing operations." A single administrator "would be more visible to all concerned and therefore more easily held accountable for agency performance . . . Agency policy and direction would more likely conform to the interest of the public, Congress and the executive branch and would result in a more expeditious and fair response to the regulated industries."

This sort of structural proposal is commonly advanced by study commissions viewing agencies from an administrative or business management perspective. Whether their implementation would in fact significantly improve agency performance, however, is questionable. Why should a single head improve the quality of a multimember agency's performance? Critics of the Federal Trade Commission's performance during the 1960s felt that its current chairman had too much power, not too little. They argued that his policies and programs served to hinder rather than further competition throughout the economy. They urged that the other members of the FTC be given more power, not less.[50] Two subsequent chairmen of the Federal Trade Commission reformed it despite their membership in a collegial body where the chairman did not possess full powers.[51] Similarly, Alfred Kahn reformed the Civil Aeronautics Board without total power; he was chairman of a collegial body with five members.

Of course, a collegial body may provoke more policy disagreements than a single head. But whether such disagreements are desirable depends upon the substantive policy at issue. For example, collegial disagreement with Kahn's airline deregulation policy might have hindered needed reform; disagreement with the policies of his predecessors at the CAB might have promoted it. Dissenting commissioners can direct attention to problems with majority policy when a court reviews an agency decision. Indeed, dissenting commissioners may encourage new agency policies, while a single head of an agency may strongly favor the status quo. This tendency is aggravated because a single head depends more heavily upon existing agency staff than does a collegial group. Thus, it is difficult to say abstractly whether moving from a collegial body to a single head will promote reform.

The other recommended structural change—that the president have authority to replace agency chiefs at will—rests upon the view that the president feels less "responsible" for the actions of an independent agency. He is more likely to take responsibility for decision of an agency wholly within the executive branch. Here too, however, one must doubt the significance of the change. There is little indication that the president requires agencies wholly within the executive branch whose chiefs serve at will (such as the Federal Energy Administration or the Bureau of Mines) to act more responsibly or "better" than independent agencies such as the Federal Power Commission or the Civil Aeronautics Board (which was reformed through presidential appointments). Moreover, in certain instances such as the Federal Communications Commission (as the Ash Council notes), independence of the president is highly desirable.

The major weakness in these and other similar proposals for structural change, however, is that they are designed to be policy neutral. They assume that improved agency structure will automatically bring about improved performance. Yet there is little evidence that this is so. On the contrary, structural change appears irrelevant to the making of major changes in substantive agency policy—to determining whether an environmental tax should be adopted, whether trucking regulation should be abolished, or whether collective bargaining should augment regulation of workplace safety.

A related set of managerial proposals seeks to improve agency planning, coordination, and performance. The Office of Management and Budget, for example, recently claimed that it had "identified the single, most important problem in the regulatory process as the lack of consistent and effective policy oversight of regulatory decisions by the heads of regulatory agencies . . . The officials who signed regulations often had no idea of what was in them. Those who wrote regulations were not held accountable for their actions."[52]

To rectify these management deficiencies, President Carter in 1978 proposed that agencies be required to publish semiannually an agenda of upcoming, significant regulations, including costs; to set a deadline for completion of each action; to establish an internal office of regulatory planning and management to oversee the coordination of agency activities; to have the agency head approve personally any significant regulation; to write regulations "in plain English"; and to review its rules periodically to ensure their continuing effectiveness. Whether these proposals increase agency efficiency or create more red tape remains to be seen. But, regardless, they are not intended to bring about major substantive reform.

Supervisory Proposals

Not surprisingly, there are three different sorts of proposals that would restructure relationships within the government to give others more authority to supervise agency performance. Some would give more supervisory power to Congress, others to the president, and still others to the courts.

Congress. The most popular current proposal would give one or both houses of Congress an opportunity to veto any major rule of an agency after it is promulgated but before it takes effect. Those favoring the veto point to the enormously broad power that Congress has delegated to the agencies: the FCC is to award licenses on the basis of "the public interest, convenience, and necessity"; OSHA is to ensure "safe" and "healthful" places of employment; the FTC is to eliminate "unfair and deceptive" practices. They claim that more narrowly drafted regulations are impractical, yet the public's elected representatives ought to influence directly or check the manner in which that power is exercised.

The veto, they claim, provides a desirable, practical check on the growing power of the president and the agencies. The size of government has increased exponentially since 1789. The knowledge explosion has made it nearly impossible for Congress to cope with the needs of the electorate. Congress must respond flexibly to specific problems, yet finds it difficult to generate detailed expert factual information and is captive to what the executive branch tells it about the need for legislation. Thus, the only practical way for Congress to set legislative policy within the "separation of powers" framework is for it to delegate broadly and then to disapprove agency actions that it does not like.

Those opposing the veto argue that it will, in practice, become a congressional staff veto. Agencies in self-defense will have to seek the advice of congressional staff *before* promulgating a rule, and participants will therefore try to convert that staff before approaching the agency. Since Congress has no set procedures for doing so, the parties will thereby circumvent agency procedures designed to allow all parties to see and comment upon one another's claims. Moreover, all the special interests will look to Capitol Hill for a second bite at the apple. The rules likely to be debated or vetoed are those as to which affected groups have sufficient political power to attract a committee chairman's attention. Thus, Congress might be more likely to intervene where an agency seeks to regulate powerful private interests. Further, the existence of the veto would make it difficult to plan. An ICC chairman could not plan to introduce a comprehensive procompetitive reform of trucking regulation, for his pricing regulation might be approved while his entry regulation was vetoed. Finally, the political effect on the members of Congress is itself uncertain. A veto might give them more power, but also may lead their constituents to hold them directly responsible for all the actions of the bureaucracy.

Although legislative veto provisions have been enacted with increasing frequency and nearly three hundred appear in different pieces of legislation (particularly appropriations bills), their constitutionality is in question. Every recent administration, whether Democratic or Republican, has argued that the veto is unconstitutional. They claim that it violates the "presentation clause" of the Constitution—the clause that requires all legislation to be presented to the president for his approval or veto prior to becoming law.[53] They also argue that the one-house veto violates Article 1, Section 1 of the Constitution, which requires all legislation to secure the approval of *both* houses of Congress. Of course these clauses only apply to "legislation." But Congress can only exercise legislative power (with certain specified exceptions), and therefore it cannot constitutionally exercise a veto unless it is a form of legislation.

The proponents of the veto find this reasoning too formalistic. Given its reasonableness and desirability, the Constitution's language should be given a sufficiently broad interpretation to allow it. The Court of Claims decided by a vote of four to three that a one-house veto was constitutional,[54] but the United States Court of Appeals for the Ninth Circuit recently ruled against its constitutionality.[55] The Supreme Court has not decided the question.

Aside from legislative veto proposals, Congress might be encouraged to use its oversight power more frequently and effectively. Congressional oversight of airline and trucking regulation has helped bring about significant change. Yet how to institutionalize the process is unclear. The subcommittee of Congress directly charged with the responsibility of overseeing a particular agency's work sometimes finds it difficult to carry out detailed oversight. The very fact that the subcommittee is involved with the agency on a regular basis means that its members and staff develop an interest in preserving the regulatory status quo just as does the agency itself. The subcommittee and the agency deal with the same parties, they are subjected to the same arguments, and they begin to see the issues in the same way. In fact, CAB oversight hearings were not conducted by the Aviation Subcommittee, which has direct legislative jurisdiction over the CAB, but by the Administrative Practice Subcommittee—a subcommittee that has no legislative authority and that had not previously been involved in airline regulation. The subcommittee's hearings were effective—a fact that suggests that oversight by "outside" committees is desirable. But it is not practical to have committees of Congress continually seeking to oversee matters within the jurisdiction of other committees.

Some have suggested that the Budget Committee or the Appropriations Committee should carry out oversight and that they should do so by insisting that each agency justify its *entire* budget, not just the incremental increase, each year ("zero-based budgeting"). Yet justification can readily turn into boilerplate. Moreover, these committees do not have the time or tools to conduct a CAB-type investigation of many agencies, and they could not do so very often.

Others have proposed a special Congressional Office on Regulatory Oversight, with a director and staff, managed by six congressmen and six senators.

Given the rivalrous nature of Congress, however, it is unlikely that a group will readily share policy responsibility. Nor can the staff answer regulatory questions—which are not policy neutral—without policy direction. Thus, the product of such an office would likely depend upon the views of its chairman or majority. If such an office created an agenda, decided to develop a coherent overall intellectual framework, and carried out the painstaking, elaborate, and often unglamorous detailed work needed for individual agency investigation, reform might well come about. But there is nothing in the simple creation of the office that suggests this will happen.

The president. Proposals that would strengthen the president's power to influence agency policies have been made in the past (by Redford)[56] and more recently by Lloyd Cutler and Senator Roth, who argue that the president has become unable to coordinate policies among the executive branch and independent agencies. With the support of the American Bar Association, they propose a statute that would allow the president to direct an agency to take up and to decide any regulatory issue within a specified period of time or to modify or reverse an agency rule or policy. In other words, the president himself, acting under certain procedural constraints, could reverse most agency policy making. Presidential action would be subject to congressional review either through a legislative veto process or by requiring Congress to renew the president's authority at regular intervals.[57]

The reason a statute is required is that most regulatory statutes delegate power not to the president but to the agency head. Thus, the president cannot overrule the agency head on a particular matter, but can only dismiss a regulator who displeases him. Andrew Jackson, for example, could not overrule his secretary of the treasury when he refused to withdraw public funds from the Bank of the United States, but he could (and did) fire him. The result is that agency heads in practice have considerable autonomy, for presidents are unwilling to fire a major public official except over a very important matter. Some who hesitate to undermine this agency autonomy still seek to increase coordination by encouraging groups of regulators and White House officials to meet regularly to discuss policy matters.[58]

There is much to be said for the Cutler proposal. It would allow the president to bring about increased policy coordination among agencies, to prevent major departures from his policies, and to prevent actions that he would consider seriously mistaken. It would also involve him more directly in regulatory matters, providing increased opportunity for major change. And since the Council of Economic Advisors and the Bureau of the Budget have great influence on the White House staff, in these areas changes might be in a procompetitive direction.

On the other hand, the proposal has its problems. For one thing, will it mean that groups adversely affected by agency action simply come to the White House for a second opportunity to defeat it? For another, even if a president is less willing to protect a special interest than is, say, a subcommittee chairman, his agenda is still highly political. Arguably, political considerations should not be brought to bear piecemeal upon individual agency regulations. Moreover, why is the president's policy likely to be so much more sensible than the agency's? The president may have higher-quality advice available in the Council of Economic Advisors or the Bureau of the Budget, but the agency has many more facts at its disposal and is more familiar with them. Would the proposal require a much larger White House staff? Further, if the president follows the advice of his economists will he inject economic considerations where Congress specifically did not want them? In the final analysis the direction that any reform takes under the proposal depends upon the substantive policy directions preferred by the president. The proposal itself produces little pressure to move in any one direction.

The courts. Senator Bumpers and many other critics of the regulatory process would have the courts examine the rules, regulations, and legal decisions of agencies with greater care.[59] At present, courts tend to reverse such agency decisions if they are arbitrary or outside the authorizing statute. In practice, courts defer to agencies on many legal matters, the exact degree of deference depending upon a host of factors, including the nature of the legal decisions at issue.[60] The basic object of Senator Bumpers' proposal is to encourage more active court review and less deference.

The aim of this proposal is to assure agency fidelity to congressional statute. Agency decisions will have to be more carefully supported in the record, and agency employees will have to be more careful. Judges will be encouraged to learn more about the technical bases for agency decisions—to learn statistics, if necessary, and to understand scientific language and reasoning. Fewer irrational agency decisions will take effect.

Bumpers' proposal, while popular in the legislature, has its drawbacks. Even if its intent is only to send a signal to the courts to defer less to the agencies, how much less deference ought there to be? Would one want, for example, to insist that judges rehear the merits of, say, the "separations manual" for allocating the joint costs of telephone service? Do the courts have the time or the resources to examine such decisions de novo? From a political perspective, one cannot be certain which groups will be favored. The business community, for example, might like to see OSHA take greater care, but it may feel that greater scrutiny of the Nuclear Regulatory Commission means only longer delay in issuing licenses. From the perspective of regulatory policy, the effect of the proposal is also indeterminable. As the example of natural gas regulation makes clear, it is sometimes the courts, not the agencies, that seek to expand the scope of regulation. By slowing down agency proceedings and examining more closely the relation of the agency decision to the authorizing statute, will stricter review mean less experimentation? Will it make agencies hesitate to look for new but less restrictive ways to carry out their mandate?

One's skepticism about the ability of this and other structural proposals to solve the major problems of regulation arises out of our discussion of the defects in regulation which are embedded in the system and with which an intelligent, well-meaning administrator cannot effectively deal. Why, then, should an intelligent, well-meaning judge or congressman or president be able to deal with them any better? And if regulatory reform therefore means significant substantive reform in many areas, simply giving increased supervisory power to a judge or congressman or president provides little assurance that those reforms will come about.

New Institutions

Proposals have been made to create various new institutions designed to help overcome the problems of regulation. These proposals are only tangentially relevant to the types of regulatory problems we have discussed.

An administrative court. The Ash Council recommended creating a separate administrative court, similar to the tax court, to review administrative decisions of the securities, energy, and transportation agencies.[61] Forty years earlier the American Bar Association had recommended the creation of a similar court that would handle agency adjudications and many of the agencies' licensing functions as well.[62] The principal objectives of such proposals are: (1) to secure better review of agency decisions and promote uniformity of decision-making processes and results among agencies; and (2) to relieve the agencies of many time-consuming adjudicatory tasks and allow them to concentrate on policy-making and managerial functions.

The critics of these proposals argue that these objectives would not be achieved. The court's limited jurisdiction might restrict its appeal to highly qualified judicial candidates. Moreover, to remove adjudications from the agencies is to remove much of their basic work. Familiarity with individual cases helps agencies determine proper policy, and the ability to make policy in individual adjudicatory proceedings gives the agency flexibility. Thus, there is no guarantee that removal of the agencies' adjudicatory powers would produce better policies.[63] To remove the agency's power to award licenses and place it in a court may simply prevent an agency from coordinating complimentary policies without curing the problems that make individual decisions so difficult. Finally, even if freeing the agency from its adjudicatory burden gives it more time to set policy, that policy will not necessarily be better. With more time, the FPC in the 1960s would have continued to hold down natural gas prices; the CAB's rate policies would have remained restrictive; and the FCC would have continued to find it impossible to devise fair and effective licensing rules.

A technical review board. Some students of the regulatory process, noting the difficulty that agencies and courts have in making technical analyses, have proposed the creation of new institutions to perform or to evaluate technical work. Ackerman, for example, would create a board of experts in technical disciplines to act as advisors to agencies or judges.[64] And a well-known scientist, Arthur Kantrowitz, has urged the creation of a Science Court, composed of experts who would hear arguments and then issue a statement of the scientific facts relevant to a policy controversy.[65] Such evaluations and advice make better decisions and would help the courts decide when an agency decision was unreasonable.

Critics of these proposals have raised several questions.[66] Who will serve on such panels? Why will they reach better results than an agency itself? Can controversy among experts be narrowed down or resolved easily? How often can one separate out from a major policy issue the "value" questions and the "factual" questions, the scientific questions that can be resolved and the scientific questions that cannot be resolved? Can a panel properly evaluate technical studies and judge whether they are being used properly or misused by the agency, without a thorough knowledge of the particular regulatory proceeding and issue? Will the panel become sufficiently familiar with the details of the regulatory proceeding? Would it prove nearly as useful to provide judges with scientifically trained law clerks who could help them evaluate the technical soundness of an agency's decision?

The ombudsman. Many foreign countries, several states, and a handful of American cities have successfully used ombudsmen to deal with complaints concerning abuse of governmental power. The ombudsman classically investigates, criticizes, publicizes, and recommends change in administrative practice, but he cannot himself change any administrative act.[67]

Ombudsman-like functions are now performed at the federal level but not by an ombudsman. The power to examine agency procedures and practices, for example, rests in the hands of the congressional committees, the Office of Management and Budget, and the Administrative Conference of the United States. The power to investigate and to prosecute criminal misbehavior on the part of public officials is vested in the Department of Justice. The obligation and the power to investigate citizen complaints—to cut through red tape to produce action, and to correct individual instances of injustice—belongs to individual senators and congressmen, who help secure their own reelection by serving constituents in this way.

Proposals to create an ombudsman rest upon the view that doing so would be inexpensive. It would provide a formal, visible method for citizens to complain, and the office would be, and would appear to be, nonpolitical. These facts, and experience elsewhere, suggest that an ombudsman will focus upon individual instances of injustice and will affect only very indirectly the matters of substantive regulatory policy.

A consumer protection agency. For many years consumer advocates have urged the creation of a Consumer Protection Agency (CPA), which would advocate the consumer's position before regulatory agencies and legislative bodies. It would make recommendations for additional legislation and it would force to the attention of regulatory agencies facts favorable to the consumer's point of view.[68]

Those opposed to the agency have argued that it is simply an additional governmental bureau, unlikely to cure the problems of too much bureaucracy. They fear the potential political power of its head, who would become the chief consumer spokesman.

The merits of the proposal depend in large part upon the extent to which one perceives the problem of inadequate representation as responsible for the inadequate performance of regulatory agencies. It is true that it is difficult to organize consumers so that they can be represented by private counsel. And public interest lawyers often have inadequate resources, while industry lawyers have far greater financial resources at their disposal. The CPA would tend to redress that balance. Yet doing so will not necessarily cure the substantive problems of regulation.

In any event, legislation creating a CPA nearly passed Congress but it was defeated in the House of Representatives in 1978. Since that time, support for it has diminished.

Encouraging Substantive Reform

The generic proposals most compatible with this book's analysis are those that encourage substantive reform, and, in particular, substantive change toward less restrictive alternatives. These proposals are of two sorts: (1) those that encourage the agencies to adopt more competitive or less restrictive proposals, by imposing an ''impact statement'' requirement; and (2) those that encourage Congress and the president to examine regulatory programs individually and in detail. The latter are more likely to produce significant results.

Impact Statements

The National Environmental Policy Act (NEPA) requires that agencies produce an environmental impact statement before taking action that threatens significant environmental harm.[69] The act requires only that the agency study the issue and prepare a statement, not that it act one way or the other. Nonetheless, as enforced by the courts, the act has made agencies far more sensitive to environmental problems and has probably halted many agency projects that would have caused environmental damage.[70] NEPA's success has led regulatory reformers to propose other impact statement requirements, designed to influence the substantive direction of agency policy.

The most significant proposals would encourage agencies to adopt less costly or less restrictive methods of regulation. President Ford, by executive order, required the agencies to write an ''inflationary impact statement.'' The agency would determine how much its proposed action would raise costs and whether there were alternative, less costly ways of dealing with the problem.[71] President Carter withdrew this order, substituting an order requiring a ''regulatory impact statement.'' Before the agency takes any major action, it must write a statement setting out the action's objectives and alternative ways of achieving them. It must then justify its action as better than any alternative.[72]

Congress has also recently considered the impact statement approach. Senator Ribicoff's reform bill would have agencies consider the economic (along with the noneconomic) consequences of major rules.[73] Senator Kennedy introduced legislation that would require a "competitive impact statement." Before an agency could take an action that would lessen competition substantially, it would have to show that satisfying the agency's statutory objectives required that action rather than a less restrictive alternative.[74] Senator Eagleton's bill would require agencies to consider performance standards rather than design standards. And Congress recently enacted a law that tells the agencies to pay particular attention to small business.[75]

In addition to their ability to focus the agencies upon factors currently of interest to Congress, the strength of many of these impact statements is that they provide a justification for the Office of Management and Budget, the Council of Economic Advisors, the Council on Wage and Price Stability, and the Department of Justice (Antitrust Division) to intervene in agency proceedings and to present their views. These agencies are institutionally disposed to stress the need for competition, the importance of incentives, and the difficulties of classical regulation. Their presence in the proceeding can force the agency to take more serious account of these considerations. Thus, the Council on Wage and Price Stability has intervened in several agency proceedings and shown that the agency's proposed action would have involved costs out of proportion to probable benefits.[76] Intervention based upon the impact statement can also force the White House staff to pay attention to issues and decisions that might otherwise pass unnoticed. Involvement by the Council of Economic Advisors in some major regulatory proceedings, for example, has led the White House to develop a firm position, which, in turn, has strongly influenced the agency's decision toward less restrictive regulation.[77] Finally, if the impact statement is reviewable in court, action that is unreasonable in terms of the statement can be set aside. Thus, the Justice Department might urge the courts to set aside ICC action that impeded entry into the trucking business on the grounds that the ICC had not written (indeed, could not write) a competitive impact statement showing that a restrictive entry policy was needed to carry out the purposes of trucking regulation.[78]

There are several major weaknesses of the impact statement approach. (1) It is difficult to find a single factor, or even a small number of factors, that *all* agencies would do better to focus upon. The ICC, for example, might do better to focus on the need for competition, but that is not so serious a problem for OSHA. (2) The final decision remains with the agency. (3) It is not difficult to write a plausible justification for almost any decision along the lines required by the statement. By now it should be clear that classical regulation, even when far too restrictive and undesirable, is never without plausible justification. In every instance one can find claims, evidence, and argument that will support regulation. Weighing of arguments and careful judgment is needed before concluding that a particular regulatory program or action is undesirable. Thus, it will not be difficult for agencies to reach a decision and then to write whatever impact statement is needed to justify it. The temptation for the agency to do so will be great, because its staff, through inertia, will tend to favor existing regulatory directions. And in many agencies it is common practice first to reach a decision and then to have a special opinion-writing section compose a statement in justification.[79]

The more specific the impact statement requirement, the more likely it will influence agency action. Those requiring specific focus upon the environment, cost increases, or even competition are likely to prove more effective than those requiring a search for better alternatives. Nonetheless, the impact statement approach risks creating a significant amount of additional bureaucratic paperwork and consultant studies with only a small change in substantive results.

Encouraging Step-by-Step Reform

The generic proposals most compatible with the approach outlined here are those that encourage step-by-step, detailed examination of individual agencies. Detailed congressional oversight, for example, helped bring about airline and trucking deregulation. Executive branch study, when combined with congressional support, has also recently brought about major change in the railroad and banking industries. But how can Congress and the executive be encouraged to continue to conduct this type of oversight and reform? The major proposal advocated as a way to do so is "sunset" legislation. Because of certain serious drawbacks in the basic sunset concept, however, modifications of that plan have also been seriously considered.

Sunset proposals. Sunset legislation is designed to force Congress to consider regulatory reform on an agency-by-agency basis. It provides that an agency, together with its rules and regulations, will simply cease to exist as of a certain date unless Congress specifically enacts legislation that extends the agency's life. The threat of extinction should lead Congress to reconsider the need for a regulatory program before it disappears. Typically, sunset legislation also provides a comprehensive set of criteria, which Congress, after investigation, is to use in determining whether the agency's life should be prolonged.[80] Several states, including Colorado[81] and Florida,[82] have adopted sunset laws. Congress has occasionally inserted sunset provisions into laws creating new regulatory agencies, such as the Federal Energy Administration, which was to have expired on June 30, 1976.[83]

There are two major problems with the sunset approach. First, there is no guarantee that Congress will address itself seriously to the reform question and undertake the detailed work required. It may well simply reenact the old program automatically, as it did with the Federal Energy Administration. Or pressed by the demand for quick action, it may simply attack administrative waste without examining the fundamental objectives of the program. Second, the approach may condemn to extinction those agencies that are the subject of serious political controversy. It is far more difficult to pass legislation through Congress than to stop legislation from being passed. To give an obvious example, a few senators can filibuster and prevent a bill's enactment. Even without a filibuster, a determined minority can take advantage of time pressures, the committee system, and floor rules to delay or halt unfavorable legislation. The proponents of sunset laws seek to use this very fact to force serious reexamination of agencies. Yet the obverse side of the coin is that a minority within Congress could destroy the Federal Trade Commission, OSHA, or virtually any other agency. These defects suggest that the sunset approach needs modifications.

Agency-by-agency review: "high noon." Despite the attractiveness of a proposal for regular review of regulatory programs, whether it is possible to institutionalize step-by-step, program-by-program reform is uncertain. Any generic approach that hopes for success, however, should contain several elements. First, the proposal must lead those in positions of political authority—both in Congress and in the executive branch—to focus upon the problems of a particular program and to look for major improvements. Reform must catch the attention of those in power. They must know that they will have to take a position on the issues raised by a particular regulatory program. Thus, a forcing device is needed to convince those in authority that the reform of a specific program will be on their agenda. Second, those in authority must be willing to participate in or to supervise directly the detailed work necessary to evaluate the program comprehensively and to develop alternative proposals. They must carry out detailed, complex, time-consuming work. Third, that work must be guided by an intellectual framework. Those in charge cannot simply set out to "improve" an agency's performance. Rather, they must continuously test the existing program against arguably preferable alternatives, and, in particular, alternatives that are less restrictive and rely to a greater extent on the marketplace.

One might model a proposal containing these elements after sunset legislation, modifying sunset to overcome its major weaknesses. In 1979 Senator Kennedy introduced a bill with this aim. It contained the following provisions:[84] (1) The president is instructed to review regulatory programs according to a schedule that specifies two or three programs for scrutiny each year for ten years. (2) The president must take advice from a special committee, which will carry out the review and formulate detailed proposals for change. This committee will include as members the chairman of the Council of Economic Advisors, the chairman of the Council on Wage and Price Stability, the chairman of the Federal Trade Commission, and the attorney general. It will also include the secretary of labor, the president's consumer representative, the head of the agency currently under review, and several other members of the president's choice. The president might appoint, for example, members of Congress. (3) The mandate of the committee would encourage it to use a framework similar to the one presented in this book. It would have the committee and the president consider, among other things, how to achieve the goals of the program in less restrictive or nonregulatory ways, including the use of taxes, penalties, market-based incentives, bargaining techniques, disclosure, and the creation of new liability rules. (4) The proposals for change developed by the president must be transmitted to Congress and to the committees normally charged with supervision of the agencies at issue. (5) The proposals will remain in committee for one year, after which they, or alternative proposals developed by the committee, will be automatically discharged for a vote upon the floor of the house. They would be privileged on the floor, thus receiving priority attention. Since any member could offer the president's original reform proposals as an amendment, the president is guaranteed to vote upon those proposals after one year.

This proposal seeks to embody the three essential elements described above in the following ways. First, the attention of the president and members of Congress is attracted primarily by the legislative trigger. The president is required to study a particular agency and propose reforms, but that requirement on its own would likely produce yet one more staff report without further action. The automatic discharge from committee, however, means that opponents of a reform plan cannot stop it in committee. That fact automatically places the president's proposals on the congressional agenda for action. And the probability of action will encourage the president to make a serious reform effort. At the same time the "automatic discharge" and "automatic floor vote" requirements force the relevant congressional committees to take the issue seriously, for unless they come up with reasonable alternatives or defense of the status quo, the president's proposals are likely to be adopted. The knowledge that there will be a floor vote on a matter makes an enormous difference to a senator or congressman. Of the thousands of items and bills before Congress, only a few reach the floor; those that do will attract the attention of most members and the issue will be taken seriously. At the same time, because only a *vote* is required, rather than the disappearance of the agency (as in the sunset proposal), there is little risk that a congressional minority can destroy an existing regulatory program.

Second, detailed study and hard work is encouraged by the establishment of an executive-branch commission with members who will tend to favor regulatory reform. It is encouraged by the prospect of legislative action held out by the legislative "trigger." Knowing that Congress is likely to take the matter seriously means that the executive branch is more likely to do so. In addition, the rivalrous nature of the legislative and executive branches, together with the jurisdictional possessiveness of congressional committees, will encourage hard work, for the committee members will know that a solidly based and documented report by the executive body can be overcome—and their own participation will be relevant—only if they engage in equally detailed work. Each group has an incentive to receive credit for reform and therefore to outperform the other.

Third, the members of the executive branch committee will be chosen to increase the likelihood that procompetitive reform will take place. The Justice Department, the Council of Economic Advisors, the Council on Wage and Price Stability, and the Federal Trade Commission are all, for institutional reasons, likely to favor competition and to be suspicious of classical regulation, regardless of who is president or which party is in power. Thus, a committee with representatives from these bodies is more likely than most to approach regulatory reform using an intellectual framework of the type presented here—a framework that sees classical regulation as a weapon of last resort and looks for less restrictive ways to deal with problems thought to call for regulation.

Of course, there is no guarantee that this or any other generic proposal will lead to meaningful reform. Depending upon the political climate, neither the president nor Congress may take the requirement to produce reform proposals seriously. Committee meetings may be attended only by low-level staff; the president's recommendations may not be significant; the congressional committees may oppose change and command a majority of congressional votes. Nonetheless, although one must remain skeptical of the ability of any generic proposal to bring about broad-scale regulatory reform, this type of proposal seems as likely as any to provide an institutional base for continued interest in reform of particular programs. And it stands some chance of producing action. The action, one hopes, will be of a sort consistent with the framework set out in this book. Indeed, that framework has been created to help those interested in meaningful, substantive regulatory reform to design just such specific proposals.

Appendixes
Further Reading
Notes
Index

Appendix 1
The Regulatory Agencies

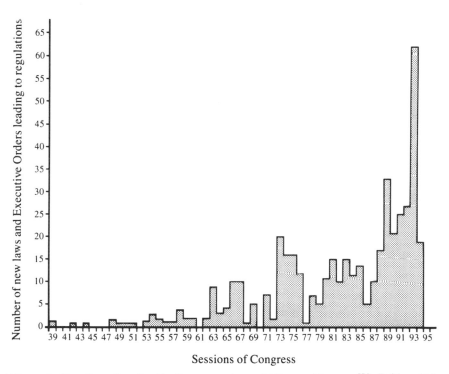

Figure 4. Creation of authority for current regulations. (*Source:* W. Buhler, *Calculating the Full Costs of Government Regulation,* obtained from the General Accounting Office [preliminary data, 1977], Management Design, Inc.)

Table 12. Federal regulatory agencies controlling prices and services.

Organization	Year established	Regulatory function
Interstate Commerce Commission	1887	Controls prices, routes, and service practices of surface transportation companies, including railroads, trucks, bus lines, oil pipelines, and domestic watercarriers.
Federal Power Commission (now in the Federal Energy Regulation Commission of the Department of Energy)	1930	Regulates wellhead gas prices and wholesale prices of natural gas and electricity sold for resale in interstate commerce.
Federal Communications Commission	1934	Sets prices for telephone and telegraph service, controls entry into telecommunications and broadcasting within the United States.
Federal Maritime Commission	1936	Controls fares and scheduling of transocean freight shipments.
Civil Aeronautics Board	1938	Regulates airline passenger fares, controls entry of airlines into city-to-city air routes, and provides subsidies to local service.
Postal Rate Commission	1970	Establishes classes of mail and rates for those classes; sets fees for other services.
Energy Regulatory Administration (in Department of Energy)	1974	Regulates wellhead oil prices and refinery, wholesale, and retail prices of petroleum products. Specifies allocation levels for wholesalers and retailers of crude oil, residual fuel oil, and most refined petroleum products produced in or imported into the United States during a period of energy emergency.
Copyright Royalty Tribunal	1976	Sets fees and charges on copyright materials.

Source: P. MacAvoy, *The Present Condition of the Regulated Industries* (1979), gathered from *The Challenge of Regulatory Reform: A Report to the President from the Domestic Council Review on Regulatory Reform,* Washington, D.C., 1977, at 50–51.

Table 13. Regulatory agencies concerned with health, safety, and the quality of the environment.

Organization	Year established	Regulatory function
The Packers and Stockyards Administration, U.S. Department of Agriculture	1916	Determines plant conditions and practices in livestock and processed-meat production.
The Food and Drug Administration, Department of Health, Education, and Welfare	1931	Licenses and controls the labeling of foods and drugs.
The Agricultural Marketing Service, Department of Agriculture	1937	Determines standards for most farm commodities and also sets minimum prices for milk in some areas.
The Federal Aviation Administration, Department of Transportation (DOT)	1948	Operates air traffic control systems and sets safety standards for aircraft and airports.
The Animal and Plant Health Inspection Service, Department of Agriculture	1953	Sets standards, inspects, and enforces laws relating to meat, poultry, and plant safety.
The Federal Highway Administration, DOT	1966	Sets safety standards for interstate trucking services.
The Federal Railroad Administration, DOT	1966	Sets safety standards for interstate railroad transportation.
The National Highway Traffic Safety Administration, DOT	1970	Sets safety standards for automobiles.
The Environmental Protection Agency	1970	Develops environmental quality standards and approves abatement plans operated by state agencies to curtail individual industry pollution emissions.
The Consumer Product Safety Commission	1972	Sets product safety standards.
The Mining Enforcement and Safety Administration, Department of the Interior	1973	Sets mine safety standards.
The Drug Enforcement Administration, Department of Justice	1973	Controls trade in narcotics and drugs.
The Occupational Safety and Health Administration, Department of Labor	1973	Sets and enforces workers' safety and health regulations.

Table 13. *Continued*

Organization	Year established	Regulatory function
The Nuclear Regulatory Commission (reorganized from the Atomic Energy Commission)	1975	Licenses the construction and operation of civilian nuclear power plants and other uses of nuclear energy (formerly the Atomic Energy Commission).

Source: P. MacAvoy, *The Present Condition of the Regulated Industries* (1979), obtained from *The Challenge of Regulatory Reform: A Report to the President from the Domestic Council Review on Regulatory Reform,* Washington, D.C., 1977, at 50–54.

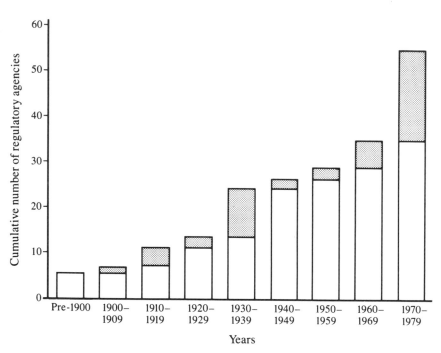

Figure 5. Growth of federal regulatory agencies. (*Source:* M. Weidenbaum, "The Trend of Government Regulation of Business," paper prepared for the Hoover Institute Conference on Regulation, Stanford University, July 9, 1979.)

Table 14. Federal agencies concerned with fraudulent practices and the security of financial institutions.

Organization	Year established	Regulatory function
Board of Governors of the Federal Reserve System	1913	Regulates commercial banks to reduce bank failure rates.
The Federal Trade Commission	1914	Administers laws concerning fraudulent and deceptive sales practices.
The Federal Home Loan Bank Board	1932	Supervises federally chartered savings and home savings and home financing institutions.
The Federal Deposit Insurance Corporation	1933	Supervises insured banks.
Securities and Exchange Commission	1934	Regulates investor information and securities exchange transactions.
Securities Investors Protection Commission	1970	Supervises and insures stock exchange transactions.
Farm Credit Administration	1971	Controls credit disbursed through the farm credit system.
Commodity Futures Trading Commission	1975	Sets terms and conditions for future contracts and the exchanges trading such contracts.

Source: P. MacAvoy, *The Present Condition of the Regulated Industries* (1979), gathered from *The Challenge of Regulatory Reform: A Report to the President from the Domestic Council Review Group on Regulatory Reform*, Washington, D.C., 1977, at 50–51.

Table 15. Regulation by state commissions.

Industry	Number of states regulating prices[a]	Number of states regulating entry
Electricity (private)	49	35
Electricity (public)	17	12
Electricity (cooperative)	29	23
Natural gas retailing (private)	49	36
Natural gas retailing (public)	17	11
Telephone	50	38
Airline service	21	25
Common-carrier trucks	47	45
Contract-carrier trucks	42	43
Railroad transportation	44	26

Source: P. MacAvoy, *The Present Condition of the Regulated Industries* (1979), gathered from *1976 Annual Report on Utility and Carrier Regulation* (National Association of Regulatory Utility Commissions, Washington, D.C., 1977), at 392, 488, 594, 612, 615.

a. Sales to ultimate consumers.

Note: All totals include the District of Columbia.

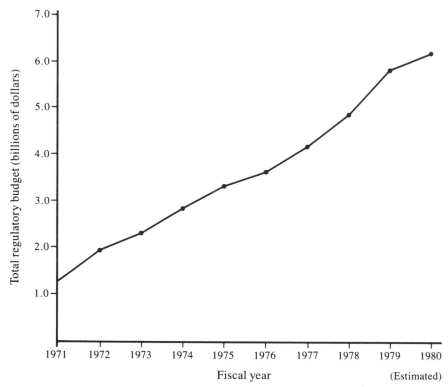

Figure 6. Federal regulatory growth. (*Source:* M. Weidenbaum, "The Trend of Government Regulation of Business," paper prepared for the Hoover Institute Conference on Regulation, Stanford University, July 9, 1979.)

Table 16. Cumulative growth of federal regulations pages in the federal register.

Year	Number of pages	Cumulative pages
1936	2,599	2,599
1937	3,445	6,044
1938	3,160	9,204
1939	5,007	14,211
1940	5,307	19,518
1941	6,877	26,395
1942	11,134	37,529
1943	17,553	55,082
1944	15,194	70,276
1945	15,508	85,784
1946	14,736	100,520
1947	8,902	109,422
1948	9,608	119,030
1949	7,952	126,982
1950	9,562	136,544
1951	13,175	149,719
1952	11,896	161,615
1953	8,912	170,527
1954	9,910	180,437
1955	10,196	190,633
1956	10,528	201,161
1957	11,156	212,317
1958	10,579	222,896
1959	11,113	234,009
1960	14,479	248,488
1961	12,789	261,277
1962	13,226	274,503
1963	14,842	289,345
1964	19,304	308,649
1965	17,206	325,855
1966	16,850	342,705
1967	21,088	363,793
1968	20,072	383,865
1969	20,466	404,331
1970	20,036	424,367
1971	25,447	449,814
1972	28,924	478,738
1973	35,572	514,310
1974	45,422	559,732
1975	60,221	619,953
1976	57,072	677,025
1977	65,603	742,628
Projected 1981		Over 1 million

Source: W. Buhler, Calculating the Full Costs of Government Regulation, Office of the Librarian, Federal Register, 1978.

Appendix 2
A Note on Administrative Law

Modern American administrative law grew out of the government's efforts to regulate private economic activity in the last part of the nineteenth century. Its original objective was to control government incursions upon private liberty and property interests by relying upon the judiciary to confine agency powers to those granted by the legislature. Thus, judges would scrutinize agency decisions to make certain they conformed to the agency's legislative mandate. The agency was required to follow procedures that would prevent it from straying beyond the bounds of the statute and that would help judges determine whether in a particular case it had done so.[1]

Using these standards, judges overturned many agency actions until the New Deal. At that time the judiciary, while using the same standards in principle, began in practice to show far greater deference to agencies. The agencies were left with few checks on their discretion, except the check of "professional discipline."

Between 1945 and 1965, by way of reaction to excessive agency freedom, Congress passed, and the courts enforced, the federal Administrative Procedures Act (APA). This act imposed certain procedural constraints upon federal administrative bodies—whether located in the executive branch or in independent agencies. Its basic object was to achieve "fairness" rather than "control." It forms the basis of current federal administrative law. Recently, it has been interpreted and supplemented by statutes and regulations that increase the participation of various interest groups—particularly the public interest bar—in agency proceedings, to the point where some scholars have argued that current law consists of the APA's fairness model, supplemented by a public interest model of proper procedure.[2]

In any event, the APA is not the sole source of administrative law. Agency decisions typically must conform to the Constitution, the substantive law authorizing the agency's action, the procedural requirements of the APA, any procedural requirements contained in the agency's authorizing statute, the agency's own (procedural and substantive) rules and regulations, and certain "common law" administrative law requisites of, for example, consistency. Obviously, the specific legal requirements depend upon the particular program and upon the content of each of these relevant sources of law. Nonetheless, it is possible to make a few generalizations about the basic legal, procedural requirements.

First, nearly all agency decisions (including any legislatory decisions) are subject to court review to determine that they do not violate the Constitution and that they fall within the authorizing statute. Many statutes delegate broad authority to the administrator. However, exercises of this discretion are also subject to review to determine whether they are reasonable. In fact, the APA sets out several standards for review of agency action. Depending upon the proceeding, a court may have to decide whether a finding is "unsupported by substantial evidence," or "arbitrary, capricious, an abuse of discretion." The intricacies of applying these standards are best overlooked here. The reader can take "reasonableness" as an approximate standard of review for every exercise of agency discretion, while recognizing that many difficult questions (how much deference should be shown the agency, how the court is to *know* whether a decision is reasonable) have been ignored. Even so broad a standard, however, affects the way in which an agency conducts its task. As has been shown, for example, it is sometimes difficult for an agency to show that a negotiated standard is reasonable, for the major characteristic of negotiation is not that its result is "reasonable" but that it is "agreed upon." Moreover, the difficulties of courts deciding whether highly technical decisions are reasonable are so great that court efforts are frequently criticized, sometimes as too intrusive, sometimes as not intrusive enough.[3]

Second, most agency decisions (and thus most regulatory decisions) fit one of four procedural models created by the APA and related statutory and decisional law. These four models vary, depending upon whether the agency uses formal or informal procedures and upon whether it is engaged in adjudication or rulemaking. In fact, most procedural requirements arise out of lawmakers' viewing the agency as a "little court," engaged in adjudication, or as a "little legislature," engaged in making rules.

Formal adjudication. When the agency adjudicates formally, it decides a particular case or controversy on the basis of a record. The agency provides a type of trial. There is an impartial decison maker, and the parties present evidence, often witnesses, who can be cross-examined. The agency cannot go outside the formal record in making its decision; its ability to consult outside people is strictly curtailed.

The requirement to adjudicate formally may be imposed by the Constitution, a statute, or by agency rules themselves. The procedure is basically designed to apply *preexisting* rules to a particular case. Its strength lies in its ability to determine individual facts. Yet rules can grow out of adjudicatory proceedings, and some agencies, such as the National Labor Relations Board, use adjudication almost exlcusively, even to promulgate broad general policies. Agencies such as the FCC use adjudication to award licenses. Indeed, much allocation takes place within the procedural framework of formal adjudication.

Informal rulemaking. When agencies enact rules, they do so almost exclusively through the APA's "informal rulemaking" procedures. Those procedures, applicable to all important rules, essentially require no more than "notice and comment." The agency must first publish a notice in the Federal Register stating the content of the rules it proposes to adopt. It then must allow all interested persons to submit comments. After receiving those comments, the agency can promulgate a final set of rules.

Until recently, the agency was free to consult anyone it chose about the rule's content. It might consult formally or informally. There was no formal record. The procedural model was the legislature, which holds hearings before enacting a bill, but whose members also engage in private, informal consultations.

More recently, however, the courts, noting that agency members (unlike legislators) are not elected, have begun to impose stricter procedural requirements on informal rulemaking. These requirements are aimed at making it easier for a judge to determine if a rule is reasonable—a difficult task if the supporting evidence has been obtained off the record. In various ways, the courts have inhibited off-the-record consultations and insisted that the agency provide adequate opportunity for the major contending parties (including the agency) to answer the arguments of the others. These requirements have led in many areas to hybrid procedures, best described as a written dialogue among the agency and parties, eventually leading to the promulgation of rules supported by a written justification and publicly disclosed information.[4] Most standard setting follows informal rulemaking or hybrid procedures.

Formal rulemaking. Occasionally a statute requires that an agency promulgate a rule only after a "hearing on a record." If so, the agency typically will follow procedures like those for formal adjudication. These will include notice, an impartial decision maker, opportunity to present and cross-examine witnesses, decision based on a formal record, and judicial review based on that record. Most ratemaking proceedings take place in accordance with these procedures. Though a Supreme Court decision casts doubt upon whether the APA itself actually requires formal rulemaking for ratemaking,[5] most agency procedural rules still provide these formal procedures for rulemaking.

Informal adjudication. Most other agency decision making, including the millions of decisions made by civil servants in their offices every day, can be classified as "informal adjudication" and are subject to few procedural requirements. Most of them can be reviewed in court for reasonableness and for conformity with the statues and Constitution. In some instances an agency may be put to some trouble to show that it acted reasonably in light of the statute's language, particularly, for example, if a statute requires environmental impact to be taken into account. Yet most informal adjudications are left unreviewed by the courts.

Occasionally, the Constitution itself may transform an informal adjudication into a more formal one, because the Constitution imposes "due process" requirements when the government takes from a person his "life, liberty, or property." [6] The process "due" typically involves notice, opportunity to present arguments and evidence and to cross-examine witnesses, an impartial decision maker, and possibly legal counsel. [7] When these requirements apply, however, is a matter of much legal dispute, revolving around whether the government is in fact taking something from someone. Is, for example, a welfare payment or an education something to which a person is entitled and which the government, therefore, cannot take away without due process? Or is it a privilege given to a person by the government, which the government can then take away with fewer procedural protections?

One might summarize these procedural rules as providing persons with certain minimal procedural expectations. When agencies make decisions of importance, they are likely to be subject to the following general procedural constraints:

1. they must give notice of what they intend to do well in advance of their doing it;
2. they must provide reasons for their action and publicly present evidence supporting it;
3. they must allow affected parties to present arguments and evidence;
4. they must overcome court review of showing through argument and evidence that their position is reasonable.

Although these requirements are minimal and administrative law is generally flexible, these points should be kept in mind. First, the law generally imposes greater protections and procedural requirements when the government orders someone to do something or takes something from someone than when the government gives someone something, such as a grant or a benefit. Regulation involves the former, not the latter, activity. Second, the procedural rules mean that lawyers play an important role in all regulatory proceedings. Lawyers tend to look for solutions that are procedurally fair, or treat like persons alike, or that preserve past expectation more than they provide economically efficient solutions. Third, complying with procedural requirements takes time. They may indeed add to the problem of delay.

In any event, it is important to recognize that these procedures are *not* the regulatory process itself. They act as a *constraint* on that process along with other constraints.

Further Reading

Introduction

Landis, J. *Report on Regulatory Agencies to the President Elect.* Subcommittee on Administrative Practice and Procedure of the Senate Committee on the Judiciary, 86th Congress, 2d Session. Committee print, 1960.

MacAvoy, P. *The Crisis of the Regulatory Commission.* New York, 1970.

—— *The Present Condition of the Regulated Industries.* New York, 1979.

Noll, R. *Reforming Regulation.* Washington, D.C., 1971.

Posner, R. "Theories of Economic Regulation." *5 Bell Journal of Economics and Management Science* 335 (1974).

Stigler, G. "The Theory of Economic Regulation." *2 Bell Journal of Economics and Management Science* 3 (1971).

1. Typical Justifications for Regulation

Hayek, F. "The Use of Knowledge in Society." 35 *American Economic Review* 519 (1945).

Kahn, A. *The Economics of Regulation: Principles and Institutions.* New York, 1970.

Robinson, J. *The Economics of Imperfect Competition.* London, 1933. Books 2 and 4.

Scherer, F. *Industrial Market Structure and Economic Performance.* 2d ed. Chicago, 1980.

2. Cost-of-Service Ratemaking

Bonbright, J. *Principles of Public Utility Rates.* New York, 1961.

Kahn, A. *The Economics of Regulation: Principles and Institutions.* New York, 1970.

Klevorick, A. K. "The 'Optimal' Fair Rate of Return." *2 Bell Journal of Economics and Management Science* 122 (1971).

Lorie, J., and Hamilton, M. *The Stock Market.* Homewood, Ill., 1973. Sections 2 and 3.

Scherer, F. *Industrial Market Structure and Economic Performance.* 2d ed. Chicago, 1980. Chapter 18.

3. Historically Based Price Regulation

Benes, R., et al. *Problems in Price Control: Pricing Techniques.* OPA History Series, Washington, D.C., 1947.
Mills, D. "Some Decisions of Price Control in 1971–1973." 6 *Bell Journal of Economics and Management Science* 3 (1975).
Slawson, W. "Price Controls for a Peacetime Economy." 84 *Harvard Law Review* 1090 (1971).
——— "Price Controls in a Cold War." 19 *Journal of Law and Contemporary Problems* 475 (1954).

4. Allocation under a Public Interest Standard

Anthony, R. "Towards Simplicity and Rationality in Comparative Broadcast Licensing Proceedings." 24 *Stanford Law Review* 9 (1971).
Cole, B., and Oettinger, A. *Reluctant Regulators.* Reading, Mass., 1978.
Friendly, H. *The Federal Administrative Agencies: The Need for a Better Definition of Standards.* Cambridge, Mass., 1962.
Noll, R., Peck, M., and McGowan, J. *Economic Aspects of Television Regulation.* Washington, D.C., 1974.
Quinlan, S. *The Hundred Million Dollar Lunch.* Chicago, 1974.

5. Standard Setting

MacAvoy, P., ed. *OSHA Safety Regulation: Report of the Presidential Task Force.* Washington, D.C., 1977.
Wilson, J. "The Politics of Regulation." In J. McKie, ed., *Social Responsibility and the Business Predicament.* Washington, D.C., 1974.

7. Individualized Screening

Breyer, S., and Stewart, R. *Administrative Law and Regulatory Policy.* Boston, 1979. Chapter 6.
Calabresi, G. *The Costs of Accidents.* New Haven, 1970.
Schelling, T. "The Life You Save May Be Your Own." In S. Chase ed., *Problems in Public Expenditure Analysis.* Washington, D.C., 1968.
Zeckhauser, R., and Nichols, A. *The Occupational Safety and Health Administration—An Overview.* U.S. Senate Committee on Governmental Affairs, 95th Congress, 2d Session. Appendix to Volume 6: *Framework for Regulation* (1978).

8. Alternatives to Classical Regulation

Areeda, P., and Turner, D. *Antitrust Law.* Boston, 1979.
Bork, R. *The Antitrust Paradox.* New York, 1978.
Calabresi, G. *The Cost of Accidents.* New Haven, 1970.

Coase, R. "The Problem of Social Costs." 3 *Journal of Law and Economics* 1 (1960).

Demsetz, H. "When Does the Rule of Liability Matter?" 1 *Journal of Legal Studies* 13 (1972).

Fletcher, G. "Fairness and Utility in Tort Theory." 85 *Harvard Law Review* 537 (1972).

Lange, D., and Taylor, F. *On the Economic Theory of Socialism*. New York, 1964.

11. Mismatch: Excessive Competition and Airline Regulation

Douglas, G., and Miller, G., III. *Economic Regulation of Domestic Air Transport: Theory and Policy*. Washington, D.C., 1974.

U.S. Senate Committee on the Judiciary, Subcommittee on Administrative Practice and Procedure. *Civil Aeronautics Board Practices and Procedures*. Washington, D.C., 1975.

12. Mismatch: Excessive Competition and the Trucking Industry

MacAvoy, P., and Snow, J., eds. *Regulation of Entry and Pricing in Truck Transportation*. Washington, D.C., 1977.

U.S. Senate Committee on the Judiciary. *Federal Restraints on Competition in the Trucking Industry: Antitrust Immunity and Economic Regulation*. Washington, D.C., 1980.

13. Mismatch: Rent Control and Natural Gas Field Prices

Breyer, S., and MacAvoy, P. *Energy Regulation by the Federal Power Commission*. Washington, D.C., 1974.

Willrich, M. *Administration of Energy Shortages: Natural Gas and Petroleum*. Cambridge, Mass., 1976.

14. Partial Mismatch: Spillovers and Environmental Pollution

Ackerman, B., et al. *The Uncertain Search for Environmental Quality*. Philadelphia, 1974.

Baxter, W. *People or Penguins: The Case for Optimal Pollution*. New York, 1974.

Dales, J. *Pollution, Property, and Prices*. Toronto, 1968.

Friedlaender, A. *Approaches to Controlling Air Pollution*. Cambridge, Mass., 1979.

Kneese, A., and Bower, B. *Managing Water Quality: Economics, Technology, Institutions*. Baltimore, 1968.

15. Problems of a Possible Match: Natural Monopoly and Telecommunications

Charles River Associates. *The Economics of Competition in the Telecommunications Industry*. Report no. 338. Cambridge, Mass., 1979.

Demsetz, H. "Why Regulate Utilities?" 11 *Journal of Law and Economics* 55 (1968).

Kahn, A., and Zielinski, C. "New Rate Structures in Communications." 97 *Public Utilities Fortnightly* 19 (March 25, 1978).

Sichter, J. "Separations Procedures in the Telephone Industry: The Historical Origins of a Public Policy." Unpublished paper, 1977. Available from Prof. A. Oettinger, Harvard University.

Waverman, L. "The Regulation of Intercity Telecommunications." In A. Phillip, ed., *Promoting Competition in Regulated Markets*. Washington, D.C., 1975.

17. Generic Approaches to Regulatory Reform

American Bar Association Commission on Law and the Economy. *Federal Regulation: Roads to Reform*. Washington, D.C., 1979.

Breyer, S., and Stewart, R. *Administrative Law and Regulatory Policy*. Boston, 1979. Chapter 8.

Cutler, L., and Johnson, D. "Regulation and the Political Process." 84 *Yale Law Journal* 1395 (1975).

Gellhorn, W. *When Americans Complain: Governmental Grievance Procedures*. 1966.

President's Advisory Council on Executive Organization. *A New Regulatory Framework: Report on Selected Independent Regulatory Agencies* (Ash Council Report). Washington, D.C., 1971.

Stewart, R. "The Reformation of American Administrative Law." 88 *Harvard Law Review* 1667 (1975).

U.S. Senate Committee on Governmental Affairs. *Study on Federal Regulation*. 6 vols. Washington, D.C., 1977–78.

U.S. Senate Committee on Governmental Affairs and Senate Committee on the Judiciary. *Reform of Federal Regulation: Joint Report*. S. Rep. 96-1018, Part 2. Washington, D.C., 1980.

Notes

Introduction

1. Interstate Commerce Act of 1887, 24 Stat. 379, now 49 U.S.C. § 1 (1976).

2. Wallace and Penoyer, *Directory of Federal Regulatory Agencies,* Washington University Center for the Study of American Business, working paper no. 36 (1978).

3. P. MacAvoy, *The Present Condition of the Regulated Industries* (New York, 1979), chapter 1.

4. See President's Committee on Administrative Management (Brownlow Committee), *Report of the Committee with Studies of Administrative Management in the Federal Government 39–41* (Washington, D.C., 1937).

5. U.S. Commission on Organization of the Executive Branch of the Government, *The Independent Regulatory Agencies: A Report with Recommendations* (Washington, D.C., 1949). U.S. Commission on Organization of the Executive Branch of the Government, *Legal Services and Procedures* (Washington, D.C., 1955).

6. J. Landis, *Report on Regulatory Agencies to the President-Elect,* U.S. Senate Comm. on the Judiciary, Subcomm. on Administrative Practice and Procedure, 86th Cong., 2d Sess. (Comm. print, 1960).

7. President's Advisory Council on Executive Organization, *A New Regulatory Framework: Report on Selected Independent Regulatory Agencies* (Washington, D.C., 1971).

8. See, e.g., H. Friendly, *The Federal Administrative Agencies: The Need for a Better Definition of Standards* (Cambridge, Mass., 1962); U.S. Senate Comm. on Governmental Affairs, *Study on Federal Regulation,* 6 vols. and appendix, 95th Cong., 1st Sess. (1977); American Bar Association Commission on Law and the Economy, *Federal Regulation: Roads to Reform* (Washington, D.C., 1978); and the extensive bibliography of prior studies listed in ch. 2 of this A.B.A. report.

9. P. MacAvoy, *supra* note 3; M. Weidenbaum, "The Trend of Government Regulation of Business," paper prepared for Conference on Regulation at the Hoover Institute, Stanford University, July 9, 1979, at 7.

10. See Sommers, *The Economic Costs of Regulation: Report for the ABA Commission on Law and the Economy* (New Haven, 1978); Weidenbaum, *supra* note 9, at 15.

11. Arthur Anderson & Co., *Cost of Government Regulation Study for the Business Roundtable* (March 1979).

12. W. Buhler, "Calculating the Full Costs of Government Regulation," paper available from the Federal Paperwork Commission or from the author at Management Design, Inc. (1978).

13. P. MacAvoy, *supra* note 3.

14. P. MacAvoy, *supra* note 3.

15. See generally R. Smith, *The Occupational Safety and Health Act* (Washington, D.C., 1976); A. D. Pietro, "An Analysis of the OSHA Inspection Program in Manufacturing Industries, 1972–1973," U.S. Dept. of Labor (Washington, D.C., 1976); A. Nichols and R. Zeckhauser, "Government Comes to the Workplace: An Assessment of OSHA," *The Public Interest* (Fall 1977).

16. See Comptroller General of the United States, *Report to the Senate Committee on Commerce,* CED 76–121 (July 7, 1976); *Motor Vehicle Safety: A Report on Activities,* DOT-HS, 801–910 (Washington, D.C., January 1, 1975, December 31, 1975); S. Peltzman, *Regulation of Automobile Safety* (Washington, D.C., 1975); and P. MacAvoy, *supra* note 3, at 130–140.

17. See, e.g., U.S. Senate Comm. on the Judiciary, Subcomm. on Admin. Practice and Procedure, *Civil Aeronautics Board Practices and Procedures,* Subcomm. Report, 94th Cong., 1st Sess. (1975) [hereinafter referred to as the *Kennedy Report*]; P. MacAvoy, *The Crisis of the Regulatory Commissions* (New York, 1970); R. Noll, *Reforming Regulation* (Washington, D.C., 1971); S. Breyer and P. MacAvoy, *Energy Regulation by the Federal Power Commission* (Washington, D.C., 1974).

18. See S. Breyer and R. Stewart, *Administrative Law and the Regulatory Process* 489 (Boston, 1979).

19. See generally R. Stewart, "The Reformation of American Administrative Law," 88 *Harv. L. Rev.* 1667 (1975); Breyer and Stewart, *supra* note 18, at 478–530.

20. See J. Freedman, "Crisis and Legitimacy in the Administrative Process," 27 *Stan. L. Rev.* 1041 (1975). See generally Stewart, *supra* note 19; Breyer and Stewart, *supra* note 18, at 103–105.

21. 5 U.S.C. § 552 (1976).

22. 5 U.S.C. § 551 et seq. (1976).

23. See Dunlop, "The Limits of the Regulatory Process" (unpublished paper, 1975); P. Aranson, "The Uncertain Search for Regulatory Reform," at 24 (unpublished paper, University of Miami Center for Law and Economics, 1979).

24. See F. Bator, "The Anatomy of Market Failure," 72 *Q. J. Econ.* 351 (1958).

25. This description paraphrases R. Merton, "Bureaucratic Structure and Personality," in *The National Administrative System: Selected Readings* 379, D. Yarwood ed. (New York, 1971), describing Max Weber's view. See also L. von Mises, *Bureaucracy* (1944).

26. See A. Downs, *Inside Bureaucracy* (Boston, 1967); Aranson, *supra* note 23.

27. Ch. 706, 52 Stat. 973 (repealed 1958).

28. Pub. L. No. 85–726, 72 Stat. 731 (1958). This act was substantially amended by *The Airline Deregulation Act of 1978,* Pub. L. No. 95-504, 92 Stat. 1704 (1978), codified in scattered sections of 49 U.S.C.

29. 8 & 9 Vict. c. 20 (1845); 17 & 18 Vict. c. 31 (1854).

30. 5 U.S.C. §§ 551–559, 701–706 (1976).

31. For an effort to define regulation and its place among other governmental activities, see J. McKie, "Regulation and the Free Market: The Problem of Boundaries," 1 *Bell J. Econ. & Mgmt. Sci.* 6 (1970).

32. See discussion in, e.g., R. Posner, "Theories of Economic Regulation," 5 *Bell J. Econ. & Mgmt. Sci.* 335 (1974).

33. See, e.g., M. Bernstein, *Regulating Business by Independent Commission* (Princeton, 1955); S. Huntington, "The Miasmus of the ICC: The Commission, the Railroads, and the Public Interest," in *Public Administration and Policy: Selected Essays,* P. Woll, ed. (New York, 1966); H. Ziegler, *Interest Groups in American Society* (Englewood Cliffs, 1964); T. Moore, "The Effectiveness of Regulation of Electric Utility Prices," 36 *Southern Econ. J.* 365 (1970); G. Stigler and C. Friedland, "What Can Regulators Regulate? The Case of Electricity," *J. Law & Econ.* 5 (1962); Breyer and MacAvoy, *supra* note 20; M. Conant, *Railroad Mergers and Abandonments* (Berkeley, 1964); S. Peltzman, "An Evaluation of Consumer Protection Legislation: The 1962 Drug Amendments," 81 *J. Pol. Econ.* 1049 (1973); and Arthur Anderson & Co., *supra* note 11.

34. See A. Bentley, *The Process of Government* (Bloomington, 1908); D. Truman, *The Governmental Process: Political Interests and Public Opinion* (New York, 1951); G. Stigler, "The Theory of Economic Regulation," 2 *Bell J. Econ. & Mgmt. Sci.* 3 (1971); S. Peltzman, "Toward a More General Theory of Regulation," 19 *J. Law & Econ.* 211 (1976).

35. See R. Posner, "Taxation by Regulation," 2 *Bell J. Econ. & Mgmt. Sci.* 22 (1971).

36. See Nichols and Zeckhauser, *supra* note 15.

37. See Stigler, *supra* note 34; Peltzman, *supra* note 34. The relative strength of producer and consumer groups might depend upon the number of persons in the group, information costs, and organizing costs. Peltzman, *supra* note 34.

38. Interest group theories, as causal explanations of either the historical origins of regulation or the actions of regulators, suffer several drawbacks. Where they are limited to producers, they are often inaccurate. They cannot fully explain environmental, health, safety regulation, or even traditional utility and transportation regulation. While such a theory may help explain the origins of railroad regulation, it does not explain airline regulation, which arose not as a method of cartelizing the industry but, rather, as an effort to stop corruption in the awarding of airline subsidies.

If the theory is expanded beyond producers, it risks becoming nonpredictive and nonexplanatory. All regulatory rules and programs benefit some group or other. One could "explain" any deviation from "optimal" regulation as a response to the political power of the affected group. This criticism can be avoided only if the theory is strong enough to predict in advance precisely how and when regulators would respond to political pressures, but so far it is not.

Finally, although these theories wisely direct attention to the political dimensions of the regulator's or legislator's tasks, they tend to overlook the extent to which nonpolitical factors affect the content of regulation. While some regulators are politicians, many are not; they are not elected; and they do not seek to maximize votes, for doing so would help them personally only indirectly. Similarly, one cannot in fairness view legislators as interested only in the political support of those who favor or oppose particular measures. The merits of those issues play an important role in political argument. Thus, the airlines were deregulated over the strong opposition of both the carriers and affected labor unions. At the same time, AT&T seems unlikely to secure enactment of legislation designed to reverse certain regulatory actions with which it disagrees. In neither instance can "pure politics," considered in terms of the political strength of the affected parties, account for the legislative result.

39. See W. Niskanen, *Bureaucracy and Representative Government* (Chicago, 1971). Numerous related articles are listed in P. Aranson, *supra* note 23, ch. 2, n. 42. See also J. Buchanan and G. Tullock, *The Calculus of Consent* (Ann Arbor, 1962); M. Olson, *The Logic of Collective Action* (Cambridge, Mass., 1965); J. March and H. Simon, *Organizations* (New York, 1958). See also A. Downs, *Inside Bureaucracy* (Boston, 1967).

1. Typical Justifications for Regulation

1. The list of "market defects" discussed in this chapter does not treat separately one justification for regulation—namely, "income redistribution," which some have thought an important basis for regulatory action. The decision not to treat income redistribution separately is based upon several considerations. For one thing, it is typically difficult to evaluate the redistributive consequences of regulatory decision making. The effort, for example, to help small towns by cross-subsidizing airline costs may or may not help those who are poor. The users of small-town service may, in general, be richer than those who use transcontinental service. Indeed, those persons who use natural gas to heat their homes and thus are helped by price controls on gas may or may not be richer than those forced to turn to other higher-cost fuels due to a regulation-induced shortage. Regulatory statutes, despite their broad language, rarely call for pure income redistribution. Further, virtually every regulatory program has redistributive effects, and could be claimed to benefit some group of people who arguably are worse off than some other group that the decision harms. Thus, pure redistribution as a justification would impose little or no standard upon regulatory actions. Finally, "redistributive consequences," like other justifications not treated in this chapter, is better left as a rebuttal argument by those supporting a program. Often, it will not be made. Thus, for example, when airline regulators sought to force an increase in transatlantic charter rates, their objective was basically redistributive; they feared the bankruptcy of Pan American Airlines and they were trying to help Pan American and its employees. It is unlikely, however, that they would have advanced such a claim as justifying forcing Pan Am's competitors to charge higher charter fares, simply because the action, even if it could be shown to help "the poor," would not have been seen as a legitimate justification for regulatory intervention.

2. For a sampling of the literature dealing with the economic justifications for regulation, see A. Kahn, *The Economics of Regulation: Principles and Institutions,* 2 vols. (New York, 1970, 1971); R. Posner, "Natural Monopoly and Its Regulation," 21 *Stan. L. Rev.* 548 (1969); G. Stigler, "The Theory of Economic Regulation" 2 *Bell J. Econ. & Mgmt. Sci.* 3 (1971); H. Demsetz, "Why Regulate Utilities?" 11 *J. Law & Econ.* 55 (1968).

3. The economist's model of a perfectly competitive market assumes that (1) individual sellers are unable to affect market price by varying output, (2) resources move freely among productive uses, (3) sellers produce identical products, and (4) actors in the marketplace possess perfect information about prices, technology, and consumptive choices. Several conclusions that flow from these assumptions are illustrated in Figure 7. When a firm first enters the market, the owner finds that he can sell his product for price P_i. This, in turn, leads him to expand his output to X_i units, where the price it

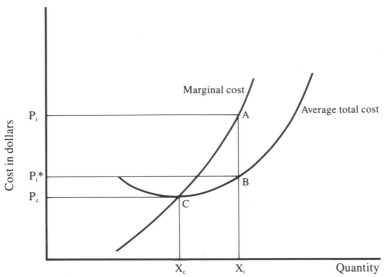

Figure 7. The competitive model.

can obtain in the marketplace is equal to the cost of producing the last unit of output (i.e., the marginal cost of $X_i = P_i$). At output levels below X_i the owner earns revenue in excess of his costs and it pays to expand; at levels above X_i it costs the seller more to produce additional units than he can recoup in the marketplace, and output will be cut back. Where the firm is able to produce at output X_i and price P_i, it earns profits exceeding total costs (Profits = Revenue − Costs = AREA OP_iAX_i − AREA OP_i*BX_i = AREA P_iABP_i*). The availability of such profits will prompt new firms to enter the industry until price has been pushed down to P_e and no firm earns supranormal profits (the average cost curve reflects the rate of return necessary to keep firms in the industry). At this point price equals marginal and average costs and each firm will produce at the minimum point of its average total cost curve. For an intuitive discussion of these concepts in a public-utilities setting, see A. Lerner, "Conflicting Principles of Public Utility Rate Regulation," in P. MacAvoy, ed., *The Crisis of the Regulatory Commissions* (New York, 1970), at 18–29. See also A. Kahn, *supra* note 2, vol. 1, at 65–70. The classic exposition of the welfare economic model of production is F. Bator, "The Simple Analytics of Welfare Maximization," 47 *Am. Econ. Rev.* 22 (1957).

4. A monopolist differs from a competitive producer in that he can unilaterally affect price by varying his level of output. If he charges the same price to all consumers, he will restrict output to the point where marginal cost equals marginal revenue (the latter term is the difference between the price paid by the marginal consumer and the decrease in revenue from reducing the price charged to every other consumer). In Figure 8, a competitive market would generate output Q_c at price P_c while monopoly results in output Q_m and price P_m. The monopoly price exceeds marginal cost by the length of segment BD and the monopolist benefits by increased profits (vis-à-vis the competitive solution) of P_mBCP_c-ADC. For a more extensive treatment, see R. Posner, *Economic*

Analysis of Law, 2d ed. (Boston, 1977), at 195–205; or F. Scherer, *Industrial Market Structure and Economic Performance,* 2d ed. (Chicago, 1980), at 14–17, 229–236. See also pp. 13–16, 213–238. The ambitious reader should consult J. Robinson, *The Economics of Imperfect Competition* (London, 1933), esp. bks. 2 and 4.

5. Consumer surplus is the difference between the price consumers actually pay for a good and the maximum price that they would have been willing to pay to obtain the good. In Figure 8, competitive output Q_c generates consumer surplus P_cAE, while monopolistic output Q_m results in consumer surplus P_mBE. The difference between these quantities P_mBAP_c consists of an income transfer from consumers to producers of P_mBCP_c (known as the producers' surplus) and a net loss of consumers' surplus of BAC. This latter quantity is the absolute or "deadweight" loss to society due to monopoly.

Price in excess of true social costs also creates misperceptions concerning the relative values of producing monopolized and competitive goods. Artificially high prices in one sector of the economy will lead consumers to purchase fewer of those goods than is efficient. As a result, insufficient resources will be allocated to the monopolized sector and society will fail to produce as much as it could. For a lucid illustration of this proposition see F. Scherer, *supra* note 4, at 17–20.

6. A natural monopoly differs from an ordinary monopoly (the type illustrated in notes 4 and 5) in that its average total costs decrease throughout the relevant range of output. Average total costs exceed marginal cost at all points and there exists no output at which a monopolist is able to recoup his total investment by setting a single price

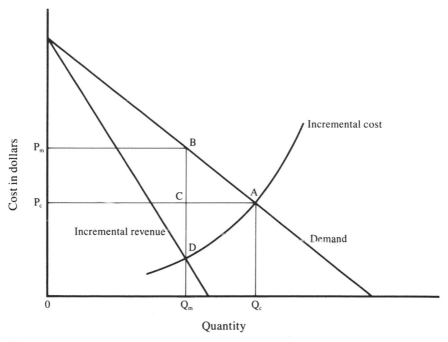

Figure 8. Monopoly.

equal to marginal costs. This is indicated in Figure 9. Government intervention to increase output from Q_m (the monopoly output) to Q_c (the competitive output) would require payment of a subsidy to the monopolist of $(P_s\text{-}P_c) Q_c$ in order to allow him to cover his total costs.

7. This is called the X-efficiency loss from monopoly. See H. Leibenstein, "Allocative Efficiency vs. 'X-Efficiency,' " 56 *Am. Econ. Rev.* 392 (1966); W. Comanor and H. Leibenstein, "Allocative Efficiency, X-Efficiency and the Measurement of Welfare Losses," 36 *Economica* 304 (1969).

8. The seminal article is R. Lipsey and K. Lancaster, "The General Theory of Second Best," 24 *Rev. Econ. Stud.* 11 (1956–1957). See also E. Mishan, "Second Thoughts on Second Best," 14 *Oxford Econ. Papers* 205–217 (October 1962); O. Davis and A. Whinston, "Welfare Economics and the Theory of Second Best," 32 *Rev. Econ. Stud.* 1 (1965); as well as the collection of papers appearing in 34 *Rev. Econ. Stud.* 301–331 (1967).

9. The greater the independence of the sector in question from the rest of the economy, the greater the likelihood that imposition of competitive forces will have a positive effect. See Davis and Whinston, *supra* note 8; E. Mishan, *supra* note 8; and F. Scherer, *supra* note 4, at 28.

10. Strictly defined, price discrimination is the sale of individual units of the same product at different prices, independent of any differences in the cost of production.

11. Generally, three types of price discrimination are distinguished. *First degree (or perfect)* discrimination describes the situation where the monopolist charges each consumer the maximum price he or she is willing to pay for the good. As such, the monopolist acquires the entire consumer surplus accruing from production of the good and expands output until price equals marginal cost. Under *second degree* discrimination, the monopolist is only able to set a finite number of prices and charges consumers

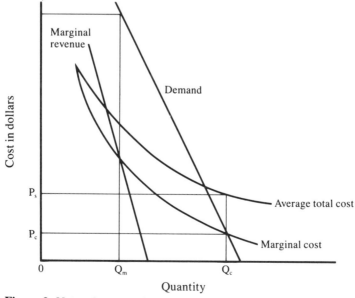

Figure 9. Natural monopoly.

the highest price they are willing to pay. *Third degree* discrimination obtains where the monopolist is able to divide consumers into two or more groups with distinct demand functions. The monopolist charges each group a distinct price and expands output until the marginal revenues generated by the two (or more) markets is equal. The above distinctions were developed by A. C. Pigou and appear in *The Economics of Welfare,* 4th ed. (London, 1962), at 275–289. For a relevant illustration of third degree discrimination see A. Kahn, *supra* note 2, vol. 1, at 137–140. See also P. Steiner, "Peak Loads and Efficient Pricing," 71 *Q.J. Econ.* 585 (1957).

12. The perfectly discriminating monopolist will always expand production to the competitive equilibrium. The second-degree monopolist will usually expand output beyond the nondiscriminating monopoly outcome. The output decision of a third-degree monopolist will depend on the shape of the relevant demand and cost curves. See J. Robinson, *supra* note 4, at 179–202, esp. 188–195. Demand elasticities, however, are notoriously difficult to estimate.

13. See "Economic Analysis of the Telecommunications Industry," Charles River Associates, Report 338.01, ch. 4 (Cambridge, Mass., 1979).

14. H. Hotelling, "The General Welfare in Relation to Problems of Taxation and of Railway and Utility Rates," 6 *Econometrica* 242 (1938); J. DuPuit, "On the Measurement of the Utility of Public Works," *Annales des Ponts & Chaussées,* 2d Ser., 8 (1844), reprinted in *International Economic Papers* 2 (London, 1952).

15. A single-price monopolist confronted with the cost and demand curves depicted in Figures 10 and 11 will not build the bridge, since there is no one price at which his revenues will cover total costs. If the monopolist is permitted to price discriminate perfectly, his revenues increase (Figure 10) to $OADQ_c$. He will build the bridge as long as $P_sAB > BCD$. Even imperfect discrimination (Figure 11) will permit construction of the bridge as long as $P_xFGP_y > HIJK$. Here consumers are left with consumers' surplus equal to $EFP_x + FBH + HKJ$. Alternatively, the government could build (or subsidize a monopolist to build) the bridge (Figure 10) at cost P_cDCP_s. Such an action will be socially justified as long as $AP_sB > BCD$. Otherwise, social benefits accruing from building the bridge will not cover costs.

16. On the difficulties of determining criteria for public investment, see, e.g., E. Mishan, "Criteria for Public Investment: Some Simplifying Suggestions," 75 *J. Pol. Econ.* 139 (April 1967), and Mishan's reply to critics in 78 *J. Pol. Econ.* 178 (1970).

17. A. Bierce, *The Devil's Dictionary* (1957 ed.), at 107.

18. But see R. Posner, *supra* note 2, at 564.

19. See generally on matters of fairness in this area A. Okun, *Equality and Efficiency: The Big Tradeoff* (Washington, D.C., 1975).

20. Moreover, the "natural monopolist" may be the firm that arrived first in the field, rather than a firm that outcompeted its rivals. The "unfairness" of the fact and the foreclosure of the field to others partly account for the ethical attractiveness of ideas such as those of Demsetz and Williamson to allow firms to bid for monopoly franchises. See Demsetz, *supra* note 2.

21. An economic rent can alternatively be defined as the excess revenue over and above the minimum amount required to keep a factor in its current use.

22. See e.g., P. Douglas, "The Case for the Consumer of Natural Gas," 44 *Geo. L.J.* 566 (1956).

23. See A. Kahn, Economic Issues in Regulating the Field Price of Natural Gas, 50 *Am. Econ. Rev.* 506, no. 2 (1960).

24. See *Building the American City,* Report of the National Commission on Urban

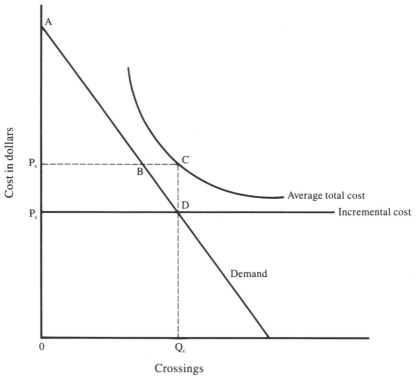

Crossings

Figure 10. The fixed-cost problem (I).

Problems to the Congress and the President of the United States, 91st Cong., 1st Sess., House Doc. No. 91-34 (1968).

25. See S. Breyer and P. MacAvoy, "The Natural Gas Shortage and the Regulation of Natural Gas Producers," 86 *Harv. L. Rev.* 941 (1973).

26. The two seminal articles in this area are F. Bator, "The Anatomy of Market Failure," 72 *Q.J. Econ.* 351 (1958); and R. Coase, "The Problem of Social Cost," 3 *J. Law & Econ.* 1 (1960). For a very readable account of the literature see E. Mishan, "The Postwar Literature on Externalities: An Interpretative Essay," 9 *J. Econ. Lit.* 1 (1971).

27. In this case, the cost that should be internalized is the expected value of damage per train trip (since fires caused by sparks do not occur on every trip). However, the courts have generally not seen the problem this way. See *LeRoy Fibre Co.* v. *Chicago, Milwaukee and St. Paul Railway,* 232 U.S. 340 (1913). See also R. Posner, *supra* note 4, at 38–39.

28. See F. Bator, *supra* note 26, at 358–360.

29. See generally G. Calabresi and A. Melamed, "Property Rules, Liability Rules and Inalienability: One View of the Cathedral," 85 *Harv. L. Rev.* 1089 (1972); H. Demsetz, "Toward a Theory of Property Rights," 57 *Am. Econ. Rev.* 347 (November 2, 1967); and F. Michelman, "Pollution as a Tort: A Non-Accidental Perspective on Calabresi's Costs," 80 *Yale Law J.* 647 (1971).

30. R. Coase, *supra* note 26.

31. See J. Buchanan, "An Economic Theory of Clubs," 32 *Economica* 1 (1965); and M. Olson, *The Logic of Collective Action: Public Goods and the Theory of Groups* (Cambridge, Mass., 1965).

32. There are two essential factors at work here. The first is that enjoyment of benefits accruing from successful bribery of producers ofttimes cannot be limited to those who paid for them (nonexcludability of consumption). This, in turn, gives rise to incentives for individuals (the "free-rider" problem) to strategically misrepresent their preferences so that they might enjoy all the benefits without bearing any costs. Unfortunately, such behavior often causes socially beneficial activities to be forgone. On the first problem see F. Bator, *supra* note 26; and J. Buchanan, *supra* note 31. On the free-rider problem see R. Posner, "Theories of Economic Regulation," 5 *Bell J. Econ. & Mgmt. Sci.* 335 (1974); G. Stigler, "Free Riders and Collective Action: An Appendix to Theories of Economic Regulation," 5 *Bell J. Econ. & Mgmt. Sci.* 359 (1974).

33. This is Calabresi's suggestion. See Calabresi, *The Costs of Accidents, A Legal and Economic Analysis* (New Haven, 1970).

34. See Coase, *supra* note 26, at 11–12. See also *Spur Industries, Inc. v. Del E Webb Development Co.,* 108 Ariz. 178, 494 P.2d 700 (1972).

35. The classic article on the information problem is F. Hayek, "The Use of Knowledge in Society," 35 *Am. Econ. Rev.* 519 (1945).

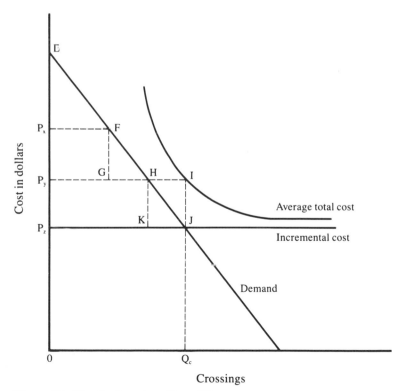

Figure 11. The fixed-cost problem (II).

36. When an individual initially considers buying a product (such as a car, a watch, or a house), he is usually unaware of all the prices that various sellers are currently charging. To obtain the lowest price, he must identify potential sellers and consult them to learn their prices. The search process is not costless, however, and the consumer must weigh the potential gains against the cost of searching. The greater the dispersion of prices among sellers and the greater the dollar amount of the purchase, the greater the potential benefits of searching. In general, the consumer will buy information ("search") until he reaches the point at which the expected incremental gain from additional searching equals the incremental cost of conducting the search. Alternative methods of providing information are justified where their cost is lower than that of private searches. See G. Stigler, "The Economics of Information," 69 *J. Pol. Econ.* 213 (1961). For an interesting variation on this discussion, see M. Spence, "Job Market Signaling," 87 *Q.J. Econ.* 355 (1973).

37. Even if subsequent users of the information, once generated, can obtain it "free," there may be adequate incentive to provide it without patent or copyright protection. Much depends on whether a producer believes its production will give him a substantial advantage over his competitors. These and related issues are fiercely debated in the areas of patents and copyrights. See F. Machlup, *An Economic View of the Patent System* (Washington, D.C., 1958); S. Breyer, "The Uneasy Case for Copyright: A Study of Copyright in Books, Photocopy, and Computer Programming," 84 *Harv. L. Rev.* 281 (1970).

38. See *Abbott Laboratories* v. *Gardner,* 387 U.S. 136 (1966).

39. P. Nelson, "Information and Consumer Behavior," 78 *J. Pol. Econ.* 311 (1970), distinguishes two general classes of goods. *Search* goods are products whose quality attributes may be determined by inspection. Items such as clothing, garden tools, and barbells fall into this category. *Experience* goods denote those items whose quality attributes can only be determined through purchase and consumption. For example, one cannot assess the quality of canned lima beans without eating them—nor can one assess ex ante whether a particular automobile is a lemon (even automakers with good reputations make lemons). See G. Akerlof, "The Market for 'Lemons': Quality Uncertainty and the Market Mechanism," 84 *Q.J. Econ.* 488 (1970); and P. Nelson, "Advertising as Information," 82 *J. Pol. Econ.* 729 (1974). The functional difference between these categories is not great where the consumer makes repeated purchases over time. One can easily sample all brands of lima beans and settle on the best price/quality combination with little sacrifice. However, where a one-shot purchase is contemplated, the differences may be substantial—and in some cases irrevocable. With search goods there is little danger of incorrect decisions, since all relevant attributes are known prior to purchase. Such is not the case with experience goods. For example, one cannot protect ex ante against negligent automobile design which might dramatically increase the likelihood of serious injury. Nor can one assess the probability that particular employment might lead to cancer ten or twenty years hence.

40. In addition to problems that arise where consumers have imperfect information concerning product quality, there is also the problem that *even in the presence of perfect information* individuals may still inaccurately evaluate the magnitude of the risks they face. See, e.g., Calabresi, *supra* note 33, at 56; and T. Schelling, "The Life You Save May Be Your Own," in S. B. Chase, ed., *Problems in Public Expenditure Analysis* (Washington, D.C., 1968).

41. See R. Pitofsky, "Beyond Nader: Consumer Protection and the Regulation of

Advertising," 90 *Harv. L. Rev.* 661 (1977); J. Ferguson, "Consumer Ignorance as a Source of Monopoly Power," 5 *Antitrust Law & Econ. Rev.* 2 (29) and (3) 55 (1971–72); and R. Posner, "The Federal Trade Commission," 37 *U. Chicago L. Rev.* 47 (1969).

42. Hearings on § 2 and § 1760 before a subcommittee of the Senate Committee on Interstate and Foreign Commerce, 75th Cong., 1st Sess. (1937). For a brief account of regulation at this time, see U.S. Senate Comm. on the Judiciary, Subcomm. on Admin. Practice and Procedure, *Civil Aeronautics Board Practices and Procedures,* Subcomm. report, 94th Cong., 1st Sess., 31–35 (1975) [hereinafter referred to as the *Kennedy Report*].

43. Aviation: Hearings on H.R. 5234 and H.R. 4652 before the House Comm. on Interstate and Foreign Commerce, 75th Cong., 1st Sess., 76 (1937).

44. See *Kennedy Report, supra* note 42, at 61–62.

45. See *Kennedy Report, supra* note 42.

46. See National Industrial Recovery Act, 48 Stat. 195, 196, 15 U.S.C. 703 (1933) § 3 (declared unconstitutional in *A.L.A. Schechter Poultry Co.* v. *United States,* 295 U.S. 495 (1934).

47. For a sample of the developing literature on the sustainability of natural monopoly see G. Faulhaber, "Cross-Subsidization: Pricing in Public Enterprises," 65 *Am. Econ. Rev.* 966 (1975); J. Panzar and R. Willig, "Free Entry and the Sustainability of Natural Monopoly," 8 *Bell J. Econ. & Mgmt. Sci.* 1 (1977); and W. Baumol, E. Bailey, and R. Willig, "Weak Invisible Hand Theorems for the Sustainability of Multiproduct Natural Monopoly," 67 *Am. Econ. Rev.* 350 (1977).

48. Of course, government action here might lower costs by lowering risks, but that claim can be made of a host of cartel and other anticompetitive agreements.

49. See F. Scherer, *supra* note 4, at 205–212.

50. For a further discussion and some illustrations see F. Scherer, *supra* note 4, at 335–340.

51. See P. Areeda and D. Turner, *Antitrust Law* ¶ 711 (1978); Areeda and Turner, "Predatory Pricing and Related Practices under Section 2 of the Sherman Act," 88 *Harv. L. Rev.* 697 (1975).

52. In such a case, exit of firms from the industry is appropriate, since they are replaced by firms who can satisfy societal needs at lower costs.

53. 15 U.S.C. ¶ 17 (1976), labor organization; Capper-Volstead Act of 1922, 7 U.S.C. §§ 291–292 (1976), farming; Fisherman's Cooperative Marketing Act, 15 U.S.C. §§ 521–522 (1976), fishing.

54. See, e.g., S. Breyer and P. MacAvoy, "The Federal Power Commission and the Coordination Problem in the Electrical Power Industry," 46 *S. Cal. L. Rev.* 661, 680–682, 685–687, 688–694 (1973).

55. See Breyer and MacAvoy, *supra* note 25, at 665–669.

56. See generally, F. Scherer, *supra* note 4, at 174–175, 506–509, 563–569.

57. U.S. Federal Power Commission National Power Survey (1964); Breyer and MacAvoy, *supra* note 25.

58. See Calabresi, *supra* note 33.

59. For a descriptive example see K. Arrow, *Essays in the Theory of Risk Bearing* 142–143 (1971).

60. See R. Gibson and M. Mueller, *National Health Expenditures, Fiscal Year 1976,* 40 Soc. Security Bull. 3, no. 4 (April 1977).

61. See M. Feldstein and A. Taylor, *The Rapid Rise of Hospital Costs,* Staff Report of the Council on Wage and Price Stability, Executive Office of the President (1977).

62. See Conference on Health Planning, Certificate of Need, and Market Entry, Regulating Health Facilities Construction (1974).

63. G. Brannan, "Prices and Incomes: The Dilemma of Energy Policy," 13 *Harv. J. Legis.* 445, 447 (1976).

2. Cost-of-Service Ratemaking

1. See, e.g., Natural Gas Act, 15 U.S.C. § 717e (1976); California Public Utility Code § 451 (1975); New York Public Service Law § 26 (1968); Wisconsin Statutes § 196.03 (1977). The Supreme Court has stated that rates are "just and reasonable" which "enable the company to operate successfully, to maintain its financial integrity, to attract capital, and to compensate its investors for the risks assumed." *Federal Power Commission* v. *Hope Natural Gas Co.,* 320 U.S. 591, 605 (1944).

2. Taxes need not be included if the commission determines its allowance for company profits on a pre-tax, instead of a post-tax, basis. And commissions' practice of making a separate determination of taxes has been criticized as distorting its efforts to calculate the cost of capital. See G. Hempel, "Public Utility Regulation, Financial Leverage, and Earnings Per Share," 88 *Pub. Util. Fort.* 17–26 (August 5, 1971).

3. In summary form, the regulator applies three basic formulas:

$$\text{Profit} = \text{Pr}_t = r_t \left(\Sigma_0^t I - \Sigma_0^{t-1} D \right) \tag{1}$$
$$\text{Revenue Requirement} = RR = OC_t + T_t + D_t + \text{Pr}_t \tag{2}$$

Prices are then set so that:

$$P_{x_1} Q_{x_1} + P_{x_2} Q_{x_2} + \ldots + P_{x_n} Q_{x_n} = RR \tag{3}$$

where t = the test year, and x_n = a particular product or service provided by the firm. All other terms are defined in the text.

4. Compare, e.g., Natural Gas Act, *supra* note 1. Commissions can sometimes circumvent this procedure by granting interim rate relief pending a hearing on the validity of the new rates. See "Interim Rate Relief," 87 *Pub. Util. Fort.* 51–53 (May 27, 1971).

5. Where costs rise, existing rates will be insufficient to cover costs and still provide an adequate rate of return. Utilities will thus seek to increase their revenue accordingly through increased prices. Where costs fall utilities will reap a temporary windfall. Should the magnitude of this unearned surplus become too great it is likely to prompt a rate investigation.

P. Joskow, "Pricing Decisions of Regulated Firms: A Behavioral Approach," 4 *Bell J. Econ. & Mgmt. Sci.* 118 (1973), posits that the regulated firm's decision to seek a price increase depends on the growth rate of earnings per share achieved by the firm in the current and previous year, on the level of interest coverage realized in the current year and the likelihood of getting a rate increase approved by the commission if a request is made. The firm's decision to voluntarily reduce rates generally results from moral suasion by members of the public or politicians, though involuntary "forced regulation'' (that is, a rate decrease mandated by the commission) also remains a real possibility.

6. "The primary concern of regulatory commissions has been to keep *nominal prices from increasing* . . . Formal regulatory action in the form of rate of return review is primarily triggered by firms attempting to raise the level of their rates or to make major changes in the structure of their rates." P. Joskow, "Inflation and Environmental Concern: Structural Change in the Process of Public Utility Price Regulation," 17 *J. Law & Econ.* 291–327 (1974).

7. Occasionally critics have judged commissions primarily upon their ability to achieve this fifth objective. Thus, in the early 1960s Dean Landis of the Harvard Law School noted the Federal Power Commission's large backlog of cases on its docket and concluded that "without question" the Federal Power Commission represents the outstanding example of "the breakdown of the administrative process." S. Breyer and P. MacAvoy, *Energy Regulation by the Federal Power Commission* 68 (Washington, D.C., 1974). Similarly, the Civil Aeronautics Board in the 1970s developed an elaborate set of pricing rules, the primary virtue of which lay in their ability to process cases speedily. In both instances, administrative efficiency was purchased at a heavy price. See chs. 11 and 13.

8. For an extensive discussion of the rate base and related issues see J. Bonbright, *Principles of Public Utility Rates* 159–237 (New York, 1961).

9. See, e.g., *Smyth* v. *Ames,* 169 U.S. 466 (1898); *McCardle* v. *Indianapolis Water Co.,* 272 U.S. 400 (1926). But see *Missouri ex rel Southwestern Bell Telephone Co.* v. *Public Service Commission of Missouri,* 262 U.S. 276 (1923), Brandeis, J., dissenting. See also A. Kahn, *The Economics of Regulation: Principles and Institutions,* vol. 1 (New York, 1970).

10. Under ordinary accounting practice, assets are carried in the firm's books at their original cost, not their replacement value. To some extent replacement cost may become easier to calculate as a result of Securities and Exchange Commission requirements that firms adjust their accounts for inflation. See S. Brav, "Replacement Cost Accounting for Electric Utilities," 101 *Pub. Util. Fort.* 20–25 (May 25, 1978); and W. Carleton, "Rate of Return, Rate Base and Regulatory Lag under Conditions of Changing Capital Costs," 50 *Land Economics* 145 (1974).

11. See L. Lyon and V. Abramson, *Government and Economic Life: Development and Current Issues of American Public Policy* 680–709 (Washington, D.C., 1940).

12. *Federal Power Commission* v. *Hope Natural Gas Co.,* 320 U.S. 591 (1944).

13. See J. Bonbright, *supra* note 8, 178–180.

14. See, e.g., B. Regland, "Compensating for a Shortcoming of the Historic Rate Base," 101 *Pub. Util. Fort.* 21–26 (March 2, 1978); L. Mullen, "Adjusted Price Index Numbers—An Aid to Regulation," 87 *Pub. Util. Fort.* (May 13, 1971) 19–23.

15. "Rates which enable the company to operate successfully, to maintain its financial integrity, to attract capital, and to compensate its investors for the risks assumed certainly cannot be condemned as invalid, even though they might produce only a meager return on the so-called 'fair-value' rate base." *FPC* v. *Hope Natural Gas Co.,* 320 U.S. 591, 605 (1944).

16. Provided that the bond is held to maturity. Should a bondholder seek to recoup his principal prior to maturity, he will sell at either a premium or a discount which reflects the then-current rate of return.

17. Depreciation over time does not change this example. If $10 million was raised

initially, but the plant has been depreciated to $6 million, $4 million has been raised from consumers as a "depreciation" charge. That $4 million either was returned to investors as a "return-of-capital," diminishing the historical amount they have invested, or it was kept by the firm and reinvested for them. If the latter, the historical investment by the firm remains at $10 million though part of the $10 million is invested in new equipment.

This simple principle can prove complex as applied in practice, given the likelihood of continued new investment by the firm in various assets, the existence of several different sources of investment funds, and the fact that rates are usually stable for several years at a time. See Kahn, *supra* note 9, at 117–122; B. Jaffee, "Depreciation in a Simple Regulatory Model," 4 *Bell J. Econ. & Mgmt. Sci.* 338–41 (1973); P. Linhart, "Depreciation in a Simple Regulatory Model: Comment," 5 *Bell J. Econ. & Mgmt. Sci.* 229–232 (1974); R. Sussman, "Depreciation Revisited," 85 *Pub. Util. Fort.* 31–35 (February 26, 1970).

18. This outcome is reached as follows: If s equals the number of new shares that must be issued, p equals the price of these shares, and the firm seeks to raise $2,000,000, then:

$$sp = 2,000,000. \tag{1}$$

Similarly, the total number of shares (old and new), times the price, must equal the market value of the stock after the sale (which is equal to the total profit pool):

$$(20,000 + s)\, p = 3,200,000 \tag{2}$$

$$= 20,000p + sp = 3,200,000$$

Substituting (1) into (2) yields:

$$20,000p + 2,000,000 = 3,200,000 \text{ or}$$

$$p = 60 \tag{3}$$

Substituting the market price of $60 into (1) yields the conclusion that s = 33,333 or, in other words, the utility must sell 33,333 additional shares at $60 to raise $2 million for new investment. The original shareholders now own 20,000 out of 53,333 shares, or 37.5 percent of the equity.

19. Some economists have tried to determine the economically proper rate of return, given some of the distortions in a free-market system that regulation introduces. Alvin Klevorick, for example, shows that if the regulation leads a firm to overinvest, its rate of return should not be equated to the market cost of capital. Indeed, Klevorick suggests that various regulatory distortions make it difficult to determine any "economically optimal" rate of return. See Klevorick, "The 'Optimal' Fair Rate of Return," 2 *Bell J. Econ. & Mgmt. Sci.* 122 (1971).

20. The two most cogent statements of this view appear in *FPC* v. *Hope Natural Gas Co.,* 320 U.S. 591 (1944); and *Bluefield Waterworks and Improvement Co.* v. *Public Service Commission,* 262 U.S. 679 (1923): "The rate-making process under the

Act, i.e., the fixing of 'just and reasonable' rates, involves a balancing of the investor and the consumer interests . . . The investor interest has a legitimate concern with the financial integrity of the company whose rates are being regulated . . . By that standard *the return to the equity owner should be commensurate with returns on investments in other enterprises having corresponding risks.* That return, moreover, should be sufficient to assure confidence in the financial integrity of the enterprise, so as to maintain its credit and to attract capital." *FPC* v. *Hope Natural Gas Co.,* 320 U.S., at 603 [emphasis added]. "A public utility is entitled to such rates as will permit it to earn a return on the value of the property which it employs for the convenience of the public equal to that generally being made at the same time and in the same general part of the country on investments in other business undertakings which are attended by corresponding risks and uncertainties; but it has no constitutional right to profits such as are realized or anticipated in highly profitable enterprises or speculative ventures . . . A rate of return may be reasonable at one time and become too high or too low by changes affecting opportunities for investment, the money market and business conditions generally." *Bluefield Co.* v. *PSC,* 262 U.S., at 692–693.

21. Testimony of Georgia K. LeDakis, Mississippi River Transmission Corporation, Federal Power Commission Docket No. Rp. 72–149, at 31 (November 1972).

22. Testimony of J. Rhoads Foster, Phase 8, Domestic Passenger Fare Investigation of the Civil Aeronautics Board. See U.S. Senate Comm. on the Judiciary, Subcomm. on Admin. Practice and Procedure, *Civil Aeronautics Board Practices and Procedures,* Report, 94th Cong., 1st Sess. (1975), at 121–123 [hereinafter referred to as the *Kennedy Report*].

23. See testimony of Georgia K. LeDakis, *supra* note 21, at 44. Whether or not utilities are less risky than investments in industrial stocks is debatable. See, e.g., H. Mulle, "Some Testimony on Risk. The Case for the Utilities and Regulation," 97 *Pub. Util. Fort.* 22–27 (January 15, 1976).

24. See generally E. Solomon, "Alternative Rate of Return Concepts and Their Implications for Utility Regulation," 1 *Bell J. Econ. & Mgmt. Sci.* 65–81 (1970); S. Myers, "The Application of Finance Theory to Public Utility Rate Cases," 3 *Bell J. Econ. & Mgmt. Sci.* 58–97 (1972). For a highly readable introduction to portfolio theory see J. Lorie and M. Hamilton, *The Stock Market* (Homewood, Ill., 1973). For a more sophisticated overview see M. Jensen, "Capital Markets and Evidence," 3 *Bell J. Econ. & Mgmt. Sci.* 357 (1972). For further discussion of the comparable earnings method, see H. Leventhal, "Vitality of the Comparable Earnings Standard for Regulation of Utilities in a Growth Economy," 74 *Yale L. J.* 989 (1965).

25. For an intuitive illustration and explanation of the Discounted Cash Flow Method see *Re New York Telephone,* 12 NY PSC 19, 92 PUR 3d 321 (1972) concurring opinion of Commissioner William K. Jones, reprinted in W. Jones, *Regulated Industries,* 2d ed. (New York, 1976), at 142–151. See also "Note on the Discounted Cash Flow (DCF) Method of Determining the Cost of Equity Capital," in Jones, at 131–152. Sophisticated treatments of related issues may be found in E. Solomon, "Alternative Rate of Return Concepts and Their Implications for Utility Regulation," 1 *Bell J. Econ. & Mgmt. Sci.* 65 (1970); and S. Myers, "The Application of Finance Theory to Public Utility Rate Cases," 3 *Bell J. Econ. & Mgmt. Sci.* 58 (1972).

26. Thus, the investor's required rate of return (i) will contain both a dividend component (y = Dividend amount ÷ Stock price) and an expected annual growth component (g) such that i = y + g.

27. See, e.g., J. McDonald, "Required Return on Public Utility Equities: A National and Regional Analysis, 1958–1969," 2 *Bell J. Econ. & Mgmt. Sci.* 503 (1971).

28. See note, "An Earnings-Price Approach to Fair Rate of Return in Regulated Industries," 20 *Stan. L. Rev.* 287 (1968); L. Ross, "Comments on the Earnings-Price Note," 21 *Stan. L. Rev.* 644 (1969).

29. See Markowitz, "Portfolio Selection," *J. of Finance* 77–91 (March 1952); Sharpe, "Capital Asset Prices: Market Equilibrium under Conditions of Risk," *J. of Finance* 425–442 (September 1964); and Lintner, "Security Prices, Risk, and Maximal Gains for Diversification," *J. of Finance* 587–615 (December 1965).

30. For an explanation and proof see M. Jensen, "Capital Markets: Theory and Evidence," 3 *Bell J. Econ. & Mgmt. Sci.* 357 (1972).

31. Note that many investors are satisfied with a portfolio whose performance parallels a standard indicator such as the Standard & Poor's Market Index. Indeed, a significant (and skeptical) segment of the investment community believes that it is impossible to consistently beat the average, absent inside information. The continued vitality of Mutual Funds, however, indicates that an equally significant group believes the averages can be beaten. For a skeptical but entertaining view of the process see Burton Malkiel, *A Random Walk Down Wall Street* (New York, 1975).

32. See W. Breen and E. Lerner, "On the Use of β in Regulatory Proceedings," 3 *Bell J. Econ. & Mgmt. Sci.* 612 (1972); S. Myers, "On the Use of β in Regulatory Proceedings: A Comment," 3 *Bell J. Econ. & Mgmt. Sci.* 622 (1972).

33. R. Ibbotson and R. Sinquefield, "Stocks, Bonds, Bills, and Inflation: The Past (1926–76) and the Future (1977–2000)," Financial Analysts Research Foundation (September 1977).

34. Although the investor is guaranteed a *nominal* 8 percent return, inflation may reduce his *real* return considerably below this figure.

35. R. Vandell and J. Malernee, "The Capital Asset Pricing Model and Utility Equity Returns," 102 *Pub. Util. Fort.* 22–28 (July 6, 1978).

36. A beta of 1.0 means that a 1 percent increase in the return on the market will produce a 1 percent increase in the return on the asset. A beta of less than 1.0 generally connotes a less risky investment. See Lorie and Hamilton, *supra* note 24, at 211–227.

37. See S. Myers, *supra* note 25; E. Bailey and R. Coleman, "The Effect of Lagged Regulation in an Averch-Johnson Model," 2 *Bell J. Econ. & Mgmt. Sci.* 278–292 (1971); and A. K. Klevorick and W. J. Baumol, "Input Choices and Rate-of-Return Regulation: An Overview of the Discussion," 1 *Bell J. Econ. & Mgmt. Sci.* 162–190 (1970).

38. See, e.g., P. Joskow, "Inflation and Environmental Concern: Structural Change in the Process of Public Utility Price Regulation," 17 *J. Law & Econ.* 291–327 (1974); Bailey and Coleman, "The Effect of Lagged Regulation in an Averch-Johnson Model," *supra* note 37.

39. See Kahn, "Inducements to Superior Performance: Price" in Samuels and Trebing, *Performance under Regulation* 88 (East Lansing, 1968); T. Brophy, "The Utility Problem of Regulatory Lag," 95 *Pub. Util. Fort.* 21–27 (January 30, 1975); T. Hyde, "Overcoming Regulatory Lag; The High Cost of a Low Rate of Return," 95 *Pub. Util. Fort.* 34–36 (February 27, 1975).

40. See P. Joskow, *supra* note 38.

41. For a discussion of the behavioral dynamics of the rate-setting process, see P.

Joskow, "The Determination of the Allowed Rate of Return in a Formal Regulatory Hearing," 3 *Bell J. Econ. & Mgmt. Sci.* 632 (1972).

42. See, e.g., McKie, "Regulation and the Free Market: The Problems of Boundaries," 1 *Bell J. Econ. & Mgmt. Sci.* 7 (1970).

43. The New Mexico Public Service Commission has undertaken a unique experiment in this area. The NMPSC developed a standardized method of determining the utility's return on equity. This is called the Cost-of-Service Index (CSI). Every three months the NMPSC examines the utility's investment, operating expenses, and revenues. If the utility's computed return on equity falls outside the allowable range of 13.5–14.5 percent of ROE, base rates are automatically adjusted to the nearest limiting value. Thus, if ROE falls to 10 percent, rates will be adjusted to earn a projected 13.5 percent in the next period. If rates exceed 15 percent, they are lowered to 14.5 percent, and so forth. No adjustment is made if the ROE falls within the allowable zone, nor is the utility able to recoup losses from subnormal periods. The utility may keep any profits earned in excess of the 14.5 percent maximum, but will have to continually improve its efficiency to sustain supranormal returns. One attractive feature of this system is that efficiency gains are split between the consumers and the utility. The utility retains all supranormal profits; the public receives lower energy rates. The system has apparently also reduced the utility's cost of capital and relieved both the utility and the NMPSC of significant administrative costs. See A. Parker, "Evaluation of the New Mexico Public Utility Rate Indexing Experiment," in W. Sichel, ed., *Public Utility Rate Making in an Energy Conscious Environment* 97–114 (Boulder, 1979); and *Public Service Company of New Mexico,* Case 1196, 8 PUR 4th 113 (1975).

44. See, e.g., "Salaries to Utility Owners Scrutinized," 86 *Pub. Util. Fort.* 47–49 (August 27, 1970). But see *Latourneau* v. *Citizens Utility Company,* 125 Vt. 38, 209 A.2d 307 (1965), in which the court reversed a utility commission's disallowance of the $70,000 paid to a president who spent an average of two days a week on company affairs. The court held that this amount was not "out of line" with the salaries paid other utilities.

45. The Supreme Court has stated in respect to the commission's ability to disallow operating expenses: "The Commission is not the financial manager of the corporation and it is not empowered to substitute its judgment for that of the directors of the corporation; nor can it ignore items charged by the utility as operating expenses unless there is an abuse of discretion in that regard by the corporate officers." *Missouri ex rel South Western Bell Telephone Company* v. *Public Service Commission of Missouri,* 262 U.S. 276, 289 (1923). Thus, commissions found it easier to exclude from operating expenses for rate-fixing purposes certain charitable contributions (*Pacific Tel. & Tel. Co.* v. *Public Utilities Commission of Calif.,* 62 Cal. 2d 634 [1965]); political advertising (*South Western Electric Power Company* v. *Federal Power Commission,* 304 F.2d 29 [fifth circuit 1962]); lobbying expenses (*Pacific Tel. & Tel.* v. *Public Utilities Commission of Calif.,* 62 Cal. 2d 634 [1965]); and excessive advertising and promotional expenditures (see *Southern California Gas Co.,* 35 PUR 3rd 300, 309–13 [Cal. P.U.C. 1960]) than to consider operating expenses more directly related to production costs.

46. See *Missouri ex rel South Western Bell Telephone* v. *Public Service Commission of Missouri, supra* note 45.

47. The Long Island Lighting Company, for example, in a rate proceeding attempted to measure efficiency trends compared with other companies. It submitted in-

formation related to the number of employees per 1,000 customers, per $100,000 of operating revenue (measured in a variety of ways), and comparisons with various bureau of labor statistics indices. The New York Public Service Commission did not explicitly state how it used this information but it referred in its opinion to the "superior record" of Long Island Lighting Company's performance. See I. Stelzer, "Utility Pricing under Inflation, Competition, and Environmental Concerns," 86 *Pub. Util. Fort.* 17–23 (December 3, 1970).

48. This issue was much debated 40 years ago. See, e.g., L. Lyon and V. Abramson, *Government and Economic Life: Development and Current Issues of American Public Policy* (Washington, D.C., 1940). A. M. Spence points out that since the regulated monopolist is not free to vary its prices, it is difficult for it to discover what price/quality combination the consumer prefers. See A. Spence, "Monopoly, Quality, and Regulation," 6 *Bell J. Econ. & Mgmt. Sci.* 417 (1975).

49. H. Averch and L. Johnson, "Behavior of the Firm under Regulatory Constraint," 52 *Am. Econ. Rev.* 1052 (1962). See more recent discussion by Alvin Klevorick, "The 'Optimal' Fair Rate of Return," 2 *Bell J. Econ. & Mgmt. Sci.* 122 (1971); and "The Behavior of a Firm Subject to Stochastic Regulatory Review," 4 *Bell J. Econ. & Mgmt. Sci.* 57 (1973). For a more intuitive discussion of the Averch-Johnson effect see F. Scherer, *Industrial Market Structure and Economic Performance,* 2d ed. (Chicago, 1980), at 485–486.

50. Since the demand for electricity is generally inelastic, an increased price level will yield the utility increased revenue.

51. See the discussion of the effect in P. Joskow and R. Noll, *Regulation in Theory and Practice: An Overview,* second rev. draft (March 1978).

52. See, e.g., Spann, "Rate of Return Regulation and Efficiency in Production: An Empirical Test of the Averch and Johnson Thesis," 5 *Bell J. Econ. & Mgmt. Sci.* 38 (1974). But see McKay, "Has the Averch Effect Been Empirically Verified?" Social science working paper 132, California Institute of Technology (1976). See generally Joskow and Noll, *supra* note 51.

53. In a study of 103 electric utilities, Joskow found that firms not involved in the formal hearing process saw their profits increase from 1961 through 1966, when production costs tended to fall. Their rates of return began to fall until 1970, when they leveled out. When costs began to rise and the profitability of the firm fell toward the level allowed by the commissions, the firms began to seek rate increases and requested commission proceedings. P. Joskow, "Inflation and Environmental Concern: Structural Change in the Process of Public Utility Price Regulation," 17 *J. Law & Econ.* 291 (1974).

54. See *Kennedy Report, supra* note 22, at 111.

55. See the discussion in the *Public Utilities Fortnightly,* July 20, 1978, at 48, Jan. 19, 1978, at 38, and Jan. 17, 1974, at 49.

56. See Joskow, *supra* note 53, at 291–327. In addition to adjustment clauses as weapons for dealing with inflation, Joskow refers to the possibility of using a future, rather than a past test year.

57. See, e.g., L. Taylor, "The Demand for Electricity: A Survey," 6 *Bell J. Econ. & Mgmt. Sci.* 74 (1975). See also authorities cited in note 70 *infra.*

58. The elasticity of demand is the proportionate rate of change of the quantity demanded (q_1) divided by the proportionate rate of change of its own price (p_1) with other prices and income held constant:

$$\text{Elasticity} = E_1 = \left| \frac{p_1}{q_1} \cdot \frac{\Delta q_1}{\Delta p_1} \right|$$

where Δq_1 = the change in quantity demanded and Δp_1 = the change in price. Consumers' total expenditures on q will decrease as p decreases if the elasticity is less than 1, will remain the same if $E_1 = 1$, and will increase as p decreases if E_1 is greater than 1. Products that exhibit an $E_1 < 1$ are said to have inelastic demand and those with $E_1 > 1$ have elastic demand.

In practice, this difference is very important. Consider a hypothetical air route between X and Y. Initially, the price is $50 per trip ($p_1$), 100 people ($q_1$) make the trip each day, and the airline's revenue is $5,000. Suppose the airline files for a $5 reduction in the fare. If the CAB's demand elasticity ($E_1 = .7$) is to be believed, then the price change will prompt 7 additional trips and the firm's revenue will *decrease* to $4,815. However, if the economist's estimate ($E_1 = 1.2$) is used, then total trips increase to 112 and the firm's revenue will *increase* to $5,040. Thus, an agency operating under an incorrect assumption of inelastic demand might disallow beneficial price decreases (and vice versa). The reader should also consider the effect that various elasticities have on consumer surplus. See Chapter 1, note 5 *supra*.

59. See *Kennedy Report, supra* note 22, at 123.

60. See the statement of Harry Kimbriel, Kennedy Hearings, March 4, 1975, at 2234.

61. See Kahn, *supra* note 9, vol. 1, at 123–158; R. Galligan, "Rate Design Objectives and Realities," 97 *Pub. Util. Fort.* 30–32 (May 6, 1976).

62. See F. Hayek, "The Use of Knowledge in Society," 35 *Am. Econ. Rev.* 529 (1945).

63. The rule was first derived by Frank Ramsey. See F. Ramsey, "A Contribution to the Theory of Taxation," 37 *Econ. J.* 47 (1927).

64. Compare the discussion of this problem in relation to community and television pricing in J. Ohls, "Marginal Cost Pricing, Investment Theory and CATV," 13 *J. Law & Econ.* 439 (1970).

65. For a discussion of the theoretical issues surrounding long-run incremental cost ratemaking, see W. Baumol, "Ratemaking: Incremental Costing and Equity Considerations," in H. Trebing, *Essays on Public Utility Pricing and Regulation* 137 (East Lansing, 1971); and A. Froggatt, "Incremental Costing in Practice," *id.* at 151. W. Baumol and A. Walton, "Full Cost Pricing and Regulatory Practice," 82 *Yale L.J.* 639 (1973).

66. See Kahn, *supra* note 9, at 166.

67. Kahn, *supra* note 9; Baumol and Walton, *supra* note 65.

68. See, for example, the discussion about the effect of comparative prices for truck and rail on the allocation of shipping resources between them. R. Harbeson, "Toward Better Resource Allocation in Transport," 12 *J. Law & Econ.* 321 (1969). But see Levin, "Allocation in Surface Freight Transportation: Does Rate Regulation Matter?" 9 *Bell J. Econ. & Mgmt. Sci.* 18 (1978).

69. See S. Breyer and P. MacAvoy, "The Federal Power Commission and the Regulation of the Field Price of Natural Gas," 86 *Harv. L. Rev.* 941 (1973).

70. See Kahn, *supra* note 9, at 87–122. For other methods of allocating capacity costs see E. Troxel, *Economics of Public Utilities* 441–463 (New York, 1947). See also the collection of articles in A. Laurence and D. Aigner, "Modelling and Forecasting

Time-of-Day and Seasonal Electricity Demands," 9 *J. Econ.* 1–240 (January 1979); *Annals of Applied Econometrics* 1979–1.

71. A survey of the economic literature on the subject is contained in P. Joskow and R. Noll, "Regulation in Theory and Practice: An Overview," at 26–30 (draft, 1978). See, e.g., J. Dreze, "Some Postwar Contributions of French Economists to Theory and Public Policy," 54 *Am. Econ. Rev.* 4–64 (June supplement, 1964), describing the pioneering work of Boiteux. See also R. Turvey, "Peak-load Pricing," 76 *J. Pol. Econ.* 101 (1968); J. Wenders, "Peak-load Pricing in the Electric Utility Industry," 7 *Bell J. Econ. & Mgmt. Sci.* 232 (1976); Panzar, "A Neoclassical Approach to Peak-load Pricing," 7 *Bell J. Econ. & Mgmt. Sci.* 521 (1976); and P. Joskow, "Electric Utility Rate Structures in the United States: Some Recent Developments," in W. Sichel, ed., *Public Utility Rate Making in an Energy Conscious Environment* 1–22 (Boulder, 1979).

72. The problem will be more complicated if one asks whether the plant cost should be the cost of existing plant or the cost of new plant. Arguably, when plant costs are rising, prices should reflect the cost of building new, additional plants. Regulators, however, will typically use historical costs here.

73. See, e.g., M. Telson, "The Economics of Alternative Levels of Reliability for Electric Power Generation Systems," 6 *Bell J. Econ. & Mgmt. Sci.* 679 (1975); Panzar, *supra* note 71; J. Vardi, J. Zahavi, and B. Avi-Itzhak, "Variable Load Pricing in the Face of Loss of Load Probability," 8 *Bell J. Econ. & Mgmt. Sci.* 270 (1977). See also M. Crew and P. Kleindorfer, "Peak-load Pricing with a Diverse Technology," 7 *Bell J. Econ. & Mgmt. Sci.* 207 (1976); and C. Cicchetti, "The Design of Electricity Tariffs," *Pub. Util. Fort.* 25–33 (August 28, 1975).

74. See, e.g., Crew and Kleindorfer, *supra* note 73.

75. The development of a workable consumer demand model is considered essential by many who favor peak-load pricing. See, e.g., J. Wenders and L. Taylor, "Experiments in Seasonal Time-of-Day Pricing of Electricity to Residential Users," 7 *Bell J. Econ. & Mgmt. Sci.* 531 (1976). .

76. See, e.g., G. Mathewson and G. Quirin, "Metering Costs and Marginal Cost Pricing in Public Utilities," 3 *Bell J. Econ. & Mgmt. Sci.* 335 (1972); D. Miller and M. Gerber, "The Technology of Load Management Rate Structures," *Pub. Util. Fort.* 41–44 (June 3, 1976).

77. See Joskow, *supra* note 71. In addition to Joskow, Wenders and Taylor discuss some of these experiments in the paper cited above, note 75.

78. Robert Lande, in an unpublished paper, "Peakload Pricing of Electricity: A Framework for Massachusetts Implementation," uses these experiments with a wide range of cost assumptions to test the practicability of all peak-load pricing for Massachusetts. He concludes that a shift to such a system is likely to be cost effective for commercial and industrial but not for residential users.

79. See Joskow, *supra* note 71.

80. Joskow, *supra* note 71; I. Stelzer, "Utility Pricing under Inflation, Competition, and Environmental Concerns," *Pub. Util. Fort.* 17–23 (December 3, 1970).

81. In fact, any regulatory tendency to hold rates low may encourage utilities to set peak prices lower than off-peak prices, for off-peak demand is less elastic. The firm can then lower its overall rates and still achieve higher profits. See E. Bailey and L. White, "Reversals in Peak and Offpeak Prices," 5 *Bell J. Econ. & Mgmt. Sci.* 75 (1974).

3. Historically Based Price Regulation

1. See generally A. Weber, *In Pursuit of Price Stability; the Wage-Price Freeze of 1971* (Washington, D.C., 1973); W. Slawson, "Price Controls for a Peacetime Economy," 84 *Harv. L. Rev.* 1090 (1971); "Price Control in a Cold War," 19 *Law & Contemp. Problems* 475 (1954); and the Series on Historical Reports on War Administration; Office of Price Administration (1947).

2. See R. Hall and R. Pindyck, "The Conflicting Goals of National Energy Policy," *The Public Interest* 3–5 (Spring 1977); P. MacAvoy, *Federal Energy Administration: Report of the Presidential Task Force* (Washington, D.C., 1977); R. Smith and C. Phelps, "The Subtle Impact of Price Controls on Domestic Oil Production," 68 *Am. Econ. Rev.* 428 (May 1978); S. Breyer, "Comment: The Subtle Impact of Price Controls on Domestic Oil Production," 68 *Am. Econ. Rev.* 434 (May 1978). For a comparative perspective see C. Watkins and M. Walker, eds., *Oil in the Seventies: Essays on Energy Policy* (Vancouver, 1977); and K. Dam, *Oil Resources: Who Gets What How?* (London, 1976); "Symposium. Comparison of Energy Policies," *J. Comp. Econ.* 95–208 (June 1978).

3. See S. 1391, 95th Cong., 1st Sess. § 111, *Hospital Cost Containment Act of 1977, Hearings before the Subcomm. on Health and Scientific Research of the Senate Comm. on Human Resources,* 95th Cong., 1st Sess. 3, 7–9 (Washington, D.C., 1977).

4. R. Benes et al., *Problems in Price Control: Pricing Techniques,* ed. P. Frank and M. Quint, OPA History Series (Washington, D.C., 1947), at 21.

5. A. Letzler, "The General Ceiling Price Regulation—Problems of Coverage and Exclusion," 19 *Law & Contemp. Problems* 486, 492 (1954).

6. 36 *Fed. Reg.* 15, 727 (August 17, 1971).

7. The output substitution, quality deterioration, and behavioral effects discussed here are also characteristic of Soviet-type planned economies. Output quotas, price rigidity, and widespread shortages must be dealt with on a daily basis by Soviet enterprise managers. An outstanding and highly readable account can be found in R. Powell. "Plan Execution and the Workability of Soviet Planning," 1 *J. Comp. Econ.* 51 (1977).

8. Chamber of Commerce of the United States, *The Price of Price Controls* 19–20 (Washington, D.C., 1951). M. Kosters, *Controls and Inflation: The Economic Stabilization Program in Retrospect* 95 (Washington, D.C., 1975).

9. R. Dickerson, "The 'Freeze' Method of Establishing Ceiling Prices," in Benes, *supra* note 4, at 42.

10. Benes, "Formula Pricing," *supra* note 4, at 75–90.

11. A. Lifter, "Pricing by Specific Authorization," in Benes, *supra* note 4, at 91.

12. See 60 Stat. 664 (1946).

13. Raw agricultural commodities were exempted from controls. Transportation costs were constricted by utilities commissions, which under ordinary cost-of-service ratemaking principles would allow the pass-through of increasing costs. Manufacturers who charged prices for delivered products that included freight were severely squeezed while their competitors who charged FOB prices were not. See R. Olson, "Adjustments and Other Special Problems under the General Ceiling Price Regulation," 19 *Law & Contemp. Problems* 539 (1954).

14. While import prices could have been controlled in the same manner as domestic prices, the fear of loss of supply of strategic or essential materials and the effects on

foreign relations led to more lenient price treatment. See S. Nelson, "OPS Price Control Standards," 19 *Law & Contemp. Problems* 554, 563 (1954).

15. Nelson, *supra* note 14, at 560; Olson, *supra* note 13, at 540–544. See S.R. 29, which allowed the regulators to pass through authorized cost increases to avoid a "replacement cost squeeze." 16 *Fed. Reg.* 5011 (1951).

16. 65 Stat. 135 (1951); Nelson, *supra* note 14, at 567–570.

17. Olson, *supra* note 13, at 542; Nelson, *supra* note 14. See F. Wolf and F. Keller, "Problems of the Industry Earnings Standard," 19 *Law & Contemp. Problems* 581 (1954).

18. See 6 C.F.R. 101, 37 *Fed. Reg.* 1237 (January 27, 1972).

19. See note 2 *supra* and J. Langdon, Jr., "FEA Price Controls for Crude Oil and Refined Petroleum Products," *Twenty-Sixth Annual Institute on Oil and Gas Law and Taxation,* Southwestern Legal Foundation (1975), at 55–100; and "Domestic Crude Oil Production—The FEA Regulatory Framework," *Twenty-Eighth Annual Institute on Oil and Gas Law and Taxation,* Southwestern Legal Foundation (1977), at 1–63.

20. See M. Feldstein and A. Taylor, "The Rapid Rise of Hospital Costs," Staff Report of the Council on Wage and Price Stability, Executive Office of the President (1977).

21. See generally Wolf and Keller, "Problems of the Industry Earnings Standard," 19 *Law & Contemp. Problems* 581 (1954).

22. A. Auerbach, *OPA and Its Pricing Policies* 22 (New York, 1945).

23. Several issues along these lines are discussed in J. Langdon, *supra* note 19; and S. Wakefield, "Allocation, Price Control and the FEA: Regulatory Policy and Practice in the Political Arena," 21 *Rocky Mountain Mineral Law Inst.* 257–284.

24. J. Zwerdling, "Pricing Techniques," 19 *Law & Contemp. Problems* 522, 531 (1954).

25. OEP Economic Stabilization Regulation No. 1, Sec. 3(a)(2): "If a seller delivers or offers a commodity or service which he did not previously deliver or furnish, he can determine his ceiling price either by (i) applying to his current direct unit cost or to his net invoice cost the percentage markup he is currently receiving on the most nearly similar commodity or service he sells, or (ii) using the ceiling price prevailing for comparable commodities or services in the same locality," 36 *Fed. Reg.* 16515 (August 21, 1971).

26. Of course, if a firm was already using its capacity fully, it would have to invest in new capacity, and the regulator would have to decide whether increased investment costs should be reflected in higher allowed prices.

27. The fact that "markup" rather than "return" is at issue does not change the principle, for marking up simply covers return plus an allowance for depreciation and other final costs.

28. See D. Cavers, *Problems in Price Control: Pricing Standards,* Office of Temporary Controls OPA General Publication 7, 27–91 (1947); Wolf and Keller, *supra* note 21, at 598–600.

29. See A. Lifter, "Pricing by Specific Authorization," in Benes, *supra* note 4, at 91.

30. Memorandum from H. A. Kwitok to Alfred Auerbach: "Your note of April 17, regarding price of new goods," dated April 21, 1942, quoted in Lifter, *supra* note 29, at 97.

31. 6 C.F.R. 300.409 (1972), 37 *Fed. Reg.* 26818 (December 16, 1972), as amended at 37 *Fed. Reg.* 28123 (December 21, 1972).

32. OPACS Price Release, RM 691, July 9, 1941.

33. C.P.R. 22, 16 *Fed. Reg.* 3562 (April 26, 1951).

34. See the discussion of the cost-based Korean War "industry earnings standard" in Wolf and Keller, *supra* note 21, at 596–602.

35. Dickensen, "The 'Freeze' Method of Establishing Prices," in Benes, *supra* note 4, at 31, 32.

36. That cost changes will occur if pass-throughs are not allowed is readily seen from Figure 12. Initially, producers' costs are such that they supply the good according to S_0. With demand D, the initial equilibrium is (Q_0, P_0) and the market is cleared. Now suppose costs increase, shifting the supply curve to S_1. In an uncontrolled market, price would rise to P_1 and the quantity produced would decrease to Q_1. However, if cost pass-throughs are not allowed—and price is limited to P_0—then suppliers are willing to produce only Q_1 while consumers continue to demand Q_0. A shortage equal to $Q_0 - Q_1$ results and the regulator must decide how to allocate the good.

37. Lifter, *supra* note 29, at 118.

38. J. Robinson, "OPS and the Problem of Small Business," 19 *Law & Contemp. Problems* 625, 638 (1954).

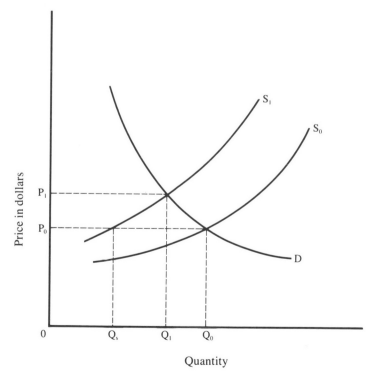

Quantity

Figure 12. Cost changes in the absence of pass-throughs.

39. 36 *Fed. Reg.* 21788 (November 13, 1971).

40. D. Mills, "Some Decisions of Price Control in 1971–73," 6 *Bell J. Econ. & Mgmt. Sci.* 3, 33 (1975).

41. The OPA had such a tool available in its power to set "dollars-and-cents" prices. Yet it was reluctant to do so, for fear that if the uniform price were too high it would create an umbrella, but if it were too low it would create hardship. See Auerbach, *supra* note 22.

42. See T. Manning, *The Office of Price Administration* 59–62 (New York, 1960); Olson, *supra* note 13, at 548–560. During World War II the OPA promulgated a regulation stating that "price limitations . . . shall not be evaded whether by direct or indirect methods." *Revised Maximum Price Regulation* No. 269, § 5, 7 Fed. Reg. 10708 (December 22, 1942); reissued with amendments 8 *Fed. Reg.* 13813 (October 8, 1943). While the generality of the statute and the criminal sanction undoubtedly inhibited evasion, the Supreme Court nonetheless found it unconstitutional in *M. Kraus & Bros., Inc.* v. *United States,* 327 U.S. 614 (1946). A similar statute was enacted during the Korean War along with a nonexclusive list of practices considered evasionary in nature. See also the 1971 regulations 36 *Fed. Reg.* 21788 (November 13, 1971).

43. See Manning, *supra* note 42, at 18.

44. Office of Emergency Preparedness, "Weekly Summary Report, Nov. 2, 1971, through close of Business, Nov. 9, 1971." See also *Stemming Inflation: The OEP and the Ninety-Day Freeze* 121 (Washington, D.C., 1972); Weber, *supra* note 1, at 106–111.

45. See Letzler, *supra* note 5, at 497–498, for a list of the elaborate record-keeping requirement during the Korean controls. One firm estimated it had to process a million purchase orders and invoices to make up the necessary records; another spent 21,000 man hours on record-keeping requirements. *The Price of Price Controls, supra* note 8, at 14–25.

46. A. Flory, "Field Administration in OPS," 19 *Law & Contemp. Problems* 604, 621 (1954).

47. See *The Price of Price Controls, supra* note 8, at 22; Nelson, *supra* note 14, at 574.

48. R. Hall and R. Pindyck, "The Conflicting Goals of National Energy Policy," *The Public Interest* 3–15 (Spring 1977).

49. See Kosters, *supra* note 8, at 106–107. Kosters found no particular weakness in investment during the 1971–73 period, but he notes that controls were in place only a very short time.

50. Kramer, foreword, "Price Control in a Cold War," 19 *Law & Contemp. Problems* 475, 476 (1954).

4. Allocation under a Public Interest Standard

1. The distinction between "natural" scarcity and "artificial" scarcity created by government is itself obscure, for all scarcity comes about in part through a decision not to allocate the product through the use of market prices.

2. See, e.g., Communications Act of 1934, 47 U.S.C. § 309 (awards of licenses must serve the "public interest").

3. *Ashbacker Radio Co.* v. *FCC,* 326 U.S. 327 (1945); 47 C.F.R. § 1.572; *Johnston Broadcasting Co.* v. *FCC,* 175 F.2d 351, 357 (D.C. Cir., 1949). These authorities

are thought to preclude the award of television licenses by auction or lottery. But see *Cowles Florida Broadcasting, Inc.*, 60 FCC 2d 372, 37 RR 2d 1487, 1564 n. 27 (1976), dissenting statement of Commissioner Robinson.

4. If each applicant is identical in every respect, then allocation by auction or lottery is fair. However, in most circumstances this is not the case.

5. See H. Levin, *The Invisible Resource* 5, 15–26 (Baltimore, 1971). For the table of allocations, see 47 C.F.R. §§ 73.601–73.610.

6. This principle, known as the DuMont plan, was advanced by an early advocate of a fourth national VHF network. See R. Noll, M. Peck, and J. McGowan, *Economic Aspects of Television Regulation* (Washington, D.C., 1974), at 101; and S. Besen, "The Economics of the Cable Consensus," Office of Telecommunications Policy, Executive Office of the President, November 17, 1972 (mimeo), at 15–18.

7. For example, the CAB not only had to decide whether to award the route, but also whether to allow the carrier to fly nonstop. Ofttimes, the board would grant the route but tack on a required intermediate stop—say, Scranton, Pennsylvania, on a New York–Chicago route. Although such an award reduced the commercial value of the route to the airline, it furthered several CAB objectives—minimizing the competitive impact of new entry and guaranteeing service to small communities.

8. FCC Form 301 (application for construction permit).

9. See Federal Aviation Act § 401(d)(1), 72 Stat. 754 as amended by 76 Stat. 143, 82 Stat. 867, 49 U.S.C. § 1371.

10. See *Ashbacker Radio Co.* v. *FCC,* 326 U.S. 327 (1945).

11. In *Johnston Broadcasting* v. *FCC,* 175 F.2d 351, 356, 357 (D.C. Cir., 1949), the court stated: "The inquiry must reveal which [applicant] would better serve [the public] . . . interest . . . To illustrate, local residence may not be an essential qualification. But as between applicants otherwise equally able, local residence might be a decisive factor . . . [Thus,] findings must be made in respect of every difference, except those which are frivolous or wholly unsubstantial, between the applicants, indicated by the evidence and advanced by one of the parties as substantial."

12. The CAB has changed many of its procedures as a result of airline deregulation. References in this chapter are to prederegulation procedures and remain illustrative of the way in which regulatory agencies will deal with the type of problem presented.

13. For a good description of how the FCC selects issues and seeks to order criteria, see R. Anthony, "Towards Simplicity and Rationality in Comparative Broadcast Licensing Proceedings," 24 *Stan. L. Rev.* 1, 33–36 (1971–72).

14. The CAB used a prehearing conference to sort out the relevant issues. The FCC seeks to specify certain issues as "important" but then allows shifts in individual cases through motions by the parties to add, to modify, or to delete issues.

15. See, e.g., *Alabama Citizens for Responsive Public TV, Inc.,* 62 FCC 2d 755 (1977); *Midwest St Louis Inc.,* 62 FCC 2d 889 (1977); *CBS, Inc.,* 49 FCC 2d 743 (1974). Since the FCC, in *Policy Statement on Comparative Broadcast Hearings* 1 FCC 2d 393 (1965) [hereinafter cited as *1965 Policy Statement*], sought to simplify the issues, much of the evidence now enters the record in the form of affidavits and pleadings (e.g., motions to add issues) rather than in the hearing itself.

16. See the Administrative Procedure Act, 5 U.S.C. §§ 702–706, and 47 U.S.C. §§ 155 (d) (7), 402, for the statutory provisions specifically governing review of FCC decisions.

17. Note, for example, the FCC's temptation to allow violations of procedural rules

of fairness to govern the award of licenses. Indeed, the major instance in which the FCC denied an existing station a license renewal ultimately stemmed from an improper ex parte contract that a former officer had made many years previously. *Greater Boston TV Corp.* v. *FCC,* 444 F.2d 841 (D.C. Cir., 1970). See also *WKAT, Inc.* v. *FCC,* 296 F.2d 375, 381–84 (D.C. Cir., 1961); *Sangamon Valley TV Corp.* v. *United States,* 269 F.2d 221 (D.C. Cir., 1959). Indeed, more than half of the handful of TV licenses ever revoked were revoked for this reason. See J. Abel, C. Clift, and F. Weiss, "Station License Revocations and Denials of Renewal, 1934–1969," 14 *J. of Broadcasting* 411 (1970), updated by the author; H. Geller, "A Modest Proposal for a Modest Reform of the FCC," 63 *Geo. L.J.* 705, 712 (1975).

18. An important distinction between the FCC and these two agencies is that the FCC does not regulate prices.

19. Cf. *Continental Airlines* v. *Civil Aeronautics Board* 443 F.2d 745 (D.C. Cir., 1971).

20. See W. Fruhan, *The Fight for Competitive Advantage* (Boston, 1972).

21. See 47 C.F.R. §§ 73.202 (FM), 73.606 (TV). The television table of assignments was adopted in the FCC's *Sixth Report and Order,* 41 FCC 148 (1952).

22. See H. Levin, *supra* note 5, at 75–77, 91, 98.

23. *FCC* v. *Allentown Broadcasting Co.,* 349 U.S. 358, 361–62 (1955).

24. R. Anthony, *supra* note 13, at 9, 85, n. 424, and 85–87.

25. The FCC has developed several "priorities" for choosing deserving cities. These include: (1) to provide a primary (AM, FM, and TV) service to all communities lacking them; (2) to provide each community with at least one local AM, FM, and TV broadcast outlet; (3) to provide at least two AM, FM, and TV services to each community; (4) to provide each community with at least two local broadcasting outlets for each service. Once these priorities are not determinative, cities are selected by comparing their populations, existing broadcasting outlets, geographic locations, and so on. See *Policy Statement on Sec 307(b) Considerations for Standard Broadcast Facilities Involving Suburban Communities,* 2 FCC 2d 190, 191 (1966); *Sixth Report and Order,* 41 FCC 148, 167–69 (1952) (TV); Anthony, *supra* note 24, at 86, n. 427; *Tri-County Broadcasting Co.,* 40 FCC 2d 171, 174–178 (1971).

26. See, e.g., *New York Times,* "Week in Review," November 12, 1978, at 6, for a discussion of efforts by the FCC in a license renewal proceeding to force New York stations either to move to New Jersey or to open studios there. See also, e.g., *FCC Oversight Hearings before the Subcommittee on Communications,* 94th Cong., 2d Sess., 51–53 (1976), statement of Rep. Andrew Maguire, Dem.-N.J.

27. See *FCC* v. *Allentown Broadcasting Co.,* 349 U.S. 358 (1955).

28. For a survey of the "localism" policy and its effects, see "Options Paper, Prepared by the Staff for Use by the House Subcommittee on Communications, 95th Cong., 1st Sess.," 45–65 (1977).

29. R. Noll, M. Peck, and J. McGowan, *supra* note 6, at 99–120.

30. *Id.*

31. J. Landis, *Report on Regulatory Agencies to the President-Elect,* 86th Cong., 2d Sess., 53 (New York, 1960).

32. H. Friendly, *The Federal Administrative Agencies: The Need for a Better Definition of Standards* 54, 53–73 (Cambridge, Mass., 1962).

33. Anthony, *supra* note 13, at 39.

34. U.S. Senate Comm. on the Judiciary, Subcomm. on Admin. Practice and Pro-

cedure, *Civil Aeronautics Board Practices and Procedures*, Report, 94th Cong., 1st Sess. (1975), at 83 [hereinafter cited as *Kennedy Report*].

35. CAB Staff, "The Domestic Route System," 53 (1974).

36. W. Jones, *Licensing of Major Broadcast Facilities by the FCC* 48–50 (Washington, D.C., 1962).

37. *Kennedy Report,* at 83–84.

38. H. Friendly, *supra* note 32, at 58.

39. Compare the statement of Commissioners K. Cox and N. Johnson, *Broadcasting in America and the FCC License Renewal Process: An Oklahoma Case Study* 32 (Washington, D.C., 1968): "We have not, and we do not, urge the Commission to evaluate the content and quality of television programs. We do believe, however, that the Commission can and should consider the character and quantity of a station's local efforts as they relate to the needs and interests of its community." Does the second sentence not represent an effort to escape the constraint imposed by the first?

40. *Johnson Broadcasting* v. *FCC,* 175 F.2d 351, 359 (D.C. Cir., 1949).

41. The commission is reluctant to take any action that might constitute "censorship" forbidden both by the First Amendment and § 326 of the Communications Act. See, e.g., *Formulation of Policies Relating to the Broadcast Renewal Applicant, Stemming from the Comparative Hearing Process* 66 FCC 2d 419 (1977).

42. See M. Spence, "Job Market Signaling," 87 *Q.J. Econ.* 355 (1973).

43. *1965 Policy Statement* 1 FCC 2d.

44. Indeed, the United States Court of Appeals for the District of Columbia has rejected out of hand even the hint of such a subjective approach when it reversed *Cowles Florida Broadcasting, Inc.,* 60 FCC 2d 372, 37 RR 2d 1487 (1976). See *Central Florida Enterprises, Inc.* v. *FCC,* 598 F.2d 37, 44 RR 2d 345, 359 (D.C. Cir., 1978): "Even were we to agree (and we do not agree) with the Commission's trivialization of each of [the challenger's] advantages, we still would be unable to sustain its action here. The Commission nowhere even vaguely described how it aggregated its findings into the decisive balance; rather, we are told that the conclusion is based on 'administrative "feel." ' Such intuitive forms of decision-making, completely opaque to judicial review, fall somewhere on the distant side of arbitrary."

45. "Comment," 43 *U. Chicago L. Rev.* 573 (1976). See also, *Report of the FCC to the Congress of the United States re the Comparative Renewal Process* 41–42 (1976).

46. Compare *Mid Florida Television Corp.,* 33 FCC 2d 1, 10 (1972), in which a 14 percent stockholder with 100 percent interest in two distant radio stations received a "slight" demerit but also received the award, with *Gilbert Broadcasting Corp.,* FCC 76D-31 (1976), in which a 25 percent stockholder with majority interest in three distant radio stations received a "substantial" demerit which cost him the license. If the decisions are consistent, the "scale" was all important.

47. See Anthony, *supra* note 13, at 43, n. 250. Compare *Henderson Broadcasting Co.,* 63 FCC 2d 433, 468 (1976), in which a hearing officer suggested that diversification is primary, with *Mid Florida Television Corp.,* 33 FCC 2d 1, 21 (1972), in which it was shown that integration preference can outweigh slight diversification preference to the opponent.

48. R. Noll, M. Peck, and J. McGowan, *supra* note 6, at 113.

49. These standards were proposed for comment in 27 FCC 2d 580 (1971). The FCC also has proposed "processing" standards for determining which initial and renewal applications will be sent up to the full commission for review. Unless the re-

newal application is sent up, it will be processed by the commission staff and automatically granted. These standards require the applicant to propose at least 5 percent local programming and 5 percent informational programming (news plus public affairs). 47 C.F.R. 0.281 (a)(8)(i). See B. Cole and A. Oettinger, *Reluctant Regulators* 133–242 (Reading, Mass., 1978).

50. R. Noll, M. Peck, and J. McGowan, *supra* note 6, at 110–111.

51. *1965 Policy Statement,* 1 FCC 2d, at 400, 401, 404.

52. *Cowles Florida Broadcasting, Inc.,* 60 FCC 2d 372, 37 RR 2d 1487 (1976).

53. S. Quinlan, *The Hundred Million Dollar Lunch* (Chicago, 1974).

54. *Kennedy Report,* at 81–82.

55. Commissioner Robinson refers to a comparative TV license renewal case that was only at the Review Board stage but had cost the challenger $2 million and the licensee $1.5 million. *Cowles Florida Broadcasting Co.,* 60 FCC 2d 372, 37 RR 2d 1487, 1566 n. 34 (1976).

56. For a discussion of these procedures, see Anthony, *supra* note 13, at 33, 34.

57. The doctrine of *Edgefield-Saluda Radio Co.,* 5 FCC 2d 148 (1966) requires the commission to waive its filing deadlines if an untimely submission raises public interest questions.

58. See Florencourt and Harrington, "Report to the Chairman of the FCC from the Task Force on Delegation" (1975), at 56–60.

59. The Review Board acted on 128 such petitions in 1971; 106 in 1972; and 224 in 1973. Thirty Review Board decisions were brought to the commission for review in 1971; 12 in 1972; and 43 in 1973. Florencourt and Harrington, *supra* note 58, at 42.

60. See *id.* at 76ff. for the review practices of the commission.

61. In *Mid Florida Television Corp.,* Docket 11083, the winning party presented 11 witnesses, including the mayor, to attest to the civic virtue of the principal owner. Tr. 673ff. The record contained more than 50 pages of letters of commendation as well as the glossy photographs. *Mid Florida Petition to Enlarge the Issues* (April 27, 1967).

62. See, e.g., *Henderson Broadcasting Co, Inc.,* 63 FCC 2d 433, 456 (Initial Decision, 1977).

63. For good examples of how evidence apparently excluded by the *1965 Policy Statement* in fact enters the record in the form of pleadings and affidavits attached to petitions to enlarge issues (heard by the Review Board), see, e.g., *Alabama Citizens for Responsive Public TV, Inc.,* 62 FCC 2d 755 (1977); *Midwest St. Louis, Inc.,* 62 FCC 2d 889 (1977); *CBS Inc.,* 49 FCC 2d 743 (1974).

64. FCC Form 301, Section IV-B, at 10 (1977).

65. See *Thomas Broadcasting Co.,* 62 FCC 2d 496 (Rev. Bd., 1976).

66. See *Cairo Broadcasting Co.,* 63 FCC 2d 586, 589 (1977).

67. See *Ascertainment of Community Problems by Broadcast Applicants—Primer,* 41 *Fed. Reg.* 1372 (January 7, 1976).

68. B. Cole and A. Oettinger, *supra* note 49, app. B.

69. Compare the effort of the commission to scrutinize the record for program information in *Cowles Florida Broadcasting, Inc.,* 60 FCC 2d 372, 37 RR 2d 1457, 1539–44, 1559 (1976), *modified* 62 FCC 2d 953 (1977), *rev'd sub. nom. Central Florida Enterprises Inc. v. FCC,* 598 F.2d 37, 44 RR 2d 345 (D.C. Cir., 1978), *Modification and reconsideration* denied 598 F.2d 58, 44 RR 2d 1567 (D.C. Cir., 1979).

70. In *Mid Florida Television Corp.,* Docket 11083, of the 572 pages of the five parties' *proposed findings of fact and law,* 281 were devoted to these issues.

71. See 47 U.S.C. § 155 (d)(5).

72. See, e.g., *Greater Boston TV Corp.* v. *FCC,* 444 F.2d 841 (D.C. Cir., 1970), *cert. denied* 403 U.S. 923 (1971).

73. Florencourt and Harrington, *supra* note 58, at 93–96.

74. *Kennedy Report,* at 81–103.

75. H. Friendly, *supra* note 32, at 64–68. See also B. Schwartz, "Comparative Television and the Chancellor's Foot," 47 *Geo. L.J.* 655 (1959).

76. See R. Noll, M. Peck, and J. McGowan, *supra* note 6, at 113.

77. *Kennedy Report,* at 83–84.

78. *Applications of Biscayne Television Corp.,* 11 RR 1113 (1956); *Sunbeam Television Corp.* v. *FCC,* 243 F.2d 26 (D.C. Cir., 1957); *Applications of Biscayne Television Corp.,* 22 FCC 1464 (1957).

79. "The Commission is not bound to deal with all cases at all times as it has dealt in the past with some that seem comparable . . . and changes of viewpoint, if reasonable, are recognized as both inescapable and proper." *1965 Policy Statement,* 1 FCC 2d, at 393.

80. H. Friendly, *supra* note 32, at 63.

81. Florencourt and Harrington, *supra* note 58.

82. J. Freedman, "Review Boards in the Administrative Process, 117 *U. Pa. L. Rev.* 546, 554 (1969).

83. Anthony, *supra* note 13, at 37, 38.

84. See Commissioner Robinson, dissenting in *Cowles Florida Broadcasting Co.,* 60 FCC 2d 372, 37 RR 2d 1487, 1559 (1976).

85. Anthony, for example, proposed a limited number of explicit objective standards related to concentration and integration. Anthony, *supra* note 13, at 70.

86. B. Schwartz, *supra* note 75, at 690–694. See generally W. Williams, "Impact of Commissioner Background on FCC Decisions, 1962–1975," 20 *J of Broadcasting* 239 (Spring 1976). Williams concludes that much of the variation in FCC policy and standards is a function of the president in power at the time.

87. See Kennedy Hearings—Testimony of Ralph Nader, *Kennedy Report,* at 173–175.

88. *Sangamon Valley Television Corp.* v. *United States,* 294 F.2d 742, 743 (D.C. Cir., 1961).

89. *Massachusetts Bay Telecasters, Inc.,* 295 F.2d 131 (D.C. Cir., 1961).

90. *Kennedy Report,* at 77–100.

91. 47 U.S.C. § 307(d).

92. See 47 U.S.C. § 301. See also 47 U.S.C. §§ 304, 309(h).

93. *Hearst Radio, Inc.,* 15 FCC 1149 (1951)(WBAL).

94. The commission found that WBAL's programming suffered from "an overabundance of commercial programs and commercial religious programs" until a few months before renewal, when it reformed. *Id.,* at 1177.

95. Before the *WHDH* case in 1969, the commission revoked or denied renewal of six licenses. Two of these concerned construction permits (the stations were not broadcasting), three were abandoned by their owners, and one was denied renewal because of unauthorized transfer of control. See J. Abel, C. Clift, and F. Weiss, *supra* note 17. About seventy radio stations had their licenses revoked or renewals denied, out of 9,400 radio authorizations. See *id.;* also, *FCC 41st Annual Report FY 1975,* at 97.

96. See *Greater Boston Television Corp.* v. *FCC,* 444 F.2d 841 (D.C. Cir., 1970),

cert. denied 403 U.S. 923 (1971). Jaffe referred to the decision as "a desperate and spasmodic lurch toward 'the left.' " Jaffe, *"WHDH:* the FCC and Broadcast License Renewals," 82 *Harv. L. Rev.* 1693, 1700 (1969).

97. *Office of Communication of The United Church of Christ* v. *FCC,* 425 F.2d 543 (D.C. Cir., 1969); *Lamar Life Broadcasting Co.,* 25 FCC 2d 101 (1970). However, in this case it was effectively the Court of Appeals that denied the renewal. See Geller, *supra* note 17, at 712–714.

98. See Abel, Clift, and Weiss, *supra* note 17, as updated for television by interview with David Weston of the Renewal and Transfer Division of the FCC Broadcast Bureau, August 1977.

99. See *Policy Statement Concerning Comparative Hearings Involving Regular Renewal Applicants,* 22 FCC 2d 424, 425–26 (1970); *Formulation of Policies Relating to the Broadcast Renewal Applicant, Stemming from the Comparative Renewal Process,* 27 FCC 2d 580 (1971).

100. *Citizens Communications Center* v. *FCC,* 447 F.2d 1201, 1213–14 nn. 35, 36 (D.C. Cir., 1971). See also *Citizens Communications Center* v. *FCC,* 463 F.2d 822 (D.C. Cir., 1972).

101. 27 FCC 2d 580, 582 (1971).

102. See *Report of the FCC to the Congress of the United States re the Comparative Renewal Process* (1976).

103. *Report on Renewal Policies, supra* note 99.

104. *Cowles, supra* note 69, 62 FCC 2d, at 955–956. While the Court of Appeals reversed in an attempt to limit the extent of the renewal expectancy, it ultimately recognized that such expectancy comports with the Communications Act, if properly articulated by the FCC. 598 F.2d 58, 44 RR 2d, at 1574.

105. Comment, 43 *U. Chicago L. Rev.* 573, 592–597 (1976). See also, H. Geller, "The Comparative Renewal Process in Television: Problems and Suggested Solutions," 61 *Va. L. Rev.* 471, 492–496 (1975).

106. *Cowles, supra* note 69, 37 RR 2d 1556 (1976), Commissioner Robinson, dissenting. The commission later modified its language to characterize Cowles' record as "substantial" (62 FCC 2d, at 955) and granted Cowles special consideration as a result of this record. The Court of Appeals reversed on this point (598, F.2d, at 57–58, 44 RR 2d, at 369–370), but later modified its opinion, leaving the door open for the commission to articulate a rationale for granting renewal expectancies on the basis of average past performance (598 F.2d, at 60–61, 44 RR 2d, at 1574–75).

107. *Kennedy Report,* at 78.

108. *Id.,* at 95–96.

109. The Court of Appeals in *Cowles, supra* note 69, called such a policy "a plausible construction of the 'public interest.' " 598 F.2d, at 60, 44 RR 2d, at 1574.

110. See *Report of the FCC to the Congress of the United States re the Comparative Renewal Process,* at 32 (1976).

111. This tendency is strongest when the agency is responsible for initially creating these expectations.

112. The courts have also encouraged the FCC to take this matter into account. See *Carroll Broadcasting Co.* v. *FCC,* 258 F.2d 440 (D.C. Cir., 1958).

113. See, e.g., *Report of the FCC to the Congress of the United States re the Comparative Renewal Process,* at 41–46.

114. A sample of 35 comparative hearing cases between 1952 and 1965, for example, reveals that winning applicants proposed dedicating an average of 31.5 percent of their time to local, live broadcasting. They *actually* devoted less than 12 percent of their time to such programs. The difficulty of enforcing program promises arises not only out of the FCC's tendency to grant renewals but also out of its limited ability to prevent station owners from transferring their licenses to others. *Moline Television Corp.,* 31 FCC 2d 263, 272 (1971). See 47 U.S.C. § 310(d) (1976). Jones estimated that 9–12 percent of authorizations changed hands each year. *Supra* note 36, at 169–174.

115. See B. Cole and A. Oettinger, *supra* note 49, at 228–241.

116. *Citizens Communications Center Inc.* v. *United States,* 447 F.2d 1201 (1971) (CCCI); 463 F.2d 822 (1972) (CCCII).

117. Consider renewed insistence of the U.S. Court of Appeals for the District of Columbia on rigidly applying the *1965 Policy Statement's* structural characteristics in the renewal context, expressed in its recent *Cowles* opinions, *supra* note 69, 598 F.2d at 54–55 (n. 87), 44 RR 2d, at 350–352, 360, 367–371, esp. n. 83.

118. The U.S. Court of Appeals for the District of Columbia highlights this intractability while discussing the *Cowles* case as follows: "First we note there was no direct inquiry into whether Central's proposed service would be 'superior' or even just 'substantial.' The Commission rejected that question as too speculative, preferring to rely on those structural characteristics identified in the 1965 Statement. These it supposed were less susceptible of puffery than representations concerning further programming. That is probably correct. The fly in the analysis in [sic] that the Commission judges incumbents largely on the basis of their broadcast record, to which there will be nothing comparable on the side of a challenger in any case. The 'comparison' thus necessarily ends up rather confused. For at the end of a hearing the Commission is left on the one hand with a series of comparative findings pertaining to integration, etc., and on the other hand with a wholly incommensurable and noncomparative finding about the incumbent's past performance. Of course the incumbent's past performance is some evidence, and perhaps the best evidence, of what its future performance would be. But findings on integration and minority participation are evidence as well, and are both *the only evidence comparing the applicants and also the only evidence whatsoever pertaining to the challenger"* 44 RR 2d, at 366–367 (footnotes omitted). The court goes on to insist that such a "confused" comparison is mandated under the current statutory framework. See 44 RR 2d, at 367, n. 83.

119. *Kennedy Report,* at 95–96.

120. *Report of the FCC to the Congress of the United States re the Comparative Renewal Process* (1976).

121. Several bills that would permit competition to displace much existing federal regulation of the communications industry were introduced during the first session of the 96th Congress. The Van Deerlin Bill (HR. 3333) would increase the free market's role in determining the development, introduction, and availability of technologies and services that use the electromagnetic spectrum by a dramatic reduction in the jurisdiction of the FCC (indeed, the FCC would be replaced by a new agency, the "Communications Regulatory Commission") and introduction of user or "spectrum fees." These fees would cover the cost of processing the license and reflect the scarcity cost of the spectrum. Traditional regulations would be retained to the extent that market forces are unable to protect the public interest. Senator Hollings introduced a similar bill (S. 611)

in the Senate on March 12, 1979. The Hollings Bill also incorporates the spectrum fee proposal of the Van Deerlin Bill, though it generally seeks to achieve reform within the framework of existing law.

5. Standard Setting

1. The National Traffic and Motor Vehicle Act of 1966, as amended 15 U.S.C. § 1381 et seq. (1976).

2. 5 U.S.C. § 553 (1976).

3. 5 U.S.C. § 706 (1976).

4. *SEC* v. *Chenery Corp.*, 332 U.S. 194, 198, 203 (1947).

5. See S. Breyer and R. Stewart, *Administrative Law and Regulatory Policy* 394–445 (Boston, 1979).

6. *United States* v. *Florida East Coast Ry. Co.*, 410 U.S. 224 (1973); Breyer and Stewart, *supra* note 5, at 481–500.

7. Breyer and Stewart, *supra* note 5.

8. See *Action for Children's Television* v. *FCC* 564 F.2d 458 (D.C. Cir., 1977).

9. See Breyer and Stewart, *supra* note 5, at 509–510.

10. *Vermont Yankee* v. *Natural Resources Defense Council*, 435 U.S. 519 (1978).

11. Following the imposition of the nationwide 55-mile-per-hour speed limit as a fuel-saving measure in January 1974, the number of auto accident fatalities dropped markedly. There were 45,196 fatalities in 1974, compared with 54,052 in 1973. See DOT/NHTSA, *Motor Vehicle Safety 1977: A Report on Activities under the National Traffic and Motor Vehicle Safety Act of 1966 and the Motor Vehicle Information and Cost Savings Act of 1972, January 1, 1977–December 31, 1977.*

12. The Society of Automotive Engineers (SAE) is a professional society, which provided an open forum for exchanging technical information about auto safety. As NHTSA began to rely upon SAE to develop its standards, industry members of SAE gradually became more guarded in their comments, reducing the value of the SAE as a source of information for the agency. See J. Gotbaum, L. Seale, R. Barusch, M. Delikat, and L. Masouredis, in "The Standard-Setting Process in the National Highway Traffic Safety Administration" (unpublished report prepared for NHTSA, December 19, 1977) [hereinafter referred to as Gotbaum]. This chapter relies on that study for much of its factual information.

13. P. Harter, "In Search of OSHA," *Regulation* 33–34 (September/October 1977).

14. *Id.*, at 34.

15. See generally R. Zeckhauser and A. Nichols, *The Occupational Safety and Health Administration—An Overview,* U.S. Senate Committee on Governmental Affairs, app. to vol. 6, "Framework for Regulation," 95th Cong., 2d Sess. (December 1978).

16. 18 U.S.C. § 834 (1976).

17. See *Boyce Motor Lines* v. *United States,* 342 U.S. 337 (1952).

18. P. MacAvoy, ed., *OSHA Safety Regulation: Report of the Presidential Task Force* (Washington, D.C., 1977), at 17–19.

19. See 34 *Fed. Reg.* 11, 148 (July 2, 1969), 35 *Fed. Reg.* 7187 (May 7, 1970), and 35 *Fed. Reg.* 16, 927 (November 3, 1970).

20. See "Softface v. Model 1974 Steel System," NHTSA engineering systems' staff. See generally Gotbaum, *supra* note 12.

21. Agency staff believe that the agency did not take adequate account of the nature of the industry. Because there were many small firms with little technical sophistication, lead times were inadequate. The result is that the braking systems req ed by the standard were blamed for accidents, which in turn led many to lose confidence in the agency. See, e.g., S. Scheibla, "Federally Mandated Brake Standards May Be a Safety Hazard," *Barron's* 4 (November 28, 1977). See generally Gotbaum, *supra* note 12, app. E.

22. See, e.g., *Nash v. Volpe,* No. 177–33 (DDC 1973), in which a representative of Ralph Nader convinced the court to order the promulgation of Uniform Tire Quality Grading Standards by a stated deadline.

23. Consider, for example, the following estimates of the cost of airbag protection. $87—NHTSA's estimate for a lap-shoulder belt system. $197—an Allstate Insurance Co. consultant's estimate for airbag protection of the front-seat positions in a six-passenger car with lap belts. $210—NHTSA's estimate for airbag protection of the front-seat positions in a six-passenger car with lap belts. $300—General Motors' and Chrysler's estimates for airbag protection of the front-seat positions in a six-passenger car with lap belts. $358—Volkswagen's estimate for airbag protection for front-seat positions with lap belts. $86—Volkswagen's price estimate for the passive belt restraint system. Center for Auto Safety, "Airbags: Facts and Figures," at 2.

24. The task force consisted of representatives of the Department of Ttransportation, Environmental Protection Agency, the Energy Research and Development Agency of the National Science Foundation, and others.

25. *Chrysler Corp.* v. *DOT,* 472 F.2d 659, 676 (6th Cir., 1972).

26. See *Nash* v. *Volpe, supra* note 22.

27. Virginia Knauer, after taking a survey of consumers in early 1972, wrote NHTSA insisting that it require manufacturers to give consumers the information that the survey showed they wanted. See Gotbaum, *supra* note 12, at 56.

28. *B. F. Goodrich* v. *DOT,* 541 F.2d 1178 (6th Cir., 1976).

29. *Chrysler Corp.* v. *DOT,* 472 F.2d 659 (6th Cir., 1972).

30. Final-stage manufacturers must certify that the finished truck meets the standard.

31. Less aggressive brakes are now allowed. 41 *Fed. Reg.* 8786 (March 1, 1976).

32. After a court set aside the NHTSA brake standard as arbitrary, *PACCAR, Inc.* v. *National Highway Traffic Safety Administration,* 573 F.2d 632 (9th Cir., 1978), NHTSA determined that it could not legally promulgate a new antilock brake requirement unless it could prove that the resulting antilock systems would work reliably in practice. NHTSA feels that it cannot certify this to be true of existing mass-produced equipment. Thus, it is unable to enforce an antilock requirement. See 43 *Fed. Reg.* 48, 646 (October 19, 1978). Nonetheless, many manufacturers include antilock devices as a "delete option" in trucks. And a significant number of truck drivers appear to be selecting the option. Interview between Martha Malkin and Duane A. Perrin, NHTSA engineer, November 27, 1978.

33. Before NHTSA promulgated any proposed rule for truck brakes, for example, truck owners—the American Trucking Association—cooperated extensively with the agency. They wished NHTSA to force manufacturers to install the safety equipment. Once NHTSA's proposals began to take a different form, the ATA stopped cooperating

and became a formidable opponent of the final standard. It joined as a petitioner in the *PACCAR* litigation. Interview between Martha Malkin and Duane A. Perrin, November 27, 1978.

34. The courts have sometimes rejected claims that a standard impeded competition in companies where, for example, the competition involved appeared unimportant. See *Chrysler Corp.* v. *DOT* 515 F.2d 1053, 1058 (6th Cir., 1975) (competition in the size of headlight lamps). In *H&H Tire Co.* v. *DOT,* 471 F.2d 350, 354–355 (7th Cir., 1972), the court stated that it agreed with the government that the fact that a regulation may cause economic hardship does not make it unreasonable. Nonetheless, it set aside the retreaded-tire standard because the agency had not adequately investigated the effect of cost increases upon retreaders. The court stated that the agency had overlooked "the fact that if economic analysis were to show that retreaders would suffer severe economic hardship, either by being forced out of business or by being priced out of their market, the retreaders' customers would also suffer."

35. Houdaille approached many legislators with its claim of unfair treatment. The agency agreed to reexamine its cost/benefit analysis of the bumper standard, even though it felt that fuel economy standard constraints would make steel bumpers obsolete.

36. See *Radiant Burners* v. *People's Gas Co.,* 364 U.S. 656 (1961).

37. To be more specific, judicial review will test (a) whether the proper procedures were followed, (b) whether the standard is arbitrary, capricious, or an abuse of discretion, and (c) whether the standard complies with the agency's authorizing statute.

38. See James Wilson, "The Politics of Regulation," in J. McKie, ed., *Social Responsibility and the Business Predicament* (Washington, D.C., 1974), at 164.

39. 35 *Fed. Reg.* 106 (January 3, 1970).

40. 35 *Fed. Reg.* 16840 (October 31, 1970).

41. 36 *Fed. Reg.* 1913 (February 3, 1971).

42. 36 *Fed. Reg.* 17343 (August 28, 1971).

43. *Wagner Electric Co.* v. *Volpe,* 466 F.2d 1013 (3rd Cir., 1972).

44. See, e.g., *Home Box Office* v. *Federal Communications Commission,* 567 F.2d 9 (D.C. Cir., 1977). See also, *Moss* v. *Civil Aeronautics Board,* 430 F.2d 581 (D.C. Cir., 1970).

45. See *Vermont Yankee* v. *National Resources Defense Council,* 435 U.S. 519 (1978). See also the discussion of the "Hard Look" doctrine and the procedural requirements imposed by boards in Breyer and Stewart, *supra* note 5, at 291–309.

46. In *B. F. Goodrich* v. *DOT,* 541 F.2d 1178 (6th Cir., 1976), petitioner complained that NHTSA had "dumped" documents into the public record after the final comment date. NHTSA responded that those documents were simply part of the record that had to be prepared prior to review. The court rejected petitioner's claim that this practice violated its procedural rights. 541 F.2d, at 1184.

47. See *Chrysler Corp.* v. *DOT,* 515 F.2d 1053 (6th Cir., 1975).

48. See Gotbaum, *supra* note 12.

6. Historically Based Allocation

1. The research work for this section was done by Judith Greenberg, a graduate student at Harvard Law School. Many of the oil allocation examples are drawn from

work that was submitted as a paper, "Rules, Goals and Notions of Legitimacy: A Study of the Federal Energy Office, 1974" (Masters thesis, Harvard Law School 1979). I gratefully acknowledge her help.

2. See Greenberg, *supra* note 1, at 16; *Hearings on Petroleum Product Shortages before the Senate Comm. on Banking, Housing, and Urban Affairs,* 93rd Cong., 1st Sess. (May 7, 1973, testimony of W. V. Barton, National Farmers Union); (May 8, 1973, testimony of R. Mason and R. J. Peterson); (May 9, 1973, testimony of L. G. Rawl and A. M. Card of Exxon and Texaco).

3. See *BNA Energy Users Report,* March 7, 1974, at A-4; *id.,* April 11, 1974, at A-9 and A-13.

4. 38 *Fed. Reg.* 34426, § 200.46 (December 13, 1973).

5. See 39 *Fed. Reg.* 5775 (February 15, 1974).

6. 39 *Fed. Reg.* 1933, § 211.11(c) (January 15, 1974) 39 *Fed. Reg.* 5775 (February 15, 1974).

7. *BNA Energy Users Report,* December 20, 1973, at A-14; cf. 39 Fed. Reg. 1933 (January 15, 1974).

8. See, e.g., *Hearings on the Farm Fuel Situation before the Senate Comm. on Agriculture,* 93rd Cong., 2d Sess. (July 24, 25, 1974).

9. Greenberg, *supra* note 1, at 29.

10. Interview by Judith Greenberg at Art Shaw, FEO Region I director of operations, April 11, 1979.

11. *BNA Energy Users Report,* February 28, 1974, at A-35.

12. See 3 Staff of the Federal Trade Commission, *An Evaluation of the Mandatory Petroleum Allocation Program* 21 (1974) [hereinafter referred to as *FTC Evaluation*].

13. Interview with Art Shaw, *supra* note 10.

14. "Agricultural production," for example, was further defined to exclude chewing gum and liquor. 39 *Fed. Reg.* 15971 (May 6, 1974).

15. Greenberg, *supra* note 1, at 20.

16. *New York Times,* February 6, 1974, at 21.

17. See *BNA Energy Users Report,* November 29, 1973, at A-39.

18. See 39 *Fed. Reg.* 1936 § 211.27 (January 15, 1974).

19. See *BNA Energy Users Report,* March 14, 1974, at A-14, 15.

20. *Id.,* January 24, 1974, at G-12; *id.,* February 7, 1974, at A-5.

21. *Id.,* February 7, 1974, at A-5.

22. *Id.,* February 28, 1974, at A-22.

23. *New York Times,* February 28, 1974, at 1.

24. 39 *Fed. Reg.* 1935 § 211.14(a) (January 15, 1974).

25. *BNA Energy Users Report,* April 25, 1974, at A-15.

26. *Id.,* April 11, 1974, at G-1.

27. Greenberg, *supra* note 1, at 41.

28. See *BNA Energy Users Report,* May 30, 1974, at A-11.

29. See *New York Times,* January 31, 1974, at 18; *FTC Evaluation, supra* note 12, at app. B-4; *BNA Energy Users Report,* March 14, 1974, at A-15; *Hearings on Market Performance and Competition in the Petroleum Industry before the Senate Comm. on Interior and Insular Affairs,* 93rd Cong., 1st Sess., at 557–560 (testimony of G. Potvin, December 5, 1973).

30. *Id.,* at 32, 60 (testimony of J. Stewart; A. Moore). *Hearings on Efficiency of Executive Agencies with Respect to the Petroleum Industry before a Subcomm. of the*

Senate Comm. on Government Operations, 93rd Cong., 1st Sess., at 13 (testimony of F. Allvine, November 29, 1973).

31. *New York Times,* January 31, 1974, at 18. *Id.,* February 6, 1974, at 1.

32. 39 *Fed. Reg.* 1934 § 211.13(b) (January 15, 1974).

33. See Cong. Comm. Rep. No. 628, 93rd Cong., 1st Sess., at 1, 2 (1973).

34. See 39 *Fed. Reg.* 1927 § 205.24(d) (January 15, 1974).

35. *Atlantic Richfield Co.,* 1974 *EMEA* ¶ 20,163.

36. *General Gas & Oil Co.,* 1974 *EMEA* ¶ 20,155.

37. Greenberg, *supra* note 1, at 47–51.

38. See 39 *Fed. Reg.* 1934 (January 15, 1974).

39. FEO, Region I, Industry Advisory Bulletin No. 9, April 1974.

40. Interviews by Judith Greenberg with Hugh Saussy, Deputy Director of FEO, Region I, April 5, 1979; and with Art Shaw, *supra* note 10.

41. Case No. 01-002364 on file in FEO Region I office.

42. See, e.g., Case No. 01-005052 on file at FEO Region I office.

43. Compare Case No. 01-004548 with Case No. 01-005052 on file at FEO Region I office.

44. Compare Case No. 01-002647 with Case No. 01-001791 on file at FEO Region I office.

45. See Greenberg, *supra* note 1, at 56.

46. The FEO regularly declared that its regulations were "emergency" regulations and dispensed with various procedural requirements. See, e.g., 38 *Fed. Reg.* 34415 (December 13, 1973). Procedures throughout were highly informal, relying upon conferences between administrators and applicants. See Greenberg, *supra* note 1, at 60–62, 75–76.

7. Individualized Screening

1. The magnitude of the potential harm (should an "accident" occur) is also an important parameter. For example, it may be worthwhile to attempt to screen out even the smallest risk where potential losses are great (for example, nuclear plant meltdown), yet not worth the effort in terms of time and money where the damage is small *and reversible*.

2. Federal Food, Drug, and Cosmetic Act of 1938, 21 U.S.C. §§ 301 et seq. (1976).

3. 21 U.S.C. § 342(a)(1) (1976).

4. See Merrill, *Government Regulation of Carcinogens in Food* 8 (1978), reprinted in National Academy of Sciences, Committee for a Study on Saccharin and Food Safety Policy, *Food Safety in the United States* (Washington, D.C., 1979) [hereinafter referred to as NAS Study II].

5. 21 U.S.C. § 346 (1976).

6. See Merrill, *supra* note 4, at 13–14; 39 *Fed. Reg.* 42743 (December 6, 1974).

7. 21 U.S.C. § 348 (1976).

8. See 21 C.F.R. 171.1.

9. This is the famous Delaney Clause, 21 U.S.C. § 348(c)(3)(A) (1976). It reads: "No additive shall be deemed to be safe if it is found to induce cancer when ingested by man or animal or if it is found, after tests which are appropriate for the evaluation of the safety of food additives, to induce cancer in man or animal." It has led to

controversy because it apparently bans any substance, no matter how beneficial, if that substance produces no matter how small a risk of cancer. See NAS Study II, ch. 2.

10. Merrill, *supra* note 4, at 17.

11. NAS Study II, *supra* note 4, ch. 2.

12. The statute excepts from the definition of food additives those "generally recognized, among experts qualified by scientific training and experience to evaluate . . . safety, as having been adequately shown through scientific procedures (or, in the case of a substance used in food prior to January 1, 1958, through either scientific procedures or experience based on common use in food) to be safe under the conditions of intended use." 21 U.S.C. § 321(s) (1976).

13. 21 U.S.C. § 321(s)(4) (1976). Whether the government granted an informal "sanction or approval" before 1958 often raises a difficult factual issue. See Merrill, *supra* note 4, at 22.

14. 21 C.F.R. 182.

15. In the case of a substance that has been GRAS for a long time and that poses no immediate danger, the FDA may issue an interim rule allowing its continued marketing, pending approval. See 21 C.F.R. 182.10(d). The formal approval proceeding will require the additive to meet the hurdle of the Delaney Amendment—which it does not have to meet so long as it is GRAS.

16. 21 U.S.C. § 342(a)(1) (1976).

17. This can cause serious problems, because packaging material may contain carcinogens. If molecules migrate to the food, even to the extent of one part per trillion, it may run afoul of the Delaney Amendment, which some believe forbids the addition of even one molecule of a substance to food if any dose of that substance (even a very high one) leads any test animal to develop cancer. See NAS Study II, ch. 2.

18. Animal drugs are regulated under the Animal Drug Amendments of 1968, 82 Stat. 342, 21 U.S.C. § 360(b) (1976). Pesticides are regulated under the Federal Insecticide, Fungicide, and Rodenticide Act, 7 U.S.C. §§ 136 et seq. (1976). Both these areas of regulation can raise problems similar to those encountered in screening direct food additives.

19. This step is particularly important in the case of GRAS substances, for the burden of proof rules make it difficult to get a new additive approved, while the procedures mandated in the statute make it difficult for the FDA to remove an item previously given formal approval; but the FDA has wide discretion in determining whether an item is GRAS.

20. There are, of course, legal rules designed to separate judicial and prosecutorial functions within the agency; so the mere bringing of the proceeding does not necessarily mean that the agency will win. Yet, in practice, it usually does win. See S. Breyer and R. Stewart, *Administrative Law and Regulatory Policy,* ch. 8 (Boston, 1979).

21. This referral is required by statute, 42 U.S.C. § 2039.

22. See 10 C.F.R. 50.58

23. See generally P. Hutt, "Food Regulation," 33 *Food Drug Cosmetic L.J.* 501 (1978).

24. For an example of the type of claim in the area of drug regulation, see S. Peltzman, "An Evaluation of Consumer Protection Legislation: The 1962 Drug Amendments," 81 *J. Pol. Econ.* 1049 (1973).

25. See Hutt, *supra* note 23, at 525–528, and sources there cited.

26. See particularly, Peltzman, *supra* note 24, for drug-related examples.

27. 199 *Science* 162 (January 13, 1978). These chemicals fall within the strictures of the Toxic Substances Control Act of 1976, 15 U.S.C. §§ 2601 et seq. (1976).

28. "Food Additives: Competitive, Regulatory, and Safety Problems," Hearings before the Senate Select Committee on Small Business, 95th Cong., 1st Sess., 42, 52, 57, 502–503 (1977).

29. Hutt, *supra* note 23, at 574. See also President's Science Advisory Committee, *Chemicals and Health* 65 (National Science Foundation, 1973).

30. Federation of American Societies for Experimental Biology, "Evaluation of Health Aspects of GRAS Food Ingredients," 36 *Federation Proceedings* 2519, 2527 (1977) [hereinafter referred to as FASEB Report].

31. "Chemical Carcinogens: The Scientific Basis for Regulation," 201 *Science* 1200 (September 29, 1978).

32. See *U.S. Council on Environmental Quality, Sixth Annual Report* 26–28 (Washington, D.C., 1975); Hutt, *supra* note 23, at 575.

33. This fact is true of many other diseases, substances, and reactions. See FASEB Report, *supra* note 30.

34. See Mack, Pike, and Casagrande, "Epidemiologic Methods for Human Risk Assessment," paper available at the National Institute of Medicine, at 1749.

35. Even if one could follow such a large group for twenty years, one is still left with the problem of identifying effects that may not become apparent until the second, third, or fourth generations.

36. This can be seen from a four-fold table often used by statisticians and epidemiologists (see Table 17). This table assumes that 10 percent of the general population uses saccharin. Thus, of 200 controls, 20 use saccharin. If, in fact, saccharin doubles the risk of getting cancer, the ratio of saccharin users who have cancer to all saccharin users must be twice as great as nonusers who have cancer to all nonusers (in the table 80/100 = twice 120/300). This fact, in turn, means that the ratio of users to nonusers among those with cancer (80/120) is twice that among the group taken as a whole (100/300). An epidemiologist, finding the facts to be as depicted in the table, would conclude that saccharin doubles the risk of a person getting bladder cancer.

37. See Mack, Pike, and Casagrande, *supra* note 34, at 1754. See generally NAS Study II, *supra* note 4, ch. 5.

38. The more complex the study, the greater the amount of time it takes to complete. When a potential carcinogen is at stake, time can mean lives—such that refined screening tests can only be bought at a substantial price. See Committee for a Study on Saccharin and Food Safety Policy, *Saccharin: Technical Assessment of Risks and Benefits,* Report No. 1, 3–90, 3–91 (National Academy of Sciences, 1978) [hereinafter referred to as NAS Study I].

Table 17. Saccharin use and incidence of cancer.

	Saccharin users	Nonusers	Total group
Cancer victims	80	120	200
Controls	20	180	200
Total group	100	300	400

39. See NAS Study II at 5–9, 5–10; NAS Study I at 3–89 to 3–91; Newill, *Methodologies of Risk Assessment,* in *Annals of the New York Academy of Sciences* 413.

40. See generally NAS Study II, ch. 5; A. Lilienfeld, *Foundations of Epidemiology* (1976).

41. FASEB Report, at 2536.

42. Many commentators have argued that there is no minimum safe exposure to carcinogens.

43. FASEB Report, at 2536.

44. Office of Technology Assessment, "Cancer Testing Technology and Saccharin," app. I (1977).

45. See the discussion in NAS Study I, 3–61 to 3–73.

46. FASEB Report, at 2545–46.

47. NAS Study II, at 5–20.

48. NAS Study I, at 3–72.

49. NAS Study II, at 5–22.

50. *Id.,* at 5–27.

51. 76 Stat. 780 (1962).

52. An "indication" is a particular use of a particular drug. Cooper, "The Quality of Advice," 2 *Philosophy and Technology of Drug Assessment* 269 (Smithsonian Institution, 1971) [hereinafter referred to as Cooper.]

53. *Id.,* at 232.

54. See *id.,* at 269 et seq.

55. 21 U.S.C. § 360g (1976).

56. See Breyer and Stewart, *Administrative Law and the Regulatory Policy,* ch. 6 (Boston, 1979).

57. See, e.g., *SmithKline Corp.* v. *FDA,* 587 F.2d 1107 (D.C. Cir., 1978).

58. FASEB Report, at 2527–28.

59. The Atomic Energy Act requires that an application for a nuclear power plant license be submitted to a board of non-NRC experts. This board, the Advisory Committee on Reactor Safeguards (ACRS) reviews the application and submits a report, which becomes an influential part of the hearing record. 42 U.S.C. § 2039 (1976); see 10 C.F.R. 150.58.

60. See *Seacoast Anti-Pollution League* v. *Costle* 572 F.2d 872 (1st Cir., 1978).

61. See generally Cooper, *supra* note 52. The judgments made in this section also reflect my experience as a member of the National Academy of Sciences Committee on Saccharin and Food Safety Policy (1975).

62. See FASEB Report, at 2557–59.

63. FASEB Report, at 2529–32.

64. *Id.*

65. FASEB Report, at 2529–34.

66. FASEB Report, at 2532.

67. See Pub. L. No. 95–203 (1977), 91 Stat. 1451. Congress postponed the effective date of an FDA ban on saccharin and asked the NAS to examine the health risks and benefits of its use.

68. NAS Study I, ch. 3.

69. NAS Study I, ch. 4.

70. NAS Study I, draft August 7, 1978, "Benefits of Saccharin," at 31.

71. NAS Study I, at 4–37.

72. FASEB Report, at 2544.

73. Christensen and Luginbyhl, *Registry of Toxic Effects of Chemical Substances* (1975). Such substances include gum, glucose, sucrose, and starch. FASEB Report, at 2545. See also the list of carcinogens in Hutt, *supra* note 23, at 560–562 (e.g., egg yolk, rice, caffeine, vitamin D_2).

74. See Miller, "Acrylonitrile," case study prepared for NAS Panel II, October 1978.

75. 430 F.2d 891 (D.C. Cir., 1970).

76. 567 F.2d 9 (D.C. Cir., 1977), cert. denied, 434 U.S. 829, rehearing denied, 434 U.S. 988 (1977), but see *Seacoast, supra* note 60.

77. See Cooper, "The Role of Regulatory Agencies in Risk-Benefit Decision Making," speech given at Animal Health Institute, October 26, 1978.

78. See Hutt, *supra* note 23, at 561.

79. See Cooper, *supra* note 52.

80. See NAS Study I, ch. 4.

81. See Draft Report of the Advisory Committee on Environmental Health and Safety Regulations to the Dept. of Commerce for the Domestic Policy Review on Industrial Innovation, December 20, 1978, at 24–25.

82. See O. Eckstein, *Water-Resources Development: The Economics of Project Evaluation* (Cambridge, Mass., 1958); *Design of Water-Resource Systems,* Harvard University Study (Cambridge, Mass., 1962).

83. See Kneese, "Benefit Analysis and Today's Regulatory Problems," paper presented at Public Interest Economics Foundation Conference, October 12–13, 1978, at 5. See generally O. Herfindahl and A. Kneese, *Economic Theory of Natural Resources* (Columbus, 1974); E. Mishan, *Cost-Benefit Analysis* (New York, 1976); Advisory Committee on the Biological Effects of Ionizing Radiation, "Considerations of Health Benefit-Cost Analysis for Activities Involving Ionizing Radiation Exposure and Alternatives," ch. 3 (National Academy of Sciences, 1977) [hereinafter referred to as NAS Cost-Benefit Study].

84. See NAS Cost-Benefit Study, *supra* note 83.

85. See S. Breyer, "The *Vermont Yankee* Case and the Nuclear Power Controversy," 91 *Harv. L. Rev.* 1833 (1978).

86. NAS Cost-Benefit Study, *supra* note 83, at 68.

87. There is considerable economic literature on this point, which lies at the heart of modern welfare economics. See, e.g., E. Mishan, "Arrow and the 'New Welfare' Economies—A Restatement," 1958 *Econ. J.* 595; or P. Samuelson, 1958 *Econ. J.* 539. Cf. F. Michelman, "Norms and Normativity in the Economic Theory of Law," 62 *Minn. L. Rev.* 1015 (1978).

88. See E. Mishan, *Cost-Benefit Analysis* (New York, 1976).

89. Mishan, *supra* note 88.

90. See Kneese, *supra* note 83, at 5.

91. See, e.g., Public Interest Economics Foundation, Conference on the Benefits of Governmental Health and Safety Regulations, October 12–13, 1978 (remarks of Joan Claybrook, administrator, National Highway Transportation Safety Administration).

92. For a discussion of the difference that ethics suggests between the identified individual and the statistical risk, see C. Fried, "The Value of Life," 82 *Harv. L. Rev.* 1415 (1969).

93. See R. Gallman, "Human Capital in the First 80 Years of the Republic," 67 *Am. Ec. Rev* 27 (1977).

94. See R. Zeckhauser, "Procedures for Valuing Lives," 23 *Public Policy* 419 (1975).

95. See E. Mishan, "Evaluation of Life and Limb: A Theoretical Approach," 79 *J. Pol. Econ.* 687 (1971).

96. See R. Zeckhauser and A. Nichols, *The Occupational Safety and Health Administration—An Overview*, Comm. on Governmental Affairs, U.S. Senate, 95th Cong., 2d Sess., app. to vol. 6, *Framework for Regulation* (Washington, D.C., 1978).

97. Thus, estimates of dollar value of a life, based on what a large group of individuals would pay for a small reduction in risk among them, vary considerably. See Thaler and Rosen, "The Value of Saving a Life: Evidence from the Labor Market," in N. Terlecky, Jr., *Household Production and Consumption* 265 (1975) ($340,000); R. S. Smith, "The Feasibility of an 'Injury Tax' Approach to Occupational Safety," *Law & Contemp. Problems* 730 (1974) (over $1 million).

98. Blumquist, "Value of Life: Implications of Automobile Seat Belt Use" (unpublished, March 1977) ($260,000); also cited in Kneese, *supra* note 83, at note 8.

99. Note that a major justification for intervention in the first place is that individuals are unable to correctly assess the magnitude and impact of incremental risks. The probity of the studies cited in the text decreases as the magnitude of this miscalculation increases.

100. See T. Schelling, "The Life You Save May Be Your Own," in S. Chase, *Problems in Public Expenditure Analysis* (Washington, D.C., 1968).

101. See generally Council for Science and Society, *The Acceptability of Risks* (London, 1977).

102. Cooper, *supra* note 52, at 9–10.

103. *Id.*, at 8.

104. *Id.*, at 10.

105. The Delaney Amendment does not necessarily remove all discretion from the administrator. It requires the FDA to deem an "additive" unsafe "if it is found to induce cancer" in man or animal, 21 U.S.C. § 348(c)(3)(A) (1976). Yet a substance is not an "additive" if it is "generally recognized as safe" in U.S.C. § 321(s) (1976). Thus, it is in principle possible for the FDA to consider an additive that saves thousands of lives, yet imposes a tiny risk of cancer on a few, as GRAS and therefore not subject to Delaney. Alternatively, the amendment says "it" must be found to "induce cancer," but if a few molecules of a substance are found in food, has "it" been found to induce cancer when pounds of it are necessary to induce cancer in a rat?

106. See L. Lave and E. Seskin, "Air Pollution and Human Health," 169 *Science* 723 (August 21, 1970).

107. See D. Bok, "Section 7 of the Clayton Act and the Merging of Law and Economics," 74 *Harv. L. Rev.* 226 (1960).

108. See S. Peltzman, *Regulation of Pharmaceutical Innovation: The 1962 Amendments* (Washington, D.C., 1974).

109. The FDA required double-blind tests for all drugs, but it proceeded to remove only those drugs that the NAS panel called "ineffective." See Breyer and Stewart, *supra* note 20, ch. 6.

110. Only where the item in question happens to be the *most* risky possible alter-

native is it certain that removal must necessarily reduce total risk. Otherwise, there remains some chance that removal could actually make things worse. Clearly, the magnitude of this risk will depend both upon the number of alternatives available and the type of risk in question. However, it is a real consideration that must be recognized by regulators.

111. See "Who Chooses Chemicals for Testing?" 201 *Science* 1202 (September 29, 1978).

112. See NAS Study II.

113. See FASEB Report, at 2553.

114. This less restrictive alternative partially shifts the screening process from the regulator to the individual. This recognizes that, in many cases, a regulator is no better equipped to make the decision, and thus it should be left to the individual.

8. Alternatives to Classical Regulation

1. Cf. R. Bork, *The Antitrust Paradox* (New York, 1978).

2. The Federal Trade Commission and the Justice Department, however, may enter litigation resulting in a decree that creates a small regulatory system.

3. Sherman Act § 1, 15 U.S.C. § 1 (1976); Clayton Act § 3, 15 U.S.C. § 14 (1976).

4. Sherman Act § 2, 15 U.S.C. § 2 (1976).

5. *Id.*

6. Clayton Act § 7, 15 U.S.C. § 18 (1976). The Antitrust Laws also include the Robinson Patman Act's prohibitions against "price discrimination," 15 U.S.C. § 13 (1976), and the Federal Trade Commission Act § 5, 15 U.S.C. § 45 (1976), which forbids "unfair" trade practices.

7. This rule was first enunciated by Chief Justice White in the famous case of *Standard Oil Co.* v. *United States,* 221 U.S. 1 (1911).

8. See generally the merger guidelines of the Dept. of Justice, 1 CCH Trade Reg. Rep. ¶ 4510 (1974).

9. This discussion is obviously a highly oversimplified account of a complex area of the law. The reader should see generally P. Areeda and D. Turner, *Antitrust Law,* 6 vols. (Boston, 1978–80), or P. Areeda, *Antitrust Analysis* (Boston, 1974), ch. 1, for further details.

10. See generally the debate about predatory pricing in P. Areeda and D. Turner, "Predatory Pricing and Related Practices under Section 2 of the Sherman Act," 88 *Harv. L. Rev.* 697 (1975); F. M. Scherer, "Predatory Pricing and the Sherman Act: A Comment," 89 *Harv. L. Rev.* 869 (1976); P. Areeda and D. Turner, "Scherer on Predatory Pricing: A Reply," 89 *Harv. L. Rev.* 891 (1976).

11. See R. Posner, "A Statistical Study of Antitrust Enforcement," 13 *J.L. & Econ.* 365, 374–381 (1970).

12. It should also be noted that the undesired activity will continue to occur while the issue is adjudicated. This temporal separation of the remedy from the detection of the wrong only compounds the injury to the competitive process.

13. See S. Breyer, "The Problem of the Honest Monopolist," 44 *Antitrust L.J.* .95 (1975).

14. See the *Standard Oil* case, *supra* note 7; cf. C. Kaysen and D. Turner, *Antitrust Policy: An Economic and Legal Analysis* (Cambridge, Mass., 1959).

15. See Areeda and Turner, *supra* note 9, at vol. 1, § 2C.

16. But see *Grosso* v. *United States,* 390 U.S. 62 (1968); *Marchetti* v. *United States,* 390 U.S. 39 (1968), where the Supreme Court held that gambling tax statutes requiring gamblers to register and pay an excise tax on winnings effectively forced disclosure of federal and state criminal offenses and thus impinged on Fifth Amendment privileges against self-incrimination.

17. See *California Bankers Association* v. *Schultz,* 416 U.S. 21 (1974).

18. 12 U.S.C. § 2801 et seq. (1976).

19. 15 U.S.C. §1601 et seq. (1976).

20. See generally Article 9, Uniform Commercial Code; see also the Federal Election Campaign Act of 1971, 2 U.S.C. § 431 et seq. (1976), requiring the disclosure of campaign contributions. It is unclear whether its object is to discourage certain contributions or to inform voters in order to allow them greater choice.

21. See Securities Exchange Act of 1934, 15 U.S.C. § 781 (1976).

22. See Federal Food, Drug, and Cosmetic Act, 21 U.S.C. § 301 et seq. (1976).

23. See Truth in Lending Act, 15 U.S.C. § 1601 et seq. (1976).

24. J. Gotbaum, L. Seale, R. Barusch, M. Delkat, and L. Masouredis, "The Standard-Setting Process in the National Highway Transportation Safety Administration," app. D at 7 6n. 9 (unpublished paper, December 1977).

25. *Id.,* uniform tire quality grading section, at 11–20.

26. See 1 L. Loss, *Securities Regulation,* 121–128, 2d ed. (Boston, 1961, supp. 1969).

27. *Id.*

28. 15 U.S.C. § 1601 et seq. (1976).

29. See S. Surrey and P. McDaniel, "Tax Expenditures: Current Developments and Energing Issues," 20 *B.C.L. Rev.* 225 (1979); S. Surrey, *Pathways to Tax Reform: The Concept of Tax Expenditures* 155–174 (Cambridge, Mass., 1973); "Appendix: A Note on Regulatory Taxes" sets out a useful framework for analyzing the problem.

30. In other words, the regulator must determine how much pollution is presently emitted, how much damage this causes, what level of damage is socially acceptable, and to what extent emissions must be curtailed to bring the damage within socially desired limits.

31. See R. Hall and R. Pindyck, "The Conflicting Goals of National Energy Policy," *The Public Interest* 3 (Spring 1977).

32. Of course, such an allocation would fail to allocate the rents to the consumer, since the price of old oil would rise to the world price. Where the value of these rents can be estimated, they can be recaptured for the consumer through the use of a tax on producers' profits. Such a scheme will produce a different distribution of the rent among consumers than would a tiered price scheme. In a tiered-price situation, all of the rents are appropriated by those consumers who are lucky enough to obtain old, cheap oil. Under a tax scheme (depending on how the proceeds are distributed) it is likely that a larger number of consumers will share the benefit.

33. Assume that a producer has Q_1 of old oil to sell, that this oil cost him P_c per unit output (a total of $P_c \cdot Q_1$), and that the world price is P_w (see Figure 13). Then, in the absence of a windfall profits tax, the producer can sell his "cheap" oil at the world price of P_w, yielding revenue of $P_w \cdot Q_1$ and a windfall profit of $(P_w - P_c) \cdot Q_1$. This is the amount that a tax would seek to recoup. In the text, the *upper bound* of the tax refers to P_w, the *lower bound* refers to P_c, and the optimal per-unit tax is the difference

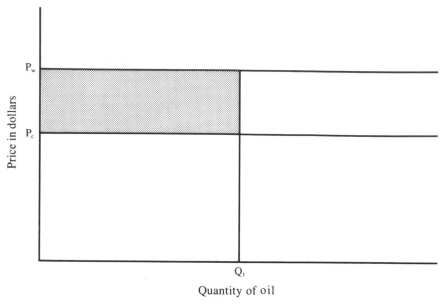

Figure 13. Setting tax levels.

between these two quantities ($P_w - P_c$). The demand and cost curves have been simplified for the purposes of illustration.

34. D. Drapkin, "Taxes as a Substitute for Regulation: Comment," 10 *Growth & Change* 53, 54 n. 5 (1979).

35. See 124 *Cong. Rec.* 55703 (April 17, 1978) (statement of Senator Kennedy).

36. The information on marketable landing rights is drawn from an interview with CAB staff member Ben Hurst, June 21, 1979.

37. The CAB has the power to grant an agreement immunity from the antitrust laws where the "public interest" requires. See 49 U.S.C. § 492 (1979).

38. There is, of course, a basic question concerning whether private entities (the airlines) should be permitted to allocate a public resource (landing slots at publicly owned and operated airports).

39. In principle, if the entering firm would bid the slot from its owner for $1 million, the owner, in not selling, loses $1 million in forgone income—a cost to it equivalent to the cost to the new entrant. Still, raising the capital required for new entry will add to the burdens of the new entrant. Moreover, if the present owner refuses to sell, it may obtain the advantage of less competition, yet the mixture of motives may be too subtle and complex for the antitrust laws to unravel.

40. This idea is embodied in the "Coase theorem," discussed in Chapter 1. Briefly, if bargaining were costless, it would not matter whether victims, manufacturers, or others paid for accidents or pollution. That is to say, it would not matter in terms of how resources would be allocated. If pollution (or accident) victims were required by law to suffer without compensation from manufacturers, they would bribe manufacturers to reduce pollution (accidents) as long as the cost of those measures was less than the cost of the harm they avoided. If manufacturers were required by law to compensate

pollution (or accident victims), they would take precisely those same measures in order to minimize their own costs. In fact, if all those affected in any way could without difficulty pay others affected, a cost-minimizing point would be reached—only those accidents (pollution) would exist that cause harm less costly than the measures needed to avoid them. The fact that transactions and bargaining are not costless, however, means that liability rules can make a considerable difference. See R. Coase, "The Problem of Social Cost," 3 *J.Law & Econ.* 1 (1960); G. Calabresi, *The Cost of Accidents: A Legal and Economic Analysis* (New Haven, 1970). A considerable literature has grown up around the Coase theorem. In the accident area, see, e.g., G. Calabresi, "Transaction Costs, Resource Allocation, and Liability Rules: A Comment," 11 *J.Law & Econ.* 67 (1968); H. Demsetz, "When Does the Rule of Liability Matter?" 1 *J. Legal Studies* 13 (1972). For criticism, see D. Regan, "The Problem of Social Cost Revisited," 15 *J.Law & Econ.* 427 (1972) (criticizing Coase's bargaining model); R. Epstein, "A Theory of Strict Liability," 2 *J. Legal Studies* 151 (1973) (arguing for more adequate consideration of "causation" as a factor in liability).

41. The "right" degree is the degree to which "safer" products are unjustified because the cost of making them safer exceeds the costs of the accidents that additional safety will prevent.

42. See, e.g., *Henningsen* v. *Bloomfield Motors, Inc.*, 32 N.J. 358, 161 A.2d 69 (1960); *Greenman* v. *Yuba Power Products, Inc.*, 59 Cal. 2d 57, 377 P.2d 897 (1963); *Seely* v. *White Motor Co.*, 63 Cal. 2d 9, 403 P.2d 145 (1965).

43. This would be so if buyers undervalued the costs or the likelihood of accidents with power mowers. If they did not, they would avoid mowers or shop for safer mowers. Producers would have as much incentive to make safer mowers as if they themselves paid the cost of the accidents.

44. G. Calabresi and A. Mclamed, "Property Rules, Liability Rules, and Inalienability: One View of the Cathedral," 85 *Harv. L. Rev.* 1089 (1972).

45. See R. Posner, *Economic Analysis of Law* 138–41, 2d ed. (Boston, 1977); R. Posner, "Strict Liability: A Comment," 2 *J. Legal Studies* 205 (1973); R. McKean, "Products Liability: Trends and Implications," 38 *U. Chicago L. Rev.* 3 (1970); cf. G. Calabresi and K. Bass, "Right Approach, Wrong Implications: A Critique of McKean on Products Liability," 38 *U. Chicago L. Rev.* 74 (1970).

46. See, e.g., J. Buchanan, "In Defense of Caveat Emptor," 38 *U. Chicago L. Rev.* 64 (1970); Posner, *supra* note 45; M. Bernacchi, "A Behavioral Model for Imposing Strict Liability in Tort: The Importance of Analyzing Product Performance in Relation to Consumer Expectation and Frustration," 47 *U. Cinn. L. Rev.* 43 (1978).

47. See, e.g., G. Fletcher, "Fairness and Utility in Tort Theory," 85 *Harv. L. Rev.* 537 (1972); Epstein, "A Theory of Strict Liability," 2 *J. Legal Studies* 151 (1974); J. Steiner, "Economics, Morality and the Law of Torts," 26 *U. Toronto L.J.* 227 (1976).

48. This assumes that the houses were purchased *after* the airport began emitting noise. Had the homeowners been there first, a shift in liability rules which grants them compensation would simply (and equitably) restore the ex ante wealth distribution (prior to the airport's invasion and impoverishment of the homeowner).

49. See R. Keeton, "Entitlement and Obligation," 46 *U. Cinn. L. Rev.* 1 (1977).

50. For discussion of the bargaining process in labor relations, see A. Cox and J. Dunlop, "The Duty to Bargain Collectively during the Term of an Existing Agreement, 63 *Harv. L. Rev* 1097 (1950); A. Cox and J. Dunlop, "Regulation of Collective Bar-

gaining by the National Labor Relations Board," 63 *Harv. L. Rev.* 389 (1950); A. Cox, D. Bok, and R. Gorman, *Cases and Materials on Labor Law* (Mineola, 1977).

51. See, e.g., 15 U.S.C. § 17 (1976) (labor organizations); 7 U.S.C. § 291 (1976) (farming); 15 U.S.C. § 521 (1976) (fishing).

52. See J. Dunlop, "The Limits of Legal Compulsion" (unpublished paper, November 1975).

53. See, e.g., R. Zeckhauser and A. Nichols, "Occupational Safety and Health Administration—An Overview," in Senate Comm. on Governmental Affairs, *Study on Federal Regulation,* 95th Cong., 2d Sess., 161 (1978); American Enterprise Institute Report, "OSHA Safety Regulations" (May 6, 1977); U.S. Interagency Task Force on Workplace Safety and Health, *Making Prevention Pay* (Washington, D.C., 1975) (report of Labor Dept. and OMB Task Force).

54. See Zeckhauser and Nichols, *supra* note 53.

55. Dunlop, *supra* note 52.

56. Zeckhauser and Nichols, *supra* note 53.

57. See S. Kelman, Regulating Job Safety and Health: A Comparison of the U.S. Occupational Safety and Health Administration and the Swedish Worker Protection Board (diss., Harvard University, 1978).

58. *Id.*

59. The workers themselves may prefer immediate wage benefits, discounting the risks of accidents; wage improvement may be easier to measure and to communicate in union elections than safety improvements; the persons most needing the protection may be less influential than union political officers.

60. See generally L. Bacow, "Regulatory Occupational Hazards through Collective Bargaining" (April 3, 1978) (study prepared for U.S. Dept. of Labor).

61. Bacow, *supra* note 60.

62. Kelman, *supra* note 57, at 230.

63. Interagency Task Force Report, *supra* note 53.

64. See A. Pigou, *The Economics of Welfare* (London, 1962); W. Baumol, *Welfare Economics and the Theory of the State* (Cambridge, Mass., 1965); O. Lange and F. Taylor, *On the Economic Theory of Socialism* (New York, 1964).

65. The major difference between a price system and a centralized command economy is the tremendous amount of information that must be gathered in the latter case in order for the administrators to correctly set prices equal to marginal cost.

66. See authorities cited in note 64 *supra.*

67. J. R. Nelson, *Marginal Cost Pricing in Practice* (Englewood Cliffs, 1964); M. Crew, "Electricity Tariffs," *Public Enterprise* 258–283, ed. R. Turvey (Harmondsworth, 1968).

68. Whether such instructions will be followed in an enterprise with a primary objective of, for example, producing electricity is debatable. See M. Roberts and S. Farrell, "The Political Economy of Implementation: The Clean Air Act and Stationary Services," in A. Friedlaender, ed., *Approaches to Controlling Air Pollution* (1978).

69. A. Bierce, *The Devil's Dictionary* 107 (1957).

70. See, e.g., P. Saraceno, "The Italian System of State-Held Enterprises," 11 *J. Int'l L. & Econ.* 407 (1976–77).

71. See R. Pryke, *Public Enterprise in Practice* (St. Martin's, 1972). Similarly many critics fear that nationalization will lead to substantial X-inefficiency through the

muting of the profit motive and the absence of the managerial discipline engendered by the competitive marketplace.

72. See, e.g., Bevan, "The Nationalized Industries," in *The Economic System of the U.K.* 439, 441, ed. D. Morris (1977): "Since [1967] the [British] nationalized industries had been used separately as blunt instruments of macroeconomics management to the complete eclipse of the allocative rules so painstakingly developed in the 1960's."

73. M. Stewart, *The Jekyll and Hyde Years: Politics and Economic Policy since 1964,* at 32 & n. 1 (London, 1977).

74. Roberts and Farrell, *supra* note 68.

75. See J. Osborne, "New York's Urban Development Corporation: A Study on the Unchecked Power of a Public Authority," 43 *Brooklyn L. Rev.* 237 (1977). See generally J. Garner, "New Public Corporations," 1966 *Public Law* 324 (1966); W. Quick and L. Wein, "A Short Constitutional History of Entities Commonly Known as Authorities," 56 *Cornell L. Rev.* 521 (1971).

76. R. Fabrikant, "Pertamina: A Legal and Financial Analysis of a National Oil Company in a Developing Country," 10 *Tex. Int'l L.J.* 495 (1975).

77. See Garner, *supra* note 75.

78. See J. Wilson and P. Rachal, "Can the Government Regulate Itself?" 46 *The Public Interest* 3 (Winter 1977).

9. General Guidelines for Policy Makers

1. See generally C. Schultze, *The Public Use of the Private Interest* 16–27 (1977).

2. See F. Hayek, "The Use of Knowledge in Society," 35 *Am. Econ. Rev.* 529 (1945).

3. See C. Kaysen and D. Turner, *Antitrust Policy: An Economic and Legal Analysis* (1959).

4. Schultze, *supra* note 1, at 16–17.

5. S. 1391, 95th Cong., 1st Sess., § 111; *Hospital Cost Containment Act of 1977: Hearings before the Subcomm. on Health and Scientific Research of the Senate Comm. on Human Resources,* 95th Cong., 1st Sess., 3, 7–9 (1977).

6. Cf. Public Health Service Act § 1352, 42 U.S.C. § 300 n. 1 (1976) (establishing procedures and criteria to be used by state health planning agencies in considering proposed delivery systems).

7. See, e.g., Howell, "Certificate of Need in Massachusetts," app., in 1 *Regulation as an Instrument of Public Administration* § 12 (February 27–28, 1978) (report of the JFK School of Government, Harvard University).

11. Mismatch: Excessive Competition and Airline Regulation

1. I managed that investigation as the staff director and wrote a draft of the report based upon the hearings and information collected by the subcommittee. The investigation's findings are detailed in U.S. Senate Comm. on the Judiciary, Subcomm. on Admin. Practice and Procedure, *Civil Aeronautics Board Practices and Procedures,* 94th Cong., 1st Sess. (1975). This section is based heavily upon my work in connection

with the investigation and report. The subcommittee report contains or refers to extensive empirical support for most of the propositions advanced in this chapter. Page numbers not otherwise identified in these footnotes refer to the appropriate pages of the report. The factual material in this chapter is based upon that report.

2. The Airline Deregulation Act of 1978. Pub. L. No. 95–504, 92 Stat. 1705 (1978).

3. P. 129.

4. P. 145.

5. P. 29.

6. P. 30. The Airline Deregulation Act of 1978, *supra* note 2, changed the former requirement from "required by" the public interest to "consistent with" the public interest. This small change in language (along with a few others) effectively brought about "deregulation."

7. Pp. 29–31. The power to grant antitrust immunity was substantially curtailed by the 1978 act.

8. Pp. 31–35.

9. P. 46.

10. Pp. 46–48.

11. The CAB estimated demand elasticity at .7.

12. P. 115.

13. P. 79.

14. These figures understate the problem, because after three years, pending applications were dismissed as stale. Pp. 81–82.

15. P. 83.

16. P. 82.

17. Pp. 86–87.

18. The board itself may have felt that it was behaving improperly, for its chairman at first denied to the investigating subcommittee that there had been a route moratorium. He reversed his position only when confronted with virtually irrefutable evidence. P. 85.

19. The board's procedures from 1969–75 suffered from other instances of impropriety. In one instance, the board improperly terminated investigation of unlawful campaign contributions and placed the files in a safe hidden from the sight of those who might have pursued the investigation. In another instance a charter company wishing to try cheap flights from Tijuana to Luxembourg was driven out of business by the board's staff improperly leaking to the press claims that the flights were unlawful and would be stopped—without giving the operator an opportunity to show their lawfulness. In fact a survey of the board's Bureau of Enforcement showed that it spent about two thirds of its resources trying to stop low-cost flights and only 3 percent looking into overcharges on other consumer complaints. These improprieties are indirectly related to the mismatch problem discussed in the text. Pp. 142–160.

20. P. 108.

21. *Moss* v. *C.A.B.*, 430 F.2d 891 (D.C. Cir., 1970).

22. CAB, Bureau of Operating Rights study, at 38, cited at 83.

23. *Id.*

24. P. 83.

25. P. 84.

26. See the Southern Tier Route Investigation, which the courts reviewed in *Continental Airlines* v. *C.A.B.*, 443 F.2d 745 (D.C. Cir., 1971).

27. *Continental Airlines* v. *C.A.B.* 443 F.2d 745 (D.C. Cir., 1971).

28. Pp. 160–176.

29. P. 127.

30. In fact, the strategy had been recommended by a Harvard Business School professor. See Fruhan, *The Fight for Competitive Advantage* (Cambridge, Mass., 1978).

31. In fact, the board had little choice, as it lacked the legal authority to control scheduling. Pp. 142–154.

32. P. 150.

33. P. 151. This was Prof. Fruhan's argument. See note 30 *supra*.

34. P. 152.

12. Mismatch: Excessive Competition and the Trucking Industry

1. This chapter reflects research conducted by William Blumenthal while a student at Harvard Law School and while a member of the staff of the United States Senate Commerce Committee. That research was also in part based upon work by the Senate Judiciary Committee, published as *Federal Restraints on Competition in the Trucking Industry: Antitrust Immunity and Economic Regulation,* 96th Cong., 2d Sess. (April 1980).

2. American Trucking Association (ATA), *1978 Financial Analysis of the Motor Carrier Industry* 9 (1979) [hereinafter referred to as ATA].

3. J. Richard Jones, *Industrial Shipper Survey—Plant Level* 85 (U.S. Dept. of Transportation, September 1975). Senate Comm. on Commerce, *Intercity Domestic Transportation System for Passengers and Freight,* 95th Cong., 1st Sess., 162 (Comm. print, 1977) [hereinafter referred to as SCC].

4. See SCC, *supra* note 3; D. Wyckoff and D. Maister, *The Owner-Operator: Independent Trucker* 2 (Lexington, Mass., 1975).

5. There are about 3,000 regulated contract carriers, but only 308 have annual revenues greater than $500,000. They account for about 3 percent of intercity truck ton-miles. See Senate Comm. on Commerce, *The Impact on Small Communities of Motor Carrier Regulatory Revision,* 95th Cong., 2d Sess. (Comm. print, 1978) [hereinafter referred to as SCC2]; ATA note, *supra* note 1; C. Taff, *Commercial Motor Transportation* 114, 4th ed. (1969).

6. See ATA, *supra* note 2; special commodities carriers deal almost exclusively in truckload shipments. See SCC2, *supra* note 5, at 13–14.

7. See ATA, *supra* note 2, at 6.

8. See SCC2, *supra* note 5, at 94; Economic Research Committee of the Regular Common Carrier Conference, *1971 Cost/Revenue Analyses* 8 (1973).

9. See, e.g., SCC2, *supra* note 5, at 13.

10. The entry standard for contract carriers is less rigid than that for common carriers, rates are negotiated; and the ICC has only minimum rate power. See SCC2, *supra* note 5, at 16; 49 U.S.C. §§ 309(b), 318(b) (1963).

11. *Forbes,* December 18, 1978, at 75.

12. Markets for truckload carriage have even fewer economies of scale, for there are fewer terminals and there is less need to consolidate shipments.

13. See American Trucking Association, *American Trucking Trends* 28–29 (1976).

14. See S. Warner, "Cost Models, Measurement Errors and Economies of Scale in Trucking," in *The Cost of Trucking: Econometric Analysis* 1, ed. M. Burstein (1965); R. Koenker, "Input Demand by Regulated Trucking Firms," 25 (Univ. of Illinois, February 1974).

15. See S. Warner, *supra* note 14; D. Wyckoff, "Factors Promoting Concentration of Motor Carriers under Deregulation," 13 *Transp. Research F.* 1 (1974).

16. See S. Warner, *supra* note 14; Lawrence, "Economies of Scale in the General Freight Motor Common Carrier Industry: Additional Evidence," 17 *Transp. Research F.* 169 (1976).

17. See American Trucking Association, *Motor Carrier Regulation—The Issue in Perspective* 6 (1975), for the figures based on the entire trucking industry. The four-firm concentration ratio is 10 percent and the eight-firm is 14 percent. The ratios for the LTL general freight segment are based on Trinc Transportation Consultants, *Blue Book of the Trucking Industry* (1978).

18. See, e.g., A. Friedlaender, "Hedonic Costs and Economies of Scale in the Regulated Trucking Industry," in *Proceedings of a Workshop on Motor Carrier Economic Regulation* 33, National Academy of Sciences (1976); R. Klem, "The Cost Structure of the Regulated Trucking Industry," in *id.* at 141; R. Koenker, "Optimal Scale and the Size Distribution of American Trucking Firms," 11 *J. Transp. Econ. & Policy* 54 (1977).

19. See G. Chow, "The Cost of Trucking Revisited," in *Proceedings, supra* note 22, at 57; S. Warner, *supra* note 14; M. Lawrence, *supra* note 16. For reviews of studies see G. Chow, "The Status of Economies of Scale in Regulated Trucking: A Review of the Evidence and Future Directions," 19 *Transp. Research F.* 365 (1978); Senate Comm. on Commerce, *The Impact on Small Communities of Motor Carriage Regulatory Revision,* 95th Cong, 2d Sess., 104 (1978).

20. See 49 U.S.C. § 316(e) (1963). The ICC can prescribe only minimum rates for contract carriers.

21. Truckers historically copied the railroads, which set rates through associations, or traffic conferences, until forbidden to do so by the Supreme Court. *U.S.* v. *Trans-Missouri Freight Ass'n,* 166 U.S. 290 (1897). In *Georgia* v. *Penn. R.R. Co.,* 324 U.S. 439 (1945), the Supreme Court held that the ICC could not, by approving these associations, immunize them from the antitrust laws. Congress then passed the Reed Bulwinkle Act, specifically allowing the ICC to grant antitrust immunity (49 U.S.C. 5b).

22. They are listed by the ICC at 49 C.F.R. § 1104.1(b) (1977). See C. Taff, *Management of Physical Distribution and Transportation* 378–380, 5th ed. (Homewood, Ill., 1972).

23. See C. Taff, *supra* note 5, at 380.

24. The independent action is filed by the rate bureau on behalf of the individual carrier. See C. Taff, *supra* note 5, at 381.

25. G. Davis and C. Sherwood, *Rate Bureaus and Antitrust Conflicts in Transportation* 73–76 (New York, 1973).

26. J. Meyer et al., *The Economics of Competition in the Transportation Industries* 214 (Cambridge, Mass., 1959).

27. C. Barrett, "The Power of the Protest," *Traffic World* 96 (September 21, 1968). See also a DOT staff study, Gerber and Thebodeau, *Factors Influencing ICC Disapproval of Motor Carrier Rates with Special Attention to the Role of Rate Bureaus*

(1976), suggesting that only 5 percent of protected independent filings for *lower* rates are successful.

28. Based on data contained on tape and submitted by the Rate Bureau to the Senate Committee on the Judiciary (1978).

29. The concentration ratios on many individual routes are high, probably as a result of ICC restrictive entry policy. See W. Blumenthal, "Anticompetitive Threats in Motor Coverage under Alternative Regulatory Regimes," 56 (Harvard Law School paper, 1979), data compiled from Senate Judiciary Comm. tapes, see note 28 *supra*.

30. *Id.*

31. Cf. F. Scherer, *Industrial Market Structure and Economic Performance* 199, 2d ed. (Chicago, 1980).

32. 49 U.S.C. § 307(a) (1963).

33. *Pan American Bus Lines Operations*, 1 M.C.C. 190, 203 (1936). Whether the ICC must take so restrictive a position is legally doubtful. See *Sloan's Moving & Storage Co.* v. *U.S.* 208 F. Supp. 567 (E. D. Mo., 1962). As a result of legislation passed in 1980, the entry standard is less restrictive. See Motor Carrier Act of 1980, Pub. L. No. 96–296, 94 Stat. 793. For a discussion of the new act, see K. Feinberg, *Deregulation of the Transportation Industry*, Practicing Law Institute (Washington, D.C., 1981).

34. See generally *H C. Gabler, Inc., Extension*, 86 M.C.C. 447 (1961); *Metler Extension*, 61 M.C.C. 335 (1952); *Nygren Transportation Co., Extension—So. Dakota*, 61 M.C.C. 349 (1952).

35. Cf. *Atlanta–New Orleans Motor Freight Co.* v. *U.S.* 197 F. Supp. 364 (N. D. Ga., 1961).

36. See Senate Comm. on Commerce, *The Impact on Small Communities of Motor Carriage Regulatory Revision*, 95th Cong., 2d Sess., 23 (1978); Senate Comm. on Commerce, *Intercity Domestic Transportation System for Passengers and Freight*, 95th Cong., 1st Sess., 73 (1977).

37. *Id.*

38. See 49 U.S.C. § 306(a)(1); statement of John Snow, Hearings before the House Subcomm. on Surface Transp. of the Comm. on Public Works & Transp., *Regulation of Carriers Subject to the Interstate Commerce Act*, 94th Cong., 2d Sess., 3–4 (September 14, 28, 1976).

39. In 1977 the ICC approved 58 percent of 340 merger applications. Data supplied by John Surina, ICC Bureau of Economics, by telephone to William Blumenthal, April 1978. In 1969 the ICC approved 90 percent of 334 merger proposals. J. Johnson, *Trucking Mergers* 163 (Lexington, Mass., 1973).

40. American Trucking Association, Brief and Petition, "Accounting for Motor Carrier Operating Rights," before the Financial Accounting Standards Board of the Financial Accounts Foundation, at 5 (July 14, 1972).

41. This was calculated by William Blumenthal from data on computer tapes supplied by the ten major rate bureaus as part of their continuous traffic study.

42. American Trucking Association, Brief and Petition, "Accounting for Motor Carrier Operating Rights," before the Financial Accounting Standards Board of the Financial Accounting Foundation, at 6 (July 14, 1972).

43. Council on Wage and Price Stability, "The Value of Motor Carrier Operating Authorities," 7 (June 9, 1977).

44. T. Moore, "The Beneficiaries of Trucking Regulation," 21 *J.Law & Econ.* 327, 342 (1978).

45. Blumenthal, *supra* note 29, at 105.

46. Calculated by Blumenthal, *supra* note 29, from American Trucking Association, *1978 Financial Analysis of the Motor Carrier Industry* (1979).

47. E. Miller, "Effects of Regulation on Truck Utilization," 12 *Transp. J.* 11 (1973). See also Federal Highway Administration, *Annual Truck Weight Study* (1972), cited in P. MacAvoy and J. Snow, *Regulation of Entry and Pricing in Truck Transportation* 25–26 (Washington, D.C., 1977).

48. S. Sobotka and T. Domencich, "Traffic Diversion and Energy Use Implications: Another View," cited in P. MacAvoy and J. Snow, *supra* note 47, at 189, 196.

49. N. Jones, Jr., "On Removing Operating and Empty Backhaul Restrictions," in P. MacAvoy and J. Snow, *supra* note 47, at 215.

50. See discussion in Senate Comm. on Commerce, *The Impact on Small Communities of Motor Carriage Regulatory Revision,* 95th Cong., 2d Sess., 70–75 (1978).

51. J. Snitzler and R. Byrne, "Interstate Trucking of Fresh and Frozen Poultry under the Agricultural Exemption," Dept. of Agr. Marketing Research Division, MRR-244 (1958); J. Snitzler and R. Byrne, "Interstate Trucking of Frozen Fruits and Vegetables under the Agricultural Exemption," Dept. of Agr. Marketing Research Division, MRR-316 (1959).

52. W. Allen, S. Lonergan, and D. Plane, "Examination of the Unregulated Trucking Experiences in New Jersey," DOT mimeo (July 1978).

53. Council on Wage and Price Stability, "The Interstate Commerce Commission's Staff Analysis of the Costs and Benefits of Surface Transportation Regulation," (January 1977). See also D. Daryll Wyckoff, "Motor Carrier Regulation—Some Unanswered Questions," Speech to Ohio Chapter of the Transp. Research Forum (December 17, 1974).

54. T. Moore, *Trucking Regulation: Lessons from Europe* 41, 44 (Washington, D.C., 1976).

55. S. Joy, "Unregulated Road Haulage: Australian Experience," 16 *Oxford Econ. Papers* 273 (1964).

56. J. Sloss, "Regulation of Motor Freight Transportation: A Quantitative Evaluation of Policy," 1 *Bell J. Econ. & Mgmt. Sci.* 327, 351 (1970); D. McLachlan, "Canadian Trucking Regulations," 8 *Logistic & Transp. Rev.* 59 (1972); J. Palmer, "A Further Analysis of Provincial Trucking Regulation," 4 *Bell J. Econ. & Mgmt. Sci.* 655 (1973).

57. See, e.g., American Trucking Association, *The Case Against Deregulation* (1972); J. Spychalski, "Criticisms of Regulated Freight Transportation: Do Economists' Perceptions Conform with Institutional Realities?" 14 *Transp. J.* 5, 11 (1972).

58. See B. Nadreen, *Transportation Mergers and Acquisitions* (1962); J. Johnson, *Trucking Mergers* 55 (Lexington, 1973).

59. See ATA, *supra* note 2; *General Increase, SMCRC* I. & S. ICC Docket no. M-29772 (November 27, 1978).

60. *Oversight of Freight Rate Competition in the Motor Carrier Industry: Hearings before the Subcommittee on Antitrust and Monopoly of the Senate Judiciary Comm.,* 95th Cong.; 2d Sess., 877 (1979) (statement of ICC Chairman O'Neal) [hereinafter referred to as Kennedy Hearings].

61. *Id.,* at 892–897.

62. Individual firms would not necessarily want to increase costs, for prices would rise only when industry average costs rise. But the industrywide Teamsters National

13. Mismatch: Rent Control and Natural Gas Field Prices

1. See Natural Gas Policy Act § 121, Pub. L. No. 95–621, 92 Stat. 335 (1978); see also *New York Times,* November 10, 1978, at D14.

2. *Hearings on Federal Power Commission Oversight—Natural Gas Curtailment Priorities before the Senate Comm. on Commerce,* 93rd Cong., 2d Sess., pt. 2, at 346 (1974) [hereinafter cited as Curtailment Hearings].

3. Staff of the Senate Comm. on Interior and Insular Affairs, 93rd Cong., 1st Sess., *Natural Gas Policy Issues and Options,* at 25 (1973) [hereinafter cited as Gas Policy Issues and Options].

4. Federal Power Commission, *National Gas Survey* 1, at 59–60 (1975) [hereinafter cited as FPC *Survey*].

5. Statement of John Nassikas, chairman of the FPC, before the Subcommittee on Antitrust and Monopoly of the Senate Committee on the Judiciary, 93 Cong., 1st Sess., 50 (June 26, 1973).

6. S. Rep. No. 94–191, 94th Cong., 1st Sess. (1975); FPC *Survey* 1, *supra* note 4, at 69–70. With a few exceptions, the major gas producers are not integrated with pipelines or firms in other parts of the gas industry.

7. *Gas Policy Issues and Options, supra* note 3, at 25.

8. *Id.,* at 25.

9. J. Muys, "Federal Power Commission Allocation of Natural Gas Supply Shortages: Prorationing, Priorities and Perplexity," 20 *Rocky Mt. M.L. Inst.* 301 (1975) [hereinafter cited as FPC Allocation].

10. P. MacAvoy, *The Crisis of the Regulatory Commissions* 156 (New York, 1970), quoting Champlin Oil & Refining Co., Docket No. G-9277, at 458 (FPC 1969) (testimony of M. A. Adelman).

11. See S. Breyer, "Taxes as a Substitute for Regulation," *Growth & Change* 39 & n. 1 (January 1979).

12. Statement of John Nassikas, *supra* note 5.

13. See E. J. Neuner, *The Natural Gas Industry* (Norman, 1960); L. Cookenboo, *Competition in the Field Markets for Natural Gas,* Rice Institute Pamphlet, Monograph in Economics, vol. 44, no. 4 (1958); C. Hawkins, *Structure of the Natural Gas Producing Industry,* in *Regulation of the Natural Gas Producing Industry* ed. Keith C. Brown (Baltimore, 1972); P. MacAvoy, *Price Formulation in Natural Gas Fields: A Study of Monopoly, Monopsony, and Regulation* (New Haven, 1962). For a more recent assessment of the competitive situation, see statement of John Nassikas, *supra* note 4.

14. FPC *Survey* 1, *supra* note 4, at 62.

15. M. Willrich, *Administration of Energy Shortages: Natural Gas and Petroleum* (Cambridge, Mass., 1976), says 46 percent. See FEA, *The Natural Gas Shortage: A Preliminary Report* 2 (August 1975) [hereinafter referred to as FEA Preliminary Report].

16. FPC *Survey* 1, *supra* note 4, at 142.

17. FEA Preliminary Report, *supra* note 15, at 2. See also American Gas Association, *Gas Facts 1973,* at 67.

18. FPC *Survey* 1, *supra* note 4, at 19.

19. FEA Preliminary Report, *supra* note 15, at 2.

20. FPC *Survey* 1, *supra* note 4, at 175.

21. American Gas Association, *Gas Facts 1973*, at 66, 69. FPC *Survey* 1, *supra* note 4, at 175 (table 6-15).

22. All the numbers in the preceding few paragraphs are rough estimates, and obviously change somewhat from year to year and from publication to publication.

23. 15 U.S.C. § 717 et seq. (1976).

24. 347 U.S. 672 (1954).

25. C. Hawkins, *The Field Price Regulation of Natural Gas,* at 223 (Tallahassee, 1969) [hereinafter referred to as Hawkins].

26. See P. MacAvoy, *Price Formation in Natural Gas Fields* 243–273 (New Haven and London, 1962).

27. Rising trends in costs of inputs and falling trends in productivity per unit of drilling are reported in National Petroleum Council, *U.S. Energy Outlook,* ch. 4 (1972).

28. Kitch, "The Permian Basin Area Rate Cases and the Regulatory Determination of Price," 116 U. Pa. L. Rev. 191, 195–196 (1967).

29. *Brown's Dictionary of North American Gas Companies,* Zane Chasten Edition, 91st ed. (New York, 1977), at 7. Actual curtailments amounted to 3.77 tcf, somewhat less than the 4.0 tcf figure given in table 1, p. 329 of the draft. See "An Examination of Regulation in the Natural Gas Industry," in Senate Committee on Governmental Affairs, 95th Cong., 2d Sess., *Study on Federal Regulation,* app. to vol. 6, at 664 [hereinafter referred to as the Ribicoff Report].

30. FPC Press Release No. 21454 (June 6, 1975).

31. The amount of backup purchased varied from year to year, but at no time between 1947 and 1954 did it fall below 14.5 years backlog. P. MacAvoy, "The Regulation-Induced Shortage of Natural Gas," 14 *J.Law & Econ.* 172 (1971).

32. *Id.,* at 171–175.

33. FERC, *Gas Supplies of Interstate Natural Gas Pipeline Companies, 1976.* In 1976 the ratio fell to 8.6.

34. This assumes that distributing companies or pipelines wished to buy more than 10 years or so worth of reserves—a reasonable assumption, given past behavior.

35. American Gas Association, *Historical Statistics of the Gas Utility Industry, 1966–1975,* table 3.

36. This has been changed by the 1978 Energy Act, specifically the Natural Gas Policy Act, 15 U.S.C. §§ 3301 et seq. (1978).

37. See Ribicoff Report, *supra* note 24, at 689, for useful statistics.

38. The figure was 12.0 tcf in 1975 and 11.4 tcf in 1976. FERC, *Interstate Gas Supplies, supra* note 33.

39. See Breyer and MacAvoy, *The Natural Gas Shortage and Regulation of Natural Gas Producers,* 86 *Harv. L. Rev.* 941, 962.

40. Hawkins, *supra* note 25, at 37.

41. *Id.,* at 26, 78.

42. U.S. Senate Comm. on the Judiciary, Subcomm. on Administrative Practice and Procedure, 86th Cong., 2d Sess., *Report on the Regulatory Agencies to the President-Elect* 54 (Comm. print, 1960) (Landis Report).

43. Breyer and MacAvoy, *supra* note 39, n. 52 at 955. See, e.g., A. Kahn, *The Economics of Regulation* 1, at 79–83 (1970).

44. Breyer and MacAvoy, *supra* note 39, n. 53 at 955.

45. The five areas were: (1) the Permian Basin (Texas and part of New Mexico); (2) Southern Louisiana (including the offshore area in the Gulf of Mexico); (3) Hugoton-

Anadarko (part of Oklahoma and Kansas); (4) Texas Gulf Coast; and (5) Other Southwest (Mississippi, Arkansas, and parts of Alabama, Texas, and Oklahoma).

46. In *Permian Basin Area Rate Proceeding,* 34 F.P.C. 159 (August 5, 1965), the commission set a new gas ceiling price of approximately 16.5 cents per mcf. In *Southern Louisiana Area Rate Proceeding,* 40 F.P.C. 530 (September 25, 1968), it set a new gas ceiling price of 20.0 cents per mcf. The interim ceilings had been 16.0 cents and 21.0 cents, respectively.

47. Permian Basin Area Rate Proceeding, 34 F.P.C. 159, 194 (1965).

48. FPC Allocation, *supra* note 9, at 301–309.

49. 45 F.P.C. 570 (April 15, 1971).

50. *Id.,* at 572.

51. Opinion No. 606, 46 F.P.C. 786 (October 5, 1971).

52. Opinion No. 634, 48 F.P.C. 931 (October 31, 1972).

53. 49 F.P.C. 85 (January 8, 1973).

54. 49 F.P.C. 583 (March 2, 1973).

55. Curtailment Hearings, *supra* note 2, pt. 2 at 285.

56. Arthur D. Little, Inc., *Report to the Office of the General Counsel, General Motors Corporation: Implications of Natural Gas Consumption Patterns for the Implementation of End-Use Priority Programs* (1974).

57. FPC *Survey* 1, *supra* note 4, at 19.

58. Willrich, *supra* note 15, n. 44 at 227.

59. *Arkansas Power and Light Co.* v. *FPC,* 517 F.2d 1223 (D.C. Cir., 1975). *State of Louisiana* v. *FPC,* 503 F.2d 844 (5th Cir., 1974).

60. *Pacific Gas and Electric Co.* v. *FPC,* 506 F.2d 33 (D.C. Cir., 1974).

61. See generally Willrich, *supra* note 15, at 90–100. "Even though the winters of 1976–77 and 1977–78 were severe, extraordinary relief petitions have dropped to a mere trickle. Approximately 20 were filed for 1975–76, three in 1976–77, and none for 1977–78. The reasons: The gas 'customers realized that they couldn't get blood (or gas) from a stone (the commission).' " (Remarks of J. Solters, FERC Staff, in a conversation with N. K. Alexander, May ?, 1978; reported in a paper by a third-year student, Harvard Law School).

62. *Pacific Gas and Electric Co.* v. *FPC,* 506, F.2d 33, 97 (D.C. Cir., 1974).

63. See the 1978 Energy Act cited in note 36 *supra.*

64. FERC, *United States Imports and Exports of Natural Gas,* 1977; FERC, *Gas Supplies of Interstate Natural Gas Pipeline Companies,* 1976; supplementary material from *New York Times,* November 3, 1978, at 65–66 (material printed during *New York Times* strike).

65. "Plentiful Cheap Gas Is Riding a National High," *Boston Globe,* March 23, 1979, at 1; *BNA Energy Users' Report* 230:21 (January 5, 1978). In 1974 natural gas accounted for 54 percent of all energy consumed by U.S. manufacturing plants; in 1976 the proportion was 49 percent. U.S. Census Bureau, *Fuels and Electric Energy Consumed* (1978).

66. *New York Times, supra* note 64; *BNA Energy Users' Report, supra* note 65.

67. H.R. 6831, 95th Cong., 1st Sess., § 1401; *The National Energy Act: Hearings before the Subcomm. on Housing and Community Development of the House Comm. on Banking, Finance and Urban Officers,* 95th Cong., 1st Sess., 2, 198–202 (1977); H.R. Rep. No. 95–496, 95th Cong., 1st Sess., 3, at 4, 74 (1977).

68. England has dealt with the rent control problem by nationalizing its gas trans-

portation and distribution companies and combining them to form a single nationalized distributor. This distributor can both capture rents and allocate efficiently because it possesses monopoly power and the power to discriminate in price on both the buying and selling sides of the market. Thus, it can offer differential prices to producers based upon their production costs, offering prices equal to incremental production costs for producers at the margin. It can then ration the gas by selling it to whoever offers the highest price—a market solution. The nationalized firm itself, however, keeps the rents and uses them for public purposes; they do not go to private producers. Thus, a nationalized system meets the objective of those who see regulation in this area as necessary to prevent private producers from keeping excessive rents for themselves. See Dam, "The Pricing of North Sea Gas in Britain," 13 *J.Law & Econ.* 11 (1970). Nationalization, however, is no panacea and has severe problems of its own (see Chapter 8).

14. Partial Mismatch: Spillovers and Environmental Pollution

1. The virtues of taxes or marketable rights in this area have long been advocated by economists. See, e.g., A. Kneese and C. Schultze, *Pollution, Prices, and Public Policy* (Washington, D.C., 1975); A. Kneese, *Economics and the Environment* (Dallas, 1977); W. Baumol and W. Oates, *The Theory of Environmental Policy* (Englewood Cliffs, 1975); J. Dales, *Pollution Property and Prices* (Toronto, 1968). For an introduction to the question, see R. Stewart and J. Krier, *Environmental Law and Policy* 564–612 (Indianapolis, 1978). For an excellent collection of essays related to the subject, see A. Friedlaender, *Approaches to Controlling Air Pollution* (Cambridge, Mass., 1978) [hereinafter cited as Friedlaender].

2. One very rough (and controversial) estimation concluded that the discounted benefits of the Clean Air Act's automobile standards (if complied with) from 1975 to 2101 is $137 billion. See E. Mills and L. White, "Government Policies toward Automotive Emissions Control," in Friedlaender, *supra* note 1, at 362 [hereinafter cited as Mills and White]. As measured by the cost of compliance, cleaning up the water pollution is a still larger problem. In 1974 the EPA estimated compliance costs with the 1972 Water Act at $342 billion. L. Ruff, "Federal Environmental Regulation," in app. to vol. 6, "Study on Federal Regulation," Comm. on Governmental Affairs, 95th Cong., 2d Sess., 255, 305 (1978) [hereinafter cited as Ruff].

3. See A. Kneese and B. Bower, *Managing Water Quality: Economics, Technology, and Institutions* (Baltimore, 1968).

4. For an excellent introduction to the technical background of environmental pollution, see A. Kneese and C. Schultze, *supra* note 1, at 11–29.

5. See Mills and White, *supra* note 2, at 348; Ruff, *supra* note 2, at 288.

6. A. Kneese and C. Schultze, *supra* note 1, at 3.

7. 42 U.S.C. § 4701 et seq. The act was passed in 1970 and significantly amended in 1977. For a description and discussion see Stewart and Krier, *supra* note 1, at 340–475.

8. For a description of how this standard was created see J. Davies and B. Davies, *The Politics of Pollution* 184–185 (Indianapolis, 1975).

9. 42 U.S.C. § 1251 et seq. For discussion of the details of this act see Stewart and Krier, *supra* note 1, at 505–536.

10. Ruff, *supra* note 2, at 283–299.

11. Ruff, *supra* note 2; Mills and White, *supra* note 2, at 368–378.

12. Ruff, *supra* note 2, at 299–309.

13. For purposes of clarity, "emission" or "effluent" or "discharge" will refer to the physical substance that is emitted from the source into the air or water. The word "pollution" will refer to the harm that the discharge causes.

14. Arguably there is a "threshold" below which emissions cause no pollution damage. See Roberts and Stewart, Book Review, 88 *Harv. L. Rev.* 1644, 1650. Of course, what counts as "damage" may vary from place to place: one may want perfectly clear air in the Grand Tetons but not care about a little haze in downtown Detroit.

15. I. Gutmanis, "The Generation and Cost of Controlling Air, Water and Solid Waste Pollution: 1970–2000" (Washington, 1972), cited in Kneese and Schultze, *supra* note 1, at 19–21.

16. Estimates by EPA and CEQ cited in Senate Comm. on Governmental Affairs, Study on Federal Regulation, vol. 6, 95th Cong., 2d Sess., 190 (1978) [hereinafter referred to as Senate Study].

17. See, e.g., H. Jacoby et al., *Clearing the Air: Federal Policy on Automotive Emissions Control* (Cambridge, Mass., 1973), and see the detailed discussion of abatement costs in D. Dewees, "The Costs and Technology of Pollution Abatement," in Friedlaender, *supra* note 1, at 291.

18. Kneese and Schultze, *supra* note 1, at 20–21.

19. Some groups would value the benefits from reduced pollution highly enough that the term "cleaner than necessary" would lack operative meaning.

20. A. Kneese, *Economics and the Environment* 51–94 (New York, 1977).

21. Senate Study, at 191, citing Kneese and Schultze, *supra* note 1, at 82.

22. R. Stewart and J. Krier, *supra* note 1, at 517. See also B. Ackerman et al., *The Uncertain Search for Environmental Quality* 223–281 (New York, 1974), and other sources cited in Stewart and Krier at 517, n. 66.

23. See Federal Water Pollution Control Act, § 301, 42 USC 1251 et seq. (1977).

24. See M. Roberts and S. Farrell, "The Political Economy of Implementation: The Clean Air Act and Stationary Sources," in Friedlaender, *supra* note 1, at 152.

25. Compare Mills and White, *supra* note 2, at 352–355, with Ruff, *supra* note 2, at 284.

26. See generally D. Rubinfeld, "Market Approaches to the Measurement of the Benefits of Air Pollution Abatement," and comments in Friedlaender, *supra* note 1, at 241.

27. M. Roberts and R. Stewart, *supra* note 14, at 1649.

28. See the earliest discussion of the advantages and limits of modeling in B. Ackerman et al., *The Uncertain Search for Environmental Quality* (New York, 1974).

29. This process is further complicated by the fact that individual air sheds do not necessarily follow political boundaries.

30. H. Beal, "Comment," in Friedlaender, *supra* note 1, at 182–188.

31. Kneese and Schultze, *supra* note 1, at 88.

32. See Dewees, *supra* note 17, at 291, 297.

33. See Ackerman, *supra* note 22.

34. Roberts and Farrell, *supra* note 24, and W. Drayton, "Comment," in Friedlaender, *supra* note 1, at 230.

35. The state implementation plans may themselves consist in part of general, sim-

ple standards, but by the time they are actually enforced, they are likely to consist of highly individualized "compliance schedules" tailored to the needs of individual firms. See Roberts and Farrell, *supra* note 24.

36. See Roberts and Farrell, *supra* note 24, at 161–164. Even where the standards are general in principle, they are made specific through the issuance, after regulation, of an Enforcement Compliance Schedule letter, which tailors the requirements to the needs of the individual firm; see Ruff, *supra* note 2, at 303.

37. Kneese and Schultze, *supra* note 1, at 63.

38. Roberts and Farrell, *supra* note 24, at 165.

39. W. Drayton, "Comment," in Friedlaender, *supra* note 1, at 230, 237.

40. Ruff, *supra* note 2, at 287.

41. For one thing, the penalty may be less than the money saved by the manufacturer who does not install the equipment—particularly since he can increase his profits by investing that money elsewhere. For another, the manufacturer may face nearly as large a penalty for a small degree as for a large degree of noncompliance. See Downing and Watson, *Enforcement Economics in Pollution Control* 26 (EPA 6001J-73-14, 1973); cf. D. Dewees, *Economics and Public Policy: The Automotive Pollution Case* 131 (Cambridge, Mass., 1974).

42. The compliance schedules themselves may be so complex that their enforcement raises major difficulties. The 1975 decree negotiated with Jones & Laughlin Steel Co., for example, in sixty pages required the company to build basic oxygen furnaces and shutdown oven-hearth furnaces by the end of 1974, to bring coke ovens into compliance by April 1974, to reduce smoke emissions on a detailed schedule, to "exercise good faith and make all reasonable efforts" to comply with emissions limitations, to rehabilitate coke-oven stacks on a detailed schedule, to design and build an "enclosed quench car" to capture emission, and, if it worked, to build and install four more. See Senate Study, *supra* note 16, at 196. Note the highly detailed individualized requirements, the technological uncertainty, and the use of flexible standards such as "reasonable" that will make the question of compliance difficult to answer.

43. C. Ditlow, "Federal Regulation of Motor Vehicle Emissions under the Clean Air Act Amendments of 1970," 4 *Ecology L.Q.* 506 (1975).

44. This has been documented by Roberts and Farrell, *supra* note 24.

45. *Id.,* at 158–160.

46. See D. Tundermann, "Economic Enforcement Tools for Pollution Control: The Connecticut Plan," paper presented at Environmental Study Conference Briefing, "Tax and Fee Approaches to Pollution Control," May 26, 1976.

47. Roberts and Farrell, *supra* note 24, at 155. Stewart and Krier, *supra* note 1, at 494.

48. Mills and White, *supra* note 2.

49. See Dewees, *supra* note 41, at 126. See also Mills and White, *supra* note 2, at 380–384; Dewees, *supra* note 17, at 325–330.

50. Mills and White, *supra* note 2, at 380–384.

51. The Clean Air Act directly applies especially stringent emissions limitations to new sources. See Clean Air Act Amendments of 1977, § 111, 42 U.S.C. § 7401 et seq. (1977). Stewart and Krier, *supra* note 1, at 503. The EPA has wrestled with the problem of new entry into areas that are not in compliance with ambient standards—about half the country. It has developed a complex set of "trade-off" regulations, which allow a

new firm to enter by paying for cleaning up significantly more pollution than it will cause. See 41 *Fed. Reg.* 55525, 55528 (1976), 40 C.F.R. 51–18 (1978). The extent to which these regulations allow entry in practice is not yet known.

52. See generally R. Stewart, "Judging the Imponderables of Environmental Policy: Judicial Review under the Clean Air Act," in Friedlaender, *supra* note 1, at 68.

53. Ruff, *supra* note 2, at 301–302.

54. See W. Baxter, *People or Penguins: The Case for Optimal Pollution* 73–78 (New York, 1974); C. Schultze, *The Public Use of the Private Interest* 53–54 (1977); L. Ruff, "Price Pollution Out of Existence," *Los Angeles Times,* December 7, 1969, at 67.

55. See W. Baxter, *supra* note 54, at 65–68, 75.

56. C. Schultze et al., *Setting National Priorities: The 1973 Budget* 368–373 (Washington, 1972). W. Baxter, *supra* note 54, at 76–77.

57. While it is generally thought that these rights will wind up in the hands of polluters, it is also conceivable that private individuals or environmental groups may purchase rights in order to reduce total pollution below the level deemed acceptable by the government. Such a tactic might aid lobbying efforts to reduce the number of rights in the future, since the groups could volunteer to relinquish their (purchased) rights in return for a lowered maximum threshold.

58. See Dales, *supra* note 1; Stewart and Krier, *supra* note 1, at 587–591.

59. See, e.g., A. Spence and M. Weitzman, "Regulatory Strategies for Pollution Control," in Friedlaender, *supra* note 1, at 199.

60. See Senate Study, *supra* note 16, at 210.

61. This is certainly true to the extent that firms compete for resources within the airshed, river district, or other pollution jurisdiction. Where firms can locate in another "rights area" (assuming rights are allocated on a state, county, or regional basis—and not nationally) without undue competitive disadvantage, the fear of anticompetitive harm is minimized. For example, a lumber company that acquires all the pollution rights for its sawmill in a pollution rights district encompassing thousands of acres of forest land might effectively prevent other companies from carrying out milling operations in the area. This might force other firms who want to use the forest land to adopt a higher cost process (or the same process made more expensive by the need to transport the lumber out of the jurisdiction before processing) or even not to enter the industry at all. On the other hand, the anticompetitive harm resulting from one paperclip manufacturer monopolizing the rights in a rights district is likely to be small. Other paperclip manufacturers are likely to be able to locate elsewhere with little ill effect.

62. See *Otter Tail Power Co.* v. *United States,* 410 U.S. 366 (1973); *Associated Press et al.* v. *United States,* 326 U.S. 1 (1945).

63. *United States* v. *Aluminum Co. of America,* 148 F.2d 416 (2d Cir., 1945).

64. See *United States* v. *Terminal R.R. Ass'n of St. Louis,* 224 U.S. 383 (1911).

65. Of course, rights do not have to be permanent. Indeed, limited-life rights (say five years) have many advantages. They allow the government to directly control the number of rights available (without having to go out on the "open market" to purchase them) and permit new entrants to get a fresh crack at purchasing new rights. Indeed, governments may want to set up quasi-futures markets in pollution rights to allow them to judge the future value of such rights as well as to provide firms to plan over longer periods of time. A countervailing factor is that firms are likely to develop fairly estab-

lished perceptions over time as to what will constitute "acceptable pollution." To the extent this occurs, governments will find themselves unable (for political and equitable reasons) to make drastic changes in the amount of rights available for sale at the beginning of each new rights period.

66. See Senate Study, *supra* note 16, at 210.

67. See Anderson et al., *Environmental Improvement through Economic Incentives* 145-191 (1977).

68. Mills and White, *supra* note 2, at 398.

69. For a comparison of fees and marketable rights, see Ackerman, *supra* note 22.

70. See "Proposal for National Charges on Emissions of Sulfur Oxides," in Environmental Law Institute, *Effluent Charges on Air and Water Pollution* 52-57 (1973).

71. C. Schultze et al., *supra* note 56, at 373.

72. Mills and White, *supra* note 2, at 398.

73. *Seventh Annual Report of the Council on Environmental Quality* (Washington, D.C., 1976).

74. Kneese and Schultze, *supra* note 1, at 70-90.

75. Senate Study, *supra* note 16, at 191.

76. Senate Study, *supra* note 16.

77. Ackerman et al., *supra* note 22; See Roberts and Stewart, Book Review, *supra* note 14, at 1655.

78. Kneese and Schultze, *supra* note 1, at 5.

79. The details of the European systems are contained in Organization for European Cooperation and Development, *Pollution Charges—an Assessment* (Paris, 1976); See also Anderson et al., *Environmental Improvement through Economic Incentives,* ch. 3 (Baltimore and London, 1977); Senate Study, *supra* note 16, at 205-209.

80. This is an informal estimate made at a seminar at Harvard University in 1976. Detailed comparative estimates of the effectiveness of the systems had apparently not been made.

81. Anderson, *supra* note 79, at 66, cites detailed proposals by The Fee Systems of Cambridge, Blair Bower, and Alan Kneese.

82. See B. Yandle, "The Emerging Market in Air Pollution Rights, *Regulation* 621 (1978).

83. See J. Foster, "The Size and Price of Emission Offsets," paper presented at 71st APCA annual meeting, Houston, Texas, June 25-30, 1978 (No. 78-125 EPA); T. Clark, "A Market for Air Pollution," *National Journal* 1332 (August 19, 1978); Senate Study, *supra* note 16, at 213-217.

84. See, e.g., Drayton, *supra* note 39, at 234; Spence and Weitzman, *supra* note 59, at 218, n. 7.

85. Roberts and Farrell, *supra* note 24, at 161.

86. Drayton, *supra* note 39, at 237.

87. Anderson, *supra* note 79, at 97-100. See generally Ballinger, "Instruments for Water Quality Monitoring," 6 *Environ. Sci. & Tech.* 130, 130-133 (1972).

88. Kneese and Schultze, *supra* note 1, at 110.

89. This description is based upon the source in note 80 *supra;* see also OECD Report, *supra* note 79.

90. See, e.g., *Portland Cement Ass'n v. Ruckelshaus,* 486 F.2d 375 (D.C. Cir., 1973), cert. denied, 417 U.S. 921 (1974); *Kennecott Copper Corp. v. EPA,* 462 F.2d 846 (D.C. Cir., 1972).

91. Cf. Drayton, *supra* note 39.

92. See OECD Report, *supra* note 79; also *supra* note 73.

93. Kneese and Schultze, *supra* note 1, at 57; Senate Study, *supra* note 16, at 206.

94. See the discussion in Anderson, *supra* note 79, at 145–191.

95. Anderson, *supra* note 79, at 157–160.

96. "Proposal for National Charges on Emission of Sulfur Oxides," Environmental Law Institute, *Effluent Charges on Air and Water Pollution* 52–57 (1973).

97. This assumes he realizes that he is paying most of the abatement costs through higher product prices.

98. The Japanese have developed a compensation system of this sort for cancer victims. See J. Gresser, "The 1973 Japanese Law on the Compensation of Pollution-Related Health Damage: An Introductory Assessment," 8 *Law in Japan* 92 (1975).

99. This is the Senate Committee's recommendation. See Senate Study, *supra* note 16, at 201.

100. This problem could be avoided by initially issuing a large amount of short-term rights (say, for two years) along with an announcement that the total stock of rights will be progressively reduced by 10 percent each time new rights are issued. This method would allow firms to become accustomed to the new regulatory regime, while minimizing economic dislocations. Environmental objectives would have to be partially deferred in the short term. The added administrative costs of frequent auctions would probably be offset by other benefits.

101. The firm may well go out of business because it chooses to sell its rights to another firm. But in that case the owners of the selling firm are well compensated. They would not object to such a scheme. They might well object to a scheme that gave them no initial allocation and forced them to go bankrupt.

102. U.S. Constitution, Art. 1, § 7. This subsection draws heavily upon a student paper written by F. Mullan that closely analyses the administrative details of tax and fee systems.

103. See Internal Revenue Code § 162(f) and § 164 (1979).

104. For example, the auto companies have argued that they do not see civil penalties for failing to meet fuel efficiency standards as taxes. Thus, they will strive to meet those standards, rather than pay. See, e.g., *Hearings before the Senate Finance Comm. on the Energy Tax Act of 1977*, 95th Cong., 1st Sess., pt. 2, at 147 (1977).

105. See S. Cnossen, *Excise Systems: A Global Study of the Selective Taxation of Goods and Services* 62–66 (Baltimore, 1977).

106. See Internal Revenue Code § 4064(c),(d)(3) (1979).

15. Problems of a Possible Match: Natural Monopoly and Telecommunications

1. See T. Moore, "The Effectiveness of Regulation of Electric Utility Prices," 36 *S. Econ. J.* 365 (1970); G. Stigler and C. Friedland, "What Can Regulators Regulate? The Case of Electricity," 5 *J.Law & Econ.* 1 (1962). These studies were done at a time when production costs fell due to technological change.

2. A summary of empirical results in the 1960s and 1970s is contained in P. MacAvoy, *The Present Condition of the Regulated Industries and Prospects for Regulatory Reform* (1979).

3. To some extent those who found regulation ineffective, note 1 *supra,* compared

the prices of regulated with unregulated electricity companies. The latter, however, may have kept their prices low for fear of attracting regulation.

4. H. Demsetz, "Why Regulate Utilities?" 11 *J.Law & Econ.* 55 (1968).

5. Sometimes firms would bid unrealistically low prices in order to get the franchise, and then immediately seek a rate increase. This franchise regulation was no easier in practice to carry out than cost-of-service ratemaking. For an account of its difficulties, see W. K. Jones, *Regulated Industries, Cases and Materials* 28–31, 2d ed. (1976). See also, J. Sichter, *Separations Procedures in the Telephone Industry: The Historical Origins of a Public Policy* 13–14 (1977).

6. For a discussion, see Charles River Associates, "The Economics of Competition in the Telecommunications Industry," ch. 4, report no. 338 (July 1979).

7. For an overview of the telecommunications and recent FCC decisions, see the agency's report in Docket 20003: *In the Matter of Economic Implications and Interrelationships Arising from Policies and Practices Relating to Customer Interconnection, Jurisdictional Separations, and Rate Structures,* 61 FCC 2d 766, 793 (1976). This report, which concludes that the limited competition permitted by the FCC in the last decade has greatly benefited the consumer, is reprinted in *Domestic Telecommunications Common Carrier Policies: Hearings before the Subcomm. on Communications of the Senate Comm. on Commerce, Science, and Transportation,* 95th Cong., 1st Sess. 143–249 (1977) [hereinafter cited as Senate Hearings].

8. See Senate Hearings, *supra* note 7, at 95–99, 115–119 (submission of FCC Chairman Richard Wiley); P. Berman and A. Oettinger, "Changing Functions and Facilities: The Politics of Information Resources," 28 *Fed. Comm. Bar J.* 227, 242–254 (1975).

9. *In the Matter of Use of the Carterfone Device in Message Toll Telephone Service,* 13 FCC 2d 420 (1968), recon. denied 14 FCC 2d 571 (1968). See A. Kahn, *The Economics of Regulation: Principles and Institutions* 2: 140–145 (New York, 1971), for a discussion of this decision. Since *Carterfone,* the FCC has in several cases taken action that reaffirms and extends its initial ruling. See Senate Hearings, *supra* note 7, at 101–104. The resulting "interconnect industry" has, however, experienced financial difficulties and has only recently begun to prosper. Compare Salomon Brothers, *The Telecommunications Supply Industry* (July 1977), with Salomon Brothers, *Telecommunications and the Emerging Communications Equipment Industries* (September 1978); see also "The New Telephone Industry," *Bus. Week* 68 (February 13, 1978).

10. This bill, first introduced toward the end of the 96th Congress and later revised and reintroduced in March 1979, would replace the FCC with a new Communications Regulatory Commission and would lessen regulation in both the telephone and broadcasting industries. In particular, Sec. 101 would require regulation "only to the extent marketplace forces are deficient." See, e.g., "House Panel Offers Plan to Deregulate Communications," *Cong. Q.* 1547 (June 17, 1978). "The Communications Act of 1978," *Regulation* 13 (September/October 1978).

11. See Charles River Associates, *supra* note 6.

12. Statistics provided by AT&T, January 1979.

13. Senate Hearings, *supra* note 7, at 162–163.

14. Charles River Associates, *supra* note 6, table 1-1 (1979).

15. Charles River Associates, *supra* note 6, at ch. 5, p. 57.

16. *Id.,* at ch. 5, pp. 57–60.

17. See, e.g., Mantell, "An Econometric Study of Returns to Scale in the Bell

System," prepared for the Office of Telecommunications Policy and submitted as Bell Exhibit 40 in Docket 20003 (1974); Vinod, "Application of New Ridge Regression Methods to a Study of Bell System Scale Economies," Bell Exhibit 42 in Docket 20003 (1975); Vinod, "Nonhomogeneous Production Functions and Applications to Telecommunications," 3 *Bell J. Econ. & Mgmt. Sci.* 531 (1972); Sudit, "Additive Nonhomogeneous Production Functions in Telecommunications," 4 *Bell J. Econ. & Mgmt. Sci.* 499 (1973). See also AT&T's "Multiple Supplier Network Study," reprinted in Senate Hearings, *supra* note 7, at 438–448.

18. Charles River Associates, *supra* note 6, at ch. 4.

19. See L. Waverman, "The Regulation of Intercity Telecommunications," in *Promoting Competition in Regulated Markets* 201, 223, ed. A. Phillips (Washington, D.C., 1975).

20. See, e.g., "Statement of Richard R. Hough," in *Hearings on the Communications Act of 1978*, Bell System Statements 10–16, a compilation of Bell System testimony given before the Subcommittee on Communications of the House Committee on Interstate and Foreign Commerce (July and August 1978).

21. *Id.*, at 12.

22. Charles River Associates, *supra* note 6, at ch. 4, pp. 43–65.

23. *Id.*, at ch. 4, pp. 53–54.

24. Charles River Associates, *supra* note 6, collects in chapter 5 an impressive series of studies showing a low rate of technological innovation in regulated industries. However, many of these studies deal with competitively structured industries, and the Bell System has been highly innovative. A review of the evidence collected suggested that whether innovations of telephone technology would increase or decrease in the presence of new entry is not proved either way.

25. See note 24 *supra*. Whether a new entrant, eroding economies of scale but stimulating competitive response, will bring about more research or less is hotly debated among economists, with empirical evidence produced on both sides of the issue.

26. See J. Sichter, *Separations Procedures in the Telephone Industry: The Historical Origins of a Public Policy* 13 (1977).

27. "The effect of the judicial process and decisions on state regulation during its formative years was, to summarize a complex situation, devastating." *Id.*, at 11. See also J. Bauer, *Transforming Public Utility Regulation* 64–65 (New York, 1950); *Missouri ex rel Southwestern Bell Tel. Co.* v. *Missouri Public Service Commission,* 262 U.S. 276, 289 (1923).

28. Sichter, *supra* note 26, at 11; Bauer, *supra* note 27, at 65. One consequence of judicial review was the incredible length of the proceedings. As a result, "telephone cases are used as a horrible example by commentators on the rate making process." "Comment: The Direct Regulation of AT&T," 48 *Yale L.J.* 1015, 1019, n. 29 (1939). In 1930 Justice Frankfurter could attack the Court's fair-value approach by writing of a New York confiscation case that had begun in 1919 and, 62,864 pages of testimony later, was still unresolved. F. Frankfurter, *The Public and Its Government* 95–108 (New Haven, 1930). For the chronology of this and a similar Chicago case, see the concurring opinion of Justice Brandeis in *St. Joseph Stockyards* v. *U.S.,* 298 U.S. 38, 88 (1936).

29. Part of the charge covered the telephones AT&T supplied to the companies. For a critical analysis of these transactions, see Federal Communications Commission, *Proposed Report: Telephone Investigation* 167–199 (Washington, D.C., 1938).

30. This consideration also influenced the development of nationwide rate-averag-

ing, a phenomenon that evidently pleased the newly created FCC when it first began to regulate interstate rates in the 1930s. See Wheat, *Some Interstate Telephone Rate Problems* 8 (Washington, D.C., 1937) (address before the Federal Bar Association).

31. The companies agreed to bill their customers for long-distance calls and retain 25 percent of the revenues. See, e.g., *Southwestern Telegraph and Telephone Co.* v. *City of Houston,* 268 F. 878, 884 (S.D. Texas, 1920).

32. In 1910 Congress passed the Mann-Elkins Act, 36 Stat. 539 (1910), which provided for a weak form of price regulation, but few cases were brought and the net result "may well have been to relieve the wire carriers of any effective governmental control." Note, "The Telegraph Industry: Monopoly or Competition," 51 *Yale L.J.* 629 (1942).

33. Sichter, *supra* note 5, at 99.

34. 47 U.S.C. § 151 et seq. (1970).

35. See the FCC's description of its prior processes in the TELPAK case, Docket 18128 38, Pike and Fisher, R.R. 2d, at 1121, 1146–47. See also the complaint of Bernard Strassburg, *Case Study of Policy-Making by the Federal Communications Commission, re Competition in Intercity Common Carrier Communications* 3 (1977 draft report prepared by the Urban Institute): "Regulation . . . was largely ineffective, if not controlled by AT&T by virtue of its ability to orchestrate supply, demand innovation, and obsolescence in telecommunications."

36. The impetus of a change came in 1930, with the Supreme Court's decision in *Smith* v. *Illinois Bell Telephone Company,* 282 U.S. 133 (1930). One of the issues in *Smith* was the Illinois Commission's failure to "separate" the company's intrastate and interstate property when it set rates. The Court stated that "while the difficulty in making an exact apportionment of the property is apparent, and extreme nicety is not required, . . . it is quite another matter to ignore altogether the actual uses to which the property is put." *Id.,* at 150–151. Presumably, this meant that long-distance toll rates ought to be increased, in order to reflect the fact that long-distance calling utilized local plant. The Justices retreated from their initial position in *Lindheimer* v. *Illinois Bell Telephone Company,* 292 U.S. 151 (1934). The District Court had allocated local *revenues* as well as plant and expenses to interstate services. Thus, the allocation did not lead to a reduction in local rates (or an increase in toll rates) because the reduction in costs assigned to the intrastate jurisdiction was offset by a reduction in revenues. The Court, however, approved the procedure. For a discussion of *Smith* and *Lindheimer* and their impact on separations, see Sichter, *supra* note 5, at 63–89.

37. A. Kahn and C. Zielinski, "New Rate Structures in Communications," 97 *Pub. Util. Fort.* 19, 22 (March 25, 1978).

38. A history of the various plans agreed upon over the years is traced in *National Association of Regulatory Commissioners* (NARUC-FCC Cooperative Committee on Communications), *Separations Manual* 5–8 (1971). See 47 U.S.C. § 410(c) (Joint Negotiating Board). See also *Competition in the Telecommunications Industry: Hearings before the Subcomm. on Communications of the House Comm. on Interstate and Foreign Commerce,* 94th Cong., 2d Sess., 105–126 (1976) (testimony of Paul H. Henson) [hereinafter referred to as *Telephone Hearings*].

39. See dissenting opinion of FCC Commissioner N. Johnson, FCC Docket No. 18866, 26 FCC 2d 247, at 262 (1970).

40. See concurring opinion of FCC Commissioner N. Johnson, FCC Docket No. 16258, 9 FCC 2d 30, at 129 (1967).

41. U.S. Department of Justice, "Initial Comments of the U.S. Department of

Justice," 3 (July 1978) (submission to the FCC for use in its investigation concerning the desirability of a long-distance monopoly).

42. Statistic provided by AT&T, December 1978.

43. Charles River Associates, *supra* note 6, ch. 1, p. 8.

44. Kahn and Zielinski, *supra* note 37, at 20.

45. For an overview of some of the issues presented by private-line competition, see, e.g., Comment, "Recent Federal Actions Affecting Long Distance Telecommunications: A Survey of Issues Concerning the Microwave Specialized Common Carrier Industry," 43 *Geo. Wash. L. Rev.* 878 (1975). See also *Telephone Hearings, supra* note 38.

46. *In the Matter of Allocation of Frequencies in the Bands above 890 MC.*, 27 FCC 359 (1959), 29 FCC 825 (1960). See also A. E. Kahn, *The Economics of Regulation*, vol. I, 24, n. 11 (New York, 1970).

47. 27 FCC, at 413–414.

48. 27 FCC, at 411–412.

49. 29 FCC, at 825.

50. *In Re Applications of Microwave Communications, Inc.*, 18 FCC 2d 953 (1969), recon. denied, 21 FCC 2d 190 (1970). See also Kahn, *supra* note 46, at 132–136.

51. 18 FCC 2d, at 959.

52. *Id.*, at 960–961.

53. *Id.*, at 966.

54. *In the Matter of Establishment of Policies and Procedures for Consideration of Applications to Provide Specialized Common Carrier Services in the Domestic Public Point-to-Point Microwave Radio Service*, 22 RR 2d 1501 (1971), recon. denied, 23 RR 2d 1501 (1971), aff'd sub nom. *Washington Utils. and Transp. Com'n v. FCC*, 513 F.2d 1142 (9th Cir., 1975), cert. denied, sub nom. *Nat'l. Assoc. of Regulatory Utility Commissioners v. FCC*, 423 U.S. 836 (1975).

55. 22 RR2d 1503. The subsequent history of DATRAN is indicative of the financial problems besetting the specialized carriers (problems they have yet to overcome). DATRAN went bankrupt in 1976 and blamed its demise on AT&T's allegedly anticompetitive behavior. It filed an antitrust suit against AT&T. See Senate Hearings, *supra* note 7, at 1174 (testimony of Herbert Jasper).

56. 22 RR2d 1546–51.

57. *Id.*, at 1553. In 1976, in its Docket 20003 Report, the FCC contended that SCC competition had, indeed, expanded the market for private-line services. See Senate Hearings, *supra* note 7, at 225. While it is true that private-line revenues have grown significantly since 1971, the increase might be attributable to a diversion of business from MTS and WATS, rather than market stimulation due to the presence of the SCCs.

58. 22 RR2d 1556–57. Indeed, the FCC explained, "AT&T has vast competitive resources, and it is likely that it will succeed in obtaining a very substantial portion of the large potential market." *Id.*, at 1553.

59. *Id.*, at 1584.

60. In 1976 the suspension period was increased to 5 months. Act of August 4, 1976, Pub. L. No. 94-376, § 2, 90 Stat. 1080 (amending 47 U.S.C. § 204 (1976)).

61. *In the Matter of Amer. Tel. & Tel. Co. Charges, Classifications, Regulations, and Practices for and in Connection with Private Line Services and Channels*, 34 FCC 244 (1961), 34 FCC 217 (1963), recon. denied, 34 FCC 1094 (1963).

62. The tariff provided for reduced rates per mile as the number of channels fur-

nished between a given pair of points increased. The subscriber could obtain a discount of up to 28 percent—that is, 28 percent below the total charge that would accrue if individual users collectively ordered the same number of channels. 34 FCC at 316.

63. 47 U.S.C. § 202(a) (1976) provides: "It shall be unlawful for any common carrier to make any unjust or unreasonable discrimination in charges, practices, classifications, regulations, facilities, or services for or in connection with like communication service, directly or indirectly, by any means or device, or to make or give any undue or unreasonable preference or advantage to any particular person, class of persons, or locality, or to subject any particular person, class of persons, or locality to any undue or unreasonable prejudice or disadvantage."

64. 34 FCC, at 317.

65. However, the FCC pointed out that AT&T had so far lost only $1.7 million in revenues to private microwave, but its discounts had cost it $6 million in lost revenues. *Id.*, at 318. The FCC used the wrong comparison, however. It should have compared the $6 million not to what AT&T *did* lose to microwave, but to what it *would have lost* if it had kept its prices high.

66. *In the Matter of Amer. Tel. & Tel. Co. Tariff FCC No. 250, TELPAK Service and Channels*, 37 FCC 1111 (1964), 38 FCC 370 (1964), recon. denied, 38 FCC 761 (1965), aff'd sub nom. *American Trucking Ass'n* v. *FCC*, 377 F.2d 121 (D.C. Cir., 1966), cert. denied, 386 U.S. 943 (1967).

67. TELPAK consisted of 4 discount schedules, ranging from 12 circuits (''A'') to 240 circuits (''D''), with the discount increasing with the number of circuits.

68. 37 FCC, at 1115–16.

69. *In the matter of TELPAK Tariff Sharing Provisions of Amer. Tel. & Tel. Co. and the Western Union Telegraph Co.*, 23 FCC 2d 606, 613 (1970), rev'd on other grounds sub nom. *Amer. Tel. & Tel. Co.* v. *FCC*, 449 F.2d 439 (2d Cir., 1971).

70. 37 FCC, at 1117.

71. *In the Matter of Amer. Tel. & Tel. Co. Charges, Regulations, Classifications and Practices for Voice Grade/Private Line Service* (*High Density–Low Density*), 55 FCC 2d 224 (1975), 58 FCC 2d 362 (1976), 59 FCC 2d 428 (1976).

72. 55 FCC 2d, at 228.

73. 58 FCC 2d, at 371.

74. 59 FCC 2d, at 433–434.

75. *In the Matter of Amer. Tel. & Tel. Co. Long Line Dept. Revisions of Tariff FCC No. 260 Private Line Service Series 5000* (*TELPAK*), 38 RR 2d 1121 (1976), 40 RR 2d 1289 (1977).

76. AT&T contends that cost-based pricing will lead to significant increases in residential rates—perhaps by as much as 79 percent. See its 1975 Residential Cost Study, reprinted in Senate Hearings, *supra* note 7, at 460–470. In its Docket 20003 report, the FCC suggests that this fear is overblown, particularly since the carrier has yet to suffer adversely from the (admittedly limited) competition it currently faces. *Id.*, at 171–180, 220–231. In any event, value-of-service ratemaking is not immune from attack on other grounds: the fact that it supposedly benefits *all* residential users (regardless of need) at the expense of *all* business users (regardless of their needs), and the fact that the excessive charges to businesses are eventually reflected in consumer prices anyway.

77. Brief of Bell System Respondents, at 18 (March 12, 1973). For a complete derivation of the test, see W. Baumol, O. Eckstein, and A. Kahn, ''Competition and Monopoly in Telecommunications Services,'' 15–16 (1970) (memorandum prepared for AT&T). Their report is reprinted in the *Industrial Reorganization Act: Hearings before*

the Subcomm. on Antitrust and Monopoly of the Senate Comm. on the Judiciary, pt. 2: *The Communications Industry*, 93rd Cong., 2d Sess., 1333–49 (1973) [hereinafter cited as *IRA Hearings*].

78. 38 RR 2d 1163. The FCC certainly knew that it would be impossible for AT&T to set *all* rates at LRIC, yet it wondered why "Bell does not . . . address the obvious question of why it does not make overall (aggregate) use of its long-run incremental costs philosophy." *Id.*, at 1182. And while it spent most of the decision worrying that residential rates might increase if the LRIC methodology were used, it failed to consider the real problem—that rates might increase even more in its absence.

79. *Id.*, at 1169–72.

80. *Id.*, at 1213.

81. *Id.*, at 1206, 1204; the FCC later agreed to reconsider the TELPAK part of its holding, but by that time AT&T had already decided to continue the tariff. 40 RR 2d 1308.

82. *In the Matter of Bell System Tariff Offerings of Local Distribution Facilities for Use by Other Common Carriers*, 46 FCC 2d 413 (1974) aff'd sub nom. *Bell Telephone Co. of Pennsylvania* v. *FCC*, 503 F.2d 1250 (3d Cir., 1974), cert. denied, 422 U.S. 1026 (1975).

83. 46 FCC 2d at 426.

84. *In the Matter of Regulatory Policies Concerning Resale and Shared Use of Common Carrier Services and Facilities*, 38 RR 2d 141 (1976), 39 RR 2d 765 (1977), aff'd sub nom. *AT&T* v. *FCC*, 572 F.2d 17 (2d Cir., 1978). For a discussion of some of the issues facing the commission, see Comment, "Resale and Sharing of Private Line Communications Services: AT&T Restriction and FCC Regulation," 61 *Va. L. Rev.* 679 (1975).

85. See, e.g., *In the Matter of the Application of Packet Communications, Inc.*, 43 FCC 2d 922 (1973).

86. 38 RR 2d 168–183.

87. *Id.*, at 186.

88. *In the Matter of MCI Telecommunications Corp.*, 34 RR 2d 539 (1975), 37 RR 2d 1339 (1976), rev'd sub nom. *MCI Telecommunications Corp.* v. *FCC*, 561 F.2d 365 (D.C. Cir., 1977), cert. denied sub nom. *FCC* v. *MCI Telecommunications Corp.*, 434 U.S. 1040 (1978).

89. 34 RR 2d 539.

90. 37 RR 2d 1352.

91. *Id.*, at 1352, 1357.

92. *Id.*, at 1359–60.

93. 561 F.2d 377. See also 47 U.S.C. § 214(c) (1970).

94. *Id.*, at 379.

95. *Id.*, at 380. *In the Matter of Petition of AT&T Co. for a Declaratory Ruling and Expedited Relief*, 42 RR 2d 789, 817 (1978), rev'd sub nom. *MCI Telecommunications Corp.* v. *FCC*, 580 F.2d 590 (D.C. Cir., 1978), cert. denied, 439 U.S. 980 (1978).

96. 22 RR 2d 1552.

97. Statistic provided by AT&T, January 1979.

98. Statistic provided by the Common Carrier Bureau, FCC, January 1979.

99. Half was an extraordinary gain. In 1975, MCI lost nearly $70 million on revenues of $7 million. See the company's 1978 annual report, at 12.

100. The FCC opened the domestic satellite market to new carriers in 1972, but

placed certain restrictions on AT&T's ability to compete with them. See *In the Matter of Establishment of Domestic Communications—Satellite Facilities in Non-Governmental Entities,* 35 FCC 2d 844 (1972), 38 FCC 2d 665 (1972). Existing systems are still in the start-up phase; Satellite Business Systems, which is jointly owned by IBM, COMSAT, and Aetna Life and Casualty, is scheduled to begin operations in early 1981. See "Communications Dogfight," *Dun's Review* 48 (June 1977).

101. See Charles River Associates, *supra* note 6.

102. See E. Zajae, *Public Utility Pricing: A Confrontation of Equity and Efficiency* 55–60 (Bell Labs, 1979); W. Baumol, E. Bailey, and R. Willig, "Weak Invisible Hand Theorems on the Sustainability of Prices in a Multiproduct Monopoly," 67 *Am. Econ. Rev.* 350 (1979). D. Panzar and R. Willig, "Free Entry and the Sustainability of Natural Monopoly," 8 *Bell J. Econ. & Mgmt. Sci.* 1 (1977).

103. See Charles River Associates, *supra* note 6, at ch. 6, pp. 5–9. The report also discusses other variations of the nonsustainability thesis not discussed here.

104. See Baumol et al., *supra* note 102, at 1343–44.

105. Cf. Charles River Associates, *supra* note 6, ch. 4.

106. See R. Baseman, "Open Entry and Cross-Subsidy in Regulated Markets," paper discussed in Charles River Associates, *supra* note 6, at ch. 1, p. 16.

107. See Charles River Associates, *supra* note 6, ch. 3.

108. It has been estimated that 73 percent of AT&T's rate base involves costs currently allocated in accordance with separations procedures.

109. See, e.g., Senate Hearings, *supra* note 7, at 285–286 (statement of John deButts). One solution might be to require the SCCs to defray part of local service costs, but it would be administratively difficult to allocate those costs as well. Cf. Communications Act of 1978, *supra* note 10.

110. See Charles River Associates, *supra* note 6, chs. 4–5; P. Berman and A. Oettinger, *The Medium and the Telephone: The Policies of Information Resources* (Cambridge, Mass., 1976).

16. From Candidate to Reform

1. Pub. L. No. 95-504, 92 Stat. 1705 (1978). See Chapter 11 *supra.*

2. Under the Airline Deregulation Act, the Civil Aeronautics Board will cease to exist on January 1, 1985. *Id.*

3. The Securities and Exchange Commission abolished fixed rates for stock brokers' commissions by administrative order.

4. Much of the information in this chapter was gleaned from the author's experience as staff director of the investigation of the CAB conducted in 1975 by the Subcommittee on Administrative Practice and Procedure (chaired by Senator Edward M. Kennedy) of the Senate Committee on the Judiciary.

5. R. Caves, *Air Transport and Its Regulators* (Cambridge, Mass., 1962).

6. G. Douglas and J. Miller, III, *Economic Regulation of Domestic Air Transport: Theory and Policy* (Washington, D.C., 1974).

7. M. Levine, "Is Regulation Necessary? California Air Transportation and National Regulatory Policy," 74 *Yale L.J.* 1416 (1965).

8. W. Jordan, *Airline Regulation in America* (Baltimore, 1970).

9. This latter subject is discussed and described in numerous books on the legislative process. See, e.g., M. Olsen, *The Logic of Collective Action* (Cambridge, Mass.,

1965). The fact that the subject matter is "regulation" does not change the basic political analysis.

10. U.S. Senate Comm. on the Judiciary, Subcomm. on Admin. Practice and Procedure, *Civil Aeronautics Board Practices and Procedures*, 94th Cong., 1st Sess. (1975).

11. *Id.*, at 41.

12. *Id.*, at 42–45.

13. *Id.*, at 40–58.

14. *Id.*

15. *Id.*, at 67–68.

16. Airline Deregulation Act of 1978, *supra* note 1.

17. Generic Approaches to Regulatory Reform

1. For discussion of many of these proposals, see the six-volume study by Senator Ribicoff's Committee on Governmental Affairs, *Study on Federal Regulation* (1977–78).

2. J. Landis, *Report on Regulatory Agencies to the President-Elect*, Subcomm. on Admin. Practice and Procedure, Senate Comm. on the Judiciary, 86th Cong., 2d Sess. (Comm. print, 1960).

3. President's Advisory Council on Executive Organization, *A New Regulatory Framework: Report on Selected Independent Regulatory Agencies* (Washington, D.C., 1971) [hereinafter referred to as the Ash Council Report].

4. Senate Comm. on Government Operations, "The Regulatory Appointments Process," in *Study on Federal Regulation* 1, 95th Cong., 1st Sess. (January 1977), at 7.

5. *Id.*, at xxxi (finding number 1).

6. Common Cause, for example, has compiled a lengthy study showing that more than half of all commissioners over a period of years came from the regulated industry (or law firms associated with it) and more than half accepted such employment after completing their terms as commissioners. See generally S. Breyer and R. Stewart, *Administrative Law and Regulatory Policy* 138–144 (Boston, 1979).

7. See Breyer and Stewart, *supra* note 6, ch. 7.

8. See, e.g., *International Harvester Co.* v. *Ruckelshaus*, 478 F.2d 615, 647–650 (D.C. Cir., 1973); Breyer and Stewart, *supra* note 6, at 509–511.

9. See *Goldberg* v. *Kelly*, 347 U.S. 154 (1970).

10. See *Perry* v. *Sindermann*, 408 U.S. 593 (1972).

11. See *Thompson* v. *Washington*, 492 F.2d 626 (D.C. Cir., 1973).

12. See *Goss* v. *Lopez*, 419 U.S. 565 (1975).

13. See *Wolff* v. *McDonnell*, 418 U.S. 539 (1974).

14. See generally Breyer and Stewart, *supra* note 6, at 688–717.

15. See H. Friendly, "Some Kind of Hearing," 13 *U. Pa. L. Rev.* 1267 (1975).

16. Cf. L. Tribe, "Structural Due Process," 10 *Harv. C.R.-C.L. L. Rev.* 169 (1975); L. Tribe, *American Constitutional Law* 503–504 (Mineola, 1978).

17. Harvard Center for Criminal Justice, "Judicial Intervention in Prison Discipline," 63 *J. Crim. L.C. & P.S.* 200 (1972).

18. See D. Baum, *The Welfare Family and Mass Administrative Justice* (New York, 1974); J. Mashaw, "The Management Side of Due Process: Some Theoretical

and Litigation Notes on the Assurance of Accuracy, Fairness and Timeliness in the Adjudication of Social Welfare Claims,'' 59 *Cornell L. Rev.* 772 (1974).

19. See G. Frug, "Does the Constitution Prevent the Discharge of Civil Service Employees?'' 124 *U. Pa. L. Rev.* 942 (1976); R. Rubin, "Job Security and Due Process: Monitoring Administrative Discretion through a Reasons Requirement,'' 44 *U. Chicago L. Rev.* 60 (1976).

20. See R. Hamilton, "Procedures for the Adoption of Rules of General Applicability: The Need for Procedural Innovation in Administrative Rulemaking,'' 60 *Calif. L. Rev.* 1276 (1972).

21. Federal Food Drug and Cosmetic Act, 21 U.S.C. § 301, § 371e (1976).

22. R. Hamilton, "Rulemaking on a Record 6: The Food and Drug Administration,'' 50 *Tex. L. Rev.* 1132 (1972).

23. See S. Rep. 96-1018, pt. 2, "Reform of Federal Regulation,'' Joint Report of the Senate Committee on Governmental Affairs and the Committee on the Judiciary, 96th Cong., 2d Sess. (1980) [hereinafter referred to as the Ribicoff-Kennedy Report].

24. This is Kenneth Culp Davis's comment in a letter to the Senate Judiciary Committee, quoted in the Ribicoff-Kennedy Report, *supra* note 23, at 51.

25. See *Portland Cement Association* v. *Ruckelshaus,* 486 F.2d 375 (D.C. Cir., 1973).

26. The Supreme Court has restricted the power of the courts to impose real procedures in informal rulemaking. *Vermont Yankee Nuclear Power Corp.* v. *Natural Resources Defense Council, Inc.,* 435 U.S. 519 (1978).

27. See generally Barry Boyer, "Trade Regulation Rulemaking Procedures of the FTC,'' Report to the Administrative Conference of the United States by the Special Project for the Study of Special Rulemaking under the Magnuson-Moss Warranty/Federal Trade Commission Act (unpublished, 1979). See especially the data appendix at 89.

28. The 96th Congress criticized the commission at length, seriously criticizing the quality of its performance.

29. 567 F.2d 9 (D.C. Cir., 1977), cert. denied, 434 U.S. 829 (1977).

30. 564 F.2d 458 (D.C. Cir., 1977).

31. Previously it was thought that *informal* rulemaking allowed agencies to consult when and with whom they wished. They need not decide on the basis of a record. Like a legislature, the agency would ask for comments but need not decide on the basis of comments publicly provided.

32. See Senate Committee on Governmental Affairs, Study on Federal Regulation (6 vols., 1977–78).

33. See Ribicoff-Kennedy Report, *supra* note 23.

34. See Chapter 14 *supra; Moss* v. *CAB,* 430 F.2d 891 (D.C. Cir., 1970), ended the practice.

35. The Domestic Passenger Fare Investigation, discussed in Chapter 11 *supra.*

36. R. Stewart, "The Reformation of American Administrative Law,'' 88 *Harv. L. Rev.* 1667 (1975).

37. *Id.*

38. *Id.* See also J. Landis, *The Administrative Process* (New Haven, 1938).

39. See, e.g., T. Lowi, *The End of Liberalism* (New York, 1969); R. Fellmeth, *The Interstate Commerce Commission: The Public Interest and the ICC* (New York,

1970); J. Turner, *The Chemical Feast* (New York, 1970); G. Stigler, *The Citizen and the State: Essays in Regulation* (Chicago, 1975); and numerous others.

40. See Stewart, *supra* note 36; Breyer and Stewart, *supra* note 6, at 32–35 and ch. 10.

41. See Administrative Practice and Regulatory Control Act of 1979, S. 1291, 96th Cong., 1st Sess. (1979).

42. See, for example, the liberalization of requirements of standing, ripeness, and reviewability discussed in Stewart, *supra* note 36; and Breyer and Stewart, *supra* note 6, at ch. 9.

43. See the Freedom of Information Act, 5 U.S.C. § 552 (1976).

44. See the Government in the Sunshine Act, 5 U.S.C. § 552b (1976).

45. See the President's Committee on Administrative Management, *Report of the Committee* (Washington, D.C., 1937).

46. See U.S. Commission on Organization of the Executive Branch of the Government, *The Independent Regulatory Commissions: A Report With Recommendations* 4 (Washington, D.C., 1949).

47. See U.S. Commission on Organization of the Executive Branch of the Government, *Legal Services and Procedures* (Washington, D.C., 1955).

48. Landis, *supra* note 2.

49. Ash Council Report, *supra* note 3.

50. See P. Elman, Administrative Reform of the Federal Trade Commission, 59 *Geo. L.J.* 777 (1971).

51. See S. Breyer and R. Stewart, *supra* note 6, ch. 8.

52. Senate Comm. on the Judiciary, *Hearings on Regulatory Reform,* Pt. 1, 96th Cong., 1st Sess. (1979), at 61.

53. See H. Bruff and E. Gellhorn, "Congressional Control of Administrative Regulation: A Study of Legislative Vetos," 90 *Harv. L. Rev.* 1369 (1977); H. Watson, "Congress Steps Out: A Look at Congressional Control of the Executive," 63 *Calif. L. Rev.* 983 (1975); Breyer and Stewart, *supra* note 6, at 96–98.

54. *Atkins* v. *United States,* 556 F.2d 1028 (1977).

55. *Chadha* v. *Immigration and Naturalization Service,* No. 77-1701 (9th Cir., 1980).

56. See E. Redford, *The President and the Regulatory Commissions,* prepared for the President's Advisory Committee on Government Organization (1960).

57. See L. Cutler and D. Johnson, "Regulation and the Political Process," 84 *Yale L.J.* 1395 (1975). The proposal is limited to policy determinations, not awards of individual routes or licenses in order to minimize the possibility of special favoritism for individuals. But see A. Morrison, "Should the President Control the Regulators?" *Washington Post,* November 2, 1978.

58. See Ribicoff-Kennedy Report, *supra* note 23.

59. S. 111 added as an amendment to S. 1477, 96th Cong., 1st Sess. (1979).

60. L. Jaffe, *Judicial Control of Administrative Action* 546–594 (Boston, 1965). But see A. Morrison, "Should the President Control the Regulators?" *Washington Post,* November 2, 1978.

61. See Ash Council Report, *supra* note 3.

62. A.B.A. Special Committee on Administrative Law, "Report of the Special Committee," *Annual Report of the A.B.A.* 721–793 (1936).

63. See Breyer and Stewart, *supra* note 6, at 398–420.

64. See B. Ackerman et al., *The Uncertain Search for Environmental Quality* 147–161 (New York, 1974).

65. A. Kantrowitz, "Controlling Technology Democratically," 63 *American Scientist* 505 (September–October 1975).

66. See, e.g., Callan, "The Science Court," 193 *Science* 950–951 (1976); Abrams and Berry, "Mediation: A Better Alternative to Science Courts," *Bull. Atom. Scient.* (April 1977).

67. See generally W. Gellhorn, *When Americans Complain* (Cambridge, Mass., 1966); W. Gellhorn, *Ombudsmen and Others* (Cambridge, Mass., 1966).

68. See, e.g., Senate Report on the Consumer Protection Organization Act, S. Rep. No. 92-1100, 92nd Cong., 2d Sess. (1972).

69. 42 U.S.C. §§ 4321 et sèq. (1976).

70. See generally R. Stewart and J. Krier, *Environmental Law and Policy,* 2d ed. (Cambridge, Mass., 1978).

71. Exec. Order No. 11821, 39 *Fed. Reg.* 41501 (1974), as amended by Exec. Order No. (1949), 42 *Fed. Reg.* 1017 (1976).

72. Executive Order No. 12044, 43 *Fed. Reg.* 12663 (1978).

73. See Ribicoff-Kennedy Report, *supra* note 23.

74. S. 1291, 96th Cong., 1st Sess. (1979).

75. See Ribicoff-Kennedy Report, *supra* note 23, at 23–31.

76. See J. Miller and S. Yandle, *Benefit-Cost Analyses of Social Regulation: Case Studies from the Council on Wage and Price Stability* (Washington, D.C., 1979).

77. The Carter administration secured modification of proposed cotton-dust safety regulations issued by the Department of Labor. Whether this was desirable is a matter of controversy. L. Cutler, "Who Masters the Regulations?" *Washington Post,* October 18, 1975, A. Morrison, "Should the President Control the Regulators?" *Washington Post,* November 2, 1978.

78. There is case law suggesting that even without an impact statement requirement, agencies may take anticompetitive actions only when there is no "less restrictive alternative." U.S. Senate Comm. on the Judiciary, Subcomm. on Admin. Practice and Procedure, *Civil Aeronautics Board Practices and Procedures,* 94th Cong., 1st Sess. (Comm. print, 1975). Yet this rule is often honored in the breach. An impact statement requirement would strengthen it.

79. See Breyer and Stewart, *supra* note 6, at 769.

80. See, e.g., S. 2812, 94th Cong., 1st Sess. (1975); S. 3318, 94th Cong., 2d Sess. (1976).

81. Colorado was the first state to enact sunset legislation, which went into effect on April 22, 1976. Forty-three agencies (36 of which regulate occupational licensing) are subject to the law, which limits agency lifespan to six years, during which time it will be subject to legislative review or renewal; see, e.g., Title 24, Section 34–104 of the Colorado Revised Statutes (Supp. 1978).

82. Title 1, Section 11.61 of the Florida Revised Statutes (Supp. 1979).

83. 15 U.S.C. § 761 note (1976).

84. S. 1291, 96th Cong., 1st Sess. (1979).

Appendix 2: A Note on Administrative Law

1. See generally R. Stewart, "The Reformation of American Administrative Law," 88 *Harv. L. Rev.* 1667 (1975); S. Breyer and R. Stewart, *Administrative Law and the Regulatory Process* 489 (Boston, 1979).

2. See Chapter 1, n. 8.

3. See *Vermont Yankee Nuclear Power Corp.* v. *Natural Resources Defense Council,* 435 U.S. 519 (1978) and the comments on the case written by C. Byse, R. Stewart, and myself in 91 *Harv. L. Rev.* 1804 et seq. (1978). See also the discussions and sources cited in Breyer and Stewart, *supra* note 1, at 291–306, 499–522.

4. See, e.g., *Mobil Oil Co.* v. *FPC,* 483 F.2d 1238 (D.C. Cir., 1973); *Action for Children's Television* v. *FCC,* 564 F.2d 458 (D.C. Cir., 1977); Breyer and Stewart, *supra* note 1, at 499–557.

5. *United States* v. *Florida East Coast Railway Co.,* 410 U.S. 224 (1973).

6. U.S. Const. Amend. 14.

7. See, e.g., H. Friendly, "Some Kind of Hearing," 123 *U. Pa. L. Rev.* 1267 (1975).

Index

Master Freight Agreement, covering 300,000 motor carrier employees, provides a vehicle for raising industry average costs. See "The Truckers and the Feds—A Tangled Relationship," 11 *Nat'l J.* 6 (1979). Wages account for 60 percent of trucking company costs. ICC Bureau of Accounts, Statement No. I-54, *Explanation of Motor Carrier Costs* 71–79 (1954). An increase in those costs is accompanied by a proportionate increase in profits. Moore estimated that wages in the regulated sector, which is heavily unionized, are far higher than wages in exempt trucking. See T. Moore, "The Beneficiaries of Trucking Regulation," 21 *J.Law & Econ.* 327, 332–341 (1978).

63. See, e.g., *General Increase, Middle Atlantic and New England,* 332 ICC 820 (1969); *Increased Rates and Minimum Charges, South,* 335 ICC 77 (1969).

64. *SMC General Rate Increase,* 1978 Fed. Carr. Rep. (CCH) (Cases) ¶ 36,875.

65. See *New Procedures in Motor Carrier Restructing Proceedings ex parte,* MC-98, 1978 Fed. Carr. Rep. (CCH) (cases) ¶ 36,851, ¶ 36,851.08. G. Wilson, *Essays on Some Unsettled Questions in the Economics of Transportation* 149 (Bloomington, Ind., 1962).

66. C. Taff, *Management of Physical Distribution and Transportation* 362, 6th ed. (Homewood, Ill., 1978).

67. See C. Taff, *supra* note 66; also based on Blumenthal's examination of tariffs and interviews at ICC, see note 29 *supra*.

68. See *Motor Carrier Rates in New England,* 47 M.C.C. 660, 661 (1948).

69. See G. Wilson, *supra* note 65, at 157.

70. Based on Computer Tape Survey Data in Senate Commerce Comm., *supra* note 50.

71. C. Taff, *supra* note 66, at 380.

72. C. Taff, *supra* note 66, at 385.

73. Thus, as measured by weight, far less than 95 percent of LTL shipments move on class rates; the heavier shipments move on commodity rates. Blumenthal, *supra* note 29, at 87 (derived from Senate Commerce Comm. CTS tapes).

74. See *Animal Feed—Kansas City, Mo., to Chicago,* 325 ICC 147 (1965) (rated cut below fully allocated costs to fill chronically empty backhauls); *Aluminum Extrusions—Miami to Chicago,* 325 ICC 188 (1965) (rates cut to meet private carrier competition). See generally G. Hilton, *The Transport Act of 1958: A Decade of Experience* (Bloomington, Ind., 1969).

75. Senate Commerce Committee, *supra* note 50, at 112.

76. In 1974, for example, the ICC denied a petition by Consolidated Freightways to make its St. Paul–Dallas route less circuitous, cutting mileage by 37 percent. P. MacAvoy and J. Snow, *Regulation of Entry and Pricing in Truck Transportation* 21–22 (Washington, D.C., 1977).

77. Senate Commerce Committee, *supra* note 50, at 113.

78. 49 Stat. 543 (1935), 49 U.S.C. §§ 10101–11916 (1979 Supp.).

79. See D. Pegrum, *Transportation: Economics and Public Policy* 314–315, 3rd ed. (Homewood, Ill., 1973).

80. See J. Eastman, *Report of the Federal Coordinator of Transportation,* H.R. Rep. No. 89, 74th Cong., 1st Sess., 114–115 (1935).

81. *Id.,* at 127.

82. *Id.* See also, M. Fair and E. Williams, Jr., *Economics of Transportation* 488 (New York, 1959); W. Jones, *Regulated Industries* 484–487 (Brooklyn, 1967).

83. For studies suggesting that less regulation of both truck and rail would increase

the railroads' share of intercity freight, see P. MacAvoy and J. Snow, *supra* note 47, at 189–212.

84. Transportation Act of 1958, 72 Stat. 568, 572 (1958); 49 U.S.C. 10704(d) (1979 Supp.).

85. Railroad Revitalization and Regulatory Reform Act of 1976 § 205, 90 Stat. 31, 41 (1976); 49 U.S.C § 10704(a)(2) (1979 Supp.).

86. American Trucking Association, *Motor Carrier Regulation—The Issue in Perspective* 5 (1978); see also Senate Committee on Commerce, *supra* note 95, at 125; American Trucking Association, *1978 Financial Analysis of the Motor Carrier Industry* 5 (1979).

87. Data supplied to William Blumenthal, *supra* note 29, by the American Trucking Association.

88. Based on research by Thomas Berggsen, "The Case against the Case against De-Regulation of the Motor Carrier Industry" (diss., Harvard Law School, 1978).

89. See W. Miklius and K. Casavant, "Stability of Motor Carriers Operating under the Agricultural Exemption," in P. MacAvoy and J. Snow, *supra* note 47, at 271–301.

90. See T. Moore, *supra* note 62, at 33, 82 (Britain, Belgium); S. Joy, *supra* note 55, at 273 (Australia) (Australia experienced transitional difficulty).

91. U.S. Dept. of Agriculture, "Economic Performance of Motor Carriers Operating under the Agricultural Exemption in Interstate Trucking," 10 (1969).

92. R. Farmer, "The Case of Unregulated Truck Transportation," 46, *J. Farm Econ.* 389, 403 (1964).

93. See American Trucking Association, *Motor Carrier Regulation—The Issue in Perspective* (1978).

94. ATA, *supra* note 2, at 11.

95. See, e.g., Economic Research Committee of the Regular Common Carrier Conference, *1971 Cost/Revenue Analyses* 8 (1973); Charles River Associates, *Impact of Proposals for Reform of Economic Regulation on Small Motor Carriers and Small Shippers,* report prepared for DOT (July 1977).

96. See Blumenthal, *supra* note 29, at 160–162.

97. ATA, *supra* note 2, at 3, 4, 9.

98. P. McElhiney, "Motor Carrier Freight Rate Study," prepared for DOT and the Federation of Rocky Mountain States (May 1975). Although many carriers have abandoned small communities, virtually every small community receives service from some certificated carriers. Senate Commerce Committee, *supra* note 50, at app. 3. See Blumenthal, *supra* note 29, at 165–166.

99. Hearings before the Subcomm. on Antitrust and Monopoly of the Sen. Comm. on the Judiciary, 2 *Oversight of Freight Rate Competition in the Motor Carrier Industry,* 95th Cong., 2d Sess., 841 (1979) (statement of ICC Chairman Daniel O'Neal).

100. M. Pustay, "The Impact of ICC Regulation on Service to Small Communities," Bowling Green State University, mimeo (n.d.).

101. R. L. Banks and Associates, "Service to Small Communities," in P. MacAvoy and J. Snow, *supra* note 47, at 139.

102. Of the carriers surveyed in the sample, 25 percent said they would continue to offer service. Senate Commerce Committee, *supra* note 50, at 89.

103. Blumenthal, *supra* note 29, developed these conclusions from unpublished data submitted to the Senate Commerce Committee.